WHITNEY FATHER,
WHITNEY HEIRESS

WHITNEY FATHER, WHITNEY HEIRESS

W. A. Swanberg

CHARLES SCRIBNER'S SONS ❋ NEW YORK

Library of Congress Cataloging in Publication Data

Swanberg, W. A. Date
    Whitney Father, Whitney Heiress
    Includes index.
    1. Whitney family. I. Title.
CT274.W46S95   929'.2'0973   79-27455
ISBN 0-684-16448-5

Grateful acknowledgment is made for permission to quote from the following copyrighted material:

"A Cradle Song" by William Butler Yeats reprinted with permission of Macmillan Publishing Co., Inc., from *The Variorum Edition of the Poems of W. B. Yeats*, edited by Peter Allt and Russell K. Alspach, copyright © 1957 by Macmillan Publishing Co., Inc.
"The Reminiscences of Lloyd Carpenter Griscom," copyright © 1972 by the Trustees of Columbia University in the City of New York.
"The Reminiscences of Nelson Trusler Johnson," copyright © 1972 by the Trustees of Columbia University in the City of New York.
"The Reminiscences of Walter Lippmann," copyright © 1975 by the Trustees of Columbia University in the City of New York.

Grateful acknowledgment is also made to the Department of Manuscripts and University Archives, Cornell University, for use of photographs; the Yale University Library; Flora Irving; Michael Straight; Charles Howland Russell; Grayson M-P Murphy; Francis C. Lawrence, and Richard P. Delano.

Blessings on
DOROTHY

CONTENTS

BOOK I

BOOK II

LIST OF ILLUSTRATIONS

BOOK I

BOOK II

WHITNEY FATHER,
WHITNEY HEIRESS

BOOK I

"... Whitney had ... gratified every ambition, and swung the country almost at his will; he had thrown away the usual objects of political ambition like the ashes of smoked cigarettes; he had turned to other amusements, satiated every taste, gorged every appetite, won every object that New York afforded, and, not yet satisfied, had carried his field of activity abroad, until New York no longer knew what most to envy, his horses or his houses."
                                                            —Henry Adams

1. Whitney was dashing, ambitious, able, burning to make money and lots of it.

2. Flora furnished millions, true, but he wanted millions of his very own.

1. The Christening

THE CHANCEL was rich with Bermuda lilies, and the baptismal font—a mass of the same white fragrance—was surmounted by a dove hung on wires in the attitude of descending. More striking than usual at this ceremony was the irony of the subject's indifference to the honor done her. Sunlight streamed through stained-glass windows to throw shafts of colored light on a congregation of unusual eminence. The entire cabinet, from old Secretary of State Bayard on down, joined with heads of the Navy and Army, and with Supreme Court justices and leaders of Congress, in certifying by their presence the importance of the baptism of the Whitney baby. The Reverend Doctor ·Leonard took the infant from her mother, Flora Payne Whitney, remaining imperturbable despite the baby's protests. "Name the child," he said, although he knew the name perfectly well.

"Dorothy Payne Whitney," said Secretary of the Navy William Collins Whitney, handsome in double-breasted Prince Albert coat tailored by Poole's of London. The child's auxiliary godmother, Madame de Reuterskiold, wife of the Swedish Minister, beamed more prettily than Mrs. Whitney thought necessary. Flora Whitney suspected that her pregnancy had given opportunity for an affair between her husband and Madame and was later to write of her "thin tricks and allurements and purrs."

Christenings were unexciting, but this one was of such political and social importance that powerful Americans from all parts of the country gathered at historic St. John's Church on Lafayette Square, along with foreign envoys ranging from the piano-playing Baron von Zedtwitz to the ever-smiling Turk, Mavroyeni Bey. The date was April 11, 1887. The audience included those aging Civil War heroes Adm. David Dixon Porter and Gen. Philip Sheridan, and people as oddly assorted as the eighty-seven-year-old poet and historian George Bancroft, once Secretary of the Navy himself; the dashing young international lawyer, Walter van Rensselaer Berry; and English-born Frances Hodgson Burnett, without whose recent *Little Lord Fauntleroy* no library was complete. President Cleveland himself—unkindly described by young Cecil Spring Rice of the British legation as "5 feet high and 4 feet wide; he has no neck and six chins"—had united with his wife in suggesting the child's first name. The President had skipped this event, but the First Lady—the baby's godmother—was in the first row.

". . . I christen thee Dorothy Payne Whitney," Dr. Leonard intoned.

Since no one could foresee Dorothy's remarkable career, it was, as always at christenings, the parents who were honored. One could not speak of them without superlatives. They were the most social, the most generous and most sumptuously hospitable couple in Washington—also, in a sense, the most mysterious and most suspect. They had entered the capital in 1885 extruding money—Mrs. Whitney's money, not the Secretary's—and with a retinue of real estate people and architects and decorators who armed them for social assault. No sooner had the Whitneys bought the twenty-eight-room former Frelinghuysen mansion at 1731 I Street, just off Lafayette Square and a three-minute trot from the White House, than they spent $45,000 in refurbishing it. They enlarged the dining room, added a great ballroom, and finally pushed the workmen out one afternoon barely in time to have a New Year's Eve party at which "President Cleveland escorted Mrs. Whitney to dinner," she wearing "a dress made entirely of rare lace" topped off by her famous diamond tiara. No sooner had they bought their hundred-acre country place called Grasslands, out beyond Georgetown, than carpenters and decorators swarmed over it to ready it for the first cotillion. Flora Payne Whitney's career was Society. She exulted and excelled in the role of hostess to thousands. Her husband, though he never showed it publicly, detested her dependence on huge assemblages, and there was trouble between them. Flora had written to her son Harry, away at Groton School:

> Monday Mrs. Potter came and I had a big dinner of twenty-four for her that night, and the musical people came in after to rehearse for their Friday night concert. Wednesday I had my reception and there must have been six hundred people here. . . . I had my last big reception Thursday night. Over eight hundred people. When the dignitaries went away at about twelve o'clock . . . the young people danced till two

o'clock. And Harry, I was just the *youngest* there, for I had about three partners for every dance.

The Secretary of the Navy felt himself awash to the scuppers in receptions, dinners, musicales, and dances. After two years of it there was scarcely a senator, Supreme Court justice, congressman, or lowly clerk of legation from Chile or Bavaria who had not been entertained at the Whitneys'. Mrs. Whitney, said *The New York Times*, "reigned supreme; always a leader, she sounded the keynote and society followed. . . . The coming to Washington of Mr. and Mrs. Whitney was coincident with a style of entertaining which . . . had been unknown in this city." One grandiose estimate had it that "at a single party 200 gallons of terrapin soup and eighty cases of champagne disappeared." Respected arbiters of Society agreed that Flora had displaced Mrs. Sen. Don Cameron of Pennsylvania, the most brilliant hostess of the Republican Arthur regime, and had done so with such grace that the Camerons were glad to accept Whitney invitations. Everybody loved Flora Whitney—even John Philip Sousa of the Marine Band, who dedicated his "La Reine de la Mer" to the Navy's first lady. But the Secretary accused her privately of selfishness in sponsoring an endless round of entertainments that were ludicrous in their size and grandeur and destructive of their family happiness and his own peace of mind.

Everybody knew that it was Mrs. Whitney's money that paid the bills. Whitney was scarcely so self-deprecating as to proclaim this, nor were his wife and her family so crude as to publicize it. The Whitneys had been married eighteen years, they had always lived far above his modest income, his family had no fortune, hers had a great one, and people could add two and two.

At forty-six, the Secretary had lost his earlier appearance of dash— even rakishness. In person he was as charming as he was handsome—an inch over six feet, as straight and almost as well muscled as when he had rowed for Yale, his sandy mustache perfectly trimmed, his tailoring impeccable. Though he seldom smiled, he always looked congenial. With his genuine friendliness and his easy conversation, which could range from the analytical to the frivolous, he was nothing short of magnetic. Flora was six months younger, gowned in Paris and sternly corseted, her slimness having yielded to five pregnancies (one child had died). Her prematurely white hair made a striking aureole around features that were strong and vivacious rather than beautiful, and she had what one observer called "good, constant eyes and such marked qualities of candor and human sympathy that one does not wonder that she is so popular and so much loved." She was intellectual, articulate, and driven.

Whitney, though truly hospitable, was swamped with work—Navy work and work of his own that he kept quiet about. During Washington's torrid summers he remained on duty most of the time while Flora fled to cool Newport, Bar Harbor, and Lenox, sponsoring more parties there. The incorruptible old Carl Schurz had protested Whitney's selection for the cabinet, describing him as a carpet knight whose chief qualification was the $20,000 he had given the Cleveland campaign—again his wife's money. *The New York Times,* whose publisher George Jones was then deeply suspicious of Whitney, had called him "a small politician of the malodorous type, a mere dispenser of patronage and distributor of municipal spoils, and as much out of place in Cleveland's reform scheme as a ward bummer would be in a bank directory." Later, *The Times* changed its tune. Henry Adams, the elegiac student of life and of government, recovering from his wife's suicide, was also studying his friend Whitney with astonishment and admiration. Young Spring Rice, out of Eton and Oxford but a mere third secretary, had no R's and introduced himself by saying, "I am Spwing Wice of the Bwitish Legation." He first appraised Whitney as "a New York wirepuller" and "a clever lawyer who has married an enormously rich . . . lady with whose money he is gaining popularity and influence." Then he too relented, writing, "They are both perfectly kind and the reverse of snobbish," and, after describing Whitney as "the most prominent citizen of New York, whose influence with that of one or two others elected Cleveland," observed that their efforts "resulted in the election of the most honest politician. . . ." And once when Spring Rice was ill, he recorded that Whitney "carried me off in his carriage" to rest at Grasslands, with a kindness that "surpasses anything I ever dreamed of."

Flora Whitney had produced a splendid child at the age of forty-two, and the christening of Dorothy was an occasion that she could not resist expanding into the kind of public assemblage Whitney deplored. Seven hundred were invited to the reception at the I Street home. Big as it was, the house was so crowded from entrance hall to ballroom that it was touch and go finding chairs for the elderly. (Among the guests were Sally Davis, daughter of a judge, whom Flora suspected of having designs on Whitney, and Frances Halyar, a legation wife and excellent rider whose gallops with Whitney had also brought vexation to the hostess of Grasslands.) Caudle was offered containing wine and rum—this despite some Missouri women who had recently proclaimed that "the newspapers report that Mrs. Whitney . . . gave a dinner [at which] . . . alcoholic drinks were served," and "Resolved, that the Women's Christian Temperance Union of Missouri express their deep mortification." Flora's rich father, the elderly Senator Henry B. Payne of Ohio, enjoyed a nip for all that, nor did Mrs. Payne mind.

Among the gifts that the Whitney baby would grow to treasure were a silver porringer and plate from the pretty wife of the President, and a parcel from George Bancroft of the eighty-seven years and white beard. Bancroft still sat a horse with grace and had recently finished his history of the United States. The parcel contained two volumes of Milton in a fine parchment edition with a note attached:

> The accompanying parcel will be the property of Miss Dorothy Whitney from the moment that the officiating officer of the church shall say the words, "Dorothy, I baptize thee." —G. Bancroft

Flora's rich bachelor brother, Col. Oliver Hazard Payne, godfather of the child, was in Europe and Whitney himself served as his proxy. The Colonel had long since adopted the Whitneys as a second family, and they were the primary beneficiaries of his generosity—a generosity so extraordinary that it had caused newspaper comment. The three other Whitney children were there—fifteen-year-old Harry Payne from Groton, and thirteen-year-old Pauline Payne and William Payne, eleven, both from private schools in Westchester. The uniformity of the middle name was a mark of the powerful, pervasive, and unchanging family pride of the Paynes. They were, like Dumas's musketeers, all for one and one for all. Some Republicans contended that the elder Payne, a Democrat, was now in the Senate only because his son, the Colonel, had strategically distributed $100,000 in the Ohio legislature that elected him. Also, because Colonel Payne was a partner of John D. Rockefeller, some said the Colonel's brother-in-law Whitney was a tool of the Standard Oil Company. George Frisbie Hoar was referring to Whitney when he asked in the Senate, "Is [Standard Oil] represented in the Cabinet at this moment?" Indeed, rumor invariably hung around Whitney's head like a cloud. Some instinctively disapproved of a man who flew so high on money not his own. It was widely believed that he was buying his way into the White House with his wife's money.

2. Payne Money, Whitney Pride

FLORA WHITNEY was a creature of impulse, prone to inordinate admiration of a new friend until she had measured his spectrum of attractions, then likely to move on without the least unpleasantness to measure a fresh acquaintance. Individuals seldom held her interest for long. It was the excitement of crowds that she loved. She was no longer as obsessed by religion as she had been in what she now called her priest-ridden days, but even then she had been flexible in reconciling her enjoyment of the worldly with the Word. "I should die if Christ were taken away from me," she once wrote to Whitney. But she also wrote him, "After all, it is very grand in the midst of wealth and luxuries to condemn the world that gives it to you . . . but it is so much better to enjoy them with senses you are thankful for. . . ." Even Christ was to be amenable. Yet the attention she had time to give her children—especially the oldest son—was loving in the extreme. Her Thanksgiving letter to young Harry, who was lonely at Groton, was as touching in its reference to the daughter she had lost as it was warm toward the living son:

> I can never be thankful again with my whole heart as long as the frost and the cold lie on the grave of my precious Olive. Then *you* are gone and I have always a great yearning after you, that quarreling of feeling that it is so hard to be separated from you and your love, and yet it is the best thing for you to be where you are.

It is unlikely that she still had any hope of launching her husband toward the White House on a tide of terrapin and champagne. And her father, the senator, who had long pursued the presidency as Galahad sought the Grail, had given it up at last. He was seventy-seven, too old. Few in Washington would have believed it, but Flora—who at first may have had a surreptitious motive—now gave great parties simply because she loved great parties, because she strove conscientiously for recognition as Washington's most brilliant hostess and planned a similar victory in New York, which meant the nation. As for Whitney, if he had ever had presidential ambitions, he had—or thought he had—repudiated them. Ordinarily a considerate husband, he wrote to her as he sweated in the capital and she took the breezes at Lenox:

> . . . you know that it was only when you cried as you did about my decision not to come [to Washington] that I angled for another chance and took it. I had in my hands independence and wealth and by this time would have been a recognized force in New York, and have been under no necessity for the rest of my life. I gave it up! It has been what you

required, you are well adapted for it and have made a success of it, and I can go back again poor (you are rich enough, thank Heaven) and with all the elasticity and good fellowship gone out of me through care and worry over other people's business. . . .

His motivation in wanting to reject the Navy post had been admirable. He was tired of living on Payne money and had begun an enterprise that he felt sure would make him a fortune of his own. He had surrendered to Flora in the belief that he could run the Navy in Washington and quietly guide his New York affairs at the same time, and he was exhausting himself in the effort.

He had been appalled by the condition in which he found the Navy. The few American front-line ships were too weak in firepower to stand off any serious adversary and too slow to run away. Not only European but Japanese and even a few English-built South American warships excelled our own. In the abysmal Grant administration the Navy Department had been clogged with spider webs and dry rot. An effort at reform during the Arthur administration had left the department still leaky and corrupt. Purchases, instead of being concentrated under one head, were scattered through the Navy's eight bureaus. Whitney found, for example, 166 separate purchases of coal by seven naval bureaus and an order for $61,000 worth of canvas in 1883 when there was already a surplus of canvas. The senile wooden *Omaha* escaped the scrap heap where it belonged by being rebuilt for $572,000. The small 910-ton *Mohican* had cost $908,000 for repairs in twelve years—$225,000 more than the cost of a new iron cruiser. The Secretary added in his official report:

> If the $75,000,000 spent since 1868 by our Government had been used to stimulate competition . . . in the production of modern ships of war . . . the activities and agencies at the disposal of the Government would have been by this time entirely adequate to its needs. It has been wasted by Government agencies upon worthless things. The invention of the country has been discouraged. The Hotchkiss gun . . . was the product of American invention, which, when ignored and rejected by Government agencies here, found [in France] its field of development. Ericsson, whose name will always be one of the great ones . . . works now at the age of 83 without encouragement or notice at the great problems of naval warfare, and is receiving more attention and greater encouragement from other governments than from our own.

Whitney's satisfaction in scuttling his Republican predecessors did not impair his argument. The Navy was in decay after two decades of one-party rule. The United States, pretending to world prestige, would be at the mercy of a first- or second-class naval power. It would take smart work to catch up, since the building of a new steel navy required expertise and resources that the country had not seen fit to command. There were no mills yet capable of making armor, nor foundries experienced in producing modern steel guns. Whitney's thrusts drew blood from his predecessor in the cabinet, William E. Chandler. Chandler had given virtually all new shipbuilding to the aged ironmaster John Roach, a personal friend who had backed him with political contributions. Whitney had no sooner taken office than he appointed a naval advisory board to test a new Roach ship, the dispatch boat *Dolphin*, and rejected the vessel pending rectification of its faults. Among its seventy-nine defects were its failure to develop the required 2,300 horsepower and the required fifteen knots per hour, and the fact that its single gun could not be fired straight ahead.

The *Dolphin* case projected Whitney into the hottest controversy of the day. Its rejection also placed under a cloud three cruisers that the Roach yards were building. Roach brought in other "experts" who praised the *Dolphin*, while Chandler charged that Whitney's sole motive was partisanship. In the midst of the uproar, Roach, tottering on the verge of insolvency for two years, went bankrupt. The Republican press, headed by Whitelaw Reid's *New York Tribune*, loosed maledictions on Whitney—particularly painful in the case of *The Tribune* because for all their political differences the Reids and Whitneys were fast friends socially in New York. Whitney, said *The Tribune*, "has deliberately discredited American naval architects" with his "pretentious naval reforms," was making "war upon the shipbuilding industry," and was guilty of "deliberately ruining John Roach."

On the contrary, as time would tell, at long last the Navy had a Secretary who was efficiently reorganizing the department to make it accountable for its errors and working with industry to encourage development of the skills needed to build the formidable steel fleet essential to the nation's safety.

3. The Depravity of the Times

WASHINGTON BANTER had it that if one wished to hear good music, chat with a Russian envoy, enjoy fresh oysters, wild turkey, and old Madeira, hear a dramatic reading, dance all night, or meet the President, the cabinet, and the Congress, all one had to do was to attend the Whitney parties regularly. The Whitneys' liberality with wines was a far cry from the cold-water Hayes administration when "Lemonade Lucy" Hayes's White House ban on liquors affected the whole city and inspired the mournful witticism that "water flowed like champagne." To Henry Adams, on neighboring H Street, the Whitney parties were mass demonstrations rather than opportunities for quiet discourse. He liked Whitney but had abandoned Society after his wife's tragic death. Both Adams and Whitney had New England backgrounds, ties with Boston and Harvard, interest in law and politics. Adams, though crustily independent politically and professing leadership of a remarkable party of one, the Conservative Christian Anarchists, had been delighted by Cleveland's victory over the tainted James Blaine. The late Mrs. Adams had attended the same school in Cambridge (though a few years earlier) as Flora Payne, and both were notable bluestockings. Adams kept the Whitneys under observation as amazing sociopolitical specimens and doubtless heard more about them through his first and dearest friend, John Hay. Hay had married Clara Stone, the daughter of rich Amasa Stone of Cleveland and an old friend of Flora's, so that the Hays and Whitneys traded invitations, undreaming of the event that was to link their families seventeen years later.

The Whitneys had been of assistance in getting President Cleveland married to that raving beauty Frances Folsom, fifteen months after the inauguration. Flora helped Frances shop for the event, the Whitneys stood by Cleveland at the White House wedding, and immediately afterward Whitney asked to see the bride's wedding ring. She surprised him by taking it off and handing it to him. "I was afraid," he said, "that you would have some foolish superstition about taking it off. . . ." She was a year out of Wells College and just back from Europe, especially fresh and charming beside the five-by-four President, twenty-seven years her senior. The band played "Come Where My Love Lies Dreaming," and even Republicans succumbed to the romance of it. It was Flora Whitney who introduced the bride, a Buffalo girl, to a Washington Society she knew not at all.

So Frances Folsom Cleveland replaced the President's maiden sister Rose as chatelaine of the White House. Rose was rather formidable, a teacher and lecturer, author of a study of George Eliot's poetry, more intellectual but less sociable than her famous brother. Never a chatterbox, she had passed time at presidential receptions by silently conjugating Latin verbs. She was a warm friend of the Whitneys except at the time of their great social barbarism.

This occurred when they asked their friend Mrs. James Brown Potter to give a recitation at their benefit for the Training School for Nurses. Mrs. Potter was a determined amateur actress. She also had a repertoire of dramatic readings, complete with gestures, which she had collected in a book. Among them were such safely affecting chestnuts as "Paul Revere's Ride" and "The Charge of the Light Brigade." Among them also was the daring " 'Ostler Joe," a poem by George R. Sims. Whitney leafed through the book with her to make a selection. Was he, perhaps, sabotaging his wife? "Recite ' 'Ostler Joe' and you will make the hit of your life," he told Mrs. Potter.

Among the two hundred guests were the President, Rose Cleveland, and dozens of dignitaries with their wives. Some of them froze as Mrs. Potter uttered the first two lines:

> I stood at eve, as the sun went down, by a grave
>   where a woman lies,
> Who lured men's souls to the shores of sin with
>   the light of her wanton eyes. . . .

Mrs. Potter raised a provocative shoulder. It was the story of the downfall of the lovely wife of 'Ostler Joe, lured by a rake to a life of sin in London:

> Aimie listened and was tempted—she was tempted
>   and she fell,
> As the angels fell from heaven to the blackest
>   depths of hell,
> She was promised wealth and splendor, and a life
>   of guilty sloth,
> Yellow gold for child and husband [slow and tragic here]
>   —and the woman left them both.

Mrs. Potter was too intent on her interpretation to notice that some of the audience were more gripped by shock than by Aimie's tragedy. "Quick from lord to lord she flitted," she declaimed, "Higher still each prize she won. / Next she trod the stage half naked, / And she dragged a temple down." Although the story ended on a moral note with the siren's death, Mrs. Potter found that she had broken up the party. As she described it later:

Miss Cleveland rose from her chair. . . . she asked for her carriage, saying to Mrs. Whitney, as I and all present heard: "I have never been so shocked in my life." . . . everyone left the drawing room, followed her out in silence, and went home. Mr. Whitney said nothing, except that he was going to bed, and disappeared.

The Secretary in this instance was as timorous as the Navy he had inherited. Not even the friendly *Times* could forgive Mrs. Potter's grossness:

Her reading of Swinburne's [sic] " 'Ostler Joe" raised universal condemnation about the town and distressed and deeply embarrassed every man and woman in the chosen audience that had to listen to these indecent verses. . . . As an instance of the depravity of the times, it may be told that since that unfortunate night the libraries and bookstores have been besieged by people anxious to read the verses again. . . .

Headlines about the indecency easily overshadowed newspaper attention to the dispute between the United States and Canada over the Atlantic fisheries. But Joseph Pulitzer's Democratic *New York World*, which had praised Whitney's regeneration of the Navy, called it a "nine days' wonder and gossip." *The World* printed the whole poem without a blush under the subhead: "It Has Frequently Been Given in Public in New York Without Especial Comment—Was the Washington Audience Over Prudish?" Even Rose Cleveland was forgiving—the President and his lady had never taken it too seriously—as shown by a later Society note:

One of the most magnificent dinners ever served in Washington was that given by Secretary and Mrs. Whitney tonight for the President and Mrs. Cleveland. The table of polished mahogany was laid for 26 guests. . . . The claret pitchers were gold mounted, and the spoons and dessert knives were gold. The dinner cards were gilt-edged and bore the Whitney monogram. . . . There were four wines served. . . . Mrs. Whitney received her guests in a Worth gown of ivory satin. . . . There was a great diamond star at her throat and diamonds in her ears. Mrs. Cleveland appeared for the first time with her neck and arms uncovered. . . .

4. Blue Letters Are Dangerous

As SECRETARY of the Navy, Whitney commanded senior officers who with few exceptions had served in the Civil War he had avoided. It is not unlikely that he felt chagrin. Like any convert, he developed an esprit de corps zealous enough even for old salts like Admiral Porter. He inspired a change in the design of naval uniforms that brought new smartness to both enlisted men and officers. He labored to master technicalities Secretaries traditionally left to their specialists. He made an intensive study of the relative merits of the compound and the triple-expansion naval engines, reaching the conclusion that the latter more than justified its additional cost by its greater economy of operation. He started a veritable crusade to encourage American manufacturers—among them Andrew Carnegie—to make armor plate and gun forgings needed by the Navy. The pacifist Carnegie replied, "Compliments to my friend the Sec'y of the Navy who I am sorry to see trying to rob his country of one of its chief glories," and underlined a sentence in a page he enclosed from his *Triumphant Democracy*: "It is one of the chief glories of the Republic that she spends her money for better ends and has nothing worthy to rank as a ship of war." But Carnegie thought hard about the business he would lose, decided that armor plate was purely defensive after all, and wrote to Whitney later, "You need not be afraid that you will have to go abroad for armor plate. I am now fully satisfied that the mill we are building will roll the heaviest size you require. . . ."

A trifle headstrong, Whitney was aroused enough over Canadian arrests of American fishermen to urge a strong hand and use of the fleet in resolving the fisheries quarrel. When the Panamanian revolutionist Pedro Prestan seized several Americans in Colón, burned the town to the ground, and threatened to capture the Pacific Mail steamer also named *Colón*, Whitney put an edge to his message to the commander of the United States gunboat *Galena* in the harbor:

> You [are] ordered . . . to protect American interests and the lives and property of American citizens. All that is implied in these words is expected to be done by you to the extent of the force under your command. . . .

He also ordered Rear Adm. James Jouett, who was at New Orleans with the *Tennessee* and the *Swatara*, to head for Colón with a battalion of Marines. But by the time Jouett arrived there, Whitney's orders were cooler, ending, "You have no part to perform in the [local] political or social disorder . . . and it will be your duty to see that no irritation or unfriendliness shall arise from your presence on the Isthmus."

Whitney worked amicably with Republican Senator Eugene Hale of

Maine, chairman of the Senate Committee on Naval Affairs, and with Democratic Chairman Hilary A. Herbert of the House Committee on Naval Affairs, getting appropriations then regarded as enormous. He provoked Republican ire when he dared to buy British plans for a speedy steel ship similar to one built in Britain for the Japanese navy. He gave contracts to the Cramp shipyard, an organization formerly frozen out of naval work by Roach. With an eye to the future, he urged that a group of naval apprentices be admitted to the Naval Academy to compete with cadets for commissioning, and he arranged for two American cadets to study at the Royal Naval College at Greenwich. A firm believer in the political use of patronage, he hired as many Democrats as possible and even had the naval cadet son of that loyal Democratic warhorse Manton Marble transferred to the new U.S.S. *Boston,* just what he wanted. He could relax like a schoolboy during an otherwise drab cabinet meeting by passing notes back and forth with Lucius Quintus Cincinnatus Lamar, the sixty-one-year-old former Confederate officer who was now Secretary of the Interior. Whitney opened by writing, "You are looking well today." Lamar responded that what made him look so well was his meeting, after some decades, with an old sweetheart, now a widow.

> WHITNEY: Does the romance of the recollection remain after seeing her?
> LAMAR: In a degree of intensity that terrifies me.
> WHITNEY: Go slow. Let it have time. . . . Don't decide too quickly.
> LAMAR. No decision at all. An increased conviction that it would be unwise. . . . I could not introduce her to Mrs. Whitney, or Mrs. Endicott, or any of our ladies without a misgiving that they would fail to see her in her true value. And yet to my surprise, she has all the time taken a deep, anxious, and almost tremulous interest and pride in every incident of my career. She has an old letter written by me forty-one years ago. It is on blue paper. . . .
> WHITNEY: Alas! You have then talked of these old times and have been taken . . . back to that lovely time that has gone. *Beware! It has gone.* Those little blue letters are dangerous. . . . Your imagination is at work now. . . .

While Flora was at cool Bar Harbor, Whitney invited Lamar to stay overnight at Grasslands—better at any rate than the steaming city—and at breakfast read aloud to him "Marjorie Daw," the story of a ladylove even more imaginary than Lamar's.

Whitney's subtleties eluded the blunt and occasionally pigheaded President. As Henry Watterson noted of Cleveland, "Assuredly no one of his predecessors had entered the White House so wholly ignorant of public men and national affairs"; and, "Cleveland confessed himself to have had no social training, and he literally knew nobody." He now took instruction from William Whitney to remedy the first defect, and from Flora Whitney for the second. If the President could not always agree with William, he did later speak admiringly of him:

> Mr. Whitney had more calm, forceful efficiency than any man I ever knew. In work that interested him he actually seemed to court difficulties and to find pleasure and exhilaration in overcoming them. His conquest over the obstacles he encountered in undertaking to build up our navy afforded him greater delight than the contemplation of the great results he achieved. . . . his mental poise was so complete that neither passion nor irritation could lead it astray.

Nevertheless, the Whitney entertainments were so frequent and extravagant that the President began gradually to limit his own and his wife's participation in them because they seemed undemocratic and politically unwise. Whitney warned Flora not to besiege them with invitations:

> Mr. Cleveland does not consider the reputation we have for lavish hospitality and as rich people desirable for them as associates in the public eye. . . . I hope you will be quiet at Bar Harbor. . . . I do not wish to see anything in the newspapers.

Whitney enjoyed poker with friends, including the President, who once wrote to him, "Can't you spend the evening here? I think I've got about ten dollars that I feel uncomfortable about." Whitney's own poker group, known as the Road Gang, met irregularly. On one of these occasions, Watterson, that beau ideal of Democratic editors, had a table with Sen. Don Cameron, Speaker of the House John G. Carlisle, and the President. Carlisle had no card sense. On one deal Cleveland picked up a pat full house and Watterson a pat flush. Neither drew a card, of course, while Cameron drew one card and Carlisle four. *Four.* The betting was lively, with raising and counterraising, Carlisle exciting the pity of his companions because he lacked the judgment to get out. He stayed to the showdown. He then laid down four kings.

"Take the money, Carlisle . . . ," Cleveland exclaimed. "If ever I am President again you shall be Secretary of the Treasury." (Cleveland was President again and Carlisle did become Secretary of the Treasury.)

5. Are His Hands Clean?

WHITNEY WAS driving hard, losing sleep, conducting two difficult enterprises. As if his Washington duties were not enough, he often boarded a train to New York where he was mounting an extraordinary effort to make a street railway fortune of his own. He was the most politic of men, and it was not illegal but impolitic for a cabinet member under such sharp Republican scrutiny to promote a private undertaking of this magnitude. He pushed his traction project in a manner that had an appearance of secrecy. The hostile *New York Tribune* put a watch on him and embarrassed him:

> The Secretary of the Navy has spent much more time in this city recently than the general public is aware of, but he has not been occupied with naval business. Mr. Whitney has been intensely interested in the . . . scheme to obtain control of the Broadway and Seventh Avenue Railroad. . . . Mr. Whitney was in town a week ago yesterday, although few New-Yorkers discovered it. He did not proclaim his presence on the house-tops. But the Philadelphia men . . . spent hours in consultation with the Secretary of the Navy in his house at 57th Street and Fifth Avenue. Mr. Whitney returned to Washington but was soon back here again and quiet conferences . . . have been going on day after day in the Whitney mansion.

The Times was also again suspicious, commenting on its front page that Whitney might be "playing a deep game" and that he "passed a good deal of his time in this city incognito last week, consulting with his Philadelphia and New York friends."

There was a reason for the papers to look with distrust on what might otherwise appear the commendable business of promoting an efficient street railway system. An intriguer accurately named Jacob Sharp had earlier promised to do the same thing. He had offered $20,000 to each of New York's twenty-two aldermen who would approve his request for a 999-year transit franchise on Broadway. These officials met under the chairmanship of Alderman Henry W. Jaehne, a dapper dresser believed to be in the real estate business. One of Sharp's competitors offered slightly more, but his tender was partly in stock and the vote went to Sharp and spot cash by twenty to two, the latter pair refusing any and all bribes. The truth came out when the police discovered in a separate investigation that Jaehne was not a realtor but a large-scale fence who paid low prices to the underworld for stolen goods and sold them at a large profit. Caught with stolen valuables, Jaehne also confessed the wholesale bribery of the aldermen. Six of the aldermen took the first train to Montreal, where they read of their indictment and the arrest of their colleagues. The grim humor mixed with outrage over the scandal was enhanced by the suggestive name of one of the indicted aldermen: Fullgraff. One of Harrigan and Hart's popular comedies touched on the issue, showing several aldermen asleep in the Mulligan living room after a heavy Irish stew:

> CORDELIA MULLIGAN: Whatever will I do? The aldermen are all sound asleep.
> DAN MULLIGAN: Lave them be. While they sleep, the city's safe.

The Boodle Aldermen, as they were called, were not yet tried when a Philadelphia syndicate headed by Peter A. B. Widener bought a controlling interest in Sharp's Broadway and Seventh Avenue line. It was now so evident that corrupt profits could be made at the city's expense that the Philadelphians fell under immediate suspicion of working hand in glove with Sharp. The Navy Secretary's quiet meetings with them did not look well. For at least two years Whitney had tried to gain a foothold in New York transit. Was he now allied with the Philadelphians in a new effort to take the city for what cynics called a streetcar ride?

The most searching inquiry was made by *The New York World*, owned by Whitney's eccentric friend and fellow Democrat, Joseph Pulitzer. *The World* charged that the Philadelphia syndicate had already watered the stock so that on paper they had gained $6,000,000, "and for which they have paid the city not a single cent. . . . Is this not a gross swindle on the people of New York?" A *World* man interviewed Widener in Philadelphia. An affable, articulate man, Widener denied stock watering, or working with Sharp. The whole purpose of his group was to unify and improve New York's patchwork horse-car system. "We buy 2,000 kegs of horseshoes at one time," he said, pointing out the economy of large operations. "We intend putting this road and all other roads for which we can obtain privilege and consent, into a corporation to which New York capital . . . will be invited."

"What is the fact about Mr. Whitney?" he was asked.

"Well, I have an idea that Mr. Whitney is strong enough to take care of himself. I am no apologist for the Secretary. He needs none. I know his position and it is impregnable. He can bear the most rigid scrutiny. . . . It would be an absurdity for me to undertake the defense of a man who needs no defense in any place, and particularly in the city of his birth and home."

He was in error there, for Whitney was not born in New York. In any case, days had passed without explanation from Whitney himself. The " 'Ostler Joe" uproar occurred at the same time, leaving him simultaneously exposed to suspicions of depravity in both his taste in poetry and his intentions with street railways. *The World*, defending him in the poetic sphere, said it was time that he spoke up in the other matter.

> By the way, the friends of Secretary Whitney are becoming a little restless, and regret that he does not at once and effectually clear up and sweep away the persistent and, we are sure, malicious reports that connect him with the Philadelphia speculation. We believe his hands are entirely clean. But would it not be better for him to hold them up promptly before the eyes of the people in order that all may know exactly how clean they are?

Two days later, Whitney's reply was published in *The World* and all other New York newspapers. Through it ran the note of asperity one might expect of an honest man whose motives are questioned. In it he disclosed that he was a member of a group that had sought and failed to get the franchise Sharp had won. In doing so, he reminded his readers that he and his partners had merely "availed [ourselves] of the general street railroad law of 1884" and suggested that they might have been given some credit for their opposition to Sharp. When the Philadelphia men came on the scene, he and his colleagues discovered that the Philadelphians, unlike Sharp, proposed a sound and forward-looking street railway unification that would permit transfer from line to line and was entirely "in the public interest." Whitney so far had not invested in the Philadelphians' enterprise, though he viewed it approvingly and might yet do so:

> That states my exact relation to it. What effect this investigation may have upon it, and whether I shall ever join it, are as open questions for me as for any one else.
> If my connection with the transactions I have mentioned is in any respect open to just criticism I am not aware of it.

It was such an effective letter that it quieted a suspicion that would in time prove all too justified.

6. *Dependently Wealthy*

BOTH WHITNEY and Flora were anxious that Cleveland should be re-elected in 1888. Flora was delighted with Washington Society, offering as it did friendship with the most powerful people in the country as well as the sophisticated folk in the foreign legations, without in the least interfering with her freedom to visit New York, Newport, or Lenox whenever she cared to. She wanted another four years of it. "You are doing too much," her father warned her, "and you will kill yourself," but she wrote gaily to her son Harry that she was "especially *hard-of-*killing." Whitney wanted no more of it. But both hoped that President and Mrs. Cleveland could escape the brutal press treatment that Cleveland had received in the 1884 campaign.

Republicans then had seized on his courageous refusal to deny that he once might have fathered an illegitimate child by an earlier attachment to the unchaste Maria Halpin. *The New York Sun* had speculated about Cleveland as a "coarse debauchee who might bring his harlots to Washington and hire lodgings for them convenient to the White House." His rather gross appearance was easy for cartoonists to caricature spitefully. Some Republicans who could not forget that he was the first Democratic President since a civil war fought largely against Southern Democrats enjoyed implying that Democrats were still likely to be traitors. Whitney was a little peremptory in writing to Flora in the summer of 1887, when she was at Bar Harbor with the children, asking her to avoid publicity, to refrain from excessive correspondence with Mrs. Cleveland, and "Do keep your dignity." She replied immediately:

> As you kept your own counsel so closely, I knew nothing about your relations with the President. Mine with Mrs. Cleveland are very friendly, and we write to each other continually. If your appearance in the papers were always as complimentary as mine are, I don't think much damage would be done. I hate ostentation and waste and am never guilty of either in this dear little place.

Some of the tensions between them were attributable to the air of independence implicit in this letter. She lacked the deference expected of wives in the 1880s, and certainly her autonomy was due in large part to her freedom from the usual wifely dependence on the husband's income. While Flora was capable of great subtlety, she seemed at times to lack an appreciation of the tender points of a husband's pride—a weakness that may have caused him to exaggerate other relatively minor complaints he had. For example, she had gained weight, and it irked him that she—so meticulous in company—could at times appear before him in an untidy negligee. He loved to ride and sometimes had to ride alone because she was unskilled with horses and unenthusiastic about riding. He gave her sound instructions about their horses at Lenox:

> Before you ride "Cafe au Lait" have him given six or seven miles by some one else, then use the curb on him. He is indeed a brute but he needs work daily. Please give instructions to have him ridden daily by one of the men. Coachman should do it. Never mind the children, you try "Lily Rose" and if you like her, keep her yourself, it is of more importance that you should ride than they should. . . .

Of late he had suffered terrible headaches. He would scarcely have been human had he not reflected that Flora, who had all but forced him to take the Navy post he had not wanted, ought in all justice to defer to his political judgments—especially those about the President and his wife. Furthermore, it was difficult for one enduring the capital's humidity to accept dicta uttered in Bar Harbor or Lenox breezes. There was in those days no Undersecretary of the Navy, no Assistant Secretary—only Secretary Whitney. He often worked unceasingly at his desk until seven, and during the sultry season it was his habit to rise early at Grasslands to clear away deskwork before the heat struck. Now, feeling worse than ever, he begged off accompanying the President to the Philadelphia Centennial and collapsed in October. His symptoms, in addition to the severe headaches, included unsteadiness of the legs and general debilitation, frightening because he had always been strong as an ox.

He returned to his New York home and put himself in the care of his doctor and his brother-in-law, Col. Oliver Payne. Oliver, two years older than Whitney, had recently resigned as treasurer of the Standard Oil Company but remained a large stockholder. He was militarily erect, decisive, and to outsiders so formal and possessed of such seeming hauteur that Henry Flagler, another Rockefeller partner, described him as "kin to God." But he epitomized the Payne family solidarity. He loved his sister Flora with an affection so tender that some—perhaps unfairly—were later to question its normality, and his generosity toward her and her entire family for the next seven years was to become legendary. He had bought a five-towered residence at Fifth Avenue and 57th Street from Mrs. Frederick W. Stevens—estimates of the price varied from $500,000 to $800,000—and given it to Flora. (Mrs. Stevens had divorced her husband to marry the fourth Duke de Dino, of Talleyrand-Perigord, who had himself divorced his first American wife, the former Elizabeth Curtis of New York, to marry Mrs. Stevens.) The house was one of the avenue's showplaces, a combination of Queen Anne and Romanesque modes, of red brick and stone trim. Colonel Payne was also said to have given Flora a million dollars to live up to such a place as a Payne was expected to do. Even though the sum was probably much less than that, it was added to gifts he had made upon the birth of each Whitney child—added also to generous gifts from Flora's father.

But Whitney, unlike his wife, had not become independently wealthy. If he could be called wealthy at all, he was dependently wealthy. The extent to which he had permitted Flora, and himself, to become steady beneficiaries of the Payne largess might argue some flaw of character. On the other hand, it was in his favor that he was working hard to establish his own fortune and that he would have rejected the secretaryship for this reason except for Flora. As for the Colonel, he seemed to lack the perception to realize that the prodigality of his bounty toward his sister might create difficulties for his sister's husband. And above all, was it not true that Flora—in her seeming willingness to let her husband continue as a Payne pensioner to fulfill her own social ambitions—should also have been aware of the destructive effect of that dependence on Whitney's pride?

Oliver had created a *ménage à trois* pleasing to him and Flora. He had his own grand apartment on the second floor of the Fifth Avenue house, hung with his paintings. Even if Whitney had been peculiarly insensitive, which he was not, there must have been some uncomfortable realization that the house was more Oliver's—and Flora's—than his own. None of the three seem as yet to have mentioned any possible tension over this situation, much less that it might have something to do with Whitney's present illness. Now, however, Oliver was the dear friend, staying with Whitney and trying to coax him back to health. Whitney wrote to Flora, who was still at Lenox:

> I am here in N.Y. . . . . I struck a headache the day I left Lenox. . . . It laid me on my beam ends so to speak and I finally yielded to the Col.'s entreaties and came back here to consult the Oracle—
> [Dr.] Loomis has been working at me for three days and I am better, but I am not allowed (nor do I wish) to go out—nor do anything— Meanwhile precious moments fly. . . . It is a miserable good for nothing person I am— You would utterly despise me if you were here to see. . . .

He also wrote to the President, getting a kind reply: ". . . I enjoin upon you absolute freedom from any anxiety concerning your official duties and assure you that all will go well until your return." But two weeks later, when he wrote Cleveland again, he was so discouraged as to contemplate resigning:

I cannot tell you what has happened to me. I have always been strong—have worked easily and without care—lighthearted. . . . I have never in my life worried over anything—but all the same I am of no sort of use and I am not improving at present. . . .

Attached as I am to you and to the work you set me to do . . . I fear my only chance for health will come in relief from the thought of the duties I am neglecting. In the night I wake and think of them. . . . The iron clads and the harbor defence boats are delayed by my condition. . . . It would be vain for me to attempt to express the regret, and astonishment with which I write these words. . . . A week or two and I shall speak positively one way or the other.

Cleveland, who wrote his letters laboriously by hand, replied warmly: "You know so well how much aid and comfort you have been to me, and how much I appreciate and value your usefulness and association . . . that I am sure you will understand me as well as if you looked into my heart, when I ask you to consider first and to the exclusion of other things, your health and safety. . . ."

Flora came down to New York to help care for Whitney. Rumors flew. "William C. Whitney . . . is seriously ill," said *The Times*. Commodore D. B. Harmony, who had taken his place as Acting Secretary, said Whitney's trouble was simple overwork: ". . . he totally disregards his health and is now paying the penalty." There was talk that he had "fallen victim to Potomac malaria," even that "he has completely 'lost his head.'" ". . . his house [is] the center of the Administration social circle. . . . Business affairs in New York have also claimed attention, and persons familiar . . . are aware that the Secretary has made the journey to New York pretty regularly every Saturday to return on the following Monday or Tuesday." A report that he would resign was denied by the President's secretary, Daniel S. Lamont. On November 19, Flora returned to Washington and denied it herself. "He was simply overworked," she said. "He had nervous prostration. . . . He was at Bar Harbor only about a week, and a short time at Lenox. . . . Now the rest he should have taken there is forced on him."

Wherever Flora might be, there also would be parties whether Whitney was there or not. On November 25 her guest of honor at dinner on

I Street was Mrs. Stratford Dugdale, a niece of Macaulay and a friend of Spring Rice, the widowed Secretary of State Bayard taking the head of the table for the absent Whitney. On December 9, Whitney was back in his role as perfect host, looking fit, when Flora gave a dinner to honor Joseph Chamberlain, the wealthy Birmingham screw manufacturer who had been a member of Gladstone's cabinet. Chamberlain, in America to try to settle the endless fisheries controversy, wore an orchid on his lapel and a monocle on a ribbon. A widower, he had fallen in love with the daughter of Secretary of War William C. Endicott, Whitney's colleague from Massachusetts. Because of the fear that it would cost Cleveland the Irish vote, however, Chamberlain's engagement to Miss Endicott, whom he later married, was to be kept secret until after the 1888 election. Secretary and Mrs. Endicott were guests, and the British Minister, Sir Lionel Sackville West, soon to commit the international faux pas that was to send him packing home. Whitney as host had to conceal the annoyance he felt about the fisheries question and especially at Secretary Bayard, whose policy he thought namby-pamby and pro-British. By dint of herculean effort and the help of Commodore Harmony, he had finished his annual report on the Navy Department—again an able and literate accounting. In it, among many other things, he expressed satisfaction in the development of three American manufactories "necessary to the construction of armament of a modern war vessel, that of steel forgings for heavy guns, that of arms for iron-clad, and that of machine and rapid-fire guns."

With Flora's season in full swing, the Secretary often got home from his office and instructed his valet to lay out his evening clothes while he took a half-hour nap to ready himself for the night's work. So reluctant was Flora to miss an event—to fail of attendance at a gathering where who knew what fascinating things might happen—that it was a special torment when two parties of importance were held the same evening. She did her best to even the score by her frequent doubleheader evenings when she and Whitney left a dinner party to go on to a dance. When she gave her dinner that winter for the President, the cabinet members and their wives, the guests had no sooner departed than the Whitneys hurried off to a cotillion at the Levi Z. Leiters'.

7. "Gassing" with Women

ON APRIL 27, 1888, Senator Payne was one of five hundred guests at the Cramp yards in Chester, Pennsylvania, to see the gunboat *Yorktown* and the cruiser *Vesuvius* slide down the ways while Secretary Whitney looked on with some pride. These two ships had cost him great effort and anxiety, as they all did. They had cost him consultations, arguments, dinners, dances, headaches. They were soon to be followed by the *Baltimore, Charlestown,* and *Petrel,* and the year after by the *San Francisco, Philadelphia, Newark, Concord, Bennington,* and *Cushing.* Among others under construction for which he was responsible were the battleships *Texas* and *Maine,* the latter to gain sinister fame ten years later. Whitney was to spend $80,000,000 in adding 93,951 tons to the fleet—three times what any other Secretary had spent in a four-year term. Through his efforts the Navy could go to American factories for everything needed in weaponry, though Carnegie had been slow with his new plant and it was still necessary to get armor plate abroad. To Whitney must go credit for pioneering the revolution in American naval power.

But the summer came on blistering. He grew sick of Washington and had time only for a few days at Lenox, where Flora was established in comfort, though she was feeling no better than he. He had left her there after an argument over the college young Harry was to attend, Flora favoring Yale and Whitney, disillusioned with his old alma mater, preferring Harvard.

This was the time Flora picked to launch a quarrel that gained what was for them a savage momentum. Underneath the Flora of warm affection and brilliant smile was still the creature of moods, sudden tempers, suspicions. Such was her desire not to miss anything of interest that she had been incensed because William did not arrange to accompany the President's party on a trip west: "It is nothing to you that I wanted to go. 'You did not want to go!' That expresses the situation consistently with all that has gone before and that which is to come." She was not certain that it was Navy busy-ness that kept him in Washington. There was no denying that he was a dashing figure, and she censured him because on his visit to Lenox he had left her when she was indisposed and gone driving with Fanny Woolsey. He replied:

I am not going to apologize. . . . that I am not at liberty to drop a note to a lady . . . to ask her to drive with me, and take her without accountability, while it amuses me seems ridiculous. The very sensation of being watched is quite enough to take away the pleasure. . . . I may talk with a lady a few times—then it is someone else. I could certainly never be charged with an intrigue. . . . No one has been more free from such things than I am. Your happiness is what I most care for, and whatever sacrifice of inclination it calls for, will be forthcoming. But a man who works as quietly as I do mentally and represses so much needs to be let

alone to work his salvation out in his own way. Bottle him, tie him to the
house post, and one can't tell what may happen.

Although he went on to lighter things and ended the letter "Your
Lover," she was furious at his statement that it amused him to "gas"
with women, as he put it, and his unguarded suggestion that she subtracted rather than added to his pleasure. Her pregnancy with Dorothy
had been a delicate one, and she felt that he had not been sufficiently
solicitous. She raked back almost ten years in her memory to the time
when she thought that he was "gassing" a trifle too intimately with Mrs.
Hurlbert, the pretty wife of the then editor of *The New York World*, and
several women since then. She forgot that her school teacher back in
Cleveland had once praised her writing but warned her of her gift for
satire that could cut and stab. Twice in her long, long letter she paid
him compliments lost under an avalanche of scorn:

> I should think it almost funny, if it wasn't quite too pathetic, your con-
> fession of martyrdom. . . . . I really was simple enough to think that we
> had been quite happy and content with each other, and though now I
> think of it, you did have a little of the manner of the saint, and the loving
> and petting were mostly on my side. I enjoyed it, knowing you were a
> little out of health and sometimes depressed with your work and with pol-
> itics, and then I thought there was no one at the moment for you to "gas"
> with, as the list of women you enjoy that amusement with is not large. I
> imagined you were virtue sitting on the footstool at Sally Davis's divan
> amongst the other fools, and had possibly a little reaction after the inten-
> sity of the Reutershields [sic] affair. I am born a little too honest and loyal
> to understand and admire such women, and then too, one woman sees
> through another so. The thin tricks and allurements and purrs. They
> have all the same stock in trade, unappreciated lives and unloving hus-
> bands, bringing in what Wagner calls the "sympathetic motive."
> . . . . do you know I think your head was just a little turned in Wash-
> ington. Like a girl on her first season out. You had too much amuse-
> ment. There was Sally Davis on her divan dependent upon you for ad-
> vice and consultation. There was the Halyar for you to ride across
> country with and to flatter. There was the Reutershields to discuss you
> with her tears and to hold your hand while you guided her through the
> early stages of her pregnancy—what *interesting* conversations that must
> have led to. I know you think that you can control yourself and stop short
> of the danger line, but I think you went too far with Mme. Reutershields.
> I know that at a time when men are apt to be tender to their wives I was
> left most cruelly alone. You could sit for hours wiping away her tears
> (Mme. R.), but to me you could say "Well I don't suppose you would tell
> me what is the matter and I don't know as I care to know."

Whitney was not the only one who felt martyrdom. She went on:

I made up my mind—not for her sake but because I thought you were burdened with work—that I would ask nothing, so through all those long waiting days I took all those drives alone, all those weary days in bed expecting that longest hour, from five to six. I would have valued it more than those other women. My little excitement when I could first sit up to dinner . . . and the second night you stayed at Sally Davis's. . . . The months of neglect after when you never noticed me, but to find some fault with my dress, and then a positive insult to me. . . . Don't you think you carried your love of "gas" with a woman a little too far that time? . . . I seem to wonder if the reason you don't stay here is because I stop your "gas-ing" with Fanny Woolsey. . . .

The next day, obviously repenting and worried over his reaction, she wrote to him a short letter entirely pleasant and complimentary, urging him to come to Lenox the following Sunday. The Van Alen coaching party would be there for dinner, as would Elisabeth Marbury and Elsie de Wolfe: ". . . we certainly would all play: 'here comes the Chief'." The day after that, another pleasant letter, and next day still another. Whitney noted that a few of the "gas" episodes were five or more years old and that she had been brooding over them. He had received all three letters before he replied with one fully three thousand words long. He suggested that he and Flora were to some degree incompatible, since she had wept until he had agreed to come to Washington, and because she pursued a social career so shallow in its emphasis on numbers that he was forced to turn to individuals for comfort:

It is quite unfortunate for two people to be married who do not enjoy the same things. It is no reproach to them that they differ, they cannot avoid it—they never should have been put together. . . . And lest I should say something as I write that should seem hard, I will say now . . . what I have said to others many times in the last year—that you are . . . the finest woman I have ever met—but it is a fact, that we differ radically as to what we enjoy. . . . The quiet peaceful home which is the only atmosphere in which a man who works with his mind can find the necessary rest and relief, is not consistent with a woman's career—and no two people with careers ever ought to marry. I look back on what I started to be with a strange kind of lost feeling now, as though I had missed my way, and when one of the two is incapable of deferring to the wishes of the other, and the habit has grown into their daily life, it is shocking when something is struck that one really cares for, and in an unguarded moment breaks out. . . .

I have sometimes thought that we were growing together and being more happy, but it is simply that I have grown a little more acquiescent.

The greatest testimonial I have made to you of that fact was coming here [to Washington, where she had been socially successful and he had helped her to that success]. . . . You won't be able to say to me as you did once when I was struggling night and day for success, that I had brought you from position and influence to where you had none. I have given you a greater opportunity than you had at home and my debt is discharged. . . .

. . . You never care for anyone very long, and therefore, we never have a circle of friends that we enjoy, and that left you your time to entertain the rabble and pursue your career. . . . You have shaped our living at last so as to exclude everything that would really add to my enjoyment, and I am down fairly and squarely to a machine; work all day, and entertain crowds. . . . Isn't it ludicrous—our life? Who do we care for? Who have we helped to bear their burdens better by our affection and sympathy? Whose inner life have we learned to know and help? And how else shall we go down life's walks with the love and sympathy of others?

He noted that people often came to him for advice—Miss Endicott had in the matter of Joseph Chamberlain and the Irish vote; Secretary Endicott himself had come to him. Others asked him for guidance because he did his best to give them "good hard sound sense," whereas Flora scoffed at this and called it "holding hands." He seemed to concede getting in a trifle over his head with the Swedish lady:

I never did anything to justify her in her nonsense—she was a fool—I never "held her hand," "wiped her eyes," nor made love to her (for that is what you mean by such expressions). . . . You liked [the Reuterskiolds] as well as I did for a long time. . . .

It is a fine picture of me "sitting on a foot stool at Sally Davis's divan amongst other fools." . . . You are as much above her as one woman can be above another, but that isn't the reason you dislike her. It is because you thought I liked her, and I did. She was as good-hearted and bright as anyone could be, and instead of fools, she had the bright people around her. . . . I stopped because I saw myself distrusted. . . . and in return I get this deluge of insinuations, sarcasm and abuse. . . . Couldn't I easily adopt the habits of other suspected and distrusted men and make appointments on the sly . . . ? . . . it is in your mind that I [am] a dishonorable man. . . .

I fear I have not much patience with your tale of neglect, considering that there was never a woman who had less of it. . . . I am quite aware that my nerves are in danger of breaking up. At times I cannot restrain myself from intense passion on different things. If I can only get out of this life [in Washington], I shall rejoice at the deliverance, and I shall hope that in some other atmosphere we may cultivate mutual sources of enjoyment until we get a basis upon which to go down the slope together happily. Yours, W. C. W.

He mailed the letter, then regretted it as Flora had regretted hers, and telegraphed her next morning: "I WISH YOU WOULD RETURN TO ME WITHOUT READING LETTER MAILED BY ME LAST NIGHT." Three days later he telegraphed her again: "HAVE YOU DONE AS I REQUESTED ABOUT LETTER. . . . IT IS OUR ANNIVERSARY."

It was indeed their nineteenth. He always marked the date gallantly with flowers. But it was asking too much of any woman, much less one as spirited as Flora, to return unopened such a fat letter sure to contain fascinating if frightening intimacies. One must believe it likely that Flora tore open the letter all the more swiftly after receiving that telegraphed appeal to return it sealed. Their correspondence on the matter either ended there or the remainder has been lost or destroyed. They did love each other in their fashion, and the question remained whether their love could survive the new storms that were sure to break.

8. It's All Up

EVEN AS the Whitneys skirmished, the journalistic guns were being unlimbered for the presidential campaign. One of the greatest Democratic assets was Frances Folsom Cleveland, who had enveloped the homely President in an aura of romance that considerably enhanced his popularity and who had undertaken her new role with a wisdom and tact winning universal praise. She was indeed such a national favorite that less scrupulous Republicans saw how she could be transformed into a Democratic liability.

Rumors began to circulate that the President was drinking heavily, that he was surly and violent, that he beat his wife, that his treatment was so insupportable that she fled the White House and took refuge with the Whitneys. There were variations on the theme of brutality, some woven around actual events. One story had it that Henry Watterson had taken Mrs. Cleveland to Albaugh's Opera House in Washington to see Madame Helena Modjeska portray Lady Macbeth, and that when he escorted her back to the White House the President struck her drunkenly and forbade Watterson ever to return. Watterson had actually taken her to the play, along with Speaker and Mrs. Carlisle. But when they returned, Watterson affirmed, "supper was awaiting us, the President amused and pleased when told of the agreeable [evening]."

Scandalous tidbits about the presidential household were such proven circulation-getters that even Democratic papers could not resist printing them. "The fact is that, as anyone can see," Spring Rice wrote, "[the Clevelands] are a most devoted couple. . . . Mrs. Fairchild, the most domestic of Cabinet ladies [Charles S. Fairchild of New York City was Secretary of the Treasury and a close Whitney friend], was accused in *The World* of having telegraphed Conkling to institute proceedings for divorce. The next step will be Whitney, etc., etc."

The next step *was* Whitney, but this time the work of Democrats. That odd political specimen Gov. David B. Hill of New York had so powerful a yearning for the presidency that he was not above conniving at or winking at a crude attack on the incumbent, supposedly his friend and fellow party member. At the Democratic National Convention in St. Louis in June, a scurrilous eighteen-page pamphlet was distributed with the title "Cleveland . . . and W. C. Whitney—A Pair of Thieves—How They Run the Administration and Knife the Governor of the Empire State." It glorified Hill and his lately deceased ally, Tammany boss John Kelly, and accused Whitney of "hounding" Kelly "in the last hours of his protracted fatal illness." It repeatedly referred to Cleveland as "the Beast of Buffalo," a man of unspeakable orgies. It was of course a pack of lies. The delegates wisely nominated Cleveland for a second term.

Whitney suffered most of the summer in Washington heat while Flora moved with the children first to Lenox, then to Bar Harbor, and back to Lenox again. He wrote to warn her again of the inappropriateness of inviting Mrs. Cleveland to Lenox at this point: "She has a personality before the American people the charm of which [would] be all gone if she should pass one week in fashionable society—heralded as she would be. If it were after election, it would be quite another thing." In fact Flora was unwell—evidently the first sign of a heart ailment that would grow in seriousness—and he urged her to rest. ". . . you must confine yourself to lounges and the bed. . . . I was shocked at your dancing. . . ."

Not for Flora the lounge or bed so long as she could write invitations. At Lenox, where she had christened the impressive Whitney cottage "Ventfort," she presided over "one of the most important social events of the season," a lawn and archery party for two hundred women. The piazzas were laid with Turkish rugs, and music was furnished by "a

mandolin band from New York and the Germania Orchestra of Pitts-
field." Beautiful as the ladies were, *The New York Herald*'s account
said, a fitting theme for their marksmanship was, "I shot an arrow into
the air, / It fell to earth I know not where."

During the campaign, a shrewd Republican calling himself Charles
F. Murchison and describing himself falsely as a former Briton now living in California shot an arrow with perfect aim. He wrote to Whitney's
good friend the British Minister Sackville West, asking whether Cleveland or the Republican Benjamin Harrison were the better candidate.
Sackville West broke a cardinal rule of diplomats: Never offer political
opinions in the land to which one is accredited. Innocently he replied
that while both gentlemen were well qualified, he personally preferred
Cleveland. Next day, his letter was quoted in newspapers under such
headlines as "British Queen Chooses Cleveland." The State Department instantly demanded his recall, and his diplomatic career was over
at sixty. But the damage was done. Diplomacy was similarly outraged by
the Cleveland-supporting Mayor Abram Hewitt of New York City when
he turned a frosty eye on a group of Irish leaders who invited him to
review the St. Patrick's Day parade.

"We all know that the Irish vote is strong enough to elect any candidate in this city . . . ," he said. "But, for the purpose of getting that
vote, I shall not consent to review any parade, be it Irish, or Dutch, or
Scotch, or German, or English."

With such friends, Cleveland scarcely needed enemies. In 1884 he
had won pivotal New York State only by a hair's breadth. On election
night, Flora and other friends were with the President and his wife at
the White House awaiting the returns. Among them was the President's
indispensable private secretary, Daniel S. Lamont, who was to appear
later in Whitney's life—a keen politician who, as an Albany journalist,
had attracted Cleveland's attention when the latter was governor. By one
o'clock Flora was so excited that she snatched Mrs. Lamont as companion and drove by carriage to Democratic headquarters, where Whitney had already installed himself. The issue was yet in doubt. He introduced them to the party workers, and the two women returned to the
White House. It was considerably later that Whitney drove to the executive mansion, his entrance as dramatic as any Shakespearean, and said
to the vigil keepers, "Well, it's all up."

9. Vile Stories

ALTHOUGH CLEVELAND'S popular vote exceeded Harrison's by almost
100,000, New York's thirty-six electoral votes went to Harrison and with
them the election. Cleveland's loss of his own state by 13,000 votes
while Hill was reelected governor by a plurality of 19,000 made many
believe that Hill had played him false. Flora, appalled by the defeat,
was further incensed when, a month later while Whitney was in New
York, she heard that Chauncey Depew had repeated publicly some of
the mendacities about the Clevelands. She called in *The Chicago Tribune*'s Washington correspondent and gave him an interview that covered three columns of its front page:

> I have found it hard to keep still, and have several times asked Mr. Whit-
> ney to let me have my say for the public ear. My indignation has been so
> great that I could hardly refrain from rushing into print. I have held my
> peace, however . . . and would continue to do so were it not for the fact
> that at a dinner party in New York, only two weeks ago, no less a gentle-
> man than Mr. Chauncey M. Depew amused the guests by repeating
> many of the vile stories about the President's conduct toward his wife. It
> is incredible that a man of Mr. Depew's standing and character should
> give currency to such vile stories. . . . And then, they say that the Presi-
> dent gets drunk. This is as false as all the rest. He is not a drinking man.
> Sometimes he takes a bit of whiskey and water with his friends or guests,
> but he does not drink, as the word is commonly used, and I know it.
> . . . Why, they had it that Mrs. Folsom [the President's mother-in-law]
> had to fly to Europe; that the President drove his wife out of the White
> House and we had to take her in. . . . You have my permission to quote
> all I have said, and I sincerely hope that this is the last of the whole
> wretched falsehood.

The story was a sensation, much of it being quoted secondhand by
every New York paper. Cleveland immediately wrote to thank her for
"your noble defense," adding, "I feel almost guilty for bringing my
sweet girl wife within the radius of such things." Astonishingly, Whitney rebuked Flora in a letter and went so far as to write apologetically to
Depew, a fellow Yale man and good friend with whom Whitney had
been involved in a railroad enterprise. Depew, at his 45th Street home,
defended himself stoutly, saying that while he had repeated a Cleveland
tale at a dinner party, Mrs. Whitney was mistaken because "I did not
give my personal sanction to the story . . . I do not believe a word of it,
and gave expression to that disbelief at the time." "I am very sorry,"
Whitney wrote to him, "that Mrs. Whitney should have in an impul-

sive moment used your name and got you talked about." Had not the
Republican Depew used the names of the President, his wife, and
others and got them talked about, and was it an effective way to silence
a damaging story to tell it at a gathering?

One excuse for Whitney's annoyance might be his firm subscription
to the principle that since he left social matters to his wife, so she must
leave political pronouncements to him. Another reason might be found
in his liking for the charming Depew. These factors still seem insufficient to cause him to apologize to the man who owed the apology.
Could his strange solicitude have been affected ever so slightly by, Depew's enormous influence, both in his own right and through his connection with the Vanderbilts? Whitney's transit operations in New York,
to which he would soon be devoting most of his time, needed friends,
not enemies.

During their lame-duck Washington season the Whitneys entertained
as if the world was to end on March 4. At one afternoon gathering their
guests, including Mrs. Cleveland, listened to Professor H. A. Clapp of
Johns Hopkins lecture on *Romeo and Juliet*. They gave a benefit
Christmas party at which their daughter Pauline, now tall and chestnut-
haired at fourteen, was one of the sponsors. The names on their visiting
list, *The Times* said, "numbered no fewer than four thousand," and
Flora seemed determined to squeeze them all into her ballroom in a
succession of four huge receptions, at several of which they danced until
the early hours. The last was followed by the descent on Washington of
that bald-headed side-whiskered Democratic traitor (in the eyes of many
Cleveland men), Governor Hill. Hill, it was said, had neither vices nor
principles. Unscrupulous in his use of people, he did not graft, drink,
smoke, gamble, or care for women, nor did he care overmuch what political line he took so long as it won. He lived in three black frock
coats, the newest one for state occasions, the second-best for daily wear,
and the third relegated to dressing gown status, worn with slippers.

Now he wore his newest. Whitney proceeded to lionize him. In his
well-known role as conciliatory Democrat seeking to unite all factions,
Whitney was famous for cosseting dissidents and could do so without
alienating the regulars. One of his close friends in Washington was the
New York Congressman Bourke Cockran, the Tammany orator from
County Sligo who had fought Cleveland's nomination in 1884 with bitterly eloquent brogue. Now, the Whitneys feted Hill at a dinner on
February 6, the President being one of the less enthusiastic guests. Next
day, Hill was Whitney's luncheon guest, senators and congressmen by

the score being invited to meet him. Hill, of course, was getting an early start for the 1892 presidential nomination. Though he did not say so publicly as yet, he reasoned that Cleveland had been President one term, had failed the test for a second by losing his own state, and should step aside in 1892 for the best Democratic candidate, who was of course Hill. It could have been pure coincidence that both Hill and Cockran were in a position to do Whitney's traction business some good. Cockran, influential on his own, was close to the new Tammany leader in New York, Richard Croker, with whom Whitney was on excellent terms. As for Governor Hill, the State of New York exercised authority over the City of New York in controlling the legislation affecting street railways. *The New York Times* ridiculed Whitney's guest of honor and cheered the host:

> Most of [the congressmen] have heard that [Hill] wants to be President, and . . . is already at work arranging the spontaneous outburst of popular favor for him that is to sweep down all opposition in the next Democratic National Convention. . . . [Many] think they saw in the Whitney reception something more important than a "Hill boom." . . . [Whitney] is the man in general Democratic estimation who has stimulated all the activity that has been shown by the Administration. . . . He has been repeatedly spoken of as a candidate for President. . . . Mr. Whitney . . . who furnished the Democrats in Congress with a pleasant opportunity of meeting the Governor and enjoying a delightful lunch, was seen by everyone who met the Governor. He was the host and was never more affable or entertaining. It is not at all surprising therefore that [many of the guests] . . . go so far as to declare that if they have to make a choice between the two their candidate will be Whitney rather than Hill.

After Harrison's inauguration, friends called to say good-bye as the Whitneys were closing the handsome place on I Street where Dorothy had been born and where, some mathematically inclined observer estimated, they had entertained some 65,000 guests during their four years' residence. Flora was near tears. For four years she had enjoyed the proximity and availability of the White House. She cherished her reign over this city of extremes, her friendship with the rawest Westerners and the most cultivated Europeans, the glamor of foreign tongues, the latest fashions, dance steps, delicacies, and outlooks. It was a way of life that should have lasted another four years but for the gossipmongers, the liars, the Depews, and Governor Hills. Flora, so cordial and sociable that she could be happy almost anywhere where Sociely was civilized and luxurious, was nevertheless a woman of deep sentiment. She was leaving friends of a dozen nationalities. She asked her final visitors to walk back with her for a last look at the place soon to be called the former Whitney mansion. "As the little party passed through the second drawing room, a man was engaged in taking an inventory of the furniture. The sight completely unnerved Mrs. Whitney, and, breaking down for the first time, she wept unrestrainedly while Mr. Whitney tried to soothe and calm her."

Two

1. "Act Well Your Part"

THE MENTAL POISE Cleveland saw in William Collins Whitney was so evident even in his boyhood that few had predicted other than a brilliant career for him. He was born July 5, 1841, in rustic Conway, Massachusetts, in the hills west of the Connecticut River. The third of five children, he had a proud family tree, having descended on his father's side from John Whitney, who had arrived in Boston from England in 1635. The Whitneys could trace their ancestry back to Turstin the Fleming, a Norman follower of William the Conqueror, and later men of mark in England. William Whitney's father, Joseph Scollay Whitney, had a mental poise of his own. At twenty-four he was appointed "general" of militia, the title implying nothing Napoleonic but indicating qualities of leadership. He was known as General Whitney all his life, although neither battle nor training maneuvers ever came under his purview. He had a bit of the gambler in him—a trait marked also in both his sons. A devout Congregationalist and Democrat, he was so venturesome that the list of his enterprises in the space of sixteen years included keeper of a general store, bag manufacturer, postmaster, state legislator, sheriff, delegate to the Massachusetts constitutional convention, small banker, and president of a fire insurance company.

William's mother, born Laurinda Collins, had family pride of her own, being a descendant of Governor William Bradford of Plymouth Colony. She had the mettle and ability to handle a four-horse team—something that William, who loved horses, never forgot. She was also sweet and loving, a writer of prim and exact letters. The Whitneys were "small-town prosperous" enough to present the Congregational church with an organ.

William was thirteen when his family moved to bustling Springfield where his father had been appointed to the political patronage post of superintendent of the national armory. At fifteen the boy jotted in his notebook such maxims as "Act well your part. There all honor lies." In 1860 the Whitneys moved to Boston when his father was given the considerable job of Collector of the Port, an appointment granted no one without years of loyal service to the party. By then William had graduated from Williston Academy, preceded by his older brother Henry, with whom he was to keep in close touch most of his life. There were three younger sisters, Susan, Henrietta, and Lilly.

William went on to Yale, where he excelled with ease. He would have excelled to a greater degree had he not so much enjoyed the pleasures of social discussion when study was in order. Yale's faculty then totaled fifteen, tuition was $216 a year, dormitories had neither plumbing nor gaslight, and early morning classes as well as evening study were conducted by candlelight and concentrated on the classics. When Whitney was a sophomore, the Republican Lincoln became President and replaced Joseph Whitney with a deserving Republican. Hence politics, its fascinations, rewards, and perils were a part of the son's background. The family continued to live in the Boston suburb of Brookline as the resourceful General Whitney landed on his feet as president of the smallish Metropolitan Steamship Company, whose boats plied between Boston and New York.

At Yale, William could not match the style of his rich classmate and friend Oliver Hazard Payne. The meeting of these two, if not precisely historic, was and would remain momentous for them long after each had become, in his own way, a figure in history. Not that they were inseparable—not nearly as friendly as Whitney was with Henry F. Dimock of rural Connecticut and William Graham Sumner, from Hartford. Payne was two years older, a trifle impersonal, seeming always to keep himself in close rein, felt by some to be toplofty because he came from a mansion on Euclid Avenue in Cleveland and had gone to one of the most prestigious of preparatory schools. The ties between Whitney and Payne, later so strong that they could not be torn without bleeding, were loose at Yale.

As a Clevelander, Payne's progression from Andover to Yale bespoke parents as high in their regard for education as in their belief in his promise. He was the son of pioneers who had gone west, seen every opportunity in the expanding frontier, seized all of them, and squeezed them of fabulous juice. He had ambition, drive, intelligence. Whitney, the son of the sons of pioneers who had succeeded modestly and stayed on as the frontier moved away, had in Payne a friend with an appetite for success not then common at Yale. The two, both Democrats and both fascinated by politics, were casual companions for two years. Of course they traded stories about their homes and families. Payne's father, who came from a family that had been in Connecticut for several generations, was trained at Hamilton Theological Seminary in upstate New York, was a member of the bar, and was not only one of the wealthiest but one of the foremost business and political leaders in Ohio. Phenomenally successful as a lawyer, he had branched out into business and had helped found one railroad and become part owner of another, moving also from municipal office to the state senate. A skillful party leader, he had been Democratic candidate for United States senator and for governor, losing to men of stature—Ben Wade beating him for the Senate by one legislator's vote and Salmon P. Chase narrowly defeating him for governor. Oliver's mother came from wealthy and respected Ohio pioneers. Her father was the well-known Nathan Perry, who had first dealt profitably with the Indians, then found even greater success as a Cleveland merchant. The Payne home, said to have cost $100,000, was of cut stone, the finest in the city. With their three sons and two daughters, the Paynes made a family of seven who encouraged, defended, and inspired each other, never content with the ordinary.

If Oliver Payne was a shade self-satisfied, he had his jovial moments and was strong for the Union. In 1861, though his Unionist father wanted him to stay in college, Oliver left Yale and secured a lieutenant's commission in an Illinois regiment. Whitney, like most of his classmates, let others solve the problems of Mr. Lincoln, who had removed the senior Whitney from the Boston collectorship. College men were less inclined to join the army than the scantily educated, and the draft was spotty in its application, skipping Massachusetts and Connecticut entirely for one year of the war. Staying at Yale along with Whitney were Dimock and Sumner, the latter already combining the intellect and industry that were to bring him scholarly fame. Sumner, in fact, taxed Whitney for indolence, although Whitney improved his effort, wrote for the Lit, pulled an oar on the crew, was tapped for Skull and Bones, and still won honors at his graduation in 1863. Payne by then had been in uniform almost two years and was fighting in bloody skirmishes in Tennessee. Whitney went on to Harvard Law School for a year, living so pleasantly with his family in Brookline that his sisters later spoke of his warmth and affection. When he emerged from Harvard in 1864, ready to go out in the world, Oliver Payne had recovered from serious wounds received at Chickamauga. He rejoined his regiment to fight gallantly at Resaca as a colonel but was so depressed after the horror-filled Atlanta campaign that he resigned in November 1864, which influential officers could then do. He returned to Cleveland and entered the world that was made for him, business. His father gave him $20,000 as a starter—a pleasant custom the senior Payne had inaugurated with his eldest son Nathan and was to continue with his youngest, Harry—and within a year Oliver was rising swiftly as an entrepreneur in oil and iron.

2. A Liberated Woman

BY 1867 Whitney was practicing law on Wall Street in New York City in partnership with his classmate Henry Dimock, making a living and not much more. He wrote occasional editorials for the Democratic New York World, owned by Manton Marble, and now and then contributed a piece to the semiliterary magazine The Round Table. His connection with The World led him to appraise expertly the large field of New York newspapers and to improve his acquaintance with them. He early discovered the wonders that "good publicity" could perform for one's political party and also for one's personal enterprises. His skill in cultivating the press of all parties was to be of great service to him throughout his life.

When Oliver Payne came to New York on business, Whitney was a little surprised at the enthusiasm with which Payne renewed their less than ardent college friendship. In February 1868 the Colonel laid a romantic trap for Whitney by bringing his sister Flora with him. Flora was just six months younger than Whitney, twenty-six years old, at that time an age regarded as early spinsterhood. Although not truly beautiful, she was vivacious and attractive and—particularly since she was a splendid catch for a man thinking expediently of money—one might ask why she had not yet married.

The reasons were evident. She belonged to neither of the two categories of women acceptable to the male-dominated upper crust: the gently submissive or the woman who ruled but concealed the iron hand. Flora was self-assured, independent, intelligent, choosy, now and then a shade bossy. She had none of the shrinking-violet attributes considered correct for females. Warmhearted, ambitious, experienced far beyond the usual sheltered young woman, she anticipated by decades some aspects of the liberated woman of the twentieth century. After attending the Cleveland Seminary, she had spent a year at the starchy Spingler Institute in New York City, then had studied and excelled in Cambridge in special private classes for women conducted by Louis Agassiz. Returning to Cleveland, she had fallen in love with a young man whose credentials were insufficient, and at twenty-one she was sent out of danger on a two-year tour of travel and study during which she ranged from Ireland to the Levant. Her escorts were her father's friend, former governor Mattison of Illinois, and Mattison's family.

She was a compulsive writer, admitting that she simply had to write her impressions at full length and her parents could stop reading if they became bored. Her letters were thick, detailed travelogues of four thousand words or more:

> . . . take in the view, now you see the Alhambra, a fortress palace, with its crumbling walls and square towers following the undulations of the ground, set on a hill, a spur of the Sierra Nevada—below is a wild ravine, at its bottom flows the gold-sanded Darro.

"Behold me fairly in the heart of Turkey land," she began one letter from Constantinople, and a letter to her wounded soldier-brother began with typical ebullience: "You darling Ol—I hardly know which to write to, you or the bullet in you. . . ." In Paris she indulged a lifelong passion for dress: "I have the most a la mode dressmakers and milliners and have no fear but you shall find me the very latest advertisement from Paris."

Although Whitney had visited Oliver in Cleveland, he had not yet met Flora. Oliver later boasted that he "knew that if they met, they would fall in love with each other." He liked Whitney—liked also to manipulate matters political and otherwise. On this occasion he arranged for the pair to meet in the top-floor dining room of the fashionable Fifth Avenue Hotel on Madison Square, a romantic spot with a sweeping view of the city. Flora was not demure as young women were expected to be. She did not blush or drop her eyelids. Whitney long afterward described the scene:

> How you looked I plainly recall in your blue dress and with the blue and gold book in your hand when you threw down the gauntlet for a flirtation. "So you are the Will Whitney that I have had held up to me for so many years?" I must have been a little blundering at picking it up I imagine, for the attack was unexpected and bold. . . . You asked me to order for you and then criticized and complimented until my time to go. Then

the opera in a few nights and dangling our spoons over the cups of tea.
. . . And [the Colonel] the noble, good, anxious old boy hovering
around us, for I think it can fairly be said, My Dear, that ours was a
match first made in Heaven and then by the Col. . . . I was away up in
the clouds. . . .

Not too far up, for she returned to Cleveland, there were other girls,
and he did not push his suit. It appears that she had decided to marry
him but that he took too long about it: surely it was not business that
called her to New York in December. They attended the opera, among
other entertainments. The tone of her reply to his query concerning
dress and transportation had a touch of the peremptory:

> Mr. Whitney shall do as he pleases, I don't think a new hat requires a
> dress coat.
> The carriage would undoubtedly be a vast ornament to us but as I am
> in good health, I would suggest that we walk the three steps between the
> Hotel and the Opera House.

But she could also melt charmingly. "Mr. Whitney said he loved
me!" she wrote in her diary December 15. If Whitney was not averse to
marrying money, no one could say that he had purposely gone to wive
it wealthily in Padua. They took the train to Cleveland for Christmas,
announcing their intentions, and Whitney was the center of a Payne
family gathering at which he was examined, weighed, and (except for
Oliver and Flora) not approved without further study. "Goethe said he
had only *three* weeks' happiness out of his long life," she wrote to him.
"I have done almost as well as that already . . . that weekend in New
York—and this week here." She wrote archly about his earlier women
companions: "Now, my dear William, if you would only *own up* and
out with it at once it would be much better than letting it reach me in
little broken bits, it makes my agony all the longer. You might as well
send me an alphabetical list that I can refer to. . . . Papa is suggesting
a set of funeral urns to hold some of the ashes of my 'dear departed.'
You shall have a set to match." She was cruel enough to write of an old
suitor, an army general, that when he was promoted from colonel "he
left me one of his eagles and his heart. I think I have the former upstairs, but the latter I never took good care of. . . ." She confessed that
she was utterly spoiled, could not cook, and was untrained at domestic
duties: ". . . my housekeeping when it comes to a test stands something
as the authority of the Centurion. . . . I don't know a bit about money

or its value. . . . I always lose keys. . . ." She was not ready to give up fashion: ". . . we will live as handsomely and with just as much charm and attraction in our home as our good love and taste can make it." Whitney, thinking of the luxuries and servants that she took for granted, worried that he could not maintain her in her accustomed style and wrote that he felt troubled "that I got you into this scrape at all." He went to New Haven for his class dinner (he was president of his class), drank copiously of wine, and at "the pensive hour of four o'clock, we went up to the Class Ivy and sang our Ivy Song and gave some nine cheers or more. . . ." Flora, who could veer from adoration to occasional insensitivity, once wrote to him so hurtfully that he returned the letter (which she destroyed) along with a reply showing genuine anger. She replied in deepest contrition, "I can hardly believe that I wrote such a letter to you. . . . I am utterly ashamed and grieved. . . . long ago in school, that lovely Miss Hoadly said to me . . . 'you have a gift of satire, a dangerous gift, and you must be careful, it will ruin your happiness sometime if you don't guard it.' "

Flora admitted to Whitney that she could be shockingly moody—as he was later to learn personally—and at times would not speak to her mother for days. She taught a Sunday school class, revered her pastor, knew her Bible, but read secular works incessantly—Browning, Seneca, and Dickens at the moment. When Whitney defended *The Round Table* against libel charges pressed by Charles Reade because of its denunciatory review of Reade's *Griffith Gaunt*, Flora first sympathized with Reade because she had admired his *Peg Woffington*. But she came around to Whitney's side, arguing that a century earlier writers were

> starving and dying under the lash of the reviewers, and now he can't stand a few little honest words that sold his book for him; we might just as well put our literature under the control of the Government . . . as to threaten the press, if it speaks its mind. . . .

She used every wile in her effort to lure Oliver into an interest in a distant cousin who was attractive and available, bringing Whitney into the plot. Oliver the impervious rejected the bait. Flora's father and mother came separately to New York, ostensibly on other errands but also to view Whitney *in situ*, living in untidy bachelor rooms in Washington Place. Mrs. Payne at least was not wholly impressed and told Flora so. That young lady was already piqued because Whitney's letters, while affectionate, lacked the poetic flow of endearment she cherished and occasionally touched on the weather. Flora, whose letters had been

filled with avowals such as her declaration that she could "live like a
nun in her cell, with you on my crucifix," changed her tune: "We have
been together so little. Oh! what if we should be disappointed in each
other. . . . We are such strangers after all. . . ." Whitney wrote back
in such exasperation that she addressed him humbly:

> I feel as though I had ten pyramids crushing me. . . . Why did you not
> give me a good hearty shaking before, it was just what I needed. . . .
> Mama gave me such dreadful pictures of New York life and society, she
> did not mean to frighten me. . . .

At last these uncertain preliminaries were over and it was settled that
they would be married. Henry Payne bought for them a handsome five-
story brownstone house at 74 Park Avenue, near 40th Street, paying also
for its extensive remodeling and its furnishings. It was Whitney's duty to
consult with the architect, even to help choose rugs and chintzes, and
to see that the renovation would be ready so that they could move in
after their marriage. "We are just like two birds building our nest," she
wrote, "only I am the lazy one, and do nothing but sit on a distant
branch and sing about it." She urged him not to have any boilers about
the house: "Here, Sunday, I wanted a fire in the furnace, and there
wasn't any water in the boiler and it blew up, and I had a slight reproach administered to me for it."

But she did not realize how deep a problem the Payne money was to
Whitney, nor how sensitive he was over his comparative poverty—an
anguish that was to grow. "Although Father and Mother are willing to
be so generous to us . . . they can't afford more extravagances for us afterward," she wrote to him, with no idea how hurtful was this emphasis
on the Payne benefactions. She was more understanding when she
wrote:

> The Boys [her brothers] told me last night that they wanted to give me a
> Diamond Necklace as their gift together. . . . Ol . . . says it is not
> showy, but rare and *quiet*. . . . Would you rather I did not have it? The
> dear boys are lovely in their extravagance and I appreciate their desire in
> this, though I would be just as happy if they would get me crystal.

He could scarcely insist on crystal. "Why should I object?" he replied. ". . . Everything that is beautiful *ought* to be yours. . . ." But
he *had* to have money so that he could match the Payne grandeur.
With his adventurous brother Henry he took a flyer in railroad stock on

margin. The stock sank and they lost their whole investment. He was forced to write to her in deepest embarrassment:

> I have decided to give you some little thing, Flo, just as a memorial of the occasion. You have so many good friends that will be giving you beautiful things, I shall only give you a little remembrance of some sort, not to be shown as a gift, and only commemorative of the day.

It was a poorer Whitney who married Flora on October 13, 1869, at Cleveland's First Presbyterian Church in that city's most magnificent social event of the year. Among the groomsmen were Henry Whitney, William Graham Sumner, Oliver Payne, and his brother Nathan who—true to Payne style—was a rich coal merchant, soon to be mayor of Cleveland.

3. The Gambler Caught

THE PARK AVENUE house was ready and beautiful and just waiting for a succession of expensive parties when the Whitneys returned from a Niagara Falls honeymoon. There were two servants, and since Flora was a stranger to thrifty cuts of meat and bargain dresses and loved to dash off to the Catskills, Saratoga, or Cleveland when the impulse struck her, it seems clear that the Payne largess was continuing, if on a reduced scale. Since Whitney was never prosperous enough for truly luxurious living, the Paynes could choose between letting Flora live in what they would feel mean circumstances or helping out. The amount of Payne help over the years was prodigious. Whitney was to become one of the three famous husbands of the day to find such manna in marriage, the other two of whom were to become his good friends, Whitelaw Reid and John Hay. Reid married the daughter of Darius Ogden Mills, and Hay the daughter of Amasa Stone, both so rich that the incomes of their sons-in-law might be considered academic. Like Whitney, Reid could live comfortably as head of *The Tribune* and Hay as a renowned writer and diplomat, but not in the grandeur they enjoyed by courtesy of their fathers-in-law.

Whitney accepted the Payne hegemony with only occasional signs of rebellion. An obvious defense was for him to gain his own fortune as quickly as possible. During the following year he seemed to be moving toward that goal when he became counsel for the Continental Life Insurance Company, the New Jersey Mutual Life Insurance Company, the Metropolitan Steamship Company (his father's firm), and the Tredegar Iron Company in Richmond. But he moved away from it in his weakness for speculating in capricious stocks and for participating in politics. In 1870 he spoke out against Boss Tweed, then at his height. Among others who opposed Tweed and with whom Whitney became friendly was Richard Croker, as yet a minor Tammany underling. Croker, just Whitney's age, born in Cloghnakilty but raised in New York, was not unfriendly. A machinist by trade, a leader of the Fourth Avenue Tunnel Gang, he was still at twenty-nine a passable prizefighter with the level, challenging gaze not uncommon among men of the ring. The fact that Croker and Whitney opposed Tweed did not prove either an idealist. Each was a practical Democrat who knew that Tweed had gone too far and damaged the party. Whitney, however, joined the reformist group of Apollo Hall Democrats, became a leader of the Young Men's Democratic Club, and in 1872 ran for district attorney on the Apollo ticket. "William is in *politics*," Flora wrote to her sister Mollie, "and the first thing that kind of business does is to take a man away from the bosom of his family. . . . William is a natural politician. . . . He has made several speeches. . . . About a hundred Committee men are to meet here Wednesday night and you can imagine the powwow."

He lost. It was his first and last bid for elective office, though he stayed deep in politics. Along the way his education included a close-up view of the splendid Tweed edifice of corruption as it showed its first cracks and then slowly began to crumble, disclosing how willingly individuals once believed impeccable had joined in the Tweed frauds. In the middle distance was enacted the chicanery of the Grant administration in Washington, in which high office seemed largely reserved for liars and cheats. Whitney in any case was not one of those Apollo purists who left the room when a Tammany man entered. His view reflected his great amiability and was to become a large factor in his enormous behind-the-scenes political power. He believed that one could not blame the whole of Tammany for Tweed and that Democrats even in opposing factions were still Democrats. In fact, as Apollo soon languished, he was to join Tammany and become a member of its general committee.

The Whitneys' first child, a boy, was born in 1872 and named Henry Payne after his grandfather, though the Henry soon became Harry by common consent. Flora, the inveterate writer, wrote a long essay about his birth and early infancy. Although she was to have four more children, Harry remained the apple of her eye, the receiver of special favors. Flora's father gave a substantial gift on the birth of his first grandchild and namesake. Oliver Payne, who had recently sold his big Cleveland oil concern, Clark, Payne & Company, to the Standard Oil Company and had become a ground-floor Rockefeller associate, was the Whitneys' guest whenever in New York, dripping with money. In fact, Whitney himself was not a model of thrift, insisted on the finest of tailoring, and kept fine horses and a carriage. Money was a problem. He concealed the depth of that problem for a time. The Whitneys' first daughter, Pauline Payne Whitney, was born in March 1874, almost concurrent with the Panic of 1874, which shook the stock market badly. It turned out that Whitney had been speculating heavily on margin, and he was wiped out after risking good money after bad.

In the summer Flora was in Cleveland again with the two children, not overly pleased with him because his ardor had cooled, he read the paper at table, and he spoke in monosyllables—an ungraciousness doubtless due in part to money worries he had only hinted at to Flora. Before they married, he had been concerned about the reduction in luxury she would have to accept. Actually they were living very well indeed, and it came to her that he might be paying for it in excessive labor and care. She wrote to him:

> If you are working to keep up a too extravagant style of life, oh, let us give it up. I value your health and your leisure in your family much the most. Will, I would give up our home—beautiful as it is—in a moment if it would relieve you. Let us live for ourselves and not for others . . . we can always take the bedstead with us. [While she admitted that he surrounded her with all her needs, he neglected the attentions that had delighted her.] You, my husband, whom I remember as the ardent lover in the first year of my marriage! . . . I have ground my teeth to prevent angry words. . . . it added to the hurts, and hurts grow inner disappointments, and these into indifference . . . and then the angel of romance folds forever her wings. . . .

The tone of her letter was transformed instantly by one of the attentions she cherished. She broke off and continued anew:

> Oh! My *Dear!* Here Lizzie just brought me your *telegram. You Darling!* Out of my happiness now, I know how miserable I have been. . . . A thousand, thousand kisses and love, Flora

But her tone was to change again because Whitney was in such financial straits that on a quick trip to Cleveland he told her about it confidentially. She wrote to him with surprising wisdom after he returned to New York:

> I wish now you had been a little more explicit to me about your business matters. Left to myself I take a black view of it. It would be very, very hard to let Father know of your embarrassments, for he has been so kind and we know just how he looks upon speculating. I am afraid he would lose confidence in you. . . . It is a hard lesson, but it is wise to be cured young of a love of the "Street." . . . If we keep each other's love and are honest, we will in the end be the happiest.

He replied penitently, declining her suggestion that he might tide himself over by borrowing from one of her brothers:

> My Dear Girl, it has not been the fact of debt that has troubled me half so much as the fever of my efforts to get out of it, and the feeling of restraint that there was something My Wife did not know. . . . I do not want any help except the little I may—or may not—ask from you. . . . And now, My Dear, do put it out of your mind. . . . Debts are not pleasant things to have I know, but they are the lot of almost everybody— all your brothers, my brother, and Father—and almost everybody is a borrower. It is business. . . . I 'haint lost much by speculation! That isn't it. I lost by getting behind and going into politics, and . . . then I undertook to speculate it out, and then I failed—then I was a fool—of course I didn't stop until I had lost some more. . . .

He urged her to keep it from her family. Indeed his letter was hardly a model of candor. His argument that it was not speculation that caused his loss only emphasized that it *was* speculation, and his admission that it might take "a couple of years" to make good his indebtedness would scarcely classify it as a "little trouble." His statement that he might ask financial help from Flora suggested that she either had an income from the Paynes or had Payne money in her bank account. Probably Flora saw through him instantly. Yet, even granting Whitney's gambler's streak, it was surely possible that his humiliating plunge had been motivated by the desperation of a man of modest means seeking to hold his own with rich in-laws.

4. The Centennial Fraudulence

THAT SAME year, Henry B. Payne proved his determination and his popularity by his election to Congress in a predominantly Republican dis trict, with the strong help of his politically shrewd son Oliver. And in 1875, only a year after Whitney's disastrous loss, some of the Payne money must have come his way again, for he (and doubtless Flora) went to Europe. At any rate the archives of Henry Poole and Company, outfitters to the Prince of Wales, disclosed that Whitney stopped in and ordered a "dahlia-colored . . . beaver frock coat with velvet cuffs and lapels for $40." So exclusive was Poole's that one could not just walk in and order tailoring but had to furnish credentials. The Reverend Morgan Dix of Trinity Church in New York had recently called there and displayed a letter from Bishop Horatio Potter to the Archbishop of Canterbury. That had not been good enough. Dix had been required to get a letter from his banker in the City. Whitney, perhaps aided by a charm that Dix lacked, got by with a letter from one H. C. Cooper Esq. and was thereafter a steady customer.

For more than five years Whitney had worked skillfully for the Democrats and gained in importance. He knew that frail but powerful schemer, Gov. Samuel J. Tilden. One of his friends was a Park Avenue neighbor, the former Apollo man William H. Wickham, a gem merchant who became mayor in 1875 and appointed Whitney corporation counsel at $15,000 a year. The office was an important one and the salary substantial for the time—$3,000 more than the mayor's—though a mere driblet to corporation lawyers of the Payne or Tilden stamp. He was little enough known to outsiders so that *The Herald* gave his specifications: ". . . a man of about thirty-five years of age [he was 34], of good presence and very agreeable manners" who "distinguished himself [at Yale] by his brilliancy"; while *The Tribune* humiliatingly miscalled him "John C. Whitney." He reorganized his new office, being confronted by a gigantic workload—some 3,800 lawsuits against the city, most of them pressed by people who had been given contracts by the now fallen Tweed Ring. "The just presumption was that everything was fraudulent," Whitney observed, one example being his settlement for $50,000 of the $2,000,000 claim for Ring printing and stationery. Before he had only observed political corruption. Now he was confronted by the chapter and verse of its results.

In March 1876, Flora presented him with their third child, William Payne Whitney. In June he was a delegate to the Democratic National Convention in St. Louis along with such men as Mayor Wickham, Manton Marble, Tammany boss John Kelly, and rich August Belmont. "Henry B. Payne, of Ohio, Suggested as the Most Available Candidate," the then-Republican-leaning *New York Times* headline reported. Availability indeed was Whitney's father-in-law's outstanding characteristic, for—without forgetting his considerable political skills—the presidency seemed a toplofty vision for a freshman Congressman. While the New York delegation was instructed for Tilden, there was nothing to prevent Whitney from doing favors for Payne, who would have enjoyed the House speakership if the presidency eluded him.

It was a commentary on the breadth and variety of the nation that, during the convention, Yale had its commencement in New Haven while in Montana Gen. George Crook had a "spirited fight with Sioux Indians" in which eight soldiers were killed. *The Times*, whose revelatory articles had been instrumental in bringing down Tweed, put the Democrats along with the Sioux: "Thanks to Tammany and an unlimited supply of bad whisky . . . there have been brawls, fisticuff encounters, and men crazed with liquor roaring themselves hoarse for and against Tilden. . . ." The Republican *New York Tribune* was as scornful: "There were three genuine fights of the old-fashioned Democratic kind in the Lindell House. . . . One of the Tammany roughs drew a pistol on a Tilden Missourian right in the great hall of the Lindell and proposed to put an end to him and his Tildenism together."

But murder was kept off the agenda as the Democrats compromised their monetary quarrel by naming the greenbacker Thomas A. Hendricks as running mate to the hard-money Tilden. Whitney had corresponded with his father-in-law about the latter's chances for the presidency and speakership and had introduced him to the puissant Manton Marble. Now after the convention, August Belmont and his equally Democratic son Perry stopped off in Cleveland with Whitney to visit with Congressman Payne at the mansion on Euclid Avenue. It seems likely that Whitney was enlisted by Payne to push the older man's presidential hopes and fortunes. The two were alike in their fascination with politics, and Whitney had much to offer a man who was a big fish in Cleveland but a minnow in New York. Personal acquaintance with important eastern Democrats could be of value to him. The Whitney genius at political strategy, for which he was later to win national fame, was now well known in New York and by his father-in-law in Ohio.

Whitney stumped New England for Tilden in this bitter campaign which raked up the animosities of the Civil War and made a burlesque of the electoral system. It seemed so clearly a Democratic triumph on the day after the election that Republican papers conceded, the Republican candidate Rutherford B. Hayes admitted defeat in his diary, and Tilden announced a victory dinner for forty. Alas, it became clear that

Hayes had 185 certain electoral votes, Tilden 184, and that the out-
come depended on three states still under Republican carpetbag rule,
Louisiana, South Carolina, and Florida. Votes no longer counted. One
Louisiana official sent word that Tilden could win that state for
$1,000,000, an offer the upright Abram S. Hewitt, chairman of the
Democratic National Committee, rejected even when the sale price was
reduced to $200,000. In the end, of course, the Democrats were
cheated and Hayes was in the White House. The celebration of the nation's centennial with this fraudulence embittered some Democrats for
life, but not the resilient Whitney, now a party leader coming into
prominence.

Flora's incessant trips to Cleveland and elsewhere were less a sign of
marital unrest than of her addiction to activity. Their letters were
usually warm and affectionate. One had to accept her as she was, bow
to her whims, be ready for surprises. Though she confessed that before
her marriage she had been "priest-ridden," she discovered new heroes
from time to time and now she fairly worshiped Henry Ward Beecher in
his secular status. The charge that he had committed adultery with Mrs.
Tilton, which was spread in discreet language across all front pages and
was the subject of delighted gossip all over the nation, shook her somewhat, but she had decided that one such sin could hardly damn so exalted a man. A great talker, she would discourse on any subject that
came into her head, including Beecher, though adultery was then a
topic never discussed between the sexes. Though Whitney's daring in
this respect was later to be demonstrated in the "'Ostler Joe" incident,
he was sensitive about Flora's conversational freedom and wrote to her
while she was still in Cleveland, "I do hope you will not talk the
Beecher matter over with men."

In May 1877, when her youngest child William was only a year old,
she decided to go abroad with her brothers Nathan and Harry. Harry,
her youngest brother, had graduated from Yale four years after Whitney, studied law at Columbia, and practiced in Cleveland despite a
serious lung affliction. A change of climate and physicians might do
him good. Flora took with her Harry and Pauline, aged five and three,
leaving Willie with his governess and a wet-nurse. She did this although
she was pregnant again, expecting to be back in a few months.

Her third brother, Oliver, now spending much of his time in New
York, kept Whitney company. "I really think the Colonel loves me,"
Whitney had written to Flora, "and I begin to feel a tenderer feeling for

him than I used to." His tone suggested that Oliver had hardly been his *fidus Achates* and that until recently Whitney could get along very well without him. "The Colonel and I never saw much of each other in College," his letter went on, "and it is very strange I think that he should have carried away so kindly a regard for me, as you have led me to believe he had." Now, however, they were good companions, taking the boat ride around Manhattan on Sundays and occasionally driving out to Jerome Park to dine. Two of Whitney's three sisters had married and now lived in New York, Susan being the wife of Whitney's former law partner and old friend Henry Dimock, Lilly married to the rising banker Charles Tracy Barney. Whitney, a fond family man, went occasionally to Boston to visit his aging parents, his brother Henry, and his invalid sister Henrietta.

In Paris, Flora stopped at Worth's to buy dresses not only for herself but for her sisters-in-law Lilly and Susan. "Please send me your number of gloves," she wrote to Whitney, "or better still a *glove*. I can get beautiful two-button gentlemen's gloves for Fifty Francs, Ten Dollars a dozen *here.* . . . If Ol. is with you, send his number too. I invested in Fifty Dollars worth of cravats for you both this morning. . . ."

Intending to return in September, Flora stayed on because of her brother's failure to improve. Whitney had to do without his wife and two of his children at Christmas that year. On January 22, 1878, Flora gave birth to her fourth child, a daughter, in some European city, probably London, where Harry was taking treatment from Sir William Jenner, physician to Queen Victoria. A fortnight later, on February 8, Harry Payne died at Menton on the French Riviera, aged only thirty-three. Flora sailed home with her brother Nathan and her children, with the sad knowledge that Harry's body was in the hold of the ship, but eager to see her husband and show him their infant girl. She had been gone for nine months. The girl was named Olive, after Flora's brother Oliver, the middle name of course as always being Payne.

5. *The cam-Payne for Payne*

WHITNEY WAS an efficient corporation counsel, credited with saving the city at least $20,000,000 in his defense against the endless claims of those who sought to profit from Tweed. He was a workhorse in what had traditionally been a hive of drones. "I am not a quick, rapid, facile man at all," he had warned Flora. "I do what I do by means of hard work. . . ." He was interested enough in his public reputation to keep scrapbooks of newspaper clippings about himself. Since a part of his duty was to see to the city's arrangements with its various privately owned surface and elevated railways, he learned a great deal about this hodgepodge of rail lines—knowledge that was later to bring him millions. He was reappointed by two succeeding mayors, both of course Democrats.

Power interested him more than principle. He seems to have moved along politically in the city's faction-ridden democracy with a cool propensity for throwing in with the faction that would do him the most good, yet always working for unity. Elected along with him to the Tammany General Committee was his friend Richard Croker, who had served one term as alderman and was now coroner. Croker's rough camaraderie contained the slightest tinge of menace, but his shrewdness along with his steady view of politics as a system of rewards for the faithful made him a man on the rise.

Even before 1880, it was evident that Henry B. Payne was again fulfilling his function of availability for the presidency. His failure to be reelected to Congress had been a heavy blow to his status as a contender, and his age—nearly seventy—would seem to have finished him off. This he did not concede. His spirit of determination—already a visible heritage in his son Oliver and his daughter Flora—was to reappear again markedly in the Whitneys' daughter Dorothy. With a little luck he might have won the nomination. Everybody liked him, he looked easily ten years younger than his true age, which he no longer publicized, and critics suggested that he made a point of walking and gesturing with brisk and youthful movements when under political observation.

Tilden, the unquestioned party leader at sixty-six, seemed out of the running because of a stroke that had shattered his health, caused an eyelid to droop, and his speech to slur. He was so sly and secretive that not even his closest political allies—and Whitney was one of them—knew his intentions. The year before, Whitney had joined a group of prominent Democrats in a visit to Tilden's new stone mansion in Yonkers. When Tilden appeared, he beckoned and said, "Come this way, Mr. Whitney." Honored, he followed Tilden up the stairway to the tower, sure that the old man was to confide important political matters in him. Instead, reaching the top, Tilden only gestured proudly and said, "You can see Staten Island from here."

The Democrats appeared to have a good chance if they nominated a strong candidate. "The campaign opens lively," *The New York Herald* observed as the national convention opened in Cincinnati in June. "Whether it will end cam-Payne is now a mooted point." "Mr. Whitney's relationship to Henry B. Payne," said *The Tribune*, "puts him under suspicion with many of being here in Payne's interest. . . ." Payne was there with his wife, his remarkable affability on free display. Oliver Payne, lacking the paternal grace, was in the background with what some thought a conspiratorial air, and Flora, who would never have missed witnessing this effort to put her father in the White House, was surely somewhere in the wings. Whitney himself, a Payne man from the start, waited impatiently for the word from Tilden, who had stayed in New York and was still undeclared.

"The most absurd statements are made today by those who are working for Payne," *The Times* observed. "His son, who asserts that he is merely a spectator, but who is really doing his best to secure his father's nomination, declared today that the Ohio delegation was solid for Payne. Fortunately for him, no friend of Thurman [Allen G. Thurman also had strong Ohio backing] was near. . . ." Payne's opponents made much of his age, one calling him "an attenuated, dried-up old fossil." Actually, the Democrats' catastrophic old fossil was Tilden back in New York, scheming for the office his frail body could never survive, insisting earlier that his first choice was Payne but now keeping silent while the convention awaited his instructions and Payne's backers began to lose confidence. Henry Payne received a telegram from a Tilden man in New York asking if he would consent to be running mate on a Tilden ticket, to which Payne could only agree. Tilden's message to the convention, when at last it came, was so ambiguously worded that it could be interpreted either as something close to a reluctant withdrawal or an offer to run if the party needed him. Whitney, disgusted with the old fox, toiled for his father-in-law. "Ex-Mayor Wickham and Corporation Counsel Whitney," a reporter noted, "each in a white hat, white choker, and a green umbrella, winked, lighted fresh cigars, and started out to peregrinate, argue, and convince." There were speculations, not entirely tongue in cheek, about the power Wickham and Whitney could wield if they could nominate and elect Payne. "These men already have the Mayor, the Corporation Counsel, and a host of minor officers. What, then, will be their position if to a major share of local patronage they are able to add the Custom House, Post Office, district attorney's office, and the rest of the federal patronage? They would absolutely dominate the metropolis."

But Tilden's maneuver had hurt Payne even more than the latter's presumed connection with the Standard Oil Company. He got eighty-one votes on the first ballot, after which Whitney worked furiously to win over more New York and Ohio delegates. He saw it was hopeless and, with Payne's consent, withdrew his name. The convention, without enthusiasm, went on to nominate Gen. Winfield S. Hancock of Gettysburg fame. The high pitch of Whitney's hopes for his father-in-law and his disgust with the man who dashed them were implicit in his comment—the comment of one who normally schooled himself not to speak ill of any Democrat:

> One of the peculiar weaknesses of Mr. Tilden as a political leader is that he gives his whole confidence to no one, not even to those on whom he must rely for the execution of his plans. . . . If Mr. Tilden had been frankly out two weeks before the convention met, we could have nominated Payne. But Tilden wasn't out even when he wrote that letter. . . . Anyhow, the old man is now nearly a physical wreck.

6. Enter Mr. Cleveland

DEMOCRATS WHO had seen the presidency lost in 1876 by theft seethed when they lost it in 1880 through the petty rapacity of one of their own. James A. Garfield won New York State, and with it the election, by a mere 21,000 votes, putting a Republican in the White House for another four years. Whitney was one of many who blamed it on John Kelly, the money-honest but power-hungry boss of Tammany. Had Kelly not sacrificed the national ticket to parochial greed and insisted on local candidates who hindered rather than helped the national ticket, Hancock would surely have won New York's 35 electoral votes and been the victor by 190 against Garfield's 179. Whitney had always given plums to Tammany and expected something in return. ". . . although an anti-Tammanyite in name," *The Herald* had said, "[Whitney] retains Tammany men in office . . . giving to the anti-Tammanyites the pleasure of his countenance and to the Tammanyites the substance of his patronage. . . ." Whitney and others were so irate at Kelly that there was secession from the Wigwam and an entirely new aspect to politics in New York.

With Abram Hewitt and others, Whitney launched a bright new reform organization, the County Democracy. In Hewitt, Whitney had a friend who was to watch him narrowly all his life, first in admiration, then in doubt, and finally in outrage. A Columbia graduate nineteen

years his senior, Hewitt had battled Tweed and later fought at Whitney's
side in the struggle for Tilden in 1876. These Democratic seventy-sixers
who had bled together were united by bonds similar to those of men
who had survived Gettysburg or the Wilderness. Hewitt was a man as
close to moral rectitude as could be found in the party. A classic example of the honest, patriotic, and altruistic businessman, he had made
a fortune as an ironmaster, came near losing it by keeping his three
thousand employees at their jobs during panic times, and was devoting
his later years to philanthropy and an often bullheaded effort to bring
integrity to politics. It was too much to ask of a man of such character to
have sweetness too, and Hewitt did not. His great energy and skill were
forever on the verge of being neutralized by his failures in tact, patience, and tolerance—qualities Whitney had in abundance. But the
two men so effectively exploited Kelly's political blunders that formerly
firm Tammanyites joined the new organization, and the County Democracy began to feel its muscle. Whitney felt strong enough to urge
that the County Democrats invite Tammany and other smaller splinter
groups to join them—in a subsidiary role, to be sure.

". . . Mr. Whitney proposes to send out a committee to Tammany
Hall," observed *The Tribune*, "and Irving Hall and all the other halls
and factions against which the new Democracy is an organized protest,
and ask them to abandon their own organizations and unite with the
new concern. It is not possible that Mr. Whitney is serious."

Whitney was serious indeed, demonstrating one of the great passions
of his life—to see all Democrats united, if possible under Whitney.
Kelly for a time was livid. In his Tammany sheet, *The New York Star*,
he hinted that Whitney had been corrupt in his choice of attorneys to
argue cases for the city, had planned to bribe Tammany aldermen, and
had used his influence in the city's dock department to benefit his father's firm, the Metropolitan Steamship Company. It would be risky to
place credence in these charges, since they appeared in none of New
York's less blatantly partisan journals, but they did add to the evidence
that Whitney had expanded his political influence well beyond the
limits of the powerful office he held and had become one of the city's
top Democratic leaders.

Tammany for a time was eclipsed by the strong new County Democracy. As a delegate to the 1882 state party convention at Syracuse,
Whitney sought out the Albany Democratic leader Daniel Manning
and found him chatting with a portly companion whose pardon Whitney begged while interrupting them long enough to tell Manning, "The

man who can defeat the Republicans worst [for Governor] is that buxom Buffalonian, Grover Cleveland." "Mr. Whitney," Manning chuckled, "let me introduce you to Grover Cleveland of Buffalo." Cleveland, whose first impression of Whitney could thus have hardly been unfavorable, was nominated and elected, a success due in large part to Whitney's ability to bargain with Boss Kelly and bring in Tammany. Whitney resigned as corporation counsel the day after the election, after more than seven years in the post.

". . . the expenses [of the department] were reduced by me about forty percent during the first two years . . . ," he reported, "and have been still further reduced since."

While his conduct of the office was generally approved, the quality that aroused greater interest was his virtuosity in political organization and tactics. No one could touch him in his ability to heal wounds, to bring the quarreling factions together at critical times, as he had done in the election of Cleveland as governor. Obviously he loved politics, loved the role of the planner and tactician who works out of view of the audience, advances the pawns, and crowns the kings. But now politics would have to take second place. He was out to make his own fortune, to end his financial subservience to the Paynes (including his own wife Flora), to be his own man again.

1. Crashing the Gates

WHITNEY RETURNED to the private practice of law and, with Flora, worked skillfully for two objectives, wealth and social prominence. Despite the bitter complaints he was later to make about Flora's weakness for parties of regimental size, he had no objection to Society as such. It appeared that he was transferring his political talents to the *beau monde* with the purpose of making a social success that would be pleasant of itself but would also aid his financial climb. The Whitneys had arrived at a time when New York Society was in fierce contention over the question of admitting into its ranks those newcomers overflowing with affluence but considered lacking in lineage and taste. The outsiders, one of whose leaders was Mrs. William K. Vanderbilt, were storming the gates. The seigneurs, whose unquestioned leader was Mrs. William Backhouse Astor,* had conducted a defense that was beginning to falter. One of the battlegrounds where the issue would be decided was No. 660 Fifth Avenue at 52nd Street, where Richard Morris Hunt had just completed for the Vanderbilts an immense mansion patterned after the Chateau de Blois. Its purpose was to eclipse the huge brownstone of the Astors at Fifth and 34th—to make Mrs. Astor take notice, to force her to accept the Vanderbilts into the gilded arena to which she held the key.

Both coteries barred politicians, especially Democratic politicians, unless they had prominent redeeming traits. Among the few who qualified were August Belmont, Abram Hewitt, and Whitney. The Whitneys, by reason of their own undeniable charm and their well-planned entertainments, had fought their way past the outer fringes of the Vanderbilt faction, though not yet into leadership. This was fast work con-

---

* More accurately, she led a relatively extravagant portion of that complex social network and was herself not above criticism by Knickerbocker matrons for her addiction to jewelry and for her husband's grandfather's profession as butcher in Germany.

sidering their newness in the city and New York's tendency to ignore a considerable family tree unless it had taken root, grown, and branched out in New York, no Cleveland tree being recognized. The Whitneys knew the Vanderbilts well. William K.'s older brother Cornelius and his large family had been Park Avenue neighbors until they moved uptown, as so many in Society were doing. Their oldest son Willie went to Arthur H. Cutler's private school for boys, as did young Harry Payne Whitney. The dynasty was founded by the burly roughneck Commodore Cornelius Vanderbilt, who had started as a Staten Island ferryman and amassed a fortune with steamships and railroads. It was passed on through his son William Henry, now sixty-two, and to *his* sons, Cornelius Jr. and William K., both a few years younger than Whitney.

Mrs. William K. Vanderbilt was born Alva Smith in 1853, daughter of a prosperous Mobile planter. Plump, not beautiful, but massively determined, she had been educated in France and had met and overpowered Willie at White Sulphur Springs. Her resolution to assume social leadership was close to mania. She lacked the charm of Mrs. Astor, whose rejection of the Vanderbilts was blamed mostly on the late Commodore's plebeian origins. He had died only recently in 1877 and was well remembered for uncouth behavior and shocking language. Although he had left $94,000,000, the greatest fortune of the time, the Vanderbilts had been unable to live him down. Mrs. Astor, a Schermerhorn who could trace her family back for generations and could claim no taint of either vulgarity or commerce, could admit Alva Vanderbilt, two decades her junior, to the elect by visiting her or merely leaving her card. This she had resolutely refused to do. Now Mrs. Vanderbilt planned a great costume ball for March 26, 1883, as a housewarming—a trap intended to snare Mrs. Astor. The question that transfixed Society in both factions was: Would Mrs. Astor come, or permit her pretty daughter Caroline to come, and thereby publish to the world her acceptance of the Vanderbilts?

While the Vanderbilts' acceptance would not automatically mean the validation of all other nouveaux such as the Whitneys, it would set a precedent and would surely mean entrée for many of them. Hence, in the world of fashion, the Vanderbilt ball assumed the aspect of a crucial judgment equivalent to that of a Supreme Court decision in law. The ball had been announced early in February, and the Society newspaper writers had been growing more excited about it as the day approached.

Whitney was already prominent in a skirmish over the same principle: whether the old Knickerbocker aristocracy based on family, tradition, and cultivation could exclude from the opera applicants of the big-
business or robber-baron class who generally had more money and
diamonds and were building palaces uptown. Almost all the boxes at the
city's only opera house, the small Academy of Music on Irving Place,
were owned by the old families. "Conservatives cherished it for being
small and inconvenient," Edith Wharton noted, "and thus keeping out
the 'new people' whom New York was beginning to dread and yet to be
drawn to." The nouveaux, many but not all of whom were less interested in opera as art than as a social function, thereupon formed a corporation, the Metropolitan Opera Company, Ltd., in which each of
sixty-five founding members subscribed to $15,000 in stock, which en-
titled him to a box in the new house when it was completed. Among
the leaders in this enterprise were William K. Vanderbilt (or, some said,
Alva), Cornelius Vanderbilt, J. Pierpont Morgan, and Whitney. The
massive Metropolitan was nearing completion at Broadway and 40th
Street. Was it a token of capitulation when the William Backhouse
Astors subscribed for a box? William K. (or, some said, Alva) was committed for two, although until then his passion for yachting had taken
priority over his interest in music.

So the suspense over the ball was building to a marvelous pitch. "The
Vanderbilt ball," said *The Times*, "has agitated New York society more
than any social event that has occurred here in many years. . . .
scarcely anything else has been talked about. . . . It has disturbed the
sleep and occupied the waking hours of social butterflies, both male and
female, for over six weeks. . . ."

The Times well knew that it concerned more than mere butterflies,
since the issue involved nothing less than the pride and peace of mind
of many captains of industry as well as their conjugal harmony. The de-
nouement was anticlimactic. Young Caroline Astor, assuming that she
would be invited, organized with her friends a dancing group in which
they would appear as pairs of varicolored stars. They bought costumes,
worked at their act until they were delighted with it, and Caroline
would have been crushed had she been excluded. Alva Vanderbilt knew
how to capitalize on such emotions: "Hearing of Miss Astor's plans,
Mrs. Vanderbilt intimated to common friends that, alas, it would be
quite impossible for her to invite the young lady, since the Astors had
never paid her a call. Mrs. Astor, admitting for once that her hand had

been forced, summoned her carriage, left her card at the shining new portal, and thus made the Vanderbilts forever free of Best Society."

Best Society would never be the same. The presence at the ball of Mrs. Astor's satellite, the fat social arbiter Ward McAllister, attired as the Huguenot Count de la Moie, confirmed the Vanderbilt victory. Since 1,200 had been invited, Fifth Avenue was more snarled with equipages than ever before in history, several magnificent carriages were slightly damaged, and two coachmen had a fistfight. Inside the enormous structure, Mrs. Vanderbilt was triumphant as "a Venetian princess taken from a picture by Cabanel." Her husband was the Duc de Guise, wearing "yellow silk tights, yellow and black trunks, a yellow doublet, and a black velvet cloak embroidered in gold." The Cornelius Vanderbilts were as splendid, she clad as "the 'Electric Light,' in white satin trimmed with diamonds, and with a magnificent diamond head-dress," he as Louis XVI in "fawn-colored brocade with silver point d'Espagne." (The city's costumers and dressmakers were exhausted. Seventeen guests appeared as Louis XVI, seven Mary Queen of Scots, and eight Marie Antoinettes.) Whitney's friend Abram Hewitt was costumed as "King Lear while yet in his right mind," while pretty Mrs. James Brown Potter, pre-" 'Ostler Joe," was here an innocent Madame Favart. The sensation of the evening was the Hobby-Horse Quadrille, in which dancers clad as equestrians performed caracoles on life-sized horses which were "covered with genuine hides; had large, bright eyes, and flowing manes and tails; but were light enough to be easily and comfortably attached to the waists of the wearers, whose feet were concealed by richly embroidered hangings."

Since there were more than a thousand present, and the newspapers could give space to the costumes of only the leading hundred or so, it was a sign of rapid social progress that the Whitneys were described at all: "Mr. W. C. Whitney wore a very becoming black velvet costume of a Marquis of the old regime, with rich lace jabot and cuffs and a powdered wig, and Mrs. Whitney, as 'Mme. Thermidor,' wore a piquant dress of the Directory."

Ex-President Grant, whose esteem for money perhaps mattered more to him than the subtleties of the social struggle involved, was a guest with Mrs. Grant, neither of them in costume. It was easily the grandest and most expensive ball ever held in America, and worth every penny, propelling the lady from Mobile into the social sunlight and confirming her belief in her course. She was to continue her bold maneuvers in pursuit of social prestige and was to commit what some thought the parental outrage of the century.

The Whitneys meanwhile were following their own less melodramatic course of social climbing. They had both shifted to Episcopalianism—moves that may have been in response to pious reflection but that raised their social status. Whitney's club memberships already included the Union, Knickerbocker, Yale, University, Manhattan, and Democratic, and he was to go on to set some kind of record in this realm. Flora patronized the more fashionable charities. Far from pressing the willingness she had shown to economize by getting rid of the expensive Park Avenue house, she now considered that house unsatisfactory because it had no ballroom and was overcrowded when the guests exceeded a hundred.

Whitney's sponsorship of the new opera, however, was an entrance into financial as well as social circles, which required three years of intermittent attention, some of it in the form of gatherings at the homes of the respective sponsors. In this way he came to know, among many others, old William Henry Vanderbilt, his son-in-law Hamilton McKown Twombly, and his two sons Cornelius and William K.; J. Pierpont Morgan, William Rockefeller, Darius Ogden Mills, the broker Henry Clews, and James Gordon Bennett, publisher of *The New York Herald*. Music had new charms for a somewhat out-of-pocket attorney no longer on the sunny side of forty when it offered a friendly connection with men of such power.

Two months after the Vanderbilt ball, Whitney met with the other founding members at the all-but-completed Metropolitan Opera House. Each sponsor was now assessed another $5,000 to finance the completion of shops that were to be rented out on the Broadway side. But at last the Metropolitan, costing $1,732,978.71 ($1,200,000 less than the new Vanderbilt palace) opened October 22, 1883, with a performance of *Faust* sung in Italian by a cast headed by Christine Nilsson and Italo Campanini. The Whitneys occupied Box 63, one of the best. If the building was ugly outside, its interior had a grandeur reflecting the wealth of its sponsors. No European house could rival its capacity of nearly four thousand seats. Its acoustics were perfect except for the odd circumstance that the singers could scarcely hear their own voices in the huge space. "Essentially," one observer noted, "it was a semicircle of boxes with an opera house built around them, a private club to which the general public was somewhat grudgingly admitted."

2. *Bear Up, My Dear*

EVEN AS he had danced at the Vanderbilt ball, Whitney had been planning his bid for the Broadway surface railway franchise. He failed, as has been seen, because of Jacob Sharp's liberality toward the aldermen. A third bidder for the franchise was a group including Thomas Fortune Ryan, a prosperous Wall Street broker. It was this group that had made an offer to the aldermen that was rejected in favor of Sharp's more attractive bribe. It would be unfair to assume that Whitney had made an offer, but one could say fairly that after his seven years of intimacy with city affairs and close acquaintance with city officials, it would have been a greater tribute to his honesty than to his sense of political and business realism if he had been the only one who went to the Board of Aldermen with merely a smile and handshake.

At the same time, so enterprising was he, Whitney joined a group including William H. Vanderbilt, Andrew Carnegie, William Rockefeller, J. P. Morgan, and H. McK. Twombly in the promotion of a railroad through southern Pennsylvania aimed at breaking the monopoly of the powerful Pennsylvania Railroad. Except for Carnegie, these men were all fellow sponsors of the Metropolitan Opera. It is not unlikely that in his many meetings with them over problems of opera construction and contracts, his abilities had become so evident that they hired him. Whitney was a minor investor, putting $20,000 in the road as against such sums as $5,000,000 by Vanderbilt, the promoter-in-chief, and the same amount by a group headed by Carnegie. But he was one of its top managers, entrusted with such vital assignments as getting the necessary legislation through the state capitol, without which the new road could not be undertaken. Occasionally he went to Harrisburg as a sort of lobbyist-in-charge—a profession seldom burdened by conventional ethics.

The combine's aim to break the Penn monopoly was not inspired by regard for the public interest but by the Vanderbilts' intention to invade a profitable territory* and the Rockefellers' drive for lower freight rates that would assure them greater oil profits. As for Carnegie, he was aroused because the Pennsylvania had raised by 20 percent the rate on coke, which he needed for his steel works; he also wanted to sell rails and other steel equipment to the new road. The knowledge of the

---

* A further Vanderbilt motive was revenge on the Pennsylvania for building a railroad along the west side of the Hudson, which competed with the New York Central's east-shore line.

millions behind the Vanderbilt project, and the fierce opposition to it of the Pennsylvania, was likely to make it difficult to get it approved by the legislature without extreme persuasion. Whitney finally got it through the legislature, then had to exert more solicitation to get a reluctant governor to sign it—a considerable feat. He was working with three of the greatest businessmen of the era, Carnegie, Vanderbilt, and Morgan (though Morgan, four years older than Whitney, had not yet reached his peak), and he developed a lifelong affection for Twombly.

Was there some family tension that caused Flora to go to Europe without him at this time? Not necessarily, in view of her impulsive need for travel and the constant temptation of the White Star steamers leaving New York. She wept and so did he as he saw her off on May 23, 1883, with the four children. He wrote her fondly two days later and again two days after that:

> There is nothing prettier in the world than your relation to your children, the unaffected love between you and them. . . . [After seeing her off] I drove immediately to the Opera House meeting at the Casino. . . . I got away from there in time to go to the Opera House with George Whitmore and Cady [the latter the architect of the Metropolitan], and looked over the choices. . . . Thence to Delmonico's in time to meet the man from Philadelphia . . . for use with the governor, on our Bills. We dined well, talked business all the time, and I sent him off to Harrisburg at eight thirty, and until twelve thirty I was at the council meeting of the University Club—a wrangling, jangling affair, for which I was in a capital mood. I contributed my fair share. . . . When I got home at one o'clock, and drew up a chair under the gas light and took a cigar without a book, I was mad enough to have gotten into a fight with the balance of the Universe. . . . I had had enough for one day—the family—the Opera House—the Pennsylvania—the University Club—and no time to think till I should go to bed.

Shortly after she left, Whitney attended a dinner at the home of the former Democratic Congressman Roswell Pettibone Flower, a rich broker, and learned to his astonishment that Flower was earnestly trying to build a presidential boom around himself. It was difficult to take him seriously, because of the lisp that seemed to go with his name—he called himself "a plain bithnethman." Besides, Whitney occasionally advised Governor Cleveland on political matters and already saw the governor as a contender. Another guest was Joseph Pulitzer, who only a fortnight earlier had purchased *The New York World*, thereby displacing Whitney's good friend the former editor of the paper, William Hurlbert. Whitney, writing to Flora, felt sympathy for Hurlbert:

His home of twenty years is broken up and every tit-bit of elegance by which he was surrounded goes with it all. . . . what a pity such a man should have anything to do but to grace and adorn life. . . . Pulitzer [is] six feet two or three inches, sharp-faced with bushy hair and scraggy whiskers . . . antagonizing people at dinner, however, a sharp fellow, hard working and probably keen as a briar. . . . I knew him well in Seventy Six and we talked over the old campaign. . . . The real amusing part of the dinner to me was to discover that Flower is a candidate for the *Presidency*. These men all seemed to know it, and it made me laugh to myself how Flower had lately when we met wanted my opinion as to who ought to be the nominee of the party, and I had innocently talked over with him everybody but himself. I really congratulate myself that I never caught the disease . . . Though men have often talked to me of Governorships and even, some fools, the Presidency. . . . As for me, I am delighted to be out of it all. I enjoy much more the entertainment of private affairs.

If that last was true, had he attended this thoroughly political meeting at Flower's because his private affairs—his city traction plans—required political influence? He went on to tell Flora that she was not generally as considerate toward him as to others but that she was coming around:

You are a curious compound, My Dear, your genial nature and your bright spirits would make you like everybody, but a more critical person at bottom, easier irritated at little uncongenial contacts, never was made. Idealizing everybody at first, and then seeing them through and through. Your loving nature that craves affection and love from others has saved you from . . . well, never mind what from. At all events it tided us over until we began to grow together and love each other for what we were and not for what you thought I was. Now and then though, My Dear, the sweets go all around for a week or two without getting any of them on my plate. I generally know where the antagonism started, and just how you feel. . . . My consolation is that I honestly believe that with most men you would have been absolutely miserable. . . . The "Yales" beat the "Harvards" at baseball yesterday.

Soon after writing this letter he was stricken to learn by cable that his youngest child, five-year-old Olive, had contracted diphtheria and died in Paris on June 5 and that Harry and William were in the grip of the same disease. Flora, the compulsive writer, kept a long, touching diary, hour by hour:

The only time [Olive] spoke when I could not understand her was about twenty minutes before she died. "Mama, hold my hand," rang in my ears. I went away and when I returned to see her she had on her steamer dress, a crown on her head of white rosebuds, garden pinks and white flowers at her feet, with a bunch of pinks in her clasped hands.

Then I was free to go to Harry, the first time since he was brought in [to the *Maison de Santé*] Monday morning. . . . Can it be I who paces up and down? Is that my Olive lying on that white bed with candles at her head . . . the little face as though she must breathe . . . the eyes sunken, the sweet mouth and nostrils black; but the head and the little ears charming and the expression as though she was dreaming in a soft still way.

There were cables from the Paynes in Cleveland to their daughter, from Oliver Payne and from Whitney to Flora as he packed to catch the next boat:

BEAR UP MY DEAR WE MUST YOU MUST FOR ME AND I WILL FOR YOU. . . . I MUST SEE HER FACE ONCE MORE REMEMBER THIS IN MAKING ARRANGEMENTS

Whitney, enduring the seven-day voyage in fear that all of the three other children might also die, arrived to find them safe, Pauline never touched by the disease and Harry and Willie recovered. He had his last look at Olive, who had been placed temporarily in a glass-topped coffin. He took a lock of her golden hair, which was later found in his papers, and sent her body home for burial at Woodlawn Cemetery in New York.

Flora was distracted with grief, haunted by the guilt that can strike in such circumstances: *If* she had stayed at home with the children, it would not have happened. In Paris with the Whitneys was Flora's good friend from New York, Ellen Hopkins. They were joined in Paris also by Oliver Payne, come to do what he could to comfort Flora.

With him Oliver brought that old Payne family friend and eccentric master-of-all-the-arts, Alexander Gunn. Whitney had first met Gunn in Cleveland nine years earlier. The two men henceforth were to be linked in warmest affection, one that seemed incongruous in view of the vast differences between them.

Gunn was forty-five, plump, nearsighted, and benign, looking older than his age, as Whitney looked younger than his forty-two. The well-educated son of a wealthy Cleveland family, his parents now dead, he had sown his wild oats in Europe as a young man. In 1879 he had astounded his many friends by giving up his merchandising business and "retiring" to a religious colony. He had gone to Zoar, sixty-five miles south of Cleveland, to join a commune founded there in 1818 by Bavarian Separatists and to find "sanctuary from the clamors and empty ambitions of the world." His immediate motivation had been a broken love affair.* The discipline at Zoar was flexible, but he strained it to the limit, exciting controversy among the faithful. While he was not the only member of this agrarian colony who cultivated fruits, vegetables, and roses and occasionally tended a gaggle of geese, he was surely the only one who also owned a dress suit and an excellent small library, ordered champagne by the case, retained membership in Cleveland's dignified Union Club, and while in New York stayed (by courtesy of a friend) at the millionaire-infested Union League Club. He had a catholic taste for liquors vinous, spirituous, or fermented. He liked to surprise the Paynes and other friends by sending them Zoar pickles or melons in season and a goose or turkey at holiday time.

With Oliver, Gunn, and Mrs. Hopkins, the Whitneys sought restoration in Switzerland. Whitney was fascinated by Gunn, though Flora later said jealously that he showed most interest of all in the attractive Ellen Hopkins: ". . . in Europe when I was broken hearted and really out of my mind, all you and Ellen thought of was to get away with each other and 'gas'." Gunn's inclination to accuse himself of stupidity and failure spiced his humor with cultivated irony. He was a loyal Democrat who subscribed at Zoar to *The New York World* among other papers and could enliven discussions of politics—especially after champagne—by drawing apt parallels from history or literature. His broad learning and discrimination in the arts perhaps reminded Whitney that in his own preoccupation with politics and business he had let such appreciation slide. Although Colonel Payne had begun (as had the Whitneys) the collection of European paintings that was now a mark of New York social distinction, his grasp of the arts was less sure than his comprehension of Wall Street.

At Ragatz, which Flora had described at length during her tour twenty years earlier, she took the waters while Whitney read Shelley to Gunn on the great veranda of the casino, with the Alps spread out before them as far as the eye could reach. Oliver, for all his generosity, was not the man to whom one would read Shelley, and the Gunn-Whitney congeniality may have left his nose a little out of joint. They moved on to Lucerne, then to Como. Did Payne money pay for this long excursion? In Strasbourg in September the Colonel and Gunn left the Whitneys and headed homeward, Gunn thanking them for a sum-

* One of the current Zoar pamphlets alleges that the lady was Flora Payne, but this is contradicted by Gunn's own writings.

mer that, "though shattered by a great calamity, yet has left so much
that cannot die and shall not be destroyed." The Whitneys returned in
October, the children going back to school, Whitney resuming his work
with the Vanderbilt group, and Flora going miserably to Lenox. "I do so
hope," she wrote to him with her usual flair for vivid expression, "you
won't lay it up against me that I was so unendurably cross last Sunday.
. . . I don't see how I am to get much better. I am afraid I will wear
out your patience and love at last and then what will become of me?
After a great sorrow if one is to live long, they ought to be able to grow
new hearts and new brains."

3. Standard Oil Intrigue?

FOR ALL his talk to Flora about his delight in being freed from politics,
Whitney reentered politics on two fronts. First, he pulled strings to help
his father-in-law Payne become a United States senator from Ohio.
Then Whitney, with Hewitt, revitalized the County Democracy in New
York and took a leading role in the 1884 effort to elect a Democratic
President. In addition to his close acquaintance with every Democratic
leader, Whitney was on good terms with many of the powerful New
York newspaper proprietors including Bennett of *The Herald*, Reid of
The Tribune, Dana of *The Sun*, and Pulitzer of *The World*. He was,
unless the terms were synonymous, both a political expert and a con-
noisseur of public relations.

Late in 1883 Henry B. Payne again took aim at the White House,
this time via the United States senatorship, senators then being elected
by the state legislatures. Whitney's good work for him in 1880 might
well have borne fruit but for the Machiavellian tactics of Tilden. Alexander Gunn, back at Zoar among his vegetables and flowers, was watching the Ohio contest. He had sent Flora *The Rubáiyát of Omar
Khayyam* to allay her melancholy, and to Whitney *The Meditations of
Marcus Aurelius*. He wrote to Whitney that Oliver was "deep in politics," working for his father's election, and that the senior Payne was not
too old for high office:

Think of Talleyrand and Thiers . . . . Palmerston, Bismarck, and Gladstone—all men who held the rod of empire until extreme old age. Mr.
Payne is younger than most men of fifty—his strong intelligence is rip-
ened into the rarest type of wisdom.

Young or not, he was attacked again because of his alleged ties with Standard Oil. Whitney had cultivated Joseph Pulitzer and was ready to make political use of his sensational—and sensationally successful— Democratic *World*, which took the whole nation as its political province. Whitney wrote to Pulitzer in behalf of Payne: "It is becoming . . . important to us as a party. We don't want to carry the Standard Oil Co. unless we have to," adding:

> The attack on Mr. Payne has done him more good than harm because it has cleared up a fact . . . that Mr. Payne has not now, nor has ever had any interest—not to the extent of one cent in the Standard Oil Co. nor any thing to do with it or its affairs. . . . The controlling men . . . are well known in Ohio and are known to be republicans.
> John Rockefeller
> William Rockefeller
> H. M. Flagler
> are the three most important men in it. . . .

Whitney did not mention that Oliver Payne, a Democrat, was as important in the Standard company as Flagler. Nor did he say that Oliver was going to such lengths to elect his father that if the latter did not sympathize with Standard, then Oliver was fighting his own company. The elder Payne, whatever his party label, was a corporation man devoted to business interests. He had once been, if he was no longer, a Standard stockholder.

Pulitzer at times enjoyed exercising his rich capacity for malice. *The World* story boosting Payne did not appear. At this very time the news came out that the Whitneys had acquired the former Stevens mansion at 2 West 57th Street in what was now the grandest part of Fifth Avenue. To Pulitzer the Standard Oil Company was perhaps the only corporation more contemptuous of the public good than the Vanderbilts' New York Central Railroad. Either Pulitzer overlooked Whitney's letter or was not impressed by it. *The World* featured a story headed "The Recent Fifth Avenue Purchase for William C. Whitney," and a subhead that hurt: "What it is to Have a Millionaire for a Father-in-Law." Speculating on who had paid for the house, the body of the story also trampled on Whitney's advice: "The latest and probably the most correct story . . . is that Mr. Henry B. Payne, of Ohio, and of the Standard Oil Company—Mr. Whitney's father-in-law—bought the property for $600,000 for his daughter."

Since this appeared only two days before the Ohio legislature was to elect a senator, Whitney may well have ground his teeth. The Standard company steadily maintained unrighteous influence in the state capitol at Columbus, having recently had "in its direct employ a member of the House, a member of the Senate, an ex-member of the House, and three outsiders." But the legislature was believed to be influenced most of all by some $100,000 Oliver Payne was said to have distributed, and it elected Henry B. Payne to the United States Senate. John D. Rockefeller's leading biographer, defending his subject, declared, "It seems clear that money was spent with inexcusable lavishness by the Payne managers; that probably some of it was used corruptly, though proof is lacking; but that it was Oliver Payne's money, and not a cent of it the Standard's."*

The World, unaware of this, a little late in the day applauded Payne's election, saying editorially, "Henry B. Payne . . . is a man whose Democracy has always been of the best and purest quality. . . . His opponents charge him with being a monopolist, but there is no evidence whatever to support this allegation beyond the fact that his son . . . is identified with the Standard Oil Company."

The great fortunes being made in this virtually taxless boom era often required the rich to think anxiously about how to spend enough money to keep from stumbling over it. Whitney, who never had this trouble, was constantly with people who did. The new house made him look like a multimillionaire, whereas he had scarcely started making his first million. One can only speculate in what proportions this princely gift was intended as a social establishment to assuage Flora's anguish, to repay Whitney for his political aid, and to furnish Oliver with a capital address when he was in New York.

The house had four stories, filled four city lots, and its ballroom—a feature required by the very fashionable and very rich only during the last decade or so—presaged a new social future for Flora. Until then it had been enough to rent Delmonico's or Sherry's for splendid events, a practice now considered niggardly. Unlike the old brownstone mansions, which Mrs. Wharton thought "coated New York like a cold chocolate sauce," this one shone with red brick and stone trim and had soaring gables, wide bays, and an impressive entrance. Oscar Wilde had earlier ridden up Fifth Avenue and shaken his head at the endless blocks

---

* The admirable Allan Nevins, Rockefeller's biographer, changed his emphasis from that in his biography of Cleveland, published eight years earlier, in which he wrote: ". . . when [Senator Payne] took his seat in 1885 his title was tainted with impudent corruption. Officers of the Standard Oil had supplied his managers with huge sums to bribe the legislature. . . ."

of brownstone and commented that New York was an imposing but gloomy city:

> The Stevens mansion suddenly broke upon his view. The sun was shining upon its red brick sides, and the golden devices from its many peaks glistened in its rays. Then Mr. Wilde's face brightened. At last he murmured, "That house seems like a voice crying, in this wilderness of dark art, 'Brighter days, brighter days, brighter days.' "

Certainly Flora and William Whitney (who had heard Wilde lecture at the Merchants' Club) hoped it would bring them brighter days. It was on the southwest corner of an intersection that had a great mansion on each corner: that of the Collis P. Huntingtons on the southeast, the Hermann Oelrichses on the northeast, and on the northwest corner the biggest of the lot, the huge rambling brownstone of those friends of the Whitneys, the Cornelius Vanderbilts. "Without a guide, one could never find his way through the [Whitney] house," *The World* said, "for the rooms are set in every out-of-the-way nook and corner, and open into other rooms which are never suspected to exist."

One room that surely existed was Oliver's room, or more likely, Oliver's apartment, into which he moved his furniture and his art collection. Indeed, in a sense that could escape only the thickest-skinned, it was Oliver's house. He deeded it not to the Whitneys jointly but to his sister Flora. It cost $200,000 to make alterations and to collect furniture, rugs, and artwork for the building, and the added cost of such things as a larger staff of servants and more splendid horses and carriages must have been considerable. Above all this was the amount it would now cost to entertain in the grand style that both the house and Flora demanded, and that now involved her in an intense activity that helped to dull the ache over Olive.

Moderation and discrimination were no easier in social life than in business in the post–Civil War era of swift expansion, mechanization, and the exploitation of seemingly limitless resources. The rewards held out for shrewdness in enterprise were dizzying. The opportunities for wealth heaped new incentives on the old Poor Richard ethic of work and success—an ethic repeated by Emerson, stressed in the McGuffey Readers, dramatized in 135 novels by Horatio Alger promising that wealth was the reward of virtue, and preached by the Baptist exhorter Russell Conwell, who in his famous "Acres of Diamonds" lecture urged Americans, "I say, get rich, get rich!" Conwell himself became a millionaire giving the lecture six thousand times. Success was not the bitch-goddess. Success was the energetic and patriotic exploitation of America's God-given opportunities.

True, Henry Adams scoffed at the general conception of what constituted success and how success generally manifested itself. His more worldly brother Charles Francis Adams had met and conducted business with many of the successful and said sweepingly, "a less interesting crowd I do not care to encounter. Not one that I have ever known would I care to meet again either in this world or the next; nor is one associated in my mind with the idea of humor, thought, or refinement." And the Knickerbocker Theodore Roosevelt was to put the thought in different words: "I am simply unable to make myself take the attitude of respect toward the very wealthy men which such an enormous multitude of people evidently really feel."

But these were minority voices. Henry Ward Beecher, whom Flora so much admired, regarded poverty as most often the fault of its victim, felt a dollar-a-day wage sufficient for a worker with a family of five so long as he did not smoke or drink beer, and said in a sermon, "generally the proposition is true, that where you find the most religion you find the most worldly prosperity." And Whitney's old classmate and fellow Bonesman William Graham Sumner, now a professor at Yale and still a frequent guest of the Whitneys, viewed the accumulation of wealth in economic terms that both Whitney and Flora welcomed. Sumner, the preacher of laissez faire and social Darwinism, had little time for the "unfit." He preached the virtues of the solid middle class but saw the rich as the greatest benefactors because they started the wheels of progress and kept them going for the benefit of all:

> They may fairly be regarded as the naturally selected agents of society for certain work. They get high wages and live in luxury, but the bargain is a good one for society. There is the intensest competition for their place and occupation. This assures us that all who are competent for this function will be employed in it, so that the cost of it will be reduced to the lowest terms. . . .

Sumner had trouble with Yale's president Noah Porter over some of his teachings. Whitney supported his old friend and was so irate at their common alma mater for such philistinism that he planned to send his sons elsewhere. Indeed, Sumner, though entirely honest and independent in his thinking, became the most popular of Yale's professors among the householders in the most expensive stretch of Fifth Avenue between 34th Street and Central Park. One Yale benefactor doubled his contribution because "Yale College is a good and safe place for the keeping and use of property and the sustaining of civilization when endangered by ignorance, rascality, demagogues . . . communists, butlers, strikers . . . and fanatics of sundry roots and sizes." And John D. Rockefeller said in a Sunday school homily:

> The growth of a large business is merely a survival of the fittest. The American Beauty rose can be produced in the splendor and fragrance which brings cheer to its beholder only by sacrificing the early buds which grow up around it. This is not an evil tendency in business. It is merely the working-out of a law of nature and a law of God.

4. What Was Whitney's Motive?

ALEXANDER GUNN had a different view of roses. He had at Zoar eighty-three named varieties, from Olga of Wurttemburg to Gloire de Dijon and was adding to them yearly. "I watch the papers for news from home," Gunn wrote to Whitney from San Francisco, where he was visiting, "and notice all the 'pros and cons' in regard to Mr. Payne. It looks as if my prediction . . . would come true. 'Glamis thou art, and Cawdor,' and if Mr. Payne could be president, I would say, like the prophet of Israel: '*Nunc dimittis.*' " But if Gunn saw expanding power ahead for Macbeth Whitney, he admitted dread at the prospect of old Payne entering a furious political struggle for the presidency. "The place he now has will beautifully round off a noble and useful life, even if that high seat does not come to him."

Payne had redundantly made clear that his new senatorial status did not cancel his presidential availability. As it turned out, his only chance had come and gone in 1880. When the Democratic National Convention opened in Chicago in July, *The New York Herald* man wrote, "I confess it is difficult to diagnose the situation in New York. Mr. Manning does not appear sincere in his advocacy of Cleveland. . . . Whitney really hankers for Payne. . . ."

It can be assumed that Whitney was in closest touch with his father-in-law, who was also in Chicago. Next day, Senator-elect Payne saw that he had no chance, withdrew, and Whitney declared, "If our [New York] delegation will present the name of Mr. Cleveland with any degree of unanimity, he will, in my opinion, be nominated on the second ballot."

His reputation for accuracy in political judgments was borne out when Cleveland was nominated on the second ballot. Whitney's political skill was recognized when, under Sen. Arthur Pue Gorman of Maryland, he and Daniel Manning of Albany became the leaders of the Cleveland campaign. This was a task—an arduous one—traditionally undertaken by politicians seeking political rewards. Why, if Whitney intended to quit politics after the presidential campaign, did he accept this grueling labor? An explanation would also have to be found for his contribution of $20,000—one of the biggest—to the campaign fund, even if the money came from the Payne coffers. Whitney was now so busy politically that he dropped out of the Vanderbilt project in Pennsylvania, which seems to have disappointed him in the meagerness of its rewards.* That left him with his somewhat neglected law practice and his city traction project—still hardly more than a plan but one in which he had great hope.

Here his motivation becomes puzzling. It will be remembered that he declined a place in the cabinet, but that Flora was so eager to go to Washington that she wept and he gave in, accepting the Navy post. He later held this against her because "I had in my hands independence and wealth and by this time would have been a recognized force in New York. . . ." Why then was he acting in every way like a man seeking political rewards in Washington?

One could speculate that Whitney might have been willing to accept office, and great power, on the off chance that Senator Payne became President. But this he knew from the start to be next to impossible, and also his $20,000 campaign contribution came after Cleveland's nomination. His mention of "independence and wealth" and power in New York of course referred to his traction designs. Such a project was deeply enmeshed with politics and the exertion of influence. Certainly if he took a leading role in electing the first Democratic President since the Civil War, and dropped $20,000 into the plate and refused Washington rewards, he would still be a persona most grata among the Democratic politicians in New York City and would be a "recognized force" there. His service to the party nationally would be rewarded in the city to the advantage of his traction plan. But this of course is a guess—not proof of devious schemes.

* That entrepreneurial struggle was ultimately settled by a Morgan-sponsored compromise between Vanderbilt and the Pennsylvania Railroad advantageous to them both. The railroad through rugged southern Pennsylvania was left unfinished after some two hundred lives had been lost in its construction. Fifty years later, this roadbed, with tunnels, became part of the Pennsylvania Turnpike.

The question seemed academic when the discovery of Cleveland's earlier affair with the widow Halpin enabled the Republicans to lampoon a Democratic campaign that was billed as a crusade for reform and to use a devilish marching song:

> Ma! Ma! Where's my pa?
> Gone to the White House,
> *Ha! Ha! Ha!*

The Democrats, who had lost through fraud in 1876 and poor management in 1880, seemed doomed to lose in 1884 because the candidate had been discovered to have a living, breathing, illegitimate child.* Republican papers the country over labored the theme of adultery, but few could equal the description of Cleveland in Dana's *New York Sun* as "low in his associations, leprous with immorality, perfidious, whose name [is] loathsome in the nostrils of every virtuous woman and upright man. . . ." The Democrats countered with newly discovered letters written by the engaging Republican candidate, James G. Blaine, suggesting his involvement in unsavory railroad deals. Blaine had actually ended one of his missives, "Burn this letter," embarrassing such Republican papers as Reid's *Tribune* in their efforts to picture Blaine's secret bargaining as exemplary. The campaign sank lower when a few Democratic papers falsely claimed that Blaine, as a young schoolteacher, had been brought forcibly to the altar by the angry kin of his bride, whose child was said to have been born before the traditional interval. The child had since died. Interested Democrats examined the tombstone and reported that a vandal, obviously a Republican seeking to hide Blaine's guilt, had chiseled away the date of birth—to which Republicans logically countercharged that it was the Democrats who did the chiseling in order to erase the record of the child's perfect legitimacy.

It seemed impossible that finical Americans would elect as their President an admitted adulterer, a bachelor now also advertised as a dissolute drunkard. It was here that Whitney, with the urbane drive for Democratic unity that had become his hallmark, brought telling results. He was aided by Pulitzer's *World*, which day after day featured vivid variations on the theme of Blaine's villainy and his status as footboy for the rich. Soon after election day it became apparent that the result again

---

* Cleveland never acknowledged fathership but did acknowledge intimacies with Mrs. Halpin. He did not believe the child to be his but contributed to its support.

hinged on New York State. It took three days to determine that Cleveland had won the state by only 1,149 votes. Five hundred and seventy-five votes the other way would have elected Blaine. Anyone who had influenced 575 votes could be said to have elected Cleveland. William C. Whitney had elected Cleveland. And Joseph Pulitzer had elected Cleveland.

5. Whitney and Pulitzer

WHITNEY AND Pulitzer had embarked on a friendship fated to encounter heavy weather. The Pulitzers were guests of the Whitneys at Lenox. Pulitzer sometimes visited with Whitney on Sundays to talk politics—a testimonial to Whitney's conversational gifts, for the publisher could not abide bores of any party. Probably it also showed recognition of Whitney's social standing, for Pulitzer, despite his concern for slum dwellers, sought advancement in the fashionable world. They made an odd pair. Pulitzer was towering, angular, dark-bearded, long-nosed, intense, and often disheveled; he spoke excellent English with a Hungarian-German accent. Against this intensity the amiable Whitney, six years older, appeared almost languid. Whitney, an old companion of *The World* when Marble ran it, knew that Pulitzer had performed not one miracle but two in the eighteen months between his arrival in New York from St. Louis and the election of Cleveland. He had taken a dying newspaper and transformed it into an enormous profit maker; and he had forced those who had ridiculed him to realize that in that short space he had become the nation's leading Democratic publisher. He was suddenly a power.

More than that, he introduced a totally new concern for social justice and a flat disagreement with William Graham Sumner's theories about the benefits bestowed by the rich. *The World*'s cannonades against the excesses of wealth excoriated Whitney's good friends. Some said that Pulitzer lived in the biggest of glass houses, since he resided not in the slums but in Gramercy Park, wore silk underwear, and would soon be a millionaire himself if he had not already reached that status. These critics missed the point. Pulitzer had no objection to wealth and its responsible enjoyment. He simply insisted that the rich should observe certain rules. They must make their money honestly. They should spread it not in vainglorious show but by paying good wages as well as heavy taxes on incomes, inheritances, and luxuries. While the taxes were to be measures of the future, Pulitzer himself observed the other strictures, being forever honest about money (if sometimes less so in his journalism), a generous if outrageously demanding employer, profuse in his charities, and obsessed with ideas for improving the country. Already almost a nervous wreck at thirty-seven, losing his eyesight, he was impossible to live with, unreasonable toward his wife, tyrannical toward his children, but capable of great charm when so inclined.

His similarity to Whitney seemed to end in the fact that both were Democrats. A Magyar-Jew from a cultivated Hungarian family, he had come to this country penniless, tasted American freedom with the delight of one who knew European despotism and yet saw room for vast improvement. He had arrived in New York at a time when Fifth Avenue poodles wore gem-studded collars while in lower Manhattan a million people lived in tenements "reeking with poisonous and malodorous gasses," as *The World* described them, "whose underfed occupants groped their way along dark and filthy passages swarming with vermin." He knew that in the Tenth Ward some 650 people were packed into each acre of ground, and the crush increased with every incoming boat bringing cheap labor for the capitalists—worse than Calcutta. Men were glad to work for a dollar a day,* a day being at least twelve hours. Women and children toiled for half that. Until Pulitzer arrived, the ghetto, for all the political attention it received, did not exist. He rediscovered it and held it under Fifth Avenue's nose. *The World* steadily attacked "the low upper classes," the "vulgar wealthy," and "the watered-stock aristocracy," warning, "Does Fifth Avenue forget that it is flanked by the tenements of Eleventh Avenue and Avenue B, and outnumbered 1,000 to one in point of mere numbers?"

The World poured fire on the corporations and the moneyed set of which the Whitneys were part and parcel. About Jay Gould, off on his yacht *Atalanta:* "His daily expenses are as much as the wages of 200 workingmen in [his] employ. . . . One bottle of his choice wine costs more than a Missouri Pacific laborer can spend for food for his family in two weeks." (True, Pulitzer was searching Europe for Johannisberg Cabinet Blue Seal 1862 and 1868, and would later have a yacht bigger than *Atalanta*, but he paid his people well.) *The World* commented acidly on the indigence of William H. Vanderbilt, who until recently had escaped all taxation by swearing that his debts exceeded his income, and whose granddaughter was later to become Pulitzer's daughter-in-

---

* But wages were generally even lower in Europe.

law. It assailed the Vanderbilts *en bloc* for corrupting legislators, under-paying workers, overcharging shippers and passengers on their railroads, and watering the stock so that the family fortune now reached $200,000,000. It declared that this amount would make a gold ingot weighing 350 tons, which would take 7,000 men to lift and 25 freight cars to haul. It excoriated the Vanderbilt headman Chauncey Depew for warning that America was threatened by communism and anarchism:

> Mr. Depew . . .[might have] pointed out to the greedy corporations and monopolies of which he is so brilliant a representative that there is no Communism in the country and can be none except through the insane folly of corrupt wealth.

The World lampooned New York Society's adulation and imitation of British aristocracy, the competition in baronial halls and ballrooms, the knee-breeched footmen behind gilt chairs, the maroon livery of the house of Vanderbilt and the blue livery of the house of Astor, the lorgnettes at the opera, the coats of arms. One man on *The World* staff specialized in exposing fake escutcheons. He discovered that Whitney's neighbor Collis P. Huntington (who started as a peddler before striking the railroad bonanza) had an escutcheon oddly featuring a buffalo and that the late president of the defunct American College of Heraldry and Genealogy was an "unfortunate ex–Sing Sing convict." (Though the Whitneys had a coat of arms, they seem not to have exploited it.) The paper observed that at the opera, "Mr. W. H. Vanderbilt, W. K. Vanderbilt, Jay Gould, and others had valets stationed before their doors" and called it "an insult [to] American freemen by a show of shoddy aristocracy that is made nowhere else in the world." *The World* assailed "the sordid . . . ambitious matchmakers, who are ready to sell their daughters for barren titles to worthless foreign paupers." Hence it managed a good word for the usually reprehended Astors (some of whose fortune came from tenement rents) when their daughter Caroline married "a plain American," Orme Wilson, cheered "All honor to her," and even reproduced the Astor coat of arms, with its lion rampant and motto *Semper fidelis*. Pulitzer knew that all categories of his audience shared human curiosity about goings-on in the mansions of the rich. His *World* often seemed schizophrenic in publishing on page one or two full-dress accounts of social events in the homes of moguls who were denounced on the editorial page.

Politically Pulitzer was far ahead of his time. Whitney was eminently a man of his time, well disposed toward humanity but unexcited about the ghetto, not really offended by stock watering or political corruption but still a game player who, in the Navy office, was to defend its probity out of sheer competitive zeal, party loyalty, and patriotism. But Pulitzer, above all a devoted Democrat, could overlook a few flaws in one who had worked so effectively for the party as Whitney. When Whitney was proposed for the cabinet, there was a storm of criticism, mostly Republican but also from Mugwump reformers fearful of his links with the corporations and his supposed ties with Standard Oil. *The Springfield* [Mass.] *Republican* said he "would scarcely be considered if it were not for his wealthy father-in-law. . . . There will be serious criticism . . . on the ground that he represents the Standard Oil Company and corporate monopoly." *The World* replied:

Mr. Whitney, if he should go into the Cabinet, would be chosen on his merits as a Democrat of unblemished character, fine abilities, and unquestionable fitness. He has given evidence of his capacity in an important public office in this city in which he set his face against all jobbery. . . . He is a life long Democrat. His father, General Whitney, was one of the most prominent Democrats of Massachusetts and one of the best of men. . . . shall [Whitney] be excluded from office solely because he is rich? . . . As to the Standard Oil Company, a man may as well be held responsible for the crotchets of his great-grandmother as for the investments of his wife's relations.

Four

1. "I Must Make Some Money"

So WHITNEY became Secretary of the Navy, and he and Flora were united in Washington with Senator and Mrs. Payne. While they had all abandoned the effort to make Payne President, President making was nevertheless a fascinating occupation, especially if one had a likely candidate in hand. One can be sure that it did not fail to occur to the Paynes, including Flora, that Whitney, with four years in the cabinet added to his already strong credentials, might be more successful. It occurred to many others and was a subject of newspaper speculation. Shortly after the Whitneys went to Washington, Oliver Payne resigned as treasurer of Standard Oil, citing his "need for a rest" after almost twenty years of hard service. Seven months later, at the very time that Standard's new ten-story skyscraper at 26 Broadway was completed, Oliver moved to New York, living in his suite at the Whitney home but planning a mansion of his own nine short blocks up Fifth Avenue at 66th Street. His move, and his history of political potency in Ohio, inspired a story headed HARD CASH IN POLITICS in *The New York Herald*'s most roguish style:

> A politician of national prominence . . . whispered recently in a *Herald* reporter's ear: "Did you know of the big fact that Colonel Payne, of Ohio, has come to New York to take up permanent residence . . . ?"
> "No; what of it?"
> "And has joined the County Democracy?"
> "Well, what of that?"
> "Why, this is what there is of it, that he is a millionaire son of a millionaire Senator and brother-in-law of Secretary Whitney, of our mighty nav-ee. . . . This millionaire's brother-in-law [Whitney] may be a presidential quantity in 1888, and New York is a pivotal state, and this man has a genius for modern politics. He's got a purse that is inexhaustible, a silent tongue, a capacity for the organization and manipulation of

men. Keep your weather eyelid turned on these parties and you will see
something of what is going on in this country. . . ."

Of course, *The Herald*'s unnamed wiseacre was mistaken in that
Cleveland was renominated and lost—a fact that moved Whitney even
higher on the small list of presidential possibilities.

While Flora could comment delightedly on Dorothy's progress ("she
has cut two more teeth and has learned the trick of laughing aloud.
. . . she is squealing out on the piazza now"), it was her first child who
was decidedly her favorite. Whitney too seemed excessively indulgent
toward Harry—a fact that later may have played a part in the alienation
of the second son—and had written to Flora: "Altogether, My Dear, I
think we can look forward to our down hill side of life with more than
the usual complacency—if these children do not murder our happiness—I am not afraid of Harry, he is cautious, and his judgment is, I
think good about people, and Will, will I hope, be [as wise], but Pauline, withal so affectionate and sweet, is headstrong and decided and I
always fear for her."

Meanwhile, Whitney and Flora quarreled over the college to which
Harry was to be sent. Out of patience with Yale, Whitney wanted Harry
to go to Harvard, and Oliver Payne was in agreement. Flora, who had
taken a dislike to Harvard years earlier when she studied in Cambridge,
would not hear of it. Whitney was aroused because Flora seemed to
have no reasons favoring Yale as specific as his reasons against it, but
she was near Groton and had Harry's ear while Whitney in Washington
could only write him urging Harvard: "You must not be influenced by
your Mother about such a thing. If I had graduated at Trinity, she is so
sentimental that she would think it was the place for you, her early girl
associations are Yale, two brothers going there. . . ." Flora, seeing
Harry weekends and writing him such inflammatory appeals as "Are you
still a fighting Yale man?" had the propaganda advantage. Whitney,
furious when Harry went to Yale, wrote to her:

> You are quite unconscious of the fact that when you have settled any-
> thing in your own mind as you want it, you are entirely incapable of
> reasoning upon it. Your contribution to a discussion is impatient, irrita-
> ble denunciation and sarcasm—you never deliberate. . . . You really
> know nothing about Yale as I do. You have heard the Colonel and me
> condemn its narrowness and stupidity. You have heard its cleverest Pro-
> fessor [Sumner] talk about it in your presence. You have seen the Colo-
> nel and me absent ourselves for years from the College Meetings, but

. . . you deliberately write me that the only thing you have heard me say
. . . in favor of Harvard, is that "more gentleman's sons go there."

As Whitney's Navy term neared its end, he was importuned to run for
governor of New York. Ahead of him, if he was interested, lay a brilliant career in politics with an excellent chance for the presidency. He
turned his back on it. Now he was determined to do what he had
planned and failed to do in 1884—make great golden piles of money.
From the very time of their courtship, his letters to Flora had displayed
his vulnerability to the advantage she—and all the Paynes—held over
him simply because of their money. It was an advantage he was determined to erase. "I look back on what I started to be," he had written to
her, "with a strange kind of lost feeling now, as though I had missed my
way."

While he was still in the cabinet—three months after those embar
rassing inquiries made by *The World* and other newspapers—Whitney
had joined forces with the Widener group and with Thomas Fortune
Ryan. They had bought out Sharp and become the leading traction
men in the city. But there were many surface lines still under independent control. Whitney's syndicate intended to get them all, one by one,
and to add new ones. It was an immensely complex undertaking, involving not only separate franchises but separate parcels of property—involving also contests and lawsuits. Whitney, after his long service as corporation counsel, knew it all by rote. For this reason, but even more
because of his enormous political influence, he was head of the group,
although Widener and his associates apparently furnished most of the
beginning capital. As for Ryan, he was unexcelled as a stock market operator, and this was primarily a stock operation. Born in poverty in
Virginia, Ryan was ten years younger than Whitney and had risen rapidly from broker's clerk a dozen years earlier. Tall, genial, flashy in
tailoring but quiet of speech, he was such an indefatigable worker that
Whitney later was able to take several months' vacation each year without worry. Ryan, Whitney later said, was "the most adroit, suave, and
noiseless man" he had ever known and if he kept his health was sure to
be "one of the richest men in the country."

Not for them the vulgar methods of Sharp. "William C. Whitney
would not soil his fingers by personal contact with aldermen," observed
Burton J. Hendrick in his study of the syndicate's operations, "but dealt
always with one or two men at the top. In return for these favors he did
not distribute common bribes but paid huge lawyers' fees, gave tips on

the stock-market, and let favored people in on the ground floor." Before very long his friends Richard Croker, now boss of Tammany and the city, and Bourke Cockran would be in the surface railroad business in a small but profitable way.

Whitney took afternoon rides in Central Park, meeting others who rode there, including the Reverend Doctor W. S. Rainsford, rector of St. George's Episcopal Church in Stuyvesant Square. Rainsford, whose senior warden was J. Pierpont Morgan, was nevertheless so politically liberal that he was thought radical in his time.

"Mr. Whitney," he said as they rode together, "I suppose you will be our next President."

"Oh, no," Whitney replied. "I am done with politics. I must make some money. Mrs. Whitney has money; I have none. I am going into New York street railroads."

"Well, they are in such a tangle you will need a lot of legal work. Whom will you engage?"

"Well, I have engaged Carter. He is of course good and able, but I am going to engage Root."

"Why are you changing?"

"Well, Carter tells me what I cannot do, and [laughing] Root what I can."

This endorsement of cunning shocked Rainsford. "The standards of right and wrong in public duty were low," he later reflected. "The man who made money was listened to and was popular. How he made it did not matter."

2. A Bigger Ballroom

FLORA WHITNEY was a victim of the canon forbidding a woman of "means and quality" to have a profession or career, or even a college education. Her whole duty was to marry advantageously, have children, and be satisfied with Society and culture. Had custom permitted it, Flora would in all probability have made an outstanding professor, writer, lawyer, cleric, or businesswoman. Her ambition, ability, and energy equaled that of her father or her brother Oliver, but she was denied their outlets. She did have a function in Society that would have more than satisfied most women but that failed to measure up to her inordinate expectations, especially in view of her occasional disappointment in Whitney. Her passion for prominence had shone savagely in her earlier charge, as he put it, "when I was struggling night and day for success, that I had brought you from position and influence to where you had none." It was a judgment so humiliating that it alone would have broken up many marriages. Probably few other than he were aware of her random onslaughts of wretchedness and temper, which at times she could end with winning self-reproaches. While most women in her circle obediently accommodated themselves to the code, they lacked the inner drive that swelled Flora's frustration.

. . . All except Mrs. William K. Vanderbilt, the redoubtable Alva, whose overload of ambition and social aggressiveness was pushing her into a kind of madness.

Mrs. Cornelius Vanderbilt (born Alice Gwynne, daughter of a prosperous Cincinnati attorney), across 57th Street from the Whitneys, had six children and accommodated. Her husband was six years older than William K. and had inherited $2,000,000 more from their late father (and Whitney's sometime business associate), William II. Her husband was now head of the Vanderbilt family, owners of the great rail lines soon to be known as the New York Central. Alice was said to resent that Alva acted as if William K. (or to be strictly accurate, as if *Alva*) were head of the family. The great ball with which Alva had captured headlines and forced the surrender of Mrs. Astor should in all justice have been given by the Cornelius Vanderbilts, new house or no. There was no holding Alva in her place. On a Mediterranean cruise in their great yacht (named *Alva*), the William K. Vanderbilts called on, and were received by, the Sultan of Turkey, and in India they had been feted by the mighty. The nonyachting Cornelius Vanderbilts were grand enough to lease for a holiday Hatfield House in Hertfordshire from the Marquess of Salisbury, but still there was no catching up with Alva. While Alice was a woman of determination who was to become formidable in her later years, she was the loser in this contest. William K. was reasonable—much more entertaining than the serious, business-preoccupied Cornelius. But Alva was totally unreasonable.

Flora Whitney kept her sanity, but the end of the Washington interlude left a great emptiness in her life. She found herself unable to fill it with the concerns of four children, charities, house decorations, travel, dress, the purchase of bibelots, paintings, and tapestries. In the end—indeed almost immediately—her competitive spirit took command, and she focused on leadership in Society rather than mere membership in its upper echelon. She had quickly captivated Ward McAllister ("McAllister was delighted with my gown," she had exulted, "said it was admired all over the house."). She had led Society in Washington. Why should she not lead it in New York, with Mrs. Astor nearing sixty and showing her age?

Flora could scarcely have failed to weigh the Whitney social advantages against the nearest competition across 57th Street. While she was on the most cordial terms with Alice Vanderbilt, and all the Vanderbilts, her own background of education and travel, as well as her personal warmth and ability as a hostess accustomed to entertaining cultivated people of many races, were unmatched in New York. As for Cornelius, it was true that he was solid, considerate, upright (except in business), and, unlike most hard workers, enjoyed dancing. The fact remained that his schooling had ended when he finished a private New York academy at eighteen and went to work as a clerk for a Vanderbilt-connected banking house. His diction was not always flawless, and, although he was very intelligent, his store of knowledge beyond the New York Central had its limits. For all his millions, his cultivation fell short of Whitney's. But among the occupants of the palaces on the other three corners of Fifth and 57th, the Vanderbilts were the Whitneys' closest friends. Cornelius and Alice were faithful members of Flora's church, St. Bartholomew's on Madison Avenue, whereas Whitney still stood by Grace Church downtown. The Vanderbilt children played with the Whitney children—although Harry was now at Yale and showing occasional interest in the Vanderbilts' fourth child, Gertrude.

So, after the Whitneys quit Washington and enjoyed Europe, William still found himself propelled into a whirl of entertaining of which he did not approve. He was not alone among busy New York husbands who stayed in town much of the time while their families were at the resorts. The Whitneys' 57th Street home was unused (often except by Whitney) during parts of the spring, summer, and fall seasons when the rest of the family followed the flight of fashion to Lenox, Newport, or Bar Harbor. Their handsome cottage (a Society term denominating a huge and luxurious home far from the Opera and Horse Show) at Lenox was the scene of garden parties. At Newport they had leased the former William R. Travers villa on Narragansett Avenue. At Bar Harbor they had no permanent place but rented one by the season, and thus far they had no winter retreat in the south but were looking into the matter. Flora's wealth, augmented by the legacy of a wealthy aunt, amounted to something less than $3,000,000 plus her property, but this sum was a comfortable one when servants were paid $16 a month, filet mignon was 19 cents a pound, men's shirts 60 cents, and ladies' fine high-button leather shoes $2.25. John Jacob Astor had spoken truth when he remarked with only a trace of irony, "The man who has only a million is as well off as if he were rich."

The Whitneys were separated often enough to suggest not that they were estranged but that their differences made occasional separations salutary for them both. But Whitney was one of the sponsors of the New Year's Ball at the Opera House in 1890, at which the Clevelands were present and "Mr. Grover Cleveland brought in Mrs. W. C. Whitney and sat next to her." There were three hundred servants in livery. A four-set Sir Roger de Coverley was danced before supper, *The World* said, and went on maliciously: "Mr. McAllister danced with Mrs. Robert Goelet and Mr. Cornelius Vanderbilt with Mrs. W. C. Whitney, although the Vanderbilts and the Whitneys are said to be struggling now for social supremacy." *The World* also pointed out that "the millions of dollars represented by the good clothes and the jewelry of half a dozen such women as Mrs. William Astor, Mrs. Cornelius Vanderbilt, Mrs. W. K. Vanderbilt, Mrs. Bradley Martin and Mrs. W. C. Whitney are simply past computation." Newspaper description of the attire of the more socially important women among the seven hundred present scarcely missed a button or tassel:

> Mrs. William C. Whitney wore a Worth gown of yellow sicilienne with a semi-train of gold-dotted tulle, and front and side trimmings of gold lace headed with garlands of blue corn flowers. The gold lace and corn flowers on the corsage were arranged to form a V at the waist and filled in with tulle. A sapphire-blue sash fell on the back skirt from the belt. The broad collar encircling her throat was formed of innumerable small diamonds representing leaves, with a large sapphire in the center of each, clasped together at the back and front with sapphire buckles.

The stunning Mrs. Frances Burke Roche, separated from her husband and whom gossips would later link with Whitney, was clad as "an ideal Russian empress, the yellow hue of her gown suiting her brunette beauty admirably." Flora's involvement in competitive Society had recently been underlined when she planned alterations in her Fifth Avenue house: "The ballroom . . . although a handsome room, was entirely too small." She called in architects who, by an exterior extension and the incorporation of the Red Room, more than doubled its size to allow for larger parties. She now had one of the half-dozen biggest private ballrooms in New York, but so rapidly were such amenities being expanded that one could not hold such a rank for long. The Vanderbilts across the way, who perhaps had more reason for feeling cramped considering their six children and twenty-seven servants, began an expansion of their already huge pile by pushing it through to 58th Street, displacing five townhouses that had been there. When completed, it was the largest private home in the city. It was finished off with a porte-cochere on the 58th Street side with sixteen-foot wrought-iron gates made in France. Among the many new features were a vestibule described as "conspicuously larger than the Supreme Court of the United States" *and* a grand ballroom sixty-four by fifty feet, larger even than the Whitneys' new one. Nevertheless, Flora introduced her new ballroom by giving a fete for twenty of the year's prettiest debutantes; then by treating the Thursday Evening Club to an elaborate musical program, "the vocal numbers being rendered by Herren Reichman, Kalbach and Fisher and Frauleine Traubmann and Huhn of the Metropolitan Opera Company," the singers being followed by "a dance to music by the Hungarian Band"; then by opening the Easter season with a cotillion for two hundred guests ranging from the Vanderbilts across the street, the McAllisters, Whitelaw Reids, and Stuyvesant Fishes to a bevy of debutantes and their escorts.

Despite Reid's late savagery in his *Tribune,* he and his wife were frequent guests of the newspaper-wise Whitneys, perhaps also because he and Whitney had joined in a stock enterprise. Reid, born in Ohio, a Civil War correspondent who had later taken over Greeley's paper, had married Elisabeth Mills despite the opposition of her father, Darius Ogden Mills. Reid had not prevented his wife from spending Mills's money lavishly on a Madison Avenue palace and a country estate in Westchester. The Reid-Whitney stock enterprise was their investment, along with Mills and a few others, in the remarkable Linotype machine invented by Ottmar Mergenthaler. Mechanical typesetters were in the air, several others being "perfected" by their inventors, and Mark Twain lost thousands invested in a similar but faulty machine. The former Navy Secretary who had studied the compound and triple-expansion engines picked the right typesetter, for Mergenthaler's was to sweep the field at great profit.

3. Impropriety in Europe

THE CLEVELANDS lived scarcely a mile away from the Whitneys on Madison Avenue near 68th Street. Cleveland was now attached to a

Broad Street law firm headed by Whitney's close friend Francis Lynde
Stetson, an Amherst graduate and former County Democracy stalwart
who was soon to grow rich in handling the legal work of the J. P.
Morgan house. Yet there was little social communion between the
fashion-pursuing Whitneys and the more sedate Clevelands. The former
President had a small circle of close friends. His bulk as well as his inclinations made him shy of ballrooms. Preferring fishing, he bought a
vacation place on Buzzards Bay and had little to do with the smart set.
"Whitney is in on many things and I hope is adding to his riches," he
wrote to his former Postmaster General, William F. Vilas.

Whitney had taken his good friend (and Cleveland's presidential secretary) Daniel Scott Lamont into the traction syndicate in a managerial
role. Lamont was another dependable man, which gave Whitney the
opportunity to indulge his penchant for travel. In 1890 he sailed for
Europe with Flora, their daughter Pauline, and Whitney's sister and
brother-in-law, the Charles T. Barneys. At sixteen, Pauline was tall, attractive, and had her mother's friendliness and energy. She had been
educated in the social arts—in courtesy, penmanship, grace of movement, the dance, the civilities of the ballroom and the opera, and the
responsibilities of a guest and of a hostess. Now, in the care of a tutor-
governess, Elise Moevis, she was to study French, art, music, and similar subjects as she made a two-year tour more disciplined than the one
Flora had made in her youth. So many American girls of wealth were
marrying titled Europeans that it could be conjectured that she was
being readied for such an event, should it happen.

After Pauline had left with her tutor, the four adults set out to enjoy
themselves at shopping, the theater, the opera, and the races. Barney,
ten years younger than Whitney, was born in Cleveland and hence had
a background similar to Flora's, though of less wealth. A graduate of
Williams College, he was doing well as a New York banker. But their
pleasure was drowned in discord, which Whitney later blamed on Flora:
"I had dragged the party around after you, first to London and then to
Paris. You were cross and hard to please until the whole attempt at a
party had proved an absolute failure. . . ." Flora's version of the start of
the difficulty is not to be found. By chance they had met the darkly
beautiful Mrs. Arthur Randolph, a widow whom they had known in
New York and Bar Harbor. Whitney became so incensed at Flora's ill
humor, according to his story, that for a time he had left her and the
Barneys and joined with Mrs. Randolph in a shopping or pleasure tour
of their own. This so angered Flora that the Whitney-Barney excursion

was left in ruins. Lilly Barney, Whitney's sister, went so far as to say that Mrs. Randolph was "thoughtless" in taking so much of his time, which seemed also an oblique criticism of her admired brother and his excessive interest in women. Along the way, Whitney was measured by his London tailor and attended the races at Ascot, where he caught one William Day in the act of trying to steal his black pearl pin, valued at $1,000, and stayed to see Day get three months at hard labor.

The degree of the impropriety would depend on the length of time he and Mrs. Randolph were together, which is not known. Obviously it was not overnight but was more than a mere half-hour stroll. That Whitney would behave in this manner showed not only utter impatience with Flora but some disregard for the feelings of the Barneys. But according to the mores of the time—especially severe in relation to women—Mrs. Randolph's behavior was a trifle shocking. That she knowingly would take Whitney away from his wife and friends—people she also knew—suggested two things: that she was more than ordinarily attracted to him and that she was not a slave to convention.

Whitney returned in July on the *Majestic*, apparently before the rest of the party, met by reporters as always. They noted that he had "a select coating of ocean tan upon his cheeks and a choice specimen of English coating upon his back." He denied their suggestion that he might have any influence in naming the next mayor or that he wanted to be President, insisting, "I . . . want to be considered hereafter as out of politics." He laughed at an earlier story in *The World* built on rumors that he had conspired against Richard Croker and would soon take Croker's place as boss of Tammany: "I would not if I could supplant Richard Croker in any position that he might hold. I have great admiration not only for the ability of Mr. Croker but I also have implicit confidence in his honor and integrity." While Croker was no Tweed, the words *honor* and *integrity* seemed immoderate. Things had changed indeed. The tone of the interviews combined with other indications to suggest that Whitney was now the real power in Tammany and hence in New York City—so powerful that it was not preposterous to think of him as planning to unseat Croker, though he professed to be so friendly with him.

He soon joined Flora at Newport, where he was seized by rheumatism in the shoulder and by a continuation of the quarrel that was equally painful. Although Mrs. Randolph was to appear later in Whitney's life, he now declared, "It is no deprivation to me if I never see her again." Flora insisted that he had been more than friendly with her. He denied this and accused Flora of damaging Mrs. Randolph's reputation. He left Newport and went to the spa at Richfield Springs, New York, seeking relief both from rheumatism and quarrel, and wrote to Flora:

> . . . between us unfortunately, there is a barrier which I am not able to step over . . . you have done [Mrs. Randolph] a great injury. Scandal wags its tongue at every pretty woman almost. . . . you have been talked to by various women, as one who was assumed to be her friend . . . and your manner and words have injured her. . . . She was companionable, and bright spirited and I enjoyed her socially. Why shouldn't I? . . . Well! We have made quite a failure of it but for the sake of the children and society we will say nothing. As I have said before it is not the fault of either of us. We do not enjoy the same things and never will. I have tried not to be in the way of your love for society, and on the contrary to be a help, if possible. You on the contrary cannot meet me half way, and let me have friends. . . . The great god society is absorbing. . . .

His antipathy toward Flora's mass entertainments was consistent, and his daughter Dorothy was later to sympathize with this attitude. Without exculpating Whitney, it seems that the life the Whitneys had led since their marriage was more to Flora's taste than his, that she had usually had her way, and that in the instance of the Navy post he had sacrificed four years of his life to her wishes. Whitney's argument—was there a trace of cunning in it?—was that since he disliked Flora's huge gatherings but went along with them for her sake, in return he should be permitted to "have friends." His preference for small gatherings and warm friendships was sound enough. There seems no evidence, however, that any of the friends of whom Flora complained were men, since her only recorded protests concerned Mrs. Hurlbert, Ellen Hopkins, Madame Reuterskiold, Frances Halyar, Sally Davis, Fanny Woolsey, and now Mrs. Randolph. This was a serious quarrel, lasting for many weeks while he remained away at two different spas. All of Flora's letters concerning the matter seem to be lost, so that her arguments must be divined from his replies. His attitude at first was one of resignation, that they should stay together for the sake of the children and of appearances. But at the end he apologized for taking such "serious offense":

> Now nothing of what you thought happens to be true. I do not care for anyone but you, and whether I am here or elsewhere I am miserable and wretched if you are not happy. People cannot have lived together as we have without having become very dependent upon each other, and the

trouble with us is, we are both very set in our ways, and do not give and take as we should. . . .—Your Will

But he put their relations on a basis of comfortable habit rather than ardor, and he did not specifically deny having had affairs with women whom he might not "care for" in eternal domesticity. The evidence so far, plus evidence to come, suggests that he did have such affairs but conducted them with discretion enough to keep gossip meager though not nonexistent. And the fact was that he was infatuated with Mrs. Randolph, a circumstance that created a problem indeed.

4. *The Four Hundred*

REPORTERS, RUMORS, politicians, and offices were pursuing Whitney. He seemed to reject them all, being preoccupied with money getting. Henry Adams classed him with Tilden and Hewitt as a man "who played the game [of politics] for ambition or amusement, and played it . . . much better than the professionals, but . . . who felt no great love for the cheap drudgery of the work." Whitney's traction affairs had begun to prosper as the reform-bent County Democracy, in which he had been a driving force with Hewitt, faded away. Work on his new Broadway line, where cable power was to replace horses, was soon to begin, employing more than three thousand men, *The Times* noting, "and of these nearly all . . . are Tammany voters [and there is] a small army of political foremen to see to it that the job does not proceed with too great haste." Abram Hewitt, who had taken a special but unavailing interest in city transit during his mayoralty, gave Whitney a sample of the Hewitt plainspokenness when Whitney went to Europe again in 1891 and chanced to meet him at the Bristol Hotel in London. "Hello, Hewitt," he said, "are you going back to the States soon?"

"No," Hewitt snapped.

"Well, you ought to go back and take the nomination for the presidency. You deserve to get it."

"You ought to go back," Hewitt growled, "and stand trial for the Metropolitan Street Railway operations. You deserve to get a jail term."

Implicit in the outburst was Hewitt's disillusionment with the man whom he had believed a political reformer. But so carefully did Whitney make his transit moves that so far only Hewitt, the insider, combined such discernment and outrage.

With Harry Whitney at Yale and Willie (now called simply Payne) at Groton, Pauline was enjoying Europe, attending the first performance of *Parsifal* at Bayreuth, meeting American friends unexpectedly, growing used to being introduced to titled people. Dorothy Whitney, now four, was old enough to become aware of the age separation from the other children that almost had the effect of placing her in a younger generation. She had sat on Joseph Pulitzer's lap and tugged experimentally at his beard on his last visit before his tortured nerves, insomnia, and worsening eyesight drove him to consult European physicians. Flora, defying a heart irregularity that should have slowed her down, was building the Whitney social position by attending, usually with her husband, all the great affairs and giving great ones of her own. Ward McAllister's book *Society As I Have Found It* had just appeared with such sentiments as "In planning a dinner the question is not to whom you owe dinners, but who is most desirable," and "If you want to be fashionable, be always in the company of fashionable people." Flora was not such a snob and had been most democratic in Washington, and yet McAllister was expert and a good friend, and she now seems not to have gone out of her way to invite unrefined intellectuals. True, among her friends were Elisabeth Marbury and Elsie de Wolfe, who were not wealthy and gave "simple little Sundays" at the smallish Irving Place house they shared. But both Miss Marbury, a lecture impresario, and Miss de Wolfe, an amateur actress also gifted at interior decoration,* were hostesses and conversationalists of finesse, approved by McAllister. Isabella Gardner, the talk of Boston, whom the Whitneys had evidently met abroad, was an occasional guest while in New York. In a different category was the tall and voluptuous Mrs. Paran Stevens, whose acrobatics on the social ladder had amused those securely at the top.

The former Marietta Reed, daughter of a prosperous grocer of Lowell, Massachusetts, she had at nineteen married the wealthy and much older widower Paran Stevens of Boston. Stevens's money came from his string of small hotels, to which he added his part ownership of the fashionable Fifth Avenue Hotel on Madison Square in New York— the same hotel where Whitney and Flora had met in 1868. Here also the Prince of Wales had stayed while he visited New York in 1860. Mrs. Stevens had met him during that time—a fact about which some who disapproved of her provocative qualities said, "Of course." An obstacle to her climb was Stevens himself, who was interested not in Society but

---

* She was later an expensive Society interior decorator and invariably a leader in the best-dressed list.

in racehorses. His death in 1872, when she was forty-nine and looked much younger, freed her for the completion of her design. She visited England with her daughter Mary (known as Minnie), who had inherited her mother's allure. They made a stunning pair, and indeed Mrs. Stevens was also interesting, witty, and generous. An expert contriver, she arranged another meeting with the prince, and such were the attractions of the two American women that they were invited to Sandringham, to Marlborough House, and were accepted in British Society. Minnie's status as an "innkeeper's daughter" was, if not quite forgotten, overlooked. She rejected the proposal of an elderly duke and married Capt. Arthur Paget, grandson of the Marquess of Anglesey. Paget's meagerness of estate scarcely diminished Mrs. Stevens's triumph, since he came from a titled family and was an intimate of the Prince of Wales, and her brilliance was conceded by New York hostesses who now hastened to send her invitations.*

The new Mrs. Paget knew the American Jerome sisters, one of whom had become Lady Churchill, the other Lady Leslie, and was *au courant* with British Society otherwise unconnected with America. Mrs. Stevens, who now divided her time between her Fifth Avenue home at 28th Street, and Newport and London, was a lively conduit between New York and English worlds of fashion. Flora and Mrs. Stevens were close friends. It would be surprising if the Pagets were not among those whom young Pauline Whitney visited in Europe, surprising also if the Whitneys did not contemplate the possibility that Pauline might make a similarly exciting matrimonial catch.

For years Ward McAllister had talked of the *crème de la crème,* the Four Hundred who really counted in New York Society, without naming them. The Four Hundred of course were those elect who could be crowded into Mrs. Astor's ballroom. Curiosity about their identity far exceeded that about the Triple Alliance or Mr. Edison's newly patented Kinetoscope. Newspaper people now tended to laugh at McAllister as the most egregious of snobs who sprinkled his speech with mincing "Don't-you-know's." But there was no question that he had won over Mrs. Astor (who could be no less than Number One of the Four Hundred) and that McAllister had long held some standing as a kind of steward or majordomo of the mighty.

---

* Mrs. Stevens appeared as Mrs. Lemuel Strothers in Edith Wharton's *The Age of Innocence.* As a girl, Mrs. Wharton, then Edith Jones, had been courted for a time by Mrs. Stevens's son, Henry Leyden Stevens.

But who were the remaining 399? The question obsessed Society reporters, it tormented the less assured members of the gilded set who wondered if they were in or out, and it engrossed the poor, who could gaze in envy or admiration from a distance. Nine years earlier *The World* had published the names of New York City's millionaires, and buyers had fought for copies. In 1892—not to the proletarian-oriented *World* but to the sedate *Times*—McAllister specified, at the time of Mrs. Astor's momentous annual ball, the individuals who made up the Four Hundred. This was the time of all times to unfold the secret, since one's position was largely dictated by Mrs. Astor and it could be assumed that all or nearly all of those at her ball were of the elect. The Whitneys were there, of course, Flora in "lemon satin with tulle rufflings and draperies," and Mrs. Burke Roche also was present. Mrs. Astor, whose hair had never been abundant, wore her black wig and many jewels. She enjoyed welcoming guests while posing before her portrait, done by Carolus-Duran. Yet she had "pleasant cordial manners," the no-nonsense George Templeton Strong had been charmed by her, and there was something engaging in the way she "unaffectedly enjoyed her undisputed position."

McAllister named only 307 (including himself and his daughter), which gave the opportunity to many of the disappointed to feel sure that they were among the 93 he failed to name. He was derided as "Make-a-Lister," but it was one of the most eagerly read stories since Appomattox. The Whitneys were safely on the list, to be sure, as were Cornelius and Alice Vanderbilt. No one suggested that Alice was delighted that her sister-in-law Alva and her husband William K. were skipped, but it could be taken as certain that Alva, if not her husband, was in a passion. Chauncey Depew, who although president of the New York Central was really a Vanderbilt employee, was named. The other two palace dwellers at Fifth and 57th, the Oelrichses and the Huntingtons, were not listed, nor was Mrs. Paran Stevens, or the Whitelaw Reids or, of course, the Pulitzers. Paul Dana of *The Sun* was the only newspaperman admitted. The names of Whitney's sisters and their spouses, the Henry F. Dimocks and Charles T. Barneys, were missing, as was that of Oliver Payne. But then, others among the missing were the J. P. Morgans, who made it easily in money, family, and grandeur, but failed in the qualification of effort, important to McAllister. One had to work hard, give parties at a great clip to satisfy him, and the Morgans did not.

Hence the list honored the possession of the social graces along with an admixture of "family" and the considerable wealth and effort it took to entertain grandly. Anyone who was on it could name a dozen others who were on and should be off and as many who were off and should be on. Its names, with a few exceptions, denoted English ancestry. It was anti-Semitic, excluding the rich and cultivated August Belmonts. It was anti-Irish save for a half handful of the starchiest of the lace-curtain Irish such as the Kernochans and Kanes. It was so anti-Italian that not an Italian name appeared. It was anti- almost everything else except for a few of the old Dutch families—Van Rensselaers and Roosevelts and some but not all of the nouveau-riche Vanderbilts. It leaned toward people who had had money for at least two generations, who had inherited wealth and whose present incomes came from professions regarded as correct—banker, broker, lawyer, importer, manufacturer, "clubman," architect, dealer in real estate. Although many on the list came from parents who had been "in trade," it tried to exclude people still demeaned by such an occupation, though exceptions were made for such as the William D. Sloanes (he being a carpet and furniture dealer who had married a Vanderbilt daughter). Not a clergyman appeared among the 307, and only one professor—Dr. (and Mrs.) Francis Delafield, professor of medicine at Columbia. Theodore Roosevelt, aged thirty-four, was passed over though other Roosevelts appeared. Anne Morgan was on the list without her parents. George Bend, head of the Stock Exchange, and his wife Elizabeth—good friends of the Whitneys—went unmentioned while their beautiful daughter Amy and their other daughter Beatrice, attractive but not beautiful, were listed.

The list was an excellent subject for ridicule as well as a target for those with seriously democratic instincts. The newspapers as a rule did not dare to lampoon it openly, although there were back-handed comments particularly in *The World*. A considerable opposition centered around the humor magazine *Life*, which for several years had discovered much of its fun in the extravagances of Society. On the publication of McAllister's *Society As I Have Found It*, a *Life* cartoon showed a policeman with two top-hatted drunks in hand, answering the captain who asked him what he had: "Society as Oi have found it, sorr." *Life*'s best artist, Charles Dana Gibson, was only twenty-five but brilliant, and merciless toward the high-flyers, one of his cartoons alleging that the Four Hundred had "all style and no brains," another caricaturing McAllister in gown and pantalettes, leading a great flock of geese, each wearing coronet and jewels.

It was typical of Whitney's thoughtfulness (perhaps also of his undimmed Democratic loyalty) that he asked his traveling daughter Pauline to call on Pulitzer at Baden-Baden, where he was taking the cure. The World, which in 1884 had so gloriously supported and elected Cleveland, had backed away in coolness in disastrous 1888—something Whitney did not want to happen again.

Pauline found Pulitzer "so very melancholy of late that they did not know what to do." The Whitneys and Pulitzers had the same New York physician, the fashionable Dr. J. Woods McLane, and the Whitneys had their own health worries. Flora, who evidently had tried to conceal from Whitney the growing gravity of her heart condition (probably in part because she was fearful that he would curtail her social program), had an attack in the spring of 1892 that could not be hidden. Indicative of her impulsiveness and her network of ties with New York Society was her knowledge—and Whitney's—that the only chance for rest lay in flight to Europe. Whitney had a peculiarly strong sense of privacy in some personal matters for a man who so cultivated the press when it could be useful to him, and he looked on illness as a private affair. No mention was made of Flora's condition when he sailed with her on April 13. He had been in correspondence with Cleveland for weeks about the 1892 outlook. Now before sailing time he ignored David B. Hill, said Cleveland should be the nominee, and seemed more concerned with social issues than was customary with him:

> . . . the issue of the Democratic party . . . is tariff reform—not free trade, not the destruction of our industries in any way . . . but relief from overprotection . . . from enriching a few at the expense of the many, and from extravagance in public expenditures. . . .

He was, it was true, enriching himself at the time in a way later alleged to be at the expense of the many. Flora took to her bed in a suite at the Hotel du Rhin on the Place Vendôme where she was attended by a specialist. They were joined in Paris by Pauline, nearing the end of her tour, and by Oliver Payne, always solicitous about his sister. Oliver at fifty-three was heavier, but well groomed and self-assured. He had long since taken possession of his four-story mansion at Fifth Avenue and 66th Street, waited on hand and foot by servants, so that he was no longer at the Whitney home for extended stays. While he had quit the Standard management and had no firm office hours, he was still a heavy holder of the company's stock and had branched out into railroads, steel, tobacco, and other stock holdings. He was said to be thirty times a millionaire and gaining fast, simply by shrewd activity in the market.

On May Day, when it had been threatened that the Anarchists would riot, Whitney (perhaps with Oliver) walked the streets of Paris and exhibited typical conservative feeling:

> The city was extremely quiet. Of course people had been asked to stay within doors and there was not the same crowd that one generally meets there on the boulevards. . . . The police and militia were many of them in citizens' dress, and I think that the slightest attempt at disturbance would have been promptly quelled. I regard the order preserved on that day as another triumph for the French Republic. . . .

Whitney, at least, had been told the real gravity of Flora's heart problem—that there was no guarantee that she might not die at any moment, while on the other hand she might with luck and care live on for a considerable time. He treated her with a consideration that seemed to reflect true affection—the affection and admiration for her gifts that had so long alternated with his exasperation at her obvious faults. She replied in kind as she always did when he was more than ordinarily attentive. She soon fretted over his absence from business and from the growing preconvention political activities. They both badly wanted Cleveland to be nominated and elected, though Whitney hoped to limit his own involvement in the campaign. Since Oliver was with her, Whitney crossed the Channel to buy polo ponies for Harry, on top of a fine hunter, Beni-Hassan, which that never-neglected young man had been given just before his parents left for Europe. (Among the nice things they enjoyed doing for Harry had been to supply fifty theater tickets when he brought some classmates down from Yale.) In London Whitney also took surreptitious lessons in driving a tallyho, a sport much in fashion and excelled in by several of his friends including Col. William Jay and James Van Alen. To Flora he wrote that unless she was much improved he would prefer not to return home but would rejoin her:

> . . . I found myself so uncomfortable away from you that I had rather go back [to Paris] and let the business of politics go to thunder. . . . I shall be wretched & miserable & have no peace & I shan't really do anything—while you are sick. . . .

She replied that the doctor was gratified at her improvement and now permitted her to sit up. "I am sure you will not feel there is any danger in leaving me, and the necessity of your being at home is so great that I should feel in continued reproach to myself. . . . It is a kind of crime to be sick & one must expiate it by oneself. I have had alas so much of it. . . . A lovely trip to you." Oliver telegraphed that he could safely go. Whitney, still honored for his service to the Navy, was dined at the Savoy by the American naval attaché, Captain Emory. He replied to Flora, confessing his instruction in coaching: "I have been taking a few lessons from Tiffany. I may as well tell you because I presume somebody has seen us together, though of course I didn't want it talked about. He compliments me & thinks I will make a good driver. It has kept me pretty busy going out twice a day to Battersea Park, where we could maneuver to our heart's content. . . ." He urged her to have Oliver and her nurse take turns reading to her fifteen minutes at a time to break the monotony. He signed himself, "Your ancient & honorable lover," and sailed on the *Majestic*, to be met in New York May 18 by a flock of reporters and his son Harry, whom he was so delighted to see that "I grabbed the boy & kissed him in sight of all." "I think," he told the reporters, ". . . that Mr. Cleveland will be the choice of the Democratic party at Chicago." At home he received an uproarious welcome—and flowers—from five-year-old Dorothy.

"It seems she was expecting the pink doll you had written her about," Whitney wrote to Flora, "& I had to dart around today & make up for my past shortcomings. She is quite a different child from what she was three months ago—strong, ruddy, & full of life & strength." There was bad news too. Willie, the nice Vanderbilt boy from across the street, was desperately ill with typhoid, certain to die—and he was a fellow student with Harry at Yale. "McLane says Willie got it on their trip to Chicago," Whitney reassured Flora, "—not at N.H. [New Haven], he says there is none in N.H. now." Willie died, and all the Whitneys except Flora and Dorothy went to his funeral.

5. Whitney in Command

WHITNEY HAD an uncanny knack for appraising sentiment and was confident that Cleveland could be elected and that Hill could not. Hill, recently elected to the Senate, had taken care, with the cooperation of Croker, that the agreeable Rosewell P. Flower replaced him as governor. The New York Hill men had held their notorious "Snap Convention" in February, three months ahead of the usual time. The Cleveland supporters, surprised and unprepared, were outnumbered, and the Hill partisans, including Croker, controlled the convention and named Hill delegates. They might have won in any case, but the flavor of chicanery was strong. Fairchild and other irate Cleveland men organized their own "Anti-Snap" state convention and nominated Cleveland delegates a week before Whitney returned. Their convention, however, was clearly irregular and had no chance for recognition at the national convention scheduled for Chicago in June. The suicidal tendency of the Democrats was even more violent than usual. What it portended was a vicious battle of factions in Chicago that would sunder the party and assure the reelection of Harrison.

Flora wrote from Paris that she was so well that she and Oliver would soon leave for Venice: "I have a big box of Cotillion favors—the value only 280 dollars. Col. says to ask you should I declare them or bring them through." He was consulted about cotillion favors when he had his hands full of blood-lusting Democrats. He was in danger, for in backing Cleveland he was opposing both Croker and Hill, who could hurt him in his traction enterprise.

". . . nothing better could be done," Cleveland wrote ten days before the convention, ". . . than to have Whitney pretty well to the front in the matter of management and organization."

He knew that on the previous day Whitney had held a meeting at his home of a dozen leading Democrats from ten states* who had brilliantly—if a trifle despotically—planned the convention's organization and management. They had chosen in advance the more important convention committees—even the temporary and permanent chairmen. At Chicago, Whitney did not go "pretty well" but entirely to the front. From handsome headquarters at the Palmer House and his own suite at the Richelieu, he made himself the acknowledged leader and, it was said, "held the fate of the gathering in his hand." Hill's backers repeated their litany that Cleveland had had two nominations, had failed in the second, and should now step aside. Their greatest complaint was that Cleveland had left many efficient Republicans in office whereas Hill could be depended on to sweep them out and distribute the spoils. The two men's detestation for each other was well known. The detestation spread to the opposing factions. With the party so fragmented, defeat seemed certain no matter who was nominated.

From Bellagio, where Flora had moved with her brother after Venice, Whitney heard that both of them were well: "The Colonel is really

---

* Among them were Don M. Dickinson of Michigan, Francis Lynde Stetson of New York, W. F. Vilas of Wisconsin, William F. Harrity of Pennsylvania, and Josiah Quincy of Massachusetts.

enchanted with the place. . . . Ol sits on the porch at six-thirty evenings watching a pretty Russian Countess writing her letters, and waiting for the evening boat with the Paris Herald." It was one of many letters he had received over the years from Flora, writing from a place of scenic and climatic perfection while he boiled and suffered. He was, however, at the top of his political game. To both Democratic and Republican newspapermen present it seemed that Whitney—handsome, amiable, the glass of fashion as always—had been born, educated, and tempered expressly for this Chicago test. His success, and his magic in handling the press, could be read in headlines and comments in the newspapers of Chicago, New York, and Washington:

> "This Mr. Whitney is the Prince Charley, the Young Pretender, of this celebration." (*Chicago Tribune*, June 21, 1892). "WHITNEY IN COMMAND" (*New York Tribune*, June 19). "Mr. Whitney has shown himself to be a consummate master of politics." (*Washington Post*, June 19). ". . . Mr. Whitney is the only Cleveland manager . . . with the skill, experience and party acquaintance especially needed to ensure the triumph of his chief. . . ." (*New York Tribune*, June 19). "He was unfailingly polite . . . an easy mannered man of the world, and he talked with an amazing readiness and fecundity of ideas." (*New York Herald*, June 20). "Croker is sleeping a little more easily since Whitney told him that he was not expected to [abandon] Hill in the Convention, but that if he would loyally support Cleveland in the campaign Tammany would be recognized as the only Democratic organization in New York." (*New York Herald*, June 22). "Mr. Whitney came over to the Palmer House this morning . . . and was given an ovation." (*New York Times*, June 19). "Ex-Secretary of the Navy Whitney / Has Handled his Forces in So / Masterly a Manner that Victory / Appears to be Almost / in His Grasp" (*New York Herald*, June 20).

And *The Chicago Tribune* mistakenly suggested that the Whitney charm and the Payne money made a powerful combination: ". . . Oliver Payne has never found enough to do for his handsome friend."

On the contrary, as will be seen, the Colonel had turned against Cleveland, and Whitney got no help from that quarter. Whitney, a truly great mediator, succeeded at Chicago in avoiding a Democratic explosion by removing the fuse. His counsel at this most precarious of all conventions was so sage that someone called him the "Fool Killer," a tag that stuck. As he sniffed the breezes of contention it became plain to him that the Hill forces were weaker than generally believed. They had lost delegates from other states who were offended by the patent trickery of the Snap Convention. There was a national feeling for the blunt honesty of Cleveland that Hill did not enjoy. A careful head count convinced Whitney that even with the New York delegation solid for Hill, Cleveland would still get at least six hundred votes on the first ballot—enough to nominate him. Why, then, try to deny Hill the New York votes? Cleveland might be irked at the seeming lack of support in his own state, but Whitney was quite willing to let Hill have this feather in his cap in the greater cause. Give Hill New York, Whitney counseled, and escape a bloodletting. This tactic afforded the only chance to win over the Hill men between convention and election day and to carry always unpredictable New York State.

And lo, the wonder of wonders, the final exquisite touch: The exigencies of the convention dovetailed so nicely with Whitney's New York traction enterprise that one might think—and one could not exclude the possibility—that he had reentered politics for this specific purpose. His favor to Hill would be appreciated. His assurance to Croker that Tammany would be recognized as New York City's only Democratic organization was a great favor to the boss, who always returned favors.

The idea affronted Fairchild and Whitney's other Anti-Snap friends who wanted to fight for a piece of New York, but Whitney not only prevailed but kept their friendship. Cleveland was nominated on the first ballot. "Dear Bill Whitney!" Henry Adams wrote to John Hay. ". . . Whitney will be President in '96."

"My dear Will," Flora wrote to him (she was now in Newport, he back in New York), "We had a discussion at the breakfast table as to when you would come. Dorothy said 'I think Sunday morning' & when the postman brought your letter we all lost. Harry said, 'I just know he will be thrust into the chairmanship. . . .' I don't see how you can keep up this great strain and not break under it. They will never let up on you until after the fourth of November."

But Whitney declined Cleveland's entreaties that he head the Democratic National Committee. William F. Harrity was given that post, though for Harrity it approached the honorary because Whitney led the campaign itself with all his headlong energy, aided by Dickinson of Michigan. It was the nation's only election in which the candidates of the two major parties were President and ex-President. President Harrison's running mate was Whitelaw Reid, who had subtly campaigned for that nomination in his own newspaper and who became so certain of victory that he invited friends to visit him in Washington after March 4. Harrison won sympathy when his wife died in October, and Whitney's efforts for party unity got little help from the bullheaded Cleveland, who

was truly lacking in political tact. "When I am with you," he had writ
ten Whitney, "I am carried off my feet by your persuasive way of putting things, by your enthusiasm and by your friendliness and willingness. When I leave you, my intuitions and strong opinions are revived
and things look very different." Alas, Whitney could not always be with
him. He was irate because Whitney pressed him to pay reasonable attentions to the New York Hill men, an essential if the state was to be
won. Cleveland wrote to his friend William Bissell:

> The policy of truckling conciliation . . . has resulted in its legitimate
> fruit, and I am now urged to send for Murphy and Sheehan [Edward
> Murphy of Troy and William F. Sheehan of Buffalo, Hill supporters
> allied with Croker] and conciliate them. Whitney wrote me a letter he
> wanted me to send to Murphy and I declined to do it, whereupon he
> wrote me a very petulant and unpleasant letter. He was here yesterday
> and we had a little talk—nothing unpleasant, but I can see that he is not
> satisfied and he seems to be on the point of exploding.

So stubborn was Cleveland that Whitney wrote to him sharply, "You
do not realize, I think, that you were nominated against the united
voice of your State organization and that their pride is in a state of
serious irritation. . . . You cannot carry this State without that feeling
is removed. . . . If you think it best not to even write a friendly letter to
the Chairman of your State Committee . . . I had better stop where I
am." He did succeed in luring the vacationing Cleveland to New York
for a "conciliation" meeting with Murphy, Sheehan, and Croker during
which Cleveland smote the table with his fist and refused to make any
pledges of patronage with an emphasis that did more honor to his
honesty than his diplomacy. Surprisingly, the tension was broken by the
amiability of Croker, whom Whitney had won over, and the meeting
ended without rancor. George F. Parker, who worked under Whitney,
observed that his "marvelous powers of concentration, amounting almost to genius" were given to the Cleveland campaign, adding: "Business, social duties, —everything that can engage the attention of a man
in the prime of life, rich, ambitious, ingenious, active, full of energy
. . . were put aside for the duties of the movement."
Whitney drove himself mercilessly, running a headquarters at the
Hoffman House with seventy-five workers, attending conferences, pla-
cating upstate Democrats, comparing notes with Dickinson, stopping at
Newport to visit Flora and the family en route to meetings in New England, raising money for the campaign, getting a good contribution

from father-in-law Payne but not a sou from brother-in-law Payne. The latter's quarrel with Cleveland is not known; a man of power, his expectations of government favor were high and the President could be brusque with such people. At Newport Whitney got a large donation from his friend James J. Van Alen that would return to haunt him. Van Alen was regarded by some as "second-order both in wealth and social standing." His Democratic persuasion and his eccentricities were disadvantages weighing against his Knickerbocker ancestry, his father's distinction as a cavalry general in the late war, and his stupendous marriage. His wife, who died in childbirth, had been Emily, one of the three daughters of Mrs. Astor. The Astors had so opposed the match that General Van Alen had challenged Astor to a duel, causing Astor to apologize, but he nevertheless absented himself from the wedding ceremony. James Van Alen's Oxford education had imbued him with a reverence for things English, made him a collector of English clocks, furniture, and pewter, and—more unusual—caused him to affect a monocle and to lard his conversation with archaisms such as *forsooth, prithee, 'Zounds, egad,* and *varlet.*

Van Alen at any rate was an arresting diversion in Whitney's campaign drudgery during which he thanked God that Pulitzer and his *World* were heartily with Cleveland, shook a thousand hands, smiled a thousand smiles, wrote a thousand letters, caught trains on the run, attended windy dinners, and lost sleep. One would so much like to think this grinding labor done solely for principle and loyalty that it is with reluctance that one leans to the opinion that Whitney was also thinking of Whitney—not, after all, surprising this side of paradise. While he was now wealthy in his own right, a later rumor that he contributed something like $250,000 to the campaign seems exaggerated. But when betting favored the Republicans, Whitney, the incorrigible gambler, was at least confident that the Democrats would win. He joined a pool at the Fifth Avenue Hotel aimed at using a half million dollars to change the odds. He urged Croker to join, and when the boss replied that he had no money, Whitney said, "I'll put you in for a hundred thousand dollars." According to the story, Whitney later gave Croker $100,000 as his winnings.

"I shall come to town Wednesday," Flora wrote to him, "as I really cannot bear the excitement. . . ."

Cleveland's smashing victory by 277 to 175 electoral votes*—and his

* Cleveland's popular vote in round numbers was 5,556,000 against Harrison's 5,175,000.

clear triumph in New York State—was a Democratic conquest that could hardly have occurred had not Whitney called the tune over both convention and campaign. If ever one man put another in the White House, it was in that election of 1892. "I went to Clevelands Tuesday night to watch for the returns," Flora wrote to her father, "and at one o'clock Mrs. Lamont and I got into my carriage and drove down to the Hoffman House. . . . we found them all there as jubilant as boys. Illinois had just been conceded. I shook hands with Croker and he said, 'Well, I am glad for Mr. Whitney's sake.' [Will] has the warmest congratulations . . . on the success of his hard work—and no one knows outside of his family what hard work it [was]."

6. *"Dear Flora Is Quite Ill"*

WITH CLEVELAND'S election—the most decisive since Lincoln's reelection in 1864—the recognition of Whitney's quarter century in politics overflowed in cascades of admiration. His popularity, after some inevitable recession during the four-year interregnum since his work for the Navy won national acclaim, was at its height across the country. He was urged for a cabinet post that would lead naturally to the presidency in 1896. "The probable future of this man affords an interesting study," *The Atlanta Journal* editorialized. "He is not yet fifty years of age [he was fifty-one]. He is qualified for any office in the land." Much of his fascination lay in the knowledge that he had outmaneuvered and brought into line the acknowledged masters of expedient politics—Hill, Croker, Murphy, Sheehan—without losing his sheen as the gifted amateur of dash and light touch who seemed to perform his miracles without their resort to threats, deals, and horse trades. This was a romantic conception to a large degree, due in part to the handsome Whitney's total lack of the plug-ugly stigmata of the "boss," but it prevailed. Cleveland in gratitude was ready to offer him virtually anything in the presidential power to give, starting with the post of Secretary of State and the mission to England. ". . . Mr. Cleveland asked for an expression of my willingness as to holding office," Whitney said later, "in a letter that I shall always prize more highly than I would any office."

"I see so much of you in the newspapers," wrote Alexander Gunn, who had recently sent cucumber pickles to the ailing Mrs. Payne in Cleveland. ". . . I rejoice to see your name honored, for I know better than any who write of you, your real greatness, your kind heart."

Whitney declined office on the ground of Flora's poor health and his own business affairs. Flora was indeed a worry, no more able to abstain from party giving and party going than a bluebird could cease flying. Before the election she had featured first Paderewski and then Adamowski at vast gatherings, then given a dinner and musicale at Newport, her grounds being "illuminated most beautifully," for guests including the William Jays, William K. and Alva Vanderbilt, Perry Belmont, and the Count and Countess Divonne. After the Newport season she was at Lenox "for a rest." But resting came hard, for one thing because she was excited about the election and came to New York to watch it, for another because she was planning Pauline's debut. Pauline, at last returned from Europe, a young lady simply bursting with the kind of energy that could make every moment one of suspense, was hardly a restful companion.

Her debut was celebrated at the New York home on December 10 with a reception for which *The World* said 1,000 invitations were sent out, *The Herald* 1,500. The Whitneys had installed a "wide double electric-lighted awning" at the entrance. The J. P. Morgans, who were among the guests, had been first in New York to discard gas and use electric lights throughout their house on Madison Avenue, which had no ballroom and, though handsome, could not compare in pretentiousness with that of the Whitneys. "The house has been too often described to call for any further details of its embellishments," *The Herald* said, making do with a condensed appreciation: "The tapestried halls, with their broad staircases; the long ball room, whose hangings and woodwork were brought from a French chateau, and the drawing room, with its wealth of rare paintings, were all decorated with flowers, orchids and American Beauty roses abounding." Flora, "ablaze with diamonds," wore "an empire costume of heavy yellow silk veiled with black lace," while Pauline "looked very distinguished in a lovely white silk French gown," wearing no jewels whatever. *The World*, enthusiastic about the electoral exploits of the Fool Killer, so far forgot its preoccupation with equality that it made allusion to the famous "Hundred and Fifty" who constituted the cream of the Four Hundred and left no doubt that the Whitneys were among them.

Pauline, who would be nineteen in March, was thus launched into the winter series of parties, operas, and balls, with the eyes of Society on her escorts and interested speculation as to whom she might marry. Most interested of all were Flora and Whitney—until early in January when Flora suffered a heart attack that sent her to bed with stern orders from Dr. McLane that she must have absolute rest.

She was forbidden to fret over plans for Dorothy's sixth birthday party on January 23. She lay in a great bedroom away from the noises of the street, flooded with sunlight, and surrounded by the heavy furniture and ornamentation of the time. All the children now except for Dorothy must have known the seriousness of her condition. It seems unlikely that this supercharged woman could discipline herself to be a good patient, to merely lie and rest. Yet she improved somewhat and was permitted to be bundled into a sleigh for a ride in snowy Central Park. But immediately after her own fiftieth birthday on January 25 she took a turn for the worse.

A heart specialist, Dr. Charles McBurney, was again summoned, but neither he nor Whitney nor Oliver Payne now had much hope. ". . . our Dear Flora is quite seriously ill," Whitney wrote to her sister, Mrs. William Bingham, in Cleveland. "She is brave and does not herself talk of it and we cannot let her know we see it. . . . Col. thinks you should intimate it to your Father and Mother." President-elect Cleveland wrote to him, "The cloud that hangs over your household casts a somber shade over ours. . . ." Flora certainly was not unaware. Strangely, her will had not been executed. On January 31, Francis Lynde Stetson was called in and she signed in a firm hand a will leaving her entire estate of about $3,050,000 to her husband. Dorothy wrote many years later, "I was taken into her little sitting room—on the upper floor of our big New York house—to say good-bye. She was lying on a couch—that is about all I remember—but she must have been very ill, for it was the last time I saw her." Dorothy was then sent away with her governess to Lakewood, New Jersey, to shield her from the sad experience. Pauline was home, Harry and Payne were called from school, and relatives arrived from New York and Cleveland. During the night of February 4–5, 1893, there was only time for an attending nurse to call Whitney from bed, and at 2:55 A.M. Flora "passed peacefully away in her husband's arms a minute after he reached her bedside."

"The elegant mansion . . . where Mrs. Whitney reigned a social queen," *The World* said on its front page, "has become a house of mourning, and the man who could have any office in the gift of President-elect Cleveland and would accept none is prostrated by the bier of a dead wife." In keeping with the Whitney rule of privacy, no outsider except for Whitney's close friend and traction aide, Daniel Lamont, had known of the seriousness of Flora's heart ailment. "For four years," Whitney later wrote to Cleveland, "this terror has been in front of me, and I have been capable of only spasmodic effort." That would have included their 1890 quarrel over Mrs. Randolph and unexplained but bitter differences they had in 1891, but Whitney had earnestly sued for peace on both occasions. Lamont took charge of all funeral arrangements. Whitney, who had once wept on seeing Flora off to Europe and had later kissed his twenty-year-old son in public, was not one of the emotionless iron men.

The funeral was at St. Bartholomew's Church, where the choir sang Flora's favorite hymn, "Hark, Hark, My Soul," and not a member of the family was dry-eyed—above all, Oliver Payne. Flowers included those from the irrepressible Mrs. Jack Gardner of Boston, whose interest in men of dash and handsomeness (such as Whitney) was incessant. Pallbearers included Cleveland and eight others, six of them on the List: Cornelius Vanderbilt, George Peabody Wetmore, E. Randolph Robinson, H. McK. Twombly, Thomas F. Cushing, and Buchanan Winthrop. Among the mourners were four ex-mayors of New York and many justices, cabinet members, and senators. Others were Chauncey Depew, of the historic newspaper quarrel with Flora because of his remarks about Cleveland, and Ward McAllister, who had lost his own wife. A special train of three Wagner palace cars waited at nearby Grand Central Station to take the funeral party to Woodlawn Cemetery in the Bronx, where Flora was buried next to Olive in a grave "walled and floored with marble." To the Paynes—that family of pride, solidarity, and affection—her death at fifty came after the deaths of Harry at thirty-two and Nathan at forty-eight, leaving only two of their children, Oliver and his youngest sister, Mrs. Bingham.

3. Whitney built the navy the nation needed.

4. Flora accused him of other interests.

5. Sen. Henry B. Payne, ever available.

6. Dorothy Payne Whitney, about four.

7. Alice Gwynne Vanderbilt, wife of Cornelius, is seen as "Electric Light" at her aggressive sister-in-law's ball. *Below:* The Cornelius Vanderbilt house on Fifth Avenue, the city's biggest.

8. Cornelius appeared at the same ball, as Louis XVI. Below is his magnificent Newport cottage, The Breakers, where the Whitney and Vanderbilt families were ultimately joined.

9. At Whitney's celebrated 1901 ball, jockeys rode in on papier-mâché horses to hand out favors. *Below:* The gabled Whitney mansion at Fifth Avenue and 57th Street where Dorothy spent her childhood.

10. Mrs. Astor *(center)*, the unquestioned leader of Gilded Age Society, could admit or exclude eager candidates. The Whitneys became favorites of hers and made fast progress.

11. J. P. Morgan gave Whitney a hand.

12. Thomas Fortune Ryan, a loyal ally.

13. P. A. B. Widener, another partner.

14. Boss Croker, a Whitney intimate.

15. Joseph Pulitzer—first friend, then foe.

16. Whitelaw Reid, a fellow speculator.

17. Chauncey Depew broadcast scandal.

18. Finley Peter Dunne, alias Mr. Dooley.

19. King Edward's favorite mistress, Mrs. George Keppel, was a chic Whitney guest who, years later, introduced Dorothy Whitney to the king.

20. The marriage of the Duke of Marlborough to Consuelo Vanderbilt was scarcely made in heaven, but it brought the duke a badly needed $10,000,000.

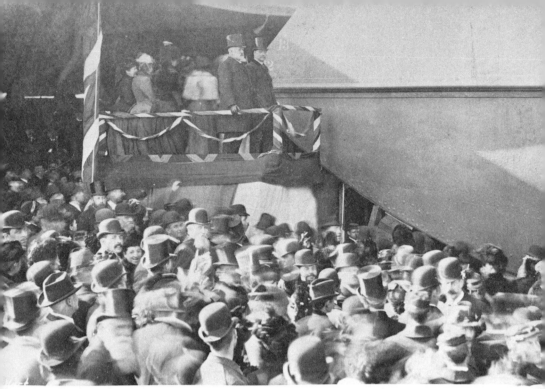

21. Whitney (*at right on platform*) christens battleship slated for sinister fame: the *Maine*.

22. Mrs. Potter of the shocking poesy.

23. Ward McAllister invented the 400.

24. President Cleveland praised the "efficiency" and "mental poise" of Whitney, and joined him at poker. And the pretty first lady (*right*) learned about capital Society from the fashionable Flora Payne Whitney.

25. David B. Hill—no vices, no principles.

26. Elihu Root, Whitney's artful attorney.

27. Delmonico's (*below*) was one place where Whitney met the slippery Colonel Mann.

28. Colonel William d'Alton Mann was gossip and blackmailer extraordinary.

29. The dramatic Gertrude (*shown in tableau*), whose marriage was to have a strong effect on Dorothy's views.

30. The Whitney cottage at Lenox.

31. *Below:* One interior in the fifty-room Whitney Aiken place, which also had a racetrack.

32. *Below:* The country place at Old Westbury, and *(above)* its "quarter-mile" stables.

33. Part of the sixty-three-foot ballroom of the mansion at 871 Fifth Avenue, whose exterior is shown below. Whitney built it as a setting for his second wife, who never put foot in it.

Five

1. Dispensing the Patronage

Two WEEKS later Whitney left by train for Florida with Harry, Payne, Pauline, and Oliver Payne. Dorothy, as usual, was the stay-at-home because of her age. "Since the death of his wife," The Times said, "Mr. Whitney has been prostrated and his brother-in-law, Colonel Oliver H. Payne, has wished him to take a Southern trip."

In Jacksonville they met ex-Senator Payne and Howard Melville Hanna and boarded the steam yacht Comanche, owned by Hanna. The latter was a brother of Mark Hanna and part owner of the thriving family enterprises, which included coal, iron, shipping, banking—and traction. Although the Hannas were Republicans, they and the Paynes had grown up together in Cleveland and were good friends.

A mutual friend of the Paynes, Hannas, and Whitneys was Alexander Gunn. His charm was so compelling that Mark Hanna and other Cleveland potentates made occasional trips to Zoar to enjoy Gunn's companionship, his champagne, and his superb rose garden. That there was talk of Gunn aboard the Comanche on its leisurely Caribbean cruise is as certain as was the daily rising and setting of the sun, and in fact Whitney was urging Gunn to accept a European consulship, which could be arranged with the President. Whitney did not think his friend was precisely wasting himself at Zoar but felt that he would enjoy a long European stay.

What with Whitney's charm, his social credentials, his election wizardry followed by family tragedy, his alliance with Croker, and his appearance of remaining mysteriously aloof while great offices begged for him, newspaper comment about him was inevitable. He was more publicized than many important officeholders, a form of flattery that seemed not to annoy him. When the Comanche put in at Nassau after steaming as far south as Barbados, newsmen noted that the governor and his wife, Sir Ambrose and Lady Shea, conveyed their respects but refrained from holding a formal reception for the party because of Whitney's mourning. A *Times* reporter who later interviewed him when the yacht docked at Brunswick, Georgia, noted, "His stateroom was found thick with papers containing all the political news." He returned to New York, *The Tribune* thought, "physically rejuvenated, but still bearing traces of his grief." There were rumors that Cleveland had at last lured Whitney into his cabinet. Other rumors said the two had quarreled, that "Mr. Cleveland had broken numerous promises made to him in the late campaign and that his self-respect would not permit him to have anything more to do with the President politically." *The Times*'s rumor that Cleveland and Whitney were estranged was balanced by *The Tribune*'s later rumor that they were deep in plans to make Whitney governor of New York in 1894 and President in 1896:

> It has come to be generally believed that [Whitney's] own personal ambitions lead in that direction and that he had the successorship to Grover Cleveland in his mind's eye when . . . by a series of brilliant maneuvers [he] succeeded in [electing] Mr. Cleveland. . . .

Declining office himself, he seized the power offered him in naming others. Chief among them was Lamont, who became Secretary of War a great deal richer than when he had gone to work for Whitney's traction company; he was to be in some degree Whitney's "man" in the cabinet. Whitney highly approved, if he did not suggest, the appointment of Hilary A. Herbert, his congressional friend from Cleveland's first term, to the Navy. He urged Walter Q. Gresham, designated as Secretary of State, to make use of Lamont's advice and experience. Whitney was pressed by office seekers as if he held high office himself. He was often in correspondence with Lamont about patronage and policy and was able to fill less important posts with friends. His intimacy with prominent Democrats in every state, built up during the campaign, added to his influence. Now in 1893 the panic was much on his mind, with great banks and railroads collapsing and the stock market (in which he was heavily involved) badly hurt. He did not sound decidedly unlike a candidate when *The World*, introducing him as "not only one of the most sagacious politicians but one of the ablest business men of the country," published a long interview in which he followed Democratic scripture. He blamed the trouble on the tariff and silver purchase act of the Harrison administration, and he uttered sentiments sympathetic with labor:

If the country is not being drowned in a silver flood, it is, at any rate, being scared to death by the fear of such a deluge. . . . [But the] poison lies deeper. . . . our present tariff system is essentially a tax upon the producing and industrial [working classes]. . . . The tariff is assessed, not upon what men own, but upon what they eat and drink and wear. . . . a poor man with a large family may be compelled to pay more taxes . . . than an economical millionaire with only himself to keep.

But Pulitzer could turn like a tiger even on Democrats, even on Whitney. *The World* had outstripped every other American newspaper in circulation and had become a national oracle, always watched warily by Democratic politicians because of its independence and unpredictability. The administration genuflected toward Pulitzer because of his services during the election. He was not above tickling his ego by making occasional use of his immense influence. At Bar Harbor, where he spent the summer months in a house sealed against particles that aggravated his asthma and noises that tormented his nerves, he enjoyed the acquaintance of the Lawrence Townsends of Philadelphia. Townsend wanted to be secretary of legation at Vienna, a post that Pulitzer felt he would fill admirably. Through *The World*'s aggressive young managing editor, George B. M. Harvey, Pulitzer asked the President to make the appointment and it was done at once.

In fact, Harvey himself was offered the consul-generalship in Berlin—a misguided administration effort to be friendly. Harvey did not decline instantly enough to please Pulitzer, who suspected him of weakening in the total loyalty he demanded of all *World* men— suspected also that the administration was trying to steal Harvey from him. It took less than this to put the neurasthenic publisher into a rage. Secretary Lamont, all unknowing, sought to please Pulitzer by giving him a scoop and letting him know, through Harvey, that the administration would appreciate his approval of the appointment of Whitney's friend James J. Van Alen as Minister to Rome.

The World pounced with an editorial and a flurry of articles denouncing the appointment for a profusion of reasons: Van Alen lacked "public service or prominence earned." The extent of his services to the party had been to march in one Democratic parade. He was a hopeless Anglophile who had said, "America is no fit place for ladies and gentlemen to live in," and in Washington recently he "asserted that Mr. Whitney had sold him the office for the cash," said to be $50,000 in the form of a campaign donation. *The World* quoted a friend of Van Alen's as saying that the latter deserved the post because "*He paid for the office like a gentleman*," the story continuing:

Van Alen is short and fat. He prides himself on his resemblance to the Prince of Wales. . . . He wears a single eyeglass with a heavy string attached. He speaks with a weird bastard cockney, which fills Englishmen with wonder. It is the sort of English accent that a man with no talent for imitation might get from hansom-cab drivers and Strand barmaids. A prize-fighting gentleman of the Bowery was brought to Newport to train the fat off Van Alen. The fighting gentleman, called One-Eyed Connelley, said he had never met a man who seemed less fit to be on earth than Van Alen. . . . His progress has been slow in spite of his wealth. The Ambassadorship for $50,000 is the greatest bargain of his life. . . .

Whitney in anger wrote *The World* protesting its "slanderous" stories, saying Van Alen was well qualified for the post and was backed by Rhode Island's Democrats. His donation (which Whitney said was less than $50,000) was made out of party loyalty; no promise of office was involved. "Mr. Whitney usually speaks in rather softly modulated tones," *The Sun* observed. "He is not an excitable citizen." Now he was, if not excited, incensed. Cleveland stood by the appointment and wrote privately of the "frivolous statements of a most mendacious and mischievous newspaper." Van Alen was confirmed by the Senate, whereupon he surprised everyone and gained some esteem by resigning with dignity. As for Alexander Gunn, no such fuss was made about him but he wrote in his journal, "I have determined not to take a consulate which, through Will, could have been mine."

2. Within the Law

AT THIS point and until the turn of the century, Whitney possessed power in each of three unrelated spheres—the political, social, and financial—that most men would prize in any one of them. Such triunity of power was not uncommon in the almost absolutist prewar planter-aristocracy of the South, but no one comes to mind who equaled it in Whitney's time. Theodore Roosevelt was to add political power to his family prestige while always remaining somewhat modest of purse. Mark Hanna was to be one of many combining financial and political power but unheard of socially. Whitney was the sole possessor of the blessing of President Cleveland and the whole Democratic party including Boss Croker, the highest regard of Mrs. Astor, and a position in Wall Street fortified by his alliance with Thomas Fortune Ryan and the Philadelphians as well as by close relations with such men as Cornelius and William K. Vanderbilt—themselves high in social and financial power but politically inactive.

Whitney (who never in his life got farther west than St. Louis) pronounced himself "overwhelmed" as he viewed the wonders of the great Columbian Exposition in Chicago and repeated his usual denial but with an added explanation: "I am out of politics and wish to stay out. It is a time in the education of my children when I desire to be near them, and business also requires my attention."

He had given more thought to his male children than did most men of such large affairs. Harry, now in his last year at Yale and an editor of the *Yale Daily News,* was nearest his father in appearance and temperament, strapping, handsome, sociable, an excellent horseman. Payne, now a freshman at Yale, was still growing, had a wry sense of humor, but was more introverted than his brother and always fated to be somewhat in Harry's shadow. Whitney's two daughters, though they had his love, got less of his attention since his duty toward them was considered fulfilled when they were prepared for successful marriage. He was thinking of taking all of his children to Europe in the summer of 1894, a plan that did not materialize. The end of Flora's vast parties, much as he had disliked them, left a great hole in his life that he filled in part by joining and attending more clubs. His club life was more than merely social, however, for he remained a leading director of the Metropolitan Opera, was an enthusiastic board member of the American Museum of Natural History, and took an interest in the annual Horse Show. What with his inheritance of Flora's fortune on top of his own magnificent emoluments, he was now what he had long wanted to be, a rich man in his own right, spending money for things he wanted. He loved to spend money. Although there were subtler motivations, Burton J. Hendrick, who made the earliest thorough study of Whitney's financial career, said that the simplest explanation for his transformation from comparative political rectitude to robber-baron rapacity was that "Whitney had the luxurious tastes of a Medici." A later commentator said that "this extravagant side of his nature gained an overmastering control of him" and "his passion for domination and display never loosed its grip."

This kind of man—handsome, perfectly tailored, agreeable, rich, generous, socially and politically powerful—could be said categorically to be attractive to women. Whitney was surely the cynosure of ambitious and unattached women, a man who could have picked a mistress or a second wife from a line of applicants. It seems likely that his interest in women—active enough when Flora was alive—would have

heightened now. Rumor was busy enough so that to dance with a lady
not firmly attached was enough to start it. The stunning Mary Leiter
mentioned "the rumour that she was to marry the recently widowed
William Whitney," and that "the newspapermen were clamouring at
her door for confirmation or denial." She was only twenty-three, the
daughter of a former Chicago department store millionaire. She had
been one of Charles Dana Gibson's early models, and she had known
the Whitneys both in Washington and Newport. But she was not interested in Whitney, being secretly engaged to the rising Briton George
Curzon, later to become a marquess and take her to India when he became Viceroy. Whitney's passion for Mrs. Randolph seemed unob-
served. His discretion was suggested, though not proved, by the fact that
Col. William d'Alton Mann's weekly magazine of Society gossip and
genteel blackmail, *Town Topics*, was not pairing him off with eligible
women.

For it was here that Colonel Mann, who originally came from
Michigan, entered his life in an interesting, if oblique, manner. By now
Whitney certainly knew Mann, since they both frequented Delmonico's
and were good Democrats and fellow members of the Manhattan Club.
Mann, fifty-three, a red-faced, portly man with flaring gray whiskers
who always wore a frock coat and striped pants, had been a genuine colonel in the Civil War, though this was one of the few genuine things
about him. He had escaped conviction in an oil swindle before he arrived in New York to take over and revive the failing *Town Topics*. This
well-printed, slick-paper publication, which called itself "The Journal of
Society," opened every issue with "Saunterings," gossip items about Society people filling eight or ten pages and written in elegant-racy style by
"The Saunterer," who was Mann. These items were decidedly personal,
unlike the cautious and respectful tone of newspaper Society reporters.
They ranged from the highly flattering to savagery barely skirting the
edge of libel. The Saunterer commented, for example, "Mrs. Belmont
dyes her hair. Though covered with diamond rings, her hands are
wrinkled like a washerwoman's," and said of a daughter of the long-suf-
fering James Van Alen (a granddaughter of Mrs. Astor) that she "suffers
from some kind of throat trouble—she cannot go more than half an
hour without a drink." He had a special pique against Mrs. Astor, often
commenting on her burden of jewelry, wondering editorially whether
she or the actress Nelly Farren had the most, deciding that Nelly "probably has more diamond garters" and suggesting that Mrs. Astor appear at
the next Charity Ball "wheeling her jewels in a barrow." Now and then

he took off on Mrs. Burke Roche, writing once with masterly ambiguity that she appeared in recent photographs "in a very low-necked corsage in which the 'crease under the arm,' which is always very beautiful, when not unsightly, is very plainly shown." The Saunterer was expert at hinting at the sexually illicit and homosexuality. He had built up a staff of informants composed of servants and people at Society's edges so that his comments contained much of the knowledgeable. *Town Topics* was required reading among the elite, though each would have denied interest in such "trash." It was not yet generally known that Saunterer praise could be bought for a price and that Mann could be persuaded for a consideration to forget scandal. As Mann himself later put it, "I have cartloads of stories locked up in my safe that would turn New York upside down if they were published."

So far, *Town Topics* had treated the Whitneys well. Now, as a highly eligible widower, Whitney was of prime social interest and could be expected to be under the Saunterer's most alert observation.

Whitney was in some danger too of losing his reputation as a mover and shaker, a man of achievement—a reputation that had come from his years of political activity and occasional magic. If he was indeed quitting politics, what could save him from social superficiality, the worship of the baronial that was the central aim of his social circle? In any case, his generosity with Daniel Lamont was repeated with Lamont's successor, none other than George Harvey, who had decided at twenty-nine that life was too short to work for such a tartar as Pulitzer. As when he had been corporation counsel and Navy Secretary, Whitney had the gift of inspiring affection among his staff and colleagues. As a businessman he increased the affection by making the association with him highly profitable. An unusually honest young Tammany man destined to be mayor of New York, George B. McClellan, commented that "Harvey had become a sort of jackal for William C. Whitney and the latter's political liaison man with politicians." It fitted in with Hendrick's picture of the master intriguer working fastidiously through subordinates, as did his employment of such hard-fisted lobbyists as Louis F. Payn and Lemuel E. Quigg. Although Whitney retained his Wall Street office in the Mills Building, he was to be one of the first to move his uptown operations into a suite at the new Waldorf-Astoria when it was built on the very spot where Mrs. Astor had once greeted Flora and him at her annual balls. While he was still interested in the Linotype and other enterprises, including banks and railroads, New York City transit was easily his biggest and most profitable venture.

Here he had the invaluable legal aid of that keenest of all men, sharp-faced Elihu Root, who "never accepted the notion that a lawyer before accepting a cause, must be sure it is just." And here also his friend Francis Lynde Stetson invented for him and gave him the protection of the first holding company ever created. Stetson divided the traction enterprise into two, the Metropolitan Street Railway Company being the operating unit and the Metropolitian Traction Company being the holding company "which did not construct and operate street railways itself, but merely owned other corporations that did so."

The stout, round-faced Peter A. B. Widener, seven years older than Whitney, was leader of his Philadelphia associates. The smart son of a German bricklayer, he had learned the butcher trade and made his meat shop a Republican headquarters in the old Spring Garden market. He prospered as a meat supplier to the Union Army, emerging from the Civil War with $50,000 in profits, and thereafter rose from ward leader to great power in Philadelphia and Harrisburg. His lieutenant was William L. Elkins, who had moved up from grocery clerk to butter-and-egg wholesaler and then plunged at the right moment in Titusville oil, which made him rich when he sold out to Standard Oil. The third Philadelphian, William H. Kemble, was a former ward politician who had become a rich banker and henchman of the powerful Republican boss Matthew Quay. A domineering man, Kemble had once assaulted a reporter who asked to interview him and had been sentenced to a year in jail for bribing legislators—a term that Boss Quay's magic saved him from serving. With Quay behind them, Widener, Elkins, and Kemble had dominated Philadelphia politics precisely as Whitney now dominated New York politics. Quay had a financial interest in the scheme when the others set out to "unify and modernize" Philadelphia's seventeen independently operated traction lines.

Their profits were so satisfying that as their home project neared its end they sought the same deal in other cities, especially New York. New York had some thirty independent horse-drawn lines, most of them owned by wealthy families or estates, all of them a scourge to citizens wanting to get anywhere: "The cars were small, unventilated, shockingly filthy, and broken down. They were lighted by faint kerosene lamps; in wintertime, a mass of straw or hay thrown upon the floor furnished the only warmth." Each line followed its own course. Even riders traveling only a short distance often had to take several lines, pay several fares, and proceed in a zigzag. The Whitney group's plan was obviously admirable if executed honestly—to secure these and other franchises, to unify and reroute these lines, to replace the horses with steam or electric power, and to install modern, comfortable cars. The Jacob Sharp scandal had brought about legislation providing for the sale of streetcar franchises at public auction open to all. Alas, like so much legislation aimed at curbing larceny against the public, it had been attacked and rendered useless by sharp lawyers on the ground that the various surface lines had been organized under special grants prior to the new law. It will be remembered that Mr. Rainsford had been shocked by Whitney's smiling statement that he let go an earlier lawyer because he told Whitney what he could not do, "and Root [tells me] what I can." A junior lawyer who observed meetings of Whitney and his traction group noted:

> Whitney would sit at the head of the table. When the talk was spent, he would say, "Well, gentlemen, this is the thing to do," and he would state it briefly. Meanwhile Root would be writing on small slips of paper and when Whitney had finished he would say, "This is the way to do it."

In these enterprises the collaboration of the brilliant Root, later so able and honest as a public servant, was of course never criminal or illegal. Nor was it the kind of work that an attorney of high ethical sensibility would be inclined to look back on later with pride. Unfortunately, a lawyer who advises a client as to how he can stay within the law in conducting business that is manifestly unfair and disastrous to the public was then and still is within his rights. There are attorneys who refuse to take that kind of work, but Root was not one of them. He later told his good friend Theodore Roosevelt (who rather looked down on that brand of legality) that "he had great difficulty in making up his mind whether he should act as attorney for the Whitney-Ryan traction interests in New York but finally reached the conclusion that there was no reason why he should not." [*]

3. It's No All the Time

ON MAY 16, 1894, Alexander Gunn sailed on the *Majestic* as the guest of Whitney along with the Charles T. Barneys, Pauline Whitney (still wearing mourning fifteen months after Flora's death), and her friend

---

[*] Root's distinguished biographer, Philip C. Jessup, so balanced otherwise in his appraisal, seeks to defend him in this instance but can only fall back on the argument that he was within the law.

Johanna Davidge. Whitney's valet, Truelove, was in the party to care for his master's needs. Gunn, who enjoyed his own inconsistencies, could write of "these unhappy men who are rich," and "O Vanity! . . . with all your riches you may not buy a happy hour." Whitney's riches were about to buy Gunn many happy hours. Gunn could preach the blessings of the simple life at Zoar and yet revel in the sybarical. "Zoar—Monte Carlo," he reflected, "can any wider stretch lie between any other two? I love them both."

The last Whitney-Barney European excursion had been marred by the unpleasantness over Mrs. Randolph. Whitney was especially fond of his youngest sister Lilly and her husband. As for Gunn, he was an old friend linked with him by memories of Flora and all the Paynes— memories too of Olive's death in Paris. His poetic temperament, his cultivated enthusiasms and aversions, were luxuries Whitney could not expect to find in his encounters with the likes of Croker, Ryan, and Widener. Perhaps the presence of Gunn was Whitney's admission to himself that in becoming baronial he was losing touch with things of the spirit.

They shared a table aboard ship with the corporation attorney Elbridge T. Gerry, his wife, and two daughters. Whitney knew them, one might say, "of course." The Gerrys, as family-proud as the Whitneys, were almost near neighbors, having a Richard Morris Hunt–designed pink chateau on Fifth Avenue near 60th that contained a superb law library. Whitney enjoyed Thackeray and liked to read when he had time, but he had no law library and could be said to have abandoned the law for business. Gerry admitted to owning a coat of arms and had been properly excoriated by *The World* for this "anti-American advertisement."

"Will and I are converts to the new system of Mr. Gerry, which forbids water at meals," Gunn wrote in his diary. "Champagne is . . . a great improvement. . . . the table is luxuriously served—the earth is raked for delicacies of food and drink." Among the passengers with whom they chatted were the Earl of Warwick and Moreton Frewen, an Englishman who had long owned a ranch on the Powder River in Wyoming. Whitney—of course—knew the charming, capricious, Cantabrigian Frewen, an implausible soldier of misfortune. He had married (at Whitney's own Grace Church) Clara Jerome, the elder sister of Jennie Jerome who was Lady Churchill and whose thirteen-year-old son was Winston Churchill. Frewen was building a legend of sublime failure. He was a man of endless schemes both for moneymaking and for the improvement of mankind, who had failed at ranching, gold mining, the sale of timber, bats' guano, and many other business promotions. Always broke and on the verge of ruin, he invariably had a new inspiration he was sure would enrich him. He came of an old family, had excellent connections, and for a time had shared Lilly Langtry as mistress with the Prince of Wales. Through it all he was an ardent believer in bimetallism—the use of both gold and silver as monetary standards— about which Whitney was curious as a possible solution to the terrible American economic depression. Frewen had been in Washington trying to influence legislators in favor of bimetallism. Wonderfully persuasive, he had many friends among the senators and was hatching a concurrent scheme—not wholly ethical in which he asked Whitney's help. The Congress was working on a new tariff bill. While in Washington, Frewen had also sought to persuade legislators to raise the tariff on African diamonds from 10 to 30 percent. While he reasoned in complicated fashion that this would strike a blow for bimetallism, he also planned to make a quick fortune by speculating on the price differential. Whitney agreed to use his influence to help him—impelled, one hopes, on the score of bimetallism rather than aiding Frewen's private trickery, which Whitney may not have known about.

Gunn wrote that it was his group's intention to "go to London, then to Paris, then to Tours, and later to Bayreuth to hear Wagner's opera; perhaps also to Berlin and Vienna." But they landed at Liverpool, investigated Chester, looked over Warwick Castle with its Holbeins and Raphaels, and hardly more than got settled at the Bristol Hotel in London when Pauline upset all their plans. She contracted typhoid fever. Luckily it was not a serious case, but for a time she did her sightseeing from a hospital bed.

Gunn enjoyed registering at luxurious places like the Bristol as coming from "Zoar, Ohio," which usually drew stares. "We have the best rooms at this hotel," he wrote a friend. "It makes me shudder at what it costs every day, more than would suffice me a year at Zoar." His correspondent was Ludwig Zimmermann, his closest friend at the Zoar colony, who over the years received fascinating descriptions of Gunn's adventures with Whitney and others. "Mr. Whitney treats me with the most delicate and affectionate consideration," Gunn went on. "I ordered a lot of clothes at Poole's and when I went to pay, found he had paid for the whole thing. He is always buying things for me in spite of all my protests. We have carriages always in waiting to drive where we want to go, with coachmen and footmen in livery."

They made tours out from London as Pauline improved. Whitney was looking for paintings and other objets d'art and also sightseeing in a tireless and thoroughgoing manner—Windsor, Oxford, Blenheim Palace, Woodstock, Tintern Abbey, Stratford. "Mr. Cornelius Vanderbilt and his family made the two day trip to Stratford, and we traveled as only Kings travel in this country," Gunn recorded. "The Vanderbilts, despite their wealth, are most pleasant people, and we had merry times with plenty of 'cold bottles' and every luxury man can conceive." Indeed, Gunn's affection for cold bottles was steadfast. Barney, a confirmed punster, picked up Gunn's remark after viewing paintings of assorted monarchs that he disliked the "idiotic mug" of Henry IV: "I did not suppose any mug looked idiotic to you." After a boat trip to Windsor, Gunn admitted in his journal, "on the way back I drink too much Scotch whisky and Will mildly reproves me." Whitney, who found friends everywhere, dined in London with the touring Dr. McLane and his companion, the distinguished neurologist and novelist who summered at Bar Harbor, Dr. Weir Mitchell, and also with Moreton Frewen. "I am glad to hear," Whitney later wrote Frewen, "the Bill is taking shape in the matter of diamonds. I sent another dispatch . . . and it may have helped—I think it would have." Alas, even Whitney's influence failed: the new tariff kept the diamond duty at 10 percent and another Frewen scheme perished.

". . . I call with Will on the Duchess of Manchester, the Countess of Warwick, Mr. and Mrs. Sassoon," Gunn noted. The Duchess of Manchester was born Consuelo Yznaga, a Cuban heiress who had been prominent in New York Society and a friend of Mrs. Paran Stevens's daughter Minnie, now Mrs. Paget. Whitney and Gunn looked at antiquities, tapestries, sculpture, even fabrics: "Will and I go . . . to the Duchess of Sutherland's palace, where a sale of Scotch homespun is going on. . . . when Will is captured by the Duchess I slip quietly away. . . ." They visited museums, abbeys, cathedrals. They saw *The Masqueraders* ("a most vile play well played"), Sarah Bernhardt in *La Tosca*, Rejane in *Mme. Sans-Gêne*, heard Handel's *Messiah* at the Crystal Palace, and *Lohengrin* with the de Reszkes and Melba in the cast ("Prince and Princess of Wales there," Gunn observed. "Opera in parts beautiful. . . . The Swan sticks and is finally kicked off by Lohengrin. . . ."). They saw "an excellent performance of *The Mikado*."

While Whitney stayed in London to be near Pauline, he sent Gunn, the Barneys, and Miss Davidge to Paris for a week. When they returned, Pauline was much improved and was taken to a country place at

Weybridge for convalescence, kept company by Miss Davidge while the Barneys sailed home and Whitney and Gunn toured to the far north of Scotland, the homeland of Gunn's ancestors. When one landlady said she could not serve them a hot lunch because of the bank holiday, Gunn noted, "Will is firm with her and she yields meekly." They went to Wycombe "to see the old mansions where Will's ancestors lived." They visited the town of Whitney, near the Welsh border, site of "the old manor of the Whitneys." At Malvern they hunted grouse and attended church, and "Will sings the responses to the Creed with such an expression that [a woman seated nearby] boldly turns her head to see what true holy man is there." At Worcester Whitney bought flowers for Pauline and also dahlia bulbs for Gunn's garden at Zoar.

"The beer at Chipping Norton is very good," Gunn commented and wrote elsewhere, "We have been testing the new champagne—each night two bottles. It is decided that the '84 Krug is beyond the Ayala, while I insist on the reverse." A month before they were to leave, he wrote, "It is like leaving heaven to leave England and my friend; my life is so small and empty—perhaps my own fault." Gunn's life was anything but small and empty, but the boundless Whitney enthusiasm and the wide-ranging Whitney acquaintance and interests were apt to make companions feel wanting. Whitney received urgent cables from Senator Hill's henchmen in New York imploring him to be the Democratic candidate for governor in the fall. The party had declined, hurt by the panic and by some desertions to free silver, and Governor Flower, Hill's present man in the office, was too colorless to be reelected. Hill shunned the candidacy himself because if he lost it might ruin his presidential chances in 1896. The block had been offered with artful cajolery for others to lay their heads on—Daniel Lamont, William J. Gaynor, and Perry Belmont, all of whom had hastily declined. Whitney, though not aware of this byplay, cabled his refusal.

". . . I was never so kindly treated before by anyone as he treats me," Gunn wrote of Whitney as they prepared to leave. With Pauline fully recovered, they sailed on September 20. At Queenstown Whitney read that the Hill leaders had at last offered the candidacy to Governor Flower himself, who declined with dignity. When they reached New York, reporters boarded the ship and swarmed around Whitney, who puffed comfortably at a cigar. "His blue serge yachting suit and cap made him look perfectly at ease," said *The Tribune*, "and as he surveyed the circle of eager reporters he smiled and smiled and again smiled. 'What-in-the-world-is-it-all-about?' " he asked innocently. It turned out that the desperate Democrats had extended their convention at Saratoga for two days in the hope of coaxing him to be the nominee. His refusal was as firm as ever, though he said, "whoever receives the nomination will receive always my support. . . ." A deputation of a dozen-odd Democratic emissaries, among them C. C. Baldwin and J. Sergeant Cram, came aboard and besought him to save the party, saying that he was the only Democrat who could beat the Republican candidate, Levi Morton. It was no use, and they dispersed in gloom. The third deputation to meet Whitney was his own kin and friends, Harry and Payne Whitney, the Barneys, Thomas Fortune Ryan, and George Harvey. As Whitney and his party walked away, he was met by James T. Kilbreth, the Democratic Collector of the Port, a Yale man of Whitney's vintage and of course a friend. "Do you really mean it, Whit?" asked Kilbreth. "I mean it, Kil, my boy; it's no all the time. . . ."

4. Chaperoning Pauline

So DISASTROUS was the panic and so rebellious much of the electorate that President Cleveland wrote to Whitney, "God only knows the way of relief." Boss Croker had weighed the portents, observed that he was losing control in the city, resigned, and left for Europe until the storm blew over. His man Mayor Thomas F. Gilroy was still in office but would surely be ousted in the next election. As for Senator Hill, he was unable to get anyone else to run for governor so at last agreed heroically to be the victim himself, and Whitney paid him a congratulatory call and gave him his support. The President maker did his best to keep his hold on the reins of power in Washington, Albany, and New York City. The allegation that "Whitney . . . used his own knowledge of local politics as well as his prestige as a former presidential Cabinet member to obtain for a time virtual control of Tammany Hall" seems if anything to underestimate his power in the city. Mayor Gilroy was Croker's nominal successor at the moment, but The Tribune commented, "Mr. Whitney is at the Mayor's office now every day or so. He was accompanied . . . yesterday by Thomas F. Ryan, treasurer of the Metropolitan Traction syndicate. The ex 'foolkiller' of 1892 has been giving the Tammany organization, through its leader, Mayor Gilroy, a good deal of advice . . . about a candidate for Mayor. . . ."

There was no determined journalistic questioning of the propriety of Whitney, as a traction magnate seeking favors from the city, having such daily freedom of the mayor's office, along with Ryan. So charming was he that he seems to have won over editors of all parties. But the election that fall, as feared, was a Democratic disaster. Hill lost to Levi Morton by 156,000 votes, and although Hill had cushioned himself by keeping his Senate seat, he shed much of his remaining prestige. The Republicans gained a huge majority in the House, held their Senate majority, and New York City had a Republican-Fusion reformist mayor, William L. Strong, who showed his zeal by naming young Theodore Roosevelt to the Police Board. Democrats, looking toward the 1896 presidential election, could see only thunderheads.

Whitney had also to contend with rumors of his alleged romantic involvement with two different women. Gossip that he was interested in Johanna Davidge seems patently false. Miss Davidge is shown by Gunn's private journal to have been Pauline's close friend and companion in England, as she was in New York, but the talk was so persistent that both her family and Whitney himself felt impelled to make public denials. The other woman mentioned, but as yet without real conviction, was Mrs. Randolph—in this case only a wisp of smoke but a large fire. While attending the 1894 Horse Show at Madison Square Garden, Whitney was queried by reporters and he "solemnly asseverated that he was engaged to no woman."

The unhidden romance in the family was that of Pauline, who now had a serious suitor whose qualifications had to be explored. He was an Englishman, Almeric Hugh Paget, aged thirty three, thirteen years older than she. It seems likely that they had met in England through Minnie Stevens, Mrs. Paran Stevens's daughter who had married one of Paget's older brothers, Capt. Arthur Paget. The late Mrs. Stevens was said to have approved highly of Almeric who, although he was a grandson of the first Marquess of Anglesey, was one of thirteen children and unfortunately had no title himself but of course was of "distinguished family." There was the question of money. Some years earlier—the later newspaper accounts were vague about this detail and others—Almeric had, like Moreton Frewen, come adventurously to America and gone west intending to be a rancher. He had instead ended up in St. Paul, Minnesota, where he was said to have profited handsomely in real estate and insurance. His family background, not yet known to Whitney, contained sterling individuals and others whose exploits counseled caution, especially including his late grandfather, the marquess himself, who had combined wild and willful traits with others widely praised. While only nineteen, taking the grand tour of Europe, he was jailed in

Geneva for a drunken escapade when he and a few young English friends essayed to capture the town. His weakness for liquor and women was notorious, his affair with the Duchess of Rutland causing the greatest scandal. He became a dashing soldier, however, losing a leg at Waterloo and becoming a member of Parliament, Lord Lieutenant of Ireland, and finally a privy councillor. Old One Leg, as he was called, maintained grand establishments in Wales, Staffordshire, and London, was wastrel enough to be brought to court for debt, and divorced his wife after she had given him eight children, then married the sister-in-law of the Duke of Wellington, who gave him ten more.

Whitney no longer had Flora's counsel about the fitness of suitors. It appears that he arranged another tour abroad, to combine pleasure with an opportunity to appraise the man who wanted to become his son-in-law, and also to give Pauline occasion to know him better. "Will writes me to know if I can go to Rome and Egypt with them," Gunn wrote in his journal. ". . . I can only say no. But . . . Rome! To see it once again, and dip my hands in the fountain of Trevi!" When Whitney urged him by telegram, Gunn's resistance crumbled.

On December 5, 1894, Whitney sailed, again on the *Majestic*, with his son Harry (now a Yale graduate with Phi Beta Kappa honors), Pauline, Miss Davidge, Almeric Hugh Paget, Gunn, and the valet Truelove whose name, it was hoped, bespoke the spirit of Paget's quest. They were bidden bon voyage by a large group including the Barneys and Colonel Payne, the latter, Gunn noting ominously in his journal, so "serious and cold" that it appeared that their long friendship might be over. Gunn had no inkling of the reason, other than the colonel's overbearing nature and the ease with which he could take affront. Gunn was highly sensitive, and the thought cast a pall over his trip. Whitney, on the other hand, was benevolence itself. In his stateroom Gunn found "a cigar and a bottle of ancient whisky" sent him with Whitney's compliments. Paget, a man of middle height, well-trimmed mustache, and pleasant mien, sat at the Whitney table and also played cards with Pauline, who was an inveterate cardplayer and put him to rout regularly. Whitney chatted frequently with Paget, who scarcely seemed to inherit the rashness of his grandfather. Paget's father, Lord Alfred Paget, had been in the household of Queen Victoria from 1837 to his death in 1888, rising from Equerry to Chief Equerry and Clerk Marshal. Although Almeric may not have mentioned it to Whitney, his father, despite the marriage that produced thirteen children, was reputed to have been in love with the queen—a love that some members of the family claimed was reciprocated. "He was said to have worn the Queen's portrait over his heart, and even to have hung her miniature around the neck of his dog," according to the biographer of the first marquess.

Since Whitney was infatuated with Mrs. Randolph, perhaps this was one way of serving out the term of mourning he was required to observe. The crossing was rough, Miss Davidge being so ill that she was "longing for death." Dropping Paget off in England to visit his family and rejoin them later, the rest crossed Europe by train to board ship at Brindisi, spending Christmas on the Mediterranean. "At breakfast the table decked with holly and mistletoe," Gunn recorded; "a great array of presents; Pauline, Miss Davidge, Harry . . . give me pleasant things . . . at dinner we have three bottles and much merriment. . . ." At Port Said when they landed the temperature was ninety degrees and "a majestic fat lady, who in the ship was a model of perfect dressing . . . turns red, and the sweat makes a sad ruin of her painted face."

At Cairo they took sumptuous rooms at the Continental to start off a typically strenuous Whitney expedition, gorging themselves on all the arts, beauties, and pleasures. Whitney and Gunn heard the opera, dined with old Whitney friends at the British embassy, traveled through "incredible dust and antique filth" to see both howling and whirling dervishes, repeatedly visited the Sphinx and other monuments by camel and donkey, and looked incessantly at dahabeahs in search of one grand enough for Whitney. On January 17 Paget rejoined them and they all sailed up the Nile in their dahabeah for a month's excursion, dining luxuriously and waited on by Egyptian servants. Paget occasionally shot pigeons, Gunn marveled at tomatoes growing red while Zoar was under snow, and they visited the great temples at Luxor, Karnak, and Thebes: "a majesty unknown in modern architecture." Returning to Cairo, where Whitney's niece Helen Barney was added to the party, they sailed to Jatta, toured the Holy Land, saw Athens ("The prime minister of Greece visits the ship. There are national airs.") and Constantinople. Thence they made for Sicily on a steamer on which they encountered Darius Ogden Mills, co-investor with Whitney in the Linotype, and his companion Charles Crocker, son and successor of the San Francisco railroad and banking mogul.

"The attachment intensifies," Gunn wrote after watching Pauline and Paget. Paget was now addressing his most serious and courtly attentions to her, unable to do so privately because the code of the time forbade an unmarried lady to be alone with a gentleman. The whole party made an attentive audience, spying on the couple and speculating as to whether Paget seemed to be gaining ground or perhaps losing. Pauline, with her social training and two years abroad, seemed equal to the situation, not one easily overwhelmed by ardor. The climax seemed certain to be approaching when they landed at Messina and went on by train to Taormina. It did not appear that Paget's earnest appeal could continue much longer without either an acceptance or rejection by Pauline, and the suspense was considerable among the observers.

Taormina providentially furnished the perfect setting for the continuation of the drama—the centuries-old Greek theater, a spectacularly beautiful spot overlooked by Mount Etna and itself overlooking the Ionian Sea. "Mr. Crocker is very attentive to Miss Davidge," Gunn recorded, "while the other two [Pauline and Paget] withdrawn apart are earnestly engaged. It is like the garden scene in *Faust*. Mr. Mills thinks, as I do, that the crisis has been reached, and Paget knows his fate. There never could be a more poetical place for troth plighting." An hour later, as they left the theater by carriage: "Her face is filled with rosy light. I am sure the engagement is settled. . . . I hope they may be happy, for I am very fond of Pauline—and Paget is in every way a gentleman. Crocker and Mr. Mills both think the thing is settled."

Neither the young couple nor Whitney enlightened them. At Naples, Paget left for England, still keeping the secret. On tour, Whitney was his usual pleasant self, giving Gunn occasional presents—a fine bronze Narcissus, a handsome cigarette lighter. For himself, Whitney was looking for works of art and such things as an antique silver service for sixty. Could the latter be a clue signifying an intention to remarry? Gunn, despite his exposure to it, was astonished by the lavishness Whitney poured on them, the food, the vintages, the luxury of the Tramontano at Sorrento: "Vast and splendid rooms; two great saloons, a dining-room, a boudoir, an open gallery over the sea, and four immense chambers. I can hardly see the ceiling of my room, whereupon is painted a fresco of the Apotheosis of Venus. After dinner a private entertainment for us." On his earlier tour of England with Whitney he had once written, "I shudder at the extravagance in which we live. . . . Sometimes I fear an upheaval of the many poor against the few rich." Now, passing over the visible destitution in Egypt, the Near East, and Italy, he knew more vividly than the insulated Whitney that the United States itself was in terrible straits. While Whitney was enlarging his fortune, Gunn's own meager means had dwindled, as had those of most of the farmers and wage earners. The bank failures and foreclosures continued. Three million were unemployed. Coxey's pathetic army of the jobless, a painful memory, had wound its way through Ohio before reaching Washington to see its leaders arrested for walking on the grass. The railroad strike had been roughly put down when Cleveland called out the army. Gunn knew the difficulties even of the thrifty husbandmen of Zoar and occasionally felt in his heart that he was betraying these people. Between Gunn's lines could be read his regret that Whitney, so generous and considerate to his companions, seemed to waste little worry on the problems of the poor. Gunn's delight in the tour was also marred by his memory of Colonel Payne's antagonism and its possible effect on Whitney: "I fear my friend [Whitney] has not fully considered the animosity of the Colonel and it may be a dull cloud on his relations. Why should this man, once so dear a friend, stand like a cloud between me and the sun?"

In Naples Whitney received a cable from *The New York Times* asking him to comment on the *Alliance* incident. A Spanish warship in the Caribbean had fired on an American vessel of that name. Poor aim had made it a near miss. No damage was done, but feeling was growing hot over alleged Spanish inhumanity in Cuba, and Whitney let himself go in a long, belligerent statement that *The Times* front-paged, and all other papers followed suit next day. It read in small part:

> [The firing] was deliberate and with full knowledge of the character of the act. . . . It is a . . . wilful insult to the American flag and people. I do not recall so wanton an outrage as happening to any first-class power in fifty years. An apology scarcely wipes out such an affront. The truth is, we have happened to come in for a piece of the general brutality and ruffianism that holds Cuba. The thing is a relic of the Middle Ages. It is a disgrace to us that lies at our doorstep. It makes my blood boil, for one. . . .

Coming from Whitney and appearing in newspapers all over the country, the statement undoubtedly fanned the fires of United States interventionism. The jingoist *Tribune* praised him and saw him as tossing his hat into the ring for 1896. "The Naples message may be the first bulletin of a presidential canvass," *The Tribune* editorialized, although it admitted, "We may be wrong, for Mr. Whitney is a deep and wary man whose political designs are inscrutable. . . ."

It was not unreasonable to suspect his statement of indicating tentative presidential ambitions. His pugnacity was no uninformed outburst, for he had been keeping up with events in Cuba, occasionally giving

Secretary of State Gresham his thoughts by mail or telegram. The disadvantage of his own poverty and Flora's wealth no longer held. He would not have been the first politician to hold the door open a trifle and to titillate the public. His power in Tammany and his accommodation with Hill could assure him backing in New York, especially if Hill's own chances had been destroyed by his gubernatorial disaster. Whitney's jingoism about Cuba struck a popular chord and could win him votes. The Naples blast may have been a trial balloon to test the presidential breezes. When he later received the New York papers he professed to be unhappy, writing to Gresham, "I got hopping mad here all alone by myself, and as usual in such cases put my foot in the hole"—a private, not a public, retraction.

The party went on to Rome, where Gunn had time to dip his hands in Trevi while Whitney "goes to call on Princess Respoti." Gunn wrote to his friend Ludwig, "I long for Zoar. Am here in Rome . . . with everything the hand of man can furnish—so perverse is man." He cautioned Ludwig to uncover the roses, start the dahlias in pots, "and be very careful to keep the names." In Rome they met another princess—more properly a queen, Mrs. Jack Gardner. Her rich railroad-and-mining-company husband was with her but was always fated to be mentioned as an auxiliary or afterthought. Whitney and Gunn went to the galleries with the Gardners and spent one whole day with them in going by four-in-hand to picnic at Ostia, followed by a cook, waiters, tables, and food from their hotel. Driving a four-in-hand at a fast clip—strange horses at that—was a gauge of the Whitney confidence and daring, the coach careening through crowded city streets blaring its horn and making Gunn uneasy not only at the luxury and arrogance of it but also the actual risk.

A cable from Cleveland told them of the death of Mrs. Payne. That left the immediate Payne family, once numbering seven, with three survivors—the old ex-senator, the Colonel, and the youngest daughter. Pauline immediately purchased mourning attire. On to Florence, to Bologna, then on to Venice in May. Here occurred other meetings with Mrs. Jack. The Gardners annually rented the Palazzo Barbaro on the Grand Canal for several months. Whitney and Gunn first took tea with her there, then next day dined with her. Perhaps because the couple, not surprisingly, occasionally quarreled, Gardner was absent on both occasions. "We dine with Mrs. G. in the beautiful old palace, served by her people in livery," Gunn wrote, "the vast and splendid rooms filled with frescoes and rare works of art." She easily ranked as one of the world's rarities herself, and Whitney as one of the most remarkable of men. If Mrs. Jack had to be conceded an edge on him in ego and impudence, in appreciation of art and music, even in travel (she had circled the globe ten years earlier and been the first white woman to see Angkor Wat, which she reached by elephant), they were alike in fashion and energy, and she had never built a Navy or elected a President. No more than comely of feature but beautiful of figure and grace, gowned in Paris, she was Boston's most incurable coquette, having stretched her husband's patience in flirtations with dozens of men. Recently, when she had had an audience with the Pope, knowing friends had expressed concern over the pontiff's defenses against her fascinations.

She was of a susceptibility and spontaneity never quelled by the presence of others. Whitney was nearing fifty-four, a year younger than she, handsome enough for anyone, a man in the headlines being discussed as a presidential possibility, who was yet knowledgeable in the arts and could drive a coach as Ben-Hur drove his chariot. But perhaps Whitney's interests lay elsewhere. Gunn's epicene account made it clear that all the proprieties were observed: "A memorable night. Will sits on her right, and I on her left,—her plain face transparent with genius; a great woman. We then go to the opera, lighted by thousands of candles. The King and Queen come; all rise. . . ."

5. Helping Mr. Morgan

ON THE way home, probably by design rather than accident, Whitney met Croker in England. Arriving in New York with his party on May 29, 1895, after six months' absence, he told reporters that Croker was "entirely interested in his horses and [has] given up politics"—erroneous indeed. Whitney found himself regarded universally as a strong contender for the 1896 presidential nomination, which it was felt he could have for the asking. He was actively promoted by many, including Pulitzer and the newcomer William Randolph Hearst, the strapping young Westerner with the soft voice who had just taken over *The New York Journal*. Democratic National Chairman William F. Harrity and other conservative party leaders came out for Whitney. *The World*, canvassing thirty important editors in New York State, announced that twenty-six were for Whitney, the editor of *The Rome Sentinel* saying "Whitney would run like a steer in the corn." *The Tribune* heard rumors about . . .

a comprehensive program in which President Cleveland, David B. Hill, William R. Grace, Richard Croker and [others] . . . were to take part. Mr. Whitney . . . was to have the devoted and unqualified support of the Hill-Murphy State machine, the Tammany Hall organization, the Grace Democracy and of President Cleveland, Secretary D. S. Lamont and all the cuckoos of the State of New York and many other States.

When Whitney went to Bar Harbor that summer, saying as usual that he was not a candidate, he had Gunn with him again. "I am in a smooth sea in a luxurious steamer [Whitney's new yacht *Columbia*] two hundred and six feet long, furnished like a palace and flowing with Epernay," Gunn wrote. ". . . . Mr. Whitney, Colonel Harvey, and myself are the only ones on board. For us the whole machinery runs; the steamer has a crew of thirty men, besides servants." At Bar Harbor Whitney rented Mosley Hall, a magnificent estate overlooking French-man's Bay. He must surely have conferred with Pulitzer, now better sheltered there in a new soundproofed granite addition to his home called the Tower of Silence. Within a few weeks the two would be at odds.

Secretary of State Gresham had died and been succeeded by the stern Bostonian Attorney General Richard Olney. When Venezuela quarreled with British Guiana over their common boundary, Olney took Venezuela's side and invoked the Monroe Doctrine in a curt note to Lord Salisbury, the British prime minister, saying in part, "Today the United States is practically sovereign on this continent, and its fiat is law. . . ." His lordship, not accustomed to that tone, waited four months before replying in tart disagreement. Cleveland supported Olney, demanded a United States commission to determine the boundary, and added astonishing menace: "In making these recommendations I am keenly alive to the responsibility incurred and keenly realize all the consequences that may follow."

Abruptly the nation reacted in jingoist excitement that suggested a deep American desire to show muscle. Cleveland's message made headlines and was read to schoolchildren all over the land. Theodore Roosevelt, spoiling for a fight, wrote to a friend that he was ready for action, which he hoped would include the "conquest of Canada." Dana's *New York Sun* felt that anyone disapproving was "an alien or traitor" and foresaw battles in "the English Channel and the Irish Sea." *The Tribune* for once praised Cleveland and assailed the "peace-at-any-price cuckoos," and when a stock market dip caused some Wall Streeters to deprecate war, *The Times* flew at them as "patriots of the ticker" and likened them to Digger Indians who "eat dirt all their lives and appear to like it." Creaking veterans of the Civil War offered to march against the enemy. There had seldom been such national hysteria with so little cause.

Whitney, the inveterate adviser of cabinets, patted Olney on the back, writing to him, "All the State Department has needed for a long time was a strong man . . . who was not afraid to resist the encroachment of the European powers over here." He also wrote to Secretary of the Navy Herbert advocating a "strong stand."

Pulitzer seemed one of the few Americans to keep his head. He was later to approve "a little war" with Spain, but now he deplored a big one with England over such a trifle. His *World* campaign was a masterpiece of crusading, a stunner in his abandonment of his usual cut-and-thrust for a gentle invocation of reason. Day after day *The World* brought in friendly cables (at *World* expense) from Salisbury, Gladstone, the Prince of Wales, and other British leaders, followed by similar messages from Americans beginning to see the light. Flagwavers came to realize the absurdity of naval battles in the Channel, or New York harbor either, over a minor jungle boundary dispute. Olney described *The World*'s interference with official foreign relations as treason, and Roosevelt wrote privately, "As for the Editors of the . . . *World*, it would give me great pleasure to have them put in prison the minute hostilities begin." But calm was restored, and the dispute was settled by arbitration so amicable that possibly the fire-eaters were a little ashamed.

It is not uncommon to find chauvinism in people socially amiable, as Roosevelt so perfectly demonstrated. All along, Whitney had shown a touchy sense of national honor, and its reappearance now seemed genuine rather than the calculated tactics of a politician seeking the presidency. He was riding high, enjoying life once more—in love again. He cut a dashing figure at Bar Harbor during the summer of 1895 with his new yacht and his rented mansion. He called on Mrs. Randolph, who was at Bar Harbor, often enough to cause *Town Topics* to speculate about an early marriage. He gave a reception for his sister-in-law, Mrs. Henry M. Whitney*; he entertained Secretary of War Lamont and joined in a huge Kebo Club fete for Secretary of the Navy Herbert, part of the Navy having found this a pleasant place to tarry at the height of the season when the resort was filled with swells and ornamented by foreign diplomats.

---

* His brother Henry had become a traction exploiter and stock market operator in Boston as William was in New York.

Whitney's fundamental difference with Pulitzer was emphasized when the depletion of the gold reserve required Cleveland to float another loan. Pulitzer recalled that the last loan, made through a syndicate headed by J. P. Morgan, had netted the bankers close to $8,000,000. Pulitzer immediately began another *World* crusade, this one cut-and-thrust, urging the administration to sell the bonds to the public instead. In one of his front-page appeals appeared a cartoon of Morgan as an evil-looking pirate and an exhortation that Cleveland trust the people and "smash the Ring!" meaning of course the buccaneering bankers. Whitney had known Pulitzer for a dozen years, Morgan for fifteen. Whitney's even older friend Stetson, Morgan's attorney, attended the White House meeting at which Morgan's syndicate offered the loan. On the very day of the *World* blast, Whitney wrote to his cabinet confidant, Secretary Lamont, in small part:

> Personally I think it is very fortunate there is such an alliance to be had by the Government as Morgan & his great power. . . . If I were the President whatever I did I should do with Morgan. It will fail of the effect otherwise. . . .

The next day he wrote to Lamont again at even greater length and with strenuous arguments that Morgan should get the loan, that his mere name would restore confidence. His efforts for Morgan were industrious enough to raise the question (though it is pure speculation) as to whether Morgan had asked for Whitney's help. A further fillip is added to the speculation by the fact that Mrs. Randolph was a devoted worker at St. George's Church in New York and that Morgan, the senior warden there, was said to be her good friend. Morgan, who fully expected to get the loan, was disgruntled when Cleveland rejected his offer and floated a $100,000,000 public loan that was heavily oversubscribed—a success that bore out Pulitzer's rather than Whitney's theories and was also a failure of his influence.

6. *"Luxury and Heartless Pride"*

"PAULINE WRITES me of her engagement," Gunn wrote to Whitney. ". . . I am very glad—it is in every way admirable. I cannot think of anyone better than Paget."

So the audience at the Greek theater at Taormina had read the pantomime correctly. The wedding was set for November 12 at ultrafashionable St. Thomas's Episcopal Church, five blocks down Fifth Avenue from the Whitney house. Certainly the Whitneys were not overjoyed when they discovered that the marriage of eighteen-year-old Consuelo Vanderbilt to the ninth Duke of Marlborough was to take place in the same church just six days before Pauline's. It was as if two coronations were to be held at Westminster Abbey within a week. The Marlborough affair was the enterprise—no other word could describe it—that Consuelo's mother, Alva Vanderbilt, had planned and executed every step of the way. There had been two formidable obstacles to the union. One was Consuelo's wish to marry Winthrop Rutherfurd, a young attorney descended from the old Winthrop and Stuyvesant families but without title. The other was Alva's own divorce from William K. Vanderbilt on grounds of adultery, a Society scandal that occurred while Whitney was in Italy and that complicated the consummation of Alva's designs. She brushed difficulties aside and carried through a project that also involved international intrigue and long-range economic planning. Consuelo's wishes got short shrift, as she later explained:

> My mother tore me from the influence of my sweetheart. She made me leave the country. She intercepted all letters my sweetheart wrote and all of mine to him. She caused continuous scenes. She said I must obey. She said I knew very well I had no right to choose a husband, that I must take the man she had chosen, that my refusal was ruining her health and that I might be the cause of her death.

The story spun itself out in purest melodrama. Consuelo could not appeal to her adored father, who had been banished. Mrs. Vanderbilt called in her physician to assure Consuelo that her resistance was aggravating her mother's heart condition and might kill her (she was then forty-two and was to live to be eighty). In the summer of 1895 Alva took Consuelo to London, where she enlisted the aid of her old friend Minnie Paget (Almeric's sister-in-law), who easily arranged for Consuelo to meet the duke. He was twenty-four, arrogant but broke, and with Blenheim and its two hundred servants to support. The fact that Consuelo disliked him had no bearing in the matter. Alva invited him to Newport, where Richard Morris Hunt had designed her white Italian marble villa known as Marble House, Newport's greatest, costing with furnishings around $9,000,000. The duke arrived in September, while Whitney was at Bar Harbor, and stayed a fortnight, not so much to extend his acquaintance with Consuelo as to arrange his price for marrying her. The terms of the sale were embodied in a contract drawn up by attorneys on both sides, as businesslike and binding as any of those covering the Vanderbilts' railroad deals. It said in part:

> Whereas a marriage is intended between the said Duke of Marlborough and the said Consuelo Vanderbilt, and whereas pursuant to an agreement made upon the treaty for the said intended marriage, the sum of $2,500,000 . . . on which the annual payment of 4 per cent is guaranteed by the New York Central Railroad Company, is transferred this day to the trustees. And shall during the joint lives of the said Duke of Marlborough [and] Consuelo Vanderbilt, pay the income of the said sum . . . unto the said Duke of Marlborough for his life . . .

Henceforth, New York Central shippers and passengers would have another capital expense to defray. Other expenses brought the cost of the title to nearly $10,000,000, said to be more than one-tenth of Vanderbilt's fortune. But how did Alva persuade William K., who loved his daughter, to foot this bill when he disagreed with his wife on everything except divorce? Was Vanderbilt so glad to get rid of Alva that he agreed in order to assure his own freedom, or was it true that Alva held her knowledge of a Vanderbilt scandal over his head? It remained their secret. "I spent the morning of my wedding day in tears and alone," Consuelo later disclosed; "no one came near me. A footman had been posted at the door of my apartment and not even my governess was admitted. . . . My mother had decreed that my father should accompany me to the church to give me away. After that he was to disappear. We were 20 minutes late, for my eyes, swollen with the tears I had wept, required copious sponging before I could face the curious stares that always greet a bride." She looked wretched as her father escorted her into the church. The Whitneys and Paget were among the guests as Consuelo advanced up the aisle to join Richard John Spencer-Churchill, the duke. He had been visibly upset over her tardiness—were those millions to be denied him after all? As the nuptial pair stood before the altar, the choir sang:

O! perfect love, all human thought transcending. . . .

The Times called it "without exception the most magnificent [wedding] ever celebrated in this country." *The World*, much as it execrated such marriages, gave this one seven columns on the front page but with a barbed subhead, NOW SHE'S A DUCHESS, and disclosed the bride's mother's hostility toward her ex-husband and his whole family: "No member of the rich and powerful family whose name Mrs. Vanderbilt bears saw the ceremony yesterday. Even Chauncey M. Depew did not receive an invitation." Indeed the feeling between Alva and all the Vanderbilts was so bitter that the Hamilton McKown Twomblys (Mrs. Twombly was a sister of William K.), who were in Europe, stayed there in order to avoid entanglement in the feud, which became permanent.

A quip of the day was, "Here we go 'round the Marlborough bush." "Th' Jook iv Marlburrow," wrote Finley Peter Dunne in his role as Mr. Dooley, "is a young lad an' poor . . . I dunno how he done it, whether th' Ganderbilks asked him 'r he asked thim. Anyhow, it was arranged. 'Twas horse an' horse between thim. Th' Ganderbilks had th' money an' he was a jook." *Life* cartooned the duke as a ragged Columbus landing on our shores, to be met by Vanderbilt Indians offering him wampum and a daughter. Elsewhere *Life* lampooned the practice in general with a cartoon of a dazed-looking young lady bristling with jewels and captioned, "The Countess De Generett (Née Goshwatta Pyle)."

If Pauline Whitney was concerned that Consuelo's wedding might outshine hers, at any rate she was happy and not under guard. Before her wedding, Whitney gave a dinner for Paget at the Metropolitan Club; among the many guests were the disappointed Winthrop Rutherfurd, Paget's brother-in-law and sister, Lord Edward and Lady Colebrook, and Gertrude Vanderbilt, who had occasionally been seen lately with Harry Payne Whitney. On November 12, many of the Four Hundred watched Pauline walk down the same aisle in a ceremony in which no expense had been spared to make it every bit as pretentious as its predecessor. The hundreds present included the J. P. Morgans, James J. Van Alen, and the Joseph Pulitzers, disputants in another sphere. As always, Whitney favored the press, among the other editors and publishers present being old Charles A. Dana and his son Paul, the Whitelaw Reids, and the Charles Millers. Harry Payne Whitney was an usher and Gertrude Vanderbilt a bridesmaid. Dorothy Whitney, slim and pretty at eight and a half—so long the baby excluded from great events—had a public role in this one as a flower girl, wearing poplin trimmed with Russian sable and a velvet hat copied from a Dutch master. Alexander Gunn, dressed to the nines, was given a seat in the very front row so that he could better enjoy the music. He found the music superb but was miserable because Col. Oliver Payne had cut him dead. Whitney, seeming forever at ease, escorted Pauline to the church "looking very proud of his beautiful daughter, smil[ing] amiably on the people."

Inevitably comparisons were made between the two weddings. "It was Mr. Whitney's desire," said *The Times*, "that . . . the musical programme should be without equal. . . ." Whereas Alva Vanderbilt had had Walter Damrosch with an orchestra of sixty, the Whitneys had Nathan Franko with a slightly smaller group but more than made up for this with Edouard de Reszke singing "Ave Maria" with violin obbligato ("heavenly," wrote Gunn) and de Reszke with Lillian Nordica in a duet, "The Crucifix," with orchestra and organ. Each bride's train was five yards in length. Mrs. Astor, always so bejeweled that *Town Topics* said she entered any room "like a meteor" and was able to sit down with caution but could not lean back because her gems would perforate her, blessed both weddings with her presence. As Pauline walked down the aisle with her father, behind them came Mrs. Daniel Lamont on the arm of President Cleveland (who had forgotten to wear gloves), an honor not given Consuelo. Three clergymen headed by Bishop Henry Codman Potter were sufficient to join Pauline and Paget in matrimony, whereas it took the combined efforts of five, also headed by Bishop Potter, to effect the Vanderbilt-Marlborough union. There were more guests at Whitney-Paget but more curious onlookers outside at Vanderbilt-Marlborough, for it took 300 policemen to maintain order, as against 250 at the former. Consuelo betrayed "signs of nervousness," and no wonder, whereas Pauline "walked with a quiet air of self-possession most uncommon in brides" and had a "clever, riante face." Whatever other errors William and Flora Whitney might have made, they had given their children the confidence of their love and consideration.

Both brides were tall, but Consuelo was half a head taller than her duke, whereas Pauline and Paget were equal. The gifts given the new duchess were fewer than those given the new Mrs. Paget because many of the Vanderbilts excluded from the former's wedding were so furious at her mother that they omitted gifts. Each wedding was attended by the *bon ton*, but there was a difference—the Whitney gathering included politicians, not all of them at home in Society. This, *The Times* explained, "was undoubtedly due to the fact that while ex-Secretary Whitney . . . is a member of what is known as the smart set, he has also been a conspicuous figure in the public life of the United States, and may again be a more conspicuous one."

The politicians present in addition to the President included Secretary of War Lamont, Secretary of the Navy Herbert, Governor Levi Morton, the Whitelaw Reids, the William Harritys, the Abram Hewitts, and, of all people, Boss Croker in a Prince Albert, his beard neatly trimmed, his gaze even a little more hard and level than most of the many corporate rulers there. Had Flora been living, one could venture that Croker would not have been there, however helpful his presence was to Whitney's traction enterprise. The Whitney guest list was sprinkled with titled Englishmen from the embassy and the friends of Paget and Whitney—Sir Julian Pauncefote, Sir Roderick Cameron, the Earl and Countess of Essex (the latter being the former Adele Grant of New York). And Whitney's new but still unannounced love, Mrs. Arthur Randolph, a striking brunette who appeared to be in her mid-thirties and got no special attention at all, presented the bride with a modest gift, a "jewel box set with brilliants."

Diamonds, not brilliants, were the gauge of friendship here, although another simple gift, a "silver cigarette case" given the bride by Mrs. George Bend, was an ominous sign of feminine vice. The gifts "filled one of the largest rooms on the second floor of the [Whitney] mansion." In permitting the papers to list them, estimating them to be worth around a million dollars, the Whitney of some severely private feelings succumbed (as had Alva Vanderbilt) to the grossest vulgarity of the Gilded Age. His own gifts would have lightened the Egyptian national debt. He gave Pauline part of her late mother's jewels, the rest being saved for Dorothy:

> . . . a coronet fully three inches deep, composed of five rows of solitaire diamonds of large size, the interstices filled with smaller diamonds; a chain two yards long consisting of 300 diamonds . . . a two and a half inch wide collar of sapphires and diamonds . . . a collar, similar in size, of diamond hoops linked; a corsage ornament of diamonds, about four inches in length, in the form of a spray of roses. . . . a broad collar of pearls and diamonds.

To these Whitney added his own newly purchased gift, "a magnificent diamond and pearl necklace," so different from the "little remembrance, not to be shown as a gift," which he had scraped bottom to buy for Flora when he married her. Uncle Oliver presented Pauline with "three strands of superb pearls, each a quarter of an inch in diameter, fastened with a clasp of diamonds." There were scores of other combinations of gems, the J. P. Morgans contributing a "ruby and diamond bracelet" and Joseph Pulitzer's own paper admitting that he bestowed "a watch, set with rubies and diamonds." The President and Mrs. Cleveland made do with an antique silver urn, engraved with the bride's initials, and the Crokers with a "large silver-framed mirror." *The Tribune* was so frank as to describe the groom's gift, a diamond pin, as "small." Paget's means were cautiously described. It was admitted that as the

youngest of thirteen children, many of them sons, he had come to
America to seek his fortune, but that "he is today one of the principal
real estate owners in Minnesota," a place where real estate was then in
oversupply. The young couple were to abandon this demesne and make
their home in New York, where Paget had, perhaps gladly, accepted a
job with Whitney's traction syndicate. *The World*, always the upholder
of the peasantry, admitted that Paget's brother Arthur was an intimate of
the Prince of Wales but defended the Democratic Whitneys: "Yet noble
blood was not bought and sold at this wedding" as it had been, *The
World* suggested without spelling it out, a week earlier. The most free-
wheeling and refreshing comment of all came from the sometime black-
mailing Col. William d'Alton Mann, alias the Saunterer, in *Town
Topics:*

> When millionaires vie with one another in providing for their children's
> weddings the richest of floral decorations and the most elaborate and
> costly music obtainable, people of less wealth will more and more favor
> the quietest of marriages, on the principle that if one cannot compete
> well, one had better not try to compete at all. Beautiful as was the music
> at the Marlborough-Vanderbilt wedding, that furnished by ex-Secretary
> Whitney . . . was far finer. I have never heard in any church more
> beautiful music of its kind than that which filled the hour before the
> bridal party arrived. . . . To hear Nordica sing Gounod's "Ave Maria"
> with a harp obligato [sic], Edouard de Reszke in several selections, and
> Franko's excellent orchestra render Handel's "Largo" with the organ and
> harp, was a musical treat that I shall long remember. And yet the music,
> exceptional as it was, was not prized or even thoroughly enjoyed by the
> majority of the guests. They had come there to see and be seen, to gossip
> about the Horse Show, to criticize one another's gowns, and to compare
> Miss Whitney with Miss Vanderbilt as a bride. [During the music] I
> found myself repeating "Cast not your pearls, cast not your pearls," etc.,
> etc.

At the reception at the Whitney house, catered by Sherry's and attended by 150, the two cabinet members and Bishop Potter sat with
President Cleveland and Whitney, taking precedence over Croker. The
feast included "Oeufs Brouillés aux Truffes" and "Carré d'Agneau à la
Bourgeoise," and among the wines, Irroy '89. When it was all over,
Whitney had had the kind of day that entitled him to slippered ease in
the evening, but he did not tire easily. He abandoned Mrs. Randolph
for the sake of appearances and turned up that evening at the Horse
Show at his friend Stanford White's splendid new Madison Square Garden, with Turkish rugs and wicker chairs in his box. Here he was

among friends—always among friends. Scores of the wedding guests greeted him, among them Alva Vanderbilt, the William Jays, Col. and Mrs. John Jacob Astor, and Governor and Mrs. Morton. As for Gunn, his greatest fear was that Colonel Payne's hostility would turn Whitney against him. Because of Payne's snub, Gunn did not stay as planned with Whitney but retreated to the Union League Club, writing to Whitney: "I think it best to go home today. . . . Of course I knew the Colonel no longer cared for me, but I did not know before that his resentment was so bitter." He permitted himself an unhappy outburst against New York in his journal: "I do not belong there. It is the resting place of luxury and heartless pride. Some near and most dear friends are there; but oh, the hard, brutal, corroding riches that flaunt in the face of the poor!"

Ironically, money worries called him back to New York a week later. His modest primary investment, one that he had counted on to see him through, was in danger. "I feared to lose the amount," he wrote. "Every hand seemed against me, and, in despair, I went up to see my friend [Whitney]. I was received with a kindly, affectionate enthusiasm. I told my troubles, and without any effort he solved the difficulty . . . and made an advance on my hopes of $800. . . . I make record here of the deep sense I have of his goodness."

7. The Fool Killer Foiled

THE PASSING of Flora had severed the closest link between Whitney and Oliver Payne. Although the Colonel was still the generous "Uncle Oliver" to Whitney's children, Whitney had been annoyed by Payne's rejection of Cleveland in 1892, and he may have resented Payne's treatment of Gunn. It seems unlikely that Whitney did not ask Oliver the reason for his hostility. Whatever the reason was, Whitney did not share it but continued his kindnesses toward Gunn, at this time sending him a new bicycle to help him get around Zoar—a contrivance that so often threw the nonathlete that he gave it up. Oliver's extreme generosity toward the Whitney children seems to have included a somewhat proprietary attitude toward them, and it is not impossible that Whitney for his part may have wished that Oliver could have kept his gifts on a somewhat lesser scale of grandeur so that Whitney could have had the father's rightful place as first in munificence. Surely Flora had not kept secret from Oliver the episode concerning Mrs. Randolph in Europe, since there had been some gossip about it and Flora and Oliver had later had that long European holiday together. But it had not alienated the Colonel enough to prevent him from joining Whitney on a fishing trip in Canada. Was Oliver resentful because Whitney was no longer the poor relation who needed help but was reaching toward financial equality with him in part because he had inherited his sister's fortune, as well as owning such enormous popularity? It would not be the first time a benefactor had disliked losing that role and being outshone by his former dependent.

Whitney's son Harry was studying law at Columbia University, and the two occasionally dined together at one of Whitney's clubs. Whitney now had a discreet and admiring private secretary, Thomas J. Regan, and still another "confidential" secretary, the former *World* man Harry Macdona. He took at least three months of leisure each year but read a detective novel every night to quiet his brain so he could sleep. Sometime in the winter of 1895–96 he broached to Harry the subject of marrying Mrs. Randolph, but Harry was opposed to it. By then, Flora had been dead for three years. Harry's opposition, according to later evidence, took less account of Whitney's own loneliness than of Harry's feeling that Flora's replacement by another woman would be difficult for him and the other children to accept. Whitney was responsive enough to this argument so that he postponed his plan, a considerable personal sacrifice.

His contemplation of marriage at that time, shortly before the presidential preliminaries were to begin, did not necessarily imply that he had ruled out all thought of the highest office. Gunn, visiting Crocker in San Francisco and riding around the state in the Californian's private railroad car, found some Western newspapers urging Whitney for President but wrote to him that he did not believe any Democrat could be elected: "Nothing is strong in our party but yourself and the Globe on Atlas will be nothing to the load you will have to carry. I want you to adorn that high state, but I do not want you so sorely handicapped as you would be now." Still, some Democratic leaders thought he would accept the nomination if the party would straddle the silver question so that he could "run as a gold-standard man in the Eastern States and as a friend of silver in the West." If so, by June he seemed to abandon the idea. His son Payne, a substitute on the Yale crew, was going with the team to take part in the Henley regatta. Whitney, though important Democrats were sending him imploring telegrams or visiting him in person with appeals that he seek the nomination or at least go to Chicago and save the nation from the silver crowd, apparently decided to wash his hands of it. He would go to watch Payne at Henley and make it a springboard for a European tour. He coaxed Alexander Gunn, back at Zoar, to be his companion and reserved passage on the *Teutonic* sailing June 17.

But the party appeals kept coming. By June 15, when Gunn was in Cleveland ready to come to New York, Whitney was uncertain about sailing. "More country saving and another postponement," Gunn grumbled in a letter to his friend Ludwig. "I had only five telegrams from New York yesterday." On June 16 Senator Gorman called at 2 West 57th Street and pressed Whitney with such fervor that he yielded and telegraphed Gunn again. "I shall have an entertainment sometime next week celebrating my return from Europe," Gunn wryly informed Ludwig. "You may invite the Clodhoppers' Club. . . ."

At his home, Whitney met reporters in a smoking jacket and said he would go to the convention and do what he could. He was sorry to miss the regatta: "If my son rows in the race, I will have to be content with seeing him in my mind's eye." He and Gunn would make the European trip later. What with Whitney's Tammanyization and his accommodation with Senator Hill, perhaps it was not surprising that Don Dickinson of Michigan, who had worked so closely with him in 1892, was suspicious. Dickinson wrote to President Cleveland that Whitney had "no real intention" of going to Europe, that this had been a drama staged "for effect." He believed that Whitney was plotting with "the Bunco-man" (Hill) to take charge of the sound-money forces and make Hill the candidate.

Whitney was indeed conferring with Hill and scores of other Democrats. He had received a standing ovation at the state party convention at Saratoga. But he now confessed openly that the silverites were so strong that for him to go to Chicago was "a sort of fool's errand." He and his New York Democrats left Grand Central Station July 2 in three luxurious parlor cars more heavily stocked with food and drink than with hope. Whitney took with him his secretary, Regan, and among the large party were Thomas Fortune Ryan, George Harvey, Fairchild, and Hill. The Republicans, led by Mark Hanna, had nominated McKinley and come out for gold despite McKinley's earlier unguarded—and duly corrected—approval of silver. Whitney had hardly settled himself in his Auditorium Hotel suite in Chicago than he realized that the party's split was suicidal. He spent a week working hard at an impossibility. It was flattering to see some delegates wearing Whitney-for-President buttons, and he did what he could to stem the silver tide, but it was all over when the well-rehearsed evangelism of thirty-six-year-old William Jennings Bryan brought pandemonium to the Coliseum.

". . . [Bryan] pushed into th' air th' finest wurruds ye ever heerd spoke in all ye'er borrrn days," Mr. Dooley observed. " 'Twas a balloon ascinsion an' th' last days iv Pompey an' a blast on th' canal all in wan. I had to hold on to me chair to keep fr'm goin' up in th' air. . . ."

Whitney's enjoyment of Finley Peter Dunne at this moment could not have been wholehearted. To his moral condemnation of the silver notion as a "dishonorable" debasement of currency was added the discomfiture of the magician of 1892 having lost his talisman. Through Regan he announced that he was taking the awful step: bolting the ticket. "There are no possible conditions or circumstances that would induce me to vote for it or assist it." Indeed it was said by a Republican paper that he now favored McKinley and urged the Republicans to take the sound-money Democrats into their fold to strengthen the gold candidate. He later denied this, though it was true that Whitney was a Democrat by inheritance, always conservative, with little sympathy for Western problems. The strain to his old loyalties would have been more hurtful than the fairly simple political accommodation with such friends as Morgan and Vanderbilt.

The Fool Killer, suffering from wounds inflicted by the Fools, returned from Chicago to find that Cornelius Vanderbilt had suffered a paralytic stroke. The engagement of Gertrude Vanderbilt to Harry Payne Whitney had been announced in the spring, with the wedding set for July. It would have to wait—and so would Harry and Gertrude—until father Cornelius improved. With Harry, Whitney dined at the Metropolitan Club (known as the "Millionaires' Club") just three blocks up the street at 60th and Fifth Avenue (it had been founded by J. P. Morgan because the Union Club had enraged him by rejecting a business associate). Of course they discussed Harry's coming marriage—they got along famously—but was the father able to broach again the subject of his own coming marriage? In any case, Whitney and Harry crossed 57th Street to pass through the Vanderbilt "vestibule" of Supreme Court proportions, negotiate inner distances, and ascend marble staircases before reaching Cornelius, propped up in his sickbed, his dark muttonchop whiskers well combed as always. Chauncey Depew was already there. They found the patient improved but still weak. The straitlaced Vanderbilt's previous bedroom had faced on the Plaza, and it had troubled him to awaken every morning to see the posterior of a nude woman in bronze, bathing. The city had rejected his plea that the sculpture be removed, so he had been forced to change his bedroom, which he could choose from among dozens. The death of his son William had left the second son, Cornelius, Jr., the principal heir. Young Cornelius had upset the whole family by his romance with the vivacious Grace Wilson, whom he had been forbidden to marry on pain of being disinherited. Why, since father Cornelius and Grace's father, the cotton broker R. T. Wilson, had been fellow founders (with Whitney and others) of the Metropolitan Opera? It was not because the fortune of Wilson, who came from Tennessee, had been founded on the sale of blankets (shoddy blankets, some declared) to the Confederate Army; the New York Central pot was not calling any kettle black. Indeed the Wilsons had done so splendidly at the altar that they were called "the Marrying Wilsons": Grace's brother Orme had married Caroline Astor, her sister May had married Ogden Goelet, and her sister Belle had married Michael Herbert, brother of the Earl of Pembroke. No—the trouble was money, the Wilson fortune being modest compared with that of the Vanderbilts, the latter charging that Grace was eight years older than the twenty-three-year-old Cornelius and had vamped him for profit. This was coldly denied by the Wilsons, who said Grace was twenty-five, no more. Some of the family believed that Cornelius's insistence on marrying Grace had brought on his father's stroke. In marrying her, young Cornelius (known as Neily) lost the $40,000,000 he was to have inherited and was cut off with a million and a half.*

In any case, the father Cornelius and Whitney got along splendidly, not only because the Whitney lineage was the more impressive of the two and the fortune considerable, but because they had been friends for years, participated in scores of cotillions together, attended a hundred operas together, seen their children grow up and become friends, and had socialized in New York and Newport as well as that special occasion when they had visited Stratford-on-Avon together. Cornelius and Whitney had urged Gertrude and Harry not to be too hasty, but they gave the young couple their wholehearted blessing.

---

* This was later adjusted heavily upward when Neily threatened to sue—a move for which he was exiled from the family in a feud of many years' standing.

1. Wedding after Wedding

"McKINLEY WILL carry this [New York] State by fully 200,000 majority," Whitney said, putting his reputation as a political seer on the line before he left for Newport to attend the wedding. Less attention was paid to his prediction, which turned out as usual to be astonishingly accurate, than to the wedding. This union of a Vanderbilt and a Whitney, exciting to Society-watchers who computed and debated the relative grades of the principals in wealth, family standing, and social brilliance, had the added glamor of taking place at the Vanderbilts' many-chimneyed, seventy-room villa at Ochre Point, The Breakers, Newport. In 1885 Cornelius had bought Pierre Lorillard's cottage on that site for less than $400,000. When it burned to the ground in 1892, he had commissioned Richard Morris Hunt to replace it.*

The Breakers, patterned after a sixteenth-century northern Italian castle, approximated the nearby Marble House in cost and chilly splendor. Cornelius and his wife Alice were to be praised or blamed equally, having divided the decisions. Alice Vanderbilt was an affectionate mother, much more human than her former sister-in-law of the $10,000,000 Consuelo sale, though somewhat puritanical and sedately insistent on social rank, resolutely refusing to enter a shop. Hunt, an aging graduate of the Beaux Arts, had warned his own students, "The first thing you've got to remember is that it's your client's money you're spending. . . . If they want you to build a house upside down standing on its chimney, it's up to you to do it, and still get the best possible results." The four-story Breakers, covering almost exactly one acre of its twelve-acre site, was and is a great mass of masonry looking grandly out

---

* Hunt had also built for Cornelius's intellectual youngest brother, George Washington Vanderbilt, perhaps the most arrogant of all American castles, the 250-room French Renaissance Biltmore House, surrounded by 145,000 Vanderbilt acres near Asheville, North Carolina.

to sea, notable for fountains inside and out and for such touches as a fireplace costing $75,000 (most of it had come from Pompeii), bathrooms with both fresh and salt water, and a children's playhouse with beautiful miniature pianos and dishes that would ultimately be enjoyed by the offspring of the couple to be married there. The decorators had hung in the billiard room a painting of a nude, which the Vanderbilts had ordered draped. Cecil Spring Rice thought that Newport had "the vulgarest society in the world, 'the refinement of vulgarity.' " The Breakers, which in part bore him out architecturally, had been in use for only two years when, at noon on August 25, the wedding music began.

Every New York newspaper had sent reporters with orders to get inside if possible and see the wedding, but it appears that none succeeded and they were required to get their stories afterward from guests and servants. Because Cornelius was still feeble and in a wheelchair, the affair was kept small, there being only sixty guests, all relatives or closest friends. Harry had invited Gunn, who sent his regrets, knowing that Colonel Payne would be there. The Pagets were absent because of Pauline's pregnancy, and young Neily Vanderbilt, because of his disapproved marriage, was not invited. Only two clergymen fulfilled the churchly role, the inevitable Bishop Potter being assisted by the local Episcopal rector, the Reverend George J. Magill. Former senator Henry B. Payne, a little stooped and shrunken at eighty-six, and with less than a month to live, had sorrows to contemplate along with the joys of this occasion. Vanderbilt had already marked this event by writing "hand some checks for each individual servant of the household," thirty-five of them. Reggie Vanderbilt, Gertrude's youngest brother, was one of the ushers, all wearing frock coats with boutonnieres of lilies of the valley.

Mrs. Vanderbilt entered the Gold Room, the aptly named scene of the ceremony, on the arm of Whitney. Chauncey Depew, substituting for the ailing father, escorted Gertrude down the grand staircase to the altar where Harry waited beside his brother Payne, who was best man. The Saunterer of *Town Topics* was no more there than any of the newsmen, but one might think he had been. Considering his capacity for malice, he wrote more appraisingly than spitefully: "Miss Vanderbilt, as might have been expected from her tall figure, dark hair, and fresh rosy complexion, made a really handsome picture, although, strictly speaking, not really a handsome girl. . . ." Vanderbilt was there in his wheelchair, ready to give the bride away without rising. Dorothy Whitney was a flower girl along with Gladys Vanderbilt, her longtime play-

mate and sister of the bride—these two, now wearing gowns of white
silk fringed with lace, had dramatic careers ahead of them. At nine,
Dorothy had the white skin against dark hair, the erect posture, and
supple grace that would mark her through life. There was a faint hint of
shyness, a quality neither of her parents had—particularly her forceful
mother—and that would always remain one of her attractions. Never
would one discern in her the spirit that a few of her more standpattish
Society friends would come to define as radical or even rebellious. She
was as pretty as a picture.

Certainly she took it for granted that this marriage was destined to be
forever happy—an assumption that time would dispute.

After the vows were spoken amid bowers of lilies, roses, and gladioli,
the wedding breakfast was served in the seventy-by-fifty-foot banquet
hall. The thirty-piece orchestra, led by Nathan Franko, surprised everyone by playing "The Star Spangled Banner," Franko later explaining
that it was his own idea: "It is so rarely that an American girl of fortune
marries one of her countrymen that I thought the selection decidedly in
keeping with the occasion."

Father Vanderbilt so enjoyed the rendition of "El Capitan" that he
requested it a second time. His geniality did not rule out prudence, for
three detectives had been hired to guard the gifts, which again represented a great fortune. The gift of the bride's parents, a diamond tiara
and necklace with pear-shaped diamond pendants, bought in Paris, was
said to have cost $100,000, and the five strands of matched pearls given
by Col. Oliver Payne were valued at "nearly $200,000." Perhaps the
rumors that the Colonel had more money than social eclat and hoped to
repair the latter with the former did him an injustice, for some of his
later philanthropies were large and secret.

The Times called it "the most notable marriage ceremony and breakfast that Newport has known." Bride and groom left by carriage in a
shower of rice and hardly used old shoes. Awaiting them at the station
was a special train arranged for them by Father Vanderbilt. It consisted
of a locomotive, a combination passenger and baggage car, and one of
Vanderbilt's private cars. Earlier, Whitney had made his own arrangements for the couple's convenience:

> . . . an order was sent to [Whitney's] Lenox agents for the construc-
> tion of a camp upon [October] mountain. It was to be built and furnished
> within thirty days. With feverish excitement contractors began to work.
> Hundreds of laborers and carpenters were employed, and by working day

and night, by the aid of calcium lights at night, a large and expensive camp was completed in contract time.

The camp, in addition to a set of diamond pins, was Whitney's gift to the couple, their honeymoon retreat, to be followed by a larger gift later when they were en route to Japan. Whitney at the same time made his Fifth Avenue house available to the President as a place to greet the aged, towering, and uninhibited Chinese statesman Li Hung Chang, then visiting in New York. Li, who enjoyed an occasional pipe of opium and asked candid questions such as "the ages of the ladies who were presented to him and the salaries of the officials who were his hosts," was greeted in the Whitney great hall on August 29 by President Cleveland, Whitney, Secretary of State Olney, and others. Ten days later, Whitney and his children, including the bridal couple, were in Cleveland to attend the funeral of Henry B. Payne. One of the mourners—his presence no longer able to hurt Payne politically—was his old friend John D. Rockefeller. Gunn, despite his long friendship with the family, did not attend, again undoubtedly because of Colonel Payne. This apparently was the last time Whitney and the Colonel met on a friendly basis. Whitney had recently purchased that last seal of the sybarite, a private railroad car named *Pilgrim*, in which he traveled a few days later to Bar Harbor and put up at Malvern House. "There he met Mrs. Randolph," *The Times* said later. "His time was spent mostly with her, and the talk of an engagement between them was revived."

When it was announced by Regan, Whitney's secretary in New York, that Whitney and Mrs. Randolph would be married the very next day in what amounted to a "pickup" ceremony attended by a mere handful of friends hurriedly invited, the newspapers flew into a tumult of speculation. The couple were married September 29 at St. Sauveur's Episcopal Church. "Mr. Whitney was dressed in a long black frock coat, with lighter trousers," said *The World* "His waistcoat was white; his tie was pale blue. He stood in full view with an expression of delight and impatience. He watched the door to the right of the chancel . . . he pulled impatiently at his mustache. . . . Presently the door opened and the fascinating widow who has withstood so many suitors was in the doorway. . . . She and Mr. Whitney looked at each other across the church. She smiled, blushed vividly and dropped her eyes. He smiled, blushed slightly and threw back his shoulders. Then they advanced toward each other and met at the opening in the chancel rail."

The papers said that the only usher was Mrs. Randolph's bachelor brother, Frederick de Courcy May, and that he had some years earlier been a "prominent clubman and man about town." They did not mention that he had been a member of the socially exalted Union Club when, in 1888, he had the misfortune to kill a New York policeman in the course of an argument. Friends had hidden him in various of his clubs for a time. Then he had appeared in court, produced bail, and promptly decamped for South America, where he stayed several years until the matter blew over. Whitney was attended not by any vintage friend such as Oliver Payne or Elihu Root or Daniel Lamont but by a jovial acquaintance, Constantin Brun, the Danish Minister to the United States and a regular at Bar Harbor. None of Whitney's children was there, nor any of his closest friends or associates, not the Barneys, not the Dimocks. After the brief service there was a luncheon, and "Mr. and Mrs. Whitney will remain a week or two at the Anchorage," her mother's cottage. Their plans, *The Herald* reported, were "uncertain." They might go to Hot Springs, Whitney said, or maybe to Europe. (Actually, some days later they went to Lenox, Mr. and Mrs. Harry Payne Whitney having recently left there en route to their Pacific Coast sailing.)

2. The Family Skeleton

THE PAPERS, caught off guard, outdid each other in efforts to appear knowledgeable about the romance, reporting: "The engagement was practically announced eighteen months ago, shortly after the rumor that Mr. Whitney was to marry Miss Johanna Davidge. . . . Mrs. Randolph, it is known, wrote to friends in Europe months ago that she was engaged to marry Mr. Whitney, and those friends were not slow to communicate the intelligence to their friends in this country." Journalists wrestled over the puzzle of why Whitney, whose daughter Pauline and son Harry had been married in the grand manner, announced months in advance, should himself have been married suddenly and inexpensively: "One of the reasons for the privacy of the wedding is given as the death of Senator Henry B. Payne of Ohio. . . ." "[At Bar Harbor] last September, Mrs. Randolph was one of a small party invited by Mr. Whitney to [sail] in his yacht. At the end of the season it was announced that their marriage might occur in the spring, but this was denied by Mr. Whitney's authority." "I became engaged to Mrs. Randolph only last Friday," *The Herald* quoted Whitney as saying, "and we thought that we would take time by the forelock."

But the front pages implied that the hurried improvisation of the wedding and the absence of any announcement of the banns, along with the failure of any of the Whitney children to attend, might suggest a lack of enthusiasm on their part for his remarriage. Whitney seemed under some pressure to show that his children's absence was perfectly explicable. Pauline and Paget were at his Adirondack lodge, he said, and Pauline's "condition" forbade travel. Harry and Gertrude could not come, having been about to leave for the Orient. This did not explain Payne and Dorothy's absence. *The Times* took the trouble to check at New Haven and establish that Payne "was at his recitations at Yale [on the wedding day] as usual." But the Saunterer of *Town Topics*, who prided himself on solving all social riddles, wrote, "I do not draw the conclusion from the absence of Mr. Whitney's children . . . that they are necessarily opposed to his marriage." The wedding had not surprised him at all, he said—he had predicted it in the summer of 1895—and he delivered one of his ambiguities:

> Mr. Whitney has not been able to conceal the fact of his affection for Mrs. Randolph from his intimates from the beginning of his devotion to her, and her close friends, notably Mr. and Mrs. William Douglas and
> · Mr. Pierpont Morgan, have, doubtless felt assured, for some time, that her marriage to Mr. Whitney would certainly occur.

The Saunterer had his own sly way of hinting at impropriety without perpetrating libel—little signals that titillated his readers. A lawyer always read his racier material to see that it was worded circuitously enough to make lawsuits unlikely. Was the way in which the Saunterer linked Mrs. Randolph's name with J. P. Morgan, even with those of the Douglases in between, that kind of signal? Morgan's reputation as a secret ladies' man was by then firmly established among those well posted. But in defense of Mrs. Randolph, it might merely have been the scoundrel's signal to Morgan and/or Whitney warning them that a little money would make his comments less veiled and more pleasant.

Edith Sybil May Randolph was tall, almost as tall as Whitney, "with a perfect figure and wonderful coloring," said *The Herald*, a newspaper that had a special reason to follow her family—and was "rarely cultivated, and extremely witty and clever. Her bon mots were repeated everywhere." Born in Baltimore, she was the second of the "three beautiful May sisters," daughters of the late Dr. J. Frederick May, a family that later lived in Washington and New York. Dr. May had become a footnote in history as the man who identified the body of John Wilkes Booth, Lincoln's assassin. Edith's sister Caroline in 1877 had been spared the fate of marrying her then fiancé, the aberrant James Gordon Bennett, publisher of *The Herald*, when in his cups he urinated into the piano in her parlor before a gathering on New Year's Day. For this her hot-blooded brother Frederick had publicly horsewhipped Bennett in front of the Union Club and later fought a bloodless pistol duel with him. Some of the Mays had been guests at Washington levees given by the Whitneys during their four years there and later had known them in New York and Bar Harbor. When still hardly more than a girl, Edith May had been one of the guests aboard the yacht of the Thomas Garners when it capsized in a squall off Staten Island. Both Garners and three of the guests had been drowned, and Edith had won commendation for her efforts to save them. Later the family—quite prosperous on inherited money—had lived for a time in Europe. In Dresden Edith had met the English Captain Arthur Randolph of the Queen's Own Hussars, who had followed her back to America, where they were married in 1878. They had lived in Europe and later in Douglaston, Long Island. According to the Saunterer, the marriage "was not overly happy, and as he resigned his commission soon after and had comparatively little means, she was obliged to lead almost a retired life in a little country cottage at Douglaston. After his death, some seven years ago, she became enabled to have a small house [on 40th Street] and to spend her summers either abroad or in a Bar Harbor cottage." The newspapers followed customary prudence by omitting her age, thirty-seven, which was eighteen years younger than Whitney. Her daughter Adelaide was thirteen and her son Arthur, called Bertie, two years younger.

The socially attentive Whitney made a note, later found in his papers, that she was "well connected" in the world of fashion. She was a cousin of Whitney's across-Fifth-Avenue neighbor Hermann Oelrichs, and also a cousin of Mrs. William Jay, Mrs. Jay and her husband Colonel Jay—a member of the old New York family—having been longtime Whitney friends. Whitney's fear that there would be rumors that Flora had disliked Mrs. Randolph, which would suggest jealousy—which might suggest cause for jealousy—was demonstrated by a note he sent to President Cleveland two days before the marriage. After asking for the Clevelands' good wishes, he added:

You know how baseless scandals originate and circulate, and I therefore wish to say to you and Mrs. Cleveland that the only person from outside our immediate family circle whom Mrs. Whitney wished to have with her daily and did have with her daily was Mrs. Randolph. This at the end of her life down to the second or third day before she died.

Without precisely questioning Whitney's word, it would seem astonishing if Flora's detestation for the woman who had so outraged her (and who so outmatched her in youth and beauty) had changed to affection. Especially was it surprising in view of the lack of enthusiasm for Mrs. Randolph on the part of Whitney's three older children, who evidently had heard about the famous European incident. It seems clear that they had disapproved of the marriage, that Whitney had for some time hoped to bring them around but had failed, and that at last he had resolved to wait no longer. He had seized a time to marry Mrs. Randolph when Senator Payne's death gave an excuse for a diminution of pomp—a time also when the absence of Harry and of Pauline was accountable—and the haphazard nature of the ceremony could be explained away. The fact that the decision to marry was indeed made on the spur of the moment seemed borne out by the hurried note Whitney sent to Harry a few days before the event:

As these moments are a little summary, I wish if you & Gertrude feel inclined you wd send your good wishes to Mrs. (Arthur) Randolph by wire Tuesday morning. . . .

His doubt that Harry did feel so inclined was evident. Harry's letter, written later to "Dear Papa" from aboard the *Empress of India* bound for Japan, was scarcely enthusiastic:

Of course your marriage was a great surprise, and when it was all done it seemed harder to get along with even than the thought of it last winter. So I was very glad that we had made our plans to go to Japan. Of course it may all turn out for the best as you seem sure that it will, but I do not quite see how. . . . The house is so much Mamma's that it's hard enough to think of somebody living in it in her place without adding to that having it opened to entertainment with another hostess. . . .

The wedding being so sudden puts us all in an unpleasant light. Everyone naturally thinks that we were all away because we would not be present, and the fact that we did not hear of it till the day before does not help much. Still it may all be as you say, and turn out well.

This hardly suggests gratitude for the care that (Whitney informed Cleveland) Mrs. Randolph had given Flora, nor the affection between the two women Whitney had alluded to. Harry had disapproved of his father's marrying Mrs. Randolph months earlier, he still disapproved, and on top of that he was offended because the hurried wedding *looked* peculiar socially. Harry's letter indicates an anxiety about social correctness as well as disapproval of Mrs. Randolph. While it was decreed that the mourning period for a lost spouse must be long, there were departures from this rigidity, and Whitney should have been forgiven for cutting it short at three and a half years unless there were other transgressions not appearing on the record. The only transgressions that would seem to fit the case would be Whitney intimacies with Mrs. Randolph (or, less likely, other women) during the mourning period.

Now came the family crisis, bitter and shattering. Col. Oliver Payne was in a fury at Whitney's remarriage. Whitney legend has it that his rage was caused by his irrational worship of his late sister Flora, whose picture remained everywhere in his mansion. It is said that he called the Whitney children together (he must have written Harry, who was away for many months), denounced their father, branded him not only as unworthy and dishonorable but as a spendthrift who would leave them nothing. He urged them to disown their father, promising that if they did, he (Oliver) would shower his millions on them. On the other hand, those who chose to stay with their father would be disinherited by Oliver and would probably end up in poverty. What it amounted to was that Oliver offered to make it financially profitable for them to turn their backs on a father whom they should disown on the score of decency anyway. This skeleton was to hang in the Whitney closet for years. A further factor in the case is the certainty that Flora had forgiven Whitney for whatever transgressions might have once occurred and had left him her entire estate in a will executed only a few days before her death.

There was at least one ray of warmth and affection that penetrated this pall of dissension enveloping Whitney's time of supposed happiness. It came from Alexander Gunn, to whom he had written about his marriage before anyone else including Whitney's own family and the President. Gunn replied by sending a Zoar goose to Lenox and writing:

> I send today . . . the Michaelmas goose . . . remembering the anniversary of the 29th—the feast of St. Michael and the Angels. I will keep the day a high holiday, and turn my face to October Mountain about the time you dine, hold high my glass, and drink to you all.

Another affirmation of loyalty and affection later came from Dorothy Whitney, then "going on ten," who wrote many years afterward:

> . . . my father sent for me [and told of his marriage to] the Mrs. Ran dolph whom I had seen in Bar Harbor and thought so beautiful at the time. He said that two of his children—my sister Pauline and my brother Payne—could not forgive him for doing this and that "Uncle" as we called him, regarded this marriage as treachery to my mother—But Harry my eldest brother was unwilling to break with my father and would remain loyal to him—What did I choose to do—would I stay with my father—or go along with Uncle and Payne and Pauline? I remember so clearly this terrible moment—sitting with Papa in the long downstairs drawing room at 2 West 57th Street—and being faced with such a deci- sion—But I said—I think quite unequivocally—that I wanted to stay with him. And from this time on, the family was broken in half—Pauline and Payne with my Uncle—while Harry and I stood by Papa.

3. Broken in Half

WHITNEY AND his bride considered but put off a European honeymoon, stayed a few weeks at Lenox, spent the holidays riding at Aiken, then opened the Fifth Avenue house for the winter season. While Harry and Gertrude were still in the Orient, Whitney made them a gift of the mansion, though he and Edith were to occupy it for months until the young couple's return. Harry's reply was appreciative, but it again touched on the unsuitability of Whitney's remarriage and of his bride becoming hostess where Flora long had reigned:

> Of course if you are well fixed it is an excellent way out of the dif- ficulty. . . . We children would probably have always had an injured feeling and a sense of injustice with the present state of affairs and it might in time make us drift . . . apart, which would never do. Also, I fancy that your wife must prefer a house of her own. I am very much at- tached to the house and of course am pleased with the idea of having it, but it must not be at your expense.

This kind of quarrel was the life's blood of the Saunterer in *Town Topics*. If the family was ruptured in other ways, there still seemed to be agreement on keeping it secret—but how long could the secret be kept?

In any case, with Edith, Whitney began marriage on a footing op- posite from that on which he and Flora had lived for years, when he was in financial subordinacy. Now he was in comfortable command, as

a gentleman of the nineties expected to be. Edith was a talented rider—
a field in which Flora had failed him. It was not necessary for him to
reproach the memory of the restless, driven, loving, challenging, impulsive, emotional, polemic Flora to enjoy Edith's more balanced qualities
of serenity and affection, enhanced as they were by all the social graces,
a naturally pleasant nature, and striking brunette beauty. Nor is it likely
that she was unaware that she had made the catch of the century in
snatching this most eligible of men away from a field that could not
have been other than top-chop. The feeling toward her as a result may
not have been unanimously friendly, but Dorothy was enthusiastic: "My
new stepmother was very good to me and I loved her dearly—She was
the first person I can remember who kissed me goodnight. She brought
her two children into our home, Bertie and Adelaide Randolph—both a
few years older than I was—but this meant a family group for me and a
sorely needed sense of companionship."

Still, Edith's first year or so as Mrs. Whitney could not have been
without difficulties even as Whitney embarked on an orgy of spending
and activity aimed in part at surrounding her with suitable splendor. He
pushed the completion of the stables at Westbury. He leased the nearby
mansion of the banker James F. D. Lanier, who was spending months
in Europe, so that he and Edith could ride and enjoy the country as
they supervised construction and also planned the palace they would
erect there for themselves. With Thomas F. Ryan he began stock operations in a business that promised new profits—tobacco. On his Aiken
property rose a Southern colonial cottage that astonished the natives,
two hundred feet long, with a "wide sweeping piazza . . . fraught with
columns at every few feet rising to the second story." The reception hall
alone was thirty-six by forty feet; the fireplaces and furniture were elegant antiques for which agents had scoured the market; there was a magnificent billiard room and there were twenty-four bedrooms for guests
alone, so that with servants' quarters the house had more than fifty
rooms. The immense two-story stable building, of matching design, had
thirty-two box stalls, eight standing stalls, and room for twenty-two
vehicles, while at a distance was built a mile-and-furlong horse track.
Whitney, much like a prince succeeding to the throne, and with a new
and cherished queen to cosset, surveyed his demesne, consulted his
viceroys, bought more acreage in Westbury, and also added to his land-
holdings in Massachusetts and the Adirondacks. He imported thirteen
buffalo, two blacktail deer, and twenty antelope from Wyoming and
placed them on his stock farm near Lenox. And to replace his New

York home, he bought for "about $650,000" the Robert L. Stuart man-
sion at 871 Fifth Avenue, at 68th Street, which came on the market
after the death of Stuart, a sugar millionaire.

It was a massive four-story brownstone front building with a fifty-five-
foot frontage on Fifth Avenue and two hundred feet on 68th Street.
This was on the newer Grand Canal of Mammon farther uptown,
across from Central Park where the master and his lady could ride. It
had been built for Stuart in 1884 by William Schickel and had been
leased for a time after Stuart's death by Levi Morton, the banker and
sometime vice-president and governor whom Whitney knew well.
Whitney had of course visited the house as a guest. Although it was
only twelve years old, grand as it was, Whitney treated it as if it were in
advanced decay and gave the contract for almost entirely rebuilding it to
the Tiffany of architectural firms, McKim, Mead & White. He wanted
changes and embellishments that were to cost many times the price of
the house itself. One improvement was the addition of a large wing to
house the inevitable ballroom, sixty-three by forty-five feet and forty-
four feet high, said to be the largest private one in the city but actually a
shade smaller than the vastness of the Cornelius Vanderbilts'. Before
long Stanford White, a dynamo who loved to spend his clients' money,
would be in Europe for Whitney and others, visiting the galleries and
the palaces of impecunious noblemen, "darting from object to object,"
as Aline Saarinen later commented, "[indicating] 'this tapestry for William C. Whitney's house—that statue for the dining room of Senator
Clark.' " Wallace Irwin saw the ridiculous in the invasion of Fifth Avenue by the likes of Sen. William A. Clark of Montana, but one could
not say that his verses were totally inapplicable to Whitney:

> Senator Copper of Tonopah Ditch
> Made a clean billion in minin' and sich,
> Hiked for New York, where his money he blew
> Bildin' a palace on Fift' Avenoo.
> "How," sez the Senator, "can I look proudest?
> Build me a house that'll holler the loudest—"
> . . . .
>
> Forty-eight architects came to consult,
> Drawin' up plans for a splendid result;
> If the old Senator wanted to pay,
> They'd give 'im Art with a capital A,
> . . . .
>
> Pillars Ionic,
> Eaves Babylonic,

Doors cut in scallops, resemblin' a shell;
Roof was Egyptian,
Gables caniptian,
Whole grand effect when completed was—hell.

If Whitney had better taste than Senator Clark, there was still a class tastelessness among the rich in their vulturous descent on the artifacts of Europe, their belief in instant grandeur in the novel rearrangement of old segments. Meanwhile, although the Whitneys gave no large parties of the kind Flora had gloried in, *The Times* later said the winter was "a great social triumph" for the new Mrs. Whitney, going on ambiguously: "Her wonderful tact enabled her to steer clear of all the social complications which were beginning that winter to be puzzling and annoying. . . . She also interested herself in entertaining Mr. Whitney's political friends, with great success."

The Tribune reasoned that Whitney changed his plan to go to Europe with his wife in the spring of 1897 because he wished to "take control of the warring odds and ends of the Democracy" and "lead them to victory" in the mayoral election that fall. His position as an antisilver Democrat whose party nationally was for silver was an embarrassment to him. His purpose for the mayoral election was to unite all city Democrats, gold or silver, on the theory that the money problem had no connection with local politics. He was, as he had now been for years, the most powerful politician in the city working behind the scenes. Despite his habit in the past of giving preelection "political dinners" at which he invariably wielded influence, one he gave on July 14, 1897, aroused interest because of the stripe of his guests and their general air of secrecy. It was held at the Metropolitan Club, of which Whitney was then president (and of which Oliver Payne was also a member, requiring them now to get distant tables if present at the same time). Whitney declined to give a list of his guests, but it was known that they included Thomas Fortune Ryan, Francis Lynde Stetson, Roswell P. Flower (who was financially interested in New York traction), the Tammany file leader William F. Sheehan, the Tammany ex-mayor Hugh J. Grant, and John D. Crimmins, a Tammany contractor whose firm often did construction work for the surface rail lines.

"We didn't talk any more politics than we did religion," Flower told a reporter without winking.

The Tribune editorialized archly about the holy conversations of "Dominie William C. Whitney . . . the Rt. Rev. Hugh J. Grant, Bishop of

Tammany Hall . . . and many other divines [who] graced the session."
The Herald remarked more seriously:

> Mr. Whitney's . . . failure to state publicly his position in the coming
> campaign [has] caused some gossip among politicians. They recall the
> fact that he and his friends have been the heaviest contributors to Tam-
> many campaign funds in the past. Mr. Whitney, having a fortune in-
> vested in enterprises dependent upon public franchises, is naturally in-
> terested . . . in the character of the winning ticket. . . . he is identified
> with the street railways, and in a campaign, one of the issues of which is
> municipal ownership of franchises, [some Tammany leaders] doubt the
> advisability of listening to his advice as to the selection of the ticket.

The Herald deserved commendation for mentioning an issue, if only
mildly, that all the city's newspapers should have been concerned
about. Even *The World* seemed asleep on this one, and New York journalism was generally deficient in protecting the public interest. *The
Times*, recently taken over by Adolph Ochs but not yet regenerated, ran
a story about the complaints of the leader of the Bryan-oriented Progressive Democratic League. If it was true as claimed that the city Democracy was all for Bryan, this man demanded, "why do we hear of Whitney, Crimmins, and men of that [Goldbug] class having a say in the
councils of the organization?" The question concerned only the silver
issue and had no bearing on the need to protect public franchises. The
Croker lieutenant John Sheehan seemed to let his conscience show
when he replied, for he skipped Bryan and landed on franchises: "That
is false; they [Whitney, Crimmins, *et al.*] have absolutely nothing to say
in the organization. . . . When our boys went to Albany I instructed
them not to grant a single favor to the Metropolitan Traction Company."

It was also inquired whether Croker's return from England might not
interfere with Sheehan's campaign plans, "it being a well-known fact
that Mr. Croker is favorable to the Whitney interest." Sheehan replied—most mistakenly as it turned out—that he understood that
Croker "has no desire to assume control of the organization for the Fall
elections."

If the evidence would not satisfy a court of law, some astute observers
believed that Whitney exercised irresistible behind-the-scenes power,
manipulated the election, and put his own man in office. This was the
first election for Greater New York, with Brooklyn and other formerly
independent areas having become part of the metropolis. Though the

race might be close, indications pointed to the election of the Republican Seth Low, twice mayor of Brooklyn, a man of honesty and ability, respected except among machine politicians. He had been nominated by the Citizens' Union on a platform favoring municipal ownership of franchises and was expected to get the Republican nomination as well. Low made it plain that he meant business about the franchises, saying, "It is utterly unreasonable that because of defective legislation, these valuable grants should be given away without compensation to the city." He went further, saying that franchises already held by traction magnates should revert to the city when a change was made from horsecars to steam or electric operation—exactly the change Whitney and his few remaining competitors were contemplating.

Matthew Breen, a veteran Democratic attorney and political insider who was an observer of these events, wrote, "This utterance was [Low's] undoing. . . . At this juncture a great street railroad magnate, a distinguished Democrat, waited upon . . . a potent Republican deputy-leader, and represented to him the dire catastrophe that would befall the city if Low were elected Mayor . . . and, lo and behold! in a day or two all the Republican district leaders of the City were 'inoculated.' The feeling began to run high against Low. . . ."

As a result, Low did not get the expected Republican nomination, which went instead to Benjamin Tracy, with the vote divided among four candidates. "The distinguished Democrat," Breen went on, "having made the desired impression . . . went to Europe. . . . Croker [was now] perfectly confident of the triumph of Tammany Hall."

Croker thereupon brushed his underlings aside and took charge of the victory. Whitney did indeed go to Europe with his wife. But for Tracy, Low would have won handily.* The evidence is strong that Whitney had made Croker in debt to him and absolute boss of the city for the next four years, years of unbridled corruption. The Tammany puppet Robert Van Wyck was elected mayor. Croker held court daily at the Democratic Club. "The mayor reported there every night and sat in a corner unnoticed until Croker had finished his work, when the latter would nod to the chief executive, who would then follow his boss upstairs to receive his orders for the next day."

* Low got 151,540 votes, Tracy 101,864, and Van Wyck 233,997.

4. Tragedy at Aiken

PERHAPS WHITNEY atoned for his treatment of New York with his kindness to Gunn, who wrote to him, "You have gilded the dull evenings of my days," and privately in his journal wrote, "This man has made my life full of light and kindness. I shall never forget while life lasts." Gunn paid $18 a year rent for his cabin at Zoar and had available meat raised by the brethren, bread baked by the brethren, and beer brewed by them so that—were it not for his travels—he could live comfortably for $200 a year. Around him were Ludwig Zimmermann and a half dozen other convivial friends whom at times he called the Clodhoppers' Club and again denominated as the King and Cabinet, Ludwig being King, Gunn Minister of Agriculture, and the manure hauler Kapfel being Prime Minister. To these bucolics Gunn was an unfathomable mystery, a savant, an eccentric genius who loved Zoar but could stand it only so long before he must leave to buy books or visit the Union Club in Cleveland, or to visit friends in California or White Sulphur Springs, or to visit his great friend Whitney. His travels, except with Whitney, were expensive, as was his habit occasionally to buy such luxuries as fine champagne by the case. He had been able to continue this double life only because Whitney had saved his investment for him. Now Whitney had gone further and arranged for him to get some shares of Metropolitan Traction.

"With some of the complacency of Croesus," Gunn wrote to him, "I watch the towering flight of Metropolitan Traction. 124! Can it be that it will hold that dizzy height? . . . It takes my breath away to read in the newspapers of the vast investments you lead. Millions—like chessmen on the Board of Fortune."

Gunn had visited Whitney and his new bride at Lenox before they left for Europe and found Edith "a beautiful creature." When they returned, Gunn noted, "This week Will sends me three cases of Dagonet, vintage '86—very rare and costly." The Whitneys returned in mid-November, after Van Wyck's election but in time for that obligatory social event, the Horse Show where, *The Times* reported, "Mrs. Whitney's box . . . received much attention." While the Horse Show was a fairly artificial extension of sport, it had to be said that both Whitney and his wife did love horseflesh.

Number 2 West 57th now being occupied by the Harry Payne Whitneys, Whitney had leased the townhouse of Mrs. Oliver Harriman at 24 West 57th to shelter them until the new Fifth Avenue place was finished. Payne, unreconciled, on his visits from Yale doubtless stayed with Harry in order to avoid his father and stepmother; and he was always welcome at Uncle Oliver's place, two blocks south of Whitney's house-under-construction. The exact status of Pauline (her baby had lived only a few hours) and Almeric was more ambiguous. If Almeric was not precisely penniless, he was pinched, and money was important to them. Pauline at any rate had sided firmly with her uncle, and it was said that he had rewarded them with an expensive house at 11 East 61st Street. Yet Almeric still worked in some vague executive capacity for Whitney—not an indispensable man but doubtless kept on the job because of Whitney's hope of winning back Pauline. Thus the Pagets were exacting tribute from both sides, and their fate appeared to depend on which millionaire first lost patience with them.

From Europe the Whitneys had brought with them three English friends as guests—Lady and Sir Edward Colebrook, and Sydney Paget, an older brother of Lady Colebrook and of Almeric Hugh Paget. The Colebrooks were riders, and Sydney Paget, who had also spent some years in the Western plains, was a horse-racing enthusiast. By November 29 the Whitneys, the Colebrooks, and Paget were at Lexington, Kentucky, attending horse auctions. In two days Whitney bought the fine mare Lou Bramble for $9,000 and five other horses of lesser repute, but he denied any intention of starting a racing stable—a denial the Kentucky horse people took with salt, especially in view of the dimensions of his stable construction at Westbury. "I am not in the racehorse business," Whitney said, insisting that his new mounts would make good hunters. This seemed another aspect of the odd need for privacy that seized him at times. On December 21, the Whitneys boarded their private railroad car and left for Aiken with the Colebrooks, Paget, Edith's daughter Adelaide, and Dorothy Whitney. Another member of the party was the New York physician Dr. C. F. McGahan. Some of the very rich now took a doctor along on extended trips to rural areas—a practice at any rate less theatrical than Colonel Payne's habit of taking his barber with him when he went to Georgia to hunt.

Dorothy Whitney, who would never attain her sister Pauline's audacity, was at an age, almost eleven, when the split in her family and the hostility on the part of Payne and Pauline might have shaken her with lasting effect. It did not, for her character was firm. She later said that the fact that Uncle Oliver had disinherited her and Harry for remaining loyal to their father caused Whitney to extend himself in business so that he would leave them an estate not paltry by comparison with what Oliver could be expected to leave Payne and Pauline.

But Whitney was anything but desk-bound during much of 1897 and impressed his intimates more by his capacity to spend than to earn. It was evident that he was supremely happy in his marriage. He was enjoying life, enjoying his ability to make others enjoy. With an indulgent wife, he had entered his true metier as the host who delighted in small groups, delighted in treating his guests to every luxury of food and entertainment regardless of cost, yet was so evidently pleased about it that he seemed to do it out of hospitality rather than ostentation. A later student of the art of prodigious spending, Lucius Beebe, placed Whitney in the very top rank along with J. P. Morgan as "indisputably a magnifico . . . one who indulged the sybaritic taste of an authentic Corinthian as no American has ever done since. Mediocrity in Whitney was unthinkable."

The party had expected to return after the Christmas holidays, but the weather and the riding were so glorious that they stayed on, Whitney also planning to take his English guests on a pleasure trip in his private car. Neighbors and close friends of Whitney both on Long Island and at Aiken were the Thomas Hitchcocks, Jr., Hitchcock being as at home in the saddle as Whitney, and his wife being one of the very best of women riders. Hitchcock and Whitney were fellow members of the men-only Meadow Brook Hunt Club on Long Island—gentlemen who rode hard in pink coats after foxes and had their own distinctive evening dress, "a scarlet coat with robin's egg blue facings and hunt buttons, worn with a white waistcoat."

The Whitneys and Hitchcocks fairly covered the countryside with hoofmarks, joined at times by two other New York couples who were guests of one or the other, the Duncan Elliots (real estate) and the C. F. Havemeyers (sugar and banking). On February 21, the Whitneys and Hitchcocks left the Hitchcock cottage, liberated a captured deer, and rode pell-mell after it. Also in the party were the Colebrooks, Adelaide Randolph, Dorothy Whitney, Paget, and a few others. They had begun to spread out as they approached a rustic bridge so low that riders had to bend sharply to pass under it safely. Edith Whitney, riding this day a horse two hands higher than her usual mount, failed to bend low enough. Approaching the bridge at a brisk clip, she struck her head with sickening force against a timber and was thrown to the ground.

There were cries of dismay. The chase ended immediately and the riders dismounted and gathered around her. She was bleeding from the head, breathing but unconscious, a sight particularly shocking to her own daughter Adelaide, her stepdaughter Dorothy, and her husband of seventeen months. She was carried to the Whitney place, where Dr. McGahan—his presence proving to be providential rather than an affectation—examined her. He found a six-inch scalp wound but was more concerned about her continued unconsciousness and the fact that both arms were paralyzed, a sign of spinal damage. Whitney telegraphed two New York specialists, Drs. Charles L. Dana and C. F. Bull: "TAKE SPECIAL TRAIN AND DON'T LET THEM LOSE A MOMENT." Dana and Bull were there in thirteen hours instead of the twenty-four hours usually required for the trip.

Edith had broken a cervical vertebra. After hovering near death for three days, she recovered full consciousness to find herself immobilized in a hip-to-head plaster cast. Whitney, who had not been in his office for two months and seldom for two months before that, stayed with her two months longer until she could be moved to New York. "The journey back," Dorothy recalled, ". . . was made possible by his attention to every detail of this tragic return. . . ." He ordered a special train of four luxurious Wagner Palace cars for the journey, one of them solely for Edith and her physicians and nurses. She was lifted into it through a window, still in a cast, her head now supported by a made-to-measure metal frame. She could now move both arms somewhat, and she bravely told friends at the station that she would be back next year, riding again.

Arriving at Weehawken, she was placed in a deep-springed carriage, ferried across the Hudson, and driven home over cobbled New York streets in the same carriage. "Mr. Whitney and a party of friends walked along by the side of the carriage, removing obstacles that might cause the invalid unnecessary pain by the jolting of the wheels." Gunn wrote to her in commiseration and confided to his journal, "I will not believe that this lovely and amiable creature will not recover." But Edith made out her will seven weeks later.

For Dorothy Whitney, the vision of Edith lying insensible on the ground with blood staining her forehead, the pain and paralysis that she suffered thereafter—all made the girl react against horses, against riding. She never wanted to ride a horse again. Her father talked to her gently about it. It was tragic, he agreed, but life was filled with risks of many kinds, and if one set out to avoid them all, one might as well be dead.

He was firm under the gentleness. He wanted her to continue riding, and she did.

5. What the Transgression?

"YOU PROBABLY know that I have very close business connections in Cleveland, the home of the Standard Oil Company," the Boston lawyer W. H. Coolidge later said confidentially to Clarence Barron. "My information, and I consider it A-1, is that Oliver Payne has sworn solemnly to take William C. Whitney's wealth away from him. You probably remember that Whitney married Oliver Payne's only sister and that marriage was the foundation of his wealth as when Whitney married Miss Payne, Oliver H. Payne gave her $3,500,000 in cash and securities and a $500,000 residence in New York. . . . After his wife died Whitney married again. This angered . . . Payne, who swore that he would take away every cent from Whitney that he secured by reason of his former marriage. He got his Standard Oil stock away from him and has been pursuing him relentlessly ever since."

While Flora was not Oliver's only sister, and Coolidge's figures vary from those given elsewhere, he was right about the relentless animosity. The bitterness of this animosity—hard enough to explain in a self-willed character like Oliver—is staggering to contemplate in Whitney's own flesh and blood. Although money was not at the bottom of the feud, it was a factor. There is the possibility that Whitney's gift of the 57th Street house to Harry (after already bestowing other gifts on the bridal couple) angered Pauline and Payne, who remembered the place from their childhood, felt it as much theirs as Harry's, and bore in mind that Gertrude might very well inherit even more than Harry. But perhaps that reasoning could be turned around. Since Whitney's gift of the New York house was made eight weeks after his remarriage, might it have been by way of rebuke to Pauline and Payne for their refusal to accept his second wife?

There was the consideration that Oliver, two years older than Whitney and now in poor health, seemed slated for the obituaries much sooner than the strapping and vigorous Whitney, so that Oliver's fortune was not only much bigger but seemed certain to be divided earlier. He would die childless, and his only remaining sister had married the prosperous Charles William Bingham, so that Pauline and Payne, to whom he had been so generous as far back as they could remember, seemed his closest presumed heirs. While Edith Whitney seemed beyond child-bearing even before her accident, this was not a certainty, and in any case her children Adelaide and Bertie would come in for a share of the Whitney fortune that Oliver said would be negligible anyway. As for Almeric Hugh Paget, his marriage to Pauline may have been a true love match but it was also a good thing for him financially, and it may do him a gross injustice to entertain the idea that he felt an accommodation with Oliver would be a good thing now. Although Almeric was still in the sensitive position of being employed by Whitney, the latter seemed to regard this as a situation giving him some leverage in his effort to win back Pauline—leverage that would be lost the moment he discharged Almeric, an act that would probably alienate Pauline and Almeric permanently.

But the real mystery in the case is the exact nature of the moral transgression in connection with which Whitney felt some guilt. It seems impossible that Whitney would acknowledge that his mere remarriage after so long a period was sufficient grounds for a son and a daughter to join with Oliver against him. Surely, if that was the extent of Whitney's wrongdoing, it would be apparent to him that Pauline and Payne were thinking only of money in their estrangement from him and their affiliation with Oliver. Affectionate father though he was, would he have anything further to do with two children who rejected him solely for Oliver's millions? Nothing seems clearer than that he would not. Whitney obviously felt some culpability that rendered the estrangement to some degree morally justified; he had committed some transgression that he hoped would fade enough in the minds of the two children so that they would come back to the fold. But he was not going to wait forever. When Payne Whitney graduated with honors in June 1898—twenty months after Whitney's remarriage and four months after Edith had been injured—Uncle Oliver was at Yale to congratulate him. Whitney stayed away.

6. And Now Farewell!

WHITNEY ATTENDED the Sheepshead Bay races and bought more horses with the advice of Sydney Paget, now such a close adviser that he and his wife lived with the Whitneys. "I have always loved horses," Whitney now admitted. ". . . we have secured a small stable."

Edith Whitney remained bedridden in the care of nurses, corresponding with friends, including Gunn, by means of a secretary. She
enjoyed it especially when Whitney read to her the latest of Mr. Dooley's pronouncements or discussed with her a new building on his
Adirondack property, the progress at Westbury, or—his greatest prize of
all—the works of art being "built into" the Fifth Avenue house. While
Secretary of the Navy he had read technical works on such subjects as
marine engines. Now, Dorothy Whitney recalled, "I remember passing
the open door of Papa's room every evening and seeing him beside his
desk reading all the medical books he could lay hands on. He hoped
always to find some answer to the cruel and implacable fate that was in
store for [Edith]. . . ." She had been moved to Westbury—an undertaking requiring the most extreme care—and in July she was taken to
Bar Harbor:

> . . . her husband [has] been constant in his attendance on her, and he
> made elaborate preparations for her removal. An especially constructed
> carriage . . . having a cot inside, with a large air cushion in place of a
> mattress, carried Mrs. Whitney . . . to the Roslyn station. . . . Dr.
> McGahan, the family physician, and five nurses as well as Mr. Whitney
> and a party of relatives and friends, followed. . . . Mrs. Whitney was
> carried to a special car in waiting, and the carriage was loaded on a
> baggage-car.
> Mr. Whitney held an umbrella over his wife's head while the transfer
> . . . was made. . . . At 10:45 the special train started for Long Island
> City [where] the cars were run onto a float [across the East River] to Mott
> Haven, where the cars were placed on the tracks of the New Haven
> Railroad, and the journey was continued. The trip to Bar Harbor will be
> made in easy stages.

She stayed for two months at Bar Harbor, where "she has had bad
days when she suffered extremely from neuralgic pains, the result of the
weather. But she has seemed to enjoy living at her favorite summer
resort." On September 22, equally painstaking steps got her back to
Long Island. Whitney's yacht was either out of commission or he had
got rid of it—nothing further is heard of the yacht—so J. P. Morgan
lent his *Corsair*, to which she was transferred from a launch. The plan
was to steam all the way to Oyster Bay on Long Island with her husband, physician, four trained nurses, and eight servants, but a rising
gale made the yacht pitch painfully for her, so she was taken ashore and
moved home laboriously by train. ". . . I remember coming into her
room in the Westbury house," Dorothy recalled, "and seeing her lying

in the big bed—a smile on her face and a loving greeting to me." Her spirit was indomitable; she was determined to recover. When Whitney asked if he should rent his opera box, she replied, "Oh, no; keep the box. I shall want to use it if only for the matinees."

"I see in the 'World,' " Gunn noted in his journal, "that Mrs. Whitney is no better, and the gloomy certainty closes down that she never can be well. This is the cruelest thing I ever knew. Nature made this incomparable woman and then ruthlessly destroyed her." In December he was invited to the Whitneys in New York in the hope that he would cheer Edith and also Whitney himself, who could have used a rise in spirits. But it happened that while Gunn was there she was more unwell than usual and was unable to see him. He wrote to her:

> Think of me always, most dear friend. I would willingly give my poor fragment of life if it would make you happy. I was under your roof. You will never know how much I felt the pang that prevented me from seeing you. . . . My whole heart and soul are with you and Will.

On Long Island, what had been great farms only twenty miles from Manhattan was now the habitat of rich horse lovers. At Westbury, Whitney's nearest neighbor, the banker Edwin D. Morgan, was eliminating the inconvenience of driving four miles to church by building a "private chapel, ballroom and gatehouse combined at his country estate." At Whitney's, three hundred men had been busy enlarging the old homestead for temporary use until a new one could be built, finishing the stables, the racetrack, and a two-mile bicycle path—hurrying because no one knew how much time Edith had. In the spring of 1899 the fashionables gathered there to see the annual races of the Meadow Brook Steeplechase Association. ". . . the beauties of society were present, arrayed in their prettiest frocks and gowns, to witness the cavaliers . . . do feats of daring. . . . Mr. Whitney left nothing undone. . . . In a large marquee tent a sumptuous luncheon was served. . . . Mr. Whitney was here, there and everywhere to see that all were cared for." There were several croppers but no injuries, one event offering the newly created Whitney Cup. Edith had been placed on a high bed near a window: "All the races started and finished . . . where they could be plainly seen by Mrs. Whitney, who is an invalid."

Edith evidently sensed that this was her last entertainment. A day or two later she called in Dorothy Whitney. ". . . she asked me to stand beside her bed while she unburdened herself of something on her mind," Dorothy wrote. "She wanted to tell me herself about the facts of life about menstruation and the shock it might cause me— And so, from her—at this last tragic moment in her life, I learned that she was thinking of me and of how to help me face the future. . . ." Five days after the races Edith lost consciousness and lay insensible for two more days before she died on May 6 at the stroke of noon. "With her when she died," said *The Times*, "were her husband, her daughter, Miss Adelaide Randolph; her stepdaughter, Miss Dorothy Whitney; her stepson, Harry Payne Whitney, and the attending physician." No mention of Payne Whitney or of the Almeric Hugh Pagets. Whitney and Adelaide led the mourners at her funeral at the Garden City Episcopal Cathedral three days later. After a preliminary short prayer service at his home, they reached the cathedral in a six-coach special train he provided. Edith, who loved orchids and had been given them daily by Whitney during her long affliction, lay in a coffin covered with orchids. Among the floral offerings were those from President McKinley, ex-President Cleveland, and Governor Roosevelt. A detail that perhaps offered a clue as to their exact status of estrangement was the fact that Payne Whitney was probably there and the Pagets certainly there.* Also present was Mrs. Burke Roche who, in the calculating Society gossip that could so often be pure invention, was regarded as a candidate to replace Edith and become the third Mrs. William C. Whitney.

At the request of her children, Edith was buried beside her late first husband at the cemetery in Douglaston. She divided her modest property between her son and daughter, with Whitney as executor and as their guardian, but left some jewelry to Dorothy Whitney and bequeathed to Whitney during his lifetime the use of several magnificent tapestries she had bought in Italy. These he could use in the new Fifth Avenue home—still unfinished—which he had intended as her setting.

"God alone can account for this heavy visitation," Gunn wrote to him. "You do not mourn alone." He sent a poem, written by a "late friend," reading in part:

> And now Farewell! Night may give place to dawn,
> And birds sing on and autumn crown the land,
> But what care we, when you, our friend, are gone?

---

* The newspaper reports were unclear. *The Times* did not name specifically any of Whitney's children as attending. *The Sun* and *The World* said the Pagets were there but did not mention Payne. *The Herald* said Payne as well as the Pagets were present, whereas *The Tribune* named the Pagets but did not mention either Payne or Dorothy, and we know that the latter was there.

Seven

1. The Money Rolled In

SIX WEEKS later Whitney sailed alone for England on the *Umbria*, a decision made so suddenly that his name was not on the passenger list. Perhaps Adelaide and Bertie Randolph, who lived with him, reminded him too constantly of Edith. His activities abroad are known only from his own later brief summary, in which he said his chief purpose was to find recovery from his grief. He bought a few horses, attended the races at Newmarket, and just happened to encounter Croker there. In July, while Whitney was gone, his newly finished stables and barn were destroyed by fire despite the efforts of hose companies from Westbury, Roslyn, Mineola, and Hempstead. Stable hands saved the carriages, the race horses, and Harry's polo ponies, and the eight horses lost were the peasants of the breed, work horses. Also while Whitney was gone, his purchase of 102 more acres to add to his Westbury holdings was announced, and it was observed that "the prospect is that the hills of the upper part of Nassau County will be owned by wealthy New-Yorkers before long."

Returning in August on the *Kaiser Wilhelm der Grosse*, Whitney hurried to the Waldorf to attend to business for the rest of the day before he talked to reporters in the evening. He said he had been near prostration: "When a man almost breaks down every time a friend says a kind word to him, it is time he dropped work for a time and steadied his nerves. . . . And I did nothing in England but eat, drink, and be merry." Asked if he had had political discussions with the Boss, he protested, "I saw Croker [only] once at Newmarket for two or three minutes. . . . I had no time to say more than 'How do you do?' to him." He praised McKinley's appointment of Elihu Root as Secretary of War: "No better man . . . could have been found." It meant, though he did not say so, that even in a Republican cabinet he had two close friends, the other being Secretary of State John Hay.

Rebuilding began at Westbury—a new stable a sixth of a mile long, bigger than the one that burned, "said to be the largest and handsomest in the world," steam-heated, with electric lights and telephones, having 73 stalls and space for 116 horses in a pinch as well as fine dormitories for the dozen-odd stable hands. Two hundred men were working on roads and on a golf course—Society's newest wrinkle. More were busy on a new gymnasium building for bowling, billiards, and indoor tennis. And at long last the new mansion, 200 by 75 feet, designed by McKim, Mead & White, was started from scratch. Farms on the property raised crops that were prepared into food for the workers by a huge kitchen staff, so that the operation was compared gravely to the construction of the Pyramid of Cheops.* Whitney admired the work of John La Farge—apparently the only living and the only American artist who interested him. When he asked La Farge to paint glass panels for the house and to "do his damnedest," the independent La Farge replied that Whitney "did not have enough money to pay for what I *could* do: that I should only do what I thought was fairly fitting." Meanwhile construction had proceeded under Stanford White for almost three years on the Fifth Avenue house. Fitting together such details as stairways, balustrades, mantels, and sections of floors and ceilings removed from European edifices was painstaking work. Whitney was not pressed for living space, for abruptly he bought and renovated a pillared old mansion on sixty-seven acres near the Sheepshead Bay track, adding also sizable stables. He kept buying more horses, including the entire stable of the well-known Samuel C. Hildreth, whom he hired as trainer, and added the $40,000 filly Endurance By Right and others named Black Venus, Mr. Clay, and Kilmarnock. He studied pedigrees, firm in the belief that blood would tell. In 1899 his horses, running under Sydney Paget's colors (a technicality—his status of mourning forbade him to race on his own), won thirty-two races and prize money totaling $38,461—a paltry sum compared with their cost and upkeep. He was proud of Jean Beraud, so proud that he challenged Perry Belmont and his outstanding colt Ethelbert. At the race, Whitney wore in his buttonhole "a knot of blue in honor of Yale, Mr. Belmont . . . a knot of Harvard crimson." Harvard broke the track record and won easily. Money changed hands as Whitney shook Belmont's hand and said enviously of Ethelbert, "I believe he is the horse of the country." When Whitney's new stables at Westbury were finished, the "grooms were told in no uncertain terms

---

* Wages had risen. Whitney's construction workers were paid the union scale of $4 for a ten-hour day except for electricians, who got $3.50.

[but surely with a smile] that their safety was a minor consideration in the event of fire compared with that of the horses."

The money was still rolling in. New York traction remained Whitney's largest concern, but even his scrupulous biographer, Mark Hirsch, admitted that "tangible factual information about many of Whitney's enterprises unfortunately does not exist." Whitney did not like to keep records. He was secretive about his business affairs. Most of his stock undertakings were in complicated collaboration with others, such as his forays into American Tobacco and the automobile business, which were made with Ryan and one or another of his traction allies. He was also a director or trustee of the Morton Trust Company, the State Trust Company, the Mutual Life Insurance Company, the Fifth Avenue Trust Company, and several other organizations. But there is no telling how much of his time was spent in pure gambling in stocks that he might buy, manipulate, and sell with no interest in the companies they represented.

Through quiet stock purchases, Whitney, Ryan, and others had managed to mount a formidable threat to James B. Duke's huge American Tobacco Company, in which Oliver Payne was a powerful partner. The plan fell short of full victory because, it was said, the manipulator James R. Keene, supposed to be buying stock for the Whitney group, defected and sold it instead to Payne. Nevertheless, here was one case where Whitney gave Payne as good as he got. Whitney, who had few enemies, was said never to have forgiven Keene, though Keene had attended Edith's funeral. For all that, the skirmish netted Whitney's group millions, and thereafter, according to Duke's biographer, "six men could gather about a table and rule a great [tobacco] industry. They were: James B. Duke, Anthony N. Brady, Oliver H. Payne, Thomas F. Ryan, P. A. B. Widener, and William C. Whitney." This was purely metaphorical, since Whitney and Payne would never again meet—but once—at the same table.

Fascinated by automobiles, Whitney bought an electric car to try for himself. He then joined Ryan and a few others in buying out the Electric Vehicle Company, aiming to produce taxis as well as cars for private use. The first New York automobile show, in February 1899, had displayed gasoline, steam, and electric vehicles. The Duryea, Winton, and Pope-Hartford cars were now terrifying horses in city streets. Harry Whitney owned a gas buggy, and it would not be long before he was overtaken by a policeman (traffic policemen then rode bicycles) and arrested on Central Park West for exceeding the speed limit of eight miles

per hour. In court, "Mr. Whitney asserted that he was trying the au
tomobile for his father, William C. Whitney," and denied attaining
such speed. Unlike others, Whitney had the prevision to make legal arrangements with the holders of the Selden automobile patent when he
joined Pope-Hartford in an enterprise (characteristically, its capitalization quickly rose from $3,000,000 to $18,000,000) that was briefly profitable to him and more so to others after his death. Power-driven carriages suddenly became the playthings of the rich. Mrs. Oelrichs, Mrs.
William K. Vanderbilt, and Mrs. Stuyvesant Fish glided about in electric cars, as did the Sultan of Turkey. Whitney, however, saw automobiles correctly as a coming great industry with enormous potential
for profit. He promptly joined the Automobile Club, adding to a membership so ecumenical that he could eat at one of his clubs every day for
almost three weeks without repeating himself.*

Now that he was a widower again, banned from too obvious participation in gay Society by the inhibitory restrictions of mourning, he was
inclined to lunch and dine at one of his clubs, or at Delmonico's,
Sherry's, or the Waldorf. If it can be assumed that one's pallbearers are
picked from favorite dining companions, he ate with Ryan, Widener,
William Jay, J. P. Morgan, Hamilton McK. Twombly, and a few others
including Elihu Root when Root was in town. The touch of the boule-
vardier in him was given dignity by his many enterprises, and he was
saved from the solemnity of business by his man-about-town dash. He
was a pioneer of the Waldorf-Astoria. Oscar Tschirky, the famous Oscar
of the Waldorf, whose favor was prized by celebrities and millionaires,
was an old friend of Whitney's, who knew him when he was at the
Hoffman House and at Delmonico's and who got him to inscribe his
Waldorf Cook Book (which also contained recipes for drinks) along with
a note to Alexander Gunn. The Waldorf-Astoria,† where one could
choose among dozens of diversions including waltzing, drinking in the
vast, all-male bar, getting the world's most expensive haircut ($1.50),
listening to a symphony orchestra under Anton Seidl, dining in any of
several restaurants including the Palm Room where full dress was ob-

---

* His clubs were: Metropolitan, Union, Knickerbocker, Manhattan, Democratic, Yale, University, Century, Racquet, Jockey, New York Yacht, Suburban Riding and Driving, Automobile,
Country Club of Westchester, Downtown, Coaching, Turf and Field, and Meadow Brook Hunt.
He also belonged to the Society of the Mayflower, the New York Zoological Society, the Chamber
of Commerce, the Municipal Art Society, the National Steeplechase and Hunt Association, the
New England Society, the New York Genealogical Society, the Metropolitan Museum of Art, and
was an active director of the American Museum of Natural History—plus of course his continuing
active membership in the Metropolitan Opera and Real Estate Company.

† The Empire State Building today occupies its site.

ligatory, or promenading in Peacock Alley, was suddenly the place grandees headed for after the opera, the resort of the bluest blood, even if J. P. Morgan was occasionally seen there with women not recognized by Society.

More than Morgan, who ignored horses but was immersed in art collecting, Whitney maintained a token civic interest and a passion for nature and conservation. He found time to serve on the Grant monument committee and to head the Dewey reception committee that arranged the great welcome for the admiral.* He was of course an ardent patriot during the Spanish-American War, offering advice to McKinley on the use of the Navy. He wrote the Secretary of the Interior about a plan for forest conservation, started a quail and pheasant breeding farm at Lenox, brought moose from Canada to Lenox to see how they would fare, inaugurated selective logging on his Adirondack lands, drained swamps at Sheepshead Bay to eradicate mosquitoes (not because they were a nuisance to people but because they pestered his horses), and presented two buffalo bulls named Cleveland and McKinley to the New York Zoological Society.

2. A Notorious Burlesque Actress

The domestic affairs of a certain well-known millionaire of this city are not of the happiest. He and his elder son get along well enough, but the younger son has broken away from the pater and is living with his uncle. The married daughter inclines, like her younger brother, to lean toward her uncle rather than toward her father. Indeed, she has good cause to feel kindly toward the former, as it was he who gave her the handsome house she lives in. On the other hand, the married daughter's husband is closely associated with his father-in-law in business, but this is hardly significant, as the family differences are not questions of money or property. There is a romance behind all this that would make a capital theme for a novel. And in the background there stands, a threatening shadow, the tiny figure of a notorious burlesque actress.

THIS, IN its entirety, was the scandal-dripping opening item on the first page of *Town Topics* for February 1, 1900—the equivalent of the headlined front-page lead story of a newspaper. Obviously it referred to the Whitney-Payne feud, but placed at a different time and with some-

---

* It was rumored that Whitney joined other anti-Bryan Democrats in sending a courier to Manila to sound out Dewey as a potential presidential candidate in 1900 but gave up on Dewey, possibly because of the admiral's penchant for inept talk.

thing seemingly missing and something added. Had the Saunterer—the redoubtable Colonel Mann—gone mad, or was he on a fresh and true scent? After he took over the weekly, its quality had improved, its raffishness almost hidden under writing always competent and often graceful and witty. It was well printed and meticulously proofread. While its *pièce de résistance* was Society gossip, much of it innocuous, it also reviewed the opera, the theater, and the new books acceptably, covered Wall Street, the watering places, the sailings and arrivals, and the turf and other fashionable sporting events. It invariably carried a "poem" of six or eight stanzas, each stanza referring blithely to the foibles of a different Society figure. While none of this poetry has found its way into anthologies, its meter was impeccable, its vivacity irrepressible, and its humor usually piquant. In short, *Town Topics* was full of fun as well as dirty work. If it was not read avidly by the rich, then such advertisers as Pommery champagne, White Star Lines, Virginia Hot Springs resort, *Harper's Magazine*, and—yes—J. P. Morgan & Company—were wasting their money.

The extent of the blackmail carried on by the magazine was later shown to be immense, but this was not evident in its tone for the very reason that the blackmail was usually paid to keep such stories from being printed. The Saunterer could be flattering or critical in small ways newspapers did not dare. His willingness to come right out and say that he was sorry to see Mrs. Oelrichs "permitting herself to run to fat," or that Mrs. Eleanor Martin "is giving deadly dull dinners" was feared by the victims but rather enjoyed by many others. Although it would not have been safe to depend implicitly on everything appearing in *Town Topics*, one could by no means write it off as entirely unreliable either. Andy Logan, the authority on Colonel Mann's career, remarked on his insistence on accuracy, not out of conscience but self-interest:

> Mann was well aware that a spreader of even the most racy and amusing tales is in danger of losing his audience if his reliability becomes suspect; the Saunterer held on to his readers because he had a reputation for adhering to the truth, unpalatable as it may have been to those of whom it was told.

The item about Whitney and the burlesque actress, however, was in a different category, since no names were given. The Whitney family had been secretive about the feud with Colonel Payne, so that the item would mean nothing to most readers until names or more details were supplied. Given its prominent position, readers would be inclined to reason that illumination would come in later issues. Hence it would seem to have been a perfect plant for an effort to blackmail Whitney, who would presumably pay well to have nothing further printed. It would be quite possible for the Saunterer, accomplished as he was at insinuation, to go further into detail about the players in the drama, still without mentioning names, so that libel would be avoided but the participants would be known all along Fifth Avenue from Washington Square to the upper reaches of Central Park.

Nothing further was printed on the subject.

Since the threat of exposure was aimed chiefly at Whitney himself, and to a lesser extent at his children, of whom even the estranged ones would presumably be loath to have such a scandal rise about them, one might play tentatively with the possibility that it was Col. Oliver Payne who gave the item to Colonel Mann. One could reason that if Oliver was irrational enough to break up Whitney's family for what seems insufficient cause, and then seek to ruin him financially, this further vindictiveness was not beyond him. But this would be purest speculation, and indeed such a trick seems too paltry for Oliver, whose vengeance was measured in millions and in flesh and blood.

If it was not Oliver, obviously the scandal was known or suspected by someone outside the family circle, which would not be surprising after such a lapse of time. A servant may have heard something of it, Pauline may have dropped an unguarded remark—even Harry's tongue may have loosened after an extra cocktail—and Society had its watchers who made it their business to notice such oddities as the fact that Payne Whitney lived with his uncle and was not seen in public with his father. One suspects that more than a few had become aware of that, and that it was explained away as one of those not uncommon father-son disagreements that invariably become reconciled in the end.

But what of the things missing and added? The item indicated that the family crisis was recent, centering around Whitney's current interest in an actress. This is a discrepancy suggesting that the item was supplied by some outsider not aware of all the facts. There was no hint that it actually had begun three and a half years earlier, in the fall of 1896, when Whitney married Edith Randolph. This is the version believed by most of the descendants of the Whitneys today, and there is strong evidence to support it, such as Dorothy's later written account. There was also persistent talk later in Wall Street, heard by the indefatigable Pepys of the Stock Exchange, Clarence Barron, that Colonel Payne's animus was caused by his conviction that Whitney's marriage to Mrs. Randolph constituted an insult to Flora's memory. It is of course also possible that Whitney was having an affair with an actress in 1900—the sort of thing that was much more intriguing to an editor of Colonel Mann's kidney than a mere question of respect for a dead wife.

Did the fact that the threatening item about the actress was never followed up, and that Whitney thereafter was treated with greatest respect in *Town Topics*, indicate that he had paid blackmail? It was a fascinating puzzle about which some aspects remained unknown but about which a few more clues would emerge later.

3. Shades of Croesus

WHEN WHITNEY sailed on the *Majestic* July 4, 1900, stinging from a new miniscandal that had gotten into the papers and triumphant over two market coups that had received less attention, Gunn was his guest again. Another shipboard companion, though not a guest, was his daughter-in-law's youngest brother, Reginald Claypoole Vanderbilt. Known as Reggie, he was a Yale undergraduate not noted for scholarship, a bit unruly, fond of strong waters, crazy about horses and hence abreast of Whitney on that subject, though less prepared for the classical allusions of Gunn. Only the day before, Whitney's chestnut filly Killashandra had won the first race at Sheepshead Park by two lengths, but his mare Rush had so impugned her name, running far behind in the fourth race, that one sportswriter described her as "a mare of Metropolitan Traction speed."

It was characteristic of Whitney that he could converse with understanding and enjoyment with two such different persons as Reggie and Gunn—persons who if left together would discover that the other spoke a language foreign to him. This was one of Whitney's great attractions. Everybody liked to talk with him because he spoke their language, eloquent in a spectrum of topics ranging from politics to business to travel to art to sailing to journalism to music to horses to automobiles to hunting and fishing to law and to golf and many in between.

The miniscandal virtually ended Whitney's long and bumpy friendship with Pulitzer. *The World* had charged, in a salvo of front-page headlines, that Whitney and Ryan made improper use of the funds of the State Trust Company, which they controlled, in their own stock speculations.

Among the loans State Trust had made were $435,000 to Whitney's

sometime lobbyist Louis Payn, who now held office as the state superintendent of insurance; $1,000,000 to one of Whitney's brokerage firms,
Moore & Schley; $500,000 to the Metropolitan Traction Company; and
$2,000,000 to Daniel Shea, who was not precisely Ryan's office boy as
The World described him but was (and the point was the same) a young
secretary in Ryan's employ. In his official capacity as superintendent of
insurance Payn, a notorious corruptionist, had jurisdiction over two organizations in which Whitney had financial interest, the Mutual Life
Insurance Company and the American Surety Company. The loans
had been made while Elihu Root, now Secretary of War, was a director
and counsel for State Trust, and he approved them. It did indeed appear
that these friends and associates were excessively lenient in arranging for
each other the use of millions of the bank's money, and there was the
question as to whether the loans had been properly secured.

Payn's record had been unsavory ever since he had been a lobbyist for
Jay Gould and Jim Fisk years earlier, and Governor Roosevelt was anxious to dismiss him despite Payn's strong political backing. ". . . being
a frugal man," Roosevelt remarked, "out of his seven thousand dollars a
year salary [Payn] has saved enough to enable him to borrow nearly half
a million dollars from a trust company, the directors of which are also
the directors of an insurance company . . . under his supervision."

The Payn loan was steered by Whitney himself, who produced a pathetic letter from Payn saying that Payn had invested on margin in several stocks including Metropolitan Street Railway and Electric Storage
Battery, both Whitney enterprises. He would lose it all unless he could
get money quickly, which he was unable to attend to because "my poor
wife is lying at the point of death and I could not leave her for a day to
save myself from bankruptcy." Whitney was so disturbed about this first
newspaper attack on him of consequence since the mid-1880s when he
was Navy Secretary—and the danger it might bring to State Trust and
his own solvency—that he hurried to the *World* Building to see Bradford Merrill, Pulitzer's editor. Merrill, on Pulitzer's order, refused to see
him. Governor Roosevelt ordered an investigation by the state banking
department under Frederick D. Kilburn, whose report the governor
refused to release, saying only that it affirmed State Trust's solvency.
The enterprising *World* used its Albany magic to obtain a copy of the
Kilburn report, which it published. The report said of the loan to Shea,
certified by Root, "Beyond all question, this loan was illegal" and pronounced the other loans "illegal or objectionable." But the illegality was
not considered gross, no one lost any money, and State Trust was

warned to desist but there was no prosecution. Whitney wrote furiously
to Pulitzer:

> Your people have repeatedly published that the [$]2,000,000 loan was
> made to "an office boy" failing to state that it was guaranteed by two per-
> sons with either of them $10,000,000 [Whitney and Widener]. . . .
> To say these things about a financial institution having been informed
> as you & your people were of the motive of the person who ran in and
> out of your establishment daily—is to say the least risky business. . . .
> But I feel quite able to take care of myself against malice, so long as I
> don't get lazy—As for our relations, they began long ago when neither of
> us were so successful as now, & as you know I enjoy your intellectuality,
> and appreciate your great faculties more than almost anyone I know but I
> confess I did not suppose that such a man as Bacon wd find that the only
> office in New York he cd find an open door wd be the N Y World when
> his admitted motive was enmity to me, & to an institution in which I had
> invested nearly two millions of dollars—
> Thanks to no one but myself that he didn't injure it—
> However I have generally managed to even things up in the end and
> will do so in this case—
> In fact with some persons the balance has already been struck—*
> Yrs, W. C. Whitney

The *World* attack came very near ruining Whitney at a time when he
was in a Wall Street life-or-death struggle with antagonists including Oliver Payne. This savagery took place in the comparative secrecy of such
transactions, so that even the experts of the Street were at times confused by its ramifications. It began when Whitney's group sought to
consummate their aim to control every foot of Manhattan surface transit
by gobbling up their last remaining competitor, the sizable Third Avenue Railroad. It had long been controlled by Henry Hart, once a pawn-
broker, now ninety years old, illiterate, able only to write his own signature, but shrewd and determined. It had become an obsession with him
to hold the road, which he well knew that Whitney coveted During the
rascally Van Wyck administration Hart was of course forced to hire
Tammany contractors on a cost-plus basis in electrifying his line. The
contractors squeezed him dry, putting on the job six thousand Tammany voters of whom "only one man in ten was actually attempting to

---

* The "Bacon" Whitney mentions as an enemy was Charles W. Bacon, attorney for the man
who started the State Trust inquiry. This letter seems to have ended the Whitney-Pulitzer friendship, which had ebbed in any case since Whitney's virtual withdrawal from politics and Pulitzer's
almost complete withdrawal to the Riviera. But as will be seen, Pulitzer's son Ralph was invited to
a Whitney party.

work." One has a picture of Mayor Van Wyck taking his daily orders from Whitney's friend Croker and does not find it impossible to imagine that Croker arranged this for his friend. Hart, badly weakened, sought the aid of James R. Keene who, because of their Wall Street quarrel, now had two aims in life: to beat Whitney's horses on the track and to destroy Whitney in the stock market. Whitney had already bought some ten thousand shares of Standard Gas stock and was suddenly seen as a threat to the Consolidated Gas Company controlled by the Rockefeller group, including Oliver Payne. While Payne had only a minor interest in racing, his identity with Keene's other ambition was total. As one observer saw the battle:

> . . . James R. Keene, who was an implacable foe of Mr. Whitney, acted as one of the generals of the Rockefeller forces. He planned an attack upon the State Trust Company, around which the Whitney . . . forces rallied. Through an attorney charges were brought of improper financial methods having been pursued by the Trust Company. . . . Mr. Whitney was overextended. The Rockefellers controlled the money market. Interest rates were forced skyward. The load of the Whitney faction was growing so heavy that Wall Street expected to hear that it could no longer be carried. At this critical moment J. Pierpont Morgan came to the rescue, borrowing an immense sum in bonds from W. K. Vanderbilt. Mr. Whitney was saved. . . .

He was not only saved—he was enormously enriched in this double coup after a battle that took many weeks and held market observers spellbound. In February 1900 the Whitney group had the satisfaction of seeing the Third Avenue line go into receivership (when they picked it up) and at the same time roundly defeating the Rockefeller group. It was said that Wall Street had seen no such manipulation since the time of Gould and that "hundreds of small investors were ruined." The Whitney who at least twice in his early years had lost all but his very boots in the market was now so irresistible in his attack that he inspired admiring comment from Wall Street watchers who themselves were guessing about his precise maneuvers in traction and other fields. *Town Topics*, which only recently had been so menacing in its mention of the burlesque actress, now hailed him in its market section:

> The "Big Four"—Whitney-Ryan-Widener-Elkins—in Metropolitan executed a masterly coup in their acquisition of control of the Third Avenue, and the transaction parallels the operation by which the same quartet brought the Standard Oil crowd to terms. . . . Mr. Whitney and his

associates are in the game to stay, and the Rockefeller-Rogers-Payne contingent recognize that. . . . Mr. Whitney may lose a race on the track, but he is usually a winner in the stock market.

Had the Saunterer been a winner himself, the recipient of a Whitney peace offering? In any case, the Whitney who sailed with Gunn on the *Majestic* was surely less inclined to bemoan the State Trust scandal than to celebrate the angels who had guided him to the greatest financial triumph of his life and had simultaneously spoiled the sport of Payne and Keene. Metropolitan had beaten all rivals and now controlled every mile of the city's surface rail system. Whitney was more openhanded than ever during the crossing. "I am furnished with everything that money can buy," Gunn recorded. "My cabin on the main deck I find cost Mr. Whitney $500, and is only occupied by millionaires. Yesterday he said to me, 'You may need some money in your pocket' and gave me a $1,000 bill. Shades of Croesus, a $1,000 bill!!!" Gunn in one respect was sad because the Zoar colony, after eighty-three years, was breaking up. The younger generation was bored with its hard labors and simple communal life. It had been decided after much quarreling to divide up the land and other property, sell it, and apportion the proceeds. The great woods had already been sold for $15,000. "I shall not dare to wander in the profaned and mangled woods again," Gunn reflected. ". . . The field opposite my house is filled with implements, wagons, cider tanks, and every kind of rustic gear [waiting to be sold]. . . . Some of the old members move about dazed to see the ancient objects scattered." Although he could continue living in his rented house, the Clodhoppers' Club was disbanding and his way of life was disintegrating. "See that Adolph keeps my garden in perfect order . . . ," Gunn wrote to Ludwig, clinging to what he could.

In London he and Whitney dined with Sir Edward and Lady Colebrook ("very charming people") and paid their usual sartorial devoirs. "Poole is making a lot of clothes and Peal shoes." He admitted that he only had to be "careful not to drink too much." He crossed alone to Paris to see the great Exposition and encountered at Versailles his friends Mark and Mrs. Hanna, the former suffering from rheumatism. "At nearly every corner an orchestra," he wrote on Bastille Day, ". . . and the people dancing in the street. . . . I am beguiled by Mrs. Hanna to dine. . . ." He returned to London, where Whitney had examined the electric traction system and had encountered William K. Vanderbilt, to whom his thanks must have been profuse for Vanderbilt's rumored $10,000,000 loan which had turned the Wall Street tide for Whitney. He also gave thought to his racing establishment. In London he looked up the most famous jockey of the day, the Indiana-born Tod Sloan, who had ridden for the Prince of Wales and others, and found him in sorry shape. He had taken a nasty fall in the Liverpool Cup. "My right ear was almost torn off," Sloan recalled, "and my face so scratched and cut that it looked as if someone had used a currycomb on it." Whitney stared, then laughed and said, "Well, how does the other fellow look?" He had hoped that Sloan would ride the Whitney horse Ballyhoo Bey in the Brooklyn Futurity—America's richest race, made far more important because James Keene's Tommy Atkins was entered. Now Sloan seemed more fit for a hospital bed than a horse. Not at all, the jockey protested. He would ride Ballyhoo Bey and win with him.

Sloan, the magnifico of jockeys, had several servants, stayed at the best hotels, and traveled first class. Whitney gave him $5,000. He sailed the next day, rode Ballyhoo Bey in the Futurity at Sheepshead Bay, brought his horse into the lead in the stretch, and won going away. Whitney and Gunn sailed a few days later on the *Oceanic*, getting home to hear the glad news and in time to watch Ballyhoo Bey, with Sloan again up, run in the Flatbush Stakes. Again Tommy Atkins was entered, along with two other Keene horses. Their jockeys sought to box in Ballyhoo Bey against the rail. Sloan would not be boxed, and Whitney's horse won by a nose.

Two triumphs over the despised Keene! Whitney beamed at Sloan, who was staying at the Waldorf at Whitney's expense. "I'll give you all I have in my pocket," he said. Sloan recalled that "he pulled out a roll of notes and handed $9,000 to me, and then, after a pause, he took out his watch and gave that to me too. 'Now you have all I've got,' he added and shook my hand. What a man!" As for Gunn, he was a beneficiary of Whitney's pleasant custom of placing bets on his horse for his friends. Gunn wrote to Ludwig, "[I] have seven hundred and seventy-five dollars winnings in my pocket; some of it shall surely go into Epernay." To Whitney he wrote, "Always, when I am in touch with you, I have felt, like Antaeus, a new strength. . . . I tremble to think of the possibility of surviving you, which God avert."

4. The Renaissance Palace

I'll furnish a mansion, my latest whim
That will render all squalid the home of him

Who has dared to assert he's a claim to the throne
Which I coppered long since as my special own.

ALTHOUGH THIS lyric also was penned about Senator Clark's new home, it could apply as well to Whitney's and indeed to the whole competitive palace-building mania of the Gilded Age. Whitney's house at 871 Fifth Avenue was at last finished early in 1900, the Saunterer describing the ballroom as "perhaps the most splendid in New York. It is about four times as large as the ballroom in Mrs. Astor's house [she had moved uptown to Fifth and 65th, only three blocks from Whitney], and is quite as gorgeous and spacious as many a room in the most noted of European palaces. . . . When Mr. Whitney shall have emerged completely from his mourning he will probably give a ball in his new palace which will be the most notable that has ever taken place in New York."

"There is one man in the Democratic Party who would make a candidate who could bring out the whole vote, and more," said the hopeful Col. Alexander McClure of Philadelphia. "I mean William C. Whitney of New York. . . . He is one of the most accomplished politicians and statesmen this country has ever produced."

Colonel McClure could have saved his breath. Whitney had truly abandoned the "cheap drudgery" of politics. In 1900, for the first time since the memorable St. Louis convention that nominated Tilden in 1876, he shunned the party's national convention, which of course again nominated Bryan. In October, he was not one of the fourteen prominent Democrats, including three good friends and former Cleveland cabinet members—Charles S. Fairchild, John G. Carlisle, and J. Sterling Morton—who were pictured on front pages as announced supporters of McKinley against Bryan. Why did he not join these friends? Was it because Tammany had succumbed to Bryan, and because Croker and his mayor were soon to fete Bryan in the Hoffman House's Green Room, and because Whitney also had to pocket Bryan in return for Croker's continuing friendship?

Had his thousand-dollar bills and his Epernay corrupted even Alexander Gunn, who might not have investigated his Metropolitan stock as carefully as he should have? Not in the least, for one of Whitney's master strokes was his maintenance—despite his Tammany ties, his tricks with Metropolitan stock, and the State Trust affair—of highest repute, the halo still firm over his head. The Whitney-Gunn friendship was mutually precious. "We have been friends for more than twenty-five years," Gunn wrote to him in November. ". . . you have been my refuge in trouble and my delight in happier hours." Two weeks later he sent Whitney cornmeal such as only the dwindling husbandmen of Zoar could produce and admitted unexpectedly, "My heart is irregular, and the slightest exertion makes me breathless. Perhaps the machine is at last worn out." Whitney entreated him to come to New York. He arrived at the palace to be put in the care of the Whitney physician, Dr. Walter James.

The house had a considerable organ built into the side wall of the ballroom. "Last night, after dinner," Gunn wrote to Ludwig, "came two great musicians—Max Bendix and Hermann Hans Wetzler, the organist; I never heard such music—right here in the house . . . Chopin, Beethoven, Bach, Handel—and they did not leave till midnight."

The mansion was described in the Sunday supplements: "A RENAISSANCE PALACE"—"A Whole Interior made of Works of Art from Italy and France." . . . "Of the original structure, only the shell remains, the whole building having been reconstructed. . . ." "Works of art, antique carvings in wood and marble, tapestry and metal work which had been collected by Mr. Whitney and his agents in Europe have found permanent places in the palatial building. . . ." The entrance was guarded by heavy gates of plate glass set in iron and bronze from the Doria Palace in Rome. Once past that, "one enters the house through an old stone gateway which came from Florence." The ballroom was "brought over in sections from a castle in Bordeaux." *The Tribune* said, "Although the great rooms are hung with rare paintings and draperies, and decorated with massive carvings, there is an absence of the museum or show place effect, and despite its magnificence the Whitney place is a home." But of course it was intended as a showplace and *was* a showplace.

Time would dispute the assertion that these things collected in Europe had found "permanent place" here, since the Palazzo Doria, for example, still stands on the Corso after four centuries, though lacking its original gates, whereas 871 Fifth Avenue was to be torn down in forty-three years. Only a block south, at 858 Fifth, was the palace built by Thomas Fortune Ryan, called an "American Louvre" because of its many paintings—unusual because its side garden was embellished with a circular marble staircase brought from a doge's palace, now used as a trellis for Mrs. Ryan's roses. It was soon, as great houses go, to be replaced by a sixteen-story apartment building, as were Mrs. Astor's and Colonel Payne's and all the rest.

5. *Trouble with the Heart*

THE NINETEENTH century ended at midnight on December 31, 1900. Alexander Gunn, that worshiper of Bacchus, was forbidden by Dr. James to indulge. He also forbade Gunn to attend Whitney's grand twentieth-century housewarming on January 4, 1901, the occasion being the debut of his favorite niece, Helen Tracy Barney. Dorothy Whitney, not quite fourteen, was permitted to stay downstairs until midnight, when the party really began. Though Whitney had had the small gatherings he enjoyed and had been host for a meeting of the trustees of the American Museum of Natural History, this was the official end of his mourning, his first great social event since Edith's death. There were some four hundred guests, greeted in the salon by Whitney, his sister Lilly Whitney Barney, and his niece, dainty in white chiffon. To give hospitable and correct greeting to so many guests, without stumbling over a name, was itself an exhausting duty. It was a late ball, many of the guests arriving after hearing Melba and the de Reszkes sing *Faust* at the opera, others coming from a grand dinner at Col. John Jacob Astor's. The world of *ton* was present, from the forever queenly Mrs. Astor (almost seventy and now being challenged for leadership by Mrs. Hermann Oelrichs, Mrs. O. H. P. Belmont, and even that upstart Mrs. Cornelius Vanderbilt, Jr.) to Twomblys, Jays, Fishes, Reids, and that diverting young fellow who had recently taken Society by storm and surely made Ward McAllister writhe in his grave, Harry Lehr.

Lehr had married Elizabeth Drexel and informed her instantly that he had no interest in her—only her money. One of his capers had been to give a dinner for his friends' dogs. The Saunterer had been pitiless in his ridicule of Lehr's homosexuality, his "nauseous female impersonations," his "growing tendency to have himself photographed in petticoats. . . ." "Lehr's proud parade of his 'sissy' qualities has gone beyond the limit of tolerance." The Saunterer declared, "As Portia says of Monsieur Le Bon, 'God made him and therefore let him pass for a man.' " Homosexuality was a subject about which many Society women were ignorant, and they missed the point when the Saunterer wrote, "The full-page colored picture of Mr. Lehr in his feminine ballet costume, published last Sunday, is . . . an excellent likeness, and shows that he makes quite a pretty fairy when dressed in female apparel." Yet the malice was obvious to everybody, and the libel clear to the knowing.

Young Ralph Pulitzer, twenty-one years old, was one of Whitney's
guests, escaping blame for his father's sins. Mrs. Stanford White was in
white satin, her husband an honored guest accepting compliments for
his work, having previously spent untold millions on houses for Astors
and Vanderbilts, the Whitelaw Reids, the Choates, the Goelets, and
others (most of them here tonight), and having designed the Metropolitan, Players', and Century clubs in addition to several churches and his
largest achievement, Madison Square Garden, also to be the scene of
his murder. There was gossip about his wicked use of showgirls in the
private parties he gave in his suite in the Garden tower.

The Whitney palace was large enough so that Gunn, in a distant bedroom, could sleep undisturbed on an eighteenth-century bed. The cotillion did not begin until midnight: "One of the most original figures
was 'The Hunt,' in which three papier mâché and wooden horses,
named after Mr. Whitney's racers, Ballyhoo Bey, Prince Charles and
Kilmarnock, pranced into the room ridden by small jockeys wearing the
light blue and chocolate brown colors of the Whitney stable." The
jockeys distributed the favors—expensive hunting crops for the men,
tied with the Whitney colors, and Liberty satin jeweled sashes for the
women. Social rivalry extended even to favors, and these gifts, though
costly, were exceeded at other gatherings by such things as millinery
boxes containing smart Paris hats for the women, gold cigarette cases for
the men, and even precious jewelry. But the Whitney ball, said the forgiving *World*, was "UNPARALLELED IN SPLENDOR," "Likely to
Go Down in Social History as New York's Finest Private Function";
"William C. Whitney eclipsed himself last night. . . . Not a detail was
left untouched; nothing that money could buy or taste suggest was
spared to make a perfect entertainment for the six hundred [sic] guests
bidden."

By January 8 Gunn was well enough to accompany Whitney to the
opera to hear Jean de Reszke in *Aida*, then to go with him to Aiken for
a month, during which a Whitney representative paid $60,000 for the
famous Hamburg. Hamburg was the five-year-old son of Hanover and
the mighty Hindoo, who Whitney was sure would sire winners for him.
It was the second-highest price ever paid for a horse at public auction in
this country. Next, Whitney leased from Hal P. Headley the LaBelle
farm near Lexington, Kentucky, for the use of his horses, and bought
Van Dyck's portrait of Viscount Grandison for his music room. Although never notable for his charities, he gave $25,000 to the bicenten-
nial fund at Yale, that institution over which he and Flora had quar-

reled so bitterly.* Gunn, whose Aiken sojourn was spent in easy chairs and cautious walks, attended by a doctor and a servant, returned with Whitney to New York and was found well enough to make a last trip to a favorite city where he had many friends, San Francisco. He left with a physician at his elbow, paid and admonished by Whitney, and stayed at that great caravansary, the Palace Hotel. He was cheered by a stream of telegrams from Whitney, who at that time was making arrangements to win that most famous of all horse races, the English Derby.

Just as one way to build a street railway is to consult the needs of the public and fulfill them, and an approved way to acquire a great ancestral home is to inherit it from ancestors, so the usual way to develop a contender for the Derby was to bring a blooded horse along from infancy, training its every hoofbeat until it reached the required three-year age. Whitney did it by leasing the heavy favorite ten weeks before the race. But this was excusable, for chance had played into his hands. In England he had been a good friend of Lord William Beresford, a member of the English Jockey Club who had leased the colt Volodyovsky from his owner, Lady Meux, and raced him with great success as a two year old. Beresford, looking forward to the achievement of his ambition to win the Derby, died suddenly, and Volodyovsky's ownership reverted to Lady Meux. Harry Payne Whitney was in England at the time, looking after his father's racing interests, and apparently it was he who closed the deal after getting Whitney's urgent cable. Outbidding Sir Thomas Lipton, Whitney leased Volodyovsky, along with his stable mate Petronius, from Lady Meux for 5,000 guineas and half their winnings, Whitney to pay all expenses.

"I have your most kind telegram," Gunn wrote him. ". . . Dr. James has written me two letters in the kindest way, more like my friend than my physician. . . . I shudder when I think how much I have spent. . . . We leave for home tonight. . . . The trouble with the heart is nothing compared with at first . . . What can I say to you . . . most faithful friend." By mid-April Gunn was back at Zoar—now a semiabandoned place but with his friend Ludwig Zimmermann still nearby—fussing over his roses, now numbering 174 varieties, and planning his vegetable garden. Again he was seized by heart tremors. He fled to New York, writing to Ludwig, "Mr. W. and the doctor met me at the train, and I was taken to Mr. W.'s house with the utmost kindness and attention."

---

* In 1888, Yale had given him the honorary degree of Doctor of Laws.

Payne Whitney, who had studied law at Harvard, a few days later was admitted to the New York bar in a ceremony his father did not attend. It was as if Whitney lavished on Gunn the love he could no longer offer to Edith, Payne, or Pauline. His affection and sentiment had always been deep. He had been torn by the loss of Flora, then Edith; he was punctilious in his attentions to his aged mother, still in Brookline, and in Gunn he had found that paragon, the friend of intellectual affinity who admired and never criticized, the friend totally divorced from Whitney's business dealings, the friend tied to him by mutual memories and before whom he could drop the wariness of the maker of deals and be himself.

"I am surrounded by incredible luxury and no one could be treated more tenderly," Gunn noted. But he did not improve. Sensing the approach of death, he spoke of returning to Ohio, wanting to be buried at Zoar: "I think I should leave for home by Saturday next." Whitney urged instead, as he had for months, that he go to Bad Nauheim, of course at Whitney's expense. Gunn sailed on the *Deutschland* May 22. The Nauheim specialists found him in such serious condition that he could not take the baths and had to limit even his letter writing. "I must make a better showing for you than this," he wrote to Whitney. By coincidence, Pauline Whitney Paget, beginning a siege of illness that was to cut her life short, arrived at Nauheim a week after Gunn. She had two young daughters, Olive and Dorothy, whom her father was evidently seldom permitted to see. "Pauline has . . . sent me a most kind note," Gunn wrote to Whitney, "but the doctor has forbidden her to see me, for fear it may stir me up."

This Gunn letter was written shortly after Volodyovsky won the Derby on June 5 in a field of twenty-four starters and in the record time of two minutes, 40.8 seconds, with Lester Reiff up. The only other American whose horse had won the Derby was Pierre Lorillard, who won it with Iroquois in 1881, that horse having been foaled and raised in America. Whitney's triumph, far beyond mere sports page newsworthiness, made the front pages of even the most sedate New York newspapers. "I was rather confident of winning," he admitted. Harry, who watched the race, said, "The only disappointment is owing to my father not being here." Harry was congratulated by Croker, who never missed a Derby any more than he missed an election he was sure to win. In New York, Whitney credited Volodyovsky's trainer and telegraphed a message to Sheepshead Park that gladdened the hearts of all the sports there: free drinks for all comers, with Whitney paying the tab.

Indeed, Whitney's ship was coming in, in racing as it had on Wall Street. At the Ascot races immediately following, his Water Shed won the first race, his Kilmarnock II won the Alexandra Plate, his filly Elizabeth M won the King's Stakes, and his filly Mount Vernon won the Windsor Castle Stakes, all four ridden by the same miraculous Lester Reiff.

But Alexander Gunn's ship was departing. Never orthodox in religion or much else, condemned to inactivity at Nauheim, he could reflect over his own implausible career—his tragic romance, his withdrawal to Zoar, and for more than two decades his shuttling between the bucolic simplicities of the Ohio retreat and the grandeur and excitement—and the Epernay—of his visits with the Whitneys. His diary, meant only for his own eyes, made it plain that not once had he entertained suspicions of evil about Whitney. "Pauline came to see me," he wrote to Whitney; "she is looking very well indeed." It was his last letter. He died in mid-June, having assured Whitney, "your kindness surrounds me like a blessing."

6. Indomitable

AT SIXTY, Whitney could look back on both success and failure. He had let his reading slip, a sacrifice to money getting. His art collection was one of those referred to as "magnificent" by the newspapers, and his small Raphael (valued at $250,000) and works by Joshua Reynolds, Millet, Van Dyck, and Hoppner could not be disdained, backed as they were by a considerable collection of tapestries. But his love of politics and then horses had subtracted from his attention to the fine arts. Many of his paintings were of ephemeral fame. The wholesale raids on European art by American millionaires had resulted in helter-skelter amassments in which luck was a large factor. Whitney had given money for art, but not enough of his time and love, so that Widener far surpassed him. Even Yerkes had a more valuable collection, and Morgan of course outspent and dwarfed them all. Whitney truly loved music and retained his choice box at the Metropolitan, which he shared with great generosity, Lady and Sir Edward Colebrook always joining him in it when they visited him. He was not one of those dilettantes who arrived for the second act.

The loss of two wives—the terrible tragedy of Edith alone—would have brought bitterness and reclusion to some men. Added to this was the quarrel with Oliver Payne and the breakup of Whitney's own family. Now the death of Gunn, the friend so rare as to seem almost a visitant from outer space, had added its last touch of desolation.

In the light of all this, Whitney's crowning achievement was his indomitability. Tragedy laid him low, sorrow racked him, but he was flexible, he rebounded. He remained the glass of fashion, the man of charm, indefatigable in his cultivation of horseflesh, all the more fascinating because of his faint but unmistakable aura of mystery and the unanswered question of what he did with whatever spare evenings he had. True, it had to be admitted that after 1890 when (except for his herculean achievement for Cleveland in 1892) he had thrust aside patriotic, and even to some extent social, endeavor in his almost grim pursuit of money, some of his easy buoyancy had gone. His youngest sister Lilly and her husband Barney remained dear friends. His sister Susan and her husband Dimock—Whitney's classmate and first law partner— he saw less often, as was the case with William Graham Sumner. Yet the warmth of his personality—especially when measured against the somewhat menacing frigidity of a Morgan—was nothing less than a joy that friends later sought to analyze without entire success. He possessed *joie de vivre*, and he spread it. But to many outsiders he was best known as the owner of great horses and great houses. Henry Adams tried to encompass Whitney in one sweeping sentence, writing that "after having gratified every ambition and swung the country almost at will . . . [he] had thrown away the usual objects of political ambition like the ashes of smoked cigarettes; had turned to other amusements, satiated every taste, gorged every appetite, won every object that New York afforded, and not yet satisfied, had carried his field of activity abroad, until New York no longer knew what most to envy, his horses or his houses." He had expensive buildings on eight different properties, requiring an enormous staff of caretakers and maintenance people. They were, in addition to the two most lavish—the Fifth Avenue and Westbury places:

  • The Sheepshead Bay house with training stables, a private racetrack, and 67 acres of land.
  • The Aiken place with outbuildings, training stables, a racetrack, and 2,000 acres of land.
  • The Adirondack property of 70,000 acres of timber and 52 lakes on which he had built a baronial lodge and a golf course at Blue Mountain Lake, plus scattered buildings and a small railroad.
  • The leased LaBelle farm in Kentucky.
  • A small farm at Stony Ford, New York, used as an auxiliary to the Kentucky horse farm.

• The Lenox cottage in Massachusetts and 11,000 acres including the October Mountain preserve, cottage, and outbuildings.

He had the land acquisitiveness of his forebears in England, where land ownership and the upper class had been indivisible for centuries. Many Americans had more millions than he, but none as many acres and homes. He owned more land in the states of New York and Massachusetts than anyone except the commonwealths themselves. It took thirteen miles of fence to enclose his Massachusetts property. He owned two-thirds of the land in huge Washington Township in that state, where he had opened up many miles of private roads and was taxed on thirty buildings, fifty goats, twenty-five buffalo, fifteen horses, two cows, thirty sheep, and other animals and birds. His payment of taxes had brought the township out of debt, permitted the building of roads and schools, and made its people so grateful that the selectmen voted to remove the head of George Washington from the town seal and replace it with Whitney's. Whitney, though delighted by the gesture, declined with thanks. Washington, he said, was good enough.

7. Specimens of Fair Women

PERHAPS CONCLUDING at last that he had enough houses, Whitney turned his energies to the rehabilitation of Saratoga Springs, a town he well knew as a favorite site for state political conventions, a place where politicians could enjoy genteel illegality. This town of about 8,000 people, with many curative springs, slept soundly nine months of the year but came half awake in summer when vacationers enjoyed its waters and its coolness. In the month of August it came to frenzied life, invaded by 20,000 strangers extravagant in dress and expenditure. These were the horse people. The racing season made the month of August exciting for twenty-four hours of each of its days. It had been necessary to build extra sidetracks at the station to accommodate the many private railroad cars of wealthy racetrack patrons. Tiffany's and other smart New York stores had branches there for the season; brokers, too, with stock tickers handy. The hotels were fabulous.

Whether it was the air, the waters, or the liquors there, even true stories about Saratoga seemed inflated. Pierre Lorillard, Percival Hill, and William K. Vanderbilt gambled there with friends for three successive days and nights, taking time out only for Turkish baths. Lillian

Russell, fresh from her triumph at Weber and Fields's Music Hall, rode down Saratoga's Broadway with Diamond Jim Brady in a bicycle built for two—gold-plated. Brady himself owned more than 20,000 diamonds and 6,000 other precious stones. "Each day of the month a different set of gems was distributed over his person, flashing from collar buttons, shirt studs, necktie pin and necktie clasp, scarf pin, cuff links, belt buckle, watch-chain, and watch . . . (even his underwear buttons were bejewelled)." Harry Payne Whitney lost $125,000 to Charles Clark on one private horse wager. Victor Herbert received a handsome salary for directing the Grand Union Hotel's fifty-four-piece orchestra and lost so steadily on the horses that he was chronically broke—but here he was to write *Mlle. Modiste* with the song "Kiss Me Again" that bathed the nation in a mist of romance. E. Berry Wall, the amiably idle heir to a cordage fortune who treasured his title as Society's champion dude, enlivened one Saratoga day—and exhausted himself and two valets—by appearing on Broadway (the town's main street) between dawn and sundown in forty different changes of attire including shoes and canes. The rivalry for social supremacy between the vast Grand Union Hotel and the even bigger United States Hotel was so bitter that headwaiters from the two places had once sought to kill each other. If Newport was the home of stone and marble, Saratoga sang of mighty frame buildings whose construction had laid waste to great forests. The United States Hotel measured a quarter mile in length, enclosed a three-acre park, contained a half-acre ballroom, and had verandas so extensive, containing a thousand wicker chairs, that one lady guest in 1896 (it was said with every evidence of sincerity) had lost her way there for three hours before finding the route back to her room.

The fact that Whitney took one of the United States's separate cottages indicated that the hotel's social rating was approved. In the 1890s the spa had deteriorated, becoming in August the resort of more and more tinhorn gamblers, crooks, and prostitutes. Pulitzer had sent the reporter Nellie Bly, famous for her circumnavigation of the globe in seventy-two days, to Saratoga to write an exposé headed "OUR WICKEDEST SUMMER RESORT," which told of "Vice and Crime, Dissipation and Profligacy at This Once Most Respected Watering-Place." Hence the town's leaders were overjoyed when Whitney invested heavily there and announced his interest in Saratoga's improvement. The racetrack was controlled by Gottfried Walbaum, a disreputable gambler said to have gotten his start as a brothel keeper in New York. Whitney of course had no prejudice against gambling, feeling only that it should be conducted in good taste and elegant surroundings. He formed a syndicate, bought the racetrack from Walbaum, and added to his multitudinous memberships by becoming president of the powerful Saratoga Association for the Improvement of the Breed of Horses, known simply as the Saratoga Racing Association.

He had recently paid $75,000 for Nasturtium, the pick of the 1901 crop—the highest price ever paid for a two year old in any country. He had had two winners at Newmarket in England. He was so newsworthy that *The Tribune* made a story of it when he was seen to put two twenty-dollar bills in a Salvation Army tambourine on Saratoga's Broadway. Such was his prestige, this man of vigor and charm, this leader in business and Society who could still win the Futurity and the Derby, that he became virtually the instant king of Saratoga. As one historian saw it, the village authorities were so impressed by his "position in society and politics" that his "request" became "the equivalent of a command." He was just the man to restore to the spa its sheen of refinement without removing the vital element of pleasant wickedness.

The town was full of gambling places operating contrary to state law, indeed so openly that gaming at one of them was pictured in *Leslie's Illustrated Weekly*. By Whitney's request, the shabby ones were closed and the fashionable ones encouraged. By far the most fashionable was Richard A. Canfield's Casino—a handsome building set back among elms and edged by an Italian garden with fountains and statuary. Its interior included a splendid restaurant, more expensive than Delmonico's in New York, and, upstairs, great gaming rooms. For the five-week season Canfield employed the French chef Jean Columbin at $5,000, as well as fifty skilled New York waiters whose tips averaged $50 a day. The Casino was not for native Saratogans, who were excluded almost automatically by the prices charged in the restaurant and who were banned absolutely from the gambling rooms. It was for the moguls of New York, Boston, and Philadelphia. The legends of gargantuan betting at Canfield's have probably lost nothing in the retelling. It was said that William K. Vanderbilt lost $130,000 at roulette in a few minutes. It was said that "Bet-a-Million" John Warne Gates, after losing $400,000 on the horses in the afternoon, lost $150,000 more at faro, coaxed Canfield to double the limit, saw his luck change, came out more than $100,000 ahead in gaming by dawn, and was pleased to have cut his track losses, ready for another sporting day. Never mind—the documented extravagance of gentlemen of this class in other pursuits suggests that the truth may not have been badly punished.

Canfield, whom Whitney probably already knew and with whom he was immediately on the friendliest terms, was forty-six in 1901, heavy enough to wear a corset, loose-jowled, his dark hair parted in the middle over eyes that were amiable unless one was careless about gambling debts. He had been a professional gambler since he won $20,000 at faro at twenty-one, and he had served a short prison term in Rhode Island for sponsoring games of chance. His gambling places (he also had one in New York City and one in Newport) were beautifully appointed and said to be strictly honest. He was genteel, always dressed for dinner, was fascinating in conversation and a fancier of art, already having a fine collection of Whistlers. He "gave generously to Saratoga churches, hospitals, and charitable institutions" and was accepted as a local asset. Heady liquors mingling with choicest foods made his restaurant a place where gossip among and about the Four Hundred was so exciting that Mrs. Theresa Dean, who wrote a column for *Town Topics* signed "The Widow," spent much of the season there on the qui vive, sometimes dining with Canfield. She was a woman of conversational pyrotechnics, also known to Whitney, whose treatment by that publication was still admiring.

Whitney, who at times watched his son Harry and others gamble, apparently did not gamble himself except at the track. There, legend says, he made a characteristic gesture when his horse Goldsmith was to run in the first Saratoga Special. He said to a young bookmaker, John Walters, "Johnny, find out how many guests are staying at my place. Then get a list of all the servants, maids, waiters, barbers, clerks, everybody who has been of service to me or my guests at the hotel. Then, Johnny, bet one hundred dollars for each of them on Goldsmith and charge it to my account."

The bets for thirty-eight guests and their attendants came to about $12,000. Goldsmith won at six to one. Whitney said to Walters: "Put it in envelopes marked with my initials and leave it for each one of them."

This kind of thing made one Saratoga chronicler write of him, "There was a great Napoleonic sweep to his conquests and a quality of magic about him. . . . He was a genuine reincarnation of a Renaissance Prince. . . . Under Whitney's Midas touch, the Saratoga racetrack entered upon its most brilliant phase." Whitney was so delighted with Saratoga that he began improvements on the track, bought land nearby, and decided to end his European racing despite a new thrill—his Kilmarnock II won the $20,000 Prix au Conseil Municipal at Longchamps. "The sending of our best horses abroad depreciates the quality of the sport at home," he said. He left the £6,000 he won in the Derby stake for a benevolent British racing fund named for Lord Beresford and began selling off his racers at Newmarket.

The State National Bank affair had blown over and he had again become an object of journalistic veneration until, in the fall of 1901, he made what seemed the mistake of a Machiavellian too sure of himself. On October 22 the Croker-bossed Van Wyck administration granted the Elm Street traction franchise to the Metropolitan. On the very next day, October 23, Whitney came out for the Tammany candidate for mayor, Edward M. Shepard, saying, "No one, in my opinion, could read Mr. Shepard's Tammany Hall speech and avoid the conviction that a man of rare capacity and breadth of view had risen to claim public attention. It will be hailed all over the country . . . by the Democrats as marking the advent of a man capable of the highest order of political leadership."

Although Shepard was rated as "good Tammany," New York City was once more in a reformist mood after four sorry years under Van Wyck. Seth Low, that sworn enemy of give-away franchises, was the strongest opposing candidate. Ex-Congressman John DeWitt Warner was one of those who sounded the battle cry against the Whitney-Tammany entente. William Travers Jerome, reformist candidate for district attorney, picked up the theme, noting Whitney and Ryan's status as Croker's chief financial backers. He pledged to hunt down wrongdoers "even if their tracks lead straight to the offices of the Metropolitan. . . . No one knows better than I do that when I am attacking the Metropolitan Street Railway Company I am arraying myself against the most dangerous, the most vindictive and the most powerful influences at work in this community." In speech after speech he raked Whitney as he had never before in his life been raked: "Is it any wonder that William C. Whitney supports Mr. Shepard for Mayor when the platform on which Seth Low is running . . . [favors] public ownership of franchises? . . . Everyone who knows Mr. Whitney knows that it is a case of fight dog, fight cat with him when his interests are touched. . . ." Jerome characterized Whitney as a man who "debauches the Legislature and the City Council." He hinted at Whitney's alleged role in the nomination of Tracy and defeat of Low in 1897, saying that $100,000 had changed hands in that transaction. He called the State Trust loan to Shea "criminal." Whitney, he said, was the man "whose railroad has stolen from the people . . . $80,000,000 worth of franchises," and he made the sweeping if metaphorically confusing charge that "that man William C. Whitney has done more to corrupt public life in the United States than any other man that breathes on the face of God's footstool today." The Metropolitan had thousands of workers, Jerome added, and the company had "issued positive orders to its employees to vote against Jerome."

Both the anti-Whitney Low and the anti-Whitney Jerome were elected. Croker was overthrown at last. What did it portend for Whitney? He seemed not to worry. He had always been a subject of rumor, and indeed the most intense speculation about him now was whether he would remarry. Perhaps he knew that despite the attacks he was still— always—the possessor of a great, magical endowment of popularity that he could awaken simply by waving his wand. As vice-president of the 1901 Horse Show (Gordon Fellowes, its president, went almost unmentioned) he met with the association at the Madison Square Garden restaurant. When coffee and cigars were reached, Lander's Orchestra* struck up "The Red, White and Blue":

> All the guests rose to their feet. Then Mr. Whitney, at the head of the table, began to beat time with his long arms. He joined lustily in the chorus, and soon two hundred male voices, led by the former Secretary of the Navy, had set the festooned building all aflutter with the rattling refrain:

> > *"The Army and Navy forever,*
> > *Three cheers for the Red, White and Blue!"*

So easily did public admiration come to him. There were cheers for Whitney and cries for a speech, to which he responded with graceful nothings ("This is an unexpected call. . . . I am heartily glad, as I always am, to have this occasion come round again. . . ."). He was at the Garden daily for the show and, the Saunterer observed, "has been filling his box at the Show with specimens of fair women. Each day and evening the company was different. . . ." The most striking of them was that glamorous subject of international gossip, the Hon. Mrs. George Keppel: "Mrs. Keppel, who has been seen two or three times in Mr. Whitney's box, looked more statuesque and handsomer than ever. The gowns and furs of this 'More than Queen,' as she is now called, were superb, and she and Mr. Whitney were nearly mobbed by the curious crowd when they left the Garden on Thursday night." She had

---

* Lander's Orchestra had years earlier been given Society's imprimatur by Mrs. Astor and Ward McAllister and had played the "Dead March" from *Saul* at the latter's funeral at Grace Church in 1895.

come to America with her husband and the latter's elder brother, the Earl of Albemarle, as the guests of Sir Thomas Lipton to see the international yacht races, and her husband was taken ill in New York. She was also a guest at one of Whitney's series of informal Sunday "music dinners" at 871 at which he had no more than about forty guests. His November 17 gathering was for the purpose of "enabling people to meet the Hon. Mrs. George Keppel" and the Earl. Since 1898 Mrs. Keppel had been the favored, though not the only, mistress of the Prince of Wales (now king since January 1901), and she would remain so until his death. Her husband made no complaint about his unenviable status and seemed to regard his own abnegation as a patriotic duty. Whitney, who had met the prince and Mrs. Keppel in England (and to his credit said nothing about it to the papers), had other connections with Mrs. Keppel. She was a friend of Moreton Frewen; but closest of all were Capt. (now Col.) and Mrs. Arthur Paget, the former being Edward's closest aide and his bookmaker and the brother-in-law of Whitney's daughter Pauline. Mrs. Keppel, because of her great tact and taste, was described as "the most perfect mistress in history." She took her post seriously. She had been accepted by Edward's consort, now Queen Alexandra, she vacationed annually with Edward at Biarritz, was a welcomed guest at Sandringham, was popular among the British, and won special acclaim in France, "where the powers of a wise mistress had always been regarded with respect."

It was an interesting American foible that Society should glorify Mrs. Keppel for virtually public institutionalization of the conduct for which it had condemned Grover Cleveland and Maria Halpin to the abyss, although the latter two had sought privacy and their affair was brief. New York Society was undemocratic not only in accepting in royalty what was regarded as vulgar and sinful in the commonalty but in investing it with honor and romance, calling the lady in this instance "More than Queen." It also reflected a relaxation in the mores of Whitney, who had once cautioned Flora against "discussing the Henry Ward Beecher case with men." Indeed, one of Edward's earlier mistresses, Lilly Langtry, had been in New York in 1900 and had been well received by Society, including Mrs. Astor, even though she lacked Mrs. Keppel's elegance and had become an actress to boot—a profession still felt by many to be beyond the pale. It was now a social tenstrike in the eyes of the more sophisticated for Whitney to invite his special friends to meet Mrs. Keppel. Among his guests were Mrs. Astor—still the mother superior of Society despite her widowhood—the August Belmonts, the W. H. Douglases, the Edmund Baylieses, the soprano Milka Ternina of the Metropolitan Opera, that old Tammany warhorse but charming personality Bourke Cockran, and the fascinating Mrs. Burke Roche.

While the most beautiful woman present was necessarily Mrs. Keppel, who had turquoise eyes and a voluptuous figure at thirty-one, Mrs. Burke Roche was a strong second although ten years older and looking much too young to have a grown daughter and twin sons. She was soon to be described in *The Ultra-Fashionable Peerage of America*, a latter-day rating of social prestige, as "one of the classical and aristocratic beauties" and "the smartest horsewoman in the United States." She was a regular at Newport, a lover of Paris, and a student of Delsarte. Surely two such enthusiastic riders as she and Whitney must have ridden together—perhaps in Central Park, just across Fifth Avenue from 871. Born Frances Work, daughter of the wealthy banker Frank Work, she had married James Boothby Burke Roche, son of Baron Fermoy of Dublin. Burke Roche, another friend of Frewen's and similarly adventurous, was for a time a rancher in the West, a gold miner in Alaska, and a revolutionist in South America. He was in fact so seldom at home that in 1891 she had secured a divorce from him in Delaware, which he established as legally invalid in Great Britain, though this hardly seemed to pose a problem for Whitney if he was seriously interested in her.

Visitors could count on Whitney's taste in music, cultivated now for many years—not necessarily true of all Fifth Avenue organ owners. Henry Clay Frick, for example, was soon to build a palace two blocks up the avenue where he would lean back in deepest content as his organist rendered "Dearie, my Dearie, nothing's worth while but dreams of you." After the Whitney dinner came organ music by the renowned Hans Wetzler and piano music by Josef Hofmann, who had made his American debut at the Metropolitan in 1887 as a prodigy of eleven and was still only twenty-five.

8. *"Superb . . . Glittering . . . Spectacular"*

WHITNEY'S "MUSIC DINNERS" were the most fashionable small gatherings of their kind that winter, the envy of those uninvited, prized by true music lovers who enjoyed at one of them four musical artists including Paderewski and Kreisler. It was, said *The Tribune*, the first private engagement Paderewski had ever accepted—incorrectly, for the great Pole had played for a Whitney mass gathering in 1891. But the greatest social event of this year, 1901, was even now in Whitney's fertile brain and took place just a month later. This was the debut of his stepdaughter Adelaide, an event that he invested with unique importance. He had built 871 for Edith (if one put aside the ducal leanings of his own). He had gone over plans times innumerable with Stanford White, he had tramped endlessly through the place over gritty floors as the work progressed, seeking the ultimate in grandeur, all for Edith. She had died too soon, had never seen it. Now Adelaide, at eighteen, was so nearly the image of her mother that it could not fail to mix pain with his pride in her. One observer described her lyrically as "a tall brunette with dark eyes and a complexion like roses and cream," a description as apt for Edith. If Whitney could give Adelaide the greatest of parties in the greatest of New York palaces, it might in some measure balance the scales that had so terribly cheated Edith and himself.

"Mr. William C. Whitney is to give a ball for his stepdaughter," the Saunterer wrote. "It will be in no way inferior to the ball of last winter. . . . Already there is talk of superb favors and a general elegance that makes an invitation much to be desired."

The party was fashionably late. It was almost midnight on December 17 when guests began arriving in throngs, a substantial minority in motorcars, utterly choking Fifth Avenue, liveried footmen coming out from under wide awnings blazing with electric lights to aid them. *The World* seemed intent on repaying Whitney for earlier unkindnesses:

> The great mansion . . . was never more superbly arranged for guests. They found fairyland awaiting them. Two floors were thrown open and every inch of them bloomed with greens and flowers, pink, purple, red, white, yellow. . . . Mr. Whitney's house is cunningly arranged—not a guest has to show himself in the hallway till wraps . . . are laid aside and he is ready for the ballroom. . . . Mr. Whitney received his guests with the fair debutante at his elbow. . . . She was in simple white tulle over white silk, with a bouquet of lilies of the valley. [The various rooms were decorated with flowers ranging from begonias to azaleas, but with American Beauty roses in the ballroom.] Perhaps 5,000 in all were used. They were massed in the corners and set in great torches holding 100 blooms each, covering the walls. . . . Rows of gilt chairs encircled the beautiful room, with its wooden walls of carved and gilded oak taken from a French castle 200 years old. Up in the [gallery] Lander's Orchestra sat. There were relays of musicians so that never for a moment did waltz or two-step cease. Out in the hall was Karel Kapossy's Royal Red Hungarian band, all brave in scarlet and gold coats and black breeches, to play for supper and the promenade. . . . Everywhere hung tapestries. . . . They warmed up the marble walls and gave all the art lovers there food for

thought and admiration. Over the balcony in the ballroom hung another priceless piece, a great velvet banner blazoned with the imperial arms of France.

By 12:30 there were 550 people present—almost enough to delight the shade of Flora Payne Whitney. Informal dancing preceded the first supper—"supremes, terrapin, canvasback, salads rillettes, galantines, game, bonbons . . . and wines of the rarest vintage"—after which the cotillion began, with two leading couples instead of one. Roman Baldwin danced with Miss Randolph, who assuredly had perfected her steps for this great event in her life, and Craig Wadsworth with Gertrude Vanderbilt Whitney. Gertrude had worn sober clothing and desisted from frolic during the two years and three months since her father had died. This was her reentry into Society, as it was for the rest of the Vanderbilt children, though Mrs. Vanderbilt was to continue in weeds perpetually. The surprise of the evening came as the orchestra executed a ruffle and flourish as the signal for the "automobile figure" of the cotillion and "a huge, flower-decked automobile equipped with headlights and chauffeur and loaded with flowers" rolled into the room, carrying the favors for that figure—miniature automobiles for the women, satin automobile caps for the men. (The arrival of the automobile, certainly the first time such a thing had occurred inside a private house, brought a chorus of "Oh's!" said *The World*.) Other favors were up to the Whitney standard and included large puffed satin beaded bags and sachet muffs for the women, and horsehead-shaped cigar cutters and hunting horns for the men.

Still blazing with jewels, Mrs. Astor—Whitney long since had become a favorite of hers—of course headed the guest list. The cream of Society was there, but there were a few surprises: the John D. Rockefeller, Jrs., were present, though the senior Rockefeller had never achieved (nor perhaps sought) this echelon of Society. Charles Dana Gibson was listed as being there with his beautiful wife, the former Irene Langhorne of Virginia. Was Gibson, the great satirist of this kind of extravagance, getting material for his pen?

And—Payne Whitney was listed as being present.

But that did not prove that Payne really was there. With 550 guests invited it was impossible to establish those few who did not come, and the newspapers were simply given the guest list. It did prove either that Payne had been invited or that his father had wished to give the impression that he was invited. The two sides in the feud still agreed on one point—that it should not be publicized.

Dorothy Whitney, still too young for the party, was condemned to listen from upstairs. Her duenna, Beatrice Bend, was among the dancers, as were several young men later to become important in her life, and also Mary Harriman, the striking daughter of that railroad carnivore E. H. Harriman, whose historic battle with J. P. Morgan for control of Northern Pacific stock had thrown Wall Street into panic and had only recently been settled. Mary indeed was to have a special importance to Dorothy.

And Ralph Pulitzer was again listed as present, although Whitney had virtually sworn to take vengeance on Ralph's father. Pulitzer's *World*, which in 1885 had said that a bottle of Jay Gould's choice wine cost more than a Gould workman could spend for food for his family in two weeks, did not speculate on how many regiments of workmen could have subsisted on the small fortune Whitney had spent on this one party. Sherry's catered the affair in the grandest manner possible. The second supper was served at 4:00 A.M. It was like magic, said *The World*, the way buffet tables appeared. "They had all been set and spread and decorated with American Beauties upstairs. Then the 100 waiters whisked them downstairs and put them everywhere—in ballroom, dining-room, library, hall." "SUPERB BALL FOR MISS RANDOLPH," *The Herald* headlined. ". . . one of the largest and most brilliant of the season," said *The Tribune*. "The great function which William C. Whitney gave last year for his niece . . . was overshadowed by the superb ball given last night for his stepdaughter. . . ." "Entertainments given by Mr. William C. Whitney are always out of the ordinary," said the Saunterer. "[This] was no exception. . . ." "Glittering," said *The Sun*. "Spectacular," said *The Times*.

It was past 5:00 A.M. when the last guests said good night and ended the ritual, which *The Times* described correctly. A spectacle it was indeed for 550 guests and 100 waiters and many other assorted servants, and Whitney's reputation as a showman was enhanced. The smart young lawyer Lispenard Stewart later said that he went to such entertainments to be amused, "but it takes money to amuse me, and that is why I always enjoyed going to Mr. William C. Whitney's house. . . ." But this was the last great Whitney party, perhaps pardonable for sentimental reasons if it left the debutante Adelaide feeling better off than most orphans.

9. *Getting Clear*

SINCE THE Metropolitan Railroad's enormous profits—so largely entre-preneurial—depended absolutely on a complaisant city government, the joyride was over with Croker's defeat. Whitney began to extricate himself even before the reform regime took office. The millions the Whitney group had drained from their enterprise over the years had left it dependent on new investors coming in.

Through the years it had been the practice of his syndicate to recapitalize (with added water) whenever a new line was brought in, and to sell stock to the public at top prices before still another surface line was taken over and the process began once more. This was what Widener called "setting the table over again." Extra millions were made by watering the construction accounts as well. For example, when the syndicate built a surface line on Lexington Avenue, it cost them at the outside $2,500,000, yet they turned it over to the Metropolitan for $10,000,000. A horsecar line running for one-third of a mile on Fulton Street, owning ten rickety cars and thirty horses and losing money steadily, cost them no more than $15,000, yet they sold a million in stock in it. They did even better with the Elm Street line, which was capitalized and stock in it sold although no tracks were ever laid there. Since the syndicate now owned or leased lines running far into New Jersey and northward into New England, the profits were enormous but not subject to exact computation. A later commentator said of Whitney, Ryan, Widener, and Elkins, "In the decade from 1893 to 1902 the syndicate played upon the Metropolitan Street Railway Company as upon a stringed instrument. They watered its stock, speculated in it, cornered it, and dumped it. Profits to the four men were at least one hundred million dollars."*

Now, the Metropolitan was not yet bankrupt only because its innocent stockholders still had faith in it. The moment they lost credence and sold in any numbers, the whole water-soaked structure would collapse. The problem was to beguile the stockholders as long as possible and make sure that when the collapse came, it did not touch the promoters. To achieve this, they created an intricate corporate monstrosity whose like had never been seen before and which conferred on them benefits similar to those of a man who sees bankruptcy ahead and transfers his property to his wife.

---

*Cleveland Amory, in his engrossing *Who Killed Society?*, was under the impression that Whitney's fortune came from nickel streetcar fares.

This arrangement included the "reorganization" of the Metropolitan and the establishment of two new corporations to take over its assets. One was the Interurban, an operating company given (but only by lease!) the physical property of the railroad and required to run the lines. The other was Metropolitan Securities, a legal hippogriff entirely in the hands of the promoters. It permitted them to continue in financial control of the company and to continue dealing in its securities, but by means of marvelously clever stipulations it relieved them of legal and financial obligation.

Should Interurban become insolvent (as was inevitable), its creditors could collect only from Interurban, which owned nothing, and not from Metropolitan Securities—that is, Whitney and the rest. At the same time, $76,000,000 in new capitalization was heaped on the tottering structure. The total capitalization ballooned to $260,838,000—an impressive figure even in today's feeble dollars.

Afterward, when the law came to examine these complex transactions, it was felt that not half a dozen men in Wall Street could understand them. It was believed that this inscrutability was devised deliberately for the purpose of concealment. "In its intricacy," Burton Hendrick observed, "the scheme was the work of a master mind—commonly attributed to Whitney."

Not long after this reorganization, all books and records of Metropolitan since 1893 were destroyed by maceration, as was later testified in court.

Hence many of the syndicate's operations were hidden forever and it was only possible to reconstruct some of them by the records and testimony of others who dealt with Metropolitan. This was not the kind of capitalist efficiency William Graham Sumner had had in mind when he said that millionaires were a good bargain for society.

The wonder of it was that Whitney played his cards so skillfully that despite Jerome's charges against him—perhaps in part because they seemed politically inspired and beyond belief—his public image remained unblemished. Indeed his popularity actually was to rise during his short remaining span of life. The evil he did was to live after him, but the blame was to be obscured in the kind of endless legal wrangles that so often benefit the blameworthy.

On February 2, 1902, shortly before the Low administration took office, Whitney announced his decision to retire from business. Although he was assuredly Metropolitan's leader, his name had never appeared on its documents as an officer of the company and he had always referred to himself merely as a stockholder. The new district attorney, Jerome, for all his brave talk, could not seem to find any tracks leading to the Metropolitan. At that time, after so much promise of modernization, there were still 153 miles of horsecar lines in New York City, more than in all other cities of the United States combined. The Metropolitan was probably the largest user of horses in the world, owning 6,200 of them. In 1903 a former street railway executive, William N. Amory, declared that District Attorney Jerome's effort was a "deliberate whitewash" and brought charges against the Metropolitan, saying that its "insiders" had pocketed $90,000,000 from their manipulations. Although Amory's suit foundered—a fate that seemed predestined for litigants against the company—his attack continued after Whitney's death when he published a pamphlet, "The Truth About Metropolitan." In it he described the stock manipulation and the watering of construction accounts and said: "It was the genius of William C. Whitney that conceived the possibilities of the Metropolitan railways, and erected this monument of infamous graft. It is the skill and unscrupulousness of Thomas F. Ryan to which many of the completed deals owe their success."

By that time Whitney was beyond suing, but Ryan was still very much alive and brought no suit. Indeed, Ryan himself in a 1908 hearing frankly admitted that there had been "considerable stock-jobbing and stock-watering." The company by then had gone bankrupt, small stockholders had lost everything, and the city was saddled with a nineteenth-century surface network. For some years there were sporadic lawsuits brought by people trying to recover what they had lost. In one of them the lawyer Joseph H. Choate, once Ambassador to England and a friend of Whitney's, said:

This "debacle," this complete collapse [of the Metropolitan], only occurred in 1907, but the debauchery and corruption which had preceded it lasted many years. I do not hesitate to say that the greatest enormity committed in New York was the flotation and inflation of the Metropolitan Street Railway Company, its securities, and those of its subsidiary companies.

No one was ever prosecuted by the city, much less convicted. The nearest thing to any judgment of the Metropolitan syndicate's operations came when Ryan and the trustees of the Whitney and Elkins estates settled a lawsuit by the payment of $692,292. This was in the case of a projected small crosstown line that had never been built but had nevertheless been heavily capitalized; the people who bought its stock had paid dearly for nothing at all.

As for Richard Croker, he left politics after Seth Low's election in 1901, returned to his country place at Wantage, Buckinghamshire, bought another place in Ireland, and devoted himself to his racing stable. At length he won the Derby but was not accorded the customary presentation to the king. When he died in 1922, aged seventy-nine, his estate was estimated at better than $5,000,000. Peter Widener's palace, Lynnwood, just outside of Philadelphia, contained one of the best of the private art collections. When he died in 1915 at eighty, he was accounted Philadelphia's wealthiest man, with an estate estimated at $50,000,000. Thomas Fortune Ryan's estate when he died in 1928, aged seventy-seven, was appraised at $135,164,110.

Eight

1. Love or Hatred?

PAYNE WHITNEY, whose roommate at Yale had been Adelbert Stone Hay, oldest son of Secretary of State John Hay, had meanwhile become engaged to Adelbert's younger sister Helen. (In that respect at least he imitated his father, who had also married the sister of a classmate.) Adelbert had been killed in the strangest kind of accident the previous June—he had fallen from a third-floor hotel window during a Yale class reunion. This delayed the marriage, which took place at the Presbyterian Church of the Covenant in Washington February 6, 1902, four days after Whitney had announced his retirement. Two days before the wedding, a splendid dinner honoring Payne was given by Uncle Oliver at the Arlington Hotel in Washington, to which Whitney of course was not invited. At the time of that dinner, Whitney was among thirty guests including the Twomblys, Reids, and Burdens, who dined in New York with Mrs. Astor prior to her departure for Europe.

Although one can only speculate as to the exact status of the Whitney family feud at this point, there are clues to some of its particulars. Obviously the hatred between Colonel Payne and Whitney would follow them to the grave. Just as clearly, though Whitney was said not to be enthusiastic about Almeric Paget, by now he was doing his best to win back the affection of Payne and Pauline, with less than total success.

The question of the motives of the participants in the schism is critical. Granting the intensity of love that Pauline and Payne held for their mother, it was Harry who was Flora's favorite and who should have been most offended by any slight to her memory. It seems unlikely, if there *had* been nothing more than a quarrel about the remarriage, that Pauline and Payne's bitterness would persist nine years after Flora's death. If, on the other hand, Pauline and Payne turned their backs on Whitney with only the sordid motive of being rewarded by Oliver's millions, it seems improbable that Whitney could have kept his love for them and tried to win them back. (Supplementing this is the unlikelihood that the amiable if somewhat capricious Harry, who remained loyal to his father, could retain his love and respect for Pauline and Payne as he did unless one attributes to Harry the utterly base motive of taking satisfaction in their leaving the fold because it would mean that he would inherit more from his father.) Logic is insistent in suggesting that Whitney himself felt more heinous guilt than mere remarriage. The fact that Pauline and probably Payne attended Edith's funeral indicates that it was not the character of Edith to which they objected. Beyond this, supposition becomes more tenuous, but one is inclined to follow the French precept *cherchez la femme*, not merely because of the Saunterer's talk of a "burlesque actress" but because there seems literally no other direction in which to turn. Whitney had always been a ladies' man of the subtle rather than the flamboyant type. Burton J. Hendrick, shortly after Whitney's death, made a study of his business practices and his personality and described him as "physically handsome, loved by most men and all women." It is the sort of thing the solid Hendrick was not likely to say by way of mere rhetoric.

Like so many doings of the Whitneys, the Helen Hay–Payne Whitney wedding was front-page copy. Admission to the church was strictly by card, and Whitney, who had forgotten his, had to make an earnest speech to a skeptical policeman and produce his own calling card before the Cerberus relented. The Secretary of State, who gave the bride away, was at the summit of a distinguished career during which among many other things he had looked on the face of the dead Lincoln immediately after he was murdered, became co-author of his massive biography and was hailed for other literary works, negotiated the Hay-Pauncefote Treaty for the Panama Canal, preached the Open Door for all in China, and had dined with Queen Victoria and slept at Windsor Castle while ambassador. The church was so crowded that one could not move without jostling a senator or dignitary of even higher rank. Ambassadors from all nations were present, including the Wus from China and the Takahiras from Japan. Every member of the cabinet was there, as well as President and Mrs. Roosevelt, this being Whitney's second child married as a President looked on.

The President and his wife, with their irrepressible daughter Alice, were a few minutes late, so that the ceremony began as if they had pressed a button on being seated. Alice Roosevelt—another who, along with her father, would figure memorably in Dorothy Whitney's life—

was clad dashingly in "dark blue velvet, with a black velvet Gains-borough hat." Whitney, *The Herald* said, "looked on beamingly" and "looked as young as when he left Washington and the cares of official life years ago." Following the ushers were Dorothy Whitney and Alice Hay, "gowned alike in light gray satin crepe." The bride was a beauty and the groom, whose resemblance to Harry was marked, was "tall, broad-shouldered and athletic [and] seemed to be an example of perfect young manhood."

They seemed destined to be punctual, for the gift of the President and Mrs. Roosevelt was an antique clock, the Mark Hannas gave an Empire clock, and five more clocks came from five other well-wishers. "The bride is rich in her own right," *The Herald* went on, "and the groom will in time be one of the very rich men of the country, as an heir to a large portion of his father's wealth and that of his uncle, Colonel Oliver Payne." Evidently *The Herald* did not know that there was a schism, despite Payne's long residence with his uncle, nor that Payne might not inherit a dollar from his father unless he came around.

The Wus sensibly gave the bride a bolt of fine Chinese silk. The gift of the Stanford Whites was a little shocking—a small bronze copy of St. Gaudens's thirteen-foot nude Diana, which topped the Garden tower and had ruffled some proprieties even though three hundred feet above Madison Square.* After the wedding seventy-five of the guests went to the breakfast at the Hay home on H Street. Whitney and Colonel Payne had been able to avoid each other at the church, but not here: "A small table was spread in the bay window, at which were served the President and Mrs. Roosevelt, the Secretary of State and Mrs. Hay, Mr. and Mrs. Whitelaw Reid, William C. Whitney and Col. Oliver Payne." Despising each other, the two men not only had to glance at each other but out of courtesy to the rest as well as for the sake of appearances had to speak to each other without visible hostility. Alas, that history could not be turned back and a recording made of the conversation at that table! The President did not approve of Whitney. He was later to write about "various businessmen accused of sharp practice in Wall Street, and who . . . I believe to be bad citizens, against whom nevertheless nothing whatever criminal has been shown." And of his friend Elihu Root he wrote, "He has not the view that Taft and I take about corporations . . . about Mr. Whitney and Mr. Ryan and so forth, but that he is conscientious in his view I am absolutely sure."

---

* An enterprising man with a telescope frequented the square, charging a dime to see Diana.

Whitney's feelings toward Oliver could scarcely have been improved by his knowledge of the Colonel's gifts. Whitney had sought to repair the breach with his son, giving the bride "two rings, one a circlet of diamonds and one of diamonds and rubies . . . and also a diamond brooch." But he was put to rout by what Colonel Payne did for the bride and the young man the papers described as "his heir, as well as his favorite nephew":

- For the bride, "a diamond necklace and brooch of pearls and diamonds."
- For their honeymoon, he placed at the couple's disposal his winter home at Thomasville, "with horses and servants."
- His private car, attached to a special train, waited at the Washington depot to take them there.
- From Thomasville the couple were to go via Washington to Europe, where Oliver's enormous transatlantic yacht *Amphitrite* would be theirs for the summer.
- Meanwhile, Oliver had bought a seventy-by-one-hundred-foot lot on Fifth Avenue near 79th Street held at $525,000, on which he was building them a home estimated to cost an equal amount, "so that the total value . . . will be not less than $1,000,000."

The perpetrator of "Vers de Société" in *Town Topics* wrote truly:

> *If there ever was maiden who ought to be gay,*
> *That maiden is certainly sweet Helen Hay. . . .*

Yet one might wonder at the taste and character of a man who spread gifts in such profusion even for that time of excess, and inquire whether he did it out of love for Payne and Helen or out of hatred for Whitney.

2. The Celebrity of Saratoga

Now DOROTHY PAYNE WHITNEY was the last Whitney child remaining at home. One would think that Whitney, having lost Pauline and Payne to Oliver, and with Harry married and twice a father himself, would have lavished special attention on his fifteen-year-old daughter. He did not, indulgent though he was. In the man's world he took for granted, he had devoted sharp attention to the education and business training of Harry and Payne but little to the preparation of Pauline and Dorothy.

Dorothy's care and education were left in other hands. Like most of the daughters of the rich, she was kept from public school and sent to small private classes conducted by "Professor" Frederic Roser, an Englishman who had made a reputation, not entirely deserved, as the paragon of tutors. Among her five classmates, all of them to be lifelong friends, were three with whom she would be especially close: the petite Susan R. Sedgwick, Susan's cousin May Tuckerman, and Edith Greene. All knew each other except for Dorothy, who lived farther uptown. They met in the waiting room of the socially prominent Dr. Richard Derby on West 35th Street. Susan Sedgwick—now the widowed Mrs. Paul Hammond—remembers to this day Dorothy's arrival when the class began, and her recognition that she was the only "stranger" there. She was daunted but courageous. "Dorothy, with a sweet smile, held out her hand, saying 'I am Dorothy Whitney.' " Her acceptance by the others was immediate. Sometimes the class met at the Whitney mansion, a museumlike place noteworthy for its electric elevator.

From Society's dancing master, Dr. Dodsworth, Dorothy had learned the waltz and polka and discovered a joy in the ballroom that later was often to keep her dancing until three. She had graduated from supervision by governesses and had been given her overseer-companion, Beatrice Bend, daughter of the late George Bend who had been head of the New York Stock Exchange. Bend had died during a period of ill luck so that his family was left reduced in means. Beatrice was well paid by Whitney for this service. So strict were the conventions that a young lady was not permitted to leave the house and walk down the street, even Fifth Avenue, alone. To do so was to invite the suspicion that one was fast. Beatrice—who with her sister Amy had been listed in Ward McAllister's Four Hundred of 1892—was at least a dozen years older than Dorothy. Though lacking the dazzling blonde beauty of her sister, who had married, Beatrice was comely and fresh of face. Meticulous in dress, she was decisive, socially correct, and, under her admonitions, affectionate, the waggling finger softened by elaborate endearments: "Dear darling pet Dorothy." She helped plan Dorothy's social engagements, saw that she got her lessons, helped her with shopping, advised her on dress, and served as her chaperone. The girl saw rather little of her father, whose loss of Edith made her write in later years, "My poor father! He loved her so much—and she had brought the gaiety of life to him and to me and I see her always now with light around her."

Now that he was retired would have seemed the time for Whitney to have grown close to this daughter so young that she could have been his grandchild. But he was as busy as ever, what with the time he spent on his elaborate plans for Saratoga, his clubs, his social life, and his horses, and it was not uncommon at the time for fathers to remain fairly unacquainted with their daughters. It was a great occasion when Dorothy and her stepsister Adelaide, six years older than she, were among her father's guests one day at Sheepshead Bay, where Whitney's luxurious box was on the grandstand roof. But alas, he suffered the anguish of seeing Gold Heels, whom he had owned but sold for $1,200, win the Suburban.

His private car, *Pilgrim*, though only six years old, was less grand than the more recent models, so he retired it in favor of the new and more splendid *Wanderer*. Back home in New York by early spring in 1902 after his usual interlude at Aiken, he drove an automobile, make unknown, to Central Park with Adelaide as his companion to watch a coaching parade. Some of his time was spent on a favorite hobby—doing favors for friends. On Long Island he chartered the fast steam yacht *Arden* and issued "a standing invitation to his country neighbors . . . any race morning, [to] join him on his yacht and sail across the Sound to the Country Club of Westchester," that being near the Morris Park track where they all were heading.

Influenza had killed a few of his promising two year olds and damaged some of his best horses. Goldsmith and Yankee suffered badly, and Endurance By Right (which had cost him $30,000) had turned roarer and would never run again. Disease was only one of the risks that made racing a heavy loser even for heavy winners. But at Morris Park he ran Blue Girl, who had had catarrhal fever, and there was a "wild demonstration" in the Whitney box when Blue Girl stood off Hatasoo and won the Ladies' Stakes.

What with the succession of racing "seasons" at various tracks, if one followed the more important of them as Whitney did, the effort and expense of transporting horses from one track to another was considerable. To name only a few, Morris Park was followed by Gravesend, Gravesend by Sheepshead Bay, that by Brighton, and then, with August, came the great month-long racing season at Saratoga. Near the end of July Whitney arrived at Saratoga in *Wanderer* and occupied a handsome new cottage of his own convenient to his stables. Harry, his pride and joy, was with him, as was Harry's wife Gertrude, trying to improve her limited interest in racing because of Harry's infatuation with it. Dorothy and Adelaide had been sent to Bar Harbor to stay with Adelaide's grandmother, Mrs. May. The improvements Whitney had planned in 1901 were ready and lay before his eyes: the extra racecourse, the remodeled and enlarged grandstand, the handsomely rebuilt clubhouse, the extended betting ring, and enlarged paddocks—enhancements that one turf man thought likely to make Saratoga ultimately "the greatest racing center on the American continent."

Harry, who had been bookish at Yale, had taken to business with less zest than he took in his own racehorses and his fine string of polo ponies. But with him, Whitney was on such affectionate terms that this son seemed to compensate for other bitternesses. The two could talk about Harry's recent trip into the West and Mexico with Daniel Guggenheim to examine silver, lead, and copper mines; they had come back with deeds to nearly $10,000,000 worth of mining property. It had been arranged by Whitney, who earlier had bought a share in the fabled Tonopah mine in Nevada, had become an investor in and a director of the Guggenheim Exploration Company, and was preparing the way for Harry. He was forced to let Oliver prepare the way for Payne, whose six-story, marble-fronted house, designed by McKim, Mead & White, was rising on Fifth Avenue ten blocks north of 871. Whitney and Harry could also discuss the Reggie Vanderbilt "scandal," which varied with the telling. The most conservative version was that Reggie had dropped $100,000 at Canfield's place in New York. Another rendering said that Canfield had had in his safe $300,000 in Reggie's IOU's and was affronted because Reggie had settled at last for $130,000. No less affronted was Reggie's stern mother. As one bard had it, "Lo, the poor Reggie, ousted from his fold / For speculating with superfluous gold. . . ." But most of all Whitney and Harry could talk about horses, their common passion and one that Payne did not share. Whitney's fame was being sung in arias such as one in *The Tribune*:

> Of course, the celebrity of Saratoga is William C. Whitney. It is pretty well recognized that the great boom of prosperity that has swept over the Spa this season is due more to him than to anybody else. He has made a new racetrack, new not only in materials, but in atmosphere. Lifting it up from the semi-disrepute . . . into which it had fallen, he has completed the work which he began last year, and in two seasons has raised Saratoga racing to a plane which . . . is equaled nowhere else on this side of the Atlantic.

Or in the magazine *World's Work*:

> The apparent ease with which he accomplishes results is remarkable. No one ever saw Mr. Whitney in a hurry or knew him to give evidence of pressure or excitement even in the heat of political strife. His serenity and

composure seem beyond the influence of events. The princely character of his hospitality, the number and extent of his places of residence, are part of the gossip chronicles of the day.

And the Widow made Saratoga sound colorful and semidemocratic:

> . . . Saratoga is in full bloom. Streets, parks and hotels are filled. Turfmen, horsemen and millionaire lovers of horseflesh block the way. . . . Along the streets and on piazzas and in the hotel corridors are the women of the exclusive world, the half-world and the hidden world, bumping elbows and brushing skirts. Everything goes, and for the first time since our mothers were young Saratoga attracts all that is best, alive and alert, from all classes. . . . Newport has narrowed down to wealth and fashion—to one class; Saratoga is America's own. . . .

Whitney appeared relaxed, without care as he strolled over to the track to see his string take their exercise, pausing to "talk horse" with friends. "It is not at all unusual to see him sunning himself on a street corner, smoking a long, black cigar . . . looking quietly at the passing show. . . ." One candid photograph shows him standing at the track in derby hat and smart short coat, not young but youthful, tall, negligent, distinction with hands in pockets. Among the scores of his friends who could be counted on not to miss the Saratoga season were William K. and several other Vanderbilts, Pierre Lorillard, Perry Belmont, Peter Widener, R. T. Wilson, Jr., and Thomas Hitchcock, Jr.—the latter one of those who had seen the low-bridge accident at Aiken four years earlier and was now one of the directors of the Saratoga Racing Association. Whitney, still president, treated Hitchcock, Wilson, and eight other directors to dinner at Canfield's after which "the waiters . . . retired and all the doors were closed" and Saratoga problems were discussed in privacy. As many as ten or a dozen automobiles could now be seen at one time on Broadway, causing Whitney to suggest that "Saratoga should be like Bermuda, with all means of transportation banned . . . save horses and perhaps the bicycle." After the races, Canfield's was the center of fashion:

> Harry Payne Whitney does the playing for the family, and his father never loses an opportunity to watch the fortunes of his son. . . . Richard Canfield, probably the most remarkable man, next to William C. Whitney, presides there, but in so quiet and unostentatious a way. . . . Here, on an evening in the height of the season . . . [the] crowd is so dense about midnight that only a very small majority [sic] of those present can play.

Harry's horses won more than his father's that month—Harry's and Herman Duryea's Irish Lad won the great Saratoga Special—but Whitney was the prince of losers when his son was the winner. Six days after the last race he was aboard the *Celtic* with Harry and a few of the latter's friends, Whitney having leased a grouse-shooting box on Holwick Moor in Yorkshire. "Going away for my health?" Whitney said to a reporter, astonished that his health should be in question. "Do I look like it? . . . I am going over for a rest and to watch my son shoot." After the shooting, Whitney went down to London, where James B. Duke had frightened the British Imperial tobacco combine by invading its market, and Thomas F. Ryan had joined Duke in arranging an agreement with Imperial that included a satisfying division of world tobacco trade. Although Whitney had no part in these discussions, as one of the Big Six of American Tobacco he sat beside Duke at a banquet the latter gave his British colleagues at the Carlton Hotel October 7. There were the usual panegyrical toasts. Whitney called Duke "the greatest merchant in the world"; Duke toasted Whitney as the builder of the Navy, to which Whitney responded with gunboat-diplomacy unction, "it is such marvelous merchants as these men [indicating Duke and his companions] who make a great navy necessary to carry and protect trade which seems to know no bounds."

Meanwhile Dorothy Whitney had gone to Newport for a stay at The Breakers, where Harry and Gertrude had been married and where Gladys Vanderbilt now celebrated her sixteenth birthday, four months in advance of Dorothy's. Dorothy could remember how, when they were small children, "Gladys and I constructed a kind of private telephone system from my bedroom right across to hers"—a light rope over which they conducted imaginary conversations across 57th Street. At The Breakers, Dorothy—the friendliest of persons, distressed by the schism in her own family—made new acquaintance with the two separate and distinct feuds in the Vanderbilt family. One was of course between the formidable Alva, now Mrs. O. H. P. Belmont, and the entire Vanderbilt tribe. Through some sorcery she had managed to regain at least the sufferance of her daughter Consuelo, now the unhappy Duchess of Marlborough. The duchess returned to Newport that summer, perhaps more to escape the duke than to visit her mother, now mistress of the Belmont place, Belcourt. Taking a drive, the two encountered Reggie Vanderbilt in a carriage with his fiancée, whereupon "the mother nudged the Duchess, but the party passed without a word or sign." Immediately thereafter they met Reggie's brother Alfred

Gwynne in his new automobile. "Again there was a staring match without a word of recognition. . . ."

This feud was simpler and easier to manage than the other, which had dragged scores of more distant relatives into its opposing maelstroms. The latter was the one begun when Reggie's and Alfred's (and Gertrude's and Gladys's) oldest brother Cornelius, Jr., had married Grace Wilson. What with the belief that this had caused the elder Cornelius's stroke and shortened his life, and the general Vanderbilt dislike for the Wilsons and especially Grace Wilson, the family had since cut Grace and young Cornelius cold.

At Newport, young Cornelius and Grace had a cottage called Beaulieu not far from The Breakers. "The servants at 'The Breakers,' " affirmed *Town Topics*, ". . . have strict orders never, under any circumstances, to look at, recognize or hold conversation with anyone employed at 'Beaulieu'. . . . On the other hand, the servants of the 'Neely' Vanderbilts are threatened with instant dismissal if they ever have dealings with any of the other Vanderbilt . . . help." Both the Vanderbilts and the Wilsons had so many relatives who chose sides that the ramifications of this quarrel were extensive, and hostesses had to take careful account of it in sending invitations to parties. It was said that "The war between the Harry Payne Whitneys and the 'Neely' Vanderbilts is more bitter than the estrangement of Cornelius Vanderbilt and his mother. . . . Gertrude Whitney and Grace Vanderbilt each give the other the cut direct when passing on the avenue. . . . The 'Neely' Vanderbilt children and the Whitney youngsters do not know one another, and the governesses and footmen of each household have strict orders that these young cousins are not to meet."

On Whitney's return from England in October, he declined to discuss with reporters either politics (because he said he had retired from politics) or business (he said he was out of touch), but he was willing to talk about horses. He had not entirely withdrawn from English racing— "I have some good horses on the other side"—and was corroborated three days later when his Ballantrae won the Cambridgeshire Stakes at Newmarket. J. P. Morgan, meeting someone else on the ship, shook Whitney's hand on the pier. Whitney was so accustomed to an admiring press that he was hurt that there had been a droplet of criticism. To Grover Cleveland, now in retirement at Princeton, he wrote in elegiac vein:

> As for myself, I have been so many years in enterprises, the public mind has rather got me identified as a person given over to mere money

making, that I do not look upon myself as in condition to help politically very much by public utterances, and my activity in business has given me more or less enemies waiting to jump on me, so for a long time I have refused to be interviewed on any subject, and that is the one answer that I always give when I am applied to.

I often recall with the greatest delight our past associations and honestly believe we succeeded in doing some good.

It had the sound of a man who had enjoyed "doing some good" and, on looking back, wished he had done more. And he should not have complained. For while there were charges of corruption in the surface lines and protests about their inefficiency and crowding, some also praised his ability and foresight in linking "a series of disjointed street railways into a complete system" and said in utter seriousness, "The Metropolitan Street Railway system will ever be a monument to the energy and enterprise of Mr. Whitney."

3. Crepe on the Gates

SHORTLY BEFORE Whitney went to England, Almeric Hugh Paget had left his employ and the Pagets had closed or sold their 61st Street house and moved bag and baggage to England with their two small daughters. There they took a house in London and a country place in Suffolk. Almeric, though a member of the Metropolitan, Country, and Racquet clubs, may have been drawn by family ties and also by the fact that Pauline's heart and other ailments seemed to respond to treatment at European spas. Since Almeric and his relatives were anything but wealthy, and (as will be seen) the Pagets lived magnificently in England, it seems a safe assumption that Uncle Oliver had done well by them. Did Whitney urge them to stay in America? Did he try to visit them while in England? Were they now so estranged that they would not even see him? We do not know. We do know that the schism continued.

Whitney's lifelong fascination with the press had been capped by his purchase of the sport, theater, and scandal-oriented *New York Morning Telegraph*. This dubious sheet reveled in such headlines as "ACTRESS GOES INSANE AS CURTAIN FALLS," and "CHORUS GIRL / VALUES LOVE / AT $10,000." Its circulation and influence were small, but Whitney said he wanted to build it into news importance. This purpose could hardly be seen when he appointed Finley Peter

Dunne as editor, giving him a one-third interest and handsome salary. Dunne, his fame increasing, had come to New York from Chicago in 1900 and was much in demand as a contributor to magazines. He had become Whitney's good friend, though Dunne was a mere thirty-five and no one could fill the great vacancy left by the passing of Alexander Gunn. So celebrated had he become that one of the popular songs of the 1902 musical comedy *The Chinese Honeymoon* was "Mr. Dooley." Dunne was Whitney's guest at a performance and bowed to an applauding audience when the spotlight reached him in Whitney's box. Dunne had often written disparagingly of politicians who "warmed their feet at the Social Register," which he could now be accused of doing himself. He had no talent for editorial supervision. He seldom appeared at *The Telegraph* office, and rumor had it that Whitney cheerfully lost money on *The Telegraph* simply because it gave him an excuse to enjoy Dunne's companionship. Dunne was one of those who gave Whitney a sixty-second birthday party at Sherry's on July 5, 1903, at which the humorist read verses he had written, beginning:

> *In old New York there lives a man of very great renown*
>   *Who owns a palace in and forty houses out of town;*
> *He owns the tunnels, owns the cabs, and owns the trolleys, too,*
>   *And if you get run over, why the only man to sue*
> *Is Mr. Whitney!*

The elegant Sherry's, designed by Stanford White, was to gain notoriety a few months later when it became the scene of the banquet on horseback given by the Chicago utilities magnate C. K. G. Billings. For this the ballroom was decorated as a "woodland garden with sod on the floor, real birds singing . . . and a man-made harvest moon beaming down on the 36 guests and their mounts." Whitney, for all his love of showmanship and of horses, did not dine on them. Sherry's, on the southwest corner of Fifth Avenue and 44th Street, was directly across the avenue from its famous competitor for the carriage trade, Delmonico's. Next door but one to Delmonico's, at 5 East 44th Street, was Richard Canfield's sumptuous New York gambling establishment, which District Attorney Jerome had raided only the previous December. Canfield was luckily absent, but among the players there were the stockbroker Jesse Lewisohn, Lillian Russell's admirer, and Harry Payne Whitney. Both refused to tell Jerome of their experiences there on the ground that it might "incriminate or degrade" them, and they were ultimately upheld in their insistence on silence.

That fall, Whitney gave his remaining seventeen buffalo and ten of his elk to the New York Zoological Society. He sent his remaining eighty elk to be liberated at various points in the Adirondacks, still keeping herds of mule deer and moose at October Mountain. On Eastern tracks, from Brookline to Baltimore in 1903, he was easily the biggest winner,* with twenty-eight firsts, thirty-two seconds, and seventeen thirds, far ahead of his closest rivals, James Keene and August Belmont. Whitney won a total of $99,405 in purses, aside from whatever he may have won or lost in bets. Early in January 1904, he was away at the time of Mrs. Astor's ball, making it safe for the Payne Whitneys to attend and hence to be certified as among the elect. Whitney, along with Dorothy and Adelaide, was at Aiken, watching his horses train and riding over meadows filled with memories of Edith. He and Hitchcock had been among the earliest outsiders to choose Aiken when it was merely pleasant countryside. Now it was one of the fashionable resorts, inhabited during winter months by Vanderbilts, Iselins, Blairs, Kountzes, and others of the wealthy, but a place where Whitney was still king by virtue of tenure, magnificence, and hospitality.

He was back in mid-January for the automobile show at Madison Square Garden, an affair of immoderate interest to him. He was not one of those horsemen who hated gas buggies and did not—as did his Long Island neighbor James Kernochan—put up signs forbidding tradesmen to approach in anything but horse-drawn vehicles. He still had an investment in Pope-Hartford and also in the largest manufacturer of the storage batteries that propelled electric automobiles. Automobiles in New York State were now permitted to go eight miles per hour in the city and fifteen in the country, but in rural areas drivers were required to stop at the roadside and turn off the engine when a horse-drawn conveyance approached, sparing equine nerves. At the show Whitney saw the racer in which the forty-year-old Henry Ford had covered a mile in 39.4 seconds on the ice at Detroit, ice being the only smooth road available for such speeds. He saw the Pope-Hartford, the Winton, the Rambler, the Haynes-Apperson, and other beauties with polished brass lamps, canopy tops, and all-leather upholstery and encountered friends including Mrs. Burke Roche and Cass Canfield (no relation, the latter wished it known, to Richard Canfield). Payne Whitney showed up after his father left, thus escaping one of those embarrassing meetings.

On January 25, 1904, Whitney was at the opera with Beatrice Bend,

* He had consolidated his racing stable with that of Harry and the latter's friend, Herman Duryea.

Mrs. Harry Payne Whitney, and Mrs. Cass Canfield in his box to hear that young Italian—his name was Caruso—of whom it was actually said that given a little more seasoning he might excel the great Jean de Reszke. Caruso had made his Metropolitan debut only the previous November in *Rigoletto* and now appeared with Marcella Sembrich in *Lucia di Lammermoor.* Whitney had been one of those to whom the great opera house years earlier had been only a dream, composed in some part of snobbery and in part of genuine yearning for musical drama. He had conferred with the architect, seen the building rise after many battles, been a boxholder since 1883 (he now had Box 7 in the parterre, the best), contributed handsomely for the house's restoration after its interior was destroyed by fire in 1892, and had applauded a long line of performers—Christine Nilsson, Lilli Lehmann, Melba, Eames, Scotti, Nordica, Schumann-Heink, and now this new Italian—each of whom had piled glamor on top of nostalgia in the hearts of the more appreciative in the Diamond Horseshoe. In Caruso, the Metropolitan obviously had one of its great ones. Among some boxholders it was still unfashionable to arrive until the opera was well under way. Whitney stepped into the foyer during the first intermission to greet fresh arrivals with, "Ah, you should have heard that first act!"

Three days later, on January 28, began the slow and mysterious fall of the curtain on his own life. He was again at the opera, this time to hear *Parsifal,* though he had told his secretary, Regan, that he was not feeling well. He had come to entertain a certain impatience with doctors, feeling them limited in their knowledge, and was rather convinced that he knew his own ailments better than they. It was utterly impossible that Whitney, with his charm and wide acquaintance, could have been alone in his box unless he wanted to be alone and insisted on being alone. Yet there seems no mention of his companions, if he had any. This season had seen the Met stage the first performance of *Parsifal* outside Bayreuth. In the cast were Milka Ternina, Alois Burgstaller, Anton Van Rooy, and Marcel Journet, several of whom had been his guests at 871. He became uncomfortable enough so that in mid-opera he retired to the Directors' Room, where a passerby saw him throw aside his silk hat and cloak and lie down on a couch. Still, he had supper afterward with a "party of friends," none of them named in the newspapers. At home the next morning, Friday, he withstood the severe abdominal pains that are often a symptom of appendicitis. In clinging stubbornly to his own medical prejudices, he undoubtedly cut short his own life. Not until Saturday did he have Regan call Dr. James.

James immediately sent for Dr. William T. Bull, a surgeon who often rode with Whitney at Meadow Brook. Bull removed Whitney's appendix that evening at the Fifth Avenue mansion. But his condition worsened, and although he spoke cheerfully enough with Harry and Dorothy, he evidently realized the gravity of his condition and lamented the absence of Payne, who was at Oliver's place in Georgia, and Adelaide, still at Aiken. Telegrams went out to Adelaide, to Payne and his wife Helen, and to Pauline and Almeric Paget in Europe. Newspapermen, waiting in an anteroom, got nothing but scraps of information from servants. "HOPE FOR WHITNEY," headlined *The Sun*, making a guess. On Tuesday, Thomas Fortune Ryan called after ten and stayed until noon. Some two hours later Regan hurriedly left in a carriage and returned with a trained nurse and "two cases of surgical instruments," closely followed by Dr. Bull. Several other doctors arrived, until there was a total of six physicians in consultation. Whitney's two New York sisters, Mrs. Barney and Mrs. Dimock, arrived, followed by Elihu Root and then by Whitney's brother Henry from Boston. Still the reporters waited.

Not until five that day, February 2, did a butler, tears in his eyes, go to the company of newsmen and say, "Gentlemen, I regret to announce that Mr. Whitney died at four o'clock this afternoon."

Shocked that an hour had passed before they were given the news, they clamored for details but got none. The Whitney family reticence about their illnesses was firmer than ever. Not even the cause of death was given. Obviously the physicians were under family instructions of confidentiality, for as Dr. Bull left, he told reporters, "I have no statement to make. I can say nothing," and the other doctors likewise parried inquiries. It was speculated that news of Whitney's death had been withheld until five o'clock to prevent any ill effect on the Stock Exchange, but why could not the cause be divulged? It was two hours later, 7:00 P.M., before the men of the press were handed a short typewritten statement, evidently the joint work of Regan and Harry Macdona, totally wanting in the deathbed particulars newspapers consider indispensable to their readers:

> Mr. Whitney died at four o'clock of peritonitis and blood poisoning following an operation for appendicitis.

This was all that was given about his death. The remaining few words of the statement told of projected funeral and burial arrangements.

". . . it said nothing about a second operation," *The Times* noted, "and both Mr. Regan and Mr. Macdona positively declined to describe or discuss the progress of the disease. . . ." *The New York American*—had it oiled the palms of servants or others?—unveiled a little more, saying that the doctors had told Whitney that another operation, though dangerous, gave him his only chance for recovery: "He bade the physicians go ahead and do what they could. He arranged his affairs, bade his son, Harry Payne Whitney, and his daughter, Miss Dorothy Whitney . . . a hopeful farewell, and left messages for those of his children who were not there. . . . Mr. Whitney never regained consciousness after being put under the influence of ether."

A large bow of crepe shimmered on the great gates from the Palazzo Doria as the widowed Mrs. Cornelius Vanderbilt and her son Reggie and daughter Gladys led a throng of callers who spoke their sympathy or left cards. Harry was now the head of the Whitney family, theoretically in charge, but he was said to have taken to his bed, "giving up completely to his grief." Dorothy Whitney, who had been six when her mother died, had turned seventeen ten days before her father breathed his last.

4. Big Brained, Big Hearted

WITHOUT GETTING shot—though there was a rumor that he *had* been shot—Whitney in death drew more front-page newspaper attention in New York and across the land than anyone since the passing of President McKinley. The treatment was almost cloyingly respectful, with a tinge of perplexity and awe. Editors struggled to review a career astonishing in its brilliance and complexity, to convey a true picture of a man who seemed even more than the impressive total of his parts. The mere summation of his interests and achievements was formidable: the attacker of Tweed, the efficient corporation counsel, the disciple of Tilden who became the ally of Cleveland, the builder of the Navy, the Democratic idol who might have been President but abruptly abandoned a political opportunity others would have sold their souls for and turned hard into commerce; the traction magnate, the director or trustee in five banks, two insurance companies, a steamship line, a mining company, and ten other assorted enterprises; the member of twenty-eight clubs and societies, the sponsor of great opera, the experimenter with buffalo and elk, the grandee of Society whose lands and palaces ex-

ceeded those of European principalities and whose late-blooming passion for horses produced winners in America, England, and France.
When joined with the tragedy of the two lost wives (and the cleavage in
his family, which was not publicly known), it composed a career more
replete with action and drama than seemed possible to crowd into his
sixty-two years.

Woven through all these years were the charm, warmth, and style
that could have been best attested by the late Alexander Gunn, of whom
the obituarists had never heard—qualities brilliantly illuminated by
comparison with his contemporary, J. Pierpont Morgan, a far greater financier but a tyrant largely devoted to money and art, art and money.
Whitney was Mr. Fifth Avenue, the most popular man among its two
miles of millionaires, but with a dash of Broadway in him too—a favorite of Mrs. Astor but perhaps not above paying attentions to a burlesque
actress.

No leading newspaper even mentioned, much less tried to appraise,
the evil in Whitney, in whom Hewitt had seen "one of the most sinister
figures of his time" and Jerome had described as a master of corruption.
There was no allusion to sharp practice in traction. The highly moral
Nation said not a word about his surface railways and complained only
that "he did not fulfill his first promise" of political leadership because
he turned aside into "mere money-making." So popular was Whitney,
so firm the halo, that some later excused him on the ground that he
simply followed the business morality of the day. To do so was to forget
that the business honesty of the majority was solid but unpublicized,
probity never being given the attention paid the robber barons. It was
even an imperfect analogy to say that he watered stock as Morgan and
the Vanderbilts watered stock, for there were degrees of imposture
among the great manipulators. Some of them lightened their sins by a
measure of achievement, some eventual benefit to the nation however
much it cost.

Not so with Whitney. For all his great abilities and endearing traits
that make one anxious to give him the benefit of every doubt, the
weight of the evidence is clear that even if he entered the traction field
with the intention of building an efficient and useful transportation
system, somewhere along the line he threw the switch that wheeled
him off into wholesale stockjobbery. Whitney's power with Croker, his
activities in Wall Street, the repeated "setting of the table" for more
dupes, placed him less in the category of industrial developer and more
in the status of skillful gambler along with such figures as Ryan,

Widener, and Keene. If Morgan's chief monument was to be the Steel Corporation and the Vanderbilts' the New York Central Railroad, one had to say that for all their abuses they were in better shape and more useful to the country than the memorial on which Whitney had spent so much of his time and skill—that bankrupt ruin, that failure in public transportation, the Metropolitan Railway, which paid for the palaces and the horses.

The rumor that Whitney had been shot undoubtedly started because of the family secrecy during his last days. It made a heady addition to the legend, Whitney dying of a bullet, especially if the bullet had been fired by some jealous woman, as *Town Topics* would have preferred it. But the Saunterer was on his best behavior, writing (again in his first item), "Rarely if ever has New York in all its interests—social, political, financial, industrial and sporting—suffered such a shock. . . ."

Payne Whitney's seven-year bitterness was suspended by a gesture: he came north for the funeral. Adelaide arrived from Aiken. Pauline's absence was explained by distance and her illness, and the schism was hidden. Colonel Payne remained unforgiving. The testimonials from distinguished people in the United States and Europe were well above the common run of funerary bromides, as in Cleveland's tribute to Whitney's "extreme consideration" and his qualities that "grappled him to his friends with hooks of steel." But perhaps Henry Clews said it best: "He was big brained and big hearted. He made money and he spent it. He was not a close-fisted and hoarding man of wealth, but he liked to enjoy life himself and to see others enjoy it."

The state legislature honored him by adjourning. At the opera, before the performance of *Tristan and Isolde* on the day of the funeral, the lights were turned low as the curtains of the box that had held appreciative Whitneys for so long were slowly drawn shut. Navy flags on land and sea floated low on the staff. As the funeral procession left 871 and began its long journey down Fifth Avenue—led by six mounted policemen, the hearse drawn by plumed black horses—it was in a small way reviewing people and events in Whitney's career. It passed Mrs. Astor's mansion and that of Colonel Payne, both of them important in his life. It passed his own former home—now Harry and Gertrude's—and the three separate Vanderbilt palaces, as well as St. Thomas's Church, where so much money had changed hands. At 44th Street, "when Delmonico's was passed . . . the flag on the roof was lowered to half mast," and Sherry's across the street should have done as well. At 40th the cortege passed the office of *Town Topics*, the journal of Society. It was well known in Society that Colonel Mann for the last several years had conned many of its wealthiest men, including Whitney, in an imaginative swindle worthy of that artist in blackmail. The Colonel had told these men of his coming publication of a handsome volume titled *Fads and Fancies of Representative Americans* in which flattering pictures and text matter about them would appear. Eighty-two of them had paid sums ranging from $1,500 to $25,000 and perhaps more—the total take was said to be not far from a half million—to be included in this most pretentious of puff sheets. Whitney had paid the Saunterer $10,000. They had paid, most of them, less because they wanted to be flattered in print than because of the subtle warning that one's failure to "subscribe" would mean pitiless treatment in the weekly *Town Topics*. While some of them had things to hide, others paid up because it was the easiest way out. More was to be heard of *Fads and Fancies*, which was supposed to have been a publication marking the turn of the century but had not yet seen the light of day.

The cortege passed a dozen of Whitney's clubs scattered along the way—the magnificent Waldorf-Astoria at 34th Street, a place of Whitney sessions with Ryan and Root. It passed the great Garden at Madison Square, the skyscraping Flatiron Building across the way, and—still there this day—the Fifth Avenue Hotel where it had all started, that date with Flora, the girl from Cleveland, with whom his acquaintance with wealth had so quickly soared on wings of romance. Might he have been a different man—as honest as he was generous—had it not been for that terrible feeling of being a poor relation of the Paynes?

At last the procession halted at Grace Church, with its lacy stonework, still the height of fashion, at Broadway and Tenth. Here Whitney had for many years had a pew that he seldom occupied. The church was thronged as Bishop William C. Doane and the Reverend William R. Huntington read the Episcopal service. The pallbearers were Grover Cleveland, Thomas Fortune Ryan, Elihu Root, Hamilton McKown Twombly, Col. William Jay, Thomas Dolan, Grant R. Schley, George G. Haven, Peter Widener, and H. H. Vreeland, the latter representing J. P. Morgan, who was in Canada. While the service was simple, with no eulogy, the grandeur of wealth was in evidence: it took five wagons to haul away the flowers, and a special train of four parlor cars waited at Grand Central Station to transport the mourners to snow-covered Woodlawn Cemetery.

When Whitney was buried there beside Flora and Olive, "Payne Whitney stood erect, with set face. Miss Dorothy Whitney, who stood next to him, had to be supported all during the service. . . ." Her father had given her only occasional opportunity to know him, and now it was too late, but their brief encounters had been tender and she adored him. A daughter could not expect quite the attention Whitney gave to Ballyhoo Bey. Yet it could be depended on— he had in mind creating a third historic debut, this one for Dorothy, that would surpass the first two at 871. This daughter had a fine talent for forgiveness. She later explained that her father had only limited time to give her because he was so intent on his ideal of leaving a fortune for Harry and her that would not suffer too much by comparison with what Uncle Oliver would leave—and had already given—Pauline and Payne. On the contrary, since he retired at sixty, his horses and his houses—both liabilities rather than revenue producers—had consumed him.

How many millions had the great spender left unspent? Less than expected—less than if he had been only splendid instead of magnificent. He left a total of $22,906,222—comfortable enough but a shade below the Croesus class. He had been prudent: not a single share of Metropolitan Railways remained in his portfolio. His will made Harry sole executor, left him one-half the total, and made him guardian over Dorothy, who received $50,000 a year until her majority. She also received three-tenths of the total estate, and Beatrice Bend was allotted $10,000 a year so long as she remained unmarried and continued as Dorothy's duenna. Pauline and Payne each got one-tenth—magnanimous in view of their estrangement and the great shower of gold that Uncle Oliver would heap on them. Adelaide and Arthur Randolph were each left $250,000 in trust—a substantial fortune at the time, sufficient to keep them in luxury all their lives.

"An impression gained ground in certain quarters," said *The Tribune*, "that Payne Whitney had had a disagreement with his father. This was emphatically denied by members of the family . . . and the impression is finally disposed of by [the legacy and] certain other significant provisions of the will," pointing out that in the event of Harry's death, Payne was named as sole executor and also as Dorothy's guardian.

The Bettmann Archive

BOOK II

"Dorothy Whitney? She always takes the hard chair. . . ."
—*Ruth Morgan*

34. The round-the-world romance of Dorothy Payne Whitney and Willard Straight was enacted in scenes in Washington, Long Island, China, Italy, France, and England. Their marriage was to be short but marked by notable achievement.

1. The Perils of an Heiress

DOROTHY PAYNE WHITNEY moved back to the 57th Street house of her childhood, the home of Harry and Gertrude, her guardians until she came of age. Preferring to stay there, they sold 871—on which Whitney had worked so long and in which he had lived less than five years—to the Wall Street operator James "Silent" Smith. Dorothy was back on familiar terrain, again across the street from Gladys Vanderbilt. Her formal education was finished, but her informal education was to be steady and lifelong. It was the immediate purpose of Harry and Gertrude (mostly through Beatrice Bend) to groom her, coach her, give her a brilliant coming-out party and every possible preparation for the "right" marriage—marriage to a man who combined social distinction with wealth and, of course, impeccable character, the kind of man not to be found in every drawing room or opera box, but the kind of man a Whitney and a Vanderbilt had every right to insist upon as a husband.

Not only the right but, indeed, the duty. If Harry Payne Whitney was a trifle slapdash in other ways, he was firm in his estimate of Dorothy's social position and what it entailed. He kept in mind the Whitney family, the Whitney heraldic importance. He had been almost as upset by the hurried and paltry nature of his father's wedding to Mrs. Randolph as by having someone else acting as hostess in the house where his mother had reigned so long. These things must be done right. A girl's— a Whitney's—debut, her clothing, her introduction to the correct people, her cultivation of friendships with young men whose qualifications she must weigh carefully (along with Harry's advice), all were part of an elaborate mating ritual in which not one step must be slighted. There was nothing unusual about this, since it was woven into their social fabric and was observed, if not always so strictly, by all of their friends. What was to be unusual was Dorothy's reaction to it. She had little in common with Harry although she got along well enough with him.

There was no discernible ill feeling between Dorothy and her other brother Payne and his wife Helen, perhaps because they did not have the duties of guardianship and lived at some distance so that she saw them less often. The Payne Whitneys, of course, lived in the home Uncle Oliver had given them just above 78th Street, twenty-one blocks north of Harry's. Their country place, appropriately magnificent, was at Manhasset, a few miles west of the enormous acreage and awesome compound Harry had inherited from his father at Old Westbury. Both of Dorothy's sisters-in-law were gifted women, though Helen's verse and children's books would never equal Gertrude's solid achievement as a sculptor and patron of the arts.

Dorothy was easily the most remarkable of the Whitney children. Like her mother, she was born to wealth and social position, brimming with energy, hungry for learning, soon to be a world traveler studying and commenting on the world she traveled. Like her mother, she fell short of real beauty. The similarity ended there. Unlike Flora, who had a tendency to intimidate suitors—even the one she finally married—Dorothy was so compellingly attractive in appearance and manner that she was to number her friends of both sexes in the hundreds and her suitors by the dozens. Her smile came easily and lighted her face. Her innate cordiality was guarded by an appropriate trace of reserve, giving her time for quick measurement of strangers before the warmth fully revealed itself, as much as to say, "I like you and hope you will like me." Taller than average, she would come to prefer blue in dress to complement the blue of her eyes. Like many young women of extreme charm, the camera could sometimes libel and sometimes glorify her. Her mouth missed true delicacy by a fraction, but the smile and the musical voice were ample compensations. Her touch of shyness was not to be confused with any frailty of character. In contrast to Flora, whose abilities were wasted in the competition for bigger ballrooms and parties, Dorothy had a compassion that was ultimately to be translated into "radicalism" displeasing to her set. She was thrilled by such sonorous incitements to righteousness as Henley's *Invictus*. Although she took it for granted that she was of the elite, she shunned the more obtrusive snobberies of her circle and began her philanthropies—safely, through intermediary charities—by the distribution of her cast-off clothing to the poor.

She had inherited the better traits of both parents and—or so it seemed—none of their worst.

Dorothy was to become an heiress at twenty-one, less than four years distant. She would inevitably be a target for those fortune hunters who kept family money in mind, watched the headlines for dying patresfamilias, and had obvious designs on her since the onset of her father's last illness. Gertrude and Harry, though their marriage had not worked out ideally, should have been relatively free from such worry since each had been so amply provided for. But wealth on both sides hardly guaranteed a match based solely on love. Could Gertrude and Harry themselves be certain that they had never considered that a marriage between two large fortunes vastly increased prestige and power instead of dissipating them? There were many gradations of the fortune hunter, down to the man who sought to marry a wealthy girl 90 percent for love and 10 for money. Marriage was difficult enough without that 10 percent handicap. Gertrude, while she was still "being courted," wrote in despair:

> You don't know what the position of an heiress is! You can't imagine. There is no one in all the world who loves her for herself. No one. She cannot do this, that and the other simply because she is known by sight and will be talked about. . . . everyone she loves loves her for what she has got, and earth is hell unless she is a fool and then it's heaven. . . . The fortune hunter chases her footsteps with protestations of never-ending devotion and the true lover (if perchance such a one exists) shuns her society and dares not say the words that tremble on his lips.

Dorothy would inherit about seven million—more if the money was wisely invested.* If this was not quite vast, it was more than most Fifth Avenue fortunes, and the Duke of Marlborough had gone to considerable trouble and endured some humiliation to make a duchess of Consuelo, who brought him not much more. Society abounded with carnivores who would be delighted to marry for only a few hundred thousand. Dorothy was instructed—by Harry, Gertrude, and most of all by Beatrice Bend—that she was a delectable rabbit being circled by hungry wolves. Such counsel is not likely to foster trust in humanity. Everybody knew a few wealthy Society spinsters who had reached that estate because of their eternal suspicion of men's motives.

Yet even the careful Harry and Gertrude could not have anticipated the nature of the crises they were to face in the process of getting Dorothy married. She was intelligent, sensible, agreeable—qualities

---

* Throughout most of this narrative, the dollar was worth roughly ten of today's.

that should have saved them from worry. She was quickly to develop, however, an admiration for achievements higher and deeper than mere teacup technique or cleverness with stocks. That strong will, that sense of independence, traits not yet uppermost, were already beginning to surface. Since her mother had died when Dorothy was six, and she had barely become acquainted with her stepmother before what the family called "her accident," much of her upbringing had to be credited to her governesses before Beatrice Bend came along. Now Beatrice (Dorothy called her BB) was paid to tide her over the risky reefs of adolescence into the safe harbor of marriage. Beatrice was the fresh-faced British type, not pretty but attractive, experienced in Society, fluent in several languages, so worldly in her point of view that Dorothy's friends were surprised that she, the idealist, was so fond of Beatrice.

Perhaps Whitney had planned for Dorothy a grand tour similar to Pauline's, and if so it was Harry and Gertrude who started her out.

They sailed on the *Baltic* August 10, 1904—Harry and Gertrude, Dorothy and her impulsive friend from Roser school days, May Tuckerman, Harry's friend Rawlins Cottenet, and Beatrice and her mother, Mrs. George H. Bend. The gray-haired Mrs. Bend was born Elizabeth Townsend but was known to intimates by her nickname, Marianne. Dorothy had just come down from her brother's Newport place, the Saunterer having observed with maddening condescension, "Little Miss Whitney is a charming girl, and everybody made a fuss over her. . . ." Gertrude and Dorothy of course were still in mourning for the late William C. Whitney. The mourning canons were such that some unlucky persons with large families and elderly relatives wore weeds half their lives.

The disappointment of Harry and Gertrude's marriage could scarcely have been hidden from the observant Dorothy and surely encouraged a wary attitude toward matrimony in Dorothy herself. Harry, a man of potential brilliance who had been spoiled all his life, gave little time to business and devoted himself to his string of racehorses, to hunting, polo, Society, and to the treatment of what sometimes seemed imaginary illnesses. He was kinder to Dorothy than he seemed toward his wife, a woman of extreme sensitivity who often felt rejected.

In England they visited the Pagets at their country home in Suffolk while Harry went on to Holwick to shoot. "Almeric, Sir Edward Stracey & Olive met me at the station," Dorothy wrote in her Line-a-Day diary—which permitted anywhere from forty to seventy-five words a day depending on one's determination to compress and which she kept as faithfully as if her life depended on it—". . . & Sister was waiting on the steps of the house to welcome me." Olive, the older Paget daughter, was the second Olive to be named after Uncle Oliver, bringing to mind the family feud. The Pagets, richly rewarded for taking Oliver's side, owned a handsome townhouse in Berkeley Square as well as the Suffolk country place and were avidly social. Pauline had inherited her mother's weak heart, a condition that at times kept her in bed and sent her on frequent trips to continental spas, but it took an attack of exceptional severity to stop the house parties and card playing that were her life. From the start she seemed determined that Dorothy should marry a title— a compliment in a way, since it showed concern for her sister and perhaps a wish to have her near at hand in Europe. While Dorothy did not dislike Pauline, and there was never a trace of disparagement in the diary, there was no real enthusiasm either. Pauline could be said to have deserted their father and, like Payne, if she had not done it specifically for profit, the profit was there nevertheless.

Dorothy's enthusiasm for travel, however, was total. She had studied at Miss Spence's fashionable school for a year and had also taken a course in architectural appreciation in which she drew workmanlike sketches of famous buildings. In this, her first trip abroad, she reveled in a regimen of stop-and-go tourism grueling enough to sink most seventeen year olds deep in boredom. If her taste was yet unformed, she was in love with the Louvre and its Venus de Milo and Winged Victory, her eye was good and her impressions defensible: "What a beautiful city Paris is and how unlike New York!" She saw the difference although she could not yet analyze it closely. At Versailles she could see the originals of some of the effects architects had sought to reproduce on Fifth Avenue. The cathedral at Chartres transfixed her: "It is too beautiful for words—such stained glass I have never seen!" (Later she was to betray Chartres and call the basilica at Cologne "the most beautiful cathedral in the world!") If her exclamation points were excessive, they represented the honest excitement of a girl who was discovering in travel one of the great pleasures of her life.

In Paris Dorothy was permitted to socialize briefly with two eligible young men from New York who would reappear in her life—Charles Dana Draper, grandson of old Dana of *The Sun*, and Meredith "Bunny" Hare, a well-connected social worker. In Paris also the troupe picked up old Mrs. Vanderbilt and Gladys and made a three-car motor tour of the Loire chateau country and southward, Harry taking the three

girls—Dorothy, Gladys, and May—in his Mercedes, the others riding
in a Morse and a C.G.V. At Aix-les-Bains they watched the gambling.
"I tried my luck with five francs," Dorothy recorded, "and lost it almost
immediately!" Automobiling was great fun, she thought, "the machine
humming beautifully . . . except for the exploding of two tires."

Harry and Gertrude sailed on September 21, leaving Dorothy and
May to spend many more months in Europe in the care of BB and Mrs.
Bend. In Paris there were fittings at the salons of the grand couturières.
"Champot & Raudnitz for suits," Dorothy noted, "—Dumay for evening dress—& Reboux & Cartier for hats." She dined happily at Voisin's with Adelaide and Bertie Randolph, who had come back to England to live after Whitney's death. She had missed them both. "We
went to the English Church this morning," she wrote a trifle self-righteously, "which we like far better than the American, for it seems to be
more devotional & people go there to worship & not to show off their
new clothes." On a side trip to Amsterdam and The Hague chiefly to
see the Rembrandts, she wrote, perhaps more in bravado than involun-
tary admiration, of her liking for the gruesome *Anatomy Lesson*. She
was tireless except for the one day in twenty-seven that she spent, as her
diary put it, "on the sofa" and for which May's euphemism was a visitation of "the friend." After a stay at Nice, they stopped at San Remo and
Genoa, then traveled on to Rome. There they took an apartment and
visited the American ambassador, the sociable Bostonian Henry von
Lengerke Meyer, whom Dorothy had met at Aiken and Washington.
She was blunt about St. Peter's ("The proportions are wonderful but the
decorations horrible") and later, with May and a dozen others, had an
audience with Pope Pius X on which she commented with Episcopalian
coolness: ".   . we all knelt around him in a semicircle & he passed
from one to the other giving each of us his hand (with the emerald ring)
to kiss. . . . it was a most interesting experience."

Perhaps more interesting were the letters she received from several ad-
mirers, one of them Howland Auchincloss, who was at Yale, another
Grosvenor Atterbury, fourteen years out of Yale. Atterbury, a prominent
architect, who lightened his letters with amusing verse, was to pursue
her relentlessly and was to become GA in her diary. Dorothy corresponded with a dozen friends of both sexes back home and dutifully sent
postcards to those less intimate and to hostesses who had been kind.
May was astonished at the extent of Dorothy's correspondence and at
her determination to learn from every church, museum, and art gallery—in fact from every hotel lobby and restaurant. Dorothy on her

part enjoyed May's bubbly cheer and her fund of jokes, one of them quite risqué:

Question: Why is drinking soup with a fork like kissing a pretty girl?
Answer: Because you can't get enough of it.

"Christmas Day!" Dorothy wrote. "May and I went upstairs to Beatrice's and found she had 2 big stockings for us. . . . After we had played with our presents for some time, we drove to S. Maria Maggiore but it was so crowded & smelly there that we soon left & went to St. Peter's instead." Her deep attachment to Beatrice was evident when Beatrice left the girls in Mrs. Bend's care for a fortnight, causing Dorothy to write, "I have never felt so lonely in all my life." After the holidays, May was met in Rome by her father, come to take her home. She made the mistake of telling him the soup-and-kisses joke, causing him to upbraid her roundly for indecency and warn her not to bring such immodesty back to America.

On January 23 Dorothy wrote, "My 18th birthday! How terribly old I am getting!" and dropped the subject there. By late February she was in Sicily with the Bends, standing in the Greek theater at Taormina, where Almeric's courtship of Pauline had been the presentation of 1895, "trying to drink in the beauty of the scene. The deep blue sky & sea, the . . . brick theatre, pink in color, the green hills & the towering snowcapped summit of Mt. Aetna beyond. . . ." But Venice in the month of May was also "divine—in fact the place is Heaven itself."

With summer, Dorothy was back in Paris to meet Harry and Gertrude, who had come for their annual visit and also to help Dorothy in selecting her clothing for her coming debut in New York. ". . . first to Paquin," Dorothy wrote mournfully, "then Worth, Doucet next and lastly Callot," adding later, "it will be a relief to get away from Paris and fittings." She was not like some, including her late mother, who enjoyed every minute at the couturières. When at last they sailed in September on the *Kaiser Wilhelm II*, Dorothy had been in Europe for more than a year and only once had mentioned being homesick.

2. *Coming Out*

WHILE DOROTHY was abroad, the eccentric Episcopal clergyman C. W. de Lyon Nichols, who aspired to succeed Ward McAllister, named her as a member of the current Four Hundred in his book *The Ultra-Fashionable Peerage of America.* This recognition at eighteen! With effort and maturity she could expect membership in Nichols's superexclusive 150, which included both the Harry Payne Whitneys and the Payne Whitneys. For a man of the cloth, Nichols was singularly idolatrous of material things. He noted that "the collective contents of the jewel caskets of the ultra-fashionable set in New York society approximate closely to 170 millions of dollars." Among those women who had spent a million for jewelry he named Mrs. Astor, Mrs. Vanderbilt, Mrs. O. H. P. Belmont, and Mrs. William K. Vanderbilt, Jr. While neither Gertrude Vanderbilt Whitney nor Helen Hay Whitney qualified for this rank, each owned a half million or so worth of gems and, said Nichols, were "worthy of being entered as prize exhibitors at any lapidary's vanity fair."

Although Dorothy punctiliously observed the ceremonials of Society, she was not the gem-counting kind. She hired a personal maid, Louisa Weinstein, whom she treated with such kindness that Louisa was to stay on, a fond fixture. Dorothy resumed her activities; her appointment books were invariably filled. Her diary, however, shows no awareness of the way in which Col. William d'Alton Mann of *Town Topics* got his comeuppance. This occurred when a Mann subordinate attempted to blackmail the fashionable broker Edwin Post, and instead of paying up, Post had testified against him. By this time Mann's career of extortion had become notorious enough so that *Collier's Magazine* saw in it a muckraking opportunity that would benefit New York and also raise circulation. Mann was in Europe at the time, but so deliberately and repeatedly did *Collier's* brand him and his chief associate, Joseph M. Deuel (who was, ironically, presiding justice of the Children's Court), as blackmailers that Deuel, like Oscar Wilde in a similar dilemma, had no recourse but to fall into the trap and sue. The case had not yet come to court, but there was plenty about it in the papers, and in the meantime Mann's *Fads and Fancies of Representative Americans* was published at last. It was a gorgeous book, as indeed it ought to be, considering what it had cost its "subscribers," printed in red, gold, and black on heavy sixteen- by twenty-six-inch stock, the top and sides of gold leaf and the cover bound in green and gold morocco.

There was William C. Whitney on a two-page spread, pages 126–27. He was flattered like all the rest of the eighty-two subjects, but in a very short "biographical sketch" (with photographs only of him and his houses), for which he must have supplied the meager facts himself. It said not a word about his two wives, his children, or the nature of his business, admitting only to his ancient family tree and his famous

horses and domiciles. While a man's inclusion in the book did not necessarily mean that he had any scandal to hide, and was believed in
many cases simply to indicate his willingness to pay for the promise of
being treated without innuendo in *Town Topics*, no one could be sure
who were the fearful and who the innocent. Hence the censorious were
inclined to attach some embarrassing implication to it. But since among
the embarrassed were three Vanderbilts (two of Gertrude's brothers,
Alfred and Reginald, and a cousin), Chauncey Depew, J. Pierpont
Morgan, Thomas Fortune Ryan, President Roosevelt himself, and
many others, the embarrassment was spread out very thin and could in
fact be regarded by some as a species of distinction.

At the subsequent trial it was brought out that Harry Lehr had of late
years become a secret informant for Colonel Mann. This explained why
the treatment of Lehr in *Town Topics* had changed from venomous to
admiring. While Mann, returned from abroad, was technically not the
defendant but a witness for the plaintiff Deuel, the defense managed to
smear him and Deuel so thoroughly as blackmailers that Deuel lost his
suit and the Colonel for once seemed flustered. He had no reputation to
lose, however, so he continued to publish *Town Topics* every week as if
nothing had happened, and to be more careful in his blackmail.
Dorothy evidently preferred not to mention this sensation in her diary.
Town Topics continued to be so provocative that she, along with almost
everybody else in Society, was at least an occasional reader.

Dorothy was friendly and liked many people, but her favorite family
was easily the Robert Bacons, who lived near her on Long Island. They
were now in Washington. The senior Robert Bacon, a Harvard classmate and close friend of President Roosevelt, had been an all-around
athlete and was ruggedly handsome at forty-five. He had been a pall-
bearer at Dorothy's stepmother's funeral. His wife, Martha, very fond of
the "orphan" Dorothy, was an adviser and confidante, and their daughter Martha, a year younger than Dorothy, was one of her closest friends.
There was also young Bob Bacon, now at Harvard, who wished to
marry her. The senior Bacon had been a Morgan partner until 1902
when, some thought, he had not been at his best in the Morgan struggle
with Harriman and had been gently shed from the firm. He was now
Assistant Secretary of State under the new Secretary, Elihu Root. One
thing that was to create a difficulty for Dorothy was the fact—as yet unknown to her—that the Bacon couple, who were devoted to her, were as
earnest as their son in their hopes that she would become their
daughter-in-law.

On January 1, 1906, at their invitation, she was in Washington partaking of high-echelon holiday festivities. "Diplomatic reception at Mr. Root's house," she recorded, "—at which we all received. Met dozens of foreigners & had a wonderful time. In the P.M. automobiled with Bob B to the Country Club—-then walked for an hour. . . . Dance here in the evening—got to bed 3.30—*fine day!*" Dorothy's budding interest in government was heightened by this propinquity to the powerful. Secretary Root was fond of her. The Bacons were thoroughly at home in the genial Roosevelt White House. She did not meet the President—her meeting with him was to occur under more dramatic circumstances—but she did meet his daughter Alice, so unconventional and peppery, so frequently in the newspapers.

Three weeks later, on January 22, the night before her nineteenth birthday, Dorothy attended her first dinner dance, at the Charles Tracy Barneys' (Aunt Lillie and Uncle Charlie) at 67 Park Avenue. Among those present were at least seven young men mentioned discreetly in her diary, not as having shown romantic interest in her—never that—but as having taken tea with her, danced with her, or gone to the opera with her: Sheldon Whitehouse, Bobbie Gerry, Howland Auchincloss, Lloyd Warren, Phoenix Ingraham, Billy Hitt, and Wirt Howe. She had some of her father's reserve and a careful reader would have to scrutinize several years of her diary entries to begin to understand faint signals of doubt or appreciation for young men on her part. Wearing "a gown of white lace, chiffon and satin," she helped her aunt receive the guests and later was whirled away by Worthington Whitehouse, Sheldon's older brother, who led the cotillion with her.

The Barney home was beautifully decorated with "clusters of orange trees in full bloom and Japanese trees loaded with blossoms." It was such a gala affair ("Wonderful," Dorothy wrote in her diary, underlining it twice) that *The Herald* mistakenly thought it was her official debut. That came at a much bigger party a week later in Harry and Gertrude's spacious ballroom. Here Dorothy—undoubtedly clad in one of her Worth gowns—stood beside her thirty-year-old sister-in-law as the guests arrived and later led out across the shining floor with the same Worthington Whitehouse, a forty-year-old bachelor practiced in cotillion leading. Music was furnished by the well-remembered Nathan Franko's orchestra. A prize guest was Alice Roosevelt with her fiancé, Congressman Nicholas Longworth. One Vanderbilt feud was seen to be fading at last with the once-disinherited Cornelius and his once-traduced wife, Grace, present in the same room with Gertrude and old

Mrs. Vanderbilt. The cartloads of roses and carnations were supplied by
Rawlins Cottenet, Society's favored florist as well as a member of the
Meadow Brook—a kindly man whom Dorothy was strangely to en
counter at times of crisis in her life. For the cotillion figures, the favors
were tomahawks and Red Riding Hood capes and hats for the women,
and Indian headdresses and fur headpieces for the men. The effect was
striking when the dancers put on the headgear and the great gold and-
white ballroom became a sea of undulating colored feathers. But there
was nothing quite as impudently startling as jockeys riding in on fake
horses, or an automobile rolling into the room in obedience to the
stagecraft of William C. Whitney. Dorothy was one of some 150 New
York City Society girls certified in similar rites that winter as being of
marriageable age, but she was easily, as those who rated these functions
would put it, the most "important."

3. Such a Perfect Ideal

DOROTHY WAS a regular at Grace Church. She was beginning to diverge
slightly from conventional piety, noting about one sermon, "It was
about the angels & I had to giggle internally all the time." She was fond
of maxims expressing rebellious idealism. One of several that she wrote
in the flyleaves of her diary would have done away with beautiful
Charlies and Cologne edifices. "There is only one true religion—the
ministry of the head to the devotion of the heart. You need no priesthood here but the priesthood of conscience; you need no costly erec-
tion of churches, but the open world of God's house of worship." She
attended a basketry class and one in literature, loved informative lectures, taught a neighborhood Sunday school class of poor girls, was active in the Junior League and the Charity Organization Society. She enjoyed the theater and the opera ("Caruso in Tosca most wonderful
thing I have ever heard"), was average at tennis but excellent at riding,
and for her the dance that ended before 3:00 A.M. lacked something.
She was fascinated by young men, spending time with many of them in
that process of judicious appraisal that would presumably narrow the
field until only the right one remained.

The debutante mating ritual included five o'clock teas, sessions of
auction bridge, riding together, and occasional house parties, heavily
chaperoned, at places ranging from Tuxedo Park to Morristown to Dr.
William Seward Webb's country place on Lake Champlain to the Whit-

ney lodge in the Adirondacks. At a Tuxedo tea Dorothy improved her acquaintance with Howard Cary, who had been a suitor of Eleanor Roosevelt until bested by his Harvard classmate Franklin Delano Roosevelt. Cary lived only three blocks away, at 17 East 54th Street. There seemed no special attraction between them; Dorothy simply named him in her diary as one of the guests. She was warmer about a later house party at Hyde Park ("Wonderful ride in the P.M. with H. Cary") and then a dance at which he was one of her partners and she wrote, "*Wonderful*—stayed up till 6 o'clock." Her diary for 1906 showed tea dates with more than forty different men.

These young people had time and money to spend, took frequent travel as a matter of course, and were forever jumping into carriages or automobiles or boarding trains for New Haven, Boston, or Washington. Most of them went to Europe every summer and were at home on the great ocean liners, regularly encountering one another in Piccadilly or the Place Vendôme. Scions of our most affluent families, with townhouses in New York and country houses elsewhere (Dorothy could choose among four country houses), they took for granted servants, opera boxes, private railroad cars, yachts, horseflesh, and exclusive clubs. The young men were invariably listed in the Social Register as belonging to two or three clubs, the Knickerbocker, Racquet, Union, and New York Yacht Club being favorites in addition to their university club, be it Yale, Harvard, or Princeton. The young ladies had been forbidden to have any clubs at all, the idea of women having private clubs being considered indecent because they might then use their clubs as many men used theirs, to arrange assignations. But the irrepressible Mrs. J. Borden Harriman, always known as Daisy, aided by Gertrude and Helen Whitney and a few others, broke the taboo in 1900 by starting the Colony Club on Madison Avenue, of which Dorothy was now a member. There were free spirits such as Daisy, and such as Dorothy was to become in her own way, but it was an ingrown society. Its female members especially were protected from any real contact with the majority of the nation's 85,000,000 people—that is, those who were self-supporting and those who were poor. Still, Dorothy's chauffeur drove her over to Payne Whitney's for lunch and she noted "Ethel Barrymore was there," so at least the taboo against people of the stage was relaxing.

A few days after her debut, Dorothy seemed to come into the purview of destiny when she dined at the E. H. Harrimans' (E. H. was the enormously rich cousin of J. Borden Harriman) on East 66th Street. A part of the mating ritual was for kindly matrons to invite debutantes to dine or dance with eligible males. Old Harriman, known as the "Little Giant of Wall Street," was slight of build and not one for small talk, but one of Dorothy's closest Junior League friends was the Harrimans' daughter Mary. Two years older, Mary was a handsome brunette who had won Dorothy's admiration first for finishing Barnard College and then for urging that the League do something constructive for the city and the poor rather than just existing in luxury. One of the guests was Dorothy's friend (possibly becoming an admirer) Meredith "Bunny" Hare. Others were Edwin V. Morgan, until lately United States Minister to Korea, and his younger friend Willard Straight, also with the State Department. Straight, who was twenty-six, had so much presence, urbanity, wit, and charm that he was apt to make other young men feel cheated even had he not been more than six feet tall and very good looking. His smile united his whole face—mouth, cheeks, eyes, forehead—in irresistible warmth. He brought with him a breath of the fascination of far places, for he had been in the Orient six years, had recently returned from Korea with Morgan, and was one of those rare Occidentals who spoke Chinese. Old Harriman, who had plans for immense railroad projects in the Far East, actually found this young man's advice helpful. Straight, who had already embarked on a romance with Mary Harriman, was soon to leave for Cuba, where he would be secretary to the Minister, Morgan.

Was Dorothy impressed by him? Not according to her diary, in which she simply named "Mr. Straight" as one of the guests. In her diary, however—it had no lock—she schooled herself to be objective and contained, as if fearing that someone might peer into it.

So Willard Straight entered her life for four hours at the Harrimans' and passed out of it again. Three weeks later she left for Aiken with Payne and Helen and a few friends on board *Wanderer*, her father's private car, which was now Harry's property. Harry and Payne were hardly inseparable, but then they never had been. Still, they seemed on reasonably good terms, and at Aiken they played tennis together, both being crack players. The fact remained that there were undercurrents here that can only be surmised. One might read significance into the fact that Uncle Oliver was Dorothy's godfather, living only a few blocks away on Fifth Avenue, and yet this agreeable girl, so averse to discord of any kind, never mentioned him in her diary until the day he died.

In five weeks at Aiken Dorothy played tennis, walked (separately) with Grosvenor Atterbury, Insley Blair, and several other young men, rode regularly, and "had a fall while trying to jump Big Brother—neither of us at all hurt, but I had a long walk home." Stopping in Washington on the way north, she was sentimental enough to visit the one-time home of her parents there, whose present occupants she knew: "Lunched with Mrs. Slater at 1731 H Street (where I was born) & went with her to Senate." Always a self-improver, she also visited the Bureau of Engraving and, "Tea with Mrs. Bacon—then I automobiled in the country with Billy Hitt." Billy, who had been at her birthday party in New York, was the son of long-time Congressman Robert Hitt of Illinois, head of the Foreign Affairs Committee, whose wife was a friend of the Hays and so socially ambitious that they had a place at Newport. In fact, Dorothy's own next stay was at Harry and Gertrude's Newport place—a brief one, for she was back in New York to board the *Oceanic* for Liverpool April 24, with Beatrice, Mrs. Bend, and Dorothy's personal maid Louisa. This was an early trip, a special one, for she was to be a bridesmaid at Adelaide Randolph's wedding. She must have been delighted that Howard Cary and Harry Curtis were also aboard—particularly Cary, whom she invariably referred to in her diary by his first name, whereas Harry was always "Mr. Curtis." In view of what was soon to happen to Cary, there was later much gossip among Dorothy's friends, who said he must have known she would take the *Oceanic* and had arranged to be on it with her.

"Read aloud & talked with Howard most of the afternoon," Dorothy noted. Howard Cary was almost two years out of Harvard but evidently had not yet entered any business or profession. His mother was a sister-in-law of Mrs. James Brown Potter, whose rendition of " 'Ostler Joe" had so scandalized Washington in 1886; his father, related to that good friend of Flora and William Whitney, the novelist Mrs. Burton Harrison, was a lawyer, club man, traveler, and linguist who spoke Japanese and Russian and had written a lively account of his journey from New York to Peking.

"Walked with Howard before lunch," Dorothy wrote April 28, "and read aloud with him afterwards." That she would read aloud with a young man did not prove that they were seriously involved, but there was a degree of intimacy about reading together, and Dorothy would not share such moments with just any shipmate who came along. "Beatrice, Mr. Curtis, and I lunched on deck . . .," she wrote. "Afterward Howard & I finished 'Colonel Carter'*—next we played bridge—and walked again. . . ." Reaching London May 3, she visited the Pagets

---

* Probably *Colonel Carter's Christmas*, 1903, by F. Hopkinson Smith.

but stayed at Claridge's and on May 5 made the shocked entry: "Yesterday Howard Cary died suddenly!"

The notation illustrates the restraint she maintained in her diary, for she wrote not one more word about it in her Line-a-Day. The mystery was featured in the New York newspapers. May Tuckerman wrote to her in agitation that it was rumored among her friends that Howard had committed suicide because Dorothy had rejected his marriage proposal. The facts of the case were indeed startling. Young Cary had come to London to visit his cousin, Lord Fairfax, the only American-born British baron, who had inherited the title from an ancestor who had settled in Virginia. The two had dined together on May 3 and gone to the theater, then returned to their Kensington lodgings. Cary was perfectly cheerful and natural, Fairfax said. Yet he was found next morning in his room "with a pistol in his right hand and a bullet wound in his right temple. He was still dressed in evening clothes. There was no sign of a struggle in the room."

Dorothy was pelted with letters from American girl friends eager to know if Cary's hopeless love for her had caused him to shoot himself. "How perfectly awful about Howard Cary's death," one of them wrote. "I wish you would tell me all you know about it. Somebody told me it was because he was desperately in love with you . . . Do tell me about it, dear."

Where there was this much smoke, there may have been a small spark of fire—that is, Dorothy may have spoken well of Cary to her friends—but that there was anything more than the mere beginnings of a romance seems unlikely. The stigma attached to suicide at the time was deep; young Cary's family and friends insisted that he was happy enough and had no problems. Dorothy herself, as indicated in a later letter to her from May, could not believe it was suicide, and a coroner's investigation later called the death accidental despite the evidence. Life went on. In the meantime, perhaps luckily for her composure, Dorothy was busy having fittings at Paquin's and was a bridesmaid on May 8 when Adelaide was married at Trinity Church, Sloane Square. The groom was Lionel Lambart, thirty-three, the polo-playing second son of the late Earl of Cavan, brother of the present earl and heir presumptive to the title.

Dorothy's preparation for life continued as she crossed to Spain with Beatrice, joined her Aunt Lilly, and toured the obligatory places. Thrilled though she was by the Alhambra and the Generalife Gardens (she spent "2 heavenly hours" in the gardens), she gave it all a bare hundred words; her mother had given them an outpouring of thousands of words when she wrote to her parents from there in 1863. At the Prado Dorothy loved Velasquez, less so Murillo. The bullfight she saw was "most picturesque but horrible—although none of us turned green or felt sick. Stayed for 3 bulls."

A month in Spain, then back to London, where she resolved to memorize a Wordsworth poem every day. Here the Pagets introduced her to a young and eligible Scot, Lord Falconer (called "Boo"), who was one of those who followed her a week later to the races at Ascot, where her father had come near losing his black pearl to the light-fingered Day. Here she was joined by old Mrs. Vanderbilt and Gladys. Here, too, DeLancey Jay, great-great-grandson of John Jay, renewed a friendship with her, having met her in New York. Jay, educated at Eton and Harvard (1903), was a law graduate serving a season with the Foreign Service, as a few young Society men did. He was a secretary to Ambassador Reid. His time with Dorothy was divided with Cecil Higgins, Jack White, and the young attaché from the French embassy, R. V. Periguy, and, of course, Falconer; but Jay seemed to have the advantage. Ascot, as always since the reign of Queen Anne, was highest fashion, so Dorothy's toilette received Louisa's best attention. Mrs. Keppel, there with King Edward, remembered her entertainment by Dorothy's father in New York.

"Mrs. Keppel introduced me to the King!" Dorothy noted, pleased that his horse-loving majesty was kind and remembered her father. "After the races today DeLancey & I rode over to Winsor [sic] forest & all through the park. It was the most wonderful ride. . . ."

Wordsworth was suffering. She crossed to Paris with the Bends, had fittings and bought clothing, then "did" Germany from Bad Kissingen and Berlin to Nuremburg and Munich, finally alighting in August at the luxurious Palace Hotel in St. Moritz. Jay and Falconer showed up there to renew their rivalry for her attention as they all settled down to tennis, hiking, riding, and afternoon teas on terraces with spectacular views. So did Sumner Gerard of the Gramercy Park Gerards, and the handsome Lydig Hoyt of New York. She chatted with an Indian rajah and the Governor General of Ashanti at tea, played tennis with Baron Monaco, dined with Lydig Hoyt and Baron Max Oppenheim of Frankfurt. Not to her diary would she admit any unusual fancy, but she seemed to enjoy herself especially with the Marchese di Serramazzana Flori from Milan, perhaps because he was thirty years her senior, courtly and amusing, and he permitted her to drive his four-horse coach. He proposed marriage to her and she declined, but with kindness. A family friend, the famous New York surgeon Dr. Andrew James McCosh, aged forty-eight and married, arrived and gave a picnic. Dorothy gave a dinner party for all her friends with cotillion after: "Danced till 2.30—Splendid." One would not have suspected from her diary that she was more attracted to DeLancey Jay than to any of them. With Sumner Gerard she played golf, had tea at Hanselman's, "& drove in a cab down to the Bad to buy Town Topics." In a letter to May Tuckerman she admitted that she liked Gerard, whose qualifications included Groton, baseball and track (captain) at Yale, and service with Roosevelt's Rough Riders in Cuba. From May she got an utterly scandalous letter in which she confessed that with a friend she had discussed the question of which young man among their acquaintance would be preferable in bed.

Serramazzana and many others saw her off at the station, the next stop being Ragatz, which she described as a "lovely place," with no knowledge that her mother had been there twice, once as a young traveler, later as a bereaved mother and jealous wife. Then came one of the indulgent pastimes of the rich—stops of only a few days' duration at a series of resort hotels, each offering something unique in accommodations, cuisine, or views: Andermatt, Interlaken, Grindelwald, Vevey, Zermatt, all names ringing of glamor and exclusiveness. And finally Paris, matchless Paris, where Sumner Gerard called on her again, she had fittings with Douillet, enjoyed *Hernani*, and sailed on the *Kaiserin Auguste Victoria* September 28. Ever the learner, she explored its Marconi room and landed in New York October 6.

Bob Bacon, DeLancey Jay, and others called on her at Westbury next day, so she gave a Sunday luncheon party: "I sat next Courty [Courtlandt Barnes] & Freddie Prince. I rode all afternoon with DeLancey & he came to dinner." There followed a procession of callers: Lydig Hoyt, Grosvenor Atterbury, Sheldon Whitehouse, James Breese, Lloyd Warren, and Devereux Milburn. From Como, Serramazzana sent her a plaintive couplet: "*Je sens un rigoureux tourment, / Causé par votre éloignement*," adding in part:

"Anybody who knows you must believe in God as only he could create such a perfect ideal. . . ."

4. Love Will Come Slowly

DOROTHY'S POSITION as younger sister in the Whitney household was growing awkward. She cherished her independence and, although she got along well with Gertrude, it could hardly have been pleasant for any of them during those intervals when there was tension between Harry and Gertrude. By general consent Dorothy moved from the great Westbury mansion built by William C. Whitney for Edith and himself, now occupied by Harry and his family. With the Bends she took over the smaller (but still huge) three-story stone-and-shingle house called Applegreen only a five-minute walk distant, which Whitney had built for Harry and Gertrude after their marriage. The move was accomplished in the friendliest manner, and Dorothy often walked over to Harry's place to talk with the Whitneys or their children, Flora, Cornelius, and Barbara.

Thus, before she was twenty Dorothy was her own hostess in a spacious house with a staff of servants available for social gatherings whenever she chose—a freedom of which she made full use. In the city she still lived for a time at Harry's but was looking for her own apartment.

In sharp contrast to her late mother, she had a second existence outside Society. She enrolled for a course in political economy at Columbia, took piano lessons, had instruction in lace making, saved used clothing for the poor, helped Lillian Wald at the Henry Street Settlement, and went to Bible class at Grace Church on Thursdays. Her devotion to the opera and the theater was appreciative rather than social. She cheered Nazimova in A *Doll's House* and went with one of her gentleman friends (always with at least one other couple) to performances of Olga Nethersole, Leo Ditrichstein, Mrs. Leslie Carter, and Ethel Barrymore. She was twenty years old January 23, 1907, but said not a word about it in her diary. Surrounded by well over a score of suitors, she was giving serious thoughts to marriage. If perhaps Bob Bacon, DeLancey Jay, Sheldon Whitehouse, and Charles Draper might seem to have an edge over the rest, still she had no "steady" and her intentions were a mystery. Her notepaper, engraved with her "DPW" monogram, caused Jay to complain that he felt outraged and lonely when he observed New York installations of the Department of Public Works appropriating those same initials. Accepting the attentions of so many young men put her in danger of being considered a flirt. On the contrary, much as she liked boys, this was also her considered reaction to her shock in discovering such made-in-heaven marriages as Harry and Gertrude's to be quite unhappy and her decision to make a careful choice from a wide selection.

By her own later testimony, she placed marriage on a pedestal dangerously high. She believed in having "long talks" with young men.

It helped to appraise them. Had she taken to heart particularly her reading of Henry James's *The Ambassadors* for her book circle that winter?

The pace was fast and she loved it—the virtually all-night proms at Yale, the house parties, the New York dinner dances, the five weeks of nonstop activity at Aiken from which she returned writing, "Aiken has been so heavenly!" Again she wrote with astonishing diary brevity, "Serramazzana died today"—just the three words, then on to happier things. Although the marchese—a dedicated fortune hunter—unlike Cary had died a natural death, it might seem an ominous pattern among her suitors that could threaten to enroll her among the *femmes fatales*. She was having the experience, unnerving to some, of being a perpetual bridesmaid—less troubling to her since she was in the position of declining proposals, of bowling men over like tenpins. She filled the bridesmaid role when her dear friend and cousin Kathcrine Barney, two years older than she, married the broker Courtlandt Barnes, and again eight days later when May Tuckerman (her own age) married the broker Hermann Kinnicutt. "Tottie [Hollister] lunched with me alone," she noted imperturbably, "after wh. the annual spring meeting of the J. L. [Junior League] took place & I was elected President." No more than on the deaths of Cary and Serramazzana did she comment on her election—a considerable honor and a sign of general respect for her judgment.

Dorothy took both *David Harum* and *Anna Karenina* with her when she boarded the *Adriatic* June 19, along with BB and Mrs. Bend, for her 1907 European tour. Also aboard were Grosvenor Atterbury and Lloyd Warren, both architects and both enemies of her reading program, determined to hold her in conversation. She avoided Atterbury as much as possible despite his prestige in his field: He was too insistent, sixteen years older than she, a half-inch shorter, too dapper, and she had not the slightest intention of marrying him.

Landing at Cherbourg, she visited in Paris with her sister Pauline and with Mrs. Vanderbilt and Gladys (how tied to her mother Gladys must have seemed in comparison with Dorothy's relative freedom!) before she sailed north from Hamburg with the Bends. She was ecstatic over the Norwegian fjords, enjoyed Stockholm, its Skansen and its royal palace ("Such funny rooms—inlaid with china!"). At St. Petersburg she took tea with the American Ambassador Riddle, as well as the attentive Count Stefan Przezdziecki of Warsaw, whom she would meet again and whose name she wisely simplified to "Count P." In Moscow of all

places she ran into Bob Bacon, touring with a friend. Her diary treated
the meeting with a negligence that might have wounded young Bacon,
especially considering the lavishness of her sightseeing superlatives, perhaps here justified. She called St. Basil's "the most bizarre & dazzling
church I have ever seen." Then came Kiev, Warsaw, Budapest, and
Vienna (where she again encountered Bacon), after which she and the
Bends took a nine-day rest at the Hungarian resort at Tatra Lomnicz.

Then to Venice, where she composed a very private document:

When the right person comes along, I wonder if one has doubts, even
then. Many of us are immediately carried off our feet and swept away
into an irresistible current of love—while to the rest of us love comes
walking slowly, and yet with sure steps he overtakes us and folds his arms
about our shrinking forms. How little can we know ourselves, and yet I
feel that love would come very slowly and gradually into my heart—and
not with a sudden inrush of emotion. Of course the man one marries
cannot be all one dreams of having him—and I am fully expectant of
disappointments—I can't help longing for certain things—he must be
strong, and he must be tender—he must be honest and generous, and
also kind and thoughtful—and oh—if he will only love me tenderly, take
care of me, put his arms about me, and let [unfinished line] . . .

Married life is full of rifts and troubles of course—and I have seen too
much of life to imagine it is all a rosy dream. But if two people understand each other and each has patience and confidence—the troubles will
be cleared away, and will not become black and mysterious shadows. Perfect faith in each other—that above all things is the truest, surest foundation, and I can't imagine anything more wonderful than this sort of an
understanding between two people. Nothing then could really go wrong.

I don't think I could fall in love with a man who had no ambition and
no aim in life—because I feel a great longing to become a part of his life
and help him when possible to do his work. And then besides—if he
lacked all ambition—I couldn't admire him—and admiration for my husband would be [unfinished line] . . .

I wonder if a woman really can be a help to the man she marries. I
have always thought so until a few weeks ago, when all sorts of horrid
feelings came to me at Tatra, and I imagined that I was not apt to be
happy. If I demand so much in a man in the way of mental capacity and
desire for work and accomplishment of what is worth while—doubtless
that man will be far beyond me in every way, and after a few years I may
drop out of his life, having ceased to be of any help, and then each of us
will go our own way. Perhaps the chances of happiness would be greater
were I to marry a man with no career who would need me in his daily
life—while on the other hand a man with a good mind and the feeling of
living and being "up and doing" would stride ahead of me and never
need the hand which I would long to give. If these two were weighed in

the balance, of course I should choose happiness with the man of no
career—for surely happiness is the aim of life.

I have only seen one man that comes near to what I long for—only
one man that I would really like to marry—at least I think I would!
Sometimes I feel "oh no"—not even you—but altogether he fills up most
of the holes and niches and I know he is much too good for me.

Who, who was too good for her? Not DeLancey Jay, whom she had
crossed off the "serious" list. Possibly Sheldon Whitehouse, less likely
Charles Draper (friends described him as interesting rather than good),
most likely of all Bob Bacon, whom she had recently met on tour, the
admirer she had known and liked for years. Just out of Harvard, where
he had captained the crew, solid and likable, though not quite as handsome as his father, he was closer to her in friendship than any of the
others and was permitted to address her as "dearest Dorothy" in his letters. But still, the tone of her soliloquy was that of a young woman who
had not yet met the man who would sweep her off her feet and make it
unnecessary for her to weigh and measure and debate and ponder.

On to Paris ("I love Paris!" she wrote), where she had fittings at Worth
and Callot, bought a new Renault automobile, and joyfully foregath-
ered with the Bacons, who were visiting there while their son traveled.
With a hired chauffeur, Dorothy and Beatrice drove "all around the
Bois" in the new car, then to Beauvais to see the cathedral. When
Dorothy sailed October 3 on the *Kronprinzessin Cecelia*, she had had
fifteen weeks of almost incessant travel. She felt handicapped by an inability to translate the extraordinary pleasure she took in travel into art,
music, or even adequate words: "It hurts to drink in so much beauty
that one cannot give it out, and I, having no form of expression, almost
choke with it inside. . . . so it all just shivers inside of me."

The ship landed October 9. The country was in the grip of financial
panic. Two weeks later, her uncle Charles T. Barney's Knickerbocker
Trust Company went under. It was said (though Dorothy either did not
hear it or did not believe it) that J. P. Morgan could have tided the bank
over its crisis, that Barney tried desperately to see Morgan and was
turned away. Barney, the punster who had lampooned Alexander
Gunn's liking for mugs, went into deep depression and shot himself
dead three weeks later. "We have just heard this evening the terrible
news of Uncle Charlie's death," Dorothy recorded without mention that
it was suicide: again this strange avoidance of violence, which seemed to
"shiver inside her" in a different way and to represent an inordinate cau-

tion. She hurried to comfort her Aunt Lilly and Cousin Kate—hurried also with Beatrice to buy mourning attire. Even in tragedy, form must be observed.

5. Kings and Presidents

CHRISTMAS WAS not usually a family occasion among the Whitneys. There was no gathering of Dorothy, Harry, Payne, and their families for a great dinner with talk and singing and exchange of gifts. Dorothy instead called at Harry's with gifts for the children, then later in the day at Payne's—a drop-in affair rather than one of long preparation. This year, however, was more festive because Count Lâszló Széchényi of Budapest, Chamberlain to the Austrian Emperor, was in town to marry Gladys Vanderbilt. Dorothy was once more to be a bridesmaid, this time along with Ruth Twombly, a cousin of the bride-to-be. Ruth, being two years older, should have worried even more than Dorothy about the number of her appearances in this role, and her later spinster status was to be blamed on her suspicions that her suitors were chiefly interested in the millions she would inherit. There was talk in the gossip press that Dorothy, already known for her democratic inclinations, opposed the match, that "when Gladys Vanderbilt became engaged to Count Széchényi Miss Whitney besought her to change her mind and her fiancé," but that "Mrs. Vanderbilt senior took a hand in the argument" and let her know sharply that the match had her entire approval.

Dorothy was too tactful to have done more than express a mild opinion to Gladys before her mind was made up. But she may not have approved since she did have a suspicion of American marriages to titles and she was, though she was moving toward ecumenism, a WASP while Count Lâszló was a Catholic. Gladys had met the count in Berlin, where his father had for years been Austria's envoy to the court and where they had attended a ball given by the American Ambassador Charlemagne Tower. The wedding at the Vanderbilt home on 57th Street made a stir in the press. It was a final wrench to the dowager since Gladys was her "baby," the last of her children unmarried. Henceforth the old lady would be truly alone with her servants in the city's largest domicile even if Gertrude was still across the street. Among the four hundred guests were all the "regulars." One striking irregularity was the total forgiveness of young Cornelius Vanderbilt (he was now thirty-six) by Mrs. Vanderbilt and the family, so that Alfred, who had succeeded to seniority when his older brother was banished, stepped aside and permitted Cornelius to give the bride away. The Vanderbilt detestation of Cornelius's wife Grace had not slowed the couple's social pace, for at Cowes, King Edward had boarded their 233-foot steam yacht *North Star*, the Emperor William II and Prince Henry of Prussia had "dined beneath Cornelius's purple and white pennant" at Trave-munde, and the couple had also entertained the Grand Duke Boris and been presented to the Czarina. Old Mrs. Vanderbilt had at last recog-nized and surrendered to the social prodigy of the new century.

The groom and many of the visiting Austro-Hungarian nobility wore hussars' uniforms with epaulets, bringing to Fifth Avenue perhaps its last glimpse of Congress-of-Vienna magnificence. At the moment the vows were exchanged, Gladys would be the Countess Széchényi; the count would be $12,000,000 richer. Along with Dorothy and Ruth Twombly as bridesmaids was Gertrude's ten-year-old daughter Flora as flower girl. In the Louis XIV drawing room the marriage was performed by Monsi-gnor Lavelle of St. Patrick's Cathedral, the bond being further sanctified by a cable from Pope Pius X. The trousseau of the bride, who had stud-ied voice under Jean de Reszke, cost $75,000, and the gifts given her were as usual stupendous, Dorothy and Ruth making do with presenting her with sapphire-and-diamond jewelry. Dorothy was shocked—or amused—enough to keep a newsclipping: "It is rumored that after the Vanderbilt wedding the announcement will be made of the engagement of Miss Whitney to Ogden Mills Bishop, a son of the late Heber R Bishop." True, she had had tea with young Bishop (whose brother Courtlandt had married Beatrice Bend's beautiful sister Amy), but marriage!

As is invariably the case with bridesmaids, this marriage took away one of Dorothy's closest friends and left her own status more speculative in the eyes of birthday-counting observers. In March she was off with Harry and a party for a private car tour of Mexico and his mine holdings there. She met Harry's friend, the ruthless and efficient dictator Porfirio Diaz, whom she described innocently as "very intelligent & easy to get along with." On June 18, 1908, with the Bends, she sailed for England.

Now that DeLancey Jay was out of the running (though he still wrote to her affectionately), this tour developed into a competition between Lord Falconer and Sheldon Whitehouse (now private secretary to Am-bassador Whitelaw Reid), for Dorothy's favor, with other contenders in the wings. Her sister Pauline was advancing the cause of Falconer, whom Dorothy thought agreeable, but the erect, courtly, curly haired

Whitehouse had solid credentials. Son of a prominent New York lawyer who had gone to England regularly for the fox hunting, he had studied at Eton, graduated from Yale in 1905, was a member of the Knickerbocker and Brook clubs, and an engaging conversationalist. He escorted Dorothy with a party to the London horse show, then to see *The Merry Widow*, and both he and Falconer joined Dorothy and Pauline in an excursion to Henley.

Few members of her set had danced at Buckingham Palace, but on this trip Dorothy enjoyed a court ball enough to mark the occasion with two exclamation points in her diary. Had Whitehouse arranged it through the embassy? Was Falconer present? With whom did she dance? She does not say, she maintains her privacy, and we must be satisfied with exclamation points. She delivered a stagey bon mot to Falconer—perhaps in a moment when she was entangled in the artificiality of Pauline's circle—saying that she was thinking of naming each of her pearls after one of her dear friends. In July she lunched with Falconer and his mother, Lady Kintore, at their ancestral home, Keith Hall, near Aberdeen. Falconer, who spent much of his time shooting grouse, did not seem to fulfill that part of Dorothy's Venetian essay on the "right person" stressing ambition. Perhaps also she concluded that what he really wanted was to bolster the fortunes of Keith Hall as the Duke of Marlborough had done with Blenheim.

Indefatigable, she crossed with Beatrice to Paris, shopped furiously, lunched with Count P., boarded the express for Switzerland, and settled at the Hotel Carlo Magno across the Italian border, near Madonna. Whitehouse and Dr. McCosh had followed them and were vacationing nearby, and Whitehouse was permitted to call on Dorothy daily:

> Sheldon & I took a heavenly walk this morning in the woods. Afternoon we spent as usual, sitting under the pine trees, reading—and talking together—Sheldon & I. It has been such a beautiful day! Oh—mais les beaux jours apportent quelques fois de la tristesse.

The *tristesse* evidently arose from her fondness for Whitehouse, but again—as in the case of Jay and how many others?—she was not ready to marry him. He urged her to do so, as a later letter demonstrated. He took her rejection gallantly and departed, not giving up. The young lady was looking for someone very special, refusing men others regarded as excellent catches, unable as yet to find in real life her ideal of the Venetian essay. A few days later she recorded:

Who should suddenly appear this morning but Grosvenor Atterbury! This afternoon he & I walked down to Madonna, later meeting Pat [Dr. McCosh] & Beatrice at the Conditorei.

Although Atterbury was one of those perhaps furthest from her Venetian dream, she was kind. On September 15 she and Beatrice were in Paris again, meeting Aunt Lilly and also Pauline, who was less well than usual. Time seldom weighed heavily:

[September 18:] Had a busy morning after wh. Sheldon lunched with us here [at the Hotel Vendôme]. I stayed with Sister in the afternoon until 5.30—then Sheldon & I walked in the Tuileries & through the Louvre courts & over the Pont Neuf to see Henry IV. . . . Dined at the Ritz with . . . Sheldon. [September 19:] G. A. & I spent the morning in the Quartier Latin, walking. . . . We lunched at Foyot's. . . . In the P.M. Beatrice & Pat & Sheldon & I motored out to Versailles through the park—thence to St. Germain for tea & home. . . . Beatrice & I dined with the same two men at Prunier's & went after to "The Folies Bergeres"!!! [September 23:] In the afternoon Sumner [Gerard] & I had a foolish time going first to the toy exhibition in the Tuileries & then motoring in the Bois.

Buckingham Palace had been given two exclamation points. The three she gave the Folies Bergeres clearly showed she found them wicked but entertaining. (Wickedly too, she read that spicy novel *The Spanish Jade*.) For all her compulsion toward benefaction, she loved a good time, be it at dance, theater, or automobile racetrack. After sailing home in October, she arose at Applegreen at 4:15 to hurry over to the grandstand alone to see the start of the Vanderbilt Races founded by the motor enthusiast the second William K. Vanderbilt. She was pleased that an American car won, averaging sixty-four miles per hour: ". . . very thrilling & no bad accidents—the Locomobile with Robertson winning by 2 minutes from the Isotta." The Princetonian Jim Breese seemed to be gaining in her favor for a time, but again she fell back on an older friend: dinner in New York with Charles Draper (but no dining out alone with men as yet—Beatrice and Dr. McCosh were with them), then the theater, after which, "Election night excitements—walked along Broadway & got home at 12.30. Taft elected by [sic] 319 electoral votes . . . Hughes gov." Draper, a broker as so many of her friends were, was eight years older than Dorothy, delightful as a companion, but perhaps too much the seasoned man about town, too little interested in civic improvement, for her. It was said that never in his life had he heard "Celeste Aida" because that aria came early in the opera and he always arrived fashionably late. There was comment in the press about Dorothy's apparent difficulty in selecting a mate, but she went her own way, mixing self-improvement, the arts, charity work, and her study of young men:

> . . . [heard] the New York Symphony Orchestra with Damrosch play Beethoven's 7th Symph. to wh. Isidora Duncan danced. . . . Read tuberculosis articles all day. . . . First night of Opera—"Aida" with Destinn, Caruso & Homer—It was splendid. . . . Sumner, Grosvenor Atterbury & Willie Iselin dined with us & we went to "Mme Butterfly"—Caruso & Farrar. . . . Beatrice, Mrs. [Daisy] Harriman, Dr. McCosh & I went through the Rockefeller Institute this A.M.

Mrs. J. Borden "Daisy" Harriman, seventeen years older than Dorothy, was an eccentric, a kind and vivacious woman, worldly, but a supporter of causes then considered radical. She was to weave in and out of Dorothy's life and have some influence on her thinking. So too with Ruth Morgan, of Daisy's age, a firm member of Grace Church, officer of the Colony Club, and fighter for civil rights, who paid a compliment: "Dorothy always takes the hard chair and the drumstick." In fact, Harry was beginning to worry about the company Dorothy sometimes kept, about her alarming radicalism. "I am filled with that terribly absorbing desire to work, and help," she wrote, "and carry through something which may be useful. . . . I can't help realizing every night how much more I might have done. . . ." She hobnobbed with visiting reformers ("I had a most wonderful morning with Miss Jane Addams. I took her down to the Music School & then to the Nurse's Settlement.") With Beatrice she inspected the composing rooms of The World, The Times, The Herald, and three other papers to appraise their working conditions. Shocked to discover that some New York schoolchildren were badly undernourished, she gave $500 as a starter to help. She pressed the Junior League to take less interest in patés and truffles and more in poverty, and she joined that most outrageous of movements, women's suffrage.

So sedate and reactionary was her set that this alone was enough to stamp her as unorthodox. Actually, her reformist activity was as yet sporadic, the impulsive deeds inspired by a natural instinct for fairness and a kind heart. It would take years and some political maturity before her humanitarian efforts would gain organization. Already interested in government, she was off to Washington in January 1909, a guest of the George von Lengerke Meyers, Meyer now being Postmaster General.

Here again she encountered Willard Straight not once but twice, suggesting the possibility that it was arranged. The first occasion was at a dinner given by John Barrett, director of the Pan-American Union: "Sat by Mr. Straight & an Italian called Centaro," Dorothy noted and, two nights later, "Dinner here [at the Meyers']—sat by Straight & [George] Marvin—then dance at the White House—great fun." The kindly Meyers were taking an interest in Dorothy and quite possibly made it a point to seat her next to that remarkable young man Straight, who was at the moment acting head of the Far Eastern Bureau of the State Department. It was a title with dash, connoting a benevolent American authority in the Orient along with a grasp of complex issues. It was a title with a ring that rendered all the more prosaic those of most of the men of her set: broker, banker, architect, lawyer, realtor.

Anyone acquainted with Straight would know him quite capable of pulling strings to sit beside a young lady who attracted him. (The name of George Marvin, another State Department man, was also one that was to acquire interest for Dorothy.) Nor was it beyond possibility that Dorothy herself was interested in Straight and arranged with the Meyers to sit next to him. But in her diary, that cautious censor of impulse, on both occasions she mentions Straight as a chance dinner partner, with no comment on him whatever. Nor did she mention that she was surely the only American girl to dance at Buckingham Palace and the White House and to meet the chief of state of Mexico (not to mention dining with Lord Falconer, Count Prezezdziecki, and the acting head of the Far Eastern Bureau of the State Department) within so short a compass.

She was back in Washington (with a party including Sheldon White-house and Sumner Gerard) March 4, saw President Taft inaugurated ("*Wonderfully* impressive"), watched the parade, attended the Inauguration Ball ("10,000 people there"), then went with the Payne Whitneys to Palm Beach. They crossed to Havana, where Edwin Vernon Morgan (the same whom Dorothy had met with Straight at the E. H. Harrimans') was American Minister, and had an audience with President Jose Miguel Gómez, another head of state: "Mrs. Gomez & daughters showed us their bedrooms etc. & we all drank champagne." Three weeks later she was in Boston to visit Mrs. Jack Gardner, now widowed but in a manner of speaking still head of her own state, who warmly called her by her first name. Dorothy marveled at the art collection at Fenway Court: "I had never dreamed of such a treasure." She watched the Harvard–Columbia boat race in the company of A. Piatt Andrew, thirty-six, who had been educated at Lawrenceville, Princeton, and in Germany and become a Harvard economics professor but was now a United States government adviser on banking reform. He was awaiting the right moment to propose marriage to her. But in May she again encountered Willard Straight.

"Dined at the [Westbury] Morgans & sat by Mr. Straight & Hal Phipps," Dorothy noted. Straight wrote in *his* diary, "Sat next Miss D. W. at dinner," not bothering to mention who was on his other side. They played tennis, Dorothy writing, "Mr. Swift & I beat Mr. Straight & Mr. David Gray"—a loss Straight perhaps found humiliating, for he failed to record it. But the two were now acquainted. Straight was about to leave the State Department and go to Europe and Peking as the representative of the J. P. Morgan and E. H. Harriman interests. Dorothy was planning a trip around the world, with a stop at Peking. Straight was back on Long Island a month later and paid his first call on Dorothy at Applegreen. ". . . Mr. Straight arrived on the 4.30," she wrote coolly on June 25, 1909. "He & I rode till 8 o'clock." Straight, who had recently visited ex-President Roosevelt and seemed to have borrowed one of his favorite terms, noted his visit "at Miss D. W.'s with whom I had a bully ride."

$$\mathcal{T}wo$$

1. Beneficent Lightning

WILLARD DICKERMAN STRAIGHT was born in Oswego, New York, January 31, 1880. His tall, lean father, Henry H. Straight, taught the natural sciences at the state normal school in that chill Lake Ontario town. His tiny, energetic mother, born Emma Dickerman, taught literature and drawing there. Henry Straight was conscientious and determined, an upholder of Pestalozzi's methods. Emma Straight was a small bundle of temperament, "vividly alive to everything," a lover of literature and an artist to her fingertips. She kept an adoring diary of Willard's baby cleverness, and if she tended to spoil him and the daughter Hazel, two years younger, there soon was reason. Henry Straight contracted tuberculosis, was ordered south for his health in 1885, but died within a year.

In 1887, through a Japanese who had been her student at Oswego and later became a Tokyo school official, Emma Straight secured a teaching post in Tokyo. She had been there only a year with the children when she discovered that she too had tuberculosis. She returned with them in the summer of 1889 and left them with a friend in San Francisco while she sought recovery in Yuma, Arizona, where she died in 1890. Before her death she had arranged for two spinster friends in Oswego to adopt and care for her children—the boy and girl so badly buffeted by misfortune. Willard, now ten, became the adopted son of tall, kindly Dr. Elvire Ranier, one of the few women physicians of the time. She had her office and lived in the home of her friend Miss Laura Newkirk, who adopted Hazel, so that the two children were kept together.

This childhood torn by anxiety and tragedy had its effect, especially on Willard, who reacted with a tempestuous and unruly disposition with which Dr. Ranier, known affectionately as Auntie Doc, could not cope. He was highly intelligent, but willful and often incorrigible at school. He so loved to draw that he was sketching when he should have been working on examinations. Dr. Ranier, who believed in discipline, resorted to severity that a later student of the complex Straight personality felt was instrumental in causing his "chief infirmity"—a tendency to lose his normally powerful self-confidence when opposed by associates. When Willard at last was expelled from school, the two maiden ladies admitted that they could not handle him and sent him off as a high school junior to Bordentown Military Academy in New Jersey. Here, astonishingly, he liked his instructors, or responded perhaps to the more masculine atmosphere, worked enthusiastically, and for two years averaged over ninety-two in his grades. In 1897, after thinking seriously of West Point, he entered Cornell University to study architecture.

The young man who had been such a problem was a brilliant student, a leader of his class in enterprises of the mind and spirit rather than of athletics, at which he was only average. It is true that he won fame for his enjoyment of the absurd, and that he invented the practice among architectural students of tossing any obstreperous underclassman bodily into a tank used for stretching large sheets of paper, but his solid achievements were many. He was a popular member of a half-dozen college organizations and of Delta Tau Delta fraternity, and was soon on the staffs of both *The Widow*, the humor magazine, and *The Era*, which sought for literary excellence. He was drawing—drawing half the time. Behind their backs he drew ludicrous cartoons of professors, but he also liked to get them to pose for serious sketches. He had a talent for writing sonorous prose and comic verse as well. Much of his work appeared in *The Widow*, of which he was first art editor and then editor-in-chief, and he was given credit for changing it from a rather pedestrian publication to a witty one. He was an originator of the "Little Willie" series, famous in its day, one of which (illustrated by himself) read:

> *Little Willie hung his sister;*
> *She was dead before they missed'er.*
> *Willie's allus up to tricks—*
> *Ain't he cute?—he's only six.*

He was an impulsive young man who could range from easily aroused impatience to great kindness, friendship, and affection. He played the guitar and had a good tenor voice. When he reached his full height, he was downright dashing in appearance and manner—con-

fident, even grandiose in his view of the future. Indeed, Straight's ambition was of such size that there was a question whether he would control
it or it would control him. He was determined to be rich *and* famous
and socially prominent, nor was he willing to wait long for these advantages.

Straight worked summers to help pay his way through school. He was
a member of the bull-session group that met Thursday evenings in the
rooms of Edinburgh-born Henry Morse Stephens, a history professor
with a background of both Oxford and Cambridge who had made a
special study of India. Throughout his life Straight seemed in search of
a father to replace the one he had lost. The urbane and charming
Stephens was one of these substitutes.

Straight had a deep vein of loyalty and affection under his rather
aggressive exterior. He paid visits to his Auntie Doc as long as she
lived, and Stephens became one of his lifelong friends, as did others
including Alfred Sze, a classmate from China. From Stephens, Straight
gained his love of Kipling whom he could quote endlessly, and not a
little of the glory-of-empire spirit. When he graduated in 1901, he
decided against an architect's career. He was offered, on Stephens's recommendation, a place in the Imperial Maritime Customs Service in
Peking. This organization resulted when European nations carved out
spheres of influence in China. It collected China's customs and supervised its mails and yet was independent of Chinese control. It was
headed by an old China hand, that remarkable Englishman Sir Robert
Hart, who hired his personnel from all over the world.

The salary was $750 a year to start—considered quite generous then
in China, where it went a long way. True, the bloody Boxer Rebellion
had only recently been crushed, but fortunes were being made in
China, Straight had a feel for the Orient and a taste for adventure, and
he accepted.

When he reached China in January 1902, he was immediately sent
to Nanking, where Sir Robert had founded a school where Straight and
other candidates from various nations were taught the Chinese
language—a formidable tongue of delicate intonations. "Were one to
work eight hours a day at any ordinary and respectable language,"
Straight wrote, "one would at the end of six months show some remarkable progress. Not so with Chinese." But he had a gift for languages and
was easily the best of the students there. In the spring of 1902, though
far from perfect, he went to work in Peking as Sir Robert's private secretary, continuing his study of Mandarin.

Hart was an elderly Ulsterman, an official of great power and prestige who maintained his own brass band and entertained constantly. His headquarters was in the midst of the Legation Quarter, that fortified enclave of foreigners sandwiched between the walls of Peking's Tartar City and its Chinese City. He was surrounded by the legations of nine European nations, the Japanese, and the Americans. However they differed otherwise, these nations were alike in their determination to profit in the China trade and in their resolve not to be caught again as they had been in the Boxer uprising. There had been killing and burning here. Hart himself had escaped without his belongings—lacking even time to don the hat without which he felt naked. Now each foreign nation had a detachment of troops as part of the settlement forced on the Empress Dowager when the rebellion was quelled. Straight handled enough of Hart's mail so that he clung thereafter to English spellings such as *colour* and adopted other British usages, more perhaps because he was a romantic than out of habit. But he proved so adept at managing the entertainment—dinners, teas, and musicales—that he was assigned largely to this social work. His singing and his skill with the guitar meant that he was often an entertainer himself. "He was a good mimic," observed Edward T. Williams of the American legation, "and could imitate Paul Du Chaillu in his lecture on experience in Africa [so that] we were all convulsed with merriment." He had a habit of tardiness which he never really cured, perhaps because he would carry off his late arrivals with such éclat that he was immediately forgiven. Straight was a compulsive writer, kept a diary, and corresponded steadily and in great detail with more than a dozen people in America. To one of them he described his surroundings, illustrating his letter with his own spirited sketches:

> Legation quarter itself is a veritable fortress, surrounded by a glacis on three sides, and the Tartar City wall on the other. The weary diner-out, wandering homeward in the wee sma' hours, is halted every now and then by a sentry, and must answer "Friend," and be told in Russian, or Japanese, or Italian, or whatever else it may be, to "advance and be recognized."
>
> The streets are policed by the troops of all nations. . . . The Russians are great, hulking fellows, bronzed and hardened by exposure and much vodka. The Japanese and English are smart and natty, our own men a bright-looking crowd, the French, undersized, dirty little beggars, the Italian and Austrian sailors a fine lot of men, but the Germans! Ai ya! such a bargain-sale crowd I have never seen. Worse fitting clothes couldn't have been especially designed for them. Stupid and heavy, they

are absolutely the worst crowd in all Peking, and, for that matter, in all China.

He illustrated *Verse and Worse*, a humorous book about China by his Irish friend J. O. P. Bland. Surprisingly, in view of his man-of-the-world manner, Straight had a streak of the puritan; he liked a cigar and a drink but retained a chivalric attitude toward women that was a part of his peculiar charm. The brilliant career he sought seemed too far in the future with the Customs Service, so in 1904, when he was offered a job as a Reuter's and Associated Press correspondent in the Russo-Japanese war, he resigned. "I have burned my bridges—whist!" he wrote, "—and am off to the wars . . . with a sketch book in one hand and a pad in the other and a telegraph wire around my neck."

Sent first to Tokyo, which he remembered from his childhood, he showed appealing frankness in his private admission that he struggled between selfish ambition and innate idealism. He was more honest with himself than the young William C. Whitney, who had repeated copy-book pieties and later fleeced his transit investors. Straight, yearning for high place, loving money and what it would bring, was yet disillusioned by official corruption that he had seen and insisting that he must not permit himself to become a parasite. But he granted in his diary that this would not be easy. Much as he liked art, that must remain only a hobby: "Imagine going through life as an artist—a little brother to the rich, dawdling at Newport, trying to catch orders   a hanger-on, a tail of a retinue." Ambition, ambition! ". . . the artist is the best side, the schemer the worst side in me," he conceded. "I am afraid there is too much ambition in my cosmos to let the schemer be driven out by my better nature, hence much tribulation and many an unhappy hour, and uneasy time, for I am not true to myself."

The future would bear out some of this—not all—to the letter.

In Tokyo he joined a roistering group of correspondents that included Richard Harding Davis (trust Straight to seek out Davis!), Martin Egan of the Associated Press, Frederick Palmer of *Collier's*, and Robert M. Collins of Reuter's. For weeks they were kept in the capital, far from the war on the mainland, reduced to pestering Japanese cabinet underlings for news, becoming good friends of United States Minister Lloyd Griscom. Griscom was another to be delighted by Straight, observing, "He won his way, wherever he was, not only by his forcefulness, but by his kindness and genial disposition. . . . He was not only an intelligent man, but also had a wide culture and understood the oriental mind

almost as well as it is possible for any oriental to do so." But underneath
Straight's assurance were occasional spasms of self-doubt: "I cannot help
feeling that in some ways I am unsound. Inexperience could perhaps
explain the difficulty; it cannot excuse it." These self-questionings were
signs of his pride and ambition, his need to watch himself, to remind
himself to hew to the line, to study and to get on, to succeed. A hard
worker and a natural writer, ready to labor all night if necessary, practiced in the cynicism of the legations, he now absorbed the sophistica-
tion of the international journalists. He was entirely pro-Japanese, seeing
Russia as the aggressor in her drive to take Manchuria and Korea,
which would make Japan her vassal.

After the Japanese had won the upper hand, Straight and his colleagues were permitted to go to Korea, where he continued to meet
important people either from design or because he simply attracted
them. One was John J. Pershing, forty-six years old and still a captain, a
military attaché at Griscom's legation who was observing the war for the
United States Army. Another was the suave, forty-year-old Edwin V.
Morgan, scion of a wealthy and distinguished upstate New York family,
who was about to become the new Minister to Korea. Morgan was impressed. He described Straight as "tall, slim, with reddish-brown hair, of
unusual frankness and charm of manner, perfectly at his ease. . . . Our
friendship started from the moment of introduction. . . ."

That was Straight—a man whose magnetism was quick to bowl people over. He won his spurs as a journalist in fifteen months. Soon after,
with the end of the war, Morgan arranged for Straight to become his
private secretary with the rank of Vice-Consul at Seoul, a dull place
after teeming Tokyo. Here a kind of beneficent lightning, which often
seemed attracted to him, struck him twice in quick succession. The first
bolt flashed when a visitor at the Seoul legation was E. H. Harriman
with his wife and three daughters, Mary, Cornelia, and Carol, and two
sons, Averell and Roland. Harriman, so slight and wispy of appearance,
had one of those grandiose dreams that so appealed to the grandiosity in
Straight that the visitor became first in his pantheon of heroes. His fortune was in the neighborhood of $70,000,000; he already controlled the
Union Pacific Railroad and the Pacific Mail steamship line spanning
the Pacific. Now he planned to create a round-the-world transportation
system. This he would effect by hooking up with the Trans-Siberian
Railway (from which he would lease the rights) and, at the other end of
that almost endless track, inaugurating a steamship line from the Baltic
to New York. It was an idea that if propounded by a university theorist

might excite derision, but when suggested by the formidable Little Giant of Wall Street it had the ring of Manifest Destiny.

The Harrimans lived at the legation in Seoul. Straight saw to their comfort, accompanied them to Fusan when they left, and had opportunity to admire the alert mind and high-pompadoured beauty of the eldest daughter Mary, who was to become his ladylove.

Soon after came the second thunderball, in the arrival of Alice Roosevelt and her suite, which included her fiancé Longworth, Congressman Frederick Gillette, Senator Francis G. Newlands of Nevada and Mrs. Newlands, and others. "The Roosevelt party," Straight wrote on October 3, 1905, "came, saw and conquered. They had audiences with His Majesty of all the Koreas, and were treated with more consideration than has ever been shown to visiting royalty before. At the first luncheon the Emperor brought Miss Roosevelt in on his arm and sat at the same table. . . ." Straight got along famously with Miss Roosevelt. He wrote and illustrated a small book of the parody verse he did so well, titled "Alice in Plunderland," and dedicated it to her. There were those who considered him designing in his cultivation of the great, but Miss Roosevelt and her later husband Longworth remained lifelong friends, as did Minister Morgan. Straight's Korean interlude ended after only eight months when it became obvious that Japan, which had talked benevolently of Korean independence, was actually running the country. No legation was needed in Seoul. Morgan was recalled to Washington, and when he got his next assignment, as Minister to Cuba, he offered Straight the same post in Havana.

Straight did not want to leave the Orient, one possible reason being that he wished to be ready to help Harriman in his negotiations for a suitable connection with a Chinese line that would join the Trans-Siberian. But having tried and failed to return to Sir Robert and the Customs, he accepted Morgan's offer.

2. Discovering Xanadu

IT WAS after his return to the United States that Straight, along with Morgan, dined at the Harrimans'—the gathering at which Dorothy Whitney first met him. He was then pursuing his romance with Mary Harriman. Meanwhile Miss Roosevelt and Longworth were married at the White House and decided to start their honeymoon in Cuba. Straight got to Havana in time to make arrangements and hire servants.

Morgan later wrote, "Three days after the wedding, Alice, Nick, Willard and myself were installed in the Quinta. We afterwards accompanied the bridal pair on their triumphal progress through the island. . . ." The burdens of diplomacy had lighter moments which Straight enjoyed to the full, and his friendship with Princess Alice and her husband was cemented.

His life became complicated enough for a time to halt his diary, and the smaller details of his progress are lost. Not, however, the major moves, which show the twenty-six-year-old legation subaltern suddenly leaping into prominence. Did he make use of his friendship with Alice? We do not know. We do know that E. H. Harriman informed President Roosevelt, or someone influential in the administration, about Straight's abilities and his expert knowledge of the Far East—skills so special that Harriman thought Straight should have a key diplomatic post there.

Miracles happened to Straight that a wise novelist knows enough to avoid. He was recalled to Washington in the summer of 1906 after only a few months in Cuba. He was summoned to the White House for a talk with President Roosevelt, who was revitalizing the Foreign Service with bright young men from the Eastern colleges. It is safe to assume that by now Straight mentioned his friendship with the President's favorite daughter—which of course the Colonel may already have known about. And both admired Kipling, with whom the President was corresponding. The impetuous Roosevelt was so delighted with Straight that he invited him out to Oyster Bay, where the young man's intelligent talk impressed him further. Straight was forever after loyal to Roosevelt and his family, conscious of a great debt to the President. For he was appointed United States Consul General in the great Manchurian city of Mukden, a railroad center and crossroads metropolis of the East—an important post and also precisely where he could be of most service to Harriman in advising him how to accomplish his plan to connect with the Trans-Siberian.

There was nothing corrupt in this move. It was one of the administration's first steps in its new policy of encouraging its foreign representatives to give all possible aid to American business there, as the diplomats of other nations had long done for their own interests. The policy had the hearty approval of Straight, who believed that the only way to save China from further partition was to make heavy and benevolent, but profitable, United States financial investments there. He was filled with the general American machismo that had resulted from victory over Spain in Cuba and the Philippines, the proud national realization of world power. He shared a widespread feeling that American influence in foreign countries could only do them good, that indeed the nation had a world mission and was obligated to spread its lessons of democracy. "First and foremost," he wrote with pardonable exultation about his new post, "it's a Consulate General, and also it's at Mukden that the biggest game in the East, save Peking itself, is being played."

Before leaving, Straight spent a weekend at Arden, Harriman's 100-room castle on the highest of the Ramapos near Tuxedo. They talked business, and, as Straight commented, "Mr. Harriman asked me to keep him advised. . . ." Because the President wanted a report from him on the economic, political, and military picture in Russia, Straight traveled to his post via Europe and the Trans-Siberian. He reported on the Trans-Siberian part of the trip also to Harriman in the crisp language of the trained observer:

> [I] made the trip across Siberia and Northern Manchuria in twelve days. . . . The road although showing the effects of the heavy traffic during the war seemed in fairly good condition and the accommodation afforded was excellent. Coal, wood and coke were used as fuel, the two former mined and felled respectively not far from the line. There are sidings every five versts but the tracks are light, the ballasting scant and the average running speed does not exceed twenty-five miles an hour. . . . The 150 odd miles of road between Harbin, which is a flour milling center, and Changchun (Kunangchengtzu) the last point in the Russian sphere, is in good condition as is the portion from this point, over the Japanese road, south to Ssupingkai, a distance of 70 miles. [But from then on the line shows ravages of war and the stations are battered.] . . . a large expenditure will be necessary before the road may really be considered to be in working order.
>
> The amount of rolling stock is very limited and the accommodation is wretched. . . . It seems certain that the Russians will do everything in their power to embarrass the Japanese in the operation of the road. . . . Although at present in an unsettled state, the country is gradually recovering from the effects of the war and there should be remarkable development within the next few years.
>
> There is a strong feeling among commercial men that a line of steamers direct from the United States to North China, touching at Japan, would be profitable. The Shanghai trans-shipping charges are heavy and the delay involved considerable, and the volume of trade is increasing to such an extent that there is a demand for a better service.

The report was three times the length given here, studded with detail, admitting the problems of the developer that Harriman hoped to be (and Straight hoped to help him to be) but emphasizing the enormous agricultural and industrial potentialities of Manchuria. Straight had a keen eye, unusual in a man of such imagination, for utilitarian facts. Both the United States and Harriman had an outstanding man representing them in polyglot Mukden. As Harriman's biographer George Kennan says of Straight, "He impressed Mr. Harriman as a young man of character and force, and one whose ability and experience might make him a valuable assistant. . . ." And Straight saw in Harriman the bold, globe-girdling multimillionaire that he would like to become himself. How better to do it than to train under him—and possibly to marry his daughter?

Mukden, almost five hundred miles northeast of Peking, was once a Tartar capital, its old city still surrounded by a high wall four miles in circumference. Now it was a thriving industrial center of a half-million people. Its narrow streets teemed with tall Chinese and Koreans, small Japanese, Russians whose eyes hinted at the Oriental, and Mongolians whose whole faces shouted it. Although the Chinese far outnumbered all the rest, and the city and the whole region of Manchuria were technically Chinese, China was as usual unable to defend her interests. The Japanese had actual control of the southern part of Manchuria while the Russians controlled much of the north, each nation seeking permanent ownership.

Straight often worked from twelve to sixteen hours a day, as he was apt to do when under the kind of inspiration Harriman gave him. His Mukden office was busier and more important than some legations. At considerable expense to American taxpayers he renovated a semiruined former temple and made it into a consulate with the magnificence he fancied. He erected there a 113-foot flagpole, said to be the highest staff in China, from which floated Old Glory. He made official calls on His Eminence Hsu Shih-chang, Viceroy of Manchuria, and on Tang Shao-yi, Governor of Feng-tien, one of Manchuria's three provinces. These men knew as well as Straight that unless heroic measures were taken, Manchuria would ultimately be swallowed by the Japanese and the Russians. As Henry F. Pringle said of Straight, "He was to be the spokesman and leading proponent of the doctrine that China's territorial integrity might be preserved if American funds, in large quantities, were invested in its internal improvements."

The diary kept by his vice-consul, Harvard-educated George D. Marvin from Brewster, New York, makes it evident that Marvin enjoyed working for Straight, occasionally playing tennis or riding with him and listening to him play the guitar and sing of evenings. However casual Straight could be before an open fire, he made it a rule to uphold his own and the United States's dignity by dressing for dinner. Since their mail went over the Japanese-controlled railway to the south, their letters were opened. Straight thereupon invented a rudimentary code using profane or absurd names for various officials he disliked—the Japanese were always "the Bandarlog," Kipling's term for the monkey people— and his letters bristled with such terms as frocko-coato and hoto-batho. For officials whom he liked he often used only their middle names, as in the case of his good friend Henry P. Fletcher, First Secretary in the legation at Peking, who became plain Prather. He gave a farewell dinner to his colleague the departing German Consul, preparing a punch with chopped fruit and spirits so heady that Marvin noted its "profound cheering effect" and the Germans called it *Der schwartze Tod*—the Black Death.

Straight's ability to lighten odd moments was matched by his furious devotion to work. His reports to the State Department were careful and thorough, as were his frequent letters to Harriman. The problem of the Little Giant, Harriman, was to hook up with the Trans-Siberian from an ice-free port farther south in China through Manchurian country controlled in actuality by the Japanese and the Russians. So far the Russians had not objected, but the Japanese made it clear that they would not permit Harriman to use the Chinese Eastern line they controlled to the south. The Japanese had enough opposition from the Russians in their plan to take over Manchuria, and they wanted no competition from either British or Americans. Straight, in one of his long reports to Harriman, urged him to bypass the Japanese by building a parallel line into Manchuria:

> There is a consensus of opinion among commercial men and those in touch with the Chinese Eastern Railway . . . that a line of this sort would be a success. . . . An opposition road would tap a rich country with great possibilities for increased production, would enable the Chinese to haul over the usual routes and ship to Newchwang a port with which they have established connections, where with improved bunding it would be possible to run trains to elevators which should be erected and load in steamers for the southern or Japanese markets. Manchuria is really a new West, with cheaper labor and a soil almost equally fertile and rich in minerals. The political conditions, moreover, render the Chinese Government more likely to welcome the introduction of foreign

capital . . . and Americans should be particularly well received. I base my statement . . . on assurances which I have received from the Viceroy and which were made with every appearance of sincerity.

Things looked promising when Lord Charles ffrench, representing the large British contracting firm of Pauling & Company, and Straight's friend J. O. P. Bland of the British & Chinese Corporation came to Mukden and arranged to build for the Chinese government an extension of the Chinese Imperial Railways (the extension being called the Fakumen Railway), which would connect with the Trans-Siberian. Straight watched the proceedings scrupulously, since the Fakumen might give Harriman the entry he needed. Bland, who was also a part-time correspondent for *The London Times*, was completing a second book called *Houseboat Days in China,* for which Straight agreed to do the illustrations. The book turned out to be a considerable success, but the Fakumen Railway was a quick failure when the Japanese—the Bandarlog—let it be known that they forbade the road and the British Foreign Office refused to dispute them in the matter. On top of this disappointment, Straight, who of course *was* a trifle pushing, ruffled the feathers of William W. Rockhill, the noted Sinologue who was United States Minister in Peking and who rapped Straight's knuckles for his aggressive initiation of ideas. Straight's gaiety had its antithesis, as a close friend noted: "He frequently succumbed to fits of depression during which he hesitated about continuing the fight and seriously considered [taking] easier and more lucrative[employment]."

But he was delighted when he received instructions from the State Department to meet Secretary of War William Howard Taft when he arrived in Vladivostok in November 1907 after visiting Manila and Shanghai. Straight and Marvin carried automatic pistols as they traveled to Vladivostok via Harbin, Harbin being fully as untamed as Port Said and, as Marvin put it, the nocturnal rule in Harbin being, "If anyone speaks to you after midnight, reply automatically."

"The Secretary greeted us very cordially," Straight noted, and in an exchange in which Taft expressed hope that the United States could now do business with China as a friend, "I assured him that we could— that now is the time—and that the fruit is ripe and it is ours to pluck. With this he seemed to agree." Straight's metaphor was perhaps less idealistic than opportunistic, but it was honest. He always believed that there was no reason why the United States should not profit handsomely while saving China from her exploiters, not seeing the contradiction implied. He was eager to lay before Taft the great opportunities for American commerce in Manchuria, Taft being not only the most influential member of Roosevelt's cabinet but almost surely the Republican presidential candidate in 1908 and hence in all probability the next President. It buoyed Straight to travel in such company, and he was anguished, sullen for hours, when by design or accident he was not invited to the Russian general's dinner for the Taft party at Vladivostok. He recouped next day when, aboard the Trans-Siberian, he dined with the Tafts and gave the Secretary information about the region, its politics and possibilities and the American opportunity to prevent the Japanese from swallowing it up. The President-to-be listened to the persuasive Consul from Mukden. Thereafter he regarded Straight as an adviser so skilled on the Far East that he became a principal architect of Taft's Dollar Diplomacy policy.

Arriving in Harbin, they all walked to carriages over a red carpet between lines of Russian and Chinese infantry at present arms—a colorful panoply in a semisavage frontier metropolis—then were escorted at a full gallop by Cossack cavalry to the Grand Hotel for refreshments and champagne. Here Straight, only twenty-seven, had the honor of being toastmaster for this gathering of American, Chinese, and Russian officialdom. He loved ceremony, had a strong sense of the dramatic, and could turn a flag raising into a grand function. He toasted the United States and its representatives, then the Chinese, and lastly the Russians—a precedence that left the latter disgruntled—while the Russian band outside played the appropriate national anthems. It was a special pleasure to Straight that his friend California-born Martin Egan of the Associated Press and Mrs. Egan were accompanying the Tafts. Straight and Marvin had spent some time in the Egan compartment singing and reminiscing about the late war.

In another letter to Harriman, Straight proposed that he help finance a strong Manchurian bank that would raise American prestige and perhaps check the Japanese confidence based on their being the only first-class power involved in southern Manchuria:

> The prospect of directing the railways of a nation may appeal to you. It would, of course, be impossible to assure you that by undertaking the organization of the Manchurian Bank, you would be certain to be entrusted with the larger enterprise. Yet, although there would be many obstacles to be overcome, I personally believe that such would be the case. . . .
>
> In submitting the proposal for a Manchurian Bank, I have felt sure that the future of such an institution would be intimately identified with the

development, not of Manchuria alone, but of all China. . . . The general outline of the scheme for a Manchurian Bank has been laid before the Department of State. . . .

The young man could take in stride lordly discussions involving great nations and provinces and millions of people—a grandiosity that never left him although it existed side by side with general amiability and kindliness. He often defended such imperialist American governmental maneuvers in collaboration with a single great capitalist as the spread of democratic enterprise and the only salvation of China. But Harriman was not ready for the Manchurian Bank plunge. In May 1908 Straight began an extended—and adventurous—tour of northern Manchuria to make a personal survey of this remote and in large part lawless area. He recorded:

> [I went] by rail north from Mukden . . . up the Sungari by boat to Kirin, from Kirin by horseback to Yenchiting . . . from Yenchiting to Ninguta on the Trans-Siberian Railway, by rail to Harbin, from Harbin by boat to Habarovsk, up the Amur to Blagovestchensk, across the river to Aigun and then by horseback to Tsitsihar and by rail back to Mukden.

The hardships and perils of the tour were a measure of his enormous desire to convince Harriman—perhaps also to make himself Harriman's associate, even Harriman's successor. He visited country seldom if ever seen by Westerners. As a Foreign Service colleague later reported, Straight told him that in one place "he came upon the ruins of an ancient capital and a palace with wonderful gardens which, some suppose, may have been that described by Coleridge but located wrongly by him at Xanadu, or Shangtu as the Chinese call the place."

At Tsitsihar, Straight received a cable from Washington instructing him to return home. He hurried back to Mukden exhausted. His enterprises sometimes drove him harder than his physique could stand—a failing that was later to imperil him. "Prior to leaving Mukden," he wrote, "I had several further discussions with [Governor] Tang Shao-yi and on the night before I left [for Washington] signed a memorandum of agreement providing for a loan of $20,000,000 for the establishment of a bank and mining, timber and agricultural development and railway construction." This was not a firm contract but a preliminary agreement that he fervently hoped he could get Harriman and/or the government to fulfill, and he carried it for six weeks en route to Washington "in a small wallet tied about my neck in a silk case." Ever dramatic! He had been summoned because Harriman wanted to see him.

When he reached Washington in September, gaunt and fatigued, he conferred with Harriman with the full knowledge of the State Department. He was now given a flattering boost in station, being named acting chief of the Bureau of Far Eastern Affairs during the absence of the regular head, William Phillips. Busy though he was, he did not neglect the social pleasures. He became a member of the exclusive Metropolitan Club, attended the Bachelors' cotillions, was seen conferring at parties with senators, and lived (along with George Marvin and others) at that most swank of bachelors' quarters, 1718 H Street, a block from the former Whitney mansion at 1731 I Street.

Along the way, however, his romance with Mary Harriman had collapsed. The papers later indulged in untrustworthy gossip as to the cause of the break but seemed agreed—it assumed the proportions of legend—that it was Harriman himself who ended it. One unidentified newspaper account, found in Dorothy's papers, asserted, for what it was worth:

> The story goes that Miss Harriman had fully accepted the devotion of the young diplomat, and that they were about to break the news to that little iron man, E. H. Harriman, when he entered his home at Arden one day and found them together. "How are you, Straight?" the railroad wizard said, offering his hand. The younger man took it. "Now, Straight," went on Harriman, "I admire you very much. You're a bully good chap, and I think you have a great future in store. But I'm going to be frank with you and tell you this: I don't want you for a son-in-law."

3. On with the New

IT is unfortunate that the exact circumstances of the breach are not known, since it was later to agitate both Dorothy and Harry Payne Whitney, Mary Harriman, and Straight himself. Two things seem clear, however, one being that Mary did not herself end the romance, since if she had, it would not have assumed the somewhat equivocal aspect it later took on. The other is that Harriman and Straight, for all the possible humiliation visited on the latter, remained on the closest business terms and that Harriman was downright enthusiastic about Straight's abilities. From it emerges the interesting possibility (which is only speculation) that Harriman wrote *finis* to the courtship because his own energies were waning, he was seized beyond cure by his dream of encircling the globe by ship and rail, and that Straight was the only man who could bring the dream to life. Harriman's iron will was well known. It is not impossible that he brushed aside a courtship, since romances occur every day, in favor of this truly great, once-in-a-lifetime opportunity—the sort of thing that warmed the blood of an empire builder and would make him remembered in history. He may have reasoned that if he had consented to the match, the indispensable Straight would have been removed from this international struggle demanding every effort and thought, would be instead enwrapped in debilitating endearments, perhaps ruined for business contention by visions of his own share of the Harriman fortune, and hence rendered useless to him. Or—perhaps Straight lacked the requisite pedigree and wealth.

If Straight gave up Mary and continued the China project at Harriman's urging, several inferences are possible, all hypothetical: He was not in love with Mary after all. Or, he loved her but loved the enterprise more—could, no more than Harriman, resist the lure of this fascinating game of international business and politics, played with the great men of several nations. Or, he was simply biding his time, going along with Harriman until the grand deal was consummated, then returning to embrace his beloved. Later events made it appear most likely that his ardor for Mary had been warm but not eternal. Indeed he could not have known her very well, having been abroad most of the time. It was true that he was passionately involved in the China enterprise. In any case, he seemed to give up Mary and now began paying attentions to Katherine Elkins of Washington and West Virginia.

Miss Elkins (not related to the Elkins of William C. Whitney's traction group), though petite and attractive, had "come out" in 1903 and hence had been available for five years and was still unmarried. One had to bear in mind that Straight, since he left Cornell, had traveled so continuously that it would have been difficult for him to give any young lady the faithful attentions usually associated with serious romance. Indeed it would have been surprising, now that Mary was denied him, if he did not turn elsewhere. The fact that later caused eyebrows to be raised—especially those of Harry Payne Whitney—was that Miss Elkins, like Mary Harriman, was a daughter of immense wealth. Her father, Stephen Benton Elkins, had amassed millions through his ownership of coal properties and industrial interests, had been Secretary of War in the Harrison administration, and was now a Republican United States senator from West Virginia. His country estate, known as Halliehurst, was that state's most splendid. Miss Elkins was one of the moneyed and sophisticated set who traveled often to New York and to European watering places. "She is a great heiress," the watchful Saunterer had said of her in *Town Topics*.

Be that as it may, the failed romance with Mary did not seem to affect Straight's relations with Harriman, for they worked in strenuous cooperation during the winter of 1908–1909. Straight was serving as the intermediary between Tang, who had given him the loan agreement that had still not been picked up, and Harriman. Harriman, foreseeing other enormous expenses in his global project, was unwilling to bear the whole risk of the loan. By now, the State Department, perhaps spurred by President Roosevelt (and President-elect Taft, with whom Straight was on the best of terms), was eager to implement and in fact to enlarge Straight's plan. The negotiations were delayed by the deaths, one day apart, of the weakling Chinese emperor and the dominant Empress Dowager, which altered the power structure in China. Straight, being the only man closely acquainted with the whole complex situation, was at the center of the struggle to negotiate the loan.

It was during this interval that Straight traveled to Long Island and dined and played tennis with Dorothy at the banker Edwin Morgan's. He was in fact shuttling between Washington and New York, seeing Harriman, seeing Roosevelt at Oyster Bay and staying overnight, seeing Robert Bacon, the former Morgan partner now Assistant Secretary of State, seeing the present Morgan partner Harry P. Davison, seeing Harriman's own bankers at Kuhn, Loeb & Company. He was also calling on Katherine Elkins in Washington as well as distinguished officials there, one diary entry reading, "Dined at the [Senator] Newlands with the President, Miss Taft, Alice and Nick [Longworth] . . . ," another, "Lunched at White House and saw the President having his portrait painted by Miss Swan who was charming. Dined en famille with the Wilson's* [H. Huntington Wilson, the new Assistant Secretary of State succeeding Bacon]. After dinner went to see Mr. Knox [Philander C. Knox, the new Secretary of State] who came later to the Wilson's when with Alice and Nick we had a song fest." He also attended a bibulous farewell party for one of his fellow residents at the clubby 1718 H Street place, Capt. James Logan of the Army, and admitted to his diary that he felt rocky the next morning.

---

* Straight, like Dorothy, was uncertain in his use of the apostrophe.

At long last, after months of discussion, the State Department came up with its own plan for involvement in China. It was decided to enter strongly into Dollar Diplomacy with an effort for an American financial and influential role in China equal to that already played by England, France, and Germany. The loan to Tang was set aside for the moment. The United States would start by encouraging private American bankers to participate in a $25,000,000 loan to China which the British, French, and Germans were then negotiating for the construction of the Hukuang railways—a group of roads in the south. China feared that Yankee participation would delay the loan and only agreed when President Taft by cable pointed out a treaty stipulation assuring America such participation.

The three European nations were vexed by the United States entrance into a negotiation that had been nearly completed and now would have to be revised. The State Department, seeking impartiality in selecting the private bankers who would handle the loan, gave it to four organizations normally in competition with each other for such business: J. P. Morgan & Company, Kuhn, Loeb & Company, the First National Bank, and the National City Bank, all of New York. Harriman was still heavily involved, through his bankers, Kuhn, Loeb, and had by no means given up his global transportation scheme. This syndicate came to be known as the American Group. The Morgan firm was given the managerial role on the private side, but the State Department was to give full cooperation, adding the prestige of the government at Washington and the legation in Peking to the efforts of the American Group.

Now, especially since Straight's friend William Phillips returned to his post as chief of the Bureau of Far Eastern Affairs, the question arose as to what to do with Straight. What with his friendship with Roosevelt and acquaintance with Taft, his sponsorship by Harriman, his record in Mukden, and his central role in the whole Chinese question, his prestige had risen to the point of becoming inconvenient. He was, bureaucratically speaking, too young for such eminence. Harriman—never embarrassed about meddling in government—urged that he be made Minister to China, a flattering suggestion but a move that Straight knew would cause trouble in the department because he would be skipping over many seniors. There was talk of sending him back to Mukden, which Harriman opposed, and in fact the Mukden post, which had been a great prize for Straight three years earlier, now seemed petty for him. Harriman took it upon himself to write Secretary Knox twice, lauding Straight's ability and record and now urging that he be kept in

Washington as a needed adviser on Far Eastern problems. Harriman insisted that his own interest in the region was purely patriotic—a statement open to doubt but not entirely implausible, since he already had
more money than he could easily spend and his efforts seemed those of
a man seeking historic achievement as much as profit.

In June, Straight resigned from the department, perhaps less regret-
fully than he said, since he was given the garland for which he may
have been working all along and which he admitted "delighted" him.
He was named the representative in China of the American Group of
bankers, a post of high prestige at a salary unknown but far higher than
anything in the department. On June 25 he visited Dorothy Whitney in
Westbury, had the "bully ride" with her he mentioned in his diary, and
discussed his coming trip to China and her later journey around the
world.

4. The Chance of a Lifetime

STRAIGHT SAILED for preliminary work in Europe June 29, finding Elsie
de Wolfe, resplendently dressed, among the passengers. She had done
the interiors for the Colony Club and had embarked on a career of
charging enormous fees for such work and spending some of it in dec-
orating her own svelte figure. Straight enjoyed chatting with this aristocratic lady and would meet her again. Neither was he a snob—he enjoyed friendships with baggage smashers and coolies—nor was he a man
of the people disdaining rank and fashion. Perhaps if he *had* to choose,
it would be rank and fashion, but not without regret. His rejection of
the artist's life, which he loved, was the measure. His longing for
achievement and recognition through intelligent planning and hard
work could scarcely be condemned. Money was essential too, for his
tastes were luxurious. As his sister Hazel later observed, Willard's
clothes had to be perfect, "And this feeling for the fitness of things extended . . . to all his surroundings . . . and he always required that
the scale and appearance of his residence should be commensurate with
his own sense of the dignity of his work."

He was twenty-nine, past the usual age for marriage. It is not impossible that he was as fastidious about the marriage he would make as he
was about his tailoring and his house—quite different from saying that
love was not important to him or that he sought only money. Love, to
this bone-lonely orphan boy, was in its realm as essential as breath, but

achievement and recognition were what he would slave for and tear his heart out for. For all his sophisticated exterior, he was thin-skinned, sensitive—a weakness that would torment him—and the anguish he suffered when the Russian general in Vladivostok failed to invite him to the Taft dinner was to be repeated in other ways.

In London he continued his discussion of large affairs with important men considerably older than himself—a process likely to turn most heads. He dined with Otto Kahn of Kuhn, Loeb & Company. He lunched with American Ambassador Whitelaw Reid. He conferred with British, French, and German representatives of the consortium endeavoring to make the Hukuang loan to China—men indignant at United States intervention at this late date. He was solaced by an invitation to a great ball at Dorchester House, Ambassador Reid's leased palace in Park Lane, where, he noted, "Danced before King and Queen," and by a house party next day at which he met, among others, the Duke of Richmond and Gordon and the Earl and Countess of Craven. He went on to Bad Gastein, the Austrian spa where Harriman, in company with his wife, sought relief from ailments of his sixty-first year.

"Spent all day with the H.'s," he wrote July 20, "talking business and things in general to E.H.H. up till eleven at night." At Harriman's suggestion he went on to Hamburg where he asked the advice of Max Warburg of the celebrated banking family about the best technique for securing participation with the British-French-German consortium and swinging the loan to China. He made one of the observations typical of the alert Straight, the watchful Straight: "Much impressed by [Hamburg] harbour facilities which have made an ordinarily impossible harbour a splendid commercial port." Then on to Bad Nauheim, where he spent the day with a person identified in his diary as "K.E.," obviously Katherine Elkins. She was vacationing there in part for her health, and he noted that she did not look well. Next to Paris, where he discussed the loan problems with United States Ambassador Henry White and others. Next to London again and two conferences with Ambassador Reid. Back to Paris, to Nauheim again, then Berlin, and thence to St. Petersburg, where he evidently sounded out the attitude of Russian cabinet officials toward the Harriman plan of utilizing their rails. Finally he was aboard the Trans-Siberian, writing, "Wagon Lits cars very smelly. Food fair—wrote letters."

On this summer journey, which some likened to an eleven-day trip through hell, he talked with a retired Russian army engineer, a Colonel Kruglik, so filled with original ideas about banks, railroads, and even flying machines that Straight was fascinated and sent some of the ideas on to Harriman. He reached Peking August 18 and was met by the Prather of the Mukden code, the Pennsylvanian Henry Prather Fletcher, seven years his senior, a career man who had been a Rough Rider in Cuba and was now chargé during a change of Ministers. The two were already good friends. He moved in temporarily with Fletcher in a comfortable house next to the legation. Straight's permanent residence was to demonstrate the prestige of the representative of J. P. Morgan, E. H. Harriman, and other powerful Americans and was to consist of nothing less than a group of buildings, opulently furnished and decorated, within a compound. He had worked hard—played quite hard too—and had won his post through merit. He was beginning a task all the more formidable because it was the chance of a lifetime, the gateway to immeasurable success, one that he was to strain every nerve and all his high intelligence to bring to successful completion. The Chinese badly wanted the loan but would exert every wile to get it on the most favorable terms. The English, French, and Germans would do their best to penalize the Americans for horning in on this enterprise after they had done so much of the spadework. In Peking Straight was to negotiate, dine, dance, quarrel, and associate with a remarkable cast of characters:

There was Fletcher, a tough, sardonic bachelor, touchy and egotistical but a man with whom Straight struck such a responsive note that they worked together smoothly, and Straight— the lonely man always seeking familial affection—came to call him the Elder Brother.

There were the financial representatives of the three European nations—Maurice Casenave from France, the blind Edmund Hillier of England, and Heinrich Cordes from Germany—all considerably older than Straight, each having his own national interests to defend, three men with whom Straight must come to terms.

There were the diplomats, all huddled together in the legation quarter southeast of the Forbidden City: Sir John Jordan, Minister from England; the French Minister Pierre de Margerie; Signor Brambilla of the Italian legation, Korostovetz of the Russian, and a host of Germans, Japanese, Belgians, and Spaniards along with their attachés. They knew each other better than they knew the Chinese, and they drank together and gave occasional parties at which they sought to heal wounds they inflicted on each other during the course of business. There were the wives of most of these men, few of whom spoke Chinese, though most spoke French or English—women carried along with the tide of empire, some of them seasoned by diplomatic travels, some new at it, white women who had little to do with the Chinese and were thrown together so often at card parties, musicales, and luncheons that there were some dear friendships and some deadly feuds. Some of these people had come through the Boxer Rebellion. In fact, Heinrich Cordes had then been secretary to the German Minister, Baron von Ketteler, and, badly wounded, had barely escaped after seeing the Minister murdered. (The Germans, after it was all over, had forced the Chinese to erect a monument to the baron in addition to paying reparations.) Now some were worried over new Chinese revolutionary mutterings to the south.

There were a few of Straight's special friends: Joseph K. Ohl was the jocular Peking correspondent of *The New York Herald*, a man who usually knew what was going on elsewhere in China. Lord ffrench, a slim Irishman with huge nose and dry wit, was still representing Pauling & Company of London, still hoping to get for Pauling a large piece of Chinese railroad construction. The plump and cheery John Percy Otway Bland had come from Ulster and started as Straight did, under Sir Robert Hart. He was fond of the younger man after their collaboration on two books, published in London by Edward Arnold, and in fact had dedicated his recent *Houseboat Days in China* to its illustrator, Straight. The most enigmatic of the lot was Australian-born Dr. George Ernest Morrison, a physician who had taken his degree in Edinburgh, knocked around the world from Morocco to the South Seas, given up medicine for journalism, and become *The London Times*'s chief correspondent in China. Known as "Chinese Morrison," he had gained fame in 1894 by walking from Shanghai to Rangoon and writing a book about it. Perhaps some of his ardent imperialism rubbed off on Straight. Morrison, somewhat jealous and aloof, disliked Bland, who was his subordinate on *The Times* but who spoke Chinese (which Morrison did not) and could write rings around Morrison.

And lastly there were the Chinese themselves, the most slippery of bargainers, deeply corrupt of government, masters of the art of playing one intruding nation against another. Straight had an affection for them that was to become eroded by frustration. He was conventionally indignant over China's exploitation by other nations, and to him the commercial and exploitative motivation of the American Group he worked for was neither here nor there because it could save China. He was deeply, deeply patriotic.

And such charm! One of those he bowled over was twenty-two-year-old Nelson Trusler Johnson, a tenderfoot at the legation who would in time become Minister himself. Many years and much hard experience later, Johnson said Straight's warmth of personality impressed him more profoundly than that of anyone he had ever met in his life. ". . . he could mix with the bankers . . . then move directly from that into our little group, associate with us, pick up a guitar and improvise airs for Kipling. We would sit there fascinated by him. . . . I feel perfectly certain that Straight could have sat down with the veriest beggar and made the beggar feel at home in conversation, and then moved directly from that to the most refined, most intellectual group one could think of and felt perfectly at home with them and they with him."

Straight was never the most docile of subordinates, and his attitude toward the State Department and the Group that employed him often became impatient. He felt, probably correctly, that he knew more about China and more about Harriman's global plans than did the gentlemen in New York or Washington swivel chairs. The Group was eager to float the Hukuang loan, Harriman's dream of linking with the Trans-Siberian being set aside for the time. Straight, on the contrary, was loyal to Harriman and dedicated to the hookup idea. To the dismay of the New York Group, he began work on that, knowing that if he could effect the deal it would give him great "face" in his dealings with the other three nations over Hukuang. Straight meanwhile was disturbed by newspaper reports of Harriman's ill health.

"The press has reported your arrival in New York giving some rather disquieting interviews as to the state of your health," he wrote to Harriman. He went on to describe the Manchurian situation in detail, adding that the State Department needed a better man in Mukden to push matters there: "The present man in charge is worse than useless as far as the big game is concerned."

And then a cable on September 10 informed him that Harriman had died the previous day at Arden. It was a terrible blow to Straight on two counts: He had lost a kindly mentor and also a powerful sponsor whose continuing influence in his favor he was heavily dependent on. Except for his rumored rejection of Straight as a son-in-law, Harriman had been considerate, a father figure and also a giant of finance who took the whole world as his oyster just as Straight hoped to do. He had taken lessons from the older man. He had reviewed Harriman's career—more than that, he had been given a privilege granted to no one else, the privilege of many hours of intimate discussions with Harriman—and in some respects planned to pattern his own course after that of the Little Giant. Straight believed he was the only one to hear and understand the full scope of Harriman's plan for a global transportation network, including the connecting line through Manchuria. In a sense he now considered himself to be Harriman's heir, charged with the duty of carrying out at least the Manchurian end of it.

But the bankers—ah, the bankers, who now formed the total of the American Group! They were less interested in the fine strategy of constructing railroads in the right places than in simply making loans and drawing interest. Straight felt that Chinese regard for the United States, as a "nonexploiting" nation that had returned to China the Boxer indemnity, was at its highest and that this good opinion should be turned to account in Manchuria. He and Lord ffrench agreed on the general terms of a seven-hundred-mile line for which the American Group would handle the financing and Pauling & Company would do the actual construction.* This railroad, which Straight felt sure would be profitable whether or not any American-managed global network ever came into being, would run from Chinchou, on the warm-water Gulf of Chihli, northward through Manchuria to Aigun on the Amur. From there it would be an easy step to connect with the Trans-Siberian when arrangements were made with Russia.

This Chin-Ai project, as Straight with his knack for condensation called the Chinchou-Aigun line, startled and upset the New York Group. But Straight, after much explanation, was authorized to go ahead. The next problem was to get the Chinese to sign the agreement. But difficulties intervened, as they always did in China, and in the meantime Dorothy Whitney was about to arrive in Peking.

5. Fresh Air in the Face

WAS DOROTHY'S visit with Straight in Peking merely incidental to her round-the-world tour, or was it predicated in part on the pleasure she anticipated in a fortnight's sociability with a man in whom she was already interested? Was she in fact taking steps to encourage a romance that otherwise might never occur? Her diary can be depended on never to betray such intimate matters, or to confess herself stooping to subter-

---

* Straight brought ffrench and his firm into the deal, reasoning that Japan's violent objections to the line would cause the Chinese, in fear, to reject it themselves but for British influence. The British were allies of the Japanese. Straight counted on the British to aid their own English firm of Pauling & Company, to bring the Japanese around to agreement. But this British cooperation failed to come about. The reader is warned that only the most simplified version of Straight's complex negotiations is given here, since a full account of them would itself fill a large volume.

fuge. Indeed she was as free from guile as a human being can be. Her Line-a-Day makes it all appear an agreeable accident. Her tour was not for pleasure alone but was also aimed at educating her in foreign affairs. She had written to Elihu Root, recently Secretary of State and now senator from New York, asking his advice about people she might call on in the Far East. He replied in delighted tone, saying that he had been so fond of her father and indeed her whole family from the time she was a baby that she fell heir to his affection. He armed her with a circular letter from the Secretary of State to all officers of the department in the countries she was to visit, and mentioning officials from whom she could expect special cordiality.

This was the warm and generous side of a man of such caustic wit that subordinates feared him. Dorothy also got a letter of reference from Leigh Hunt, a State Department officer, to Dr. Morrison in Peking, introducing her as "not a mere sightseer but a close student of human events [who] is able to appreciate most thoroughly any insight you may give her into the destiny and intricate affairs of China. . . ."

Dorothy had finished her year as president of the Junior League and had read James's *Pragmatism,* Chesterton's *Orthodoxy,* and some Emerson before she began her preliminary study for her world tour. She left New York July 13 aboard *Wanderer* with Mrs. Bend, Beatrice, and the maid Louisa. She stopped in Chicago to see St. Gaudens's *Lincoln* and in St. Paul to see the La Farge frescoes in the Minnesota state capitol. Her itinerary all but absolves her of concealed romantic motivation. Rather than showing eagerness to see Straight, it suggested that she had forgotten all about him. She and her party saw American scenery all the way from the Grand Canyon to Glacier Park and Lake Louise, plus the Seattle exposition, before they sailed from San Francisco August 7 on the S.S. *Korea.* They spent two whole months touring Japan with a thoroughness unlike that of a young lady whose heart was in Peking. Although Dorothy expected superior hotels, she could abide ordinary ones, and it was rarely that she wrote as bluntly as at Nagoya: "This hotel is horribly dirty & Nagoya is rather a hole on the whole." Straight addressed her from Peking September 4, 1909:

Welcome to our city! . . . we are all awaiting you with the red carpets and brass bands straining at the leash. . . . We place the keys of the American compound in your hands— they are of brass and are very heavy. . . .

Of their five meetings—one at Harriman's, two in Washington, and two on Long Island—only the last had been tête-à-tête with time for extended conversation. Straight was still corresponding with Katherine Elkins. On October 22, six weeks after his welcoming letter, Dorothy and her party sailed from Shimonoseki to Fusan. After looking over Seoul, they shivered with cold as they crossed the Yalu in a launch. At Antung, Straight had alerted an American official to greet them, and thereafter they were aware of his kindly influence and his considerable fame in the area. He smoothed the way for them, though he could not prevent the fire in the Astor Hotel at Mukden, which drove the ladies from their rooms early in the morning—"a very fortunate escape," Dorothy noted. Much to their relief, a private railroad car engaged for them by Straight, containing one of Straight's Chinese servants, who attended them with bows and cooked for them as they rolled southward, arrived in Mukden. "Passed Shan-hai-Kwan at 8.30," Dorothy wrote, "& saw the Great Wall by moonlight." What happened, and their own reactions, can best be told by quoting from Dorothy's and Straight's diaries, and Straight's notes to her, with occasional amplification.

Dorothy's November 1 diary entry: "Arrived at 8.20 & found Mr. Straight at the station. He & Mr. Fletcher came for us later & walked along Wall to Legation where we lunched. . . . Dined with Messrs. Straight & Fletcher—Mr. Liang-Lun-Sen there—the president of the Board of Foreign Affairs. *Such* a fine day."

Straight's entry that day, in part: "Miss Whitney very charming." (So much so that Straight and Fletcher vacated their house, moved into the legation next door, and insisted that Dorothy and her party quit the Hotel Wagons Lits and occupy the vacated house, which they did.)

Dorothy, November 2: "Mr. Straight & Brambilla [Italian First Secretary] came around after lunch—& the former took us to the Lama Temple wh. is wonderfully picturesque. . . . Services were going on while we climbed along upper galleries of the Temple. Came to our new home. Harrisons [legation people] . . . & Prince Pu Lun, came to dinner. Prince Pu Lun came near being Emp. of China."

One of Peking's occasional dust storms kept the ladies indoors November 3. Straight and Fletcher played bridge with Dorothy and Beatrice, and Straight told his diary, "Ladies' presence somewhat disconcerting I find"—not disconcerting enough to keep him from writing to Dorothy next morning:

> *Qu'est-ce-que vous faites ce Matin—*
> *Le Soleil il rit au gratin.* . . .

Dorothy's November 5 entry: "*Such gorgeous days.* Mr. Straight took us this morning to the Drum Tower, wh. we climbed for the beautiful view. Then we went outside of walls to Yellow Temple. Exquisite. . . . Miss Corbett came to tiffin & went with us & Mrs. Harrison to call on Princess Pu Lun."

Sunday morning Dorothy found Straight's note:

> Bon Giorno—
> *A lunch in the campagna—*
> *what? Followed by a ride—*
> *Yes! Fresh air in the face—*
> *Isn't? Joy in the hearts of*
> *the students—*
> *Procession leaving with*
> Mr. Fletcher about 12:00 A.M.
> *ponies and lunch preceding.* . . .

Dorothy's entry: "One of the Golden Days!! Drove out to Summer Palace & after going through that glorious place took rikishas [*sic*] to the Imperial Jade Spring, where we had picnic lunch—just we five [the quintet included the ubiquitous Mrs. Bend] . . . purple hills on one side & distant Peking on the other. Long talk tonight with Mr. Straight."

Long talk. It was so long and so interesting that neither of them ever forgot it, and in fact Straight thereafter celebrated November 7 as an anniversary. It does not appear that Dorothy had time to visit Dr. Morrison for more than a moment of discussion of human events and the destiny and intricate affairs of China.

Straight's entry: "Summer Palace and Yu Chuan San. Quiet dinner and long talk by lantern light. The best day for many moons." And he addressed her gallantly in verse:

> *For time is fleeting and too fast*
> *The sands are rushing through the glass.* . . .
> *At least Your Grace should deign to smile*
> *On us who sit and mourn our plight*
> *While you are up another flight.*

Dorothy, November 11: ". . . At 12, BB, Messrs Straight & Fletcher, & I motored out to canal & rode from there to Half Way Rest Temple where we lunched in one of the courts. Rode afterwards along canal through picturesque village. . . . Best ride I have ever had. . . ."

Straight's entry: "Record breaker. Beautiful day, lunch at Wan Show

Sze—ride along the jade canal afterwards. . . . Quiet dinner en famille, with a juggler afterwards. A little music [Straight sang and
played, as Dorothy later recalled, "his own melodies to the Kipling
songs of the East—songs of the far-flung battle lines of Empire—of
vagabondage and adventure and wanderings over the sea"] . . . then
another fireside talk with D.W."

On November 13 Straight and Bland took the three ladies by train to
the Great Wall. Next day—the visitors' penultimate—Straight and
Fletcher took them by train to the Ming Tombs, where they had a picnic lunch, and, on return, they dined and Straight commented, "Quiet
evening—bad performance," meaning that he had talked too much and
stayed too late. Dorothy on the other hand described it as "one of the
best days I have ever had. Dinner alone. Mr. Straight read me his journals afterwards." His note to her was apologetic:

> *The Matinal light burned too*
> *late again last night—*
> *You must be very tired—and*
> *I feel frightfully guilty. . . . I*
> *cannot though—honestly—say that I am penitent–*
> *Your chariot awaits—*
> *As do I—your orders—*
>   W. S.

That day, their last, Straight showed the Princess, as he now called
her (only in his diary), the mansion-in-a-compound he had selected as
his living and office quarters, commenting, "The Princess went through
the house with me, and suggested here and there. It was hard not to ask
her to stay on and live there." In the afternoon the two of them rode
together: "A wonderful ride, into the sunset. Quiet dinner and a little
choking at the throat, I think." For her part Dorothy wrote, recklessly
for her, "Our last evening;—it is so sad." Next morning, after escorting
the ladies to the railroad station, Straight wrote, "the curtains fell."

Next day he wrote, "Lonely—a/c's all morning." Next: "Rather miserable." And on November 26: "Am not a very cheerful companion
these days."

$$\mathscr{Three}$$

1. Borderland

To HER cousin Katherine Barnes in Manhasset, Dorothy wrote:

We have just left Peking after spending two wonderful weeks there and I feel somehow as if those days would always stand out as the best part of our long journey around the world. We lived in the Legation there with Mr. Straight and Mr. Fletcher [this slip demanded correction] or rather we three lived in the First Secretary's house and the two men slept in the big Legation building next door. . . . Peking has a fascination which is indescribable. . . . Mr. Straight and I used to walk along the city wall at sunset time and watch the soft glow of the distant purple hills and listen to all the strange calls and cries from the city below. . . . I have never taken such rides. . . . Peking was so wonderful . . . The best part of it all was the real friendship we made with Messrs. Straight and Fletcher and they are two of the strongest men I have ever known. Every evening . . . we used to turn out the lights and sit by the fire— and then Mr. Straight brought out his guitar and sang to us. He is really a very remarkable person with a great deal of force and a really wonderful power of sympathy. He is a famous man all over China and up in Manchuria where we traveled before reaching Peking we used to hear words of praise of him on every side. . . . It is really extraordinary—the power which he and Mr. Fletcher wield in China . . . they are serving their country in a way that makes one proud.

To Straight she wrote from Hankow:

Oh Wise Man of the East: You have made us very lonely and very homesick for the purple hills and for your own companionship. I don't think I realized what a sad break our departure was going to be until I stood on the wall with you yesterday and said goodbye to the great city and the distant hills—and hardest of all, to you. And then when we stood on the station platform and the whistle suddenly blew and we all said goodbye, I had a lump in my throat that was very hard to smile away, for the veil was being drawn there over two of the happiest weeks I have ever known. . . . I can only thank you for being the sort of man you are, and I think that after yesterday morning when we burned incense for the last time together before your Buddha and we solemnly promised to have faith always that there can never be in the future such a thing as lack of understanding between us.

The same Dorothy Whitney who had taken tea and ridden and danced with so many admiring and eligible young men in New York, London, Paris, and elsewhere had been overwhelmed in a fortnight by Willard Straight. As she later confessed, "Day by day the magic of Peking grew upon us. . . . Then one day came a trip to the Great Wall and the Ming Tombs, and after that, things were forever different. The magic of China seemed to fade before the magic of a human personality."

What did Straight have that a hundred others did not have to fulfill the specifications of her Venetian soliloquy on the "right man"? There was of course his tall handsomeness, the romance of it all, his face lifted and outlined in flickering firelight as he sang pleasantly of "vagabondage and adventure" and strummed the guitar. There was his kindness and attentiveness, his ability to make a grand occasion out of an incident, the charming things he could say and write. But there was more than that. His achievements made the Charleses and the Bobs and the Jimmies back home look lazy and sophomoric. True, he was a shade older—in fact his hairline was beginning to recede—but with no "family" or fortune behind him he had struck out on his own immediately after college, had been everywhere, had held responsible positions in Washington and abroad, seemed to know everybody, and now was entrusted by such people as J. P. Morgan and Secretary of State Knox with a mission involving millions of dollars and intricate negotiations with several governments. He was intelligent, patriotic, alert, decisive, informed, musical, able, humorous—one imagines her ticking these qualities off on her fingers—and how many other young Americans could speak Chinese?

More than that, he was an orphan even more than Dorothy was an orphan. He was lonely, terribly lonely in the midst of his obvious popularity among the people of the legations. For all his touch of the debonair, there was an irresistible boyishness about him, about his loneliness. He wrote to her the very day she left:

Princesse—I thank you for coming here—and for all the sunshine you have brought us with your bonny laugh. . . . Peking will be very different now that you have gone—dearer because you have been here—and more lonely because you have been and gone. . . . Please be careful— You are very precious. . . . W.S.

That was admiring enough, but awaiting her own reaction. When he received her first letter, he replied after the manner of Sir Galahad:

I knew you wouldn't fail me Princesse. . . . Your letter greeted me this morning—another wonderful Sunday—soft and bright—and made for us to ride together—

Thank you for writing as you did— To have you say such things made me proud and happy. . . . and I ask it humbly—that I may bear your colours on my helm? . . . I cannot write the things I feel—but you understand—I think we both did that morning as we looked out over the mist shrouded city—then back to the Golden Roofs—as we walked down from the wall—and through the busy gate—to the station gate—and then for the last—turned from the bridge and the broad street—to the distant hills of "Borderland."

It is not Goodbye—is it Princesse? . . .

He was, for a man in one way so businesslike and worldly, romantic to the core. He had sung a song of his own composition, "Borderland," making that dreamlike region seem identified at once with the purple hills beyond Peking and with the affections welling up between them. He had decided to address her as "Princesse" with the French spelling. He disdained the comma, semicolon, and period and wrote in bursts separated by dashes, quite different from his business letters. And when she wrote to him, addressing him as "Dear Guardian of Borderland," sending him snapshots she had taken in Peking and ending, "what a man you are," she was coming—for Dorothy Whitney—close to promiscuity. News of affairs of the heart traveled with such speed in her set that it is impossible she did not know he had courted Mary Harriman, though she did not know how serious it had become nor how it had ended. She knew nothing about his interest in Katherine Elkins.

Mrs. Bend and Louisa had reason to feel cheated, since they had found no romance in Peking, whereas it turned out that Beatrice felt stirrings similar to Dorothy's and was corresponding warmly with Fletcher. The ladies visited Java, then sailed for Singapore. The captain took them up on the bridge, and they saw Halley's spectacular comet. Dorothy was reading *Kim* and other works of Straight's admired Kipling. In Calcutta she visited Lord and Lady Minto—they had several times visited the Whitneys in New York when his lordship was Gover-

nor General of Canada, and he was now just finishing as Viceroy of
India—and she had tea with maharajahs including that of Cooch
Behar. Straight peppered her with letters, one of them quite fishy:

> [I try] to draw you from your silent perch—a great effort, for I am no
> shark, and you are a shiner—I be-whale my fate but to no pairpoise, for I
> can no longer bass-k in your shad-ow.

He sent her a news item of his own manufacture:

REFUSES TO WORK
Strange Action of a Heretofore Docile Guitar
His Frets Too Much for Him

> Peking, Jan. 5th— Much comment has been roused in local musical
> circles by the strange obstinacy of Mr. W. D. Straight's guitar. Its frets
> are of no avail. Nothing will bring the strings into harmony.

"Now that's perfectly true," Straight commented on this item. "I
believe myself that the sensible old thing, having served you, will serve
no other."

He wrote that he would be in Europe in the spring and *must* see her
then. But all could not forever be roses. Perhaps he grew too cocksure of
her adoration. There were intimations that he might fall short of perfection. He disagreed rather flatly with her feeling about Maurice Hewlett's
novel *Open Country*, which he read at her urging, admitting that he
was "quite cross" and "I feel the chill of the Siberian air between the
plumage of my wings." She did have that weakness for ecstatic description, and in her letters concerning such things as the Taj Mahal (with
the romantic story of its creation) and her view of a huge caravan of ele-
phants and camels, she rather permitted herself to be carried away. It
was evident that he wanted their correspondence to be on a personal
plane rather than in the nature of a travelogue or book review. He
seemed above all to prefer approval, recognition, praise, such as she had
supplied so wholeheartedly when she wrote "what a man you are." It
had to be admitted that his praise for her was ardent and well expressed.
He now came close to being hurtful:

> Your letter is superlative. You have seen the most wonderful—the
> most beautiful—the most gorgeous—the most fascinating. Today I rode
> alone . . . over the Northern plain, where we went that day to the
> Yellow Temple. . . . I silliquized [he sometimes did intentional violence
> to words] —and told the scenery that it couldn't plume itself any longer—

that India had won your heart, and that [China] now lay thumbed and a little ragged, like a month-old magazine—though still on the table . . . but eclipsed by the special Indian number. I was going to say of Gullible's Travels. It would have been rather funny if I had, but I won't—because it's not true. . . . The scenery—for we've been talking about that all the time—was very hurt, and sulked out of sight in a murky dusty sunset, as I entered the northern city gate. Poor thing—it's so hard to lose face. . . . I hope you can find some wheat in this chaff—grains of sense I mean—but don't thrash me too severely.

His approval of her next letter was a trifle backhanded:

. . . I must tell you that I liked youre* letter tonight much better than the last. . . . Youre trip I want to hear about. . . . But at this long range, when the day is one long typewritten sheet, with carbon copies—I want you and youre ideas about things and the spaces in which you dance with glee—all of which goes to show, I suppose, that I'm as ungrateful as I can be. But I'm not . . . and you can write me about the price of putty during the reign of William the Silent if you wish, and I'll be delighted—only write. . . . Patience is not a virtue that I have cultivated. . . . If I did—there must have been a drought . . . for I didn't raise much.

His finely strung nature needed encouragement and approval. He was terribly anxious to finish in Peking and join Dorothy again, but the Hukuang negotiations lagged, and he was having a ghastly time with the Chin-Ai line. The Russians were now objecting, and Straight mentioned a "stormy interview with Korostovetz," the Russian Minister. Furthermore, he was impatient with the Morgan office in New York, his august superiors, as well as with the State Department, for failing to understand the situation despite his efforts to enlighten them, and he was sometimes a trifle sharp with them.

Reaching Cairo March 17, Dorothy found "30 long letters waiting here." Better yet, she encountered Theodore Roosevelt and part of his family, Roosevelt and Kermit recently having come up from their African hunting excursion to meet Mrs. Roosevelt and Ethel there. With pretty Ethel Roosevelt, then not quite nineteen, Dorothy formed an immediate friendship that was to be close and lifelong. There were many questions about Willard Straight, for whom the Roosevelts obviously had a great affection. Dorothy was delighted with the irrepressible ex-President, who lived only a dozen miles from her on Long Island and

---

* He often spelled it *youre*. Otherwise his spelling was usually exemplary.

some of whose good friends she knew, among them the Robert Bacons, the George von Lengerke Meyers, and now Straight.

Ethel and I played around together every day in Cairo [Dorothy wrote to Straight]. . . . T.R. himself was simply splendid, and I was overcome by his sitting down and talking to foolish, ignorant me, when he had hundreds of matters to attend to. . . . He sure is a great man—and I am all for him! [She and Ethel accompanied him during his interview at the Moslem University:] You should have seen us all sitting around in a small room—frightfully solemn and dignified although T.R. gave Ethel and me the wink once or twice. . . . Of course he is going to be President again—don't you think so? Then you will be Secretary of State— and U.S.A. will immediately annex China!! Banzai!!

In Rangoon she had enjoyed girl dancers, but not the sinuous belly dancer she saw in Cairo—"too awful." Reaching Rome on April 8, she ran across an orthographically interesting friend: "Talked to Count Przezdziecki & Count Ancillotto after lunch." Old suitors—seen now with different eyes. Two days later, as prearranged, she met her sister Pauline and her daughters at St. Raphael on the Riviera. "Had a grand welcome from Sister & the kids," she noted. "Olive and I walked for an hour." Pauline had not been well, but sick or well she loved to play cards and to gamble if possible, as the poet laureate of *Town Topics* observed:

Now Mrs. Paget, worthy daughter of remembered sire,
If one believes the rumor, plunges bridgewise with much fire,
Wins seven thousand dollars at a sitting; 'tis to weep,
To think how horribly expensive Pagets are to keep.

"Lord Herbert (Reggie) & Lady Alexander Paget dined with Sister & me & we played bridge till 11," Dorothy wrote. She called on the Whitelaw Reids, vacationing nearby, and after a week with Pauline left with her party for Florence, where she exercised a sensible habit: ". . . after breakfast & bath I went out by myself & walked for 2½ hours all over Florence—climbed Campanile & spent some time in Cathedral & Baptistery—then to Palazzo Vecchio—oh I love Florence."

At Settepossi's she bought a string of pearls as a gift for Beatrice, although it was not her birthday. They moved on restlessly—perhaps a little nervously because Straight would soon be coming—to Bologna, Venice, Verona, Gardone, then Bellagio. Bellagio, where her ailing mother had once rested and watched Uncle Oliver eye the Russian countess while William Whitney was achieving the 1892 miracle at the Chicago convention. Dorothy had not read her parents' letters and was not aware of it. "The weather is overcast," she observed, "& tomorrow Halley's comet is going to finish off the earth." To Straight she wrote, "And so you are really coming—are you? . . . We are really frightfully proud of you for having gotten the loan through [he had not] . . . and I'm sure that no one but you could have done it." In *The Paris Herald* she saw a front-page picture of Mr. Willard D. Straight, identified as the American negotiating a loan for China. She was at once thrilled and discomposed, as she later admitted, because she would soon meet him and she did not know quite *how* to meet him.

2. *"I Shall Be Quite Terrible"*

The sand of the desert is sodden red,—
Red with the wreck of a square that broke;—
The Gatling's jammed and the Colonel dead,
And the regiment blind with dust and smoke.
The river of death has brimmed his banks,
And England's far, and Honour a name,
But the voice of a schoolboy rallies the ranks:
"Play up! Play up! and play the game!" *

WILLARD STRAIGHT loved Kipling because of the heroic roll of his verse but perhaps also because Straight too was a believer in God and country, in honor, character, and playing the game. He had recently finished a biography of Stonewall Jackson that he thought "full of lessons on character building." "Playing the game" was a Kipling phrase he came to use to signify a code of honor and righteousness toward one's work, duty, family, and country. His jokes and witticisms disguised a man with a vein of deep seriousness, determined to make a success of life and to occupy one of its upper echelons, always with character and honor. However warm had been his affection for Mary Harriman, and whatever his precise feeling for Katherine Elkins, he was now deeply interested in Dorothy Whitney. He had telegraphed her celebrating her twenty-third birthday on January 23, when she was in Benares, and she had reciprocated, as he noted in his diary January 31: "Thirty years old today. Telegram from Princess—best of the day."

* The selection is by Sir Henry John Newbolt, also known to Straight—a contemporary and follower of Kipling, the greater poet, in his romantic imperialism and his acclaim for Britons "playing the game."

As with some who have been orphaned early in childhood, his weakness was a low frustration point that could at times defeat his abilities. This was especially true in a long-term assignment loaded with such obstacles and reverses as plagued him now. He got along famously with Maurice Casenave, his French counterpart, and well enough with the Englishman Hillier and the German Cordes—but to get these three to agree with him on every complex detail of the Hukuang loan seemed to take forever. Nor was Chin-Ai going any better, what with Russian intransigence. His anxiety to see Dorothy again added to his malaise.

The thought that every day she was getting farther away was insupportable. He was sharper with the Morgan office in New York than he should have been. He was pleased when the Douglas Robinsons—Mrs. Robinson was Theodore Roosevelt's younger sister—stopped in Peking and visited with him. Corinne Robinson had, he wrote to Dorothy, "such a quick sympathy—like yours, Princesse," adding, "The Lord made me by nature an autocrat—a tyrant—and a soldier, not a politician." But a letter he soon sent Mrs. Robinson showed his softer side. His mood of despair had grown dark enough so that he told his troubles not to Robinson but to the sympathetic Corinne. As later events were to confirm, there were times when his normally ebullient spirits sagged, the orphan in him became unbearable, and he needed motherly advice and encouragement. In this instance, Mrs. Robinson—a warmly sentimental woman who liked him all the more for it—listened to him and gave him advice that he did not specify but for which he thanked her profusely. He ended his letter by asking her to pray for him, possibly in connection with both his love and his labors.

Now he was close to agreement with Casenave, Hillier, and Cordes on a united approach to the Chinese, but the Chinese themselves were growing unreasonable. At last, deciding that they were dilly-dallying, he delivered on his own an ultimatum: If they did not close, he would leave April 28. New York was troubled by the ultimatum, which rightly should have been cleared by the home office, but he would lose face if he did not stand by it. He was given permission to travel to Paris and London in the hope that conferences there might speed the accord, which had not yet been reached despite premature news to the contrary, which had misled Dorothy. The Chinese did not close, and he left on the twenty-eighth with his Chinese manservant Chang, whom he preferred to call William. How much he was motivated by his desire to see Dorothy and how much by the exigencies of his task remains an interesting question. He had not slept well. He had negotiated unsparingly and was exhausted and bone-weary. He rested as he rode the Trans-Siberian, writing Dorothy, "I am crossing half the world to see you, Princesse. I want to see you more than I want anything else." He had no doubt about the wisdom of his move:

> I know I'm right and hence have no smiting conscience. One learns somehow as one grows older that even one's olders and betters have to be told what to do—and disciplined—particularly when they are attempting to deal with a situation about which their knowledge is remarkable only for its extreme scarcity.

In Moscow, he read in *The Paris Herald* of Mary Harriman's engagement to Charles Cary Rumsey, a New York sculptor who specialized in animal figures. "He seemed a very nice fellow," Straight wrote Dorothy carefully, "and I am sure, since she has chosen him, that he must be a fine man. I cannot tell you how glad I am for her. . . ," Reaching Berlin, he found the Roosevelt party there, the ex-President being feted by the Kaiser. One can imagine the uproarious talk he had with that voluble family. They had seen Dorothy in Cairo! She had told them of his work in Peking! It appears that here Straight permitted expediency—Roosevelt might well become President again, with important posts to distribute—to delay by some few hours his reunion with Dorothy. He attended a reception for the Roosevelts at the American embassy and joined their party in their special train to London. Here he checked in at the Morgan, Grenfell office on Old Broad Street and found that he would have almost three days off before Morgan and Davison arrived from New York. He was off like a shot for Milan, where Dorothy awaited him at the Hotel de Ville. He knocked at her door at six in the morning. She was, of course, formidably chaperoned by the Bends, but they permitted her a few minutes of discreet semiprivacy so that the young man who had come some eight thousand miles to make a proposal of marriage need not do so before an audience. She covered this with outrageously misleading unconcern in her diary ("Willard arrived at 6 this morning—so we had breakfast together at 8.30. . . .") but made amends in a statement years later:

> There were no pretenses then. After one brief word of greeting he told me why he had come. Standing against the door of our little sitting room with his hat still in his hand he poured out the yearning of his heart. . . . I, who had been living for six months in anticipation of this day, suddenly found myself weak and uncertain. Confronted with the reality I drew back in hesitation and doubt.

She did not say, but it is not impossible, that she was also troubled by the broad spectrum of Straight's moods as shown by his letters, after his perfectly angelic conduct during the fortnight in Peking. They had ranged from the pleasant and gentle and funny to the cocksure and even to a bit of the domineering. She had encouraged him in her "what a man" letters immediately after the Peking ecstasy, but as the months of separation grew, she had withdrawn ever so slightly into a tone still warm but less openly admiring. But Straight had been quite confident, and her failure to fall into his arms was a terrible disappointment.

The four—Straight, Dorothy, and the Bends—had breakfast there in the hotel suite, a meal that could not have been without constraint. Dorothy and Straight then went to the great Gothic cathedral, "where we sat for a long time," as she wrote without elaboration in her diary, and where Straight must surely have renewed his appeals. The cathedral was the proper place, for she let him know that she believed marriage to be holy, and that while she had great affection for him, she was not sure. He evidently went into some detail about his romance with Mary—possibly also with Katherine Elkins. They ended up sightseeing, driving to the Certosa at Pavia, and all four next day drove to Stresa, on Lake Maggiore, "wh. is simply too divine," Dorothy wrote. "Willard & I went over to the Isola Bella [an island in the lake] & sat there in the garden. Then he left on the 6.15 Simplon Express."

It was characteristic of her orderly mind that even in this moment of ardor she recorded the time of the train. She wrote from Stresa:

> It's just five hours, Willard, since you went away, and I have been standing on the balcony "to the north," and thinking of you as you cross the mountains tonight. It was so strange—after you left the clouds began to gather, and a mist crept over the lake, so that when the sunset time arrived we had no sunset, and now instead of a starry sky and moonlight in the waves, there is only an impenetrable darkness above and a vague undefined shadow of a lake below. So in leaving—you took light and color away with you—and after all you needn't have been afraid of the moon. . . . I'm glad—so glad—we have had these days together here in Italy . . . the land that has always meant so much to each of us in our dreams. And I wondered if you know how much I appreciate the high ideal of truth you showed me yesterday—when you told me all those things about yourself . . . after you had told me I knew that our relationship was on a higher plane and that you had given me your truth as a part of your love. . . . Goodnight—and oh, please, sleep well!

Straight answered from Paris:

The whole world seems brighter with the Great Hope that I have that you may care—that you will tell me that you love me—that we shall be together always, in body and spirit. . . . You have asked me to wait. Do you know how hard it is [?] Do you know that I can't wait long and that at any moment I am apt . . . to let the spirit of the Moyen age sweep me away—to ride for you and swing you on the saddle before me. I shall be quite terrible then—on a very big horse—and all in tin clothes. Are you not afraid?

3. *Hooroo Antung*

IT WAS Straight's misfortune that his romantic dilemma occurred during a time of crisis and decision for his immediate employer, J. P. Morgan & Company. The situation offered him enormous opportunity if he performed well, and threatened his very employment if he did not. No sooner did he reach Paris from Milan than he was caught up in a whirlpool of financial maneuverings demanding his keenest and quickest thought. Harry Pomeroy Davison, the suave, forty-three-year-old Morgan partner who was devoting much of his time to the Chinese loan, all but dragged Straight off the sleeper on the morning of May 22 and fired questions at him. Davison knew that some of Straight's dispatches to New York had been less than reverent. He was also aware of Straight's high intellect and his position as the only man in the organization with any conception of Chinese politics and the manner in which foreigners could deal with China. On the very next day, Straight was in a long and grueling conference with Davison, Theodore Grenfell (head of the London Morgan office), Warburg, five Englishmen, five Frenchmen, and two Germans, which at last resulted in the agreement of the American Group and the other three nations in their terms for the Hukuang loan.

Now all that remained was to get the Chinese to agree. Straight in a letter to Dorothy admitted that he had done much of the talking and advising in this group of hardened money men and was quite willing to take some of the credit, which he undoubtedly deserved. He dined that night, after eleven hours of the most intense work, with J. P. Morgan himself, Davison, Herman Harjes (head of the Morgan Paris office), Grenfell, and Robert Bacon, who was the new American Ambassador in Paris. Davison was elated enough to give Straight May 25 off so that he could rush to Aix to meet his beloved, whose identity Davison did not know. This was an interval in Straight's life during which he devoted his

most consuming energies alternately to business and to love as he observed tight schedules, made trains by an eyelash, and got little sleep.
He caught the night train to Aix, having telegraphed Dorothy, and also
found time to write her:

> At eight then Princesse I will come
> Looking perchance a little bum
> For, traveling in Froggy trains
> Is bad for clothes and Willie's brains—
> But what care I for sloth and ease
> A journey's woes are things that please
> When you, dear Princesse, smile and wait,
> For breakfast [illegible word]—my heart's elate
> Like Milan—dear—t'will be in Aix,
> But—tell me, have you buckwheat cakes?

Dorothy sought, with far less success, to reply in kind:

> Hello, Willard, how are you?
> Think of breakfast, just we two!
> I shall come to you at eight—
> In the reading room sedate. . . .

He reached Aix at 6:40 and breakfasted with her (having buckwheat
caix?) in her suite at the Hotel Bernascon, the proximity of the Bends
being taken for granted. He had news: He would soon make a quick trip
to New York for talks there, and he supplied her with a code that would
make their cables cheaper and more interesting:

AIKEN—I miss you frightfully.
ANTUNG—Are you well?
BORDERLAND—(Signature word conveying love).
HOOROO—Everything fine.
GRAZIA—Thanks for your telegram.
LIEBESTRAUM—God guard you always.
SHEMMO—How are things going?
TAOHSIEH—Thanks for your letter.

They sat on the terrace, they motored to Annecy for lunch, they
dined in Dorothy's sitting room, and Straight caught the 9:14 back to
Paris. Then London and more Morgan conferences, after which
Straight wrote to Dorothy before boarding the *Lusitania*:

. . . it's very late but I cannot go to ship without a goodnight word to
you. Tonight I dined with Mr. Morgan . . . and afterward Mr. Morgan
took us to his house in Prince's Gate. What a mansion he has. . . . In
these months have been such an eternity—each time I see you it is more
wonderful—each time I know more fully how wonderful you are—how
true is the magnet that has drawn me. . . . Wonder of the World—
please tell me that the Dream has at last come true.

Dorothy, now in Paris again, received from him seven ardent telegrams in quick succession and six letters. He had also arranged with a
Paris florist to send her daily lilies of the valley and one red rose which,
she assured him, "I wear . . . each day in my dress." He landed in
New York June 3 and received her cable: "LIEBESTRAUM BOY
[Straight] BORDERLAND." He took a night train to Oswego to visit his
sister Hazel and his surviving "Aunt" Laura while daylight lasted, then
boarded another night train back to New York. The next day, Sunday,
he conferred with Davison at the latter's Long Island home, then took
the Congressional Limited to Washington, where he spent all the next
day at the State Department, seeing Secretary Knox among others.
"Dined with Katherine," he noted in his diary, without recording
whether—as he must or should have—he informed her that a new affection had altered his life. He left Washington at midnight, spent all
next day hard at work at the Morgan Wall Street office and on the following day boarded the *Lusitania* on its return trip, having spent four
days in the United States. He had found time to write to Dorothy at
length, including the avowal, "I am not *in love* but I *love*—and there's
all that difference. It's very wonderful—and very terrible—it makes me
ache. . . ."

In New York he had also called on Corinne Robinson, who had
become his kindly preceptor and to whom he wrote gratefully:

. . . that you should think me worthy—and capable of giving her—all
that youre love could wish—makes me very proud—and pretty serious
with myself It's such a tremendous thing. I'm a good deal afraid. If I
should win her—the thought that she might be taken from me terrifies
me. That I suppose is the penalty of wanting with one's whole soul—It
must be an echo of that awful thing—a New England conscience which
makes you feel that you shouldn't have that which you most care for—
and that if you should win it—you'll probably have it snatched away—
because you love it too dearly. . . .

I'm going to tell her—I don't call her Dorothy to you—because I don't
to her—or to myself—I haven't the right yet—what you said—and tell
her too that we spoke of her in Peking.

Dorothy meanwhile had taken a suite at the Hotel Vendôme, started French lessons (Straight's French was better than hers), and been caught in a social whirlwind. Her dear friends the Bacons, without Bob, were now in Paris, Bacon as Ambassador. She saw them often and also a new and temporary employee of the Group, none other than George Marvin, who had been with Straight in Mukden and later in Washington. Marvin, who had a fine Roman nose and a distinguished profile, was an intelligent and admiring companion at luncheons, dinners, and at riding in the Bois. Dorothy, as if uncertain how much longer her freedom would last, was permitting herself to be escorted to Longchamps or to dinner or the opera by a parade of men. But she favored Marvin, who had no more fortune than did Straight, and on one day saw him three times (perhaps asking him discreet questions about Willard?). She was seen almost daily at Voisin, Foyot, Larue, or Pré Catelan. Straight's Peking "Elder Brother" Fletcher, now Minister to Chile, was holidaying in Paris and attentive in his crusty way to Beatrice Bend. Dorothy, who had not been home for almost a year, was approaching expatriate status. She called on a real expatriate, Edith Wharton. She had lunch and later dined with a group including Henry Adams, now seventy-two. Adams gallantly escorted her to picture galleries, undoubtedly appraising the quality of the daughter of the man famous for his horses and houses.

Straight reached Paris June 15 and had three days with Dorothy before he left for St. Petersburg and she for London. He was thereafter less pleasant with Marvin and commented on him critically in his letters, perhaps because he had heard that Dorothy and Marvin had been companionable. But at the Vendôme she made—considering her wariness—a great gesture to show Straight that he was first in her affections even if she could not yet make up her mind: She hung an expensive gold locket, containing her picture, around his neck. This ritual he remembered to the date and hour eight years later when he was again in France but engaged in war. ". . . without you paradise would be a wilderness," he wrote to her as he left for the Russian capital with his Chinese manservant. ". . . The Great God that rules us—and shapes our lives—has meant this to be. The hand of Providence—has led us together and together we must be." He did not flinch at giving the Almighty a personal interest in their courtship or asserting that Dorothy would be repudiating His express design should she reject him.

In St. Petersburg he spent five hard days calling on cabinet ministers and aides, including Foreign Minister Alexander Iswolski (the same

Iswolski who in four short years was to claim World War I: "*C'est ma guerre!*"). He sought Russian agreement to the construction of the Chin-Ai line, but received only courteous evasion and ultimate refusal. Dorothy meanwhile had joined Pauline and Almeric at their handsome country place, Deepdene, south of London near Dorking. Lord Falconer was a guest also—Pauline was fairly thrusting him at Dorothy—and others including a painter named Milbank. Almeric was now a Tory Member of Parliament, but Deepdene seemed a perpetual house party. Straight arrived there June 28, desolated to find that Dorothy, although she had been ill with a fever of 103 degrees, was posing daily for the artist. He begrudged Milbank every minute of her time and warned her that the fatigue brought on by posing could damage her health. She seemed to have turned somewhat against him at the moment, possibly ruminating over his previous romances, which in truth would have given any woman pause. He was commuting to the London Morgan office, leaving early and returning late, so that he was often reduced to sending her notes through her maid, the faithful Louisa:

> Bon Giorno—Princessa mia. . . . Before going to pose will you tell Louisa to knock on my door—and see me for a moment in the hall. . . . Today you must be kind Princessa mia. . . .

His anxiety mounted because he was soon to be sent for a longer stay at the Morgan New York office, after which he would ultimately return to China. He had good reason to suspect Pauline of plotting against him in favor of Falconer. He sent Dorothy a deluge of notes through Louisa, urging her to see him today and to marry him soon thereafter, so insistent that she reproved him. "It was good to be near you when [one of the guests, a pianist] played 'Boheme,' " he wrote humbly though she was in the same house. "Tonight I hope you'll sit with me—too . . . and this morning—will you stop to speak with me a moment as you go down to your pose?" At last her visit was finished, and with Straight she took the train to Paris on July 1—a memorable Independence Day for him except that he had to return immediately to business in London. Luckily he had kept in touch with Professor Stephens, who was vacationing in London and who now took up the cudgels for him in a letter to Dorothy:

> It is not often that an elderly professor writes to a young lady, whom he has never met. But I have been lunching and dining with Willard Straight, who can talk and think of nothing but you. Is that a valid excuse? I hope so. If not, may I be forgiven?

But, seriously, there are things I can say that Straight cannot say for himself—though I warrant he can be eloquent enough—and that no one else can say. I knew him at Cornell, when he was trembling on the edge of many things. Without parents or means he has made himself what he is. Without any backing but his own brave heart he set out to play the game [that Kipling phrase again!] and he has played it like a man. I think no one knows so well as myself what an uphill fight it has been, for nearly every one in this world has some relative or friend to aid him, while Straight has had no home influences to guide him or console him. He has kept himself clean and wholesome and brave, when many a young man would have gone down; he has steered clear of cynicism and credulity; he has made his way in the world by sheer merit, held his head high and asked no man anything. I am prouder of him and fonder of him than of any young fellow that ever came under my hand, and love him like a son, for he represents the finest type of young American manhood. Can you wonder that I wish for him the fulfillment of his heart's desire? And will you pardon me for daring to "butt in" for a dear fellow who has no father or mother to back his suit? With the hope that I may not be considered too presumptuous. . . . H. Morse Stephens

Was there ever a swain who had such pedagogical patronage? Straight would need all of it. He was pushing his suit with every idea at hand. He determined that while in New York he would see her guardian and brother Harry and request his permission to marry Dorothy. He sent Dorothy a code word, WHEE, which he would use when he had seen Harry and gotten his assent—cheeky enough when she had not given *her* assent. He sent her others—PAGLIACCI, AIDA, BOHEME, and BUTTERFLY, each opera signifying some New York decision as to his assignment, MANON meaning "If I can come for you I shall join you in Europe and we will go to China via Siberian Railroad." If Dorothy was annoyed at his temerity, she had, if she was fair, to admit that his manner of courtship was not run-of-the-mill.

He was given time later to spend six days with Dorothy (and the Bends) at Divonne, where they motored, played tennis, or Straight sketched while she read to him. They chatted with Mrs. Wharton, who was there too, and with Judge Walter Berry, who had been for so many years so close a friend of the novelist and had never married her even when he had the opportunity—the same Walter van Rensselaer Berry who had been an usher at Dorothy's christening in Washington in 1887 and remembered her mother and father. Had Mrs. Wharton, that perceptive past mistress of Eastern seaboard foibles and passions, been gifted with clairvoyance, Dorothy and Willard might have given her material for a novel in her best manner.

Straight left at 5:00 A.M. July 19 to work in Paris, then sailed from Cherbourg July 30. He had arranged with an old lady who sold newspapers to take flowers to Dorothy daily. When he reached New York, he was encouraged by her cable:

HOOROO ANTUNG HOPE YOU WON'T HAVE TOO HOT A TIME IN OLD TOWN TONIGHT GOOD LUCK LIEBESTRAUM BORDERLAND.

4. Squared and Squared Again

WHILE DOROTHY was now independent of Harry and could marry without his consent, she obviously decided that it would not hurt for Straight to put his case before her brother. Harry would of course sputter like a fuse about Straight's previous interest in another heiress, Mary Harriman. Probably Straight hoped fervently that he would not learn about Heiress No. 2, Katherine Elkins, whose association with him had occurred in Washington. Indeed it is not at all surprising that one of the factors that continued to check Dorothy's acceptance of him was the excessive number of heiresses in his life. This remained a solid fact in her thinking, though at times his immense charm made her push it back in her mind. Straight himself was so terribly worried that the Elkins romance might give people the mistaken impression that he was a fortune hunter that Dorothy, in a more pitying moment, could not help reassuring him: "Don't worry about Katherine E.," she wrote to him, "—for what does it matter whether people do know? You and I know better still! Of course she's a fine person, and I shall stick up for her always now, because she's a friend of yours—and because she helped you at one time, unconsciously perhaps to find yourself. . . ."

In his defense, whatever his previous inclinations, his ardor for Dorothy now seemed as vivid and destined as Halley's Comet; and if it came down to the vulgar matter of money, Katherine's inheritance was to be bigger than Dorothy's. Still, skeptics could say, Katherine did not have hers yet and Dorothy did. And it *was* a remarkable coincidence that he seemed to have had no serious interest in girls who were not heiresses. It could also be embarrassing to be the third heiress in the line, and to have this generally known, as it seemed certain to be. Had he ever proposed to Katherine? No one knows. Dorothy had long since told her mentor and closest confidante, Beatrice Bend, about Mary Harriman, and Beatrice had withstood the shock. The fact that not until now did Dorothy tell Beatrice about Katherine Elkins suggests that this was a complication that Dorothy herself found hard to swallow. Dorothy's letter makes it plain that Beatrice did too. So—let Willard explain it all to Harry and see what he said.

Another objection to Straight, having nothing to do with his character, was his lack of social standing, his total removal from her friends, her "set." This had not troubled Whitney when he courted Flora Payne for, pinched though he was, he had that remarkable family tree as well as the Yale-Harvard background approved by Flora and her circle. As Dorothy later put it, marriage to Straight would involve "such a complete break with the past, such a plunge into new surroundings and new circumstances, such a separation from people I loved. . . ."

As a nine-year-old flower girl Dorothy had watched Harry and Gertrude become man and wife at The Breakers. Their marriage, which had then seemed so perfect, had turned out to be an almost impersonal arrangement, Harry attending to his horses and shooting (and other women), Gertrude to her sculpture and to interest in other men. Gertrude did not seem important to Harry. He did not seem to need her. If Dorothy was certain of anything, it was that Willard, with all his faults, needed her and with an urgency that argued that his need would not quickly fade. And she wanted to be needed. Willard's need for her was the major theme of his appeals to her, one of which now came to her from New York saying, "I want you so, Dorothy mine. These dragging weeks are tearing the heart out of me." He had seen President Taft and Secretary Knox, and he had visited the Roosevelts, about whom he wrote to Dorothy:

> I watch Mrs. Teddy R. with her youngsters—and Mrs. Roosevelt with Quentin and Archie and dear Mrs. Robinson . . . and they are so sweet. Yet I can't believe that they understand each other half as well as you and I do. Teddy mixes cocktails—and she [Mrs. Robinson] comes down to dinner with an infant on her arms—a radiant mother—and I think of you coming in like that and how proud I'd be.

Twenty-three was a magic number to him, being the date of Dorothy's birthday. He thought it a splendid omen that the Morgan office was at 23 Wall Street. He was given a part-time secretary but little work to do. As time went on, he became apprehensive—actually beginning to wonder whether he would long have a job and whether he should angle for a return to the State Department. He had planned to be back in Europe well before Dorothy returned, which would be in

October, and he seemed to be arguing in opposite directions: "It seems quite probable that I shall be here to meet you when you return. . . . I am not at all cheerful, for you'll be so glad to be home again, to see all youre friends, that I'll be lost in the shuffle. . . . Please can't you arrange to come back sooner. It doesn't seem somehow that I can wait." He even wrote to Beatrice Bend urging that she and Dorothy return carlier. Dorothy, who worried about his tendency to overwork and overplay and get too little sleep—she had commiserated with him tenderly when he was temporarily ill and called him *"mio piccolo povero"*—was provoked at his audacity in "going around" her:

> Oh Willard, you foolish child to have written the way you did to Beatrice. Of course she doesn't understand what right you have to expect us to change all our plans and go home earlier to see you and I'm afraid she thinks it's somewhat fresh of you to ask it. If you and I were engaged, or even if I knew I cared, it would be entirely different. . . . Your nerves must be on edge, poor Boy. . . .

Her tone was quite different from the near-reverence with which she had addressed him in the weeks after Peking, and indeed their positions had reversed. He was at times miserable, uncertain about his job and his ladylove, unhappy too because he had played polo with some of Dorothy's friends on Long Island and "I did not distinguish myself. . . . I wanted very much to—for your sake, Wonder child. . . ." For a time he feared that Morgan would give up on the China loan entirely, which he thought tantamount to surrender: "I made up my mind that if they did, I would take no employment from any of 'em, but would ask you to wait—dear,* until we could do something less humiliating than to work for quitters. Was I right?"

It had not earlier been Willard's wont to ask her advice. He observed that in negotiations with the State Department, J. P. Morgan told Davison, "You might as well make it clear that when we want to discuss things with the United States Government we want [the Secretary of State] and not [the Assistant Secretary]," on which Straight commented, "It was not difficult to see where the real power lies in this country. . . ." Indeed, Secretary Knox traveled to New York for talks with the Group people instead of asking them to see him in Washington. Straight was delighted when the Group decided not only to continue their effort to close the Hukuang loan but to launch a new and separate

* His use of dashes, as here, was often eccentric.

enterprise of dizzying proportions. This was a projected $300,000,000 loan to China—again in company with England, France, and Germany—based on that country's reform of its now heterogeneous and chaotic currency system. It was the greatest foreign venture the United States had ever undertaken. The Group at last assured Straight—after perhaps intentionally taking him down a peg or two—that they needed him, as indeed they did.

Davison warmed toward Straight, after some weeks of crustiness, and had him out to his Locust Valley place on Long Island (not ten miles from Dorothy's) as a guest. Davison now knew the identity of Straight's beloved, with whose brother Harry he was well acquainted. He had the considerable arrogance to tell Straight that he had talked with the lawyer Lewis Cass Ledyard, an old friend of William C. Whitney's, about Straight's romance with Dorothy. Ledyard had asked "all manner of questions" about Straight, his background and character. Davison said he had vouched for Straight as much as his limited acquaintance would permit. As Straight relayed it to Dorothy:

> [Davison] did tell L. however that on the basis and with the knowledge he had of me, he'd be delighted if I were to marry his sister. . . . He made one reservation—this I tell you—that he had heard that I had been engaged . . . to Mary—and that the thought would naturally occur to Mr. L.—as to himself—that I wished to marry "a very rich girl." He told Mr. Ledyard however, that he didn't think I was that sort of a person.

This was on the basis of knowledge of Mary and not of Katherine, about whom Straight did not enlighten Davison. Katherine, in terms of her significance to logicians as well as gossips, was not twice Mary but the square of Mary again squared. Dorothy, while admiring Straight's honesty, was aware of the groundswell of rumor about her and Straight. And Straight, so sure of himself in Peking and even in Europe, was still a fish out of water in the hands of the New York financiers—nervous also because Dorothy had assured him that she would give him her answer when she returned in October. "You frighten me," he wrote to her, "—and at the same time, you lift me into the clouds. Tell me that it can only be one way—and that Ours, dear—it can't be any other." He had suddenly lost faith in Roosevelt because of his startling speeches in St. Paul and Osawatomie attacking "lawbreakers of great wealth" and embarrassing Wall Street. "I admire the man tremendously of course," he assured Dorothy, but feared he was a fanatic. ". . . I wonder if Wall

Street is corrupting me—whether . . . I have really been acquired by the interests. I'd hate to think so."

There was comment about Dorothy in the press:

> Miss Dorothy Whitney is one of the very unusual girls of the day. One of the greatest heiresses in society, she leads a quietly philanthropic life and few outside her own set know much about her. . . . In the family councils her two brothers . . . have been worsted many times when Miss Doto took the reins in her own hands. . . . Mrs. Almeric Paget . . . and Mrs. Harry Whitney have made every decent effort to marry the willful young Doto to a man of some sort. Mrs. Paget favors an English nobleman. Mrs. Whitney, like her father-in-law, favors an American. . . .

The news had spread among Dorothy's friends that she was considering marriage to Straight, and the sentiment was heavily against him, the outsider, not a member of Dorothy's set. What could the girl who had passed over such men of the inner circle as Jay, Whitehouse, Bacon, and Draper see in this stranger? Bob Bacon still considered himself in the running, his parents hoped that Dorothy would recover her sanity, and Martha Bacon felt that her dear friend was in danger of falling into the hands of an adventurer. So too did Margaret Dix, the daughter of the late rector, now married to Charles Lawrance. Straight's previous interest in Mary Harriman was well known. A formidable opposition had developed. Even the fact that he worked for J. P. Morgan—normally a high recommendation in Society—could not save him. His college background was scorned by those who saw prestige only at Princeton, Yale, and Harvard and regarded Cornell as a small rural place devoted mostly to instructing farmers.

How much worse would it be when the romance with Katherine Elkins became known? Straight bravely went out to Arden to see Mary, who was now married to Charles Cary Rumsey, in the hope that she would speak well of him. Mary was kindly, but he learned to his astonishment that Harry Payne Whitney had already been to see her. Alas, Whitney had also gone to Washington and twice interviewed Katherine (the honest Dorothy had told him about her), having long talks with her. This made it seem certain that knowledge of the Elkins matter would soon become public property. It is probable that Ambassador and Mrs. Bacon in Paris, who considered themselves almost as Dorothy's surrogate parents and whom she truly loved, let her know their feelings. The nearest and perhaps the most influential of all was

Beatrice Bend who, some thought, was in any case jealous of her cherished Dorothy, unwilling to lose her as a companion.

Straight, with real courage, had asked to see Harry and at length was invited to have lunch with him downtown. Their conversation is unrecorded, but the joyous WHEE which Straight had hoped to cable was not sent. Dorothy, with Beatrice, at length returned to Paris and then London, where she met Harry. She spent four days with him and with Pauline at Deepdene. Harry's mission was to report on his investigations and give his opinion of Straight as a prospective husband, which could not have been high. One has a picture—partly speculative but sustained by much evidence—of the brother and two sisters together in private conference, with Harry and Pauline presenting by turns the evidence against Willard Straight. It could not have been a pleasant family reunion for Dorothy. Her letter to Straight about Harry's report, doubtless out of kindness, omitted the main points at issue and said only that Harry had a high opinion of Straight as a man and also believed that Straight had been deeply in love with Katherine Elkins.

Returning to Paris, Dorothy visited the couturières ("Everything is hideous this year!" she wrote, clearly meaning more than the new designs). She saw the Bacons at least five times, once when the Ambassador called on her alone. She also saw her Aunt Lilly. It is unlikely that they urged on her the advantages of a marriage to Straight. For all Dorothy's own basic belief in him, this propaganda was telling on her. Her route to wedlock was scarcely strewn with the legendary roses. At last Dorothy sailed on the *Lusitania* with the Bends and was met in New York October 13, 1910, by a hopeful Willard Straight.

He must have realized the instant he saw her that the answer was not Yes. He was invited out to Westbury, where he stayed with the Whitneys for six days as a commuter. The answer was not Yes but it was not No as yet either. Dorothy, in the face of conflicting pressures and enormous exhortation, could not yet make up her mind. Straight was desolated. She was sorry for him when he left for Washington for a last talk with Secretary Knox, writing to him more like the mother than the Dulcinea:

Poor Boy—you've had such a long, hard tireing [sic] day. . . . I hate to think of your long trip tomorrow and all those hours on the train, and Tuesday drawing nearer and nearer! Dear Willard Boy—God bless you and keep you safe and well.

Tuesday was the day he had to sail, perhaps out of her life forever. He called on her again three times before he sailed October 25. She did not see him off. In London he worked at the Morgan office for a week. In Paris he dined with Margaret Dix Lawrance and Martha Bacon, both of them convinced that Dorothy would make a terrible mistake if she married him. He did his best—which was considerable when he turned on both charm and persuasive power—to win them over, an effort taking courage and determination. Then on, on to the Trans-Siberian Railroad that seemed to carry his fate on its rails as much as it did Russia's. From Moscow he wrote to Dorothy:

> Just a year ago . . . you left Peking, and I was one of the bluest and most hopeless people you ever saw. Here tonight I am starting out across Siberia, and you are four thousand miles away. I wonder if the orchestra tonight, when I made them play "Boheme" and "Butterfly" and "Les Fleurs Que Nous Aimons"—I couldn't have "Liebestraum"—knew that their song was carrying very far, across the snow covered fields, over the forests and the winter waves—to you. . . . even though you say the Miracle has not yet been granted. But there is that bond between us—the bond that makes me wake with thoughts of you . . . that gives you my last waking thought, and weaves you through my dreams.

5. The Loneliest Person on Earth

STRAIGHT WAS met at the Peking station November 27 by his Chinese servants, who had erected a high arch of firecrackers with a placard, "WELCOME HOME" (the word *home* struck him as ironic), and by Americans including Daniel de Menocal of the International Bank and by other nationals including Lord ffrench and Maurice Casenave. The newspapers announced his arrival, one of them calling him "Mr. Strait," which seemed fitting on several counts. He discovered that Signor Pastore, the hard-drinking Italian Minister who was not always to be taken seriously, had been talking in the hotel bar about settling with Straight for "alienating Madame Pastore's affections." All Straight had done at a party months earlier had been to stand in the way and prevent the Minister from striking Madame. This was the least of his troubles. The new American Minister, William James Calhoun, a Chicago lawyer with white mustache and cheerful mien, was a dear man, but the Elder Brother Fletcher who knew the Chinese was gone. Calhoun was new in the State Department, new in the Far East. The Chinese were undergoing a constitutional movement which it was hoped would ward off revolution, but their new Senate did not yet add appreciably to the nation's democracy but only further snarled the already shaky bureaucracy.

Straight resumed life in his palatial domicile, with outer and inner courtyards and stable at the rear, on a lane off Morrison Street. This place, a short walk into the Tartar City and beyond legation protection, he called the Sanctuary. He greeted Gwenny, a mongrel he had owned for three years. He wrote to Theodore Roosevelt in respectful protest at his animadversions on Wall Street and received a friendly if unrepentant reply: He resumed his letters to Dorothy, adding something every day, mailing them every few days, often writing four or five thousand words a week of remarkably high quality. He continued to tell her that he loved her, to address her as Princesse, Wonder Child, and Wonder of the World, admitting that his endearments tended to be similar:

> This bores you, I suppose. It must, sometimes, to be told the same thing over and over again. I wish you'd try it with me, though. I'd like to try it and see whether I'd be bored or not.

As usual he gave freely of his talents for Christmas parties given at the various legations. To Dorothy he wrote, "I wish you'd take me for a Christmas present, Wonder Child. I'd do myself in tissue paper and pink ribbons and you could wear me always." On Christmas Eve the Calhouns had a great gathering. One observer noted:

> Whilst festivities were at their height, and a Virginia reel in full swing . . . there marched into the room two highly decorated female Chinese theatrical characters, with numerous attendants. . . . These were no less than Mr. Ohl and Mr. Straight, concealed behind paint and feathers, silks and satins. . . . Soon afterwards followed an enormous Manchurian tiger, rolling its fiery eyes, licking its chaps [sic] with its blood-red tongue, and sweeping the floor with a portentous tail. Astride of the tiger was the Chinese equivalent of Santa Claus [this being Captain Heugh, a Briton]. Santa Claus now dealt out presents to the guests, each present being accompanied by a poem touching upon the personal qualities of the receiver. . . .

Straight of course was the poet, the one for Mrs. Calhoun beginning:

> *There's a lady whom we're fond of,*
> *There's a lady who is dear*

To the hearts of all us stray ones
Who are far from friends and cheer. . . .

At the French legation three nights later, eight dance numbers ranged
from minuet to mazurka and also included a highland fling performed
by "Capitaine Macalister," a Spanish dance executed by the wife of the
Minister and host, Madame de Margerie, and a cakewalk in which
Casenave strutted opposite Mrs. Russell and Straight opposite the very
pretty Mrs. de Menocal.

"A merry Christmas to you—oh Dorothy child," Straight wrote after
the Calhoun extravaganza, "and may we never be separated on another
Christmas eve! I've just returned from the American Legation where
. . . J. K. Ohl and myself . . . distributed gifts, and talked rot—where
the monde danced and was gay, and where I was the loneliest person on
the face of the earth almost—and now I am here in the Sanctuary, with
you . . . alone, just with you, at last." His insistence on the bond between them was more than a Straight conceit—a mystic connection that
brought them together in spirit despite the thousands of miles between
them. He seemed a man divided, the realist and cynic warring against
the poet and transcendentalist, his self being given over to one or the
other alternately. The unseen thread that bound him to Dorothy was
particularly strong at special times such as the twenty-third of any
month (despite the fact that her birthday came only on the twenty-third
of January) and the seventh of any month, which commemorated the
Great Day of their first mutual regard in Peking. Or a poignant strain of
music tied in with their lives—that aria from *Bohème*, or "Liebestraum"
or "Les Fleurs"—could do it instantly, or his return to a place in or near
Peking that they had visited together. His feeling that he could all but
reach out and touch her was so vivid at such times—so he said—that he
felt sure she must feel it too.

"I've been alone tonight," he wrote three days after Christmas,
"—dined in the Sanctuary and then sat and sat—and smoked and
smoked—and thought far across the World to you. Did you know that I
was thinking of you and wanting you?" On New Year's Eve he gave a
party for some sixty people ranging from the Japanese to the Dutch to
the Estonian to the Liverpudlian. "The event of the evening," said a
local journal, "was the Birthday of the New Year, which took place
behind a curtain, and was immediately thereafter heralded to the world
by the appearance of the Infant propelled in a gigantic perambulator by
its Nurse. . . . [The Infant bore a] close resemblance to a Distin-

guished Diplomat now resident in Peking, [while the Nurse was recognized as] a Beautiful Lady . . . indispensable at all social functions in the Chinese capital."

". . . I left them all," Straight wrote to Dorothy, "as the firecrackers were rattling . . . for the New Year, and went alone and stood alone in the courtyard of the Sanctuary where you and I stood that morning. . . . It was a fine New Year's Eve in many ways, for everyone had a good time. . . . I felt all through that you were with me, and that it was *our* party—and we did make people happy not just hilarious. . . ."

Later, on that first day of 1911:

> I drove to the same bridge, whence you and I started that Monday afternoon. . . . I could recall every word we said almost—to the Bell Temple where I lit two sticks of incense—one for you and one for me. Then across the fields as we went that day—to the Jade Canal—across the bridge and over the turf to the end of the "Pei"—the slab on the tortoise—where you and I had turned. Incidentally I got a stone, and succeeded—marvelusss—in hitting the same dog that had barked at you. Back along the canal to our Temple . . . where again I burned two sticks of incense—then homeward as the sun was setting, brilliant and golden—as the hills were purpling—and the evening light softening the dun fields and the naked trees by the ice covered canal. And I sang "Borderland"—child—for the first time since that Saturday afternoon, in the rain, at Westbury. You were there, weren't you Dorothy dear. . . .

His memory was infallible. He knew how to tug on the heartstrings. It could all have been the plan of a clever dissembler, knowing the odds against him, aware that he was in grave danger of losing his heiress, imposing on a young woman he knew to be susceptible to sentiment, playing the gentlest chords of nostalgia and yearning. Yet it could have been genuine too; the letters have an unmistakable ring of sadness—and a need that had nothing to do with treasure hunts or adventurers.

Dorothy bought a French Zedel, which she learned to drive and tooled around in. She had taken a suite with the Bends at the Lorraine, at Fifth Avenue and 45th Street, which made complete her domestic separation from Harry and Gertrude. In Society, the question of her intentions concerning Willard Straight easily outranked in importance the gubernatorial election and the growing break between Roosevelt and Taft. One of the deathbed utterances of Mrs. Frank Kinnicutt, mother-in-law of May Tuckerman Kinnicutt, was, "Is Dorothy going to marry Mr. Straight?" To Straight (did she want to reassure him?) Dorothy sent a gossip item, one Delphic sentence of which summed up the attitude of most of her circle: "Dorothy has not announced her engagement to Willard Straight, and while there is silence there is hope."

After being abroad for fifteen months, with rumors about her and Straight trickling across the Atlantic from Paris and London, she was under close observation. While she seemed to have lost none of her popularity, it is clear that she was regarded as an enigma, both for her efforts in behalf of tubercular children and women's suffrage and for her abandonment of common sense and tradition in becoming involved with the outsider Straight, whose status as an heiress chaser seemed generally accepted.

If she was indeed seriously interested in Straight, it was a comfort that the Roosevelts were on his side. From the ex-President and his wife and his sister Corinne Robinson down to Alice Longworth and Ethel and Kermit and Quentin they liked Straight. Dorothy, attending a dinner at which Roosevelt also was a guest, noted that he "talked ex-chesto [a term she had picked up from Straight] throughout the meal—saying quite openly that he was disappointed in Taft—that Sereno Payne [Congressman from New York and a cousin of Dorothy's mother] had a mutton-suet brain and various remarks of this kind. . . ." Roosevelt was electioneering for Henry L. Stimson for governor, and Dorothy would have voted for Stimson too "if we had woman suffrage," but Stimson lost. "One of the most interesting things about the election," she felt, "was the tremendous growth of the Socialist vote, and . . . Colorado returned four women to the Assembly there, and the State of Washington now has woman suffrage."

It was characteristic of her that she could find time for politics at this critical period in her life. Her failure to keep her promise to give Straight his answer indicated heavy doubt, and so also did her whole-hearted resumption of social life within her own set. If DeLancey Jay and Sheldon Whitehouse had gone out of her life, there were replacements. Bob Bacon and Grosvenor Atterbury renewed their efforts. Meredith "Bunnie" Hare was back in the queue along with Jim Breese and others. George Marvin, now a writer in New York, was her escort or riding partner more than Straight would have liked. A serious and mature candidate of considerable reputation was A. Piatt Andrew. On the periphery were Moncure Robinson and Devereux Milburn. The dashing Milburn was an international polo player very nearly as good as Harry, graduate of Cambridge and then Harvard Law, son of a member of the prestigious law firm of Carter, Ledyard & Milburn (of whom

Carter had been the one who had displeased William C. Whitney by telling him what he could *not* do, and Ledyard the man exercised about Straight as a satisfactory suitor for Dorothy. That was tradition for you, the old circle, ties that went back more than a month or a year). Dorothy attended the opera, the theater, gave innumerable teas, and on one shameless occasion rode as the only woman companion of three men of the queue. She danced until the small hours but always sat out the wicked and newly popular Turkey Trot and Bunny Hug.

For all that, she found time to make liberal contributions to worthy causes and to work for such organizations as the Consumers' League, the Milk Stations, and the State Charities Aid. On one occasion she spoke to a judge who was about to incarcerate an orphan working girl caught in some misdeed. She was given custody of the girl, whom she placed in a decent job in Long Island.

But those of her friends who saw this resumption of her old routine as an indication that the "Straight aberration" was ended were mistaken. On the contrary, no sooner had Straight left than she missed him terribly, as her letters make plain. He was vivid, exciting, all brains and action, yet flatteringly dependent on her. Beside him the estimable Grosvenor Atterbury and most of the rest seemed dull. She had wide interests for a woman of the time, but Straight's were wider: politics, diplomacy, music, art, reading, education, sport, journalism, finance, and foreign trade were among them, and he could deliver sage judgments on others. He seemed to fulfill important qualifications laid down in her Venetian essay, being generous, thoughtful, and fairly bristling with ambition. And unlike most men of the time, who reduced women to domestic-adornment status, he confided his problems in her, wrote her fully about his life in Peking, even asked her advice. She was aroused by a letter from Pauline urging her to stop corresponding with Straight. She did her best to counteract the feeling against him and was delighted that her childhood friend Edith Greene Lindley, as Dorothy wrote him, "having heard Mrs. Robinson talk of you . . . thinks that you are everything that I assure her you are. One more of my friends who is for you!"

She had another long conversation at Applegreen with Bob Bacon and convinced him that they should be "just friends," as she wrote to Straight: "I'm glad—so glad it has happened this way—for next to you . . . I am fonder of Bob than of any other man I know." A cheering note for Willard! She had a much shorter talk with Atterbury, who proposed, was rejected, and caught the next train to New York. "Finis!" she wrote cruelly. She contributed $25,000 to the Red Cross, though this was not one of those "radical" contributions that made her brother Payne shake his head. (There was a story, perhaps apocryphal, that Payne was asked why he did not give more money to charity, his reply being that he kept it to give Dorothy when she gave all hers away.) The canvasser who received the $25,000 Red Cross contribution was Harry Davison, long an officer of the organization. Did she add a little to the sum in the hope that her generosity might make Straight's boss look more benevolently on Straight? Was she unaware of the chain of command, and the ultimate good it might do the subaltern, when she called on Davison's boss, J. P. Morgan, at the beautiful Morgan Library on 36th Street and bade him good-bye before he left for Europe? "Mr. J. P. M. was lovely to me," she wrote to Straight. "He laughed and said he wished I would go there every single week. . . . Dear Mr. J. P. he's such a sweetie underneath the sternness." She was called into consultation when young Dr. Richard Derby, of the famous old shipping family, proposed marriage to Ethel Roosevelt and was rejected out of hand. Derby came to Dorothy, who liked him immensely (not less because Derby liked Straight), counseled him to keep trying, and urged Ethel to relent.

"He really is a wonder, Willard," she wrote, "and Ethel simply *must* marry him!" She confessed inconsistency here, since several unhappy marriages among her friends had made her even more wary of matrimony. "I'm afraid Ethel is terrified by the great wonder of marriage just the way I am," she wrote to Straight, adding significantly, "I believe in it so much Willard, that I don't dare believe in it too much—that's all. But I do get panics now and then."

Did her enrollment in Miss Mary Bird's cooking class indicate some softening? On Christmas, Dorothy drove with Bob Bacon to her brother Payne's for an indifferent lunch while Willard halfway around the world was coping with a Manchurian tiger, giving out presents. Next day, they lunched with the Roosevelt family: "T.R. was in great form, and he and Alice together are one of the funniest combinations I have ever seen. I laughed merrily from 1.30 till 4 o'clock."

But not all was merriment. She was so moved by Straight's letters that, when "Beatrice was playing the wonderful parts of 'Walkure' on the piano . . . somehow everything went to my head and heart at once and I couldn't keep away the tears. . . ." Again, when she went to the opera, "the music of Cavalleria stirred me so much that the tears came in spite of me. . . . God bless you and give you happiness, dear, dear Willard!"

6. *Game for an Empire*

AFTER THE Peking holidays, Straight's letters made plain that his most hurtful shortcoming—frustrated impatience—was getting the best of his wiser nature. He suffered from what later became known as a desire for instant gratification. He would work hard for his goal and he did not require its immediate attainment—but it had better not take very long! Not for his quivery nerves the long, patient bargaining for an objective, a virtue so obviously required in the work he was doing and also the work of the State Department, which he perhaps mistakenly felt himself qualified to serve. He possessed almost everything but patience. His brilliance and short attention span seemed to suit him for a post presenting ever-changing short-term problems that he could solve quickly.

But of course he did not yet know this. He was working on a project that lesser men would never have dared to challenge. It was so vast and unusual that its successful conclusion might not only profoundly change the world's most populous nation but would bring Straight fame and considerable fortune. "Your position certainly makes you one of the most observed public men in the Far East," wrote his State Department friend C. J. Arnell. And the Morgan firm and the entire American Group were excited about the enormous profit promised in the deal and "the necessity of regarding this transaction not as a single undertaking but as the first of what we hope may be a series of important loans. . . ." Straight wrote to Dorothy, "Between you and me . . . just you and I standing beside and laughing at ourselves—it's history . . . and big history at that—the game for an empire."

He knew the size of the stakes. He was genuinely convinced that both China and America would benefit. He tried hard to maintain his poise, but it gave way. "[Minister Calhoun] is a corker," he wrote, "sound, clear-headed and absolutely straight and fearless. And he has a nice line of profanity which I greatly appreciate. . . ." Later, in frustration, he said, "The old man doesn't know the first principles of the game he's in." Straight's problems were several:

THE CHINESE: They badly wanted the loan but detested the stipulation that there be an Occidental financial adviser who would scrutinize their use of the money in the hope of preventing the corrupt use of it. They were quite willing to have a figurehead adviser who had authority neither to watch nor advise. ". . . there's not one man in the Chinese Government," Straight wrote wrathfully, "who is big enough—broad enough—wise enough—and honest enough—to recognize either the plight his country is in—or the need for getting and taking—advice to help her out." Sheng Kung-pao, the Minister for Posts and Communications, with whom he had to negotiate, he characterized as "one of the most astute crooks in all the galaxy of the mandarinate."

THE RUSSIANS: Nothing could budge their stand against Chin-Ai.

THE BANDARLOG (JAPANESE): "They will now move heaven and earth to make trouble, for they realize that if China can put through her currency reform and that if the Four Banks had strong investments there, that China will be in a fair way to get on her feet—and that, above all else, Japan does not wish—for she hopes to exploit China herself one of these fine days."

THE MORGAN OFFICE IN NEW YORK AND THE STATE DEPARTMENT IN WASHINGTON: "I do get mad, and make personal remarks when people 11,000 miles away, who are not informed as to actual conditions . . . insist upon a certain line of action which I on the spot know to be impossible. . . ."

LONELINESS: "I have never been quite so alone before, for here I have not one single friend, who knows or understands."

THE POISONED PURLIEUS OF PEKING: "It is . . . almost as impossible for you to appreciate, as it is for me to describe, the atmosphere of pettiness and suspicion which prevails here, where everyone more or less is spying on everyone else. It is the storm centre of world politics, and the foreign community is very small. We see each other every day; there are but a few outside influences or diversions; and this all brings out the little meannesses and jealousies and the spitefulness of human nature."

Even Theodore Roosevelt continued to bother him with speeches putting him on the capitalist defensive: "He talks of the people—the honest people—and the business interests, as if they were two separate organisms. He speaks of Wall Street as an excrescence. . . . It isn't. . . . It is the pulse of the nation—and its big men are interested from selfish as well as patriotic reasons, in making the country as rich and prosperous as possible."

He worried that he sounded like a chronic complainer, which indeed he often did, though he was saved from sourness by his rich sense of the ridiculous and his panache. His underlying sense of fairness still held, as when he wrote of Calhoun, "He's a fine old chap, and I am devoted to him, but he's not quite a thoroughbred—for no man has a right to occupy such a position without doing his best, and he doesn't." The very next day he repented: "I feel sort of sorry about what I wrote about him last night." But Straight's nerves were stretching taut. His jaundiced view was evident in his comment on the ball at the Russian legation: "[It was] preceded by a well acted little French farce and a ballet, composed of young rhinocerii who gallumphed about in short skirts. . . . I was bored to tears. General dancing followed. I had half a waltz with Mrs. Russell and flirted the rest of the evening with Madame Picot, wife of the French First Secretary. Conversation very voluble, consisting in my having told her I had heard something about her—she trying to find out what it was, and I refusing to tell. Excellent practice for one's French."

At last he became so discouraged that he drafted a cable to the Group asking them to appoint another representative. He then discussed it with Calhoun, who urged him not to send it. He was, as he informed Dorothy, holding it pending further developments.

Dorothy sympathized: "What dreadful nerve racking days these have been . . . poor Willard child!" But the thought of his quitting his post, which she considered a commitment and also a test of his mettle, profoundly shocked her: ". . . please oh please—don't chuck the game ever, Willard, in a moment of intense disgust! You see things in such unswerving lines . . . But there is always before you, the patriotic duty—I know—and really if you suddenly chuck the Group you would be chucking the larger interests of the whole country." Her tone became quite firm—if not stern. During his previous tour of duty in Peking he had grown more and more anxious to see her and less and less inclined to finish his assignment. She had been aware then of his flagging zeal, and she—a woman of matchless resolve—had steadied him. She steadied him now, though she took pains to commiserate with his troubles. ". . . wouldn't I like to shake the d—— old State Department," she wrote in response to one complaint. ". . . To h—— with the State Department! Oh Willard—I feel terribly profane today and it's Sunday!"

Straight was not always a slave to consistency. Only recently he had written his old Cornell classmate Henry Schoelkopf that there was "a certain element of stability and seriousness lacking in the American character." This was visible, he added, in "[the] failure of Americans to stick to their jobs abroad, their inability to stand punishment. . . . talk to any merchant, or manufacturer who has tried to get young men to

stick to foreign agencies. . . . The men won't stick to it." Dorothy did
not know of this letter, but she clung to the theme that it was Straight's
duty to stay on the job even when the specter of disease loomed. "The
plague is now at Mukden," he wrote, "and there were three very suspicious cases in Peking early in the week. . . . Don't worry, for there's no
likelihood of our getting it here, and even if we do, remember that only
the good die young. I see a green old age ahead!" He did rather enjoy
dramatizing such things, but for some weeks there was a great scare in
Peking, which Dorothy shared. The various Ministers met in a body
with the physicians. The diplomatic quarter went into quarantine.
Straight's dog Gwenny, to his sorrow, died of poison that had been set
out for rats against the plague. It was before this tragedy that Straight
composed for a local paper a dialogue titled "The Bassill-Eye in Peking," which even experts would have mistaken for one of the pieces of
an old friend of Dorothy's father:

> "Hinnissy" said Mr. Dooley, "D'you know phwat iz a Bassill-uss?"
> "No," replied Mr. Hennessey, "I don't. Why?"
> "Becaz, Hinnissy," said Mr. Dooley gravely, "T'is a quistyun av th'
> verrah greates' moment at th' prisint time. Bassill-uss iz th' singular av
> Bassill-eye, an' Bassill-eye, Hinnissy, is far-r-r, far-r-r wur-r-rse thin any
> evil-eye yuh ivir heard of. Th' Bassill-eyes are minoot organizms lurkin'
> in th' passin' breeze, hidin' in th' shtrong brith av y'r mos' intimate
> friends, an' dodgin' behind lamp posts an' tellygraft poles t'prey upon th'
> human race. Th' Bassill-eye combine th' death dealin' powers iv high ex-
> plosives wid th' soo-av an' takin' ways av an insurance agent. . . ."

7. Good for Us

AT TIMES Dorothy's breathless but charming diary, either through haste
or lack of space, left history forever suspended, a question eternally
unanswered. Her runabout Zedel now took her to charities and
luncheons. ". . . on my way uptown ran over poor old man—awful!"
she wrote, going on, "Lunched with Eliza . . ."—leaving her victim
bloody and dying in the gutter except that one is certain that he was not
badly hurt and that she took good care of him. A victim of a different
kind was A. Piatt Andrew, with whom she visited Mrs. Jack Gardner
and Fenway Court in Boston, then attended a party for sixty-one Gloucester fishermen whom Andrew benefited. "One old fellow," she noted,
"came up to me at the end saying 'I hear that you're the daughter of
Mr. William C. Whitney, and I want to tell you that I know everything

your father did while he was in office—how he commenced building up
the American Navy—how he stamped out graft here and put in honest
men there. . . .' I was so overcome that I almost cried, and I grasped
him by the hand and told him that I loved him dearly. Dear, dear
Gloucester fisherman!"

He was especially dear after those embarrassing news stories about
Whitney's payment to Colonel Mann of *Town Topics*, and those terrible
headlines about her father during the 1907 investigation into his transit
operations: "TRACTION PAID WHITNEY'S DEBTS," "SAYS
WHITNEY GOT THE $134,000 CHECK," "HOW THE PUBLIC
LOST MILLIONS TO TRACTION CLIQUE." There was testimony
that the Metropolitan Securities Company "was mulcted of $692,292
for the personal profit of William C. Whitney" and his associates.
There were charges of such gross chicanery that *The World*, for one, ran
an editorial headed "THE BRADY-RYAN-WHITNEY DEAL" and
demanded, "Is there no public official sufficiently interested in this
crooked deal to consider whether some of the principals do not belong
in jail?" These charges undoubtedly increased her own determination to
do good, to redress the balance. But her pleasure in the fisherman's
praise conferred no benefit on her hopeful companion. A. Piatt Andrew
proposed to her as they walked along the beach, and received her kind-
liest regrets—this though Dorothy had talked with Ethel Roosevelt until
four o'clock one morning, urging the case for Richard Derby. Since
Ethel told Derby she refused to marry him unless Dorothy married
Straight, Derby threatened to go to Peking and bring Straight back. On
a trip to Washington, Dorothy met Katherine Elkins, whom she knew
slightly and who was gossiping enough about Straight so that Alice
Roosevelt Longworth was "perfectly furious," Dorothy wrote Straight,
". . . for the way she has been talking about you. . . ." Miss Elkins, it
seems, would hardly have indulged in such talk had not her relationship
with Straight been close and confiding—something near engagement.
Harry Payne Whitney, in his investigations, had felt that Miss Elkins
had looked on Straight not as a mere occasional escort but as a man
with serious intentions toward her. His intentions apparently had been
exploded by his Borderland fortnight with Dorothy in Peking.

Miss Elkins was later described by her friend that attentive Washington gossip, Major Archibald Butt, as a social "celebrity," gowned in
Paris and a friend of Alice Longworth's. Miss Elkins, Butt said, had
been smitten by the adventurous Duke of Abruzzi but had "discarded"
him by April 1909. Rumor had it that the duke's successor in her affec-

tions had been young Adolphus Andrews, a junior aide of President Roosevelt. Yet she still kept Abruzzi's picture in her locket, causing Butt to admit, "I cannot make out what is the status between Miss Elkins and the duke." She was then pursued by William F. R. "Billy" Hitt, once an admirer of Dorothy Whitney's, and Straight appeared on the scene as Hitt's rival for something less than a year. Although it did not appear to Butt that Hitt was the answer to her prayer, she was to marry him a year later. There was no engagement between her and Straight. Though Harry might not have believed it, it appeared that Straight had been a gentleman as always, hurtful though his voluntary relinquishing of the field might have been to her, and that he could be blamed for nothing more than the possibly extraneous fact that Miss Elkins, like Mary and Dorothy, was an heiress.

Dorothy meanwhile had established a closer relationship with the Davisons, exchanging dinner engagements with them, perhaps not without the hope of hearing about Straight's progress from someone else other than her suitor.

Were his blues, his mental anguish in Peking, the tantrum reaction of a man accustomed to having his own way, or were his nerves indeed so fragile? She had to discover the answer for herself. He had been delighted to get this important assignment. In Peking he lived luxuriously with a secretary and servants. He embodied the great prestige of the banking coalition he represented. His rich correspondence paper was heavily engraved with the title "The American Group," Chinese characters meaning the same, and then, "W. D. Straight, Special Representative—Cable address: Straight Peking." He was popular, invited to innumerable gatherings among colorful and cultivated people whom he often entertained with his guitar and his singing, sometimes with his cartoons. He rode, played polo well enough for Peking. He hiked, sketched, read widely, had literally scores of friends. In addition to his voluminous correspondence with Dorothy, he corresponded with his Aunt Laura and his sister Hazel in Oswego, Prather Fletcher in Chile, Edwin V. Morgan (now Minister to Uruguay), Professor Stephens and several Cornell classmates, and State Department people as well as members of the 1718 H Street club.

Was this life so terrible that he could not endure the rebuffs to be expected in his negotiations? Could he not tolerate a few more months that would either bring him the prize or at any rate prove his resourcefulness and fortitude? Was he a neurotic or was he just plain spoiled?

Dorothy made up her mind. His performance in Peking was crucial to her. She commiserated, she advised, she praised, she warned, as in these fragments from several letters:

> I know how dreadfully hard and lonely it must be for you . . . and the negotiations with the Chinese must be such discouraging work. . . . But I have great faith that you will put the loan through . . . and then—oh Willard—won't that be wonderful! . . . I can feel a sense of loneliness and discouragement-with-the-Chinese-situation running through it all. . . . Wouldn't it be the greatest triumph ever, if you won! . . . I know that you have the will to see it through. . . . Don't be too positive . . . especially with men—for it antagonizes them and really, humility is always one of the characteristics of a big person. . . . Oh Willard—don't be in a hurry to leave the Group for the [State] Department. I'm sure it's far wiser to continue for awhile in this way with Mr. Davison and Mr. J.P. . . . I think sometimes you're apt to take personal offence a tiny bit if people disagree with you—don't you, oh Willard child? . . . There are people who say you are a fine person . . . but very conceited. I try to explain that you're really not one bit proud of yourself, but just because you have lived a great deal in the East where you have absolutely run the whole show you naturally gained . . . a tremendous amount of self assurance . . . conceit isn't in your makeup at all. You see I write you everything because . . . letters have to be spontaneous if they are to mean anything. . . .

She persuaded Beatrice Bend and Ethel Roosevelt—probably others—to write to him giving him the encouragement and praise she knew he needed. He took her tutelage with good grace, as shown by these fragments from a half-dozen letters:

> . . . if ever anything comes of this it will be because you said "Steady" and because for youre sake I want to win. . . . I grit my teeth and pound the table, and know I must win for youre sake. . . . Your cable this morning rather startled me with its "please go easy on New York." . . . The "go easy" struck a . . . sensitive spot for I've had a sorter feeling in my bones that I was going a little hard. . . . Thank you . . . for reminding me that others are tired too. . . . I know and regret frightfully that I am domineering and intolerant and positive. . . . I don't think those who know me well would say that [I am conceited], for I don't think I really am. I do think that I have a good deal of self assurance. . . . I know that I'm shy—and particularly reserved—especially with people whom I think looking for a chance to knock. . . . with all due humility and recognition of . . . error [I] feel that I've managed to get along pretty well with the men with whom I work and do things—which is a fair test.

This was true, for the honesty and goodwill beneath his vast impatience were known by everyone. His frustration, far from being capricious, was an affliction almost beyond curbing, and the repression took its toll. He had trouble sleeping. He suffered from constipation, cramps in his legs, and a nervous grinding of his teeth. He felt that he was bored, bored, bored, but on the contrary it seems to have been extreme high tension: "Casenave had an enormous party last night, where I nearly screamed with ennui—and tonight I go to Max Muller's to meet Mrs. George Keppel [the turquoise-eyed lady seemed to turn up everywhere in the world] and some other hard-faced scions of the British aristocracy." On another occasion Straight was so hurt by a word of jocular chiding by his friend Lord ffrench that he left the room, upset by the degree of his own upset.

The end came so suddenly it astonished him. The problem of requiring a financial adviser was solved by appointing a Dutchman to the task who would be virtually unpublicized, thus saving China's face. On April 15, 1911, the Ministers of France, Germany, England, and the United States met with the four bankers' representatives—Casenave, Cordes, Hillier, and Straight—and the agreement (drawn up in large part by Straight) was signed with the Chinese as if there had never been the least difficulty about it. Three hundred million dollars were to be lent China, bearing 5 percent interest, the period of redemption being forty-five years, the loan to be secured by the revenue of three Chinese provinces—all this pending routine technicalities that would take some time before the issuing of the bonds. Straight cabled Dorothy the code word "RAINBOW." He wrote to her:

> The telegram went—oh Dorothy Child—and before this letter reaches you I should be started on my way. . . . The loan was signed today without any further quibbling. . . . and "Dollar Diplomacy" is justified at last. Knox and [Huntington] Wilson ought to be pleased. . . . Oh Child—if only you had been here to celebrate, but you were—for it was your Victory, and the courage you gave, and my hope for you, Dorothy mine—alone carried me through . . . and I've you to thank for all.

Her cable to him read:

GRAZIA HAPPY SHOUTING FOR JOY GOOD FOR US AIKEN LIEBESTRAUM BORDERLAND.

That afternoon nevertheless she walked in Central Park with Charles Draper; he had met her rejection of his marriage proposal better than Grosvenor Atterbury, who could not bear to see her anymore. Next day, Easter, she attended Grace Church, the scene of her father's last service, now lightened by the sense of eternal rebirth so beautifully symbolized by Straight's success after having been so near to admitting failure. ". . . I went to church singing glad hymns of praise," she wrote to him. ". . . I just want to take your hand and dance round and round like a small child at Christmas time." She stopped dancing, however, when she learned from Davison that the much smaller Hukuang loan had not been cleared. She felt (and Davison cabled this to Straight) that he should stay in Peking until it was. He replied to Dorothy:

> My—but you are such a greediness—oh Dorothy mine! So you want the Hukuang too—do you. As a matter of fact we seem to be in a very fair way to get it—and the agreement should D.V. be signed inside a week.

On the contrary, it meant that he had to stay in Peking five more weeks, during which his nervous condition worsened so that he had occasional spells of faintness. Playing polo one day, he fell from his horse at a gallop and was left a mass of bruises. At last, on May 20, the Hukuang agreement was signed. He received appropriate cryptic acknowledgment from New York:

> HOOROO BUT AIKEN SHEMMO HUKUANG BLESSINGS LIEBESTRAUM BORDERLAND.

He boarded the train May 25, 1911, with his new manservant, Ko, and wrote:

> Just seven months ago to a day I left [Westbury] early in the morning. I pray that it's a good omen—the Seven. . . . Will you take me away to Borderland, Dorothy—to *our* country, where we can be alone—where we can read and draw and talk, and share and be everything to each other— you and I. Will you make me live again, Dorothy—bring back to life all within me that's for you alone. . . . Will you make me complete, child—a half person no longer?
> This is the third day I've been laid up—influenza I guess it is—with a sore throat and headache and fever and the usual aches all over. . . . I realize that your Willard Boy came pretty nigh to being a crock, for a little more twisting on the strings would have snapped 'em, I know. . . .

8. Away to Borderland

. . . [It] seems like the fruition of all we hoped for [Dorothy wrote to
him]. . . . And you did it all yourself . . . I've never been so proud.
. . . Mr. Davison was pleased . . . adding foolish remarks about your
conferring the order of the Double Dragon on him. . . . When I think
of you being here with me again I just gasp for joy—and then the next
moment I just shiver inside and feel just as terrified of you as I used to,
last year.

ALTHOUGH DOROTHY had several years earlier taken a course in what she
described as "sex higiene," her recurrent fears about Straight the fortune
hunter and Straight the outsider seemed complicated by fears of Straight
the male. Marriage itself alarmed her. She also had a talent for fretting
over marriages that had not "turned out." She well knew that her own
mother and father, William and Flora Whitney, had been desperately
unhappy at times. Recently, Society had been breathless over the scandal surrounding Gertrude's brother Alfred Gwynne Vanderbilt. His
wife, the former Elsie French, had sued him for divorce, charging mis-
conduct in his private railway car with Agnes Ruiz, wife of a Cuban attaché in Washington. The divorce was granted, Elsie was given
$10,000,000, and Mrs. Ruiz later committed suicide. If marriage was
dangerous within one's own social circle, how much more so outside
that comforting cocoon of protection! Visiting China was splendid, but
the idea of being whisked off to Peking to *live*, away from Grace
Church, the Junior League, the Colony Club, and the Metropolitan
Opera could be unnerving. When she thought of it, most of her acquaintance with Straight was by mail. Her longest single meeting with
him had been that fortnight in Peking, when the romance of the purple
hills, the moonlight, the guitar, and the Kipling songs had done their
work. Since then it had been mostly a series of hurried visits with him,
of Straight rushing to see her and rushing away again. Did she really
know him, or had she allowed herself to be overcome by his virtuosity at
billets-doux?

If some of her fears were of her own making, some were not. She had
become increasingly maternal toward Straight. She had babied him,
and he seemed to enjoy babying more than his normal hearty masculinity would make one expect. He had, in his work, shown that worrisome
combination of brilliance and dedication on the one hand, and on the
other that fatal tendency to lose interest, to throw up his hands in
disgust. He did, like a boy, need encouragement, praise, pats on the

head to keep going. Dorothy, whether she meant to or not, had permitted herself (and Willard) to entertain the idea that she would marry him if he succeeded in China. Now that he *had* succeeded, she shrank from going through with it.

The best evidence of this was her decision to sail for Europe with the Bends June 28 without knowing whether he would be in New York or Europe at the time—a move much like escape. While he wrestled with financial details at the Morgan, Grenfell office in London, she was thrilled at Meadow Brook to see her brother Harry in the greatest day of his polo career, leading his American four in a 4½-to-3½ victory over a British team that until the previous year had dominated international polo: ". . . the most thrilling game I ever saw. Harry and Dev [Milburn] were simply wonderful."

Straight was showered with publicity in the newspapers of New York, London, Paris, and elsewhere for his part in the two great loans. *The New York Herald* ran a three-column front-page story by Ohl lavishing credit on Straight, whose photograph showed him looking grim and truculent as if his nerves were indeed ready to snap. *The Literary Digest*'s article featured a picture of an insignificant-looking man in a derby hat labeled as Straight who was not Straight and whom Straight christened as Lebbeus R. Wilfley, the Great Mistake. This flattering press notice was advantageous. It caused Harry to entertain a faintly less unfavorable opinion of Straight and tended to justify Dorothy's interest in the outsider to many of her circle. She was anxious that he make a good impression on them, writing rather self-righteously, "Please be humble with everyone. They all really know what you've done, and I know best of all."

She met him in New York when he arrived June 21 but refused to change her own sailing date, *exactly one week later*. It was as if she was glad to see him but fearful that she would yield to his entreaties if she stayed. Next day they dined with Dorothy's cousin Katherine and her husband Courtlandt Barnes. Katherine felt Dorothy to be so idealistic about marriage that she later wrote to her lovingly pointing out that men—even men of excellence—were never perfect. Dorothy that same evening—the air at Applegreen was soft and carried the scent of roses— fell under Straight's spell just as she evidently feared she would. She accepted his proposal of marriage, but with stipulations: the acceptance was to be kept confidential as yet, and the ceremony was slated for a time considerably later and at a place as yet undesignated. She wanted no carnival on the order of Gladys Vanderbilt's wedding. It was to be small, quiet, almost hushed.

Straight made a hurried trip to Oswego to visit his "aunt" and sister, then worked two days at the Morgan Wall Street offices—"two days which I still remember as a sort of a blur, with faces peering at me over the table, and my own voice replying to questions, sounding as if it came from a person some miles off." Harry Davison "very properly remarked that he might as well let me go as I'd be of no use if I stayed."

Had it not been for this dispensation, Dorothy, seeming more in flight than in love, would have gone to Europe without him. Only because of it, Straight sailed with her and the Bends on the *Olympic* June 28. Fellow passengers were the Twomblys and Dr. Walter James, who had cared for William C. Whitney and Alexander Gunn. Straight, with seeming tactlessness for a man who was to marry a pleasantly articulate woman, read aloud to her Maeterlinck's "Essay on Silence." In Europe Straight worked at the Morgan office in London while Dorothy motored through Brittany with Amy and Courtlandt Bishop. In New York, on July 20, Harry Payne Whitney formally announced his sister's engagement to Willard Dickerman Straight, the time and place of the wedding still unspecified.

The papers reacted with headlines. The romance with Katherine Elkins was still unknown to them, so blessings were due her for being quiet at this point. That with Mary Harriman was more than enough, one newspaper comment being, "Straight's old friends have always said that he would marry a wealthy girl":

> The surprise heard on all sides over Dorothy Whitney's engagement to Willard Straight . . . is most astonishing [*sic*]. This match is one of the most amazing in many years. Straight is a poor man. He has only what he has earned as Consular Agent and now diplomat. Miss Whitney . . . is the last heiress of her set remaining unwed. . . . [She] has had untold chances to marry. For five years she has been the most sought-after and most talked-of girl in New York. . . . Straight was wildly eager to marry Miss Harriman. . . .

One can understand Dorothy's determination to be abroad when the news came out. Another headline read, "STRAIGHT CHASED BY HARRIMAN, BUT LOOKS GOOD TO WHITNEY." *The New York Times* gave a banner headline to "WILLARD STRAIGHT, WHO IS TO MARRY DOROTHY WHITNEY," with a subhead, "A Career

That Reads Like Romance Is That of the Missionary's Son [*sic*] Who Became a Figure in Finance, Politics and International Affairs, and Who Won the Love of Two Heiresses." *The Times* lingered over the theme of Harriman money, Straight's rejection by the railroad mogul, and his subsequent romance with Heiress No. 2. Dorothy hoped to minimize such publicity by having a quiet wedding in an out-of-the-way place. Where? Not London, where the New York papers had correspondents and where Pauline, who had fought Straight almost from the start, might take charge. Not Paris—it was too full of New York people. She and Straight decided on Geneva, with its handsome Episcopal church and its lovely lake view. She bought her wedding dress in Paris, not even mentioning in her diary the couturière. She wrote to Straight from Caux:

> I know it's foolish to be frightened, but I just can't help it—much as I love you. . . . I have been reading over the marriage service today and oh, Best Beloved, it is so beautiful that I felt a dreadful lump in my throat at the thought of what it all meant. I think that you and I are entering into it "reverently, discreetly, advisedly, soberly and in the fear of God. . . ."

The impatient Straight's diary entry for September 5 consisted of one word: "Hell." On September 6 he wrote simply, "Heller." That day Dorothy had a splitting headache. Nevertheless, on September 7 they were married in a morning civil ceremony by the mayor of Geneva, followed at noon by an Episcopal service. "The bride . . . whose fortune is estimated at $7,000,000 . . . was given in marriage by her brother, Harry Payne Whitney, and was attended as flower girls by her nieces, the Misses Olive Cecelia Paget and Dorothy Windham Paget. . . ." She "wore a white satin costume, with old Venetian lace veil. The bridesmaids had white dresses and blue hats and carried small baskets filled with roses. The church was splendidly decorated with flowers."

Straight, who had first sought as best man Prather Fletcher and then Harry Davison (both too busy and too far away), settled on his State Department friend William Phillips, now First Secretary at the embassy in London. Among the mere two dozen guests were Harry and Gertrude, Payne (but apparently not Helen), Pauline and Almeric, Beatrice and Mrs. Bend (both weeping).

". . . very quiet & lovely," Dorothy commented in her diary. ". . . Wedding breakfast on Pauline's terrace. Left in the motor at 3 & came to Lausanne where we caught Simplon Express at 6.30—arriving here

[Stresa] at 10.45. Wonderful night bright moon." She was a stickler for the correct minute even as she left on her honeymoon. As for Straight, if he had suffered occasional lapses of zeal in Peking, his determination had never flagged during his courtship of Dorothy. He had won her at last after twenty-two difficult months.

There were hundreds of congratulatory notes by mail and wireless. Cables arrived from well-wishers as diverse as J. P. Morgan, the Roosevelts, and His Excellency Chao Erh Hsun, Viceroy of Manchuria, the latter noting the date of the marraige as "the seventh day of the Ninth Moon." There was a letter to Straight from Davison who said with unnecessary practicality that the marriage secured him for life. The group wedding picture demonstrated that the occasion lacked the joyousness usually associated with such events. The dour gaze of Harry Payne Whitney, implying that he was still scarcely reconciled to the match, perhaps had a chilling effect on some of the others. Dorothy's expression suggested relief that it was over rather than bridal delight, and the usually smiling Straight seemed to display more tension than jubilance. The muse of *Town Topics* was limping but indomitable:

> *This very day the flags wave wide o'er blue Geneva's lake;*
> *The Switzer leaves his punctured cheese to feast on wine and cake,*
> *Fireworks from every point ascend, the gladness to increase,*
> *And Vive l'Amerique, for the day, joins unto Vive la Suisse.*
> *For Dorothy becomes now Straight, oh, wisest of her clan,*
> *Built, so methinks, on much more level-headed, solid plan,*
> *To 'scape our ghastly mobs and souvenir pursuing hordes,*
> *Surely entitleth her to this most rightful of awards.*

1. Revolution

Oh! This is a song of the Wagon Lits,
How Dorothy, ffrench and W.D.,
With Louisa and Ko, in company
Went over the Steppes to try and see
Who they could do in China.

THUS STRAIGHT, the inveterate rhymester, lightened with many stanzas the long journey across Siberia. Dorothy and he, equally moved by sentiment, had spent their first night at Isola Bella because they had found it so beautiful in May of the preceding year. Then, during a week in Venice (where, sure enough, they ran into Rolly Cottenet and dined with him), a snapshot showed them in the Piazza San Marco, Dorothy charming in white dress, picture hat, and parasol, Straight smiling in white pants and shoes, dark jacket, and Panama, holding a cigar in one hand and feeding pigeons with the other. Then, after shopping in Paris, they had taken the Nord Express, which Lord ffrench, after a stay in England, boarded at Liège. They were en route to Peking, where Straight was to perfect details of the loan. It was in Venice four years earlier that Dorothy had written: "Of course the man one marries cannot be all one dreams of having him . . . I am fully expectant of disappointments. . . ."

Now she was so bereft of responsibility that she deserted her diary for four days running. They encountered Siberian snow October 2 and read Carlyle's *French Revolution* to each other across the wastes. Their compartment was comfortable, with "three electric lights." Dorothy had Louisa to care for her, and Straight had Ko, while ffrench, with no manservant at all, seemed to exemplify the decline of empire. At Mukden the point was emphasized when they were given a private car with Straight's own cook for the Chinese leg of the journey. They arrived in

Peking on October 11. They had managed to appear in the capital on the day that the Sun Yat-sen rebellion broke out in the south.

The grand Straight domicile with its high-ceilinged reception room, ample facilities, and servants brought Dorothy no hardship: "I have a lovely sunny bedroom and sitting room and bathroom—all connecting—and Louisa also has a fine suite—and W. has his own room and bathroom beyond mine. The big living room is full of lovely Chinese things."

But there were two threats. One was the visible tottering of the Manchu regime as the rebellion gained ground. "Wild excitement in the air—'end of Manchu dynasty,' " Dorothy wrote. ". . . disturbance of some kind is expected. Major Russell of the Legation guard sent W. two large revolvers. Manchus are all leaving Peking." "Mrs. Menocal came to see me this A.M. & was quite alarming in her plan for packing up in order to be ready to move to Legation if trouble occurs." The other, only passing and hardly to be mentioned, was an occasional demonstration of the Straight temperament. After only three weeks, he was for a brief time discouraged and bored by his work on the technicalities of the loan and wanting to go home, whereas Dorothy was stimulated by the excitement and eager to see what would happen.

Yet he was so fond a husband that she wrote, "Married life seems almost too good sometimes." He skated with her, rode and hiked with her, played the guitar and sang, invented outrageous rhymes, was a member of the United States polo team that lost to the British, and founded the Purple Cows, a social organization composed of the Calhouns, de Margeries, Russells, Casenaves, de Menocals, ffrenches, and Straights, meeting weekly at each house in turn. At one dinner at the Straights', "Willard drew foolish dinner cards for everyone which caused a great deal of amusement—then towards the end of the dinner the men all made funny speeches & we sang popular songs—and had a very genial time, and no one was at all tight, although you might think so, from this account." One can be sure that Dorothy herself retained all but pristine sobriety, since liquor affected her immediately and she drank with caution.

By November 5 the rebels had quietly taken Shanghai. The Straights received a note from the Minister: "In view of the uncertain condition of affairs the Legation feels constrained to advise Americans to send their valuables to the banks . . . for safekeeping." Dorothy, the instinctive republican and defender of the underdog, was thrilled when Joseph Ohl read aloud the edict giving China constitutional government. But the fact was that this so far virtually nonviolent change in government was upsetting the currency reform on which the four-power loan to China was based. Hence Straight was by no means as thrilled as she and favored retention of enough of the old government to keep order so that the loan would go forward. "This is all highly interesting in a diary to be read years afterward," he commented, "but as a honeymoon experience it's a bit thick with excitement." China was a mystery, there was no telling when the people of Peking might revolt, and there were nights when he stayed awake to keep nervous vigil.

"We have just hoisted an American flag over our compound," Dorothy reported, "& it waves a hands-off warning to any intruders. It is the first time in my life I have lived under our flag—regarding it solely as a protection. It is quite a thrilling sensation."

"OUTBREAK AT PEKING IS MOMENTARILY EXPECTED," read one headline, but the capital remained quiet. Dorothy and Straight were taking turns reading aloud to blind Edward Hillier, representative of the English bankers. There was an interesting party at the legation honoring Madame Hoo, Madame Sia, Madame Yun, and Madame Siao. On December 24, "Willard & I rode all the morning in the Happy Valley," then Minister Calhoun posed while Straight sketched him, and they all had Christmas Eve dinner at the legation—every American in Peking, sixty in all including the missionaries. "W. had Xmas tree for me last night when we got home from Legation. Sat by fire & opened presents till after midnight—wonderful surprise. Today . . . to Reeves for egg-nog. Willard & I lunched alone—& walked after to Legation to see hockey match. . . . Dined at Casenaves—Purple Cow gathering—guitar singing after."

On January 16, 1912, she recorded, "This A.M. at 12 o'clock a bomb was thrown at Yuan [Shih-kai], as he passed in his carriage. . . . It all happened only 100 yards from our house!" Straight heard the explosion and described the scene:

> Went out on the street which was almost cleared. Yuan had escaped uninjured but the Captain of his guard had been so badly wounded that he died on the way to the hospital. Soldiers were much excited and it looked for a few minutes as if we were in for some shooting. One man running down the street with a revolver in one hand and a stethoscope in another was very nearly shot by Manchu gendarmerie. . . . [Dr.] Gatrell behaved splendidly. First started by doing up two [wounded] men in our stable, then went up and tended to the two who had been dropped at the corner and in the afternoon went to the Barracks where he looked after 15

more, most of them bystanders who were however, treated in the most cruel manner by the soldiers.

The Straights spent one night at the legation for safety—a few Americans had already moved into the two-story stone building, which had an armed guard—then returned to their own compound. Ten days later they were authorized by Davison to make inquiries in Shanghai about the probable course of the revolution and then to take a short holiday in the Philippines.

In Shanghai, Straight, who seemed to know everybody, made seventy-five calls in five days, among them seeing Tang Shao-yi who had been governor at Mukden when Straight was there as Consul General; Alfred Sze, Straight's old classmate at Cornell, who was rising in Chinese officialdom; and William Henry Donald, an Australian journalist Straight had met while reporting the Russo-Japanese war and who was now an adviser to Sun Yat-sen. As they took ship for Manila, Straight was busy for a full day typing reports. At his urging, Dorothy read *The Promise of American Life*, Herbert Croly's idealistic plan for better democracy, which Straight had read with enthusiasm the previous year. Some of Croly's statements, such as "A corporation which derived its profits from public franchises . . . found the purchase of a local or state machine well within its means," may have brought her painful recollections of the charges against her father.

Indeed Croly's style was heavy for a young woman whose reformist instincts may have been submerged temporarily by the adventures of marriage. Straight applauded one of Croly's premises—that most Americans expected good government without in the least contributing to it. It was typical of him that he should take such interest in a book concerned with the betterment of American government. It was perhaps also a sign of a more personal preoccupation with politics; it is possible that he was already thinking of running for office. Now, however, he entered a spirited Shakespearean defense of an odd item of attire to which he was addicted and which Dorothy ridiculed:

> Oh! Spats, Blessed Comforters, of Linen or of Wool—
> In Gray, Brown or Pearl. For Youth and Maid
> Who trip through London in such gay parade,
> Who warm the weak'ning ankles of Old Age. Who cap
> The neatest Shoe, the smartest Tie
> Of Leather Patent, Brown or Black, low-heeled or high,
> Who through the Russian wastes, at Stations drear,

> *The Paragraphs of Travel's tedious page,*
> *Are Nemeses for Dorothy, but Willard's cheer,*
> *Oh! Spats! So Useful, and so Ornamental too,*
> *Oh! Spats! I sing this grateful ode to you.*

In Manila they were met by two of the Governor General's aides—Warwick Greene, son of Gen. Francis V. Greene, who had commanded in the Philippines in 1898 and brother of Dorothy's dear Roser-school classmate Edith Greene Lindley; and Peter Bowditch of the old Boston family. Straight, of course, knew them both—they had visited China several times, as had the Governor General himself, the Harvard-educated (as were both Greene and Bowditch) polo-playing, former Boston businessman William Cameron Forbes. If it was true that Harvard and Yale were now carrying Old Glory abroad to foreign posts, it was Straight of Cornell who had been getting the headlines and was to get more. The Straights were Forbes's guests at Malacanan Palace. Forbes spoke so earnestly that Dorothy was carried away: ". . . he is one of the most idealistic and inspired people I have ever seen . . . he makes one feel that he is a man with a real mission in the world, and in all singleness of purpose he works out the high-minded principles in which he believes." For a week the Straights were treated as visiting royalty, honored guests at dinners, an exposition, several polo matches, and a military review. Two others whom they met and who would reappear in their lives were the rugged Capt. Frank R. McCoy of the Regular Army and the Rt. Rev. Charles Henry Brent, Episcopal Bishop of the Philippines.

Straight himself, his mind turned more than ever toward techniques in government by the Croly book, saw the benevolent American rule in the Philippines as "applied Christianity." They returned by way of Japan and Korea, surprised at what seemed benign Bandarlog rule in the latter country. Straight, proud of his bride and aflame with high ambition, took pleasure in their imperial treatment on tour. J. O. P. Bland, meeting them on their return February 25, wrote of the trip, "It acted on Straight like a tonic, turning his mind from the slough of despond to the world of men and things beyond those gray walls."

2. Marines to the Rescue

FOUR NIGHTS later, as Straight recorded, he and Dorothy were dressing for an 8:30 dinner as guests of their neighbor, Dr. Morrison of *The London Times*, when they heard an uproar outside: ". . . thought it was fire crackers till . . . coolie brought word there was fighting outside between Imp[erial] Guard and Yuan's men. Went into courtyard and heard the rattle of rifle fire everywhere—bullets shrieked overhead and coolies ducked. Fire started in north of us. Matters looked bad." During a lull they got safely to Morrison's. Before they had finished dinner, the uproar increased as looting soldiers broke into a silver shop across the road. Straight returned home to rescue the maid Louisa and get night clothing, rejoined Morrison and Dorothy; then they cautiously stole along the compound wall toward the legation. They were trapped in a cul-de-sac and had no recourse but to watch. "The street was bright with the fire-glow," Straight continued. "Parties of from two to a dozen soldiers were walking or running along, carrying their bundles of loot. Every now and then they would stop to smash in some shop. . . . Across the road a large bazar and a theater were burning. After an hour and a half, 20 American Marines came for us and we started out for the Legation. Dorothy, her maid in her lap, the bags tied on behind, piled into one rickshaw and we started at double-time down the street to the Menocals. They came out on horseback, their rickshaw laden with bundles and a coolie carrying a blanket into which Menocal had piled all his wife's dresses."

After a night at the legation, Straight visited the house next morning to find "smoking ruins on all sides" but his Sanctuary little damaged. Desultory firing continued, Minister Calhoun telegraphed Tientsin for reinforcements, and on the morning of March 3, two hundred more American Marines arrived. ". . . their march into Legation Street & under the arch into the American compound," Dorothy noted, "was really very thrilling & impressive." Conflicting rumors abounded, the government insisting soothingly that a minor detachment of troops had mutinied because of a "dispute over pay." To restore order the government resorted to the traditional Chinese practice of wholesale street beheadings. "This has been a horrible day of executions," Dorothy continued, "& dead bodies are to be seen lying around in all the streets. . . . I have kept cautiously away. . . ." *The New York Herald* broke out with headlines:

PEKIN IS SET ON FIRE AND LOOTED
BY UNPAID MUTINOUS SOLDIERS;
MR. AND MRS. STRAIGHT IN PERIL

The story, by Ohl, related that "among the refugees at the American Legation are Mr. Willard D. Straight . . . and his wife, who was Miss

Dorothy P. Whitney . . . and Mr. Daniel A. de Menocal . . . and his wife, all of whom had thrilling experiences in the streets. . . . The soldiers did not attempt to interfere with them, but there was great danger from flying bullets and fire brands. . . . Mr. and Mrs. Straight saved their records and valuables, but deserted a richly furnished house, which was given over to the looters."

One of Dorothy's letters home fell into the hands of Hearst's sensation-seeking *New York American* and appeared on a full-color page under the heading, "HOW I ESCAPED THE CHINESE BANDITS," with an editorial note doubling her fortune to $15,000,000. *The New York Times* ran a large photograph of the Straights (he wore the inevitable spats) in their handsome living room and said part of the building was destroyed by rioters. The danger was real enough, and the papers did not underplay it. From Harry Payne Whitney in New York came a cable: "WE ARE GETTING WORRIED OVER SITUATION WHAT ARE YOUR PLANS." Davison in New York, who liked the Straights and possibly also reflected that their murder while on Morgan business would reflect poorly on the firm, had already informed them that they were to be replaced. Frank McKnight, the new man from the New York office, was on his way to a post that looked less like a business opportunity than an experience in warfare.

The Straights stayed at the legation for several days behind the comforting lines of Marines. The Purple Cows met despite the turbulence, and as things quieted, Straight played some "very rotten polo," in his own words. Entertaining reached a feverish pitch as the date of the Straights' departure approached—two dinner parties at their home on succeeding nights, a stag affair given by Straight, luncheon and dinner parties honoring them at the various legations and at many private homes—one, with music, at the Casenaves.

During their last week in Peking, the Straights were virtually racing from elaborate luncheon to elaborate dinner. On their last day, Dorothy wrote, "Lunched with Gatrells—only Pu Luns there. George & Mrs. Russell came at 3 & stayed a while. Later Willard & I called on Jordans [British Minister] & took a last wonderful walk on the wall."

On March 26 she wrote: "Left Peking. 79 people at station to see us off!" Aboard the Chinese railway and then the endless Trans-Siberian, her energy flagged and she all but abandoned her diary, on April 4 writing only, "Feeling so sick!" She was pregnant.

3. Back Home and Rich

ARRIVING IN Paris April 7 to be met by Courtlandt Bishop and Lord ffrench, they lodged at the Vendôme and were instantly in the swing. They lunched with the Ambassador Bacons, then with Margaret and Charles Lawrance, all of them now reconciled to Straight. Sheldon Whitehouse, now Third Secretary in Paris, called on them. Dorothy had fittings at Callot and at Rouff and sat for the painter Bradford Johnson before she and Straight crossed to London to stay with Pauline and Almeric at 39 Berkeley Square. On the fifteenth Dorothy's diary showed the deficiencies of a Line-a-Day attended in haste, saying, "The news has come today of the terrible Titanic disaster," and going on with a seeming callousness of which she was incapable, "I spent a busy morning searching for silver."

". . . I can't get the tragedy of the Titanic out of my mind . . . ," Mrs. Lawrance wrote to them from Paris. "I knew two people quite well who drowned. . . . I can't bear to think of you two sailing for home after this awful disaster."

Straight was back at work temporarily at Morgan, Grenfell at 22 Old Broad Street. He and Dorothy attended their beloved *Bohème*, Dorothy (who always credited the leading performers) dutifully listing "Cornelius, Saltzman" as the principals. Dorothy visited the Soho Club for Working Girls, with Mrs. Whitelaw Reid was a guest at an industrial evening school, and with Straight read aloud H. G. Wells's articles on the current labor unrest. "Taft & Roosevelt are having great fight for the delegates," Dorothy noted, and later, "T.R. has won Ohio delegation"; still later, "Taft was nominated yesterday!" and finally, "Dr. Woodrow Wilson has been nominated by the Baltimore Conv."

Straight was downcast when informed by Davison that he must work in London most of the summer. He was working long hours, making one business trip to Hamburg and Berlin, two others to Paris, leaving Dorothy in the hands of Pauline, which meant incessant card playing. This the Straights finally escaped by renting a spacious country home in suburban Amersham, where Dorothy was guarded by two West Highland terriers as she read *Parenthood and Race Culture* and Straight played tennis on weekends with William Phillips, now his warm friend and admirer. Straight sent her flowers on the slightest pretext or none at all. Whenever away, he would telegraph her daily. He would often telephone her at noon when he had left her in the morning and was to return in the evening, and he expected similarly close communication from her. He was nervous and uneasy when away from her, even though the separation was only for a few hours. They motored to Cliveden for tea, as Dorothy noted, with "Lady Essex, Consuelo Marlborough, Ava Astor, Fox McDonnell, F. E. Smith, Winston Churchill, Lionel Curtis of South Africa, etc." The former Consuelo Vanderbilt was serving out her last years with the unpleasant duke. The Straights dutifully rose early to see J. P. Morgan off for America. Not until August 10 did they sail on the great *Mauretania*—not quite as new as the *Titanic* but making better than six hundred miles one day through seas less dotted with icebergs.

New York! It was their first time home after eleven months of marriage, the city hot enough to make Dorothy flee almost immediately to the Catskills with Beatrice Bend, with whom she had who knows how many confidences to entrust. Straight resumed his labors at 23 Wall Street, his salary doubled as a reward for the Chinese coup. So lonely was he with Dorothy gone that he dutifully spent his second weekend visiting his sister and Aunt Laura in Oswego and from there telegraphed Dorothy plaintively that he had had neither TAOHSIEH nor GRAZIA—no letter or even a thank you note—from her. What with his loneliness and her growing discomfort, she was back in two weeks to settle at Applegreen and receive visits from friends she had not seen for many months—Ethel Roosevelt (whom Straight called the Little Princess, still unwed), Tottie Hollister, Edith Lindley, DeLancey Jay and his wife Elizabeth, Ethel Higgins, May Tuckerman Kinnicutt, dozens of others. Straight, whom Dorothy had once begged to be "humble" and who had an admitted tendency to be highfalutin when under critical inspection, was for the first time on extended view before the people who had for so long wondered about him and talked about him. It was an ordeal for which, despite his seeming self-assurance, he had surely prepared himself in every way. At least one of Dorothy's old friends, Susan Sedgwick, who dated back to Roser school days, thought he was modest and charming, that he carried it off perfectly.

With the Davisons, Lewis Ledyard, and a few others, the Straights were given that greatest of compliments to a young Morgan employee, a short evening cruise with the great man in the largest of the *Corsairs*—this despite Dorothy's known liberal tendencies and the fact that both of them supported the wild Roosevelt. It was not known that they were also reading aloud Louis Brandeis's articles in *Collier's* about the trusts. But precisely like the vested interests, the Straights bought a Packard motorcar and leased a handsome, five-story townhouse at 22 East 67th Street, just around the corner from 871 Fifth Avenue of hallowed memory, which meant hiring more servants. As the bitter canvass of 1912 approached, it appeared that Dorothy's child had a chance to be born on election day. Straight had forgiven Roosevelt, Dorothy was enthusiastic about him, and when he took a bullet from a fanatic in Milwaukee, she hurried somewhat heavily to comfort Mrs. Roosevelt and Ethel. Typically, the Colonel made a campaign speech while still bleeding, before going to a hospital, and rather gloried in it. He was coming into the most obsessed and belligerent stage of his career, but his magnetism was still unmatched, and Dorothy was thrilled to see him when he returned to Sagamore.

Just in case things went badly, Dorothy called in William H. Page, one of her father's many lawyers, and revised her will. Her child was born November 6, the day after Wilson's momentous victory, and was compensation for Roosevelt's defeat. "A boy!!" she wrote, "& he weighs 7 pounds, 14 ounces!!!!" It took her several weeks to recover. On Christmas Day, with a foot of snow transforming the landscape, Straight had a horse hitched to a cutter and the runners sang as they drove to Manhasset to visit Katherine and Courtlandt Barnes. To Straight, with his genius for inventing honors and occasions, the Barneses were eminent people if for no other reason than that it was they with whom Dorothy and he had dined shortly before Dorothy accepted his marriage proposal. "Most exquisite day!" Dorothy recorded. "Willard & I had a nice evening alone."

Though the circumstances were different, Straight was now in a position like that of the young William C. Whitney—a poor man who had married an heiress and had to adjust to the consequences, both pleasant and unpleasant. Straight had shown more short-term initiative and daring in his exploits than Whitney (or almost anyone one could name) at the same age. In the generation since Whitney had made his great bid for wealth, many opportunities had been seized and fewer streets were paved with gold. Yet Straight's successes in China far outshone the considerable progress Whitney made as he passed thirty. Straight was rightly regarded as a boy wonder. Harriman had been his model, and the effective use he had made of Harriman while the tycoon was in turn using him was the key to his triumphs. There had been luck in it, but there had also been a tremendous drive and sheer ability in

Straight's quick rise to the Group and the Morgan firm. Both Straight and Whitney possessed the asset of great personal charm, Straight's more broad and assertive, Whitney's a quieter glow, the steel underneath.

Perhaps it was the steel underneath that Straight lacked. Whitney, after suffering under the Payne hegemony, had entered private enterprise and speedily become his own man running the show, with such hardy characters as Ryan and Widener (not to mention Croker) accepting his leadership. It was not in the nature of things that Straight could be so phenomenally gifted in so many ways and not have one considerable defect. Dorothy had already discovered the one flaw that he had to surmount. It was his tendency, even at moments when victory was near, to succumb to boredom or discouragement and seek greener pastures elsewhere. It seems certain that he would have quit the thorny Peking assignment had not Dorothy held him to it.

Spasms of nerves and doubt appeared unlikely in the man who for eight years had seemed a splendid loner in his Far Eastern enterprises and had made the intrepid journey into "Kubla Khan country." But Katherine Elkins, as Dorothy knew, had helped him to "find himself." He had leaned on Corinne Robinson, on his "auntie" in Oswego. Similar support had been given him by Mary Harriman and earlier by father figures such as Professor Stephens, Sir Robert Hart, J. O. P. Bland, and Edwin V. Morgan. Roosevelt had skyrocketed him. All these people had been impressed not only by his charm but by his abilities. But the fact was that Straight had been so comparatively briefly in each of his roles—with the Customs Service, as war correspondent, his several positions with the State Department, and finally with Morgan—and in addition had changed scenes and formed new friendships, that he had not yet been forced to prove his steadfastness in the long, hard grind.

If his need for assurance was winning, it was not characteristic of the robber baron or captain of industry. Whitney had gone it alone. But Straight surmounted the embarrassment of the light purse marrying the heiress far better than had Whitney, whose humiliation over the disparity had driven him to gamble, to lose, and to lie to Flora about it. Straight seemed untroubled by his financial insignificance. One could make judicious estimates of his increases in salary, from perhaps $2,000 a year as Consul General at Mukden (plus allowances for housing and entertainment) to perhaps $3,000 at his peak in the State Department. There had been a big jump to (let us guess) $10,000, plus splendid living accommodations, as Group representative in Peking. The doubling of his salary brought it into the neighborhood of $20,000. Living in

New York was infinitely more expensive than in Peking. Twenty thousand dollars could scarcely begin to sustain the Straights' luxurious mode of life. Assuming that Dorothy's fortune was still only $7,000,000, though eight years of wise investment should have enlarged it substantially, the return from that amount should have approximated a quarter of a million dollars annually.

Hence Straight could no more assume all the family expenses than Whitney could when he moved with his bride into their Park Avenue home in 1869. The Straights, however, overcame the money problem better than had Dorothy's parents, perhaps because she had escaped most of her mother's imperiousness. She knew that Straight was in a sense a foreigner, this being the first time he had lived permanently in the United States since college. He had been accustomed for years to luxury, servants, Savile Row tailoring, polo, and clubs. He immediately joined the Downtown Club, near the Morgan office, for business convenience. Among his other clubs were the Players', the Century, and the Metropolitan. He planned with Dorothy a new mansion on Fifth Avenue. He laid out a polo field on the Westbury property, watered by underground piping. He bought a string of ponies and entered enthusiastically into this most expensive of sporting ventures (while Harry sniffed at such presumption on the part of an indifferent poloist). A picture showing him mounted, mallet over his shoulder, horse perfectly groomed and Straight if anything more so, from polished boots to white breeches and white helmet, gives an idea of his fastidiousness in dress. He harbored a somewhat shocking hope to buy a large daily newspaper, which would cost several millions.

He seems, a little prematurely, to have felt that he had served his apprenticeship in the Morgan firm, that his future there was secure, and that in Davison he had a friendly patron who could be depended upon to advance his interests. He would be reasonably secure financially when he became a Morgan partner, a post he seemed confident was in store for him.

But he did not hide behind the morning paper as Whitney had. He hitched his political wagon to Roosevelt's star, which took courage for a Morgan man but had Dorothy's firm support. "Willard came and lifted me bodily out of the old life and it fell away," Dorothy marveled. "I never even heard it fall. Almost imperceptibly things assumed new values and new proportions. . . . He tied winged sandals to my feet and I began to soar with him to new heights of exploration. Life suddenly became an adventure, a quest on which I could risk everything."

Not quite everything. Her use of the word *risk* perhaps connoted a deeper understanding. The sandals had to come down to earth and wear well on rough pavement. Dorothy, who could never match her husband's brilliance, had a fund of wisdom and long-run determination missing in him. It remained to be seen whether they could continue to pool their abilities as successfully as they had in the China project.

4. Dollar Diplomacy Perishes

THE BABY, named Whitney Willard but called Bill, was christened at Westbury by Dr. Charles Lewis Slattery of Grace Church in a ceremony totally lacking in the fanfare given Dorothy's own baptism in 1887. Only Mrs. Davison and the Courtlandt Barneses were present in addition to the parents. There was no doubt that the child had loving parents, but both were so busy that after three months of close motherly attention he was assigned to a governess for all but an hour or two daily. In this respect Dorothy followed the English nanny system, which she had objected to in her own parents, except that her child seldom saw a day without *some* motherly attention and caressing.

The Straights were both leaders in the mayoral campaign of the anti-Tammany Fusion candidate John Purroy Mitchel, to whose name Dorothy forever added the extra "l" that seemed to belong there. If she had been active in charities earlier, she now increased her work as if her domestic happiness—her overprivilege—required payment. Back she went with the Junior League, the drive for women's suffrage, the State Charities Aid, and the YWCA. She joined a committee "to care for poor children & women of the district"; she joined a Junior Fortnightly Club; she was a member of the Economics Club, hearing lectures on such subjects as socialism and the single tax; she worked for the Red Cross; she called on Booker T. Washington; she attended a Bible class and a Women's Trade Union meeting about the unemployed; and her reading club was given serious attention. The Straights attended the theater and opera; there was the usual tennis and golf and polo; they would travel to Washington on any excuse. Dorothy enjoyed a few weeks at Onteora in the Catskills or at Narragansett (she disliked fancy Newport) in the hot weather and Lenox in the autumn. Having selected William Adams Delano as their architect, the Straights began planning their new house, to be built on a plot with a forty-foot frontage on Fifth Avenue at 94th Street.

The lavish and mannered parties that had been Flora Whitney's delight were not for the Straights, both of whom deplored such formality. Straight had a habit of bringing a few people home with him for dinner, and weekends were often occasions for house parties, small but busy, divided between serious discussion and fun. People enjoyed Straight's company as much as they did Dorothy's, which meant an endless stream of guests, old friends renewing acquaintance such as Professor Stephens, Martin Egan, Joseph Ohl, and many new ones. The Straights—especially Willard—were constantly visiting the Roosevelts at Oyster Bay. They dined out with Norman Hapgood, the John Purroy Mitchels, and the Arctic explorer Sir Ernest Shackleton. In Washington they dined or visited with people interesting personally, useful politically, or both: Daisy Harriman, who was a member of the Federal Industrial Relations Commission, had a home in the capital, and "knew everybody"; Louis Brandeis, Gen. Leonard Wood, and William McAdoo among them; and Straight went with Fletcher, back from Chile, to the Gridiron Dinner. They met an old friend of Dorothy's parents, Sir Cecil Spring Rice, now fifty-four and Ambassador in Washington. In Berlin he had met the British Ambassador's daughter, Florence Lascelles, and come to say good-bye to her when he was assigned to his next post. After an hour's conversation, he said as he left her, "By the way, Miss Lascelles, will you marry me?" She replied, "Why, yes." She was now Lady Spring Rice.

Meanwhile Straight had suffered the anguish of seeing the great work of his life, the China loan, first delayed by the Chinese revolution, then wiped off the slate by Woodrow Wilson. Not *quite* by Wilson. The Group itself had grown profoundly distrustful of the Chinese ability to repay, in view of the turbulence there, but it had put the onus on the Democratic administration. The "every diplomat a salesman" idea was repugnant to many. It did not sit well that the Minister to Greece had gotten Bethlehem Steel the contract for guns and armor of a Greek fighting ship, nor that Taft's Secretary of War Henry L. Stimson had favored sending American troops to instruct Chilean artillerists as that nation requested, since this should result in the sale to Chile of American weaponry. LaFollette's *Weekly* had demanded, "Is there anything which Mr. Knox and President Taft will not give to foreign nations in exchange for 'business' desired by their friends in Wall Street?" Straight—no admirer of LaFollette—liked him less.

On March 10, 1913, Straight went to Washington with Davison to see the new Secretary of State, William Jennings Bryan. Bryan was cordial but said he knew nothing about the loan and must study it. He did so and was utterly opposed, as was President Wilson. Federal involvement in the loan, the President said, was "obnoxious to the principles upon which the government of our people rests," its terms "touch very nearly the administrative independence of China itself," and for the United States government to take part in the agreement might even end in "forcible interference." It was not Straight's fault, but the glow of his achievement was dulled, as if he had been given a medal mistakenly, and he felt that it was the Group and the administration who were the mistaken ones.

Soon thereafter Dorothy recorded, "Mr. Morgan died this morning in Rome." A fortnight later the Straights, along with the mighty of finance and politics, attended his funeral at St. George's. Morgan had lost a little money on the China venture, but his expenditures on art alone during his last years showed that he had not done badly. And a few days later, Dorothy was able to write "finis" to her most determined nuptial embassy:

> Ethel's wedding [to Dr. Richard Derby] took place this morning at Oyster Bay at 12. So simple—wonderful—all through. Nice, happy reception afterwards. Home by 3.30 so that the men played some tennis. The Lindleys are staying over. . . .

35. Willard at five, Dorothy at about ten, long before fate introduced them.

36. Dorothy's brother Payne and Harry (*shown left to right with wives*) strongly opposed such a destiny for Dorothy.

37. At the Aiken cottage, Gertrude is top left, Beatrice Bend top right, Charles Draper at the extreme left next to Dorothy. Among others is another of Dorothy's own set, Meredith "Bunny" Hare, nearest the camera.

38. At an outing apparently at the Webb place on Lake Champlain, Dorothy is surrounded by Robert Bacon (*left*), Joseph Burden, Hermann Kinnicutt, and James Watson Webb.

39. Dorothy (*left*) and "BB" at Madonna, where Whitehouse proposed marriage.

40. Straight on his adventurous tour of Manchuria, from which he returned virtually exhausted.

41. The spats-loving Straight confers with U.S. Minister Calhoun and a Chinese representative.

The three heiresses in Straight's
: Dorothy (*left, a pastel done by
aight*), Katherine Elkins, and Mary
rriman.

43. E. H. Harriman with daughters
Mary (*center*) and Cornelia at costume
ball.

44. After Dorothy's wedding, Harry (*standing, third from left*) is less than joyful, and even Dorothy and the groom seem more relieved than ecstatic. The younger man at upper right is William Phillips.

45. Bride and groom ride in Paris, Dorothy sidesaddle, as was obligatory at the time.

46. Honeymooning happily in Venice.

47. Both were orphaned, both idealists.

48. Willard's sketch of Dorothy, 1912.

Right: Sister Pauline, who did her best to break up the romance.

49. Dorothy (*left*) in China with a group including Mrs. de Menocal and Lord ffrench (*next to her*).

50. The kimonoed Purple Cows in Peking: Dorothy in the largest hat, Straight next to her.

51. A silk-hatted Straight arrives at the American legation from his mansion beyond the Tartar Wall, Peking.

52. American Marines arrived in time to save the Straights and others from a mutinous soldiery.

53. *Left:* At the entrance to the swank "1718 club" in Washington are, at top, George Marvin, William Phillips, Col. James Logan, and Straight. Gen. McCoy pets the dog, and Henry P. Fletcher is at right in a derby hat.

54. *Right*: The one and only Colonel, dear friend, maddening politician.

The Straight house on Fifth Avenue—Federal elegance without William Whitney extravagance.

56. Straight was a determined poloist, though lacking Harry's great finesse.

57. Applegreen, the Straights' Westbury house, scene of intellectual discussions.

58. The Straights with their first child, Whitney, the only one who was to remember his father

59. The entire Straight family just before the Major left for France.

60. *At Langres:* Straight, Col. Henry Stimson, Majors Grayson Murphy and Herbert Parsons.

61. Herbert Croly.

62. George Marvin.

63. Harry P. Davison.

64. Walter Lippmann.

65. Colonel House.

66. Daisy Harriman, the last nurse.

67. Ethel Derby, Dorothy's confidante.

68. Dartington Hall, Devon, where one way of life ended and another began.

69. Often a critic, sometimes a rebel, in England Dorothy sponsored a
"shocking" departure in education.

Five

1. The New Republic

TO STRAIGHT, the most fascinating man in the world was of course Theodore Roosevelt. The two were alike in brilliance, energy, and ego, though no one could match the Colonel in the latter two qualities. Both were charismatic, both yearned more than is normal for public acclaim, and each was too mentally dynamic to be satisfied unless he had several enterprises going at once. Both were now thinking of political power. While the Colonel's vast and ruthless hunger to recapture the White House was unequaled, it appears that Straight would be willing to put aside his Morgan career if politics beckoned with enough allure. Despite the Colonel's calamitous split with Taft, which had made Wilson President in 1912, there was utter magnetism in Roosevelt and what his political blessing might do for one. There were millions to whom he was a superman, millions who would follow him wherever he led.

Straight was in general agreement with Roosevelt's "New Nationalism" political program. The tag was borrowed from Herbert Croly, but the program was not radically different from that while Roosevelt was President except in his concession that corporations should be converted to the public good rather than destroyed. The imperialism of such as Rudyard Kipling, Dr. Morrison, and in fact E. H. Harriman had left their imprint on Straight, and he was in tune with Roosevelt's muscular view of America as the moral, the just, the righteous kingpin of the world. But politics had perhaps less to do with the Straights' loyalty to the Colonel than did affection. Dorothy was as charmed by him as by his daughter Ethel. Willard loved him as the man who had befriended him, the man who seemed destined for new power.

Straight, ever since *The Widow* and *The Era* at Cornell, had been fecund in ideas and expert at communicating them. His gifts as a propagandist, visible in his enlistment of Professor Stephens and Corinne

Robinson to recommend him to Dorothy as well as in his interminable correspondence with Harriman, the Group, and the State Department while in China, now had no adequate outlet. To him this was somewhat like having one's breath stopped, particularly in view of his own political ambitions, inchoate though they were. He relieved the discomfort by bringing Roosevelt together with Herbert Croly—and himself— in an unusual new political compound.

Croly's *The Promise of American Life* was an indictment of a lagging America and a blueprint for a national renaissance. He called for the abandonment of America's chaotic individualism in favor of a patriotic discipline and dedication to the national good. To him it was folly to break up large corporations simply because they gave excessive profits to the few. Corporations should instead be encouraged but controlled so that their efficiency benefited the whole population. Responsible organization of labor was part of his picture of Americans working together for a national purpose that would be universally advantageous and would do away with the "indiscriminate, individual scramble for wealth." The country should quit its isolationism and take a responsible part in international affairs.

To achieve all this, great leaders were required—especially a great President. Here was where Croly and Straight, who were not eye to eye in every respect, agreed perfectly. For a heroic figure in Croly's book was Roosevelt, who was lauded as a reformer whose "constructive mission" had been proved by his work in all the public offices he had held, from state assemblyman to President.

Straight's own patriotism was real despite its strong elements of elitism, chauvinism, and imperialism. The pioneer who had thrilled to Harriman's global dream believed, with Croly, that planning and effort could awaken the nation. He had seen with his own eyes the vacillation of American foreign policy under Taft and then Wilson. Croly's argument that the nation could not have a strong policy abroad without an equally strong policy at home impressed him as new and incontrovertible. He felt the Open Door in China to be an empty phrase unless backed by American power and money, for otherwise the nearest and most powerful—Japan and Russia—would swallow China. Doubtless he realized that the Open Door was a euphemism for intervention there, but he was able to take the comforting view that American intervention was benevolent and salutary as opposed to the rapacious intervention of others.

Who other than Roosevelt could inspire the nation to such a rebirth in spirit? The Colonel, delighted by the laudation in *The Promise*, had praised the book in *The Outlook Magazine*. He had also written Croly to applaud his general argument, saying, "I shall use your ideas freely in speeches I intend to make."

It seems likely that Straight and Roosevelt had discussed the matter before Straight called on Croly sometime in 1913 to ask him to outline what he felt would be the best way to launch his program of reform. Croly was forty-four, eleven years older than Straight—rumpled, slight, unprepossessing, with a bulbous nose supporting rimless glasses. The son of a *New York World* editor and a bluestocking mother, he had spent youthful years in Paris and gone to Harvard intermittently for eleven years before winning a degree. His terrible shyness, which caused his conversation with strangers to be impeded by dreadful silences, soon disappeared with the friendly Straight, who in any case was articulate enough to fill all gaps. As one admirer said of Croly, he "radiated a kind of moral force, and everyone felt it." The meeting of the two men was an encounter of the peacock and the crow, but they liked each other. Straight's reformist views were perhaps more hard-headed than Croly's, his aim being to make the capitalist system work more efficiently and to foster American expansion in world trade and American prestige in world councils. In these aims Taft had tried and failed, and to Straight the new President Wilson appeared the professor, the man who opposed American ventures abroad, anything but the world-shaker. It is possible also that he saw in the Roosevelt factor an opportunity for his own political advancement. But, as time would show, he had a great and continuing respect for Croly's honesty and idealism.

Croly saw that Straight longed to own a large metropolitan daily newspaper, a dream not yet attainable. "Thereafter," Croly later recalled, "I saw him frequently, and in one of our conversations we discussed a plan for a new weekly which would apply to American life, as it developed, the political and social ideas which I had sketched in the book." Once, while visiting the Straights on Long Island, Croly bemoaned the ineffectuality of *Harper's Weekly* and Dorothy said, "Why don't you get out a weekly yourself, Herbert?"

She was attracted by Croly's belief in women's suffrage, among other things. Still only twenty-six, and out of the country for several of those years, she had been full of good impulses but politically innocent until now. The Mitchel campaign had taught her much, but probably what taught her most of all was marriage to Straight. His considerable training in government and politics, his seven-year advantage in age, his quick, inquiring mind, his broad interests and experiences and his witty and articulate discussions of them, his constant introduction to her of new people and new ideas—all this was an education in itself. Under his influence, Dorothy was opening like a flower into maturity. When she asked Croly why he didn't start his own weekly, and he said, "Where would I find the money?" she gave the reply that was to involve them all in the fashioning of a new and significant political voice on which millions—her millions—would be spent.

"I will find it," she said.

"It might take five years to make the paper self-supporting," Croly warned.

"Yes, I understand. It may take longer, much longer. But let's go ahead."

This was divine music in Croly's ears. As a later associate put it, "How could it have happened that Fate should have placed an immense fortune in the hands of a woman so brave, so true, so beautiful as Dorothy Straight?" While Straight must be given credit for opening the conversations, it was Dorothy who gave them substance.

The Straight-Croly discussions widened to include some of Croly's liberal friends, Straight's tending to be less liberal and more skeptical of knight-errantry. There were few supporters of such projects in the Morgan firm. Straight tried vainly to get Davison interested (and later felt this harmed him with the firm), though Thomas W. Lamont was an exception who was to give warm cooperation. On Sunday, November 16, 1913, Dorothy wrote, "The great 'Republic' conference has taken place! This A.M. our guests arrived [at Westbury]—Judge & Mrs. Hand, Mr. & Mrs. Croly, Phil Littell & Felix Frankfurter. . . . W[illard] had the conference from 2.30 till 7." Judge Learned Hand and Littell were close friends of Croly's, the judge an outstanding liberal, Littell a Harvard classmate of Croly's, a writer and editor. Frankfurter, another Croly intimate, had a legal post with the Bureau of Insular Affairs but was soon to take a professorship at Harvard.

Thus was *The New Republic* born. For the policy of baneful drift it would substitute a new era in dynamic governmental planning. It would cater to an intellectual elite devoted to the improvement of the democracy—the enlightenment and enrichment of the nation—and would seek to enlarge that elite. It was to be imbued with the spirit of excellence, with Montesquieu's saying that "the principle of democracy is virtue." Yet its founders sought to be politically practical in building their hopes around Theodore Roosevelt, the man whom they could help elect President in 1916.

When Roosevelt in May of 1914 returned half-dead with exhaustion from his explorations in Brazil, Straight wrote to him warmly: "It seems to me that the country is weary of [Wilsonian] uplift, weary of the high moral tone upon which, we are led to believe, affairs are at present being conducted. . . . You can sound the note and enunciate the broad policy that is required and I believe the people would respond." It had the note of a bandwagon getting under way. Walter Lippmann, who at twenty-five had been brought into the *Republic* fold, had breakfast with Roosevelt at the Harvard Club. Lippmann and Frankfurter had a further discussion with him at the offices of *The Outlook,* of which the Colonel was a contributing editor. Croly, Frankfurter, and Walter Weyl—the latter also enlisted in the staff—visited Roosevelt at Oyster Bay for policy discussions. Straight probably saw him repeatedly on his own. The first issue of *The New Republic* was not to be published until immediately after the fall 1914 elections. Meanwhile every effort was made to formulate a political program with which the ex-President (who had grown more touchy than anyone imagined) could agree.

It turned out that Dorothy, in addition to subsidizing the publication, had to subsidize Croly himself at the start. He had been moderately prosperous as editor of *The Architectural Record* and owned some New York property, but he lived well, enjoyed the Harvard Club and the Players', and was embarrassed by a delayed legacy. His debt at the Harvard Club had grown so that he received a warning and had to borrow $2,000 from Judge Hand. His difficulties were solved when the Straights bought a substantial four-story brick residence he owned at 421 West 21st Street, across from the General Theological Seminary, as *The New Republic* office. They bore the expense of remodeling it "to resemble a gentleman's club," with an elaborate kitchen that was to come in for heavy use. Walter Lippmann had no doubt that Dorothy "had a strong feeling of conscience that the money she'd inherited from her father was tainted and that she must devote it to public purposes."

While all this was brewing, Straight, a newcomer in New York, was already becoming a leader among a group of businessmen who founded the National Foreign Trade Council, whose purpose was to encourage a sound foreign trade policy. As president of the American Asiatic Association he pushed for the same ends. He was instrumental in the organization of the first National Foreign Trade Convention held in Washington in May 1914. His happy faculty of combining art with life and with business came to the fore after he visited the East India Marine Museum in Salem, Massachusetts, a place dedicated to the bygone age when American clippers carried freight all over the world. Why not have a club dedicated to the revival of such trade? A revival would of course also tend to increase the Morgan loan business.

He had in mind just the building. The handsome old three-story structure on Hanover Square in New York once occupied by the Cotton Exchange was now being vacated by W. R. Grace & Company. Across the street was the new Cotton Exchange and around the corner the Coffee Exchange. Cotton was the largest item of American export, coffee the largest import, so the neighborhood was ideal. Straight leased the building and called in his friend William Delano—the architect who was building his house—for its renovation. A search was made for fine antique pieces with which to furnish it, and Straight paid handsomely for a private collection of old ship models and prints. At a Washington dinner of businessmen allied with foreign trade, he broached the idea of a club catering to men of their international interests. The suggestion was greeted with enthusiasm.

"Very well," said Straight, "the building has been found, it has been remodeled, it is being furnished, the club house is there, all that remains is to organize the membership and move in." The club, named India House, came into being and is still thriving at the same address. Straight was reproachful enough with friends who did not join so that Delano, Martin Egan, William Cameron Forbes, Frank McKnight, and Lloyd Griscom—now back in New York after his term as Minister to Japan—were among those who became members.

While Dorothy admired her husband's breadth of interests and was particularly enthusiastic about *The New Republic,* she feared that he was spreading himself too thin and wished that he would stop occasionally to catch his breath. "Willard & I had our first evening alone in eleven days," she noted on June 18. She had again called in Attorney Page, a sign that she was protecting the interests of an expected offspring. On August 2, the day after she wrote "Germany declares war on Russia" and the day before she wrote "Germany declares war on France," she made the entry, "Such a cunning little girl weighing 7-9 pounds!" The baby was thus born (at home, as Whitney had been) under the clouds of war that were forever to shadow their lives. The delighted Straight said the child should be designated "Baby B," but of course the name Beatrice had already been decided on, to honor the dear duenna.

In September Dorothy went with the children, the maid Louisa, and two other servants to Onteora. As before, her departure even for only a few days left the normally ebullient Straight unhappy, even unnerved—

a state of mind far more painful than simple loneliness. It caused in him an almost frantic need to keep in touch with her by letter, telephone, or telegraph—sometimes all three. Years earlier he had written Corinne Robinson of his fear that, if he once won Dorothy, some ghastly accident would take her away. That an adult male could be so apprehensive over a temporary separation might appear absurd were it not for the probability that it was a reopening of the wounds of his orphan childhood. Straight's Morgan colleagues and club associates would surely have been astonished that the big, aggressive, wisecracking, world-traveling explorer of Manchuria could harbor such anxieties, but to Dorothy they were a demanding, if flattering, fact of life. Perhaps it was reassuring to her as well to discover that his affection had not waned after all with the marriage to a great fortune.

He was itching to buy either *The New York Evening Post* or *The Washington Herald*—impossible because Dorothy evidently thought it best not to advance the money. She had evolved a firm policy of deprecating his occasional surrender to boredom or frustration. These, she felt sure, were the weaknesses impairing his otherwise enormous abilities—that his success depended on his determination to conquer these vagrant impulses. Although her belief in the Morgan benevolence was receding, she felt it best that he stay with that firm until he attained something nearer indispensability than he now seemed to have. She believed him capable of greatness if his vagaries of temperament could be controlled. She conceived it as her duty to help control them, and he usually placed great faith in her wisdom—even leaned on her—but there arose inevitable tensions.

A new and potentially disruptive element was the war in Europe, for he was so pro-Allies in sentiment that he could scarcely suppress his yearning to join the British army. It was inconsistent that the man who so lamented Dorothy's brief and nonhazardous absences should even contemplate absenting himself indefinitely into danger, but (like his newspaper dream) it underlined his growing dissatisfaction with his Morgan post and fitted the pattern of the past: the quick boredom, the itchy foot, even the predilection for the grandiose and heroic. Straight ended one of his yearning letters to Dorothy at Onteora:

> . . . dined with Herbert [Croly] and a bunch of Player people—after which the Winter Garden. Quite an amusing show. . . . They played the different national anthems—the "Wacht Am Rhein" got a bit of applause—and Herbert and I started a real round for the Marseillaise. I thought we might have a row. . . .

Dorothy was back after twelve days, to be met at the Weehawken station by a Straight wildly overjoyed to have her safely back. Meanwhile, plans for *The New Republic* had progressed. The free spirits of the staff had been concerned that their efforts, though subsidized by a Morgan man (or, more accurately, his wife), should not be controlled from 23 Wall Street. The Straights, astonishingly generous, agreed that the group as a whole would determine policy. Although the Straights were to be consulted in important matters of policy and management, Willard and Dorothy combined would have only one vote in editorial conferences and thus could not veto the decision of the rest. Croly wrote to Judge Hand, "The . . . vision I have of the New Republic . . . will, I fear, set angel Dorothy back some hundreds of thousands of dollars . . . but she will get a little education for her money and so will I and so, I hope, will you and the others."

Croly was embarrassed when Dorothy also *paid* for a subscription (ten cents a copy, four dollars a year). A prepublication advertising campaign brought in a mere 875 subscriptions, including hers. The first issue, appearing November 7, 1914, sold only a few thousand copies. "The New Republic is frankly an experiment," it announced. "It is an attempt to find national audience for a journal of interpretation and opinion." It was plain, undecorated, thirty-two pages, but with solid qualities of intelligence and responsibility, touching the arts as well as politics. About the war, it said with a prescience particularly applicable to Dorothy and Willard Straight: "There broke over the country a European war which the American people individually and collectively were powerless to prevent or to mitigate, yet which may have consequences upon the future . . . of the country as profound and far-reaching as our self-made Civil War."

On November 21, with May and Hermann Kinnicutt (the latter a Harvard man), Dorothy saw the Harvard-Yale football game at the brand-new Yale Bowl built to hold 80,000 spectators. Perhaps Dorothy, like the Harvard man Walter Lippmann and his companion Freda Kirchwey, who were also in the crowd, paid less attention to the game than to the hopeful search of the stadium for people carrying copies of *The New Republic*. There were not many, but Kinnicutt and Lippmann, at any rate, could enjoy the 36–0 Harvard victory. Dorothy and the Kinnicutts were back in New York at 7:45 to be met by an anxious Straight and to dine with him at Sherry's.

2. Corporals in Wall Street

ON THE Monday after the football game, Davison announced that he and Straight must go to England on the *Adriatic*, sailing Wednesday. Dorothy decided to go with them. The war was now a grim reality in England and this would be an opportunity to visit Pauline—though Pauline hardly seemed as dear to her as Adelaide was, and perhaps the truth was that Dorothy had not been abroad for two years and missed her beloved travel. (Did Willard also beg her to keep him company?)

The Straights had a table with the benignant Davison. Two days out, Dorothy wrote, "British battleship 'Bulwark' blown up off Sherness [*sic*]," and the next day the collier *Khartoum* was sunk off Hull. The *Adriatic* was cautious, moving up slowly to Liverpool and landing there December 3. Dorothy had no sooner been lodged at Claridge's and drawn a deep breath than she "spent all the afternoon at the Red Cross office packing kit bags for British soldiers. . . ."

The war had kept the unfortunate Pauline, almost never well, from her favorite continental spas. Hence she was taking the waters at Bath, where the Straights visited her and Almeric and played the inevitable auction. Straight, feeling that he was treated at the Morgan firm somewhat as a clerk and given no real responsibility, had told Davison so. At thirty-four, Straight was a young man in that company, Davison being thirteen years older with a long banking background at Guaranty Trust and himself quite young to be a partner. It seems evident that Davison liked both Straights but by now was familiar enough with Willard's temperament to have some doubts about him. For all his triumph in China, he had things to learn. J. P. Morgan & Company was not one of Mr. Woolworth's stores, where an industrious ribbon clerk could soon rise to assistant manager. It is possible that Davison took him along on this important mission not only for the help he would give but in part to satisfy his yearning for a larger role.

Straight was so eager to have *The New Republic* strike just the right note that he wrote to Croly warning him that its radicalism must be fair and sane, that it must never stoop to sensationalism or muckraking. Despite the agreed-upon limitation of his own influence, he was never shy about advancing his views. He strongly favored American military preparedness and scorned the antipreparedness men, writing, "I hope you will puncture the bunk of resolutions such as Hitchcocks [Senator Hitchcock of Nebraska] and all the Peace propaganda as thrown by Andrew Carnegie and his minions. It's all such an imposition on the public, mere chest throwing to gain credit in Nebraska by blustering about matters with which Nebraska has no concern. . . ." Nebraskans would have disputed his suggestion that they had no concern in such affairs. His own point of view was somewhat provincially Eastern, as in fact was that of almost everybody connected with *The New Republic*, and despite its effort at fairness the paper was sectional in flavor.

Dorothy had her visit with Adelaide—her stepbrother Bertie Randolph was of course in the service—while Straight and Davison often worked into the night. Davison's errand was to perfect the details of a plan whereby the Morgan firm would be the purchasing agent for Britain in America. The volume would be huge and the deal highly profitable to Morgan—this although the December 5 *New Republic* had a letter from Ray Stannard Baker warning against American exploitation of the war "to promote its own business and trade." As Straight put it later:

> I told [Davison] that if I were running his business for him and wanted to help the Allies I would suggest that they get their Ministers of Finance together, and cooperate on a joint financial policy just as they were doing in a military and naval way. He said nothing, but went that day to lunch with Asquith and Lloyd George, where he put forward the suggestion which was promptly adopted.

Thus Morgan became agent for all Allied purchases in the United States—an enormous enterprise. Straight felt that he did not receive credit for it. The Straights took Lord and Lady ffrench to dinner along with Max Müller, former Secretary of the British legation in Peking. "Streets full of soldiers—all so dark at night," Dorothy noted, and when they went to the show at the Empire, "All war references & jokes & war moving pictures." Lord Wodehouse, a member of the British polo team beaten by Harry's four, "came to tea with arm in sling from shrapnel wound—so thrilling to hear his accounts." The Straights dined also with William Cameron Forbes, who was in London with his assistant, Peter Bowditch, on one of those business missions (like Willard's) that the British felt bled them white and enriched the Americans.

". . . Lady Sybil Smith took me to Suffrage work rooms, etc., in East End," Dorothy wrote. "Sylvia Pankhurst took us about." Sylvia was perhaps the most astonishing of the militant Pankhursts, so opposed to the institution of marriage that she was later to flout the institution by bearing an illegitimate child. Ethel and Dick Derby turned up in London, as did Gertrude Vanderbilt Whitney, who had been visiting her "enemy" sister Gladys in neutral Switzerland and also looking into the possibility of founding in France at her own expense a hospital for Allied soldiers. Dorothy motored with the Derbys to Braintree to see trenches and wire entanglements constructed there against invasion. "German battleships bombarding Hartlepool & Scarborough," she observed.

On December 17 she left Willard and Davison to continue their work and sailed on the *Lusitania* with Gertrude and the Derbys. Although she was fond of Gertrude, and cherished her three children, there was a twelve-year difference in age and she was not really close to Gertrude any more than she was to any of her siblings and their spouses. Harry, with his occasional bursts of camaraderie, came closest to brotherhood despite their totally different outlooks. Gertrude, though she lived only a pleasant walk from Dorothy's place in Westbury, was in another world. Yet the two sisters-in-law were confronted by similar central conflicts that might have brought them closer. Gertrude, though she favored women's suffrage, was seldom politically active and was a Republican mainly by inheritance. It was her artistic ambitions and her friendship with long-haired Bohemian artists that the world of Society eyed somewhat askance. In Dorothy's case it was her political intensity and urge for reform that startled her contemporaries in Society who were suspicious of reform. Harry, however, regarded Gertrude's career in art more with resignation than approval, whereas Dorothy and Willard carried on an active intellectual communion. The two women might have been closer but for a temperamental gulf: Gertrude was a Bohemian herself, unhappy in her marriage, interested in many men but few women. Dorothy was the soul of propriety in things nonpolitical, possibly too nicey-nice for Gertrude, perhaps even entertaining some disapproval of Gertrude's mode of life. Dorothy was the more successful in resolving the conflict between her politics and her life in Society, being blessed with true friendliness and having many close women friends. She was perennially an officer or a leader in the Junior League—a leader and even nominated for office in the Colony Club, whose members averaged at least ten years older.

They landed December 23, in time for Dorothy to do hurried Christmas shopping for the children, "who are splendidly well & so adorable." Ethel Derby and Daisy Harriman arrived December 25 to spend several days with her at Westbury. Daisy's husband Borden had died December 1, so that the holiday was not a happy one for her. Dorothy was excessively lucky by comparison, for the tender Straight sent her a love note every day, one of them illustrated with a caricature of himself looking very gaunt due to his worry over her, another with a caricature showing him obese because of his exploits at the table. As always, he complained that she did not write him often enough and was niggardly about cables, which indeed she sometimes seems to have been.

". . . I've been tied down every minute," he wrote. ". . . *Please cable me Dorothy about yourself and the kids.* Why will you not do this—spend something on me—rather than the unemployed." (She had given to many causes, including $50,000 to Smith College, almost completing its drive for $1,000,000, and was soon to prove growing ecumenism by giving $5,000 toward the erection of St. Brigid's Catholic Church in Westbury.) He asked, as if only half in jest, whether she regarded him as too costly a plaything.

After January 3, 1915, Dorothy's diary went dead for an unprecedented three and a half months. Her handwriting in the entries, once so clear and graceful, had grown visibly hasty. The cessation may have been due to her dislike of putting down details that troubled her, or just plain weariness. During the interval, Straight returned with Davison late in January and was home only a few weeks before he was sent again to England on Morgan business, this time alone, in waters less safe than before. Straight recorded it in the form of a combined letter and journal addressed to his son (only twenty-six months old) and headed, "Diary of a Trip to London and Paris. Written for Whitney Straight, Esquire." Davison, he wrote to his son, had not been unaware of the danger:

> H.P.D. [Davidson] asked what your mother would think of it. I replied that she wouldn't like it but that if it were the game I knew that she would wish me to go. . . . The German declaration of a war zone . . . had gone into effect only eight days before. A number of merchant steamers had been sunk. The Lusitania on her last trip had hoisted the American flag which drew a mild remonstrance from Washington and ocean travel didn't look at all safe. . . . She was splendid. . . . We went through all the heart yearnings of those who part before action. . . . I am afraid she didn't sleep much that night. She showed it in the morning but there was no word, no tear, only smiles and cheerfulness. If you ever amount to anything it will be because of your Mother.
>
> We got away at ten the next morning. I last saw her as she walked cheerily down the dock as the big ship slipped along out into the stream. This I shall never forget. . . . This and the time we went through together in Peking before you were born. These are the things that knit you close, for all the fluff is stripped away and you realize how much you care.

He was a man of feeling and sensibility, trying to instill those qualities into his children. To Dorothy he wrote while on shipboard:

> . . . here I am all alone—skating over the world—I don't like it. I
> want you—I want you just as I did before on those sea-trips of accursed
> memory—when I left you to go over to see Harry—my how I ached men-
> tally and in my heart—and how books blurred in front of me—and bridge
> bored. They do the same things now. . . . But in place of uncertainty—
> thank Heaven—there is Faith and understanding isn't there Best Beloved.
> . . . But are we going on like this? Are we going to continue as privates
> or corporals or sergeants in Wall Street—when we might be captains of
> our own ship—and sail as we pleased? How about becoming editors as I
> suggested before—try this on your piano!

One might read into this a shade of doubt that the understanding,
though not the faith, was complete. He indulged his artist's eye in
another letter, chopped up by dashes as they often were, touching also
on his political philosophy:

> . . . turquoise in our wake—glistening, foaming under the bows and
> swirling alongside—purpling under the shadows of the clouds that tum-
> bled overhead—and I wanted my Sweetie—all day. . . . I read—finished
> Cramp in fact. . . . Imperial Americanism—is I believe impossible—
> that is in the sense of imperial Britain. I am sorry—for I am a born impe-
> rialist—all that Cramp says about Tolstoy and war . . . is extremely in-
> teresting—but we have a certain mission in the world—at least we ought
> to have—This too is freedom and justice and truth—we can help. . . .
> What we need is the ordering of the nation to its responsibilities—for the
> future—by showing how we have done things in the past—I don't mean
> by this any form of reaction far from it. But from the old days we may
> gather inspiration to face the modern task.

Straight reached London March 6, dined with the Pagets, and "had
quite an argument with some of . . . Almeric's Parliamentary colleagues about Anglo-American relations. Some of them got quite stuffy
when I pooh-poohed British virtue and her respect for the neutrality of
little states. It came out alright [sic] however as I assured them that the
United States was overwhelmingly pro-Ally. . . ." He commiserated
with Lord ffrench, who had finally got a large contract for Pauling &
Company, only to have it ruined by the war. He dined with John May-
nard Keynes, a Cambridge don who had contributed to *The New Republic* and was now attached to the Treasury. He called on Col. E. M.
House, "Wilson's alter ego." House had an apartment on East 68th
Street in New York, a block from the Straights, and was friendly. He

was on one of his early and quixotic efforts, approved by the President, to mediate among the warring nations and bring peace. Now he was anxious to get in touch with France's Foreign Minister Théophile Delcassé. He was "delighted," Straight noted, "when I told him of de Margerie and Casenave," both of whom knew Delcassé. Colonel House wrote in his later-to-be-famous diary:

> March 14, 1915—Willard Straight called this morning. He is a great friend of Casenave and also of Margerie, and Margerie a friend of Casenave and Delcassé, so the circle is fairly complete. I told Straight some things I wished told to Delcassé through Casenave and Margerie. This Straight promised to undertake. I wish Delcassé to know that in my opinion France is taking a big gamble in demanding peace terms that Germany will never accept unless the Allies reach Berlin. . . .
>
> Straight is to convey the thought that it will be of advantage to the Allies to have the good will of the President, and that the best way to get it is through me.

The message seemed simplistic, but Straight soon got to Paris and delivered it to both men. While abroad, he also reviewed his dissatisfaction with his Morgan post and all but reached a decision to resign, struggling nevertheless to be fair to Davison:

> It seemed to be a question of a partnership or nothing. . . . I had had some feeling that Davison wasn't particularly anxious to have me in the firm but that he preferred to use me for his own purposes outside. In thinking this I probably did him an injustice. No one could have been kinder than he—in general—though he was small in some matters, and quite ready to take to himself all the credit for ideas which came from me and which he used with great success.

To Dorothy he wrote lovingly but with his ritual of chiding: He missed her terribly and she seemed not to understand the extent of his loneliness or her cables to him would not have been so infrequent or so brief; she could have added words to them which would have meant a great deal to him. On the return voyage he encountered Capt. Frank McCoy, whom he had last seen in Manila and who was later to embark on a romance with Daisy Harriman. Straight was back home apparently early in April, still undecided about his course. Dorothy later wrote, after his death, perhaps with more sympathy than she took the trouble to show at the time:

He was forever dreaming dreams, albeit practical ones at that, and working out new ways of doing things and new things to be done. Almost every evening he would come home from the office with the same words on his lips—"I had a new idea today." In spite of myself I was forced to become the critic, for though many of the plans were sound in conception the means of execution were often not at hand. And so it was that I often had to break the blow of his disappointments. In many instances he was unable to convince his superiors of the value of his ideas and it became my task to try and prevent him from dwelling on what he considered his own ineptitude. . . . Wall Street was uncongenial and difficult for him. . . . it nearly broke his heart to see his ideas still-born because they did not promise to be immediately profitable. . . . But he was considered too radical, too much of an idealist, too deficient in business experience.

Business was normally a husband's private domain. (Flora Payne Whitney, for all her bossiness, had kept clear of *that* sphere of William Whitney's life.) In Dorothy's Venetian essay she had stressed her "great longing to become a part of [her husband's] life and help him when possible to do his work." Did she overplay that role?

In the midst of this the Germans sank the *Lusitania* May 7—an especially personal shock to the Straights because they had sailed on her, but more so because among the 128 Americans lost was Gertrude's younger brother Alfred Gwynne Vanderbilt, thirty-eight. The lonely Vanderbilt palace at 1 West 57th Street was in mourning. Theodore Roosevelt took fire at the President's cautious reaction to what the Colonel called "piracy and murder." *The New Republic*, which still hoped to carry Roosevelt's ensign in 1916, was measured, urging Wilson to avoid war if possible. But it spoke of Germany as the "world's outlaw," and its posture of neutrality, which had been losing conviction, was gone. While no one could equal Roosevelt in jingoistic fury, Straight joined him in calling for universal military training, arming to the hilt.

He did not, as was expected at the House of Morgan—an expectation that Davison for one fulfilled—dedicate every move and breath to his job. He lacked the massive concentration on 23 Wall Street that was demanded by 23 Wall Street. He did not, as he later admitted, master the complexities of the international banking business. He was too richly endowed with diverse talents, too susceptible to boredom, to funnel all his immense energies on one lone, constricting endeavor. Such things as his active club life, his polo and golf, his politics, his proprietary interest in Cornell, and his fascination with *The New Republic* subtracted much of his best thought and effort from J. P. Morgan & Company. To this was added Straight's endless yearning to own a newspaper—an end he could achieve only if Dorothy opened her purse very wide.

To her, the Morgan post, for all its disappointments, was safe. Her knowledge of his temperamental impatience, his occasional blues, and her urging that he stick to the job had held him in China in 1911. She had been vindicated. Where would he be now if he had quit? He had generously showered credit on her for it afterward. Why could he not play second fiddle under Davison for a few more years, meanwhile truly learning the business? The largest question of all was, if he left Morgan, what would he do then and how long would his volatile nature let him stay with his next choice?

On August 6 Dorothy went to Onteora, where Straight arrived the next day with Croly and Frankfurter. Strangely, they not only reviewed *New Republic* articles but also, in a circle, discussed the pros and cons of Straight's contemplated resignation. That he—and Dorothy—would permit his business problem to become a subject of such general discussion suggests the extent to which he was demoralized and searching for light.

By the time Croly and Frankfurter left the next day, Straight had still not made up his mind. He had never broken his habit of tardiness, and he and Dorothy were late on the night of August 9 when they left by car for Albany to catch the train to the civilian military camp at Plattsburg. They missed the train at Albany but by fast driving caught it at Troy at 1:40 A.M.

3. Rosewater and Pink Tea

STRAIGHT HAD strongly supported the idea of civilian military training pushed by Gen. Leonard Wood but whose very spirit had been Wood's old confrere of the war in Cuba, Theodore Roosevelt. After the *Lusitania* tragedy, President Wilson received telegrams from fifteen Roosevelt-oriented Harvard graduates including Theodore Roosevelt, Jr., Elihu Root, Jr., and Robert Bacon, Jr., Dorothy's former suitor, demanding that adequate military measures be taken, "however serious." Straight viewed international relations with a cooler eye than most of them and, remarkable for his time, had no illusions about the innocence of the British. But he saw German militarism as the great

threat, and American unpreparedness as folly. "Had England been able
. . . to throw a million men into the field on a moment's notice," he
wrote to Croly, "this war would not have been."

The Plattsburg encampment was largely composed of well-heeled,
Eastern-educated business and professional men—Straight's own class.
Mayor Mitchel of New York City was there as a private. The Roosevelt
family was well represented by Theodore, Jr., young Quentin Roosevelt, and the Colonel's son-in-law, Dr. Dick Derby. Indeed Roosevelt
himself was soon on hand. He arrived August 25, "every inch the
Rough Rider, wearing a wide-brimmed hat, a riding jacket of military
cut, breeches, and leather leggings." Through field glasses he watched a
sham battle and then a bayonet charge that made him bare many of his
famous teeth as he shouted "Bully!" Contempt for President Wilson was
scarcely concealed when Roosevelt made a speech to the assembled
recruits, saying, without needing to name names, that to rely on "high-
sounding words unbacked by deeds, is proof of a mind that dwells only
in the realm of shadow and of shame." He drew a laugh when a half-
grown Airedale approached him in fawning manner, then rolled on its
back, its paws feebly in the air, and Roosevelt said he was a very nice
dog: "His present attitude is one of strict neutrality."

"Ethel and her baby have gone off to visit Dorothy Straight," the Colonel wrote to another son, Kermit. "Willard Straight, by the way, is in
camp and has been made a Lieutenant." And he wrote to his son
Archibald, "Ethel and Dorothy were up there to look after their respective husbands, Ethel still somewhat depressed and somewhat warlike
because Dick had not been made a Corporal."

Straight, who had thought seriously of attending West Point, had had
two years at a military academy and had often regarded himself as more
soldier than diplomat, had something of a military advantage. Shortly
after he returned from Plattsburg he decided that his Morgan post was
insupportable, writing:

> The office sent me to meet Russian generals and sich [sic], made me a
> courier because I could speak French. My determination [to resign] had
> been strengthened by the fact that . . . Lord Reading and M. Homberg
> at the head of the Anglo-French Commission came over to negotiate the
> great Allied loan. I thought that I might have been of service in connec-
> tion with these negotiations, but I was asked to perform no work, and this
> rankled. Again I felt that I was being excluded. Again doubtless I was
> wrong, but I was ambitious. . . .

Although money was important, he made no mention of this but stressed, perhaps without realizing it, the lack of recognition and praise, of status, which were vital to him. Heavy sales to the Allies had already brought glorious prosperity to the United States. Straight, in speeches to various business groups, had stressed that "a great foreign trade opportunity is today presented to us" by the European war and that "our competitors are less active than . . . in the past." Now the Morgan firm was to furnish the indigent Allies with money to continue their purchases. The Straights had M. Homberg and the French commissioners and their wives as guests at Westbury, spoke to them in their own tongue, and had a social success that remained in Homberg's memory years later when he met Straight in France, and which doubtless aided the Morgan negotiations. But Straight was excluded from any part in negotiating the great $500,000,000 Morgan loan to the British and French signed on September 25. "What do Morgan and Schwab care for world peace when there are big profits in world war?" Senator LaFollette demanded, as expected. A week before the signing, on September 18, Straight's departure was made public:

> J. P. Morgan & Co. announced last night that Willard Straight, who has been associated with the firm for several years . . . will retire on Oct. 1 to pursue special studies in international law at the Columbia Law School. . . . Mr. Straight has had an interesting history for a man who is not yet 36. . . .

Straight had abilities far beyond any Morgan partner. The trouble was, they were not Morgan abilities. The artist, the writer, the politician, the "reformer," the humorist, the sometime disputant did not fit in with the dollar-chasing workhorses of the great banking house. They decided, it was clear, that his coup in China had been the result of special circumstances including his knowledge of the language and of politics there—not useful elsewhere. The firm did not urge him to stay on, as it would have had he hatched enough of those brilliant ideas for Davison to appropriate.

International law was a profession calculated to aid Straight whether he continued in his present line of work or entered the public service, which was still in the back of his mind. It was ironical that shortly before he became thus technically unemployed, the Straights moved into their new home at Fifth Avenue and 94th Street. Although it far exceeded its planned cost of $200,000 (not including furnishings), it demonstrated that Dorothy did not feel the need for grandeur that had been so strong a trait in her father. There was no Stanford White, no raids on European palaces, no walls hung with scores of paintings. Architect Delano, a Yale man (1895) with a later diploma from the Ecole des Beaux Arts in Paris, had designed a handsome, Federal-style, four-storied building with a circular main hall and a drawing room and library on the second floor. Ample space was allowed for guests and for servants, there was a small organ, and there was a solarium and garden on the roof but no ballroom. Indeed ballrooms had gone out of style except for the few remaining upholders of the tradition of parties for hundreds of people, a group to which the Straights did not belong.

Willard did not con his lawbooks for long. While he did, he drew closer to Roosevelt although *The New Republic*, seemingly without knowing it, was gradually drawing away from him. Straight was working with Roosevelt in an effort to strengthen the preparedness movement in Congress, where it had sturdy opposition. "I have just seen Ted and Willard Straight and some of the other people interested in the matter here," Roosevelt wrote to the journalist Joseph Medill McCormick, his ardent supporter in Chicago. ". . . keep in touch with Ted and Willard before committing me to anything. . . ." He also gave restrained approval to a *New Republic* editorial about him, although he disputed its observation that he overstated. "I do not believe I do overstate. . . ," he wrote to Straight. "Of course, I have got to be emphatic to attract attention. We are not in a rose-water parlor pink tea crisis at present. . . ."

But three weeks later a *New Republic* article, "The Newer Nationalism," praised much too faintly a Roosevelt speech in Philadelphia. He wrote to Straight in small part:

> Now, these statements on the part of *The New Republic*'s editors really make me feel more amiable to them than I have felt for a long time. I have felt that they were sinning against the light. But really I think I have been mistaken. I think they are nice, well-meaning geese—early Victorian geese. . . . Love to Dorothy.

He also remarked elsewhere that *The New Republic* "was run by 'three circumcized Jews and three anemic Gentiles,' and it didn't much matter which you were." That ended the uneasy accord between *The New Republic* and Roosevelt. If he was going to run for President in 1916, he would have to do it without the aid of that publication. And if Straight, still his dear friend, hoped to ride on his bandwagon, Roosevelt would first have to find substantial public support. Meanwhile, Croly had written to Dorothy: "Thank you, my dear Dorothy, for what you are doing for the staff of the paper this Xmas. They have worked well and deserve recognition. Sometime, I hope we can give it to them out of net profits, but until we can it [is] very good of you to add this much more to all you have done for us."

4. A Jellyfish Won't Fight

How COULD Willard Straight, the quondam golden boy of Wall Street, the inventor and frequenter of clubs, the intimate of mandarins, ambassadors, presidents, and captains of industry, be other than driven mad by the quiet and modesty of Columbia's campus on Morningside Heights? How could he, as he opened his lawbooks, refrain from groaning at their overpowering dullness? How could he stand the classroom drone of instructors who had scarcely been beyond the Hudson, or the anonymity of insignificant students around him? One struggles against the suspicion that Straight, after a few weeks of this, was looking wildly for some means of escape.

Less than three months after he began his law course, a group headed by Frank A. Vanderlip, president of the National City Bank, founded the American International Corporation, capitalized at $50,000,000, and offered Straight the post of third vice-president. Since the corporation aimed to find and finance large engineering projects such as railroads in foreign countries, the job seemed in his special province. It offered him that wonderful thing, recognition. There was, however, an embarrassing aspect to it. To be attracted by something new so soon would lay him open to the belief that he had taken the law course as a temporary expedient or that his resolution had flagged.

Croly advised him to accept the offer, but Croly may have divined that his heart was not truly in the law. Straight went with Dorothy to call on Roosevelt and ask his advice. It is not impossible that the Rough Rider, well knowing Straight's dynamism and the unlikelihood of his being enthralled by abstruse legal finicalities, could see in his eyes and his whole expression that the answer he wanted was Yes.

If Dorothy was upset at this new suggestion of inconstancy, it does not appear in her diary, which was blank at the time. Straight now took an office at the Equitable Building at 120 Broadway—once the address of E. H. Harriman of sainted memory, where Harry Payne Whitney now maintained an office that he visited irregularly. Straight also lured into his employ Albert H. Fiedler, who had been his secretary at the Morgan firm, and hired other help.

Perhaps it was in connection with this new employment that the Straights were in Washington at the beginning of 1916, staying with the delightful Daisy Harriman at 1709 H Street, a stone's throw from the house in which Dorothy was born. Although seventeen years Dorothy's senior, Daisy was young at heart, immersed both in Democratic politics and Society, and familiar with what was going on at the important embassies. She was a founder of Dorothy's Colony Club, she had often been a guest of the Straights, and they would surely have visited her on the ground of friendship alone. It is possible also that she knew of moves in the administration and events abroad that might give Straight advance information about construction projects for which his firm might get contracts for the financing. The American International Corporation (AIC) wanted immediate commitments and would soon have at least one large contract in China obtained through Straight's enterprise. The firm was also anticipating the huge amount of public construction that was being postponed by the European war. It was doubted that the war could last many months longer—this was an almost universal error— and part of Willard's job was to seek out such contacts for the future. No sooner had the Straights returned to New York than they entertained a Belgian mission headed by Carton de Wiart that was looking for a loan and would need even more money after the war. Straight took the Belgians over to call on Colonel Roosevelt, whose sympathy for the Belgians—and whose contempt for the President for failing to denounce the invaders of that country with Rooseveltian rage—was at full tide.

Never would Straight permit work to interfere with his celebration of the Greatest Woman in History. On January 23, Dorothy's twenty-ninth birthday, she arrived at the Fifth Avenue place late in the afternoon to find that he had arranged for her one of those special occasions in which he took boyish joy—a surprise party, with great baskets of flowers.

Straight was giving speeches on the general subject of foreign trade to groups such as the Advertising League and the National Foreign Trade Council, and a series of them at City College. The political picture was murky, with no new Bull Moose or Progressive backing appearing for Roosevelt, and Charles Evans Hughes not certain he wanted the Republican nomination for the presidency. Walter Lippmann had a long interview with President Wilson, who seemed so cordial and reasonable that *The New Republic*'s opposition to him declined. It declined still more when Colonel House invited Croly and Lippmann to lunch at the Princeton Club in New York. "We were not able to find out just what the object of the interview was," Croly wrote to Straight, "unless it was that Col. House wished to look us over. He was very cordial and seems to be reading The New Republic regularly. . . . Both Walter and I brought away a very high opinion of the man's ability and good faith."

The New Republic still had a circulation of only 24,000 but was influential among shapers of opinion. Colonel House, foreseeing a close election, was angling to bring it into the Wilson camp. On March 15, Dorothy saw Willard off on the *New Amsterdam* as he sailed with an older AIC colleague, Nelson Perkins, to explore business possibilities in Europe. A statistician and two secretaries accompanied them plus Straight's manservant, Bennett, whose first name George was never used and who might seem a luxury under war conditions but without whom Straight was lost. He had had a manservant ever since he was twenty-one. They heard en route of the sinking of the steamer *Tubantia* and were glad to reach Falmouth. Straight, who had talked with Ambassador Spring Rice, had papers that permitted them to land immediately instead of waiting in line for examination with the hoi polloi. The British were offended that America had not entered the war following the *Lusitania* sinking, but Straight, who felt the same way, got on very well with them.

In London the visitors installed themselves at Claridge's and called on some of Straight's old friends, including Lord ffrench, the Astors, and Cameron Forbes, the latter now serving as AIC agent in London with Peter Bowditch still assisting him. Warwick Greene, another former Philippine hand, was also in London working for Polish relief. Straight visited, with Cornell warmth, his old classmate Alfred Sze, now Chinese Minister to England. The newcomers called on literally scores of people—perhaps more than a hundred—who might aid their business designs: Arthur Balfour, Edward Stettinius, Hugh Gibson, and Philip Kerr among them. They discussed investment possibilities ranging from the Trans-Andean Railway and the Pernambuco trams to the construction of a sewer system in St. Petersburg. Straight kept an account of it running to 125 typewritten pages—some 35,000 words—addressed again to his son Whitney:

> Dinner with the American Ambassador and Mrs. [Walter H.] Page, the Dutch Minister Van Swinderen . . . Cora Countess of Strafford . . . Lord and Lady Cranmore. . . . Great interest everywhere in what the United States will do. Croly's cable and one from your Mother this morning . . . indicate that things are going well and that there may be a break [in relations with Germany]. We are praying for it. But I fear that a jelly fish won't fight. . . . I went to see Mrs. [Adelaide] Lambart, your

Mother's step sister. Her husband is on Admiral de Robeck's staff in the Mediterranean and has apparently had many hairbreadth escapes. She lost her brother [Bertie, whom Dorothy remembered so well] some months ago. All her friends have been killed. She was very pathetic. . . . I went to see Lady Cunard, who had been writing notes and inviting me to various entertainments. She produced the Duchess of Rutland and the beautiful and they say wicked Lady Diana Manners, with two swains. . . . I didn't care much for any of them and escaped as soon as possible.

He encountered Lady Susan Townley, whom he had known in his earliest days in Peking: "She made some rather nasty but perfectly characteristic remarks about [Americans] wanting the war to go on so that we might get rich." He worked diligently, sometimes until late at night, part of his work being transacted with wine over napery. He attended theaters, balls, and parties so that the valet Bennett must have been kept busy. One gets a picture of Straight constantly on the move, taxiing from the office of a banker in the City to call on the Chancellor of the Exchequer and then the president of the Board of Trade (he talked with both), thence to a contractor, and from there to his club or possibly Cliveden. His weekends were crowded socially, but he usually attended the gatherings with business in view. He bought shoes at Peal's. He stopped in at St. James's Club to pay his dues.

He and Perkins crossed to Paris, stayed at the Crillon, and called on American Ambassador William G. Sharp and many French officials, one of them Straight's old friend de Margerie, at whose party in Peking Straight had danced the cakewalk. But it was with Belgian officials, in exile from their invaded country, that the two AIC men discussed the most promising plans for future loans. With a party of Belgians, Straight made a motor trip into the small corner of that country near Nieuport not occupied by the Germans, hearing frequent artillery fire. His tour was just the sort to make soldiers in the trenches boil—the making of money in the war that cost them their comfort and safety—but it was a crime he was soon to expiate. Back in Paris, Straight called on Herman Harjes of the Morgan office there, which recalled to him the suspenseful days of his courtship with Dorothy: "He was most pleasant but the fact that I am no longer in the family with these men whom I am so fond of gives me a pang of regret every now and then."

Indeed he seemed to regret his resignation from the Morgan firm, which he thereafter held in the greatest respect. The two men crossed the Channel again in water so rough that Straight was sick and "felt like the Tommies [aboard] who groaned 'For Gawd's sake toike me back t' th' trenches.' " While in England he got word by cable of a *New Republic* article unfavorable to Roosevelt. He cabled in protest to Croly, who was away, so that Lippmann undertook to explain. The paper, Lippmann said, had "leaned over backward" to be kind to Roosevelt. Only recently the editors had discovered to their chagrin that they had somehow missed reading Roosevelt's *Outlook* article of September 23, 1914, which proved that he had then not only failed to advocate any American protest at the Belgian invasion but had been quite satisfied with the "old policy of isolation":

> I feel that since the New Republic had said so often that Roosevelt would have acted in a different way about Belgium than Wilson did, it was clearly our duty to eat our words and if possible make Roosevelt eat his. This is what we did in the article about which you have evidently heard rumors by cable. . . . Personally there are few things in Roosevelt's career that have shocked me as much as this revelation of how his mind works. . . .

Straight, terribly homesick, paid his usual visit to the Pagets, now at Eastbourne. Pauline, a somewhat unorthodox believer in Christian Science and also in massage, had hurled every ounce of her feeble strength into the war effort. She had turned Deepdene into a rehabilitation center for wounded soldiers and she supplied the War Office with fifty trained masseuses at her own expense. Almeric, however, had an idea that Straight could help get him opulent American directorships: "He'd like to go on the Guaranty Trust and the Eastman Kodak," Straight wrote without comment.

"Willard sails home today!" Dorothy wrote May 13, and she met him on the twenty-first—he had been gone ten weeks—then drove him out to Westbury. Roses were blooming there and friends called on the Straights all afternoon. "Supper alone—fine evening," Dorothy wrote. On July 4, Prather Fletcher and Walter Lippmann were among the guests, and Straight, after polo and dinner, read aloud the Declaration of Independence.

Dorothy had been abstaining from riding and similar exertions. They took a cottage at Southampton, where the effervescent Edith Lindley was a frequent companion, Dorothy read *Heredity and Environment,* and (after the customary raillery about the likelihood of her child being born on Labor Day) her second son was born three days in advance of that date, on September 1. "Fair hair & blue eyes & a real nose!" she exulted. When the boy, Michael Straight, was five weeks old, a German U-boat sank six ships of foreign registry off Nantucket, though all aboard were saved. Dorothy and her entourage joined a general exodus from shore places, moving back to Westbury.

Meanwhile the Roosevelt campaign had guttered and Straight and Croly had come to a parting of the political ways. Straight could not convince Croly that the Republican Hughes—whom Roosevelt supported with the faintest of enthusiasm—was the better man. *The New Republic* came out for Wilson while publishing a letter from Straight explaining why he disagreed: ". . . I agree that Mr. Wilson and the Democratic Party have enacted certain admirable pieces of legislation. I believe, however, that this Administration has lowered the prestige of the United States and in so doing has aggravated the problems which the American people will be called upon to face in connection with the world readjustment after the European War."

"STRAIGHT DIFFERS FROM NEW REPUBLIC," *The Times* headlined as if in surprise. Women's suffrage had been overwhelmingly defeated in New York State the previous year—by three to one in New York County. The almost automatic relegation of women from financial or political affairs was underlined in Straight's statement that "I have been responsible for the financial support" of the paper. *The New Republic's* own statement said that Straight "undertook to procure a specific sum with which to finance the experiment. . . ." In both declarations Dorothy went unmentioned, which she may well have preferred

5. *Major Straight*

A FORTNIGHT after Wilson's election the Straights were at the Homestead in Hot Springs. "Heavenly day & deliciously fresh, bracing air," Dorothy noted. She had a pleasant conversation with another guest, John D. Rockefeller, read *Mr. Britling Sees it Through* to Willard as he sketched, and exulted over a 103 round of golf. "News came this morning of Pauline's death yesterday in England," she told her diary November 23 and went on without comment to other matters. Pauline's illness had been so chronic and painful that perhaps her death could be called a blessing. Among those at her services were Gen. Sir Arthur Paget, Mrs. Page, wife of the American Ambassador, and the Duchess of Marlborough. The romance climaxed by the proposal at Taormina had run its course, but Almeric was to marry another American girl of wealth within five years.*

Straight had become a persuasive public speaker and had addressed groups in Chicago, Pittsburgh, and New Orleans as well as New York on aspects of international trade. He dined with the Japanese Ambassador in the line of duty, to foster projects for AIC. A Straight guest was Wellington Koo, Chinese Minister to Washington, whom Willard had known in Peking. The Straights dined at Sagamore alone with Colonel Roosevelt, for whom Dorothy's affection was still strong but her respect for his politics dwindling. They also kept exchanging dinners with Mayor and Mrs. John Purroy Mitchel. Straight, who for three years had been president of the American Asiatic Association, tired of its grubby little *Journal* and prevailed on Dorothy to finance its truly splendid successor, *Asia* magazine—good in itself and also good for business in that part of the world. The Straights dined at the Martin Egans on Park Avenue with other guests including Herbert Hoover, who had made such a reputation as Chairman of the Commission for the Relief of Belgium. On December 30, 1916, Aunt Laura died in Oswego and Professor Morse Stephens fell seriously ill with pneumonia in New York and was brought to the Straight Fifth Avenue home. He hovered near death for days before he was nursed back to health—a service he never forgot. At Willard's urging, Dorothy sat for a portrait by Walter Dean Goldbeck, a friend of Gertrude's, who painted her in stark contrast of colors, cool and self-possessed of mien.

By February 1917 Straight had been with AIC for thirteen months. It appears that on the side he was promoting business enterprises of his own. If he was satisfied, the idealist and adventurer in him was more excited by the prospects opening up as war approached with Germany. On February 3, German Ambassador Bernstorff was at last given his passports, and Roosevelt and Straight took prompt measures. Roosevelt asked permission of the administration he had vilified to form a division to take to France, asking that Straight's friend Capt. Frank McCoy, who had been a military aide when Roosevelt was President, be his chief of staff with the rank of colonel. Straight was immediately appointed by Mitchel as Chairman of the Mayor's Committee on National Defense. In this capacity he made patriotic speeches to citizens' groups and sought to bring order into the helter-skelter preparation for war. In

---

* In 1921 he married Edith Miller, daughter of the William Starr Millers of New York, who had been guests at at least two William C. Whitney parties. By her he had three daughters and outlived her, dying in 1949, aged eighty-eight.

his effort for a substantial government post, however, he acted circuitously, being more embarrassed than the unembarrassable Roosevelt by
his political position. He had attended Hughes meetings, marched in a
Hughes parade, and there was that black-and-white statement published
in *The New Republic* saying that Wilson had damaged America's prestige. It was not the best record to take to Washington while asking favors
of the Democrats. Although he was a good friend of the powerful Colonel House, and had done House a favor in Europe, he approached
House for some specific position through that influential Democrat
Daisy Harriman. House replied to Mrs. Harriman:

> Your letter in regard to Willard Straight came too late as you now
> know.
> I do not believe that place would have been a good one for him. It
> seems to me he can sometime be used to better advantage. I have a very
> high regard for him and at the first opportunity I shall suggest his name
> for service.

That was somewhat encouraging but vague. When war was declared
April 6, Straight pulled strings for a State Department post. Perhaps
feeling some penance necessary, he wrote to President Wilson admitting
that he had opposed him but assuring him that "your memorable words
that have aroused the world have made me grateful that you were elected. . . . I trust that it shall be my privilege to serve under you." The
Straights bought a country place on the Bethesda side of Washington,
evidently in the belief that he would be working there. Straight was well
acquainted with the Counselor of the State Department, Frank Polk,
who was a good friend of Mayor Mitchel's. Straight's groomsman and
tennis partner from years earlier, with whom he had kept in touch,
William Phillips, was now Assistant Secretary of State. Still Straight
thought it best to work through Mrs. Harriman, a charmer whose smile
could perform miracles. She noted in her diary April 27, 1917:

> Met Colonel House today motoring and had two minutes' talk with
> him. I managed to pour out in no time how I had just been to see Frank
> Polk at the State Department about Willard Straight's going into the
> Department to help out during the war. The Colonel said he would talk
> to F.P. tonight and Bill Phillips. . . . The Colonel is most anxious for
> the sake of the Administration, that Willard be drawn into that work in-
> stead of getting a commission in the army as he threatens to do.

On that same day, a Friday, Dorothy wrote in *her* diary: "Willard has
gone to Washington—until Monday—to take his officers' exam Sunday."

Impatient as always, he doubtless reasoned that if the State Department wanted him it could retrieve him from the Army. He made speeches to men's groups informing them of the rules of the draft. At Cornell, where he was now a trustee, he contributed an ambulance along with $600 to maintain it in France. Dorothy became an officer in the Mayor's Committee of Women on National Defense. Patriotism, if somewhat less fervent west of Pennsylvania, gripped the East. Cornell was sending to France thirty-three of its collegians so eager to fight that they contributed $9,000 to cover their expenses for six months, which, it was assumed, would easily see the war's end. They were the first to go abroad, but three Princeton units were forming and outfits from Yale and other colleges were not far behind. On May 23, Straight was commissioned a major in the adjutant general's reserve corps and assigned to Governor's Island, a fifteen-minute boat ride from lower Manhattan. Though not yet paunchy, he had gained weight, his hairline had receded still farther, and he now wore glasses, but with his height, his handsomeness, and his smile—and the attention he gave to his uniform—he made a fine figure. He had hardly arrived there before another new major, Lloyd Griscom, came to the island and noted that he was assigned for instruction "to none other than Willard Straight, only a major himself, but with the inestimable advantage of a week's longer experience."

The nation's mobilization was felt everywhere. Walter Lippmann left *The New Republic* to work in Washington with the War Department. "Gen. Pershing lands in France!" Dorothy wrote June 8, and on June 26, "*U.S. troops in France!*" Meanwhile she had presided over a large war-work committee meeting at City Hall; she led one of many teams of women who set out to collect a total of $100,000,000 in New York for the Red Cross; she was one of the committee that raised $80,000 for the French by staging a huge patriotic-musical rally for the visiting Marshal Joffre at the Metropolitan Opera House, where Gertrude Whitney arranged a "Tableau of Nations Assembled in Homage to the New Democracy" in which Ethel Barrymore appeared as America, Mrs. Arthur Scott Burden as Britannia, and Mrs. James B. Eustis as France, and at which Paderewski, Jacques Thibaud, and Louise Homer performed; along with five hundred prominent Society women, Dorothy heard a speech by Herbert Hoover at the home of Mrs. Vincent Astor and joined them all in pledging utmost food economy to prevent hunger among the Allies; and with Ruth Morgan and others, she set up a cannery under the Williamsburg Bridge for the salvaging of fresh fruits and vegetables normally discarded as slightly damaged. Straight was engrossed in paperwork at Governor's Island, usually coming home as from an office, and joining in other efforts such as the mobilization of unused land on Long Island (including Straight land) for gardens and farms.

Into this commotion of the present came an echo of the past when Dorothy wrote in her diary on June 27, "Uncle Oliver died this A.M." At seventy-eight he had long outlived his two brothers and two sisters and had virtually disappeared from public notice. Dorothy had apparently never visited him—her godfather—though he died at the same mansion at 825 Fifth Avenue, a pleasant walk south of the Straight home. With Willard she attended his small funeral at his home, then with her brothers but without Willard rode to Cleveland in Harry's private car for the burial. The Colonel had been one of the nation's wealthiest men, leaving $178,893,655. The Oswego newspaper, which kept an eye on the Straights, leaped to the conclusion that most of the estate would be divided among the remaining three Whitney children and headlined, "MRS. STRAIGHT / WILL GET THIRTY / MILLIONS MORE." Mrs. Straight evidently got not a penny, whereas Harry was left one valuable painting he had admired, Turner's *Juliet and Her Nurse*. Payne, the favorite nephew to the last, got something like $75,000,000, which made *him* one of the richest men in the country. It all revived memories of the family schism. Could Harry and Dorothy, however free they were from financial worry, see Payne thus rewarded without unpleasant thoughts about how he had won the reward? Dorothy, true to her nature, eschewed mention of money in her diary.

Certainly the Straights hoped to clarify Willard's standing with the State Department when they took the midnight train to Washington July 11. Dorothy had a short conference with Dr. Ray Lyman Wilbur of the Food Administration, but there was a gathering at the Longworths' on H Street at which Frank Polk was present along with Mrs. Harriman, George Marvin, Prather Fletcher, and a few others. The Longworths of course were as well disposed toward Straight as was Daisy, and this would have seemed the time to get some favorable word from Polk. But nothing happened. Obviously the Hughes man was not wanted by the Democrats.

Returning to Westbury, the Straights had as guests Brig. Gen. and Mrs. William Mason Wright, whom they had met in Washington. The general, a New Jerseyan who had fought in the Santiago campaign, in the Philippines, and with Funston at Vera Cruz, was to reappear in Straight's life. Willard took the Wrights on the obligatory visit to Roosevelt. The glacial romance between Fletcher and Beatrice Bend, which had been inching along imperceptibly for eight years, reached its destination in the Straight living room at Westbury on July 25, when they were married there by Dr. Slattery of Grace Church. Fletcher was forty-four, whereas Beatrice's age went unmentioned. Among the thirty guests, including Daisy Harriman, George Marvin, Maurice Casenave, and the Bishops, was William Phillips of the State Department. The newly married couple, loaded with a hamper of food and champagne given them by the Straights, left by train for Mexico City, where Fletcher was the new American Ambassador. For the first time in many years, Dorothy could not call on Beatrice and know that she would come.

On September 3 Dorothy recorded, "Willard received his orders yesterday evening to leave at once for Fort Sill." She drove him to Jamaica and he was off by train with all his duffle. It had been seven months since he had first sought to land a Washington post. Colonel House had failed him, the State Department had failed him, and now, because of his politics, he seemed sucked into that great grinding Army machine that had no thought of personalities or feelings. To see him removed from friendly, adjacent, paper-shuffling Governor's Island to distant Oklahoma seemed in a sense to Dorothy like watching him march off to battle. Some friends felt that Straight, at thirty-seven, had no right to leave his wife and three children and go careering off into a young man's war. It may have been only coincidence that General Wright (now a major general) at the same time was appointed commander of Camp Doniphan at Fort Sill, or it is possible that Wright asked for Straight to serve under him.

6. *The Music of Her Life*

IT WAS not easy for Straight to leave home even to visit pleasant surroundings, since he quickly had to cope with his separation anxiety. He still kept the seventh and twenty-third of each month as festive days, "their" days on which throughout their six years of marriage he had brought Dorothy flowers and arranged the rambunctious celebrations that she enjoyed observing as much as he enjoyed creating. En route to Oklahoma, he wrote to Dorothy from St. Louis on the fifth, saying that she should get the letter on their day, the seventh. His letter of the seventh showed him to be aching for her. On the twenty-seventh he wrote in reproach that he had had no letter from her for three days, no pictures of the children, not even an acknowledgment of his telegram on the twenty-third. He could not understand, he said, her strange failure to write when her letters meant so much to him, nor could he comprehend her niggardliness about sending telegrams. Whether there was news or not made not the slightest difference. The link between them must be steady. "I wish you'd telegraph me every Monday that you're all well, whether anyone came down, what you've been doing." He never wrote angrily or bitterly but in a tone of hurt. His separation anxiety, rather than being ludicrous, was usually childlike and touching, a reminder of earlier ordeals, and it always put Dorothy in her most motherly attitude.

Straight was assistant to the adjutant of the Thirty-fifth Division, made up of recruits mostly from Kansas and Nebraska and commanded by General Wright, with whom he was on excellent terms. There were the sometimes unpleasant inoculations to be taken and there was unpredictable prairie weather: "The wind blew a hurricane all night and the tent flapped," he wrote to Dorothy, "—and the framing creaked so that I could hardly sleep. Then there was a roaring thunderstorm—and today it's blown hard—now we are having what is known out here as a 'Norther'." There were aspects of military life that he enjoyed so long as he could check his fractious patience and receive enough of that vital tonic, recognition.

Dorothy was now so busy with war work that she was leaving the children with governesses some friends thought not too capable, returning home late and tired with letters to write to Willard and others. Keeping two spacious houses going as she was, she had a large staff: a secretary, a household manager, butler, her personal maid Louisa, a governess, nursery maid, a cook and two second cooks, kitchen maid, pantry maid, three housemaids, three laundresses, a houseman, a second man, and two summer caretakers. There was also Bennett, temporarily released from serving as Straight's valet and now listed as "clerical assistant," a supervisor of grounds and outdoor help, two chauffeurs, and several stablemen, so that the total was well over two dozen. Although Dorothy's temper could sputter when she was pushed too far, and she did not regard servants as equals, some thought her excessively forbearing with the help and that a few of them took advantage of her. Her butler, Grove, had previously worked in that capacity for Harry,

who let him go because he was somewhat dour of mien. Dorothy took
him and kept him.

Undoubtedly with Dorothy's earnest encouragement, every effort was
made to place Straight in some administrative or diplomatic role, or if
not that, in the Army general staff. His onetime press colleague in
Japan, Martin Egan (who was now, of all things, employed by J. P.
Morgan as Davison's assistant), "knew all the brass" both civilian and
military, and was doing what he could for him. Herbert Croly and Colonel House had become so friendly that Croly visited House's apartment
every week to discuss the political situation. Late in September Croly
wrote to Straight quite excitedly. President Wilson had just announced
that House was to be entrusted with the preparations for the peace conference, which it was taken for granted would take place soon now that
America was in the war. House told Croly that he wanted Lippmann to
be one of his aides and invited Croly to be present at the peace meetings:

> He . . . stated that I would have full access to the material collected by
> the [Peace] Commission and would participate informally in its delibera-
> tions. . . . If it turns out as good as it looks it means, of course, that all
> our work [in *The New Republic*] . . . will be crowned by the opportunity
> of actually having something to say about the way in which the American
> case is put at the Peace Conference; and that, furthermore, if I attend the
> Peace Conference myself, I would be in an extremely strong position to
> know what was going on and to publish a series of semi-official articles.
> . . . I am going to ask Colonel House whether he will not assign you to
> work [on the same project] in either Paris or London. . . .

In October, Lippmann wrote to Dorothy, "I suppose Herbert has told
you that the Colonel has Willard very much in mind for some kind of
semi-diplomatic, semi-intelligence work job in Europe? He spoke most
warmly again of Willard. . . ."

Indeed the Colonel always talked optimistically about making use of
Straight's abilities, but nothing seemed to happen. Straight had apparently resigned almost immediately from AIC, but he had kept his offices in the Equitable Building and had a few financial projects of his
own, to which he attended by telegram and mail to his secretary Fiedler, who remained there with a small staff. Straight was also advising on
the editorial content of both *The New Republic* and *Asia*, dealing with
Croly, in a rather lordly way, through Fiedler. "I agree with you fully
about the desirability of publishing more military stuff," Croly wrote to
him. Croly was nobody's yes-man and would always stand up for his

beliefs, but he also knew that Straight was well informed, clear-minded, and a far more interesting writer than Croly himself. Although *The New Republic* was by all odds one of the most thoughtfully patriotic publications in the country, Croly was being harassed by the intolerant super-patriotic "sentry" organizations springing up everywhere, to whom anyone who did not describe Germans as Huns was suspect. One of these complaints came from Ralph Easley of the National Civic Federation (on whose letterhead appeared the names of Harry P. Davison, Robert Bacon, Elihu Root, and others), suggesting that *The New Republic* was "insidious and dangerous," that it gave off "poisonous emanations" and might be backed by German money.

Dorothy, now at Southampton, picked beach plums with the children and canned seventeen jars of beach plum jam for the cause. Potatoes had been planted in some of her former flower gardens at Westbury, and she noted after visiting Camp Mills with five-year-old Whitney, "Dug potatoes when we returned." It was surely the first time in her life that the daughter of Flora and William C. Whitney had had a spading fork in her hands.

In October she went by train to Oklahoma for a brief visit with Willard. So far the strategy of finding more suitable employment for him had failed, but on October 29 he was suddenly transferred to Washington and charged with organizing the administration overseas of the War Risk Insurance Bureau. Enlisted men were now offered federal insurance at low cost—an offer comparatively easy to extend to soldiers still in the United States but more complicated for men already shipped abroad. Straight studied the problem and prepared a program that the War and Treasury departments, jointly in charge, approved. He took up temporary residence at the "club" at 1718 H Street but was soon to go to Europe, a prospect unnerving to Dorothy. There was hectic train travel, Willard riding to meet Dorothy in New York, Dorothy riding to meet Willard in Washington. Each had traveled that line so often that they knew individual farms along the way. Dorothy spent a week in Washington, where they mourned together the election loss of Mayor Mitchel to Hearst's candidate, Judge John F. Hylan. Dorothy went to Rock Creek Park to see St. Gaudens's brooding memorial to Mrs. Henry Adams even though it was not the most cheerful thing in her present mood. She returned to New York alone November 19 to attend a Junior League meeting and also to preside over a war-work meeting at City Hall. Terrified at first at the thought of leading a meeting, she had come around to mere nervousness. *Town Topics* thought she did well:

At the long speaker's table sat Mrs. Straight, Mrs. Charles Cary Rumsey, Mrs. Courtlandt Barnes and Mrs. Henry Moskowitz, all so simply costumed that a fashion writer would have found nothing of interest in their gowns. Mrs. Straight called the meeting to order, and in an easy manner explained the object of the gathering—the hope to establish a clearing house for the different charities. Every syllable was heard even by those standing near the door. She is far too slender now, and very tired and pale, but she has gained much in manner and self-possession since those days when as Dorothy Whitney she depended on the Bends to say and do everything for her.

They spent a weekend in New York so that Straight could see the children—"Talked to Franklin Roosevelt on train," Dorothy noted. The attachment between Dorothy and Willard was unique, spanning great differences in temperament and growing differences in politics. The differences had, most of the time, receded because few women had ever occupied so special a niche in a man's life as she did in Straight's. They had lived richly, luxuriously, mentally and adventurously together. She was, underneath, miserable with fear over his coming departure. A letter just received from Beatrice in Mexico City noted that Dorothy "sounded a little sad and discouraged" in her last. Merely to cross the Atlantic was now dangerous, and if Willard would not precisely be leading infantry assaults, he would be traveling in the war zones.

He came to New York for the last days. They went together to the Cathedral of St. John the Divine, a solemn occasion—then later to dine with the Crolys and Lippmanns and to see *Polly With a Past*, not so solemn. On December 11, 1917, Dorothy wrote: "Took Willard down to the steamer this A.M. Left him at 11 to go aboard. . . ." In the flyleaf of her Line-a-Day she copied a poem probably taken from a current magazine, dreadfully sentimental but conveying something of what she felt:

> *Be this my part*
> *Until he come again—*
> *To keep the hearth fire lighted*
> *And his name*
> *Unsullied from all stain. . . .*
>
> *But if no more he shall return to me*
> *Who is the very music of my life,*
> *My shield in strife,*
> *The laughter and the sunlight of my days,*
> *Let me give praise that thus he died*
> *The holder of his country's love and pride. . . .*

Six

1. The Germans Are After Me

Major Straight he had a date to sail across the sea,
So he got some boys to go along from out the Infantry;
They're on their way to old Berlin and they won't stop until
The Yankee lads help lick the Huns and insure Kaiser Bill,

For, (Chorus)
We're the War Risk Insurance Bureau, and we've got a job to do,
We will tell you and we will sell you the best insurance that you ever
knew,
We will bet that we will get you before our work is done,
So if you're not I N S U R E D, you'd better see us on the run.

IF STRAIGHT regretted his failure thus far to land with the State Department or the General Staff, his buoyancy rose with command and he could not resist penning this ballad of the War Risk Insurance Bureau, which ran to seven stanzas plus chorus. He may well have written music for it too, though it does not appear in his papers. Before leaving, he had thrashed out with Croly and Lippmann plans for a new political daily newspaper in Washington, along with a design for an international network of correspondents to feed it. It seems likely that Dorothy, in the emotion incidental to separation, could not refuse to aid him financially in achieving his ambition. Aside from finishing off a few individual financial enterprises of his own, he would be unemployed when he returned from the war, which it was assumed would be in a matter of months. The formation and guidance of *The New Republic* and *Asia* had stimulated him, but his great dream was still a newspaper with hundreds of thousands of readers. He was—and he knew it—a good editor and writer.

"D. stayed [on the dock] long enough to see the men and then went with a smile," he noted in his diary. "She makes me very proud and very humble." He had sixty-five officers and enlisted men under him, many of whom he had picked himself. He was to run the European end of what was believed the biggest insurance company in the history of the world, with $1,665,184,000 in policies already in force. One of his picked men was his valet George Bennett, who was in a private's uniform but whose duty in large part would be to care for the personal necessities of the major. Another was George Rennick, from Straight's office at 120 Broadway. Straight had in his cabin the wherewithal either to protect him from separation anxiety or to inflame it: a photograph of Dorothy as a little girl of about eight, one of her taken in England in the summer of 1910, one taken more recently, and also a photograph of the Goldbeck portrait, which had appeared full page in the September *Town and Country*—plus pictures of the children individually and together. With his typical thoughtfulness, he had left letters with his secretary Fiedler at his office to be sent at intervals to Dorothy, so that she would not have to wait forever for word from him, and had left notes to be attached to flowers Fiedler was instructed to send.

His boat was delayed at Halifax due to the recent vast munitions explosion there that had killed 1,800 people and destroyed a large part of the city. He did not have a high opinion of Gen. Leonard Wood, who was aboard and who gave a talk: "His ideas about future wars as if no arrangement [is] conceivable through some international agreement to make them impossible by settling world trade and expansion. . . ." His belief in international organization for peace was real and admirable, the disturbing note in his comment being the words "settling" and "expansion." What with his Kiplingesque tendencies, one has a picture of these arrangements being supervised by the great commercial nations. To Dorothy he wrote, "We're going along in convoy . . . some of [the ships] remarkably camouflaged—looking . . . like 'The Nude Descending the Staircase.' " He and Dorothy had of course attended the great Armory Show, which Gertrude had supported and at which Duchamp's painting was displayed. "This morning I went to service . . . I went for you—and I shall continue—wherever I may be. . . ." "The realization is gradually coming over me, for the first time, that the Germans are after me—not only the British ship I am on, that I am a part of the army that's fighting them." He had a natural knack of command, a genial but firm authority that his men respected, and he was proud of them:

> . . . my men have been given the most important places on the boat. They are better than any other outfit on board the boat, better dressed,

better mannered, better disciplined. . . . The more one sees of the army the more one realizes the importance of command; as the commander is, so the men are. The highest officer always gives the tone to his organization, be it Division, Brigade, Regiment or Company.

This was perhaps a little self-congratulatory as well. Certainly his men were the best dressed if they emulated him. His uniform was of the finest tailoring, without wrinkle, his boots and belt shining, his buttons and insignia resplendent. They landed in Liverpool Christmas morning: "Fine to be here and in it at last. Had our lunch baskets and luckily a bit of whiskey in the Thermos Bottle. Our Christmas dinner. . . . Bennett found me some hot water. Felt achey with a cold." While in London he arranged with Nancy Astor, who had set up a hospital in her home for recuperating American soldiers, to put an American soda fountain in it. Straight left orders with Fortnum & Mason to keep it stocked.

Achey though he was, when he reached Paris he was among friends and enjoying luxury almost sinful when one reflected that the shooting and the gassing were going on only sixty-five miles away. The area around the Place de la Concorde had been heavily infiltrated by Americans. There was the ubiquitous Daisy Harriman, working for the Red Cross. There was Ruth Morgan, working with Daisy. There was James Logan, now a lieutenant colonel on the General Staff and technically Straight's boss. There was Frank McCoy, now a colonel and also a member of the General Staff. There was Berl Ramsey, last seen at the American legation in Peking. There was Herman Harjes of the Morgan firm and his wife. There was Henry L. Stimson, now a colonel of artillery; August Belmont (son of William C. Whitney's Democratic colleague), now a major in the Signal Corps; Warwick Greene, a major in the Air Corps; Maj. Peter Bowditch, on General Pershing's staff. There was a deputation of the fighting Roosevelts including nineteen-year-old Quentin of the Air Force, whose smile was so like his father's. Quentin's fiancée was Gertrude and Harry's nineteen-year-old daughter Flora. Colonel Roosevelt, who kept closely in touch with all four of his soldier sons, warned Quentin that if he expected to hold Flora he must write her "interesting letters, love letters," and often, at least three times a week. "Write no matter how tired you are, no matter how inconvenient it is; write if you're smashed up in a hospital . . . write all the time!"

This was a reminder Straight never needed, whether living luxuriously at the Crillon as he now was or among the sandbags. For the rest of his life, with few exceptions, he wrote to Dorothy every day in the week, usually writing a half-dozen pages each night and mailing a considerable essay on his doings every third day. This he did, as he had once written her frankly from China, not only for her sake but for his, because it made him feel a little less lonely, because the act of writing was itself a precious contact. Since the speedy transportation of these letters was of urgent importance, and the Army itself did not seem aware of this, Straight arranged with Harjes to send his mail through the Morgan office, which often took advantage of friends sailing home.

Straight was immediately working hard, with a force under him augmented to thirty-four officers and sixty-five enlisted men. He had a deadline to meet. The period during which the government insured men under the original terms would expire February 12, 1918. There were now some 250,000 American soldiers in France, the number rapidly growing, and they lived in about two hundred scattered towns and villages. It would be a formidable task to reach them all in time, particularly since the Army in its inscrutable way gave him no automobiles whatever. Yet although he suffered from a bad cold and was hard pressed, he was not one to rule out social life. He lunched with Mrs. Theodore Roosevelt, Jr., Quentin, and the Countess de Chambrun, whose brother-in-law had married Nicholas Longworth's sister. He dined at Voisin's with Logan—"good old Logie," a friend for a decade. He dined with Jack Carter of Morgan, Harjes, and the Countess of Strafford. He called on American Ambassador Sharp. He dined with the Robert Blisses, Bliss being the longtime First Secretary at the embassy, also present being Countess Casteja, née Katherine Esther Garrison of Tuxedo, New York. He dined with Carton de Wiart and with the de Margeries, another of the guests being that fiery Francophile Edith Wharton. He dined with Dick Derby, now a captain in the Medical Corps; with Stimson, Warwick Greene, and Bowditch. "Too much food and good wine," he wrote at one point. "Must cut it out or I will get fat headed."

Quite often he lunched or dined with Daisy Harriman, who had worked so loyally for him in Washington. Lonely since her husband died, Daisy had found in Washington a companion in the bachelor Col. Frank McCoy. It seemed likely that she had pulled strings to get the Paris Red Cross post because McCoy was in Paris. Straight wrote to Dorothy:

> Last night I dined at Voisin's with Daisy. The old McCoy situation had recurred. Poor Daisy was in a state. [Their romance was in difficul-

ties, and she felt him unfair.] She finally talked. She had been distrait all
during dinner. I told her she must for her sake & for the sake of the real
best McCoy—hold him to the best that was in him—not condone or
forgive for an instant the other. Poor thing—she has suffered much. . . . ,
I'm afraid she cares too much. That's the trouble.

That Daisy would confide in him so personal a matter was evidence
of his underlying kindness and sympathy. Straight needed sympathy
himself, for he wrote, "But Dorothy dear—I want a letter so—Rennick
goes every day to Morgan Harjes to try to find something from you—but
no luck. My Best Beloved—are you writing?"

To Dorothy, Frances Perkins, Dean Virginia Gildersleeve of Barnard
College, and other workers-for-good, the election of Hearst's man Hylan
as mayor was a disaster. Mitchel had been the silk-stocking candidate
from Riverside Drive, Hylan the Brooklynite candidate* whom both
Mitchel and Roosevelt had reprehensibly insisted was the Kaiser's
friend. It was understandable that Hylan bore no love for Mitchel
champions. Dorothy and Dean Gildersleeve waited in the mayor-elect's
office to discuss with him the future of the Mayor's Committee.
Dorothy wrote, not without condescension:

> . . . we waited indeed!! . . . about 35 other people also had appoint-
> ments . . . and so the result was that we all stood in line and waited our
> turn. In an atmosphere of smoking and spitting, surrounded by humanity
> of every type, we waited in line for an hour and thirty-five minutes!! For-
> tunately we each had a sense of humor. . . . When we finally got a word
> with him and murmured that we represented the Mayor's Committee, he
> exclaimed "Oh—are you the committee that spent $200,000 of the tax-
> payers' money"? When we assured him that we were distinct from the
> men's committee, he impressively informed us that he could never stand
> for our attaining [sic] any financial support from the city. . . . He . . .
> finally said that he would have to think the whole matter over. . . .

Although she was occasionally described as "radical" in the gossip
columns, and Harry at times (not to her face) referred to her as "my
pink sister," she had yet to attain a political philosophy that was whole
and complete. She was working toward an ideology, hampered by a
touch of naiveté—idealism not quite tempered with practicality and

---

* The rough-hewn Hylan soon became noted for his gaucherie. After the war, when the Queen
of Belgium remarked on the beauty of the New York skyline, the mayor replied, "You said a
mouthful, Queen."

skepticism. But she was reading the news, mingling with ideologues at the weekly luncheon meetings at *The New Republic* building, often entertaining the Crolys and others of the staff at her home, and forming political opinions on better ground than she once had. She perhaps did not yet realize that as she moved gradually to the left, Straight moved gradually in the other direction.

She had Colonel and Mrs. House as dinner guests, possibly hoping that this might remind the Colonel of Willard's availability. She had been warned that troop convoys did not move with the *Mauretania*'s speed, but it hardly seemed that the voyage could take a fortnight. On Christmas, she admitted, "When Louisa came in this morning and wished me a merry Christmas I foolishly burst into tears. . . ." Next day came word that Straight had landed, and "I feel as if the world had suddenly burst into song." The weather, she wrote him,

> has been cruelly cold—12 below zero—and the suffering in New York is terrible on account of lack of coal. Shops and offices are being closed up and now we hear that the same fate has been decreed for 75 public schools. Just think what that means! In our own house in town the pipes have been frozen and there is no running water in the bathrooms—except in yours and the one directly above! . . . unless relief comes soon, life in this city will be at an absolute standstill—no light, no heat, no water—no elevators—no transportation—no nothing! . . .
>
>   . . . The poor people [have suffered] and no relief is in sight. When I discovered that we had 20 tons of coal in this house . . . I sent out 6 tons to the three Settlement houses nearby, and from there the coal was given out in bags to about 230 families! It's amusing to hear that Mr. Samuel Untermeyer has 150 tons safely stored in his cellar . . . and that Charlie Sabin has sent two carloads down to his new house at Southampton. I wonder why there are not more Socialists in the world!

When Mayor Hylan appointed Mrs. William Randolph Hearst chairman of the Mayor's Committee, Dorothy pondered whether it would be poor sportsmanship to resign. After a few meetings with Mrs. Hearst, she quietly retired from the committee. A different problem arose with Willard's sister Hazel, now Mrs. James Sanborn and living in Nutley, New Jersey. Though Dorothy was generous to a fault, she sometimes made overgenerous offers that were expected to be refused. One feels that Hazel, who was pregnant, did not observe the rules:

> I suggested to Hazel, once long ago, that she let [her son] Bobbie spend the winter with us and go to kindergarten with Whitney, which idea she seized upon with alacrity—and at the first opportunity produced Bobbie.

She herself returns to Nutley tomorrow, leaving the youngster here for good and all. It is going to be somewhat of a strain on the nurses . . . but of course it will all work out, and it's the greatest pleasure to be of such real use to poor Hazel . . . Whitney doesn't seem to take to [Bobbie] very eagerly, which makes it all somewhat more difficult—but it's fun trying to work out the problem and I'm delighted that such an opportunity has come!

Dorothy attended *The New Republic* luncheon meeting of January 7, 1918, when the October Revolution had complicated the Russian role in the war and the negotiations at Brest-Litovsk were in progress but it appeared that the Russians might fight on. Liberals cheered the overthrow of the oppressive Czarist regime, some even feeling it would strengthen Russian opposition to the Germans. "T.L. [Thomas Lamont] who is imbued with . . . enthusiasm about the Russians," Dorothy wrote to Willard, "held forth most hopefully and sympathetically on the subject of the Bolsheviki. Everyone agreed that they had done the great trick for the Allies by forcing the hand of Germany. . . . Perhaps those negotiations may stand as the turning point of the war. . . ." A Morgan partner praising the Bolsheviki! Two days later, when Wilson spoke, she added with excessive optimism:

The President's speech is really the most masterly and thrilling document of the whole war, and it certainly ought to hold Russia, if anything can, and also, strengthen and hasten the Liberals in Germany. . . . I have been singing with gladness all day, for my heart tells me that Peace will soon be spreading her beating wings over the earth, and a new day may, after all, be dawning.

2. Douglas MacArthur's Raid

SINCE LETTERS from Dorothy were literally Straight's lifeline, and regular mail took up to six weeks and saw letters chopped up by censors to boot, they used every stratagem to avoid that fate. One of their several couriers was their friend Joseph Swan (Yale '02) of the Red Cross, who sailed back and forth occasionally. Without his couriers, Straight might not have been so phenomenally efficient at running his bureau. Wheedling the necessary automobiles out of the Red Cross, he sent out ten teams of men to the scattered American units—and with Logan made several trips himself to Chaumont, Chambertin, Neufchatel, and elsewhere. "Men taking insurance," he reported. "About 95% coming in—10,000 a throw." He disbelieved the rumor that the French people were ready to quit: "Meat, eggs, butter in plenty, the people are fed, sad, but steady everywhere." He was in steady communication with Fiedler by cable, running the remainder of his business, even cabling Fiedler for cigars, of which he insisted on the best and with which he was generous. He was also *The New Republic's* only war correspondent,* sending criticism of previous issues and long analyses of the war situation as background material for Croly. He was also expert on the Far East for both *Asia* and *The New Republic.*

Still he had time to attend the wedding of Daisy's daughter Ethel to Henry Russell at the American Church. Dorothy, discovering that Daisy had left scattered debts in New York and Washington, had systematically paid them off. ". . . she is utterly irresponsible—sentimental & kind hearted," Straight wrote to Dorothy. "So she left debts. You are an angel to settle them . . . you can't change Daisy. She's a luxury." He was kind himself, helping Daisy with wedding arrangements and giving Ethel a handsome though unspecified present. Ethel, lovely in glowing white satin by Worth, was married in a ceremony performed by Dr. Billings of Groton School; "after the breakfast in our salon at the Ritz," Daisy noted, "Cole Porter played the piano and everyone sang, Ethel sitting on the floor. . . ."

It was part of the unreality of Paris-at-war that Cole Porter and Dr. Billings should be on hand to attend to two of the essentials of an American wedding. Most American popular songs were heavily sentimental on patriotic themes. It would be surprising if they did not sing that paean to the Red Cross, "The Rose of No Man's Land," which ended, "Through the war's great curse comes the Red Cross nurse, she's the Rose of No Man's Land"; another, calculated to shatter Straight's self-control, was "Just a Baby's Prayer at Twilight (For Her Daddy Over There)," the burden of the prayer being, "Oh, won't you tell my Daddy that he must take care?" "Very gay—young officers, regular New York crowd," Straight observed. "Sat next to Princess Poniatowski (Miss Crocker) very nice. . . ." The married couple had a charivari that night in the form of an air raid, as Straight and Logan discovered after returning late to the Crillon: ". . . lights went out suddenly, then crashing and when we opened windows could hear the drumming of the airplanes overhead. . . . could see shells bursting like fireflies . . . one great plane came dropping down from the air." The racket also an-

---

* Elizabeth Shepley Sergeant went to France briefly for the paper later.

nounced Straight's thirty-eighth birthday January 31. The Gare du Nord was damaged and glass glittered in the streets, but Paris continued as lively as ever: ". . . there is always the fascination of this polyglot town . . . all manner of French uniforms—from the dapper aviator—the rough Foreign Legionary—the Annamite—the Moroccan—to the old territorial in his corduroy breeches and faded blue-gray cap . . . noise, rush—young women—all Paris . . . [strolling] along—sipping beer in the shadows on the treeless boulevards—flirting—buzzing—rubber necking. It seems far from war—yet only war has made it possible."

He itched to sketch it all seriously but had no time. The view, the shades of color down the Champs Élysées to the Arc de Triomphe by early evening light transfixed him. He saw the beauty and the drama here as he had seen it in China and wrote of it with a verve that delighted Dorothy, often illuminating his letters with quick, skillful sketches or cartoons. He needed a new assignment when the insurance job would be finished. "I'm afraid that our friend Colonel House has forsaken me," he observed in a letter to Dorothy. "Please write me about it. *But don't let Herbert [Croly] or Walter [Lippmann] press the matter. It must come from him.*" The Colonel sent word offering Straight the job of liaison with the Polish National Council, which he declined. He wanted to be in the center of events, not the periphery. He sent information and opinion to Dorothy to be passed along to Croly for *The New Republic:*

The Y.M.C.A. is organized to deal with the individual soldier—the Red + to do things in a big way—for the soldier en masse. . . . the army has been too bone-headed to accept from the Red + the things it can do—& which the army—because of its congenital stupidity & red tape—should do but can't. *Spread the gospel* & get subscriptions. . . . The N.R. was dead right & it ought to give the Red + some more praise. [As for General Pershing], he being the best if not the ideal man, the thing to do is to root for him hard—hold up his hand—make criticism kind & constructive. The same thing is true of the President. He has faults—but no one else could touch him. . . .

I doubt the stories on which you are all being fed—regarding the terrible conditions in Germany. . . . I've just read the N.R. of Jan. 5th & 12th. The articles by [William] Hard are splendid! . . . Now you must not let Herbert get the economy bee. . . . The paper is just coming into its great usefulness. Hard is one of its best bets. This is no time to count pennies. . . . [Croly] is so terribly conscientious that it's always on his mind the fact that he's using your money. Talk to him & tell him to go to it.

His liberality with Dorothy's money was charming but in a good cause. He was proud of his own outfit: "Our people in the field have done a splendid job. . . . I should say they have written something like eight hundred million of insurance—it may reach the billion mark. . . . We have reached everyone—in all France . . . & they are covered—and by the date fixed." He was so popular among his men that they gave him a dinner and a commemorative scroll in which they mentioned among other things how "free with the purse" he had been when they were pinched. For want of another assignment he signed up for the American staff school at Langres. For the first time, with other novices, he was taken through trenches in a sector near Toul held by the American 42nd Division, whose chief of staff was Col. Douglas MacArthur. "I was scared green," Straight admitted in his diary, ". . . especially of gas—that terrified me. I took off my glasses and we splashed along. Two shells sang overhead—we ducked—then the buzz of an airplane and pop, pop, pop—the shrapnel with gray smoke and high explosive. . . ." In his letter to Dorothy he forbore mention of gas:

> . . . at first I was scared to death but later got used to it. . . . they gave us a nice little lieutenant who took us up to the lines. The first shells that went overhead we ducked right down—but soon I became able to judge whether they were going way on or not. . . . next four German planes started to come overhead & it seemed as if everything had broken loose—the sky was speckled with bursting shells—blue puffs for high explosives—gray for shrapnel breaking all around but below the planes which sailed about seemingly quite unconcerned.

The handsome chief of staff—just his own age—fascinated him: "McArthur [sic] . . . is a corker—the best in the business I should think." He mentioned MacArthur in four successive letters: "[He] went out last night & with a French officer—went through the barrage & went with the attack into the German trenches—and picked off an officer's helmet. It was a damn fool—but a ridiculously brave thing to do. It's a wonder he wasn't killed. Nevertheless it helps division morale to have staff officers do just such things. . . ."

The glimpse of the trenches, the sight of men under fire, the big shells whistling overhead, the German planes, the fear and the drama of it—above all, the night attack and MacArthur's exploit—were an experience that brought on a new and—to Dorothy—frightening line of thought:

The more I see of it—the more I feel that it's the duty of anyone who has any quality of leadership—to get into it—the more I am convinced that one cannot get ahead with the war if one is content with desk work. . . . The thing that MacArthur did the other night—is what one must be ready to do—not foolishly for a stunt—but for the sake of morale. . . . All of which doesn't mean that I'm going over the top tomorrow—Dorothy mine. . . .

Dorothy, in a rare burst of petulance, said that Mrs. Hearst was doing little more than spending $100,000 of the taxpayers' money. Willard's absence was hard on her of itself and also in her knowledge that his brilliance was no guarantee of wisdom, that he tended gradually to lose balance and judgment during long periods under stress. This was especially true, as she had seen, when his ambition was thwarted, when he felt that he was being deprived of an opportunity to excel. He was more perceptive and realistic than she—or Croly for that matter—in appraising political and military circumstances such as the probable disastrous result to the Allies of the Russian revolution, and the conditions inside Germany. But there were pressures on his touchy temperament that could make him react rashly, as he had in China against the State Department and against his Morgan superiors. Pride was a large factor—pride that had good byproducts, pride that could drive him to extreme effort and great achievement but that could also turn to frustration. He hated to admit that any man could do better than he. The desire to succeed, to shine, was a human one, but he had it to an extraordinary degree. Since 1914, when he first began to feel unappreciated at Morgan's, his pride had suffered almost steady rebuff. AIC had been a mistake. The State Department had not wanted him. He was without visible employment when the war should end, and offers were not coming in. He had had his day with the insurance bureau, been top dog, done well, won praise. Now suddenly he was dropped into limbo, wondering what staff school had to offer. Colonel House had disappointed him. He was shorn of his command, at loose ends, reminded that he was after all a subordinate awaiting orders from superiors.

Dorothy sought to support him, as she had when he was in China, with letters of understanding and praise. She did her best with Colonel House without making the effort too obvious. The Houses were twice her guests in January and February, but only at a luncheon at the Colonel's apartment did Straight come into the conversation. "As we were leaving," Dorothy wrote to Willard, "the Col. asked about you and when I told him of your plans he exclaimed 'that's good, I want him to do some work for me before long.' "

Dorothy had her own pressures. Hazel Sanborn, whose civil engineer husband was away on a project, joined her son Bobbie for a time as a resident of the Straight Fifth Avenue home. The love Dorothy bore for Hazel's brother did not seem to extend to Hazel. Beatrice and Prather Fletcher, back from Mexico for some weeks, also moved in. Dorothy was now working (in addition to duties with the Red Cross, a trusteeship at Teachers' College, the loan drive, the Women's Field Army, and other organizations) with the YMCA in its crash program of reorganization for war. That body had reluctantly surrendered its seamless masculinity and permitted women assistants at Army camp huts, a step that enkindled Dorothy's maternality:

> I went down to Yaphank [seat of Camp Upton] last Saturday to try the thing out. . . . I stood behind the counter for hours just giving out books—and I was surprised to find how hungry the men were for a chat with a woman. Three men poured their stories out to me, and because I was able to give one of them some really timely advice and help him straighten out a rather heartrending situation, I came away feeling that the job was absolutely vital. . . . the Junior League has accepted the challenge and on Feb 1st six hand-picked girls are going down there. . . . I am starting them off myself. . . . [The hand-picked girls arrived:] . . . we heard some extraordinary human stories. One little French Canadian, who hardly spoke any English and had been a waiter at Mouquin's, talked to me for an hour one afternoon, and then came back again the same evening! . . . We all wore bright blue smocks . . . and not a single man was fresh. . . . On Sunday night we attended an extraordinary religious service in the hut, and when I looked around and saw Jews and Christians side by side singing hymns, the dawn of a new era seemed to be breaking. . . . The Y.M.C.A. is the . . . Great Unifier . . . the embodiment of the new Spirit of Cooperation.

On Washington's birthday she took the children down to the Twombly Fifth Avenue mansion to view from second-floor windows the great parade of the 77th Division from Camp Upton, 10,000 strong, actually seeing many friends march by—DeLancey Jay, Jack Prentice, Bill Whitehouse, and her own cousin Jim Barney among them. A few days later she broke out with chicken pox. "It's too silly!" she protested, but it kept her home for five days, after which she spent a Sunday at Sagamore with three of the Roosevelts—the Colonel, Mrs. Roosevelt, and Ethel. The Colonel was still charming socially, although politically he seemed to have gone half mad with bitterness against Wilson. "He was his very best self—most interesting but not personal or vindictive," she wrote to Willard. ". . . He was apparently most enthusiastic about the Staff College. . . ."

Roosevelt was proud of his four sons in the service, all of them married but Quentin, but he knew the risks of war. He felt that Flora Whitney should go to France and marry Quentin. ". . . even if he were killed," he said, "she and he would have known their white hour. . . ."

A fortnight later Dorothy told her diary with resignation, "Children all have whooping cough, on top of measles." A great fat letter from Willard—one of those not carried by "courier"—had been violated: "Large sections . . . have been erased with acid by the Censor," Dorothy wrote, "—in fact, one entire page is completely obliterated— and paragraphs all through . . . have been blotted out. It's too tantaliz- ing for words—but some day you must call upon your memory and try to fill it all in." She attended every weekly meeting of *The New Republic* and was ready to contribute "only $10,000," as she put it—meaning $10,000 a year for ten years—for the establishment of an industrial research bureau in connection with the magazine:

> The power of the paper is really extraordinary—and I believe it is going to do more for the education of this country than any other force I know of. . . . I do believe that the New Republic is the best thing that you and I ever put over—and all the credit goes to you!

3. The Bad Week

As to Flora Whitney, Straight wrote to Dorothy:

> I see no reason why she shouldn't come over for the Red Cross or Y.M.C.A. . . . Over here she can get married and then go on with her job—as Ethel Harriman did. . . . Now there's a possibility that Quentin might be killed. For Flora's sake I think it would be better for her to be married now—and then have it happen than to have her go on engaged only. She's very young and so is he. She's more likely in the long run to get over it that way. . . . That sounds very cynical. But I think the first case is much more frequently a case of being in love with being in love— rather than the final and lasting thing.

Flora visited Dorothy to talk to her about it. She was eager to sail. But she discovered that numerous impediments were put in the way of romantic twenty year olds, that the Army frowned on love as an accompaniment to war, and she was unable to get to France. Straight was upset by Dorothy's chicken pox. ". . . it confirmed what I have been fearing all along," he wrote to her, "—that you would overdo, and get run down & then catch something. My Dorothy. . . . Please don't try to carry the whole world on your shoulders." He gave a thumbnail appraisal of the war:

> There isn't much punch on either side now. The British are more active than the French. The French are active in some sectors only—elsewhere everyone is sitting. . . . They are conserving man power until we get in really. The Germans I don't believe have much resiliency either. Everyone is down on their springs. Either there will be a political collapse on one side or the other or things will drag along till we can give the punch that is needed to win the war. But to do this we will have to get a great army. By that I mean not only a large one—but a well organized one— above all with a staff that can function—that can lose men in a strong offensive in order to save them from attrition—a 100,000 [sic] lost in a fine advance rather than 200,000 by little piddling actions without result.

He was now ensconced in shocking comfort at Langres, a town of 5,000 population 160 miles southeast of Paris. With Maj. Grayson Murphy he had rented three bedrooms at the spacious home at 19 Rue Chambroulard of Madame Floquart, whom Straight described as "squat & evil faced—like a Hogarth picture." He was delighted with Murphy, two years older than he, who had quit Haverford College to fight in Cuba, then decided on a military career and gone through West Point, *then* decided on a career in finance. Murphy had a fine head of graying hair and was almost as natty as Straight. He was wealthy and socially prominent, lived less than a mile from the Straights in New York, and was senior vice-president of the Guaranty Trust Company. He likewise had an orderly, Edward, a former factotum at the Rockaway Hunt Club, who roomed with Bennett on the third floor.

The staff school began February 23, and Straight had room 23, which he considered doubly auspicious even though 23 Wall Street had done him ill. Founded by General Pershing, who gave a speech to start the class off, it had 168 students, more than 100 of them Regular Army officers. Although Straight's reservations about Regulars were growing fast, he mingled with them without rancor and did well from the start. One was expected to learn military organization, transportation, supply, liaison, weaponry, tactics, and other specialties in three months. From 8:30 to 12:00: attend classes. From 1:00 to 4:45: write answers to theoretical problems. Then ride for an hour, tidy up for dinner at 7:00 and then study three hours or more before turning in. Straight had a cold bath before dinner in a collapsible canvas bathtub (he believed that warm baths caused colds) and after dinner would get into comfortable flannels to light up, study, and write letters. The four pictures of Dorothy and the several pictures of the children were in clear view on a dresser. Madame Floquart's rental was outrageous, but the comfort was worth it, and the immediate liking between Straight and Murphy—both married men with families—was a pleasure to them both.

"He reels off Browning—and Chaucer and Kipling at a great rate— and has quaint ideas," Straight wrote to Dorothy. "He writes little poems to his boys every Sunday."

Another companion was Maj. Herbert Parsons, former Republican Party chairman of New York County, who had married a daughter of the Henry Clewses. Less cherished was Colonel Stimson, at fifty a decade or more older than the other three. He sometimes pulled his rank. Straight nicknamed him (aside) Hotspur Hal: "Stimson is a fine fellow but he doesn't think as well [as Murphy and Parsons]. His opinions are mosaics of what he gets here and there. He furnishes the cement—the labour—the industry in selecting the proper colours—but he doesn't design. He collates. . . . He is a Rollo—who is always noble. Don't think this a criticism—it's an analysis. . . . I find that my opinions of Stimson formed long ago—when I knew him but slightly at home— have been confirmed on closer acquaintance." He was a little hard on Stimson. "Tonight Stimson & I dined in the French officers' mess. There were about twenty of 'em. They sang—very naughty songs. I translated them for Stimson's benefit. . . . He had to be polite & appear amused & yet he was terribly shocked."

"About Colonel House," he instructed Dorothy, "forget it. Nothing really worth while will ever develop from that source. . . . I'm going to try to get into the scrap. If I can do that I'll feel that I've justified myself."

Straight, so hardheaded in his appraisal of the war, *The New Republic*, and of individual men, was deeply sympathetic for the helpless victims of the struggle. ". . . went into Madame Proats Wine shop," he wrote in his diary, "—nice lady in black a son killed—husband died of sorrow, daughter dead—and 3 bottles of Maraschino 28 years old, that her husband had saved for her daughter's wedding—sitting on the top shelf. Poor lady." He had of course talked with Madame Proat and with his friendliness and pity had drawn these facts from her. "A fine old

[French] major," he noted elsewhere, "—sad but gallant—two sons gone. . . . It is always on his mind." And again: "Tonight an old French commandant, Hugon, and a Captain Loriot dined with us. The old man is a fine type. He comes from Dijon & . . . was a Lieutenant with Petain. He has lost his son—and he's sad—terribly sad—but bucks up and cracks jokes. He is really delightful. I shall never forget the scene—tonight we drank to France—& Victory. We all stood there, the candle light streaming up into our faces and our eyes filled with tears— as he spoke—of France."

His vivid imagination, fired by the drama and pathos before him, led him at times into a religious estimate of the war. It could also affect his view of his own duty as a patriot. The tragedy of Madame Proat, the gallantry of Commandant Hugon, and the daredevilry of Douglas MacArthur were inspirations showing him the direction. There were signs, too, that underlying his thinking was his gnawing memory of what he had come to see as the great reverse of his life, and his need to demonstrate his ability to rise above it. It was almost three years since he had resigned from Morgan's, and it still rankled. He seemed inwardly to agree with Dorothy's equally inward conviction that he had not truly found himself since. Now many of the Morgan men were giving a part or all of their time to patriotic causes—Davison leading the Red Cross, Dwight Morrow advising the Allied Transport Council, Edward Stettinius supervising war purchases, Thomas Lamont advising the United States Treasury. "What a really wonderful job J.P.M. & Co. is hitting up," he wrote to Dorothy. ". . . all of them leading in Public Service—it's splendid." His own public service, if not yet arduous, involved more sacrifice. He was almost envious of Grayson Murphy: "He will be powerful when he gets home—& he should be. I suppose he'll go to J.P.M. if he wants to." Yet Murphy, so civilized and able, was like many Wall Street giants in certain limitations of political vision. He had not, Straight thought, been really aware of international relations until the Russian revolution occurred, and then he thought it was something new:

> These [Wall Street] men have progressed slowly. They have made their piles by hard grinding work. They touched the high spots late—& their experience has been narrow. They judge only by their own standard measuring stick & if you don't fit it . . you're a freak. If your experience has been wider—youre a nut—if your ideas are more progressive you are a long haired reformer. If I'd never been in Wall Street I wouldn't mind—but having been there I should have liked to have made good—

though in honesty—I don't think I should have cared to if I had been
obliged to conform to their standards & habits to do it.

The wound had never healed. Perhaps one trouble was that too much
success had come to him too soon. The stripling who had excelled in
Chinese, become a social light in Peking, conferred with Japanese diplomats and Russian cabinet Ministers and American Presidents, and had
married Dorothy Whitney had come to take grandeur for granted.
Quick achievement was the norm. Any check, any defeat, was insup
portable, beyond endurance. The other creative gifts lavished on him
were forgotten, almost thrown away in what he had come to view as the
unbearable disaster that somehow had to be retrieved. Only peripherally
could the writer, the editor, the artist in him save him from the agony
of the frustrated and failed financier.

As an explorer of history, nevertheless, he was fascinated by Langres,
the birthplace of Diderot, an episcopal see since the third century, the
scene of medieval pageantry, not far from the present battle line but so
far undamaged. It was high on a plateau overlooking the brook-sized
Marne. From its crumbling walls on a properly clear day—so it was
said—one could see Mt. Blanc, another 160 miles to the southeast. The
vast Straight curiosity made him read local history and call on Monsieur
Royer, who had fought the Germans in 1870 and was curator of the
local museum and the authority on the Roman ruins, "It's a glorious
old town," Straight observed. ". . . this place was one of the strong-
holds of France . . . where Romans, Goths, Burgundians—Knights in
armour—have held forth. Up the same road men at arms have clam-
bered—Marcus Aurelius has been carried in state. . . . When the
'three Kings'—the emperors of Russia, of Austria & the King of Prussia
were concocting the Holy Alliance they stopped here for weeks—The
treaty was merely signed where G.H.Q. is." On Easter Sunday, lifted
from gloom by two letters from Dorothy, he accompanied Murphy to
the cathedral:

> The mummery of the church always irritates me—but it was so far away
> that I forgot it. I shall never forget this Easter. It is one of the great
> Easters in History. The old Cathedral was built originally in the XIIth
> century . . . it is splendid. Three of the arch bishops of Langres have
> been made Popes. It is an ecclesiastical town. The great aisle was
> packed—old men and women—young women—little children—black
> everywhere—France mourning for her sons—her husbands—her
> brothers—fallen that France might live. . . . There were young French
> soldiers in their horizon blue . . . but a larger number—officers and

men . . . who had come from the plains of Montana—from the farms of Kansas & Iowa—from our great cities—to do their part in the great war. . . . The lights were dim. It was a gray day—but in the transept the old stained glass windows shone—like jewels—the candles' mellow flickers— like stars against the purple shadow. The white & golden & red-robed fig- ures moving to and fro—the curling smoke of the incense—the crowd— kneeling—rising—sitting—the chanting of the choir boys—the pealing of the giant organ—now free & reverberating—now distant & plaintive—the drone of the service. And the thought [of] what it all meant—sorrowing, worshipping folk—the soldiers of France and America—in this centuries- old Cathedral in the heart of France—all the tradition that clustered about it—of past wars—of past deeds of valour—of past struggles for lib- erty. The thought that in sharing in their struggle—we were winning the right to share again in all that had gone before. That we who had been going our own way for the last hundred years—were now again part of the old world from which we had sprung—part of the great world now brought together & knit inextricably by this war. . . . My heart was with you, my Dorothy. We stood there until the crowd had melted away—un- til the organ stopped. I stood there with you—and I thought of the Cathe- dral in Milan—do you remember—& of St. John in New York.

Oh—my Dorothy—the days—the weeks—the months are barren and maigre without you. But in spirit we are closer than ever before. I think we both know as we never have before what we have—what has been given us. . . . God guard you—my Wonder of the World. . . .

A few days later he wrote to Dorothy that he had rejected the offer of an administrative staff post when his course should be completed and applied for combat duty. The religiosity of his attitude toward the war was balanced by his practical view of it as a foundation for future suc- cess:

Command is what I want & is what I think I could do best. I believe I could handle a Regt. or a Brigade or a Division—that is from the human and organization standpoint—not from the military yet—but that I'll get if the war lasts—which I hope it won't. . . . That is why I want to get into "operation"—or G3. . . . If I get it it will mean that . . . I shall go up to a Brigade & then to a Division. Both jobs will be dangerous. It will mean probably that I'll go over the top—in a raid—or at best be down under the German barrage & heavy shell fire. . . . One has to do this to learn the game. Then when I get back to the Corps again—if I do—of course—I'll be much safer for Corps Hdqs. are generally a long way back. Now you may wonder why I want this sort of work when the other is available. . . . I don't know that I can give you any entirely rea- sonable answer—save that that is my hunch. This is a fighting game. In our country for many years to come—the men who have been in this war will be in control. Their leaders will be the men who led them in the war—not the men who handled negotiations—not the men who managed their supply—or ran railroads—but the men who led them in battle. . . . I want to be able to talk—to say what I think & not have any man say that I stuck to safety first principles. As I wrote you before—I hate the whole thing—& am scared to death. . . . [But in] this I know I am right—& I know that you will agree. I don't like doing things by halves. . . . I am going to try to get a regiment if I can—before I get through. . . . I hate to write you this way—Dorothy dear—for I'm afraid it will worry you. . . . the Fighting Game for the present is the one that must have priority. . . . Don't you agree Best Beloved. I think of you and the kids—and think I ought to be justified . . . in taking the easy way. But I'd rather have you mourn me—& have Bill say that I died fighting over here—than to come back to you & feel that I had shirked. . . . So—my Dorothy—I'm going at it. You may be sure that I will attempt no dare devil performances. . . . I hope that I haven't been doing heroics . . . this has all been in my mind a great deal. . . . I know you'll understand and I know you'll approve. If I do go up to the front—I'll cable—"off on a trip"—and when I come back I'll cable just back home from a trip or something like that. But don't be worried. There's not such an awful lot of danger in it really. Douglas MacArthur walked right through the German barrage the other night—& was never touched.

He could not have forgotten that Theodore Roosevelt, at age thirty-nine, had performed feats with his Rough Riders in Cuba that had made him a changed political personality, an authentic hero with a great career ahead of him.

Dorothy took Whitney and Beatrice to visit the Roosevelts, informing Willard that "the Colonel was a perfect angel to them, and presented Whitney with hunting knives! One of them was the most deadly weapon I have ever seen, which Whitney brandished about in a way that made my blood curl [sic]. Beatrice was presented with buttons and medals, etc. with which she immediately adorned herself. . . . I wonder if you will ever see Quentin. Poor Flora, I'm afraid will not get to France and she is so disappointed about it—and so worried about him."

She recorded her busy days: "J.L. girls at Liberty Loan office . . . to plan canvassing. 4.30—Cosmp. Club to hear Prof. Beard speak on 'Democracy'. . . . Dined alone & then went to conference at Mary Rumsey's with Dr. Baker & Miss Wald—on City Health Bd. situation." Again: "To Brooklyn—with Mary Rumsey & Frances Perkins to speak about Council of Organizations. . . . Book Club at Mabel's—'The Earthquake'. Home to rest. Dinner with Ruth Pratt to meet French officers—then to Lloyd Warren's. Sat by Grosvenor Atterbury &

Lloyd." Thus did she chat with the architectural department among her former suitors. Again: "Caught 1 o'cl train to Baltimore . . . dined at Anne Williams' house & went to J.I.. meeting at Helen Whitridge's at wh. I spoke about Y.M.C.A. work. Came back to N.Y. on midnight train—Willard's trick!"

She was racing to keep up with her determination to help win the war and make a better world, always with her eye on the news. "Bapaume taken," she jotted breathlessly, and later, "General Foch made Generalissimo," and again, "Americans gain 1 mile," and "94 ships launched, 467,000 tons." She had long since become expert at diagnosing Willard's letters. It is clear from her own that she was disturbed at the changes in his moods and the course of events.

Despite all the Americans in France—almost a million now—the war was dragging along without decisive action, taking much longer than anyone had anticipated. She knew the despondence into which Willard could fall if things went badly or if he encountered one of those black periods when her letters were delayed. Croly had been struck by the strange contrast between what he called Straight's "independent self-assertive disposition and his craving for sympathy, for success and for approval." Croly was not aware that when Straight was tired and depressed, Dorothy had comforted him by stroking his forehead and by a less common endearment—by pressing his wrists in her soft hands, a treatment he cherished. She could not do so now and had to make it up with words. If Dorothy had a fault, it was the ease with which she bestowed praise. On Willard she poured it extravagantly, surely because she meant it and also because it was a small price to pay for his devotion, his touching need for her, his unfailing and extraordinary letters, and for the flowers that still reached her—via Fiedler—on the seventh and twenty-third of each month. The following are fragments of six of her letters:

> . . . I'm so proud of you. . . . You are such a really big person that I feel I can never truly deserve you. Never mind, I've got you just the same! . . . Thank you Willard for making our relationship so truly beautiful—it's the most nearly perfect thing I have ever known. . . . I thank God that I have been given happiness such as this. . . . Your spirit responds to the beauty around you, my Willard, and I love that imagination and poetic sense in you. [On Easter she wrote:] I have been thinking with a deep sense of humiliation of things that I have done in the past— that childish sense of having a grievance which I have so often shown you. Do you remember all those absurd occasions when you would come home late and then quite sensibly eat your dinner instead of talking—and

I would behave like a baby and become quite injured. . . . Willard—I could never be that kind of a person again—never, never—and I want you to forgive me for all the absurdities of the past. . . . [Again:] . . . before I knew you I never really understood what bigness of mind—unselfishness—generosity—courage—honor and truth—could really mean. . . . Thank you, my child—for everything—but above all for being what you are. . . .

Since the first MacArthur incident there had been hints in his letters of his distaste for mere staff desk work and his yearning for front-line action, but his request for combat duty rocked her:

Your spirit is the most magnificent thing I have ever known, and I thank God that men are made such as you. . . . Oh Willard—my heart is too full to write! . . . You know that my prayers and my love will be around you everywhere—and that somehow, God will keep you safe. I haven't yet become steeled to the thought of your possibly being ill or wounded and my not being there to help you—and the possibility of your going through suffering nearly kills me. In fact I can't yet bear the thought of your going through any of it—that Hell on earth—but of course if you must—why, I must too. . . . [Later, after a "bad week," she wrote:] Confidence has replaced fear—and I am beginning to understand that courage means optimism—and not merely fortitude. I *know* that you are going to come out of this thing—that you are not going to be killed—for somehow or other, I have always felt that you were a man of destiny.

4. Poor Quentin, Poor Flora

STRAIGHT'S "OVER-THE-TOP" letter was written during an interval when he felt well physically. He was, nevertheless, far from sound in health. He had successive colds, coughing had disturbed his sleep, he suffered cruelly from constipation, his eyesight troubled him, his teeth needed frequent attention, and he had a recurrent ailment of the shin area of his right leg, with fever. The latter was as crippling as it was mysterious. One army doctor diagnosed it as an abscess; another wondered if it might be erysipelas. The faithful Bennett—one valet who truly admired his master—would bandage Straight's leg and he did some of his study for the staff course with his leg propped high. On a doctor's order (he did not tell this to Dorothy) he skipped class attendance for two weeks and pursued his studies alone in his room. "Missed out [writing to you] last night—Dorothy mine—" he wrote, "for I came in very late from the Staff class somewhere. No I wasn't tight—Confound it—for I am to

all intents & purposes on the wagon because of this blooming leg. . . .
But *where* are your letters. I'm getting quite frantic."

On "graduation" at the end of May he got a kind letter from General
Pershing, he designed and illustrated the "quarter-yearbook" of his class,
and he listened to Grayson Murphy perform admirably as toastmaster at
the class dinner. The farewell he made to Murphy, who was joining the
42nd Division (MacArthur's), was a feeling one—hardly less so to Parsons and Stimson. Then he found again that in the Army, a major
might propose but only unseen powers above can dispose. His application for combat duty was under consideration, and he would first have
to be formally transferred to the infantry. Meanwhile he became a liaison officer on the Third Army staff at Remiremont, near the Vosges. He
was exhilarated to be sent on June 4 to the Chateau-Thierry sector to
observe some close action, having time first for a quick trip to Paris
where he dined well and had a tailor look to his uniform. "Have
thought things all out," he noted in his diary, "and if anything happens
am quite ready. It makes me peaceful inside." He composed a letter to
be sent Dorothy if he was killed:

> My Best Beloved:—May this never be sent—but if it be—it's only to
> tell you that my thoughts are with you and the children—that I have
> gone through already anything that I could go through and am quite
> ready for what may come—if it does. What we have been to each other—
> these years my Dorothy—is worth living, and worth dieing [sic] for. I
> love you everything—everything—everything—Your Willard

"I love you everything" was a usage of young Whitney's that both
parents had appropriated. From the farmhouse near Chateau-Thierry
where he was posted he described for Dorothy what he saw, his pride in
American soldiers unhidden:

> The house is rocking & the windows rattling with gun fire—& the sky
> alight. . . . All along as we came up the roads were lined with refugees
> going inland—their household goods in bundles—children & old women
> & old men—herds of cattle—flocks of sheep—scurrying before the tide of
> war. The roads full too of many troops—dusty & tired—& stragglers—not
> ours—French. Here our own Division is a joy. The Chief of Staff a won-
> der. I tell you that given half a chance—we can beat the world on our
> army. We can fly better—shoot better—artillery & everything else—&
> fight better than the others can now. . . . But half a chance means in-
> telligence at the top. . . . I found that this time I liked [the experience of
> warfare]. It didn't bother me as it had before. . . . Dick [Derby] is
> here—& Peter [Bowditch] comes today with the C. in C. . . . the maire

& all his people—beat it about four or five days ago—leaving their home
just as it stood—Some things taken—others left—and then the withdraw-
ing! (retreating) French soldiers came through and looted—and ransacked
this house, and almost everything in the town. Whatever the owners had
left—their beautifully disciplined! and sober! fellow countrymen came in
and helped themselves & made merry. . . . I saw a lot of 'em—responsible for the defense of a certain position—fairly well stewed & no officers
anywhere. . . . The more I see of our own people and the way we go at
things the surer I am that we are not admirable perhaps—but we are the
best there is—in the way of a nation—& I am prouder each day of being
an American. . . . [The Americans] shot up three different German
Divisions. . . . the artillery was absolutely accurate & played on the advancing columns like a hose and withered them. . . . Another outfit
from one of our Divisions just over from home—never heard a shot fired
in anger—after 60 hours on the road—with their machine guns in Ford
trucks—got into line—and within three hours absolutely pulverized a
Boche attack & saved Chateau Thierry . . . the poilus who were beating
it—rallied about this group of "Yankees" and held fast.

Straight indeed did seem almost a "man of destiny" in his capacity for
turning up at climactic events. By chance he was witnessing the beginning of the furiously fought Second Battle of the Marne in which, as it
turned out, his praise for the Americans was wholly deserved. It was also
in character that he should encounter a friend in his farmhouse vantage
point between Chateau-Thierry and Belleau Wood. ". . . am sitting
with a fine chap," he noted, "—the Colonel who before coming over
was Commandant of our guard in Peking. He's a dandy—we've been
talking over old China days. . . ." Soon the noise made talk impossible:

Things have not gone well. . . . In our front a Battalion has been shot to
pieces—almost all the officers gone. . . . Shells have been dropping near
our farmhouse. . . . What a night! . . . A most awful racket—the
whole house shaking—and the miserable little lamp . . . quivering
with the blasts of a heavy battery nearby. . . . I had a talk with the
surgeon—a bully chap. He'd put through something like 500 cases since
early in the morning—had been knocked down by the whizz of a shell—
shot at by machine guns from a Boche plane—had his ambulance
shelled—He was as chipper as a daisy. . . . Dick Derby I saw for a
moment yesterday he was busy with his Field Hospital. . . . All our
wounded coming thru last night had the same fine spirit—no complaints.
. . . Incidentally the French communique . . . spoke of the French
having . . . hurled them back with violence. There wasn't a Frenchman
in sight—except the artillery which supports our people. Our men did it
all!

After three days of this, in one of those miracle transformations of the war, he was on leave at the Crillon in Paris, writing to Dorothy:

> Gracious goodness Agnes! A bath in a tub. . . . Tonight we're dining at LaRue—and then doing the Casino de Paris! What do you think of that—& I've just made a cocktail in this grand apartment . . . which was last night occupied by Sir Douglas Haig [commander in chief of the British army]. . . . It's really an extraordinary feeling to come here direct as we have. But of the two—I prefer what we left. . . . No I didn't really like it—I was scared all the time—scared to death—by airplanes overhead and noises of shells & thoughts of gas—but I could go through it again & again—I think. One lives pretty keenly in those moments. . . . It is fundamental living—eating to live—drinking to live—fighting to live.

Yet the war was a part-time occupation. He continued his long-distance "supervision" of *The New Republic*. He wrote to Roosevelt urging that he read the paper, feeling that he would approve of it. Through Fiedler in New York he ran the remnants of his foreign finance business and was also in touch with Joseph Ohl of *The New York Herald* about Straight's possible purchase of that paper, which had declined badly of recent years. General Wright, whom he had known so well in Washington and at Camp Doniphan, arrived and was made a corps commander, which Straight unabashedly thought might help his own young military career. He had several talks with the general and was one of a group who dined with him occasionally at a three-star restaurant at Fougerolles, giving Wright enough attention so that—as Straight later believed—other staff officers suspected him of apple polishing. On the Fourth of July there was a celebration at Remiremont at which Straight interpreted for the populace General Wright's speech in reply to that of an aged French senator. He was proud to be selected to give a lecture at Langres on liaison, among his listeners being many Regular Army officers. He then wrote an authorized Army pamphlet on liaison, which was well received. He managed to get himself transferred to the Fifth Corps (Wright's), in the hope that this would clear the way for his command of a battalion at the front. He pulled strings among various higher officers in his effort to get line duty. He forgot to guard against his tendency to push himself so hard that his energies would be totally depleted—a special danger now because of his uncertain health. "News from the north wonderful," he recorded. "The turning of the tide, I think. 100 guns, 14,000 prisoners. . . . Peace before snow flies, without a doubt."

On July 18 came the news that Quentin Roosevelt's plane had been shot down near Chamery and he was killed, buried with full military honors by the Germans, who remembered his father. "And poor Quentin—& little Flora," Straight wrote to Dorothy. "He died game— dear boy—but it's a bad business this air man game. . . . Please go to the Colonel and Mrs. Roosevelt—I'll write them too, and to Flora."

The Colonel took it with tight lips, saying, "My only regret is that I could not give myself." Both Theodore, Jr., and Archibald Roosevelt were recovering from battle wounds. The parents received messages of sympathy from President Wilson, King George V, and Clemenceau. Roosevelt indignantly refused to cancel his attendance at the state Republican convention at Saratoga, where he was a leading speaker. He was heard aboard the train to mutter under his breath, "Poor Quinikins!" It was days later that Straight received Roosevelt's reply (written before Quentin's death) to his earlier letter:

Dear Willard, Of course the New Republic should pay no heed to anything except principle in attacking me or anybody else, and it would be thoroughly improper to shield me from attack because of friendship for you. Equally of course, you understand that I do not believe that the New Republic acts on principle save in the sense that Hearst's papers so act.

You ask me to read the paper. I have read it in exactly the same way that I have read Hearst's papers. In each case I satisfied myself that probably the majority of the articles were all right, and sometimes in each case very good; but that there were a number so poisonously bad that taken as a whole the paper was like a spring where ten or fifteen percent of sewage is mixed with the pure water. At the moment for instance the New Republic has an article praising Wilson for his Mexican policy, which no man fit to be a leader of men, a guide to patriotic conduct, can be excused for publishing; for no man who knows the facts can write such an article unless he is either a coward, or thoroughly unpatriotic, or else cynically bent on prostituting the national honor for party advantage. I remember a similar article, I think by Walter Lippmann, on the President's conduct in the Lusitania and other similar sinkings which stood on the same level of baseness. So far from regarding the New Republic as sincerely bent on hurrying the war and demanding that it be carried to a really successful conclusion, I regard it as occupying a position substantially like Hearst's. . . . Hearst's papers appeal most successfully to gutter bolshevism, and the New Republic to parlor bolshevism. . . .

Very sincerely yours,
Theodore Roosevelt

5. *Getting Down to Fundamentals*

INCONSISTENTLY FOR a husband who could be accused of excess in seeking dangers that might remove him permanently from his family, Straight accused Dorothy of excess in accepting outside activities that kept her from the children. That he had always had too many enterprises to give much of his own attention to them was irrelevant according to mores that absolved fatherhood from most familial duties. But Dorothy's compulsion to join in good works was indeed a threat to her own health and a guarantee that her children would see little of her—an odd course for one who had so keenly missed her own mother before as well as after her mother died.

". . . you're not easing off enough, not with the children enough . . . ," Straight protested. "You must give to them of yourself—not of your tired self only—but of your real thoughtful self. . . . You ought now to give them at least three full half-days a week. . . ." Her success in leading women's activities and in addressing medium-sized groups had taken courage, being a triumph of will over a naturally shy nature. Later analysts might decide that she so enjoyed the triumph and all the plaudits that went with it—hence having her own quiet counterpart of Willard's more insistent need for recognition—that she willingly left the children with servants. Each, however, had the saving grace of setting high standards for self quite apart from audience reaction.

Whitney Willard Straight, now almost six years old, had a nightly prayer: "Dear God—please keep my Daddy safe tonight—keep him safe till morning light." Dorothy, when she received Willard's cable that he was "off on a trip for one week" (the Chateau-Thierry observation), turned more than ever to the Almighty: "Oh Willard—it's so strange—and so difficult to believe that you are actually in the fighting at this moment. I'm trying to be philosophical and calm about it, but the thought of you is in the back of my mind every single moment, and I wonder sometimes how I am able to concentrate on anything. . . . The prayer for your safety is in my heart all day, and through my dreams all night—and I'm sure my love must help to protect you." On receiving his cable that he was back from his "trip": ". . . it makes my hair stand on end, and my heart stop beating. . . . How can I ever wait for your letters! . . . I love you for saying you were scared all the time. . . ."

She heeded the administration's plea that unnecessary labor be released for war work. She cut her staff of some twenty-six servants almost in half: "As a matter of fact the chauffeurs had a row anyway and one or the other had to go—so we chose Hutchinson to stay. We are getting Furlong a good place." She gave Straight a gentle reminder of a high and scarcely war-oriented expense: "The question of your polo ponies is still unsettled, but doubtless Fiedler has cabled you for permission to sell some of them! . . . Every dollar I save means a dollar more for the Red Cross and the Y.M.C.A."

In sadness she attended the great military funeral of former Mayor Mitchel, broken to bits in an army air crash in Louisiana: "Fifth Avenue—from Washington Square up to the Cathedral—was packed so tight with people that one couldn't move a step. . . . The aeroplanes came first—circling overhead—then one heard the distant strains of the funeral march—and the muffled beat of the drums—as the troops finally came into sight. . . . Finally, Mitchell's body came, borne on a single gun carriage and covered only with the American flag—and his horse, being led behind, in black trappings. The big Cathedral bell was tolling as his body was carried into the church. . . . The flowers that were dropped from the aeroplanes came from our garden at Westbury— and they fell like a benediction from on high."

An attack of colitis—a warning of overstrain—had sent her to Sloane Hospital for four days, but the funeral of one so close heightened her dedication to the men at Camp Upton: "It is the first time in my life that I have really gotten at my own people, and I wouldn't have missed the experience for anything in the world. . . . They have appointed me chairman of the Camp Work Committee for the entire country. . . . It is an enormous job. . . . but I just can't help doing it. . . ." Dorothy Straight, the suffragist, scouted the theory that the women at home suffered more than the men in the service: "The real heroes of this war are the men, not the women, and it's up to us to play a part worthy of you. . . ." She thought most of the YMCA secretaries "pretty good," but "I can't bear the pious, evangelical attitude of certain members of the organization. . . . Religion is an internal, not an external thing and I can't bear to see it flaunted. . . . When I hear them say that their first duty is to put the soldier into proper relationship with God, I want to say—'Go to H—— the soldier is far closer to God than you are'!"

The news of Quentin Roosevelt's death, so soon after that of Mitchel, struck even closer to home—a reminder that prayers were not a positive safeguard. She had a long talk with Ethel Derby, still warm despite the knowledge of each of them that Dorothy Straight and the Roosevelts were no longer in political agreement. "She was so cheerful and natural. . . ," Dorothy wrote to Willard, "and she spoke of the fact that none of the family were going into mourning . . . they have all gone right ahead, seeing people and doing everything. . . . We have been sitting here in my bedroom for about an hour—with tears streaming down our cheeks one moment, and the next, pulling ourselves up and laughing over something perfectly irrelevant—just to keep from really breaking down. Her whole feeling about Quentin's death is . . . that above all the sorrow and tragedy of it, stands out the supreme fact of his example which will inspire thousands of others. It was only when speaking of Flora that she couldn't keep the tears back, for that poor child has practically been living at Sagamore ever since the news came." And if prayers were no safeguard, she resorted to them anyway, for what else was there: "God bless you always—and may He guard you through such danger."

An example similar to that of the Roosevelts, impressive to Dorothy, and one that remained in her mind, was that of her YMCA aide, Mrs. Christian Herter: "Two days after the death of her son, Mrs. Herter called me up to talk over the work at Camp Upton—as if nothing had occurred . . . and isn't even wearing mourning. Mrs. Mo Taylor has done the same thing—so also have the Kissels—none of them wear black and all of them hold their heads high! . . . I wonder how anyone could have said that we, as a people, were soft and selfish and yellow and everything else!" She was revealing about Straight's earlier sense of defeat when she wrote him of her relief that the days with Morgan and with AIC were over:

> When I think of you these days it always seems to me that you are not only fighting for the freedom of the world but for the freedom of your own soul, too. For years you have been tied and fettered—in bondage, really—until your spirit was well nigh broken. You don't know how terribly it used to worry me. . . . Then the war came, and you cut loose from it all! Your buoyancy returned gradually, but it was not until you undertook the W.R.I. proposition that I felt the longed-for change in you, at last! Since then, your letters have confirmed it, more and more, for they have the sort of ring to them that almost makes me weep with joy! Oh Best Beloved—you are the Willard of the old China days again, only tremendously deepened and hardened—and bigger in spirit than I ever dreamed anyone could be.

She was so generally inclined to applaud and mother him that her rare instances of firmness in opposition to his wishes seemed cruel by contrast. "I really don't think that anything could be done with that paper, Willard," she wrote quite decisively about *The Herald*, which he was eying so wistfully, "for it is in too hopeless a mess and the return would never be, in any way, commensurate with the effort." And, she added later, "you would need the Rockefeller Foundation at least—to swing it. And not being the R.F. I'm afraid there is nothing for us to do but to tell Joe Ohl to go elsewhere." She received from him a letter in which he reviewed his own past and drew lessons from it for his two sons.

To say that I'd be better [at leading troops] than a lot of Battalion Commanders—which is true—is not the point—I couldn't do it to my own satisfaction—and yet I cannot do staff duty to my own satisfaction—because I haven't had service with troops. So there you are. And that brings me to my first great principle—which you must impress upon Whitney and Michael. In fact if I had the chance only to give two pieces of advice to a youngster—I would—assuming of course he was gently bred—tell him—*always to get his foundations solid—before he started to climb*—and to by constant practice and the most consistent effort—*train himself to have his bowels move each morning as soon as he was dressed.* You've no idea what these things mean. They are the foundation for success I believe—one of success in accomplishment and leadership—the other in keeping the health without which accomplishment is almost impossible.

From the latter I am suffering constantly—and it's only a question of training. As to the former—that has been my great handicap in life. I've always been finding myself in places more important than I was really competent to hold. I've never had the foundation for the jobs I've had—except perhaps the political foundation for the Chinese loan business—and for my job in the State Department. I tried to do architecture by clever drawing instead of hard study—I never really knew where I was at because I hadn't studied fundamentals. In the Customs Service I merely started. I was an amateur correspondent—and when I started—an amateur consul—able to hit the high spots—but without sound commercial sense—or a knowledge of law sufficient to handle cases had I had any. When I took on the Group I was not a banker—nor did I ever learn much about what they call "business"—organization—the complications of flotations and all that. Then when I started soldiering—instead of beginning as I should at the bottom in the training camps—I went the easiest way—deluded myself into thinking that my administrative experience would be more valuable to the Government in the A.G. Dept. than would my services as a real soldier in the line. Always I have been too hasty and anxious to hit the high spots. I've constantly beaten other men at the start—and been passed by them—as they came on up—they having taken the rocky road of hard study and grief—& I having bluffed and jumped into a position which I could hold on to—but from which I couldn't rise—because I didn't have the fundamentals. Now this is all a perfectly honest analysis and I know that it is true. In later years—I think no one has worked harder than I have—but I have always been trying to catch up on things. . . . Almost the best job I ever did after the Chinese loan thing—was the War Risk. In the Staff College I did well—but not as you fondly think—at the head of my class. . . . I think that when on my own—with other men working for me I have always done better than when I had to do the details myself for someone else. But one can't ever expect to really lead & hold positions of great responsibility—till one has demonstrated ability in minor capacities.

This candid self-analysis, though written for the benefit of Whitney and Michael, could herald an onslaught of the blues. Indeed in the same letter he mentioned that "the relationship with Davy & with J.P.M. was too close to be severed lightly—and without a real wrench." She protested, "There's a great deal in what you say, Mr. Bones—but not everything! Doesn't the mastering of fundamentals mean specialization and the infinite knowledge of detail? And aren't these things rather subversive of creative ability. . . . if you had spent years and years simply mastering fundamentals you would probably never have really accomplished as much as you have today! . . . As to the second precept—it is such a fixed habit already that it is almost funny to see the [boys] rush upstairs every morning after breakfast as if they were bent on a mission! Poor Willo—I know your troubles, and I shall certainly try to avoid them for the children."

She had as her weekend guest the ex-mayor's widow, Olive Mitchel, a visit that meant for Dorothy the most exquisite application of taste in sympathy, a gift that came naturally to her. The young and mourning Flora Whitney was with her for two days, "and we sat up until all hours discussing Life and Death and the meaning of everything." Dorothy, like Willard, was experiencing flashes of transcendental belief as she had when Willard was in China and they both seemed possessed of the same thoughts at the same time. Now she awakened at her Southampton place to look out the window and across the sea with a distinct impression that she could almost *see* Willard in France, that he must be aware of her vision of him, and must be communing with her. Once she had a "horrid, upsetting dream about you and I came within an ace of cabling you and saying 'Are you all right'?" As for Willard, he had often, in moments of yearning or emotion, felt Dorothy's presence with him as he had during his New Year's Eve party in Peking and more recently after the Easter service at the Langres cathedral, when the organ music ceased and "I stood there with you." Again, on one of the exalted twenty-thirds, he had felt it: "All day my thoughts have been with you—my Dorothy—and I've felt that you too—were thinking of me at the same time—I seemed almost able to reach you somehow."

For their seventh wedding anniversary she sent him "two foolish presents": "The socks are the first pair I have ever knitted. . . . The little gold notebook may look somewhat ladylike . . . but having heard accounts of men being saved from bullet wounds because of their carrying metal cigarette cases over their hearts, I felt that I had to send you this fancy gift as a protection! Please carry it in your pocket . . . will you Best Beloved?" Up to now she had fought to quell her instinctive opposition to his resolve to lead men into combat, feeling that she could not face her own conscience if her courage did not support rather than detract from his. Now she received a letter from Grayson Murphy* in which he strongly opposed the notion, saying it was "sheer waste" for a man so gifted in staff work—that Straight should reject the "sort of monastic frenzy that so many fine men have in these bitter days" and save himself for the settlement of postwar problems. Next came a letter from General Wright himself in which he said that Straight was "a most excellent staff officer" and that it was a "mistake" for him to seek line duty "which he is not particularly well trained for." She rebelled and wrote to Willard in a vein quite changed:

> Please, Best Beloved—it wouldn't be right. . . . I wish you would heed the words of your friends and remain in the work for which you have been specifically trained and not fly off into line service. . . . Really, Willard—it isn't sense—is it?

6. Tell Herbert

STRAIGHT GOT *The New York Times* and *The New Republic* in France, usually weeks late, and never forgot that he was *The New Republic*'s only watchdog in Europe. The paper of course did not deal in news but in opinion and interpretation. Straight had decided feelings about what these should be and was never averse to letting Croly know when he felt him wrong. To save time, and perhaps also because Dorothy was the real subsidizer of the paper and deserved to have some voice in its policies, Straight sent much of his advice through her. "Tell Herbert" was a frequent phrase in the letters she received from him.

---

* Dorothy and Mrs. Murphy had become friends in New York, trading notes about their husbands in France.

Straight was one of the keenest of observers, even though inclined at times to shoot from the hip. The first perception that had struck him was "the unbelievable thing . . . that even now after three years—the loss of billions of dollars—of millions of men—the British and French do not play together. There are two wars in France—a British and a French war against Germany. The British General staff did not advise the French of their plan for the surprise attack at Cambrai—with the result that when [French] support was needed—they didn't throw it in." Straight urged strong *New Republic* support of Pershing, whom he thought the best man available. That his advice was the same concerning President Wilson showed fairness toward the man he had opposed.

He was correct about the Russians, correct in doubting the widespread feeling that Germany was ready to collapse any day from starvation. He quickly felt the spiritual and informational hiatus between the man near the front and the editor in the swivel chair on West 21st Street or at the Players' Club. Herbert, he wrote to Dorothy, must come to France, get next to the war, learn the facts of life and death: "It would do him good. He ought to see it—even if he comes for only two or three weeks. The paper needs it." Dorothy replied, "[Herbert] feels that a trip overseas is entirely out of the question—and he told me the real reason—so confidentially that I almost hesitate to repeat it even to you. But it's this—he can't leave Louise! Apparently whenever he goes away she worries herself into a state of illness—a sort of collapse—and he is therefore quite determined not to leave her."

Straight, who had left three children as well as his wife to go overseas for the duration, could not bleed over the childless Louise's deprivation for a few weeks: "I appreciate Herbert's reluctance to leave Louise. Surely—But he can't get this thing unless he comes over here. . . . I've left you and the children—& that's your contribution—or one of 'em. It's no easier for you than it would be for Louise. . . . I wish you would read this to Herbert—& tell him what I think. Perhaps you could look after Louise while he was away."

But Straight had to give in to Croly's staying on 21st Street. He pressed Croly hard on such issues as making peace with Germany: "The N.R. must *not advocate* any settlement" with the "present German rulers," though it should stand for peace at any time with a responsible new government. Like every good editor, he thought constantly in terms of the reactions of readers: "You know that only too frequently—a man or woman . . . will damn the paper up and down—because of a certain sentence. It gets their goat. . . . As a matter of fact the same idea might have been expressed equally forcibly in another way which would not have offended. . . . Please talk this over with Herbert." He thought Croly was irked by the war and giving too much space to politics: "You might as well sit down and discuss the respective merits of various kinds of fire extinguishers while your house burned down." Croly's approach smelled too much of the brain rather than the guts: "It's only the strong stuff—not the philosophy that will get across." *The New Republic* must show "our ability to *fight—fight—fight*. That's what's going to win—not talk talk talk." He was aroused over what he felt was favoritism and incompetence in the Regular Army: "We have promoted a lot of dodoes— because they had served for years and were nice gentlemanly fellows—& made them division commanders. . . . I have an idea—though I have no knowledge—that in Washington there's a ring in the W.D. that's promoting it's [*sic*] friends—& making a lot of bum generals—and ignoring recommendations for promotion of men who have made good over here. That is criminal. It's murder. . . . Tell Herbert to emphasize this question of lives—lives—always."

He derided the "peace without victory" idea. Readers were bored by intellectual hairsplittings about diplomacy. Their overriding aim was to win the war. "I don't think we'll get [peace] without a military decision. . . . You can't win a tennis match and think of Esoteric Buddhism— but you can if you wish—make a date for such discussion during the interval between sets. Do you get me?" He could occasionally rage at the Germans who had "lusted for world power. . . . I hope they may all be crushed—and exterminated from the world . . . these pests must be exterminated." Dorothy, whose opinions were closer to Croly's, was the mediator, writing to Willard:

> Of course the winning of the war is the supreme task. . . . [But we] must see to it that the fruits of victory are made to count in the wisest way . . . and that the things which have been gained militarily shall not be lost politically. We see so vividly before us now the tragedy of our own Reconstruction effort after the Civil War. If Lincoln had lived, it would all have been different. . . . The failure of every reconstruction period stands out all through history, and we know that many fruits of victory have been left to rot on the ground. . . . You can't prepare for [peace] without thinking about it and writing about it, and that's what the N.R. is trying to do! I can understand perfectly why you get impatient with Herbert— but as a matter of fact, the trouble with him lies in his style and not in his thought . . . his primary object is to make the war count to the fullest in the long run—while yours is to win the immediate decision.

Such letters had never passed between Flora and William Whitney. *The New Republic*, the proudest achievement of Willard and Dorothy Straight, was also a measure of their advance over the Whitneys—and over Whitney's trashy *Morning Telegraph*. It marked the triumph of the humane nonpartisan view over that of the politician. Months of nonpartisan thought had gone into the paper before a line was set in type. It was now a nonpartisan political and cultural force. It had clearly outstripped its only real competitor, Oswald Garrison Villard's long-established *Nation*, both in quality and circulation. Littell's literary column was a sophisticate's delight, Hackett's reviews of books and the theater were unmatched, Alvin Johnson had added weight to the staff in economics and politics, Frank Simonds commented expertly on the war, and there was a flock of brilliant Britons who contributed regularly or occasionally, among them H. N. Brailsford, George Bernard Shaw, Rebecca West, Norman Angell, Lytton Strachey, and Virginia Woolf. A more fortuitous circulation booster was the rumor, entirely false and probably arising from the close ties with Colonel House, that *The New Republic* was an unofficial instrument of the Wilson administration. It became necessary to increase heavily the number of copies sent to the financial district, where Wall Streeters emptied the newsstands and pored over even Croly's sober sentences for clues to market movements.

Still the paper lost money and the Straights paid its losses. Their other money-loser, *Asia,* had become a handsome publication (one issue had featured some of Straight's Chinese drawings), informative, cutting away at American insularity. Dorothy's parents had lived easily and irresponsibly compared with the Straights. Whitney had escaped personal involvement in both American wars of his lifetime. For Flora, who seemed scarcely to notice that there was a ghetto, the fashionable and perfunctory charities were enough. She might, had she been so moved, have spoken out against political inequity as ably as she had denounced the campaign against Cleveland as drinker-and-wife-beater. It was not fashionable, and indeed her husband had rebuked her for that one "impropriety."

Whitney—one of the greatest of Democrats—had seldom had a nonpartisan thought in his life. Like Croker, his genius had been directed less toward political betterment than toward mere skill in elective techniques. In the end, after his horses and houses preoccupied him, his "biography" in Colonel Mann's *Fads and Fancies* had been the knell of a man whose abilities had lacked only the inspiration that could have led him to high and noble effort.

But now some of his money was doing good every week at the newsstands in *The New Republic* and every month in *Asia*. Some of his money was to achieve belated benefit in the founding of the New School for Social Research. If it was true that the Straights stood on the shoulders of reformers almost unknown in their parents' time, and that reform was at last in the air, it was still frowned on by Society. Might the Morgan firm or other potential employers have found Straight more useful if he had not backed Roosevelt, backed this wild weekly that had even printed a vulgar article praising birth control? Certainly Dorothy's career in Society would have been more easy, splendid, and useless. Her friends were now restricted either to those who had no strong objection to her "radical" activity, or were willing to overlook it on the score of her other attractions. Two of her close friends were "queer" in the same way: Daisy Harriman (who was, however, a loyal Democrat) and Ruth Morgan, already active in civil liberties. Not a close friend was Mrs. O. H. P. Belmont (the former Mrs. William K. Vanderbilt of the Consuelo sale), now a formidable feminist who advised a younger worker, "Just pray to God. She will help you."

Dorothy, who had once deferred to Willard politically, now had convictions of her own, not without misgivings. She was upset enough over the political differences between her and Ethel Derby; she wanted no such gulf between her and Willard. As Croly saw Straight, "He had little interest in speculative or critical thinking whose relationship to practical affairs was not immediate and direct. . . ." Croly's friendship for Straight, which was warm, was mitigated to the extent that Straight intimidated him, whereas for Dorothy, who seldom intimidated anyone, the editor had purest affection. "You are wonderful, my dear Dorothy," he wrote to her. ". . . There has never been a group of intellectual warriors, since the world began, who have had the kind assistance and support from a trustful friend that we have had from you." And again: "I wish I could tell you how much I admire you." Straight worried about Dorothy's liking for radical causes he felt she did not always correctly appraise. Now it was she who was attending the weekly luncheon meetings on 21st Street, joining in intellectual talk, joining also in projects Straight did not hear of until the mail reached him weeks later. He was suspicious of those radical professors James Harvey Robinson and Charles A. Beard of Columbia, whom she listened to with such respect. He protested Dorothy's contributions toward the founding of the New School. He wrote:

> . . . I'm getting a little restive and uncertain about some of these forward looking people. So many of them aren't honest. . . . They're

not like Herbert—wise and balanced and candid. . . . You mustn't [contribute to] everything. Remember you have a husband in the army to support—and [a costly magazine] like Asia! . . . Robinson and Beard wouldn't get you—I mean anyone—anywhere except in trouble—if you followed them too far. The trouble is that they in trying to shatter old conventions want to impose the convention of unconventionality.

"I love your phrase. . . ," Dorothy replied. "Your letter is full of good lines—really wonderful—and I find myself quoting them already. . . ." She had a pleasant way of turning away criticism with praise. She *did* contribute and she *did* continue to espouse the two professors. She had to follow her own conscience, although she was troubled about Willard's disagreement. Perhaps because Lord Northcliffe had been a guest at one of *The New Republic* dinners, Dorothy made headlines in London and heard about it from Willard:

> The Daily Mail today prints an article about the millionairess Mrs. Willard Straight & the "new learning". . . . Frankly I'm afraid of the damn thing. . . . Beard—I don't believe in much except as an accelerator of thought—& I'm afraid that your going to gather in a fine lot of [undesirables] who will follow the new thought. . . . However—I'm becoming a filthy conservative I'm afraid—these days. I'm sure that whatever you do is all right. But don't go too far with it my Dorothy—& don't get involved too much—with Beard et al. They are not balanced. Neither are lots of our friends on the other side—but of the two unbalanced outfits—I think that the conservative is the less dangerous. . . .

Seldom was he so admonishing. And in his ineffaceable scroll of memory he seemed to recall everything that had passed between them down to the date and hour. He thanked her for sending him a new locket with her picture inside: "I shall hate to take off this locket I've worn all these years—since you hung it around my neck that afternoon—in the Vendome—June 17ᵗʰ 1910—before we were engaged even it was—& it has never left me." And on the anniversary of their engagement: "I've lived over again that day. What a wonderful morning. My Sweetheart coming down to the old rose room in that dainty white dress—with its Dorothy blue trimmings—then the ride—with poor old Rowdy & Texas—up on the hills—& then that funny drive in the Zedel. . . . My—I shudder still to think that you might have chucked me!"

7. *Evidence of Being a Damned Fool*

BY MIDSUMMER Straight, after such promise of military success, began heading into disappointment and ultimate catastrophe. His health was a factor, but perhaps as important was the Straight grandiosity of conception, his vast intellectual and emotional involvement in the war. In Paris he had been boss of the insurance outfit, at Langres one of the brightest boys in officers' training. Now at Remiremont, on the Moselle, he was one of a large group of staff officers, most of them Regulars. While staff life safely behind the lines was generally relaxed, it had its own severity of etiquette, a basic rule being that one must stay in his own pigeonhole. Straight, with his feeling that the war was in large part his responsibility, could not adopt the approved feet-on-desk attitude of patience and resignation. He was not satisfied to stay within the modest sphere of a Reserve major, attending solely to his own limited duties. He had studied, he had watched and applied his impressive logic to this greatest conflict of all time. His role as observer for *The New Republic* lifted him out of his staff pigeonhole and made justifiable and in fact necessary a critical overview of military operations. He began to feel that he knew—not precisely how to win the war—but knew of measures that would shorten it. The science of war was merely the use of good judgment: "The more I get into this thing the more I am convinced there's no magic to it, only hard work & application of common sense."

He firmly opposed permitting American soldiers to serve under French commanders except for brief periods of emergency. He felt it a mistake that Allied and German troops had faced each other in his own sector for years without firing a shot: "One should not disturb the nesting birds—or the wildflowers," he scoffed, "—apparently for three years this particular region has been occupied by a lot of nature-lovers." The Allies were getting nowhere by just sitting there. ". . . either you make your opponent play your game—or he'll make you play his." When at last the Allies decided to pool their supplies, he commented, "This should have been done three years ago."

If there was audacity in his judgments, there was also patriotism and kindness of heart. He had written at least 5,000 words to Dorothy about the battle around Chateau-Thierry, much of it devoted to the excellence of the American soldier. The errors of officers, he constantly reiterated, were paid for in killed and wounded men. He saw the war not as an unheralded major but somewhat from the point of view of General Pershing. Occasionally the tone of his letters hinted at a yearning to lead—not merely a battalion or a regiment—but a great army, and a confidence that with combat training and a little more staff polishing he could do it well. Large visions came naturally to the man who had worked with Harriman for a globe-girdling transportation system and had participated (even though a Davison subordinate) in the American financing of the British and French war effort.

His essays at grand strategy were perhaps known to some of his staff colleagues. His advantage over most of them in travel, experience, intellect—and money—was as evident as the press in his uniform and the polish of his Sam Browne. In such a position it behooved him to be unassuming in manner and not to flaunt his chumminess with General Wright. In the staff he found an inefficiency and muddle perhaps standard in such groups but which offended the perfectionist Straight because in its small way it lengthened the war. It caused more American soldiers to die. He felt, he wrote Dorothy, that he was "merely being carried along in a great—rather aimless—eddying current." Most of the staff men did not take it as seriously as he: "I keep still—and make a suggestion here & there & then beat it for fear I'll bust wide open & make myself unpopular by getting at 'em to get a move on." In short he did *not* keep still but made suggestions, and his phrase, "I'll bust wide open," is significant. It indicates the tension under which he worked, his inward dissatisfaction with the staff.

He was so outraged at what he regarded as the incompetence of many of the upper-echelon Regular Army officers that he wrote a long, blistering letter to Assistant Secretary of State Phillips in Washington about it:

> . . . We have pot-bellied Major Generals—& incompetent brigadiers—and rotten colonels. The higher you go the worse they are. There has been some canning—but not enough. An attempt is made to bolster up a slob by giving him an efficient Chief of Staff but that won't do. These men must be ruthlessly weeded out. . . . In war morale is everything. Morale is bred by leadership. The handmaiden of leadership is discipline. Discipline is collective self-respect. The man who respects himself shaves—keeps himself clean—salutes—and then when it comes to the last test—will stick till death. . . . The men are made by their officers—a sloppy colonel has sloppy captains . . . and sloppy men. A rotten Division Commander may have some good colonels—but the chances are they will slack on him—and when his command goes into action he will lose. Yet these men are retained. They have influence. Pressure is brought to bear to keep them. Pressure that if listened to is passing for murder—murder by incompetence. It makes me sick at heart. . . .

He urged Phillips, "Use this letter as you will—even if you get me into trouble. I court it really, I feel so strongly—and don't fail to give it to Dorothy."

His hunger for recognition and advancement in rank was enormous, spurred not only by his powerful ambition but also by his determination to make his Army career aid his business comeback after the war. One jump would make him a lieutenant colonel, another a full eagle colonel, just as Roosevelt had been. But in the Army, one who "courts trouble" is not likely to be given advancement. His fluency in French made him useful occasionally to General Wright. His occasional dinners with the General at Fougerolles were not inclined to endear him to fellow staff men less acquainted with the commander. Straight no longer had such a sympathetic confidant as Grayson Murphy. He often spent evenings writing to Dorothy or planning policy for *The New Republic* rather than mixing and drinking with his colleagues. His terrible longing for Dorothy was utterly unlike the run-of-the-mill husbandly homesickness. Letters from her were as essential as the air he breathed, and when they became lost—as the Army had such a talent for doing with letters—or even a few days late, he shed his usual companionability and grew morose.

When to all this was added his insomnia, frequent coughs, fatigue, recurrent trouble with his leg, and general flagging health, the wonder was that he held up as long as he did. "Ever since we came to Paris last year," his valet Bennett noted, "the Major has not been really well— nothing serious, only a continuous run-down—and just like the Major he would never rest up long enough to really recover. When at Langres it was only [on] the strict orders of the doctor there, Major Nichols, that he would stay away from the school for a few weeks, and after that he was fine until we got to Remiremont. Twice there I got the doctor for him. . . ."

As had happened several times in China, he was only dimly aware of his decline and how near he was to cracking. One of his most charming attributes, his friendliness, turned sour. He was less cordial to his staff colleagues, saying privately that the only one he liked was Col. Horace Stebbins.

In a petulant letter to Dorothy August 4, 1918 he declared that there was ill feeling toward him on the staff, first because he was a Reserve officer, second because he had done well at Langres, and third because he was a friend of the General. In next day's letter he repented this outburst, feeling his disgust not wholly warranted, but on August 6 he turned bitter again, once more against Regular Army leadership: "Someday the names of a few men high still in military authority—should be accursed—not for wickedness—but for sheer incompetence." But as he thought more about it, he saw wickedness also. He felt that Army error was responsible for Mitchel's death in the Louisiana air crash. By August 14 he was actually making a little list—or so he wrote—of military misdoers whom he intended to expose after the war.

Gone was the logical, reasonable, delightful Willard Straight. In his place was a man whose letters conveyed affection but were clotted also with resentment toward unnamed Army powers who were hostile to him, holding him back for reasons unknown. But on August 15, a ray of light: "My orders came in today for temporary duty with a Battalion," he wrote to Dorothy, ". . . and I shall learn a lot & get the experience I really long for. . . . Then I'll stick till I'm sent for. There'll not be a peep [of complaint]—under any circumstances." He added testily that his staff colleagues doubtless had arranged it in order to get rid of him. Next day, disaster:

> Your husband—Dorothy—is a crock*—I'm afraid. Altogether a crock. I walked 6 kilometers yesterday in riding boots—and blistered my heel badly. About four this morning [it] started to hurt like blazes. I sent for a Doctor who pronounced it infected. . . . The Doctor told me that despite my buxom appearance—I must be run down or this darned heel would never have flared up as it did. He says—resistance low—ten days rest for mine. . . . just when I had my chance to do the Battalion. . . .

His brethren of the staff, he said, were glad to see him leave. "It was only after a lot of persuasion that he consented to go," Bennett noted. Straight's next letter was on Hotel de Crillon stationery. In Paris he bought white flannel pants and vest and painting articles. He had not been so exhausted and ill-humored, he admitted, since he left Mukden in 1908. Though he was overjoyed to find two of Dorothy's letters at Morgan, Harjes, his own to her—enormously long, perhaps 1,500 words—was in part a tirade against the Army for keeping him down. His disappointment and his debilitated condition had brought him to his worst siege of depression—his first exhibition of temper. Since it had become evident to him, he wrote, that the Army refused to give him credit for his work in War Risk Insurance, his fine record at Langres, and his pamphlet on liaison, he had all the more sought leadership of a

---

* "Crock," a slang word he used also after his 1911 ordeal in China, meant humorously that he was crazy.

battalion as the only way to get recognition and advancement, which would make all the difference in his postwar career. Now, just as his chance had come, he had been thwarted by a blister.

With Colonel Logan, who also got leave, and with Bennett, he left by car with chauffeur for Deauville. He was resentful even toward his old friend from 1718 H Street, wishing Logan had not come. Part of his letter to Dorothy was a fascinating essay on his conception of Army thinking, touching also on his own confidence that he had that elusive quality of leadership that could bring out the best in fighting men:

You are working for the Just Cause—giving all your thought and energy to it. You dramatize it instinctively—you think and talk of all that it means—all that it may mean . . . and you get the big view. Your letters make me feel very small and selfish. . . . You see people like myself are too close to this thing—it's too much our daily life. . . . we [in the Army] have such an infinitesimally small role that when I do indulge in the luxury of thinking—which is rarely—I rather laugh at myself for my presumption. Nor am I under any noble delusion—about going along humbly and playing the game—in a contrite spirit—thanking what Powers there be that I am privileged to serve in the Cause of Democracy. On the contrary—I am far from contrite—I am restless at the restrictions of a very unimportant position—I am intolerant of the faults which I see all about me and which are in most cases due to the lack of imagination and constructive thinking in high places. . . . The Regular Army—as is right is in control. To them this is the opportunity of which they who are capable of dreaming—have dreamed. The trouble is that most of them have no imagination whatsoever. They have in their narrow lives—and men who are now Brigadiers were in some cases captains or majors a year ago—had the muck of the Regular army enlisted man to deal with. That man was in most cases a pretty poor lot—out of a job—pulled from the gutter—in some rare cases a fine lad searching for adventure. The attitude of the officer toward the enlisted man was based on this character. The character of the soldier has changed. He's no longer a man with a thirst and looking for a job—on which he will loaf as much as he can—he has a just cause that he is fighting for. The enlisted man and in most cases the Reserve officer—feels this. Only a few of the Regulars do. . . . The result is that they are always—always missing the possibility of getting the great response that would come from this giant army of ours— if only the *tone* was there in the leadership. . . . It is like a great organ— with all manner of keys and stops . . . and tremolos—depths and chords & harmonies undreamed of—waiting for the master. The master is not here. He is not in Washington. . . . In Washington they talk a lot about music but they don't play. They strum. Here they strum—pick out a feeble tune—haltingly—and every now and then by accident—strike a fine chord. But they don't know their instrument.

The more I am with my men—the more this conviction is borne in upon me. You know them—as I do—more intimately perhaps—Best Beloved—but I know that I could reach their souls. But I know that I'll never really have the chance.

It seems likely that Straight was near nervous collapse and that the Army doctor had seen this. He grew quite wild at times in his letters, always praising Dorothy but telling her that she must know the worst of him, that he really did not measure up to her standard—that while she was letting servants go and cutting corners financially, he took the best room in the best hotel in Deauville. And what was more, he said, he deserved it after the misery he had been through.

He got little sleep the first night because the place was full of officers and their demimondaine women, laughing and clinking glasses in the next room. Next day he moved to the Roche Hotel at nearby Trouville, hoping to shake Logan, who got on his nerves and was stuffy too, keeping military secrets from him. But Logan came along, lounging about in purple pajamas and reading cheap novels. After a few days of sketching around Villauville, Straight was a new man. He wrote affectionate letters to Whitney, copiously illustrated, instructing him to read them to the younger children. "Feel much more fit with a returning sense of humor," he noted in his diary. "Seem to have had quite a case of nerves for a young fellah!" Meanwhile a more competent organist seemed to have arrived, for the Allied armies were on the move and the Germans were giving ground in several places. He wrote to Dorothy, whom he addressed as "wise lady" and "Miss chairman of all things & leader of all good works":

> Today . . . I sketched all day. . . . How I longed to have you sitting there in the long Norman apple orchard—reading. . . . The war seems far away—though one thrills at the new French advance. . . . I think . . . that the end is coming. . . . The Americans have won the war. It will be hard for some of our friends to admit that—but they'll have to. I have a shrewd suspicion that it will make for great jealousy. Surely it will require circumspection on our part—but I hope that some of our friends won't mix circumspection with blindly letting the other fellow put things over on us. . . . Tell Herbert this—though I guess he knows it. . . . Downing Street & the Quai d'Orsay will not forget in a year—the training of centuries.
>
> . . . Once I have [troop experience] I am going to keep my eyes open and try to get out of this strait jacket game altogether into something where there will be a swing. If in about six weeks—Colonel House should ask me to do something for him—I would be very likely to accept. But first I should like to earn one promotion in the tread mill. . . .

One suspects that Dorothy found a quick opportunity to pass this along to House, the *deus ex machina* who could rescue Willard from line duty. Straight was mailing this letter along with several previous complaining ones of which he had reason to be somewhat ashamed. He could have eliminated the earlier ones, but again he exhibited the honesty that was so endearing a quality:

> The sea air & sleep has done wonders. I begin to feel quite a different person—and know I am much more sane & less querulous. The letters that have been written are going on any way—though sometimes I think of tearing them up. I can look back even now and see that I not only have been, but have given written evidence of being, a damned fool. However—such as I am—I am yours, my Dorothy—& it will all go to you for the record. The war continues good. . . . if nothing turns up as I hope it may within six weeks or two months—and if Peace should come—I want to be ordered into a real job. I don't want to apply for anything—for the Union [the Army hierarchy] would turn me down— but I want to be ordered as I was in the War Risk job. . . . After all these months—over eight it is now—I want to bring you back something on a platter—not merely an "also ran."

In his next, however, he exhibited the one propensity of all that could reduce Dorothy to exasperation. It happened that the Wilson administration, under new circumstances in the Far East, had revised its policy toward loans to China, causing Straight to write:

> Above all I wish I were American commissioner at Vladivostok. That would really be taking me back to the old game again—& I should love to do it . . . since the Government has finally come around to the Loan policy . . . I should think they might take me on again.

He hoped not to go back to the unlamented Fifth Corps. On August 26, his leave over, he returned with Bennett to Remiremont, meeting George Marvin, now a liaison officer, on the train. He had met Marvin previously in France and did not feel amiable: "Hence I spent my time reading again after many years—'The Yankee at the Court of King Arthur' which I found amusing & full of a lot of philosophy & satire which I had of course wholly missed when I read it as a kid." General Wright seemed glad to see him. Two days later he was transferred to First Army headquarters at Souilly, which he described as a "dirty town in Lorraine," assigned to personnel work under Col. Robert Barber. He loathed it instantly. He had, he knew, been pulling too many strings for weeks to get a battalion—everyone from General Wright to Colonel

McCoy to Col. Billy Mitchell of the air force—and news of this pressure had got around. In the Army, he told his diary, one was a fool to "monkey with your fate." "I've lost all I've gained," he noted, ". . . and am disgusted and disgruntled. However, Barber's a good fellow and I'll make the best of a bad job."

On the contrary, he began trying almost immediately to escape Colonel Barber. Yet to Dorothy he tried to change his unhappy tune: "For two weeks—poor Dorothy dear—you've been getting wails from me haven't you? . . . from now on if I can't write more cheerfully and less selfishly—you'll get some interesting descriptions of dust & motor trucks . . . no more of this twaddle. . . . though I think you should have held me to a better line these last days & weeks. . . . oh! how I need your wise head and your comforting voice and steady judgment—my Sweetheart."

Never had he so openly admitted his failures in wisdom and his dependence on her. On September 7, their anniversary, Bennett arranged a lavish dinner with fruit and candies and even flowers. Peter Bowditch and several other officers were guests, they drank Dorothy's health with warm champagne, and Straight recalled the Greatest Event in History seven years earlier: ". . . our ride to Montreux—and the train—and then the wonderful dinner on the balcony . . . the moonlight—and the dinner the next night—at Stresa—with Isola Bella—in the quiet lake." How different things were now!

The next anniversary, he said feelingly, he would spend at home with Dorothy and the children.

8. Let's Look Things in the Face

DOROTHY MEANWHILE had taken a subordinate role in the Red Cross drive: "I have spent all of my efforts on 82nd and 83rd Streets carrying out a house to house canvass. . . ." They had raised $150,000,000 instead of the $100,000,000 that had been their goal. Although once, in her most searing profanity, she wrote, "I wish the d—— war were over," this did not imply any loss of dedication. "I made poor Fiedler's hair turn grey yesterday," she wrote later to Willard in a letter that may have added silver to his own sparse locks, "by borrowing a million dollars for investment in the Liberty Loan. You see, the loan has gone very badly. . . ."

Her ability to contribute a million dollars—five times Harry Davison's generous contribution—was only one of the things that set her apart from Willard. She had no disaster to recoup. It was easy for her to be humble, to collect from door to door, to work at times at the YMCA as Carrie Slade's assistant, although her rank equaled Carrie's. She was secure in her position, uncertain only in her worries about her husband. Straight was dreadfully insecure, clinging to her as to a life preserver. It was the Chinese loan and the Morgan connection that had impressed Dorothy's set—not the fact that he was a gifted writer and artist who had performed an emphatic cultural stroke by his part in founding *The New Republic* and *Asia* and who was deeply and intelligently concerned in shortening the war, in making it result in a better world. Mixed in and wrestling with these ideals was his practical knowledge that unless he could make his mark as a soldier, he would return to civilian life with virtually empty hands so far as Dorothy's circle—which had become his own—was concerned. The man whose meat and drink was high achievement and public recognition of that achievement was fading into an obscurity that was insupportable. Or perhaps it was something worse than obscurity—a reputation among the cognoscenti of finance as an interesting dilettante. At a dinner Dorothy attended at the August Belmonts', she was the object of complimentary remarks, to which Belmont added, "I want to tell you that she is married to a very remarkable man—a man who has been underestimated in the past, but who is rapidly going to come into his own." He could hardly have been more patronizing in his appraisal.

"Oh, Dorothy dear," Straight had written her like the most delightfully dependent little boy, "—how I wish you could spoil me a bit!"

Up to now she had spoiled him, praised him as much as was possible by mail: "I want to make you lie down and then stroke your brow and press your wrists. . . ." And about the troublesome leg: "My poor child—if only I could have been near you!" She had promptly framed a group photograph he had sent her and commented, "I love everything about you—the angle of your cap and the cut of your clothes and the shine on your boots—and the dash and spirit of your attitude—the character of your face and the dominance of your entire personality. The others look pathetic beside you and G.M. [Murphy] and it's curious how tremendously you stand out." She was delighted that his stay at Trouville restored his humor. She immediately framed the watercolors he sent her from there. But she was aroused by his longing to go to Vladivostok as American commissioner, and her response was decisive and revealing:

. . . no wonder you want to be your own master and run your own show no matter how small the show may be—I sympathize thoroughly with that point of view—but of course you must take things as they come along and make the very best of each opportunity—and the big chance will come in the long run just as sure as shooting.

I disapprove heartily of your Vladivostok idea—although of course there isn't the slightest doubt that you could be infinitely more useful out there than you could be in France—as a soldier. . . . Best Beloved—let's look things squarely in the face! The one unfortunate impression which you have made on people during these last years is the impression that you don't stick at things—that you want to have a great many irons in the fire, and that your impatience makes you rather jumpy. Rightly or wrongly this criticism is made—the only criticism that I have ever heard, in fact—and you have got to live it down by showing great stick-at-it-iveness. If you left the army now—people would only say "There he goes again"—and for the sake of your future I think it would be a great mistake. You must stick to the army and make good there first of all—and above all things—don't show your disgust by quitting. . . . for you it means sticking at your job—sowing perhaps where others reap—but making good just the same—day after day—and week after week—and in the end it will all work out.

That paragraph told much about Dorothy and Willard and the one question that had come seriously between them. He replied quite tractably:

You are quite right about sticking to it. Vladivostok was a wild dream—crazy—but fascinating—and of course I couldn't have quit the army. But there hasn't been much sticking to it . . . I've not stayed with an outfit and made my place—as Herbert [Parsons] & Grayson [Murphy] have done.

9. In Flew Enza

Bring me, dear love, those things you take away. . . .
Your voice, whose every tone
Sings in my weary brain.
Ah, leave me not alone!
But bring yourself, unchanged, to me again.

THIS WAS written by Dorothy's friend Eliza Morgan Swift and published in a popular magazine. Dorothy clipped it and sent it to Willard, whom she wanted back unchanged except in the matter of stick-at-it-iveness. Her own tenacity was infallible. "Dr. Manning at church this

A.M.," she wrote at Southampton, "dreadful hate sermon. Priscilla Auchincloss lunched with Edith [Lindley] & me & afterward we canned beach plums until 8 o'cl."* She detested the hate-the-Germans theme and was fearful that Willard was leaning in that direction.

Her Southampton efforts came after a hard week at the YMCA building on Madison Avenue, where she had an office and no salary. Hatred, or at least intolerance, was becoming endemic. *The New York Tribune* was running a series of attacks against *The New Republic*, questioning the patriotism of its editors. Dorothy had recently received a letter from William Jay Schieffelin—another stalwart of the National Civic Federation—who had heard second- or third-hand of talk at the Players' Club that made him suspect Herbert Croly of disloyalty and suggest that it might be well to intern him as a traitor. She had held her indignation in check and replied so kindly that Croly's patriotism was unimpeachable and that "the New Republic advocated our entry into the war long before we went in—and now its whole emphasis is being laid on a continuation of the struggle until an absolutely conclusive peace is made," that Schieffelin responded apologetically. She had been invited to help the 1918 Republican campaign and had declined, although Willard considered himself (albeit no party-liner) a Republican. Thrilled at the prospect of a League of Nations, she grew enthusiastic about Wilson: "Senator Lodge made a speech the other day which sounded the keynote of the Republican party opposition,—a punitive war to the limit, the complete destruction of Germany—no League of Nations possible. . . . I'm afraid T.R. will line up with Senator Lodge. . . ."

T.R. did indeed. He wrote to Rudyard Kipling describing the League as "a product of men who wanted everyone to float to heaven on a sloppy sea of universal mush."

Dorothy's friends observed that she looked tired. In one entry she noted, "Wrote to W. all night." Depression being contagious, it was not easy for her to be cheery. She even pondered the meaning of an odd dream in which Willard came into the room with his arm in a sling as though wounded, but looking quite content.

The war news at any rate was wonderful: "I have been pouring [*sic*] over my maps and marking out the line of advance to Thiancourt on

---

* There seems no record of her 1918 canning production, but in 1917 she listed "Our own produce canned" which totaled 240 quarts of vegetables, including 11 of rhubarb, 85 peas, 54 beans, 7 lima beans, 6 carrots, 38 beets, and 39 tomatoes. To this was added canned fruits including 15 jars of strawberries, 8 blackberries, 101 of grape jelly, and 8 quarts of beach plum jam. The guess is that Dorothy's kitchen staff did most of this work.

one side and to Fresnes, Combres, etc. on the other. . . . Our men seem to be able to go through anything. . . . Best Beloved: They—and not your wife—are the Wonders of the World."

Daisy Harriman, improvident as always, had come back, sold her Uplands estate in Westchester to Mrs. Twombly for $200,000, and was letting the money sift through her fingers despite Dorothy's appeals that she let Fiedler supervise her expenditures. Daisy bought a handsome house on F Street in Washington, made a social splash at the embassies, and became the benefactress of the Amazonian Colonel Batchkarova of the Soviet women's Battalion of Death. Colonel Batchkarova, still in pain from a wound in her side, was making a considerable impression in the capital. Daisy urged her to have her uniform cleaned and mended, which the colonel did, Daisy receiving a bill for $200 from the tailor. Colonel Batchkarova soon returned to Russia. She left a manuscript about her exploits for Daisy to get translated and published and a fifteen-year-old sister, Naja, who spoke little English, for Daisy to care for until Russia became safer. Daisy, torn between amusement and despair, sent Naja to a boarding school on N Street, then sailed back to France bearing Dorothy's gifts for Willard. Beatrice and Prather Fletcher had been with Dorothy again for a few days, and it developed that their quarreling was serious enough to threaten their marriage. Dorothy was out of patience with Fletcher—all the more so because he was the most reactionary of Republicans. ". . . I realize I married a perfect angel who has always spoiled me," she wrote to Willard, "—whereas Beatrice married a crabbed, selfish old egoist who crosses her at every turn."

September 27 was a great day because it began with the news that Bulgaria had asked for an armistice and ended with Dorothy accompanying Ruth Pratt to hear the President speak in New York. ". . . he said the most momentous things and actually planted the League of Nations in the forefront of all war aims," she wrote to her husband. "I was thrilled all through for he seemed to me to stand forth again as the leader of the world. Oh—if only France and England will respond and stand with him! . . . . A punitive peace will surely only lay the foundation for further wars. . . . Does this sound like bunk to you, Best Beloved—and have you become an out and out bitter-ender? I wish I could know how you feel about it all. . . ."

On a YMCA trip to Newport, where she stayed at the palace of Mrs. Arthur Curtiss James (and made private fun of Mrs. James's social grandeur), she first saw the increasingly alarming proportions of the influenza epidemic:

> . . . such a tragic thing is happening. Spanish influenza is sweeping through this place and some of the Y. huts have had to be transformed into hospitals. The condition of the sick men is perfectly pathetic, for there are not enough nurses to look after them and consequently they are dying in large numbers. Out of 400 men who were ill in one of the naval stations 60 died. . . . Poor Camp Devens has 10,000 cases of it—Upton about 1500—and practically all the other camps [are] beginning to show signs of infection. The disease is taking a very virulent form in this country—for it seems to run into pneumonia in the majority of cases, and it is spreading like wild fire everywhere.

A couplet of the day was, "I opened the winda / And in flew Enza," but that was the only humor in it. A week later Dorothy wrote, "Oh, Willard—do you really think we might get peace this year!" then again told of the contagion:

> This influenza epidemic is holding up all our work in the camps, and it is really growing very alarming—165,000 cases in the camps alone, and a tremendous increase among the civilian populations everywhere. Schools and theaters and shops are being closed, but the disease is running riot just the same. Many of our own friends have contracted it, and the mortality is so high that it is really quite frightening. I'm only thankful that it is not as bad as this in France.

And another week later:

> I am now slated to go down to Atlanta and help organize the whole southern [YMCA] department for women's work—but the trip has been temporarily postponed on account of the influenza epidemic. Oh Willard—you can't imagine how terrible it is in this country. Already 13,000 men have died in the camps alone. . . . As is always the case in such epidemics, the toll is heaviest among the poor people. . . . In Philadelphia everything has been closed for weeks—and the streets just a long funeral procession with the bodies just being carried in ordinary boxes—for coffins are now unobtainable. It's all just like a hideous plague.

10. The Blues

"I ALWAYS seem to be making brilliant starts at things," Straight wrote to Dorothy, "and then petering out—because I guess—I don't stay put—

and really go through—I don't envy Grayson & Stebbins and the rest—
but I long for a chance to have a job in which I can deliver—for I want
to make good and be a Lieutenant Colonel too—just to show that I have
not been a dilettante but have been able to perform."

He was witnessing from the rear the largely American offensive that
erased the St. Mihiel salient. He had a pleasant office in the tall-win-
dowed library of the home of an attorney, its walls lined not only with
law books but with such things ordinarily interesting to the broad-roving
Straight mind as histories of Nancy and Bar-le-Duc and the works of
Montesquieu. One of his duties was to interrogate questionable prisoners:

> On this road—the great artery—the whole life of the army [is] con-
> centrated—artillery—supplies—gasolene—barbed wire—wood—timber—
> Y.M.C.A. Fords—Staff cars—Dodges—Cadillacs . . . horse-drawn field
> kitchens—mule-drawn machine guns, ambulances, small guns, big
> guns—trucks with troops—empties coming back. . . . Dust—dust—
> dust—everywhere—motorcycles with despatch riders—whistling and
> cursing and stumbling as they tried to get through. . . . On the road I
> met a Doctor Colonel whom I hadn't seen since Peking—14 years ago—
> and on a Y.M.C.A truck was a woman speaking excellent English who
> claimed to have been governess for M. Stephen Pichon—Ministre de
> France in China in 1900. She spoke Boche, not French . . . & her
> knowledge of the details of the Peking siege were [sic] very vague—so I
> sent in a report on her & told them to have her watched. The Boche
> frequently plant their spies as they go back.

His boss, Colonel Barber, so affected him that "whenever I am with
him I nearly screech with nerves. He's a very bright—but very un-
stable—mind I think—& has the faculty which some men have of
thoroughly upsetting everyone he comes in contact with." But the Colonel paid him the compliment of making him his first deputy and chose
him as his companion to view a predawn attack from a hilltop vantage
point:

> The fire became gradually more intense—and then at 5:30 the barrage
> started. There was a continual roar—from west to east—rolling—
> rolling—punctuated by the duller sound of the heavy guns. Red rockets
> came up from the Boche lines—all along. The attack was on. Some-
> where down in that sea of mist men were going over the top—in long
> lines—and clambering over obstacles—cutting wire—sweating—curs-
> ing—struggling. Yet but for that incessant roar it seemed so beautiful in
> the waning moonlight. Then the first tinge of dawn—and day came rap-

idly. The sky was gray & gold & green—then pink & salmon—with mauve cloud banks. . . . Balloons in observation climbed up like huge beans—dotted along the front. The airplanes soared over head and went forward. Beneath us was the sea of mist still. A spire here—a row of trees there—the two walls of poplars along a highway. . . . The trees of the Argonne were silhouetted against the soft damp cloud. And all the time that roar. It became brighter—but the mist still clung in patches—like a Japanese print. . . . it was unpleasant to be merely rubber neck- ing. . . .

Many a reporter would have envied Straight's vivid gift. His dolor increased when Bennett suffered a paralyzing, perhaps fatal, injury to his spine in an automobile accident. "Poor chap," he wrote to Dorothy after visiting him at the base hospital, "I can't get the thought of him out of my mind. . . . I am quite miserable thank you—because I'm not in it—but I keep quoting Henley's poem to myself."

It's a chilly day—and wet—and I'm feeling sort of rocky—and blue. Ben- nett—not being in this show at all—not having anything save clerical de- tails to handle—all combine to make me long for a nice bright room with chintzes—and a clean smell—and silver and nice glass—and a little music & soft rugs & no uniforms—and no war—and my Sweetheart to pat my head. But that's not yet. I must confess that I look forward to these next months with horror. They'll be awful—at best—whether one be with an army Hdqs. in a town—or in the dugouts up forward. So it goes. Damn the Hun anyway.

Walter Lippmann arrived on some War Department errand and dined with Straight, who reflected, "He's going to be 150% better too [as a writer] because of the experience." Lippmann recorded, ". . . we talked far into the night hoping, planning, sometimes doubting [that victory would be put to farsighted use], but in the end renewed." But Straight could not rise from what he admitted was a slough of despond. The American troops were performing splendidly. Both Grayson Murphy and Herbert Parsons were staff officers with fighting outfits. "Everybody with their tails up," Straight wrote in his diary, "and I'm not in it." A recurrence of inflammation in his leg made him bandage it up again and walk gingerly for several days. He had an aching molar ex- tracted, and his whole head was sore. He was troubled about what he would do if the war ever got over, in the same letter saying, "I think that take it all in all . . . I'd like to go home at once & help Herbert on the N.R.," and asking Dorothy to exert whatever influence she could in Washington or with Martin Egan or with anyone who might help him to get a post in the peace negotiations—which of course would not permit him to go home at once. He thanked her for thinking him "such a wonder":

> It's lucky for you and for me that you do—You have given me everything to be thankful for—everything in the world—and I should be happy & my soul should sing all day in the knowledge that you care. That and inner knowledge that one is doing one's best—and making good—will give the armour that will turn away any shafts that the world may throw. But the trouble just now—is, and for some time has been—that the inner satisfaction of work well done is not there.

Weather: gray, gray, gray, rain, rain, rain. Health: shaky, with something between a cold and a touch of the flu. Sleep: fitful. Mood: fearfully depressed. In most of his letters now was a heavy strain of misery and resentment, a paragraph or two devoted to the same refrain: no recognition of his services, no promotion, no combat duty. These were the invariable themes, though he was inventive in orchestrating them:

> In one of the very best divisions now—practically all the Battalion commanders are youngsters—some of them twice wounded—who have been in the show from the outset. Many of 'em were 2d Lieutenants a year—& less ago. . . . I guess I'll give up trying to be a soldier—a real fighting man—& take my old bald head—& my bad eyes—& my teeth & my sore throat . . . & be a sybarite & one of the kind of staff officers that the fighting man, & rightly—despises.

He no longer made any effort to hide his disgust. He apologized to Dorothy about his complaining letters and urged her not to worry about his complaints since they were therapeutic—it did him good to get them off his chest. But they hardly made pleasant reading for her. He had, he admitted, steadily broken Army tradition, pulled strings without being discriminating about it, urged the intervention of too many colonels and generals. As a personnel officer himself whose duty it was to place junior officers on the basis of their records, he had to admit that he belonged just about where he was. He was at times like a man looking in a mirror, seeing clearly his own faults and rejecting responsibility for them.

On October 24 came a reprieve: He was being transferred to the Generalissimo's headquarters, the seat of Marshal Foch, at a town whose name was a military secret but which was Senlis, thirty miles northeast of Paris, almost a suburb. It was an assignment that most

officers would have greeted with reverence, but Straight's gloom was so
pervasive that he saw it only as a change, a chance to break loose from
Colonel Barber, whose hand he could not have shaken very warmly as
he left. "Back in Paris," he wrote to Dorothy, "—arrived late tonight.
There I am—after dinner went to the Ritz to see Daisy—for a moment.
. . . She said you were very tired & doing entirely too much. That is
what I feared—you must stop. . . . Also more of gossip. It all [seemed]
sort of crazy. I loved hearing of you & the kids—but the rest—I don't
know—I seem to have changed . . . but I felt like saying Oh Hell to it
all. . . . She's pathetic—our Daisy, but so human."

Straight had not been in Paris for weeks and had toward its luxuries
and artificialities the somewhat censorious attitude of the soldier arriving
from near-the-front inconveniences and the knowledge that many men
were dying: "More of the same atmosphere . . . old old stuff again—
back biting—quibbling. . . . Saw Davy [Davison] & Mrs. Havemeyer
. . . Ogden [Reid]—Perry [Osborn]—Lloyd [Griscom]—Martin
[Egan]—[Edward] Stettinius—everyone in the place more or less—trying to get wise to what is going on. . . . I dined with Walter [Lipp-
mann]." His handwriting, always minuscule but originally decorative
and fairly legible, was becoming extremely difficult to read. On October
29 he was established at Senlis with a new orderly named Joe, working
under Col. Theobald Mott, U.S.A., their duty being to evaluate and
pass on information and reports from the Generalissimo's staff to Pershing's Paris headquarters at 78 Rue de Varenne. Senlis was a lovely
town of 5,000 population with its fine old Church of Notre Dame, a fif-
teenth-century town hall, and handsome old private houses. At Foch's
headquarters were military missions from the other Allies, including
England, Belgium, Holland, and Italy. Flickers of interest were visible
through Straight's dejection:

> . . . I see daylight ahead I think [he wrote to Dorothy]. Here I am in a
> very nice country house in the outskirts of a well known village not far
> from Paris—have been introduced to the popots [mess] where eats the
> staff of the Marechal—& duly installed there. . . . The afternoon sun is
> streaming in through tall windows . . . and I can see in the distance—
> through the golden foliage the slim spire—that rises above the town—a
> needle pointing straight to Heaven. . . . Elsie de Wolfe in blue & white
> just drove up in a Ford ambulance—to invite us all to dinner tomorrow
> night chez Mme. la Baronne Henri de Rothschild—Truly these are the
> horrors of war. I am not quite sure of the lay of the land yet. The town is
> pretty—the living comfortable. . . . Bennett incidentally is coming on
> well. He should live—but may be paralyzed for months to come. . . .

[This is] the sort of job that would be wonderful for a junior officer—with diplomatic experience & who knew his way about. Ten years ago I should have loved it. . . . There's no work in it—it's merely getting certain dope & being polite & persona grata. . . . As it is I feel as if I have hardly the right to go breezing about in a uniform—which has been honored by so many brave men.

"I hear that Willard is on some duty at General Foch's headquarters," Grayson Murphy wrote to his family. "I am afraid it is a sort of diplomatic liaison job. Poor Willard—he tried so hard, and he is so fine and able. He would have been invaluable in the right place, and through no fault of his, his great talents have been so largely wasted on little things. Well, it has been the story of many splendid men in this war."

So fearful was the American epidemic that some people went to business with gauze over their faces and some simply stayed home. Public assemblages were forbidden. In New York this applied also to political meetings, so that Alfred Emanuel Smith and Charles S. Whitman fought their campaign for the governorship solely through the medium of the newspapers. At long last the state had given women the franchise, but it did Dorothy little good, since she had virtually given up on the Republicans nor would she vote for Smith despite his honesty, because he was a Tammany man. Perhaps she had forgotten about her father's long Tammany loyalty. While she tended toward the Democrats, the reactionary policies of Southern Democrats made her feel that a third party might be the answer, and she had, for example, contributed $2,000 to the farmer- and labor-oriented National Party candidate for Congress in Minnesota. She refused to be intimidated into inactivity by the contagion, as a typical diary entry in October showed:

Talk about Home Ef. Sch. with Harriet Pratt this A.M.—then meeting of Team Captains for War Work Campaign. Lunch Colony Club with Nathalie & Priscilla Bartlett—office all P.M. Stopped to see Bert Patchins on way to dinner at N.R.—[at which were] Col. Thompson—Lamonts— Bill Hard—Mr. Barnes—Robinson & Beard—etc. Discussion of New Sch. Hungary proclaims herself independent.

The independence of Hungary was of importance not only as a sign of a further cracking of the Central Powers but one of hope for the enemy Széchényis. The count was an officer in the Austro-Hungarian army, and Gladys, with whom the girl Dorothy had "telephoned" across 57th Street, had had her $9,000,000 in American investments appropriated by the Alien Property Custodian. (Dorothy had Gladys's Budapest address in her diary and soon would be able to write to her again.) As for William Hard, she wrote to Willard, he had "developed the most wonderful idea" for the New School "as a sort of research body, in both domestic and foreign fields," so that "we all got quite excited about it and saw ourselves starting the school at once. . . . I can never be reconciled to not seeing your face across that table, with a long cigar in your mouth." Croly and others also enjoyed cigars, and Havanas were offered with the coffee, which caused a contretemps when the poet Amy Lowell was a guest and the butler passed her by. "Herbert," she protested in her resonant baritone, "your man went by me with the cigars." "Give Miss Lowell a cigar, Etienne," Croly told the astonished butler.

Dorothy had talked to Beatrice Bend Fletcher "like a Dutch uncle," surprised that one so sophisticated socially could be so naive about some aspects of marriage, and felt that the Fletchers returned to Mexico on better terms.* She was upset because the marriages of some of her friends seemed unhappy. Mary Harriman Rumsey, she felt, was being pursued rather purposefully by an army colonel, and a banker was showing excessive interest in Ruth Pratt: "Perhaps if I were married to John Pratt or Pad, etc. I should act in exactly the same way—but being married to you, I have no heart for anyone else. I think that life is much simpler when one is deeply in love with one's husband." Nevertheless she confessed enough inconstancy to go with friends to a "very gay party at the Ritz" with her old beau, the still unmarried Charlie Draper, as her escort. They then went to the theater—by chance the one attended by President Wilson, in town for the Liberty Loan parade: ". . . the enthusiasm he aroused was simply stupendous. The theatre audience went perfectly wild. . . . He sat in a box with Mrs. Wilson (minus orchids) Colonel and Mrs. House. . . ." But elsewhere, "The President is being so abused and vilified, that the whole country is being divided into two great camps. . . . The House and the Senate have been literally roaring with 'unconditional surrender' speeches—and everybody seems so hell bent on the war that they simply won't listen to any talk of peace. . . . It is righteous anger run amuck, I think. . . . this policy of destruction would only leave an embittered, united Germany, whose resolve would be to, some day, get even—and pull off the thing that they didn't manage to get away with this time." (Miss Spence would not have approved of her appropriation of Straight usages such as "pull off" and "Dutch uncle," not to mention "hell bent.")

---

* The Fletchers remained married until Beatrice's death in 1937.

Roosevelt's letter to Willard about the "poisonous" character of *The New Republic* had scarcely pleased her, nor had his demand for the repudiation of the Fourteen Points. Indeed she thought virtually all of his latter-day politics tragically misguided. Still, "Ethel [Derby] came over to lunch, and she was just as sweet and delightful as she could be, and made me feel that our friendship could stand well the test of this dividing and troublous time. . . . [But it] isn't easy to be in a state of fundamental disagreement with the people one loves." Dorothy sought to comfort her husband:

> Your later letter—number 46 is so depressed and blue that I had to gulp pretty hard once or twice as I read it. But really, Willard—the one thing that matters is the fact of your having made good all along the line—and even though you didn't get all the fighting you wanted, or the promotion you hoped for—the actual accomplishment is there—and everybody knows it. . . . I suppose, at heart, my overmastering feeling is just unutterable thankfulness that you are safe and sound and that you have been able to serve your country as richly and fully as you have done. I thank God every day of my life for these two blessed certainties!

Meanwhile Colonel House, about to leave for France, told Croly that he had "important plans" for Straight and asked him to tell Mrs. Straight about it. "I called him [House] up immediately," she wrote to Willard, ". . . and we had a nice, friendly, little farewell word—in which I asked him to tell you that I could wish nothing better for you than the opportunity of helping him in this tremendous world game. If the thing can be pulled off as he plans it, I think it will be the second greatest event in all history. . . . Oh Willard, I dreamed of you last night again, and this time you were home for a day or two on Col. H's mission. It's always hard to come to—after dreams of this kind which make my Borderland seem nearer."

11. Anniversary of First Love

THE BEAUTY of Senlis after the dirt of Lorraine, and the novelty of his assignment, gave Straight transient diversion. He stopped in at the cathedral and made himself known to the curé, a benign little man, l'Abbé Dourlent. While there, he said a prayer "to" Dorothy, following his practice of willing her presence with him. But he soon reflected ironically on the importance, danger, and exhilaration of his new work.

For example, he and a lieutenant colonel, both Langres graduates, spent most of a morning coding a message. Now and then he was asked by Colonel Mott to gird up his courage, put on his tin helmet, and send information by telephone to the American HQ in Paris. He estimated that he was doing work equivalent to that of a Second Secretary of Legation in a banana republic. Yet he was one of the few privileged to come and go at this headquarters of all headquarters, this brain center of the Allied armies, with news from all fronts coming in constantly. The news he was hearing indicated that the war was all but over—good news, certainly, though to him it meant that he was missing the great final push and that opportunity was forever gone. His annoyance approached anger when Daisy Harriman and Mrs. House came to see Foch's chateau and viewed him along with the other exhibits.

"Poor dear Daisy," he grumbled, " she's having such a wonderful time gossiping & wearing a uniform around—& is really such a damned fool—despite all her charms—& is so bent always on amusing herself."

But think of the Italians, heretofore so lightly regarded, whipping the Austrians! "The Dagos are working themselves up into a great military nation as the result," Straight observed, "& will sing of the days of the Roman Eagles again. . . . It reads like a pipe dream. Turkey capitulating today—The Boche tumble next & I have a hunch that this tumble is going to be the most dramatic of all. The 15th of November looks like a good date to me [for German capitulation]—& my money seems safe. I'll win back enough to pay my previous bets on this subject. . . . Goodnight," he finished his letter to Dorothy, "—we are attacking tomorrow—It will be a very big party. If only I were in it—but I'm not."

On November 4 his new prediction was on the mark: ". . . it looks as if the show should be over in a week—not more—The Boche have no choice now . . . their goose is thoroughly & perfectly cooked." He thanked Dorothy for two letters: "The first one in answer to those horrid letters from Trouville. I'm sorry they weren't lost. However, it's all part of the picture. . . . the same old record of change, shifting, the rolling stone—has continued—I guess it's fate or something—and the war ends—& I've done many things—and am still a Major—& people will wonder why—if I was such a wonder as you seem to think—I didn't get a promotion." The American gains were splendid: "After lunch & again after dinner we go to Headquarters—& get the latest dope from all fronts." His mess was amusing, good practice in French. One of the French officers, learning that Straight had been in the banking business, seriously asked his advice about starting a mushroom trust. There were millions in it, he said.

Straight observed that while others could tell of their exploits on the front lines, he could say that he carried messages for his colonel, Tibby Mott. One of his troubles, he argued, at J. P. Morgan's, AIC, and in the Army too, was that he spoke French and was housebroken so that he was invariably given a front-man, handshaking, pink-tea job instead of the real thing, and people would always think that he had looked for cinches. He had to admit that there were many Regular officers who never got as near the shooting as he did, but that did not seem to help. "I hate to find myself at the end of the war in the lap of luxury—it's like going to a wonderful dinner after you've had too big a tea and no exercise."

His endless raking of these same acrid embers was unlike the letter writer who was otherwise so instinctive in his avoidance of the hackneyed and repetitious. He would have been happiest if he, like Douglas MacArthur, could have gone over the top in the darkness before dawn, staggered with his men across a starlit, shell-pocked no-man's-land, gained the German trenches, and even, if possible, shot a Boche or two before returning with a spiked helmet. The promotion—the silver oak leaves—was now all that he could hope for. He knew he had been foolish in making so many requests and solicitations. He had buttonholed so many senior officers, asking for special consideration in getting the post he wanted, that they stumbled over each other, compared notes, and became offended. One of them had mentioned to him obliquely that he, Straight, seemed to be asking a great many people for favors. At times Straight conceded all this in his diary and letters. Yet he could not subside into the stoic acceptance of disappointment that is the mark of another kind of excellence, any more than could MacArthur. He needed to protest, to be comforted. He needed Dorothy.

His blues had begun at Remiremont early in August, and after that blessed but brief remission when he rested and painted at Trouville, they had hounded him again at Souilly and were still with him in somewhat moderated or exhausted form at Senlis early in November. His mother had written of him as a small boy that "he revels in the luxury of woe." A part of many of his letters for three months had been devoted to querulous repetitions of his ill luck, the injustice with which he had been treated, and how galling it was now to be goldbricking at Senlis while Murphy and Parsons were in it at the front, experiencing the real thing. Never did Dorothy tell him that most officers would be delighted to have the misfortune to be assigned to the Generalissimo's chateau, nor did she hint that the Army after all was an arbitrary institution that she could not change, that one could not always expect one's pleasure to be consulted and must take orders with the best grace possible. Only once did she admit that she was terribly depressed herself. If this was a reminder that she had troubles of her own, it was unsuccessful for he only replied how odd it was that both of them were down on their springs at the same time.

For all that, he was still the family man, remembering his children. He wrote quite seriously to Whitney Willard Straight on his sixth birthday, violating fact a trifle by saying that just as the war began on the day Beatrice was born, "so the war came to an end—really—on your birthday," and that "should mean that there will be a new and better world—and there will be no more wars."

The next day was the seventh of November, the ninth anniversary of that glorious day in Peking when he and Dorothy—with Beatrice Bend and Prather—had visited the Jade Temple and come back to discover, in the evening, that each knew there was a bond between them. For all his affliction, he did not forget it now. But first he telephoned Colonel House, now established on the Rue de l'Université, to ask about the "important work" the Colonel had in mind for him. House was in high excitement over the news that the German peace delegation was ready to pass through the Allied lines. He asked Straight to see him next day.

Next, through Fiedler, Straight sent a cable to Croly that both the editor and Dorothy were to cheer, relieving the fear that he was a grim bitter-ender. It was in his best manner—the Willard Straight of political and editorial responsibility throwing off for the moment his own weight of disappointment, thinking instead of the terrible cost of the war, thinking of what the war should buy for everyone. He was nonpartisan, progressive, humanitarian as *The New Republic* was at its best. Incidentally he gave his opinion of the policies of his old friend Colonel Roosevelt without mentioning his name. He noted that in the elections just finished the Republicans had made gains. They were increasing their propaganda for a return to isolationism, attacking President Wilson, attacking his idea of a world program for peace:

HIS CONCEPTION OF A LEAGUE OF NATIONS AND AN INTERNATIONAL ORGA-
NIZATION FOUNDED ON JUSTICE HAS GIVEN COURAGE AND HOPE THROUGH-
OUT THE WORLD. STILL AS BEFORE TORN BY JEALOUSY AND POLITICAL JOB-
BERY THE WORLD NOW LOOKS TO HIM TO SHOW THE WAY TO THE NEW
ORDER. HE HAS OUTLINED, AND VICTORY HAS MADE POSSIBLE, AN ATTEMPT

TO REALIZE THE PRACTICAL POLITICAL APPLICATION OF THE BASIC PRINCI-
PLES ON WHICH ALL RELIGION NOT CHRISTIANITY ALONE, REST. IF THIS
CONCEPT OF A NEW WORLD BE IMPLEMENTED BY CREATING THE NUCLEUS
OF AN INTERNATIONAL ORGANIZATION TO UTILIZE AND COORDINATE AL-
READY EXISTING AGENCIES THE SACRIFICE WHICH THE WORLD HAS MADE
WILL BE CONSECRATED. IF THIS IS NOT DONE THE GREATEST OPPORTUNITY
IN HISTORY WILL BE LOST. BY VIRTUE OF THE PRESIDENT'S LEADERSHIP AND
BECAUSE OF OUR NATIONAL EFFORT WE ARE THE CORNERSTONE UPON
WHICH THIS NEW WORLD STRUCTURE MUST BE ERECTED. CHAUVINISTS AND
POLITICAL PARTISANS HOWEVER HAVE TAKEN ADVANTAGE OF THE NATIONAL
IMPATIENCE. . . . THEY HAVE ATTEMPTED TO UNDERMINE THE POWER OF
THE PRESIDENT AND TO PREVENT THE REALIZATION OF A PROGRAMME WITH
WHICH THEY HAVE NEVER BEEN IN SYMPATHY BUT WHICH THEY HAVE NOT
DARED OPENLY TO OPPOSE. THE AMERICAN JUNKER, LABOUR AND CAPITAL
ALIKE, THE PROTECTIONIST, THE CHAUVINIST ARE EXPLOITING AN AWAKENED
BUT UNTHINKING PUBLIC AND BY SPECIOUS ARGUMENTS ARE CREATING
AN OPPOSITION TO THE ASSUMPTION OF NATIONAL RESPONSIBILITIES WHICH
MIGHT INTERFERE WITH THEIR PERSONAL INTERESTS OR AMBITIONS. THE
TASK OF THE UNITED STATES HAS ONLY BEEN BEGUN. BY ENTERING THE
WAR WHEN AND AS WE DID WE PREVENTED THE DESTRUCTION OF LIBERAL
IDEALS. GERMANY HAVING BEEN DEFEATED WE HAVE NOW THE LESS DRA-
MATIC AND LESS SPECIFIC AND INFINITELY MORE DIFFICULT TASK OF MAKING
GOOD ON THE IMPLICATIONS OF OUR DECLARATIONS AND LEADING IN
WORLD POLITICAL RECONSTRUCTION. THERE IS ONLY ONE POSSIBLE LEADER,
THE PRESIDENT. . . . THERE WILL NECESSARILY BE CRITICISMS OF TECH-
NIQUE AND ADMINISTRATIVE METHODS AND DIFFERENCES AS TO THE FORM
WHICH OUR PARTICIPATION IN THE INTERNATIONAL ORGANIZATION SHALL
TAKE. BUT THIS CRITICISM MUST NOT BE TWISTED AND EXPLOITED TO OB-
SCURE OR TO DEFEAT THE PURPOSES FOR WHICH WE WENT TO WAR. TO
PERMIT THIS WOULD BE TO BETRAY EVERY MAN WHO HAS SERVED AND
EVERY WOMAN WHO HAS GIVEN. THE PRESIDENT ALONE CAN LEAD EUROPE.
WE MUST HOLD UP HIS HANDS IN ORDER THAT THOSE WHO OPPOSE HIM
HERE MAY NOT BE ABLE TO APPEAL TO THEIR OWN PEOPLE WHO BELIEVE IN
HIM ON THE GROUND THAT HE IS NOT GIVEN THE WHOLE HEARTED SUPPORT
OF HIS OWN COUNTRYMEN. [Straight urged, even ordered, Croly:] GO TO
THIS AND DEVELOP IT AND KEEP AT IT. FRAME IT SO THAT IT WILL GET
ACROSS TO THE LOW BROW. ARRANGE TO SEND TWO OR THREE THOUSAND
COPIES EACH WEEK THROUGH THE Y.M.C.A. OR RED CROSS FOR DISTRIBU-
TION TO THE A.E.F. IT IS VITALLY IMPORTANT THAT OUR TROOPS BE EDU-
CATED PRIOR TO THEIR RETURN. THIS IS A LONG PULL. . . .

Certainly no one could now suggest that Straight might hope in 1920
to ride to political power on the coattails of Roosevelt, who was likely to
regard this as redolent of *The New Republic* sewage. That evening,
Straight furnished champagne and fine Havana cigars for the officers'
dinner. The men gathered there, wearing six different Allied uniforms,

were entitled to think it was in celebration of the dispatch of the peace delegation, but it was in fact to mark the anniversary of first love. Straight described the scene:

> General Destiches—the Marshal's No. 3—a sort of Secretary & general executive—came in late—& sat next to me. He was most courteous and very communicative. . . . He said that we were at the dawn of a new era—that there would be a new world—that Mr. Wilson had made it possible . . . and that he had taken a position so elevated—that all the rest would be ashamed not to follow. . . . He spoke of the Crusaders' spirit of the Americans—and was most flattering about our army. He should be. He also said that the thing must be [ended] at once—for Bolshevism was spreading and there might well be mutiny in the German army. . . . orders had been given which would enable the [German] delegates to get through—but that aside from that nothing would be changed—& when they were once through that the show would go on as before. This was in beautiful laconic French—a historic [statement] that the school-boys will read in years to come. The soldiers' ideal!

12. Our Day Some Day Soon

STRAIGHT'S LUNCHEON in Paris with Colonel House was not precisely private, since Colonel Mott, Gordon Auchincloss, House's assistant and son-in-law, and Mrs. House were also present. But House was "very nice indeed," Straight reported, and said that almost the last person he had spoken with before sailing was "your dear wife." He did not yet know which of several assignments would be best for Straight, one of them being a mission to Austria to organize an information service for the Czechs and Jugoslavs. That night Straight dined at Larue with two old friends from all over the world, Peter Bowditch and Warwick Greene, both of them former majors now visiting pangs on Straight by wearing the silver oak leaves. What with the news that the Kaiser had abdicated and the Crown Prince had renounced the throne, it is unlikely that their dinner was entirely sedate. "So ends Germany," Straight observed. "What days these be!"

At Senlis next day, November 10, a Sunday, news came of the Kaiser's escape to Holland, of the proclamation of the German Social Democratic Republic. General Destiches came in briefly and said, "La guerre, c'est terminée," but even if he was right in a sense, it was not yet official. At dinner they all fell to the remaining six bottles of Straight's champagne, and Colonel Valcotte said, "Nos devoirs militaires sont terminés—nos devoirs sociales commencent." But still it was not official. That evening, Colonel Mott drove to the Pershing HQ in Paris with the text of the Allied armistice terms. Straight was left at Senlis to receive word from Compiègne, where the German delegates were negotiating with the victors. If the armistice conditions were unchanged, he would telegraph Paris when the agreement came and his job was done. If they were changed, he would take the text of the new terms to the city. As he waited in the library of the chateau, he wrote to Dorothy:

> When the armistice is signed I'll close this letter—This is the last line written during war time. . . . All through you have been so wonderful— from the time we first talked it out as I sat on the edge of your bed—do you remember—when you stood on the platform in Jamaica—when we were together in Washington having those cozy luncheons—when you came to the dock & inspected the war risk detachment—all these hard months since—and you've grown so tremendously . . . and been such an inspiration to all about you . . . I respect & admire you—my Dorothy—You are the Wonder of the World—I am grateful grateful that you have given me your love—My Sweetheart—I pray that I may be worthy—always—
> 5:40 A.M. Nov. 11ᵗʰ General Destiches has telephoned that hostilities will cease on Nov. 11—at 11 A.M. I have telephoned to Col. House. Been sleeping on the floor here in the library. It is Peace—Best Beloved—think what it means!

Hence Major Straight had the honor to be the first to spread the news to a waiting world of the end of the great war. He dozed until the official armistice text arrived near eleven and he headed for Paris: "As I came into town the news was percolating through the villages . . . flags were coming out. . . . The Place de la Concorde & Rue de la Paix [two fitting names this day] were already crowded at noon—Fifteen minutes later it was almost impassable for an auto." He left the text at headquarters, then saw Colonel House. The little colonel with the small neat mustache—so neat in every way—had a broad smile. Straight's job, he said, would be to help him at the peace conference to be held in Paris.

It was the post Straight had longed for, but he left the Colonel without seeming overjoyed. He would be charged with preliminary arrangements, and he would stay on for the conference itself. While *that* was in session, he would have the ear of the President's other self, Colonel House, and would also have the ringside seat that Croly had crowed about when he thought *he* would have it. Indeed it was an occasion that Straight should have been elated about, both for himself and for *The New Republic*. He was not. He seemed a man possessed with resentment. It is clear from his diary and letters that he was too weary, too run down and in need of sleep to rise above his despondency. His mind replayed the same sad record, which he passed on to Dorothy in a long and disorderly letter partly devoted to self-commiseration: His military career had ended in a fizzle; he was moving into what people regarded as a soft job and would be accused again of chasing cinches; all his friends had got their promotions—told him he was just a victim of hard luck, that it meant nothing anyway; but it *did* mean something, and he was bitter over his failure to bring Dorothy—and the children—a decoration or even a promotion.

Even old Cornelius Vanderbilt, now fifty-five, once disowned by the family, had become a colonel of engineers and won the Distinguished Service Medal. Even Mrs. Herman Harjes won a Croix de Guerre for canteen duty near the front.

Straight took a room at the Crillon and called on Walter Lippmann, who was at the same hotel. Lippmann in earlier talks with Straight had found that in him at times "loneliness was all too close to heartbreak." His record of this conversation and several later ones with Straight was combined in one letter to Dorothy so that the several conversations cannot be distinguished from each other. Also, his letter is clouded in Lippmannesque obscurity, perhaps for her benefit. It mentions "that personal loneliness which is the background of so many of us over here"; but also that Straight was deeply concerned that "those who will decide" the peace might not have the true conception of "what alone could justify it all"—that is, justify the war. Straight's diary covering the same events is by comparison with his letter to Dorothy so cool and businesslike that it seems written by a different person: "Had long talk with Walter. Organization the first problem to get it functioning right. That's my first job."

Leaving Lippmann, he fought his way unhappily through noisy gaiety from the Place de la Concorde to the Place Vendôme. In the midst of these shouting, gesticulating, singing, dancing thousands he was an island of unhappiness, again preoccupied with what he regarded as his own failure. "Many drunk in the streets," he noted, "—all nationalities sharing the honour." He dined at the Ritz with Martin and Eleanor Egan—these were also friends with mutual recollections of other times and spheres:

All afternoon the town has been on the loose. Groups of soldiers & sailors—all nations—officers, men, women—tight or nearly so—arm in arm—dancing—singing—yelling . . . I passed . . . one gang of four, arm in arm shouting "Hail Hail the Gang's All Here" at the top of their lungs. . . . Perry Osborne [the same who had been one of Dorothy's earlier suitors] turned up with a skate and a band he had collected somewhere and brought it into the dining room finally—We all sang and it was quite gay. But I hate Paris & the Ritz & the rest of it & wish to Heaven I were off somewhere with the men [of the Army]. This damned restaurant stuff galls me. Think what this day means to the world—I'm quite tired & therefore not in any trim—but it makes me serious & rather depressed when I think of the responsibility of being worthy to do what we must do.

The Egans said he must compose a cable to Dorothy from all three of them worthy of the occasion. He agreed but was so weary and dejected that he could not simulate the appropriate spirit until the next day:

MARTIN, ELEANOR JOIN IN PEACE GREETINGS. WE TOASTED YOU AND LONGED TO HAVE YOU HERE. IT WAS A WONDERFUL ENDING OF THE NEW JOB. GOING STRONG. OUR DAY SOME DAY SOON. LOVE. WILLARD

13. Armistice in Atlanta

To WILLIAM DELANO, architect of India House and the Straights' own house and a dear friend, Dorothy gave parcels for Willard before Delano sailed for France on a government mission. On November 6 she returned on the midnight train after addressing a Junior League meeting in Boston, and heard at noon on the Peking Anniversary day the false United Press report that an armistice had been signed. "Returned to [YMCA] office & all went wild," she noted. On the eighth she took another midnight train for Atlanta, her errand being to speak to the Junior Leagues of Atlanta and Washington, urging them to send girls to France for the YMCA Canteen Service. Supposing the war *was* almost over, there would long be an American army of occupation in Europe.

She caught up on back issues of her beloved *New Republic* as she rode southward. "Our troops . . . attack on 71 mile front," she noted in her diary. "In the train all day. . . . Strange sensation traveling all alone to speak in various places." She reached Atlanta on Sunday morning, November 10, in time to hurry to church before she had lunch at the Grind Hills Club with a group of Junior Leaguers, then visited Camp Gordon and had tea with the commanding general. She spent the night at a hotel—the same night Straight spent dozing on the floor at Senlis. Next morning the whistles began to blow: "It nearly drove me wild to be off by myself in Atlanta, Georgia, when the news of Peace finally came, and I spent a strange, unreal sort of day trying to take it all in. . . ." Nevertheless, to her as to multitudes of American women, the whistles and the bells and the frolicking in the streets were a sign of relief as well as joy. The shooting was over. Her man had come through it unscathed. She had an all-morning conference at the YMCA office, lunch at the Riding Club with officers of the League, and spoke in the afternoon to a crowd of Leaguers who stopped their chattering about the armistice long enough to give her an enthusiastic hearing. She went out to Fort McPherson, which had a hospital and rehabilitation center for several thousands of wounded soldiers:

> Willard—I have never seen such nice boys—so cheerful and happy in spite of being maimed and burned and everything else. . . . So many of the unreal, selfish things have been burned out of them, and one sees their naked, fundamental quality,—simplicity—courage—genuineness— and truth. I'm afraid our civil population will never win through to so much!

She could scarcely fail to be thankful that Willard had not lost an arm or a leg or his eyesight, nor been terribly disfigured as some of these men had. She lingered and had no time for dinner, having to rush to catch the 8:35 for Washington, where she spoke to an even larger Junior League audience. She received there a letter from Willard written three weeks earlier in a discouragement that dashed cold water on her own cheer and on the gaiety of the capital, still exultant over the war's end. His hurts were not the kind she had seen at Fort McPherson, but were painful nevertheless.

She lunched with William and Caroline Phillips, out of old friendship and perhaps also to explore the possibility that Willard might find a suitable place in the State Department. The Straights' suburban farmhouse would be ready and waiting if he did. One wonders whether the able Assistant Secretary, who was building a career notable for discretion, thought that Straight had enough of that quality—especially after that angry letter about Army leadership and the admission that Straight "courted" trouble. Dorothy also had an appointment with Felix Frankfurter, who was knowledgeable about government bureaus and whom she may have queried on the same subject, though this is only speculation. She dined at 1718 H Street, where she was now an honorary member in excellent standing, having paid the bill for new rugs and furniture for the "club." Here was a hive of rising government officials who might know something about a possible future place for Willard—might also have information about his present activities which would take the curse off that sad letter. She had what she called a "delightful but rather heart-achey time":

> There was quite a little singing and playing afterwards. . . . [Basil Miles and others] were very mysterious about you and greeted me when I arrived by saying "isn't it fine that Willard has been holding Marshall [sic] Foch's hand so successfully"! Bullitt—whom I also saw, and who is now working in the State Department—murmured something about "Your husband is covering himself with glory these days" but when I pressed them all for further information they became at once discreet and noncommital. I was really rather sore with Basil for not seeing my human need and helping me—by just giving me a little further news of you. . . . Washington was really in a wild state of confusion because Peace had come upon them unawares. . . . In this country we are just about as unprepared for peace as we were for war.

When she reached New York November 15 she had an odd feeling that the city had slipped quickly back into business-as-usual without giving adequate thought or observance to the wonderful thing that had happened:

> . . . it was impossible to believe that since I had left it peace had come to the world. I say it to myself over and over again and it simply doesn't penetrate my brain! I always imagined that we would all be swept away by joyousness when peace finally came. . . . Except for the first spontaneous outbreak of revelry, it has struck us all rather dumb—and there is a curious solemnity about it all. . . . I suppose at great moments one never feels really hilarious. I wish that Lincoln's spirit could descend upon this land again. . . . "With malice toward none . . . let us strive on to finish the work we are in; to bind up the nation's wounds, to care for him who shall have borne the battle and for his widow and his orphan; to do all which may achieve a just and lasting peace among ourselves, and with all nations". What a heart and mind he had! . . .
> I wake up every morning with one thought in my mind—and that is the certainty that you are safe!

Later that day she received his cable, sent so laggardly after the celebratory dinner with the Egans:

Best Beloved—a cable at last—and such a fine joyous one, referring to
peace celebrations with Martin and Eleanor and to the wonderful ending
of the new job! The last words were the best, however, "Our day some
day soon". . . . I only wish I could express [my gratitude] in some tangible way by really becoming a finer person than I have ever been before. I
want to really live my gratitude—and make it big and conscious and ever
present, for it is far beyond the power of mere words to express, and must
actually be lived to be real. Oh how I wish I could say even half of what I
feel!

On November 12, after dining with Gordon Auchincloss and learning more about his new duties, Straight faced with courage a peril as
fearsome as any he had encountered in the war. He attended at the Cas-
tiglione a celebration for Grayson Murphy (about to leave for London
on a new assignment) at which was pinned on him the Legion of Honor
to go with the new full-colonel eagles on his shoulders. This could be
construed as a torment that only a few hours earlier would have reduced
Straight to new examinations of his own errors. He would have been expected to leave as quickly as politeness permitted. On the contrary, he
outlasted the party and was so glad to see Murphy that he talked with
him at his hotel until 2:30, adding to his own arrears in badly needed
sleep.

He breakfasted with Lippmann, chatting with him about the problems of peace. His mood had changed, and he was now fascinated by
his new job. To the suave diplomat Joseph M. Grew, who was to be
secretary of the peace conference, he gave a preliminary sketch showing
how the various delegates and secretariats might be seated. In a talk with
Colonel House, he was not reticent about urging that the President
should exercise the greatest tact in view of the touchiness of the French
and British—that he should come at the express invitation of the Pre-
miers, should accept nothing in the way of honors or degrees. Straight
felt that Wilson should make a speech to the American troops in the
field, with a group of soldiers representing each division, but should not
speak indiscriminately to Frenchmen or Englishmen. House handed
him a cable saying that the President would sail on December 3 and
asked Straight to carry the news to General Pershing and to Premier
Clemenceau:

I saw Clemenceau first in his office. He spoke in English. In his little
cap. I gave him the message and then had to tell him what a great

honour it was to meet him. He was grim and grasped me by both arms and said how much he liked America. I saw General Pershing—told him I had told Clemenceau, and he said all France would know it at once. Col. House pulled one by calling General Pershing's attention to the fact that I was still a major. It'll be interesting to see if anything happens.

Straight was to serve as executive officer for Grew—excellent, an assurance of inside participation. The Colonel wanted Dorothy to come over, to take a house "where people could be brought together" in a social-political circle in which the delegates could discuss terms. Astonishingly Straight demurred on principle. "I long so to have you," he wrote to Dorothy. "Yet I have a feeling that it wouldn't be playing the game. . . . The rest of the army can't do it. . . . oh—my Dorothy—it makes me gasp—just the thought of such a possibility." He thought about it overnight and wrote her again. "Today I said nothing doing. . . . There are too many officers over here—who would like to have their wives. An influx of women will be a very bad thing for the army." Next day he ran into Harry Davison, in Paris on Red Cross business, and asked his opinion. His view changed Straight's mind, as he wrote to Dorothy yet again:

> He thought you ought to come if the Colonel wanted it—& that the criticism was part of the game—I guess that's right. Then I talked to the Colonel & he was very sweet. He told me of some of his plans and said he wanted you very much—He said you were one of the few people in America who saw the whole thing clearly & that you would be the greatest help in the world. . . . He was quite wonderful about you Sweetheart—and he's right. . . . It's really going to be a tremendous job—to get it all into shape in time. . . . General Bill Wright blew in yesterday—& I dined with him tonight. He's tired—very tired—but in good humor. He said I'd made my mistake when I transferred out of the Third Corps. He's right—but there it is—so let's forget it. Will have to learn by experience I'm afraid—and there are many years to come. . . . Christmas together—it will be too wonderful.

Let's forget it. . . . there are many years to come. Major Straight had turned a corner. Christmas together in Paris, the city so identified with the two of them, really a province of Borderland, ringing with the strains of "Liebestraum" and "Les Fleurs Que Nous Aimons," where he had devised that lovers' code and had composed that ditty about meeting her in Aix for buckwheat cakes, and where she had later—at the Vendôme on June 17, 1910—hung that locket around his neck! Life was good after all. He forgot, as he could, how exhausted he was. He arranged for Bennett, now improved, to be brought to a Paris hospital. He had lunch with Daisy Harriman without a word of criticism about her. Certainly he told her the news—that Dorothy and the children would soon be on their way to Paris.

". . . [W]orking with Joe Grew on the organization of the Peace Commission," he wrote to Dorothy, "which is a whale of a job—and hasn't been thought out at all as far as I can make out—The State Dept. apparently was [not ready] or too stupid even to do anything about it. We have no Peace—just as we had no war organization." He talked for hours with Lippmann about the complexities and nuances of getting the President and his party to adopt a program in Paris that would please the Allies and lead to lasting peace. He thought of the President as a shrewd and able but unfeeling person; House and the rest would be happier if Wilson did not come to Paris: "House is afraid of the rest of the American mission. Interesting sidelight on retention of [Secretary of State] Lansing by President—a check I think on House. He's a stinker, W.W. Old E. M. [House]is a perfect wonder."

Next morning, Sunday November 17, Straight joined Colonel House and Auchincloss in a motor tour of part of the former front, visiting Chateau-Thierry, Reims, and Fismes. Back in Paris by evening, he dined at Voisin's with Lippmann, Dwight Morrow, and several others. He forgot fatigue. He was preoccupied with the conference. "Tried to think things out. . . ," he noted in his diary. "Suggested that they all get together and make some suggestions as to conduct of Peace Conference for guidance of our delegates."

On Monday he was in bed at the Crillon with a fever. The following day, Colonel House was also ill, but as House improved, Straight got worse. The unavailing metal-covered notebook was in the breast pocket of his uniform jacket in the closet, but around his neck was the gold locket Dorothy had recently sent him. Mrs. Harriman stopped in to see him Tuesday and thereafter sat with him daily, adding her ministrations to those of his nurses. Comdr. James McLane of the Navy, medical officer of the mission, was attending him and was joined as the symptoms indicated severe influenza by Gen. William Thayer and Maj. Kenneth Taylor, the former a Johns Hopkins professor of clinical medicine in civilian life.

Mrs. Harriman met with Mrs. Egan, Lippmann, Ruth Morgan, and Dr. Thayer to consider the question: When and how should Dorothy be notified? It would be impossible in any case for her to reach Paris before the crisis. It was decided not to cable her "unless alarming symptoms manifested themselves." Straight's temperature hovered around 104 degrees, but he talked rationally with Daisy until Friday, when he became delirious. On Saturday, when signs of pneumonia appeared, Daisy cabled the news to Herbert Croly, putting as hopeful a light on it as possible. It was her kind thought that it would be less shocking for Dorothy to hear it from a friend than from the telephoned voice of a cable company employee.

14. A Long Life in a Few Years

ON THE Sunday of Willard's visit to the front, Dorothy wrote to him: "I have been wondering . . . whether it would be possible for me to get over to France in the event of your not getting home for several months. The one thing I don't want to do is to be made an exception of—and if other wives can't go, then I won't go either. I have seen too many of my own friends breaking their hearts over this thing for me to be able to wave goodbye to them and go sailing off in glory. . . ."

Letters from him still took weeks to reach her, so that she was considerably in arrears. Not until two days later did she receive his cable sent November 16 with the news that she was expected to join him in Paris with the children. Since this was at the express request of Colonel House, who would find her useful, she had no further misgivings. Indeed, the shaping of the peace was so radiant a cause that she would have been delighted to have the most minor role in it. To have this, and to have at the same time reunion in Paris with Willard, was nothing less than paradise. The bustle of joyful preparations as she made ready to sail on the *George Washington* December 3 can be imagined. The following week she received a letter from Willard written when he was at Senlis, which seemed months ago and was no longer germane.

Then, on November 25, Croly received Mrs. Harriman's cable and took it to Dorothy at her office at the YMCA. Her diary showed her effort at composure. "I have been home ever since," she wrote, "trying to keep in touch with Washington." Her next two diary entries were her last for many months. They read:

> Nov. 26: Another cable from Daisy this A.M. Katharine [Barnes] & Nathalie [Swan] have been here—walked with latter. Lunch with children. . . . A third cable came at 6 o'cl—not quite so encouraging.
> Nov. 27: Saw Ruth Pratt this A.M.—Lily Lee—Nathalie & Katharine. Ruth T., Margot & Mrs. Dix to lunch. Dreadful day. Fourth cable came

tonight at 8.30—not much change. Meeting here tonight for J.I.—Carrie Slade—Aileen Webb—Frances Riker—Susie—Nathalie—Doro—Miss Meyer—Ruth Pratt & Ethel—who spent the night.

She could have called off the Junior League meeting, but she was following the stoic example of the Roosevelts. The "Susie" mentioned in the entry—Susan Sedgwick Swann—remembers the meeting and how well Dorothy carried it off. She had Ethel Derby with her for the night—still her dearest friend despite the difference in politics. Ethel, whom Dorothy had met in Cairo after meeting Willard in Peking, when Willard monopolized her thoughts in a way so different from the way he was monopolizing them now; Ethel, who had resisted Dick Derby (now still in France) but had finally taken Dorothy's advice and married him. To Daisy Harriman Dorothy cabled November 26:

HOW CAN I THANK YOU FOR EVERYTHING YOU ARE DOING, GRATEFUL YOU CABLED WITHOUT DELAY. THINK I HAVE BEEN ABLE TO HELP. MY LOVE TO WILLARD—WE HAVE BEEN VERY CLOSE IN SPIRIT THESE PAST HOURS.

On November 28:

SO THANKFUL YOU ARE WITH WILLARD. SURE ALL WILL BE WELL. CAN YOU CABLE FULLER PARTICULARS GENERAL CONDITION ALSO WHEN INFLUENZA BEGAN. PLEASE HOLD HIS WRISTS FOR ME—IT HELPS HIM. I AM THERE WITH HIM EVERY MOMENT.

The Red Cross was now doing without Daisy Harriman, for she had abandoned it and was keeping steady vigil over Straight. The Egans, Lippmann, Ruth Morgan, Bowditch, Stettinius, Dorothy's cousin Ashbel Barney, and others called, but only briefly, since the patient was out of his head. William Delano arrived from New York with messages and parcels from Dorothy and discovered that Straight was seriously ill and delirious. Dr. Billings, who had known Straight since the time Daisy's daughter was married, called daily. Daisy jotted in her diary:

Ill as he was, his mind has been engrossed and busy with the work before him at the Peace Conference. When he could no longer write, he used to ask me to sit by him, make notes of things he wanted to bring to the attention of Colonel House. He kept thinking he was at the front.

"Rest now, Daisy," he would say, "you've got a long trip back to Paris."

Thanksgiving Day he was still semi-conscious. "Did you say this was Thanksgiving?" he asked. "Look in my dressing table," he said; "take out all the money you want to get turkeys, and give everybody a good time. I love people to be happy."

She later wrote to Dorothy, "I sat beside Willard and held his hand all those last hours, and up to 24 hours before he left, he always knew me and called me by name. Walter Lippmann and I at 11:30 P.M. [Nov. 30] realized that he was going fast. We sent a motor for Billings of Groton. . . . He came quietly into the room, stood beside the bed, made three beautiful prayers, and two minutes after he stopped Willard quietly stopped breathing. Just as he went I kissed him and said 'This is from Dorothy.' There was no struggle, no suffering so far as human sense could see, only a great weariness from the long fight."

Daisy cabled Frank Polk at the State Department:

PLEASE HAVE HERBERT CROLY . . . OR SOMEONE ELSE CLOSE TO DOROTHY STRAIGHT DELIVER THE FOLLOWING MESSAGE TO HER:

"WILLARD PASSED AWAY VERY PEACEFULLY AT 12:45 A.M. DECEMBER 1ST. I DELIVERED ALL YOUR MESSAGES TO HIM. HIS LAST REQUEST WAS THAT I SHOULD CABLE YOU HIS LOVE. ALL YOUR AND WILLARD'S FRIENDS WERE NEAR HIM AT THE LAST AND THROUGH IT ALL THEIR THOUGHTS AND LOVE HAVE BEEN WITH YOU. ANY WISH YOU MAY EXPRESS BY CABLE WILL OF COURSE BE CARRIED OUT FAITHFULLY."

It seems likely that Daisy, out of kindness, ornamented the facts a trifle and that, for example, Straight was in no condition to convey any last request. It appears that he did not expect to die. But this surely would have been his last request had he been able to make one. Dorothy's reply was the reply of one whose civility was unconquerable:

PLEASE THANK PERSONALLY FOR ME NURSES, DOCTORS AND ALL WILLARD'S FRIENDS WHO HAVE DONE SO MUCH. I AM VERY GRATEFUL FOR THE CARE AND LOVE HE HAD. NO WORDS CAN EXPRESS MY GRATITUDE TO YOU. I SHOULD LIKE TO HAVE WILLARD BURIED IN FRANCE SOMEWHERE WITH AMERICAN SOLDIERS HE LOVED AND ADMIRED SO MUCH. WILL THIS BE POSSIBLE. PLEASE DO NOT WORRY ABOUT ME. I KNOW THAT HE IS SAFE AND THAT IS ALL THAT MATTERS.

Was there bitterness in that last sentence? More likely, it was submission to a Creator in whom she firmly believed although she had for the time given up any pretense of understanding Him. Her "THINK I HAVE BEEN ABLE TO HELP" in her first cable was only one of the evidences of her belief in her ability to communicate with Willard in spirit.

She could not lightly have made the decision to have him buried in France, painfully distant. "Oh, I love Paris!" she had written before Straight came into her life—a sentiment having no bearing now. To her, the thousands upon thousands of white American crosses in France were an earnest of the international unity, the League of Nations, the better world in which she had great faith and Straight had had strong hope. Surely also she consulted the wishes of Willard himself, whose death, she was certain, was only transference to another sphere. His admiration for the American citizen-soldier had been transcendent. His description of the church service at Langres had touched on it, as had his reflections during the terrible battle at Chateau-Thierry. It was brilliantly visible in his indignation at those Regular officers who treated soldiers as offscourings of society, his feeling that they resembled a great organ only awaiting the master's touch—his belief, not openly expressed but implicit, that if he, Willard Straight, only had time and opportunity for training at the front, he could "reach their souls," touch the chords that would lead them to victory. For him to be buried among New York businessmen and burghers would not do. Let him lie among the men he had wanted so badly to lead.

Mrs. Harriman, exhausted though she was, planned and carried through the final ceremony. No gun carriage could be found in this land of gun carriages, so the chassis of a Cadillac automobile bore Straight's flag-draped coffin, his cap and sword on top, away from the Place de la Concorde. American soldiers flanked the vehicle as it rolled down the Champs Élysées. It was followed on foot by an astonishing number of friends, some of long standing, considering the distance most of them were from home. Among them were Colonel Bowditch (representing General Pershing), Walter Lippmann, William Delano, Warwick Greene, Ashbel Barney, Martin Egan, Grayson Murphy, Herbert Parsons, General McCoy, Colonel Mott, Edward Stettinius, Herman Harjes, Madame Casenave, and Mrs. Harriman bringing up the rear. "Everywhere the French," Greene wrote, "—with that special courtesy which never fails them—took off their hats as we went by . . . and all officers and soldiers whom we passed, saluted." Bishop Charles Henry

Brent, chief of the A.E.F. Chaplain Service, who conducted the ceremony, was the same whom Dorothy and Willard had met in Manila. He later commented on how many of them had first met Straight in the Far East—Bowditch, Greene, General McCoy, the Egans, Madame Casenave, and a few others in addition to the bishop himself. A wet snow fell as the procession turned into Avenue George V to the American Holy Trinity Church, where Ethel Harriman had been married ten months earlier. After the brief church service, the snow continued until the group gathered again at the graveside at the American Military Cemetery at Suresnes, beyond the Bois de Boulogne, when a brilliant sun emerged from the clouds. The bishop made a brief address, saying, "I speak of one who lived a long life in a few years"—a feeling shared by Straight's friends, as was the bishop's description of him as "knightly." Though death is expected to have sorrowful aspects, the exceptional tragedy of Straight's passing, coming at the very moment when Dorothy had been in transports of joy over the opportunity of joining him, was in the minds of all the mourners. Major Straight was consigned to Grave 1 of Plot B, Row 16. Dorothy had planned to sail on the *George Washington*—the ship that was also to carry the President and his aides—the next day.

"It will be hard to find another like Willard," Greene reflected. "He and Dorothy united more worlds, more sets, than any two people I have ever known. New York had no other couple who embraced such wide interests, who touched so many different people, who were quite such a special force in their community, and probably never will have."

"When 'Taps' was sounded by the bugler," Delano wrote, "it was a bit too much for me," adding later to Dorothy, "What his loss will be to you I can't bear to think. Dear Dorothy, if I have said anything stupidly or tactlessly pray forgive me. I am overwhelmed by my own grief and yours. . . ."

"Oh, Madam. . . ," wrote George Bennett from his hospital bed, "He had great trips planned for you to visit Langres and the different places he stayed at while over here. . . . always the Major's idea was to make everybody happy. . . . I don't think there can be in this wide world another man like him."

And Daisy Harriman added to her long, detailed letter to Dorothy, "I didn't want to take anything off, without you having said so, left the locket, ring, and identity tag on. I hope that was right?"

Seven

1. Evenings Are the Worst

STRAIGHT, IN his letter-to-be-mailed-if-killed, had said, "I have gone through already anything that I could go through and am quite ready for what may come." As it turned out, it was Dorothy who had to run the gamut of three stages of violent emotion, not unlike Dante's varying circles of hell: fear for Willard's life, then the glorious suffusion of relief in her conviction that he had come through the war safely and she would be with him for Christmas, then the final, crushing calamity. She clung to her work at the YMCA. She was inundated by sympathy, by letters, telegrams, and calls. There was an echo from an earlier age—a warm note from Dorothy's godmother, the widow of President Cleveland, now Mrs. Thomas Preston. There was, from the young Flora Whitney, the affection and especially sensitive understanding that comes from one similarly bereft. There were messages from old China and from Washington and Wall Street associates of Straight, from General Pershing, from Colonel House. There was one from Professor Morse Stephens, now dean of arts at the University of California:

> Of all the many boys I have had with me he was the one I loved the best. He used laughingly at times to call himself my "son" and no son ever was dearer to a father's heart. In the crisis of my life, when I lay sick at your house in New York, and when you two saved my life with your care, I felt like an old father cared for by loving children. And now that very pneumonia which spared me has taken him.

It was obviously at Dorothy's suggestion that Dr. Slattery, at the memorial service over which he presided at Grace Church in New York on December 6, did not specifically name Willard Straight but honored him as one of the many gallant Americans "whose faces in this life we shall see no more." Theodore Roosevelt, who was in hospital with inflammatory rheumatism, was represented by Mrs. Roosevelt and other Roosevelts including of course Ethel Derby. But he still kept up his newspaper column, in which he paid tribute to Straight. He was one, the Colonel wrote, who had every excuse to stay safely at home, but "both he and his wife had in their souls that touch of heroism which makes it impossible for generous natures to see others pay with their bodies and not wish to do something themselves."

When Straight's will was filed at Mineola, there was no indication of the size of his estate. In view of his luxurious mode of life and his somewhat flamboyant display of it,* it was not surprising that the erroneous guess accepted by the newspapers was much inflated. "STRAIGHT LEAVES $5,000,000 TO WIFE," headlined *The Sun*, with other papers following suit. The will bequeathed $100,000 to his sister, Mrs. Sanborn; $50,000 to Fiedler, and $5,000 each to Bennett and two secretaries under Fiedler, George H. Rennick and R. E. Kincaid, as well as six months' salary to his remaining several employees. The testator had understandable confidence in the wisdom of his wife, who was made sole trustee and executrix. Straight asked his wife to provide financial support for *The New Republic* during her lifetime and ten years thereafter. He also requested her to do "such thing or things for Cornell University as she may think most fit and useful to make the same a more human place"—a stipulation that caused much comment and even some indignation among loyal Cornellians. It was explained that Straight had meant no disparagement to his alma mater. It was simply that when he was a student at Cornell, with very little money, there were times when the place seemed to lack warmth. This might seem unwarranted coming from such a popular collegian, the favorite of Morse Stephens, but anyone familiar with Ithaca's long winters and Straight's terrible loneliness would understand.

Two days later the papers published a correction: "STRAIGHT LEFT ONLY $500,000": "It was said that the announcement of the size of the estate had caused some embarrassment to Mrs. Straight. . . . 'It is better at the outset to have the facts known,' said a representative of Mrs. Straight, 'than to mislead some of the beneficiaries into

---

* While he did not equal his late father-in-law in the number of his clubs, he did well enough. In New York: the Century, Knickerbocker, Players', Cornell, Meadow Brook, India House, the Links, the Brook, University, Piping Rock, Metropolitan, Recess. In Washington: the Metropolitan. In London: St. James's and the Royal Thames Yacht Club. He was a trustee of Cornell University and a fellow of the Royal Geographical Society in London.

the expectation of getting another $4,500,000 for uplift work than the Major had or intended to devote to such purposes.' "

If Straight had been a *chevalier sans peur et sans reproche* to his valet, Dorothy was as high in the estimation of her personal maid, Louisa Weinstein, who had accompanied her to European spas, traveled with her around the world, and seen the beginning, middle, and end of her romance. Louisa wrote to Bennett in Paris:

> . . . you know how very quiet Mrs. Straight is, she is more so now than ever. She is really the most wonderful woman I have ever seen [,] so sad and still keeps up her appearance as if she is interested in every thing round her, in the meantime her poor heart flowes over with grief. Little Whitney felt awful bad but Beatrice and Michael are too young to realize it. . . . The long evenings are the worst, in the daytime Mrs. Straight keeps bussy [sic] in the Y.M.C.A. office but in the evening she is allways alone, I don't need telling you the long letters she used to write him and the Joy receiving his letters and now it's all over. . . .

On January 6, 1919, Theodore Roosevelt died suddenly and unexpectedly. Dorothy, who had had no opportunity to witness the burial of her own husband, was at Oyster Bay for the funeral of this prodigious man who had been so maddening to her as a politician and so dear as a friend. The newspapers quoted the sentiments of sorrow and tribute of scores of men of varying degrees of fame, from all over the world, but no women. Even the New York streetcars and subways stopped for one minute at the time of the funeral, during which men removed their hats and all passengers observed respectful silence. At the small Episcopal church, Dorothy sat with Ethel and young Flora Whitney, surrounded by the great who came to honor the Rough Rider—among them Elihu Root, ex-President Taft, Charles Evans Hughes, Senators Lodge and Knox, and Henry Stimson. Dorothy also encountered an old friend, Assistant Secretary of State William Phillips, and a politician perhaps a little less friendly, Mayor Hylan. They would all have trouble, as it was said, trying to "get used to a world without Roosevelt in it." He was buried near the summit of a slope that looked across Oyster Bay Cove to his home on Sagamore Hill.

The Colonel might well have sided with those Junior Leaguers who blew up a teapot tempest over Dorothy's radicalism. She was again president of the organization and had been a moving spirit in a plan to set up a series of lectures to broaden the understanding of Leaguers handicapped by the rudimentary education then considered ample for females.* Some had shocked her by their ignorance. She had herself become formidably educated, entirely on her own initiative, through attending lectures and special courses since youth, constant reading, travel, and observation, marriage to the mentally stimulating Willard Straight, attendance at scores of *New Republic* meetings where one might listen to anyone from Norman Angell to Ernest Poole to Lord Northcliffe, countless weekend discussions with the likes of Walter Lippmann, Francis Hackett, and Charles Merz, and her own habit of hard thinking. One of the suggestions of a committee appointed to push the matter had been that the lectures could be given at the New School for Social Research, recently opened on West 23rd Street. Undoubtedly Dorothy had thought well of this, being one of the founders and a director of the New School and rejoicing in its commitment to a somewhat less rigid spirit of thought. After she left for Aiken late in January, a group of the Leaguers, perhaps influenced by husbands or male friends, protested that they would prefer not to be corrupted by the New School. (It will be remembered that the era of "patriotic" snoopery and suppression of free speech reached its zenith after the war.) Among the lecturers at the New School were Robinson, Beard, and Thorstein Veblen. It was complained that Veblen and Robinson had been among the signers of an appeal in *The New Republic* for funds for the defense of members of the IWW who had opposed the war and taken part in strikes. Robinson and Beard were authors of a history book removed from the Seattle public schools because of lapses in patriotism, and Beard spoke occasionally at that hotbed of socialism, the Rand School. Veblen, in a recent issue of *The Dial*, had written that "a vested interest is a legitimate right to get something for nothing."

"MRS. STRAIGHT STORM CENTER IN BIG FIGHT," headlined the semiweekly *Oswego Palladium*, which had transferred its attentions from the former most famous Oswegonian to his widow. The headline was excessive and the fuss was needless, since plans were progressing with Dean Gildersleeve to give the courses at Barnard. The slightly tart attitude of Dorothy, interviewed at Aiken, could be divined even though no word of hers was directly quoted:

> Mrs. Willard D. Straight said today that the protest had been made by only a very few discontented members of the Junior League, which has a

---

* A woman in college was still an anomaly. Barnard College itself was suspect in many eyes. Dr. Morgan Dix, late father of Dorothy's close friend Mrs. Margaret Lawrance, had fought the founding of Barnard every step of the way, quoting St. Paul: "I suffer not a woman to teach, nor to usurp authority over the man, but to be in silence. For Adam was first formed, then Eve."

membership of 1,100, and that the committee promptly voted down the protest at once [*sic*]. The matter, she said, was one of the many unimportant incidents which occur in all organizations.

Town Topics sang of it in iambs:

Again the dove of peace within the Junior League doth rest—
Methought from recent talk, from there the dove had fluttered "west,"
For Mrs. Willard Straight into the camp hurled such a bomb
As knocked it off its pedestal; completely out of plumb.
The sweet young things who make the League, with horror viewed askance
That School of Social Research Mrs. Willard would advance,
And schism raised its horrid head. They said, "We won't attend!"
At which dear Mrs. Willard said, "To ask it, heaven forfend!"

That settled, Dorothy wrote to Flora Whitney:

You have been very wonderful through everything—and I feel, somehow, that you and Quentin are more truly one in spirit than you have ever been before. You seem to be expressing him, all the time—and to be making him live through your spirit. . . . Your love for him has made you what you are—and somehow, he must know it—and be happy.

Our common pain has brought us very close—you and I, and I wish you could know how much you have helped and comforted me.

Dorothy was seeking similarly to define the immortality that she was certain kept Willard's spirit glowing in the beyond. The certainty of immortality, however, was not enough. Willard alive had been very much alive—so much so that there were those many occasions during their separations when each had felt something close to magical contact over the distance. Their life, together or apart, had been one of constant, interested, detailed communication. However distant, they had been brought close by letter, by cable, and again by something more than letter or cable, the conviction of which amounted to thought transference or telepathy. There had been those times when each had had that eerie but delightful awareness of the other's thoughts, as if each was both a transmitter and a receiver tuned exclusively to the other. Now Willard was what was commonly known as dead—a state that she did not accept in its definition of finality, the end, the stoppage of all communication.

The letters and cables of course had stopped. The trouble was, so had the telepathy.

The distress visited on Dorothy by this failure to receive any signal from him is attested by her handwriting in a green leather-bound diary for the year 1919 lettered "WDS" in gold. This was one of the gifts she had intended to present to him when she joined him in Paris. It was an appropriate accessory in her effort to reach across the pale to him with the aid of an unnamed medium.

The resort to mediums had become common in Europe and the United States in the attempt to make contact with husbands and sons lost in the war. It seems evident that Dorothy had more reason than most to hope to span the gulf and that, characteristically, she gave it serious effort. The 365 pages of the green diary are about three-quarters filled with her handwriting. On the left-hand pages are the specific questions she asked of the medium. On the right-hand pages are Willard's purported replies given through the medium. Many of the early questions bore on her effort to understand his state of being on the other side, which seemed a necessary preliminary for setting up a steady and fruitful communication. She asked also such questions as whether she could get comfort through Christian Science, the answer being a conditional yes, if done right. Another question, typical of her, was how she could best work for the political improvement of the country, the answer here being that the best course was through articles such as those in *The New Republic*. The tone of her transcription of the medium's replies at times showed skepticism as to whether she was really in touch with Willard, and elsewhere more confidence, though never real satisfaction. She was receiving letters from George Marvin, who had the special cachet of a former suitor who had also been close to Willard in China, Washington, New York, and France. Marvin seemed unaware that Straight had cooled toward him. In her last question in the diary, Dorothy asked what she should do about GM. The reply was disparaging, that M had once had ideals but was now concerned with his own material advancement and it would be best if he departed.

The green book was not filled, and it is evident that she stopped consulting mediums. She did, however, have considerable faith in Christian Science as a means of improving her own well-being. Her sister Pauline had been one of many fashionable Americans and Englishmen who had embraced Christian Science. But all of this manifested Dorothy's spiritual unhappiness, a condition acute enough so that eventually she would have to find a way to resolve it.

2. *Some Day*

EVIDENTLY GENERAL PERSHING remembered Willard Straight as a young correspondent who had talked with him in 1906 in Japan and

Korea and whom he had met again in France here and there near the front and later in Paris. Colonel House's broad hint that a promotion was in order for Straight had not been acted on, since Straight had died eighteen days later. But Straight's warmth of personality was not easily forgotten, nor was it likely that the circumstances of his death were forgotten. In April, by Pershing's citation, Major Straight was awarded posthumously the recognition he had so needed in life, the Distinguished Service Medal "for exceptionally meritorious and distinguished services."

Dorothy's diary went neglected for eight months, a record. She resumed it July 18, 1919, with no more explanation than that of sunlight breaking through a long overcast. She wrote as she rode on the train to Raquette Lake in the Adirondacks to the lodge built there by her father: "Edith came from Southampton to lunch with me. [That was Edith Lindley, her old Roser school classmate, Warwick Greene's sister.] Together we went to N.Y. & did errands. Children coming in later, just in time to catch 7.10 train." It was an all-night ride: "Arrived 7.30 at Raquette Lake & had breakfast at hotel. Came on to camp, arriving about 9.30. Too heavenly. Lay on porch after lunch—fished later & hunted beavers."

The comfort of the establishment was augmented by the help of at least two male caretakers and five women servants. There were picnics with the children and forays into the wilderness to fish and study nature: "Cooked our lunches & fished for trout—only caught one—but it has been lovely day." "Saw 7 deer & five foxes & caught one little trout." "Worked in shop with Whitney this P.M.—then after supper we fished—caught 4 big bass." "No great excitement today except that Whitney nearly cut his finger off with an axe."

One morning Dorothy devoted to reading *The New Republic*. On August 2, Beatrice's fifth birthday, there were celebrations including a race in guide boats manned by five of the servant girls, won by a kitchen maid named May. On August 6, Beatrice Bend Fletcher and her mother arrived by motorcar, which had to be parked at the road's end several miles away while they were brought the remaining distance by boat. But Beatrice and Dorothy's opportunity to discuss confidentially the crises of life with Fletcher was cut short. The very next day Dorothy noted, "Received cable from Gen. Pershing suggesting I go to France." The General (was the idea given him by Daisy Harriman?) had thought of her in the most kindly way possible. The Suresnes cemetery was still stark and unadorned, badly needing landscaping and beautification. She was invited to supervise its enrichment.

She gave it overnight thought and decided, not without fear, to accept. "I have been wanting to go as you know—for a long time," she wrote to Susan Sedgwick Swann at Stockbridge. With Beatrice and Mrs. Bend she hurried back to New York. She talked with Harry, Gertrude, and Flora. Yes—Flora would accompany her so that she could visit the grave of Quentin. There was hurried packing, a consultation with Croly about *The New Republic*. Ethel Derby and the Kermit Roosevelts called to say good-bye, the Derbys arranging to spend a vacation at the Whitney lodge, where the children had been left with the servants. Dorothy and Flora sailed on the *Adriatic* at noon August 14. Dorothy spent one shipboard morning reading *New Republics*, then fell to Galsworthy's *Saint's Progress*, Maugham's *The Moon and Sixpence*, and a book suggesting preparation for an ordeal, *Christ in You*. She was not impressed by one of Flora's companions on the voyage, a Colonel Bloomfield—"Rather dreadful!"—and herself chatted with the journalist Isaac Marcosson.

In Paris they took a suite at the Ritz, where Mrs. Harriman was staying: "Had a long talk with Daisy—& she & Flora & I dined together upstairs. They went afterwards to dance." Dorothy was in no mood for dancing. She was thirty-two years and eight months old, visiting the Paris she loved for the first time since 1912—seven years. How could she keep the memories from flooding back as if they were flashed by the hundreds on a screen? The young and eager Willard, arriving here from China, hurrying across the Channel, then taking a night train to Milan to propose marriage to her—to be put off, to show terrible disappointment in his face. . . . Willard nevertheless feeling his oats, conferring with the likes of Morgan, Davison, and Harjes and having them *listen* to him. . . . The countless smiles, glances, and intonations that had special meaning, the ridiculously perfect doggerel he invented, the coded cables that had the telegraph people suspecting them of espionage. There was the rush rush about it all, Willard breathless both when he arrived and when he left her, Willard racing around the world as if pursuing Phileas Fogg but always arranging with some old lady to send Dorothy flowers. The rides in the Bois, the restaurants, the opera, the music, the locket.

Dorothy was terrified about her mission in Paris. Now she had to face Willard's death all over again. In the morning, Sunday, she went with Daisy to the Christian Science church, then lunched with dear old Rolly Cottenet at Laurent's—the same Laurent's where Willard had a favorite table in a corner, the same Cottenet who had dined her and

Willard in Venice shortly after their wedding. There was no escaping the pangs of memory. In the afternoon she gathered all her courage and went out to Suresnes. The graves, some of them raw and still uncovered by grass, stretched in their many rows down the hillside from Mont Valérien, overlooking the Seine and Paris in the distance. Here, on Memorial Day, less than three months earlier, a still confident President Wilson had spoken to thousands, many of them wounded soldiers: "Ladies and gentlemen: we all believe, I hope, the spirits of these men are not buried with their bones. Their spirits live. I hope—I believe—that their spirits are present with us at this hour." If they could speak, the President said, they would speak for the League of Nations that would make their sacrifice worthwhile.

Dorothy's objective entry in her diary—"Went out to Suresnes alone in the afternoon"—was the bare truth telling nothing about herself. She also noted later that when she and Flora dined with the Herbert Hoovers at the Crillon, "[I] distinguished myself by fainting & being very sick." To be enclosed in those same dreadful walls was too much. Everyone was solicitous. Flora got her back to the Ritz, where Daisy came flying to care for her with tenderness and restoratives. Not until 2:30 the next day did she recover.

After that she took herself firmly in hand. She shopped with Flora at Chanel's, Jenny's, and Callot's. She dutifully visited the YMCA. She lunched at the Ritz with General Pershing and Herbert Haseltine, an expatriate American sculptor and old friend of Gertrude's. They discussed the adornment of the cemetery, which she visited again with Haseltine and Jo Davidson, who also had a Paris studio. Dorothy was ready to spend liberally of her own money to surround the cemetery with a handsome fence and a bronze entrance gate, and to build a central memorial building of stone with appropriate statuary. As she gave it thought and study, she found Paris as always crowded with old friends, some of them in connection with the war and the peace. She met and lunched or dined with them, seldom singly: with her onetime suitor Lloyd Warren, with Colonel Logan—"good old Logie"—with Warwick Greene, Joseph Grew, Jack Carter of the Harjes office, Lloyd Griscom, Judge Berry, Signor Brambilla, who had been with the Italian legation in Peking, the Frank Polks. With Daisy she lunched with Bernard Berenson and Premier Eleutherios Venizelos of Greece, after which "Berenson took Daisy & Flora & myself to Louvre to see ancient sculpture—Chaldean, Assyrian, Gothic, etc." It was part of her study for the improvement of the cemetery.

Her diary was proof of her gain in spirits. On the following Saturday she and Flora left in a chauffeured automobile for Chamery, where Quentin was buried: "Got to La Ferté for lunch—went on through Chateau Thierry, Fére-en-Tardenois to Chamery." It was more than a year since Quentin had died, and for Flora the worst of the tragedy was over, but the graveside rite was still a poignant one. "Towns all destroyed but country green & smiling," Dorothy went on. "Wonderful day." She went with Flora next morning to the American Church, where Willard's funeral service had been held, and walked home with Frank and Lily Polk. Frank Polk, who had tried and failed to land Willard the State Department job that might have changed everything; but of course it was not his fault, it was Willard's support of Hughes, his *New Republic* letter attacking Wilson that had sent him into the Army.

She conferred incessantly with the sculptors Davidson and Haseltine and with Col. Leon Kromer of the Graves Registration Command (yes, Kromer remembered Major Straight well—had heard him lecture on liaison at Langres). She shopped with Flora on the Rue de la Paix; she had the Hoovers, Ernest Peixotto, Berenson, and many others in for tea; with Daisy and Flora she heard *Tosca* at the Tuileries, with the Polks she dined with Foreign Minister Arthur Balfour, Philip Kerr (Lloyd George's secretary, later Lord Lothian, Ambassador to Washington), and Maj. Ronald Victor Courtenay Bodley of the British Army. The duty with which she was charged, and the social activity along the way—more than she had had for many months—seemed to play a part in her reassertion of heart. Perhaps she also had some consoling reflections. True, she had been the wife of Willard Straight for only seven years. But judged simply as a marriage—the accommodation of two harmonious minds and spirits, the precious moments of affection and delight as against the times of difference and discord—it had far outshone the oddly aloof and resigned and occasionally bitter union of Flora and William Whitney.

"Most wonderful & happy day," she wrote on September 5 as she departed on an errand that earlier would have intimidated her. "Took 8 o'clock train to Langres—all alone. Arrived about 1 o'clock & had 3 glorious hrs poking about town—walking on ramparts, etc." Here he had written to her:

> The horse-chestnuts are out. The grass is wonderfully green. The hedgerows are all abloom—white—& yellow—& the violets & periwinkles dot the carpet in the woods and under the hedgerows. The shadows are purplish & the ploughed fields warm & brown & soft. France is

lovely. And I'm getting a great love for this country side that I ride through—for the little nestling villages with their quaint old churches—& the grave yards festooned with metal wreaths . . . the chickens & the kids in the streets—the old men & all the women working—working—working—while the young men fight. I love to think that some day you and I and the kids can travel around through this country. For some day we must come with a motor and take a house in the old town for a while — make sketching trips around. Some day—Some day—what a lot there will be to do—Some day. Won't there be—my Best Beloved?

It had not turned out that way. Yet she was at peace: "Went to Willard's old house—11 rue Chambroulard—& to staff college—to Cathedral & all over." At the cathedral he had called it "one of the great Easters in History," had commented on the boys from American farms and cities who had earned with their sweat and courage the right to share in the traditions of this ancient town and to celebrate mass with its people. To Dorothy he had written, "In spirit we are closer than ever before." The train got her back to Paris near 10:00 P.M. She was engrossed enough to leave next day with Daisy "in a wonderful army Cadillac car—with Private Fortune from Texas as driver." They made a two-and-a-half-day tour of the battle zone between Reims and Verdun. The second day was September 7, her eighth wedding anniversary. She left it unmentioned. "Country is completely desolated & terrible," she wrote, "—white chalky hills—our road dangerous—by shell holes—walked over battlefields."

She had undergone a transformation. On the day after their return, as she expressed it in her diary, "Went out to Suresnes at 4—& had such a peaceful experience of Reality there!" She amplified it in a note written to herself on Hotel Ritz stationery:

> It is all very quieting & convincing & full of the real victory over life—I long to spend hrs & hrs just sitting by W.'s grave, & feeling the gt sense of power to love that invigorate & bless one's spirit in that place. It is all very wonderful & beautiful.

3. *Lovely Coming Up Harbor*

AT THE Morgan, Harjes office Dorothy and Jo Davidson signed the contracts for the work on the cemetery, with Davidson to execute the sculpture and supervise the project. After what she described as a "last wonderful hour" at Suresnes, Dorothy left with Flora by car with Major

Bodley as driver to see the British battlefields. At Senlis, Dorothy viewed Foch's headquarters and visited Willard's friend, the curé, M. Dourlent. She also felt it necessary to reprove Major Bodley, a married man, for pressing his attentions too vigorously on the lovely Flora—a rebuke the Major took like a gentleman and offered his apologies. Near Corbie they "[got] down into dugouts & walked over the fields of ruin & desolation. All too horrible." The Major left them at Amiens, where they caught the Paris train to Boulogne, crossed the Channel, and were at Claridge's by 9:00 P.M. There they dined with Almeric, who had in 1918 become Baron Queensborough and for whose Tory politics Dorothy had little sympathy. She had been in touch by mail and probably by telephone with her stepsister Adelaide, who had sent flowers for Willard's grave, but Adelaide was off in Dorset and Dorothy was anxious to get home to the children.

With Flora, she rejoined Daisy Harriman at Southampton, where they sailed on the great *Mauretania*. Dorothy attended a Christian Science service with thirteen others in the stateroom of a Mrs. Tweedy. Among the passengers was Sir Arthur Whitten Brown, who told of the transatlantic flight he and John Alcock had made from Newfoundland to Ireland three months earlier in a mere sixteen hours and twelve minutes. Another was that prince of predicament, Moreton Frewen, as charming and dubious as ever at sixty-six, still on the brink of financial ruin as he made one of his hundred-odd crossings in quest of a quick fortune. This time it was a Canadian land promotion—a fiasco like the rest. "Talked to Morten [sic] Frewen," Dorothy recorded, without mentioning whether Frewen had recalled that other crossing in 1894 on the *Majestic* when he had conferred with her father about his plan to make a killing on the diamond tariff.

More interesting politically was Viscount Grey of Fallodon, former Foreign Secretary now en route to Washington with his secretary, Sir William Tyrrell, to become Ambassador. He was president of the League of Nations Union and was to urge American entrance into the League. Dorothy lunched with Lord Grey and strolled the deck with Sir William. She had caught up with the newspapers and was aware of the hardening of the Senate against Wilson and the League, and of the President's transcontinental speechmaking tour which he hoped would win decisive support. By the time the *Mauretania* approached New York on September 26, Wilson had broken down and was returning to Washington, never to recover, the League a lost cause in America.

To Dorothy this was international tragedy that one might hope would be corrected in time by enlightenment such as could be found in *The New Republic* and by education such as could be absorbed at the New School. Could she, with her puritanical sense of conscience, of overprivilege, of duty toward the underprivileged, toward the republic, and toward mankind everywhere—could she really be the daughter of Society-obsessed Flora Payne Whitney and grandeur-obsessed William Collins Whitney? She alone of the four children was so concerned. While her sister and two brothers (Payne especially) had been and were to be more generous in their philanthropies than their father had been, they had never permitted philanthropy or altruism—much less reform— to preoccupy them. None of Dorothy's generation, many of whose fathers had profited in ways not downright illegal but not admirable either, were as anxious as she to make amends.

Now, not even the peril to her beloved League could tarnish the joy of returning home. "Too lovely coming up harbor," Dorothy wrote, viewing the skyscrapers of lower Manhattan where Willard had once worked. "Beatrice & Prather met me & we dined at the Plaza—we three—then later Daisy & I came down here [to Applegreen]. Found Lindleys in house." Next day: "Saw Ruth Pratt this A.M. After lunch, while Prather played tennis, Edith & I took the children to Mineola Fair." Her life resumed its customary tenor as the entries continued, day after day after day:

> Junior League office all day. Pauline Emmet & I worked hard on final decorations & Max Williams hung pictures. Lunched at Club with Daisy. Home alone tonight.

> In town all day. Worked hard at J.L.—Bd. of Managers meeting in A.M. Lunch at Belmont with Bill Delano. Finished hanging club pictures in afternoon. Brought Herbert [Croly] down for night.

In a back flyleaf of the diary, she had written the maxim "Life really is worth while as long as we do something to make it so," and she had copied Yeats's "Cradle Song":

> *Angels are bending above your white bed*
> *They weary of tending the souls of the dead,*
> *And God smiles in Heaven to see you so good*
> *And the old planets seven grow sweet with his mood.*
> *I kiss you and kiss you, with arms round my own.*
> *Oh, how I shall miss you my darling when grown.*

Cornell University

EPILOGUE

70. Dorothy and her second husband, Leonard Knight Elmhirst, at Dartington.

Epilogue

In 1920, Leonard Knight Elmhirst, president of the Cosmopolitan Club at Cornell, called on Dorothy Straight in New York on an errand of benign expediency. His club, which included students from twelve nations, was $80,000 in the hole and in danger of disappearing into it. Elmhirst, inevitably known as Limey by his friends because he was born in Yorkshire, was the son of a Church of England clergyman, a graduate of Cambridge who had served in the war and become a disciple of Rabindrinath Tagore in India. Despite his degree in history, he was studying agriculture at Cornell so that he could promote scientific farming in India. He found Mrs. Straight to be "tall and slim, all in black except for a little sable fur around her neck and a very fetching hat."

Although Dorothy was instantly sympathetic, since Willard had been interested in the Cosmopolitan Club, she took the trouble to visit Cornell not only to investigate the club but also to see what could be done to fulfill Straight's wish that she do something to make the university more human. ". . . *of course*, I'm going to help," she told Elmhirst. Their friendship was renewed in 1921 when Dorothy, after soliciting ideas about what should be done for Cornell, and visiting other campuses, began planning a union building as a memorial to her husband.

She was fairly encircled by suitors, one of them being W. Cameron Forbes, whom she had first met in the Philippines. It was her practice, when visited by Forbes or others in whom she had little interest, to have many guests on hand. This effectively discouraged personal attentions.

But Elmhirst was tall, likable, smiling, an idealist with a charm of his own. There was only one Willard Straight, but the Englishman resembled him in some ways, having a good tenor voice, some artistic skill, an ability to dash off verse, and a benevolent interest in the Orient. The benevolence was expressed not in large financial designs but in ef-

463

forts to lessen starvation in India. Elmhirst was the second of eight sons of a modestly prosperous parson-landowner, a family that had cultivated the same land in the West Riding since 1320. Two of his brothers had been lost in the war. He was on touchy terms with his stern father because college and the war had shaken his religious beliefs and he abandoned the course that had been expected of him—to succeed to the Elmhirst pulpit. He had borrowed £50 from a friend, had traveled steerage to America, and was now eking out a living by washing dishes, peeling potatoes, and doing similar chores at Cornell. He was too proud to borrow from his father.

At a campus picnic with Dorothy he was correct enough in casual clothing, but when invited to visit her at Westbury he had to skin by on a frayed suit and one passable shirt. "She was not only charming to look at," he noted, "but there was a graciousness and style about her bearing, and, withal, a very bright gleam in her eye." She became aware of his financial straits and indeed became interested in him, though he was almost seven years her junior (as Straight had been seven years older). She mentioned in passing that she missed terribly her late husband's spirited conversation. According to Elmhirst's own account, written many years later, he was deeply attracted to her, wrote to her frequently, but forbore at first pressing it to the point of romance out of embarrassment over their disparity in wealth.

Yet there was the beginning of an understanding between them. When he graduated later in 1921, having done four years' work in two, he was qualified as an agriculturist and poultry raiser on top of his Cantabrigian Master of Arts. Dorothy was true to her disinclination toward precipitate marriage. Just as she had sent Willard off alone and unplighted to China, so did she see Leonard off to India. His long stay there would be a good test of their mutual affection. Meanwhile she worked on Straight's papers, and from them (and his own recollections) Herbert Croly wrote *Willard Straight*, published in 1924. It is an engrossing biography, not pure encomium though perhaps a shade more admiring than it might have been had not Croly had such a high regard for both Dorothy and Willard. She sent copies to scores of friends.

While Elmhirst joined Tagore in rural reconstruction work in Bengal, Dorothy characteristically pressed causes to the left of those favored by most Fifth Avenue gentry. In one of them she joined Eleanor Roosevelt in promoting the Women's Trade Union League, led by the fiery, socialist, Polish-born Rose Schneiderman. Although Dorothy had long been acquainted with Mrs. Roosevelt and her husband Franklin, this seems to have been her first joint venture with Eleanor, who was three years older. Both were Roser school graduates, though not classmates, and each had once been courted by the late Howard Cary, whose death in London had been so mysterious. They were the most energetic female proponents of social reform to come from the highest echelon of Society, and to disturb many of their friends with their unorthodoxy. Dorothy raised $20,000 toward the purchase of a headquarters for the WTUL, and she and Eleanor became close friends.

Dorothy was also preoccupied with the architect William Delano, by the building of Willard Straight Hall at Cornell, in which Elmhirst aided her with his own suggestions when he returned from India in 1923. The building, completed in 1924, was the most splendid of the university unions at the time, and more than half a century later is still a handsome, impressive place. It was revolutionary then in providing accommodations for women students. One can get lost in its many rooms and corridors. It contains magnificent lounges, quiet reading rooms, a spacious theater, and both of its restaurants serve Straight-burgers as well as more exotic dishes. Of all the many buildings constructed with William C. Whitney's money, it is surely the most useful and perhaps the most "human."

Still Dorothy kept Elmhirst waiting. They were married at last, very quietly, at Westbury in 1925, to the distress of Harry, who again felt her choice of husband unwise. "Mrs. Straight's Wedding was a Surprise to the Social World," noted The World Magazine. It was a further surprise when the Elmhirsts—taking with them the maid Louisa—moved to England, bought the handsome but crumbling Dartington Hall in Devon, with 2,000 acres, and started a combined school and industrial-cultural center there.

Education, they both reasoned, should be regarded not as preparation for life but as life itself. It was Dorothy's second foray into progressive education, the New School in New York now being well established. Her own children were the first to be enrolled at Dartington. Around the school the Elmhirsts introduced farming, poultry, weaving, pottery, lumbering, orchard and cottage-industry projects that employed local people, who were also encouraged to take part in the school dances, dramas, and entertainments. The Elmhirsts did not plan a self-contained community but sought to provide a cultural focus as well as to regenerate the countryside, pay fair wages, and halt the drift to the cities.

"At Dartington," Dorothy wrote in The Junior League Magazine for the benefit of her friends back in America, "we regard the school as a part of the community in which adult education and rural enterprises of all kinds are being carried on. . . . a thorough system of cost accounting is, probably for the first time on an English estate, being put into effect. . . . Fear of elders [on the part of the pupils, known as juniors] does not exist. . . . the juniors are exposed to the intellectual as well as the practical interests of the community. Each junior makes out his own program, and so far as possible the staff remains in the background encouraging the juniors to work alone or in small groups without a senior."

British schools were founded on stern discipline, which included corporal punishment. Elmhirst himself had taken blows and beatings in the name of character development when he attended the famous Repton School in Derbyshire—a practice he now rejected. Shockingly, the Dartington prospectus read: "We expect no compulsory attendance at classes, nor are we greatly worried if the first term appears wasted in wandering about." The pupils were asked to call instructors by their first names.

It was a unique undertaking. There was no body of experience to profit from but their own. For both Elmhirsts it meant a complete break with the past—just as Dorothy had had when she married Willard and moved to Peking, just as Elmhirst had had when he worked for improvement in India.

Perhaps their ideas were a trifle *too* advanced in the beginning. Neither was conventionally pious. Dorothy's deeply religious spirit felt an emptiness in formal churchgoing and she seldom attended services. Worse, *the pupils were not required to attend church.* This was intolerable to Dartington parishioners. The clergyman was censorious, in one sermon suggesting that the school might be run by Communists. Many of the local people were suspicious of these newcomers who so mistreated tradition. Those employed by the Elmhirsts were paid more than the prevailing rate, which meant that other employers in the district grudgingly had to meet the rise. The Elmhirsts, though terribly busy, might well have given more thought to tea-and-crumpet public relations since much of their success would depend on local cooperation. When a representative of the Dartington School paper interviewed a farmer beyond the village, some bias was evident on both sides:

"I used to know [Dartington Hall]," the farmer said in a Devon dialect the paper did not spare, "but that was avore they there Elmhirses come there."

"So you've heard of us?" the reporter queried.

"Ees, us hears a goodish bit wan way 'n another."

"Mostly good, I hope."

"Well, some is an' some idn'. I daunt zay, but what tidn' purdy good for imployment an' the like o' that, but to tell'ee the truth, I daunt 'ardly knaw what you'm a duin' uv, zeem to be havin' a dabble at so many things all to wance."

"Yes, it must seem like that."

"Wan thing I yerd . . . they'd got some contraption that makes it zeem that the zuns come up long avore daybreak, so that the cocks craw an' the 'ens lay early enough fer breakfus'. . . . There zeems to be summat wrung about it to me. . . . Another thing is thaise yer electricity milkin' machines."

The farmer had also heard that immorality was prevalent at the school and that people there often ran about naked: ". . . what's this yer about what they call Noodists up there to Dartiton 'all, people walkin' about with noil un, so to spake?"

So there was a time of uneasiness and opposition. But at Dartington itself, the pupils so enjoyed their freedom that one girl was alleged to have said, "Oh dear, do I have to do what I want to do all over again today?" To one of the students, fourteen-year-old Michael Young, the school was like a heaven in which he had arrived after a considerable stay in hell. Young, whose parents were separated and poor, had been shunted from one school to another where the food was bad and scarce and a poor recitation meant a ruler across the knuckles or a blow. He arrived at Dartington after several years of almost permanent hunger filled with a quiet resolve eventually to murder one of the more sadistic masters he had had. Here there was no punishment. "And what food!" Young marveled in later years. "Apple sauce in great bowls for breakfast, with piles of cornflakes and giant jugs of milk. Roast beef without gristle, set off by crisp Yorkshire pudding. Bean shoots from China. When once Lady Astor brought Bernard Shaw, as she said to see the children at this strange establishment guzzling away under the table, like dogs, there we were at the tables, eating strawberries and cream, and not just as a special issue to impress the visitors. . . . Whereas before I had always longed for the end of the term, now I longed for the end of each holiday. Then I could get back to the wondrous slog of eating my way through three solid meals a day, every day. . . ."

Furthermore, Dorothy lavished affection on children from broken families and virtually took Young into her household. He came to understand that this was because he was poor and had only two pairs of trousers and one sweater which he had to wear every day, and because she had been an early orphan herself, in need of affection.

"She was shy, she was sad and yet she was also gay," he later reflected. "When someone made her laugh, especially by ridiculing pomposity, she would laugh and laugh and laugh, rocking until the tears streamed down her face. She always wore a hat when walking in the open air and also ran about so excitedly with the children playing chain tag on the lawn in front of the Hall in the early days of the school that . . . she laddered another pair of silk stockings almost nightly. She floated into a gathering very erect and then, instead of taking a chair, sank down onto the floor. . . . If she was sitting in a chair when others came in she would try to give it away to them, as she was always with never-ending generosity giving away her time as well as her money."

Though Dorothy was thirty-eight when she married Elmhirst, she had two children by him. There was little communication between her and her brothers, but she visited New York annually to see her friends, and a stream of them visited Dartington. For several years she paid heavy taxes both in the United States and England, but ultimately she became a British citizen. Despite the great expense of the Dartington project, her fortune was still intact in the late twenties. The Elmhirsts, both enthusiastic theatergoers, took one flyer and backed R. C. Sheriff's play *Journey's End*, in which the heroic but doomed Captain Stanhope remarked (as Major Straight had) that imagination was disastrous in a soldier in the front lines. They profited by some £500,000 in the enormous international success of the play.

The Devon people ultimately realized that the Elmhirsts, for all their unconventionality, ran an establishment of immense benefit to them and the nation. Dorothy's own children were to prove the qualifications of the school itself, since Whitney Straight went on to become head of British Overseas Airways Corporation, Beatrice an actress of internationally acclaimed talent, and Michael, after his term at Cambridge, where he was president of the Union, an editor and public official in the field of the arts.

Dorothy in middle age had the presence of a great lady combined with modesty and affection. Woman of the world though she was, loving Dartington though she did, she never quite conquered her homesickness. On rare occasions she mentioned Willard Straight, seemingly with nostalgia. In the thirties, years of world depression, she began taking Michael Young with her on her trips to America. He was astounded by his first view of New York skyscrapers, which was followed by a stay at the baronial camp in the Adirondacks and—after Roosevelt's election—by annual visits to the White House. The Elmhirsts, with their experience in promoting light industry and building rural housing at Dartington, spoke the language of Eleanor Roosevelt, who was embarking on a similar project at Arthurdale. At one White House evening, with Frances Perkins, the Henry Wallaces, Admiral Byrd, Gen. Hugh Johnson, and Louis Howe among the guests, Elmhirst, the student of medieval history, "embellished his description of Dartington with references to the manorial system, where there had been security, a sense of belonging and rootedness. . . ." So pleased was Dorothy at Eleanor's undertaking that she wrote to her, "My dear, I am going back to England so proud of my country at last." Michael Young would never forget conversations he had with an indulgent FDR any more than he would those he had privately with Dorothy when she sat back and listened to him tell of his troubles with a sympathy he had never before experienced.

From the start she had fought the prevailing impression in Devon that Dartington School was the philanthropic plaything of endless American millions. There were at first dreadful but essential deficits, which she made good. But in 1932 the Elmhirsts set up a charitable trust with sufficient capital and investments so that the enterprise could go it alone with wise administration. Dartington became famous as an advanced school, especially strong in the arts, having such occasional lecturers as Bertrand Russell, Julian and Aldous Huxley, and Rabindrinath Tagore, while among the highly qualified regular teachers were Mark Tobey in painting, Margaret Barr in the dance, and Michael Chekhov in drama. Beatrice Straight got much of her training at the busy Dartington theater. Dorothy was an avid gardener, birdwatcher, traveler, and even poet. (She achieved verse with more subtlety and technical skill—if less romantic—than her youthful effusions.) She taught Shakespeare at Dartington and occasionally lectured on the bard to hardened convicts at nearby Dartmoor, the prison made famous by Sherlock Holmes.

Herbert Croly, on his death in 1930, was succeeded as editor of *The New Republic* by Bruce Bliven, and the publication continued its distinguished interpretation of the news. There seems no other instance in which a person paying a magazine's expenses over so many years has not also controlled its opinions. The paper enjoyed an independence for which the Straights have never received sufficient credit. Michael

Straight after his graduation from Cambridge was elevated to the staff. As World War II began with a parade of Nazi triumphs, bearing out Dorothy's prediction about the unwisdom of Versailles, she had been living in England for fourteen years. In the beginning the Elmhirsts so strongly argued for a last-ditch effort to avoid war that they were called appeasers. They changed when the stripe of the Hitlerian menace became evident. Bliven noted that the "pacifist position of [*The New Republic*] must have grated on the Elmhirsts to a high degree, but never once did they make the slightest suggestion that we should alter our course." Its course was altered when the editors themselves began to fear a Fascist domination of the world.

During the war, children evacuated from London were housed at Dartington and troops were billeted at the Junior School. Dartington became a haven for distinguished refugees from Nazi terror, among them Kurt Jooss, who made it the center of his dance school and ballet, and Hans Oppenheim, who took charge of music and gave concerts in the restored Great Hall. Whitney Straight, remaining a Briton, became a wing commander in the Royal Air Force. Michael and Beatrice Straight chose to become American citizens, Michael becoming a colonel in the Air Force and, after the war, editor of *The New Republic*. Dorothy financed the paper until it was sold in 1953, by which time her contribution had averaged $95,000 a year or about $3,700,000 for 38½ years of support.

Dartington's handsome buildings and gardens vie with Willard Straight Hall in the useful employment of a part of the fortune built by a man not noted for public benevolence. The school and its magnificent gardens are visited annually by American tourists who are surprised to learn that it is the creation of an American expatriate whose wealth came largely from New York surface lines that have long since vanished.

Dorothy's brother Payne died in 1927 at fifty-one after a tennis-induced heart attack. He was one of the richest Americans, the third largest taxpayer after Henry Ford and John D. Rockefeller, Jr., leaving almost $200,000,000. He was buried not near his late father but on his own estate. Harry died in 1930, aged fifty-eight, at 871 Fifth Avenue, his father's mansion, which Harry had sold and then bought again. His funeral services were at his mother's church, St. Bartholomew's, and he was buried at Woodlawn.

Dorothy outdid the rest in longevity as she did in good works, continuing her friendship with surviving Roser classmates, with Ethel

Derby and others in America as long as she lived. On the night before her death, in 1968 at the age of eighty-one, she followed "with complete concentration" a television debate about arms for Nigeria. She was forgiven her lack of appreciation for the established church. After a musical service in the Great Hall at Dartington—its roof had been gone when she bought it, decay was rampant, but she had made it splendid again—her funeral ceremony was held at the Anglican church in the village. She was cremated and her ashes scattered in her own Dartington garden, where Leonard's ashes were later to join hers. The four longest-surviving children of Flora and William Whitney were even more separate in death then they had been in life, Pauline resting far across southern England near Dorking, Payne 3,000 miles away in Manhasset, and only Harry (except for the almost forgotten Olive) accompanying the shades of his parents at Woodlawn.

NOTES

Notes

THERE has been one previous biography of Whitney: *William C. Whitney, Modern Warwick,* by Mark D. Hirsch (Dodd, Mead, 1948). While I would not agree with all of Mr. Hirsch's conclusions, his book is thoroughly researched, an invaluable source to which Whitney's daughter Dorothy gave aid in correspondence with the author. There is no biography of Dorothy Whitney Straight Elmhirst, and characteristically she avoided all but essential mention of herself in the biography of her first husband, *Willard Straight* (Macmillan, 1924), written with her help by her late husband's close friend Herbert Croly.

Luckily, many of the letters between William C. Whitney and Flora Payne Whitney, before and after their marriage, are extant, as are even more of those between Dorothy Payne Whitney and Willard Straight, from their first acquaintance until Straight's death. In fact, since both Dorothy and Willard kept diaries for much of their adult lives, and preserved also their correspondence with other friends and relatives, and since both usually wrote clearly and at length, we have virtually as complete and vivid a picture of them and their activities as it is possible to have. These diaries and many thousands of letters, now preserved at Cornell University in the Dorothy Whitney Straight Elmhirst Papers, form a part of the basis of Book I of this narrative, dealing with Dorothy's parents, and a much larger part of Book II, dealing with Dorothy and Willard.

Letters and papers cited below without mention of source are from this extensive collection at Cornell. In some letters quoted, unnecessary paragraphing has been closed.

Among the hundreds of other books consulted, many of them cited in the Notes that follow, those found most extensively useful were Herbert Croly's *Willard Straight,* Dixon Wecter's *The Saga of American Society* (Scribners, 1937), Louis Graves's *Willard Straight in the Orient* (New York: Asia Publishing Company, 1922), Wayne Andrews's *The Vanderbilt Legend* (Harcourt, Brace, 1941), Charles Forcey's *The Crossroads of Liberalism* (Oxford University Press, 1961), Allan Nevins's *Grover Cleveland: A Study in Courage* (Dodd, Mead, 1933), and Charles Vevier's *The United States and China, 1906–1913* (New York: Greenwood Press, 1968).

The New York Public Library's fine collection of *Town Topics* turned out to be a rich source of information as well as innuendo. Much of the research was done at that library, the Yale Library, and the New York Public Library's newspaper collection at its annex on West 43rd Street. Additional light was gained about the Straights from Columbia University's Oral History Collection. Sources consulted (other than personal interviews), and abbreviations for them and for the leading characters where abbreviations are used, are as follows:

Croly: WS. The biography of Willard Straight mentioned above.
CUOH: The oral history collection at Columbia University.
DPW: Dorothy Payne Whitney.
DWS: Dorothy after her marriage to Willard Straight.
DD: Dorothy's diary.
DWSE Prs: The Dorothy Whitney Straight Elmhirst Papers at Cornell.
FPW: Flora Payne, later Flora Payne Whitney.
Hirsch: The biography of William C. Whitney mentioned above.
NYH: *New York Herald.*
NYMT: *New York Morning Telegraph.*
NR: *New Republic.*
NYPL: New York Public Library.
NYT: *New York Times.*
NYTrib: *New York Tribune.*
NYS: *New York Sun.*
NYW: *New York World.*
SD: Willard Straight's diary.
TT: *Town Topics.*

BOOK I

Pages 3 to 7:

Christening: *Washington Post, Washington Evening Star,* Apr. 12, 1887. "Thin tricks": Flora to WCW, Oct. 1, 1888. Gwynn, Stephen (ed.), *The Letters and Friendships of Sir Cecil Spring Rice,* 2 vols., hereafter cited as *Spring Rice* (London: Constable, 1929), I: 72, July 29, 1887. "I christen thee": *NYT, NYTrib,* and *NYW,* Apr. 12, 1887. Whitney New Year's Eve party: *NYW,* Jan. 1, 1886. Flora to Harry: Feb. 20 and 27, 1886, letters combined. Mrs. Whitney "reigned supreme": *NYT* obituary, Feb. 6, 1893. 200 gallons of terrapin soup: Allan Nevins: *The Letters of Grover Cleveland* (Houghton Mifflin, 1933), 299; hereafter cited as Nevins: *Cleveland.* WCW's bitter letter is dated Oct. 7, 1888. "Good, constant eyes": *Chicago Tribune,* Dec. 7, 1888. "A small politician": *NYT,* quoted in *NYTrib,* Oct. 16, 1887. "Spwing Wice": Mrs. Winthrop Chanler, *Roman Spring* (Boston: Little, Brown, 1934), 204. "Wirepuller" and "clever lawyer": *Spring Rice,* I, 70–71, 63; WCW's kindness: the same, p. 72. Missouri WCTU: *NYT,* Dec. 4, 1886. Bancroft gift: *NYW,* Apr. 12, 1887. Hoar's remark: Allan Nevins, *John D. Rockefeller,* 2 vols. (Scribners, 1940), II: 104.

Pages 8 to 10:

"I should die": Flora to WCW, Jan. 24, 1869. "After all": Flora to WCW, Jan. 13, 1869. "I can never be": Flora to Harry, Nov. 26, 1885. "You know that": WCW to Flora, Oct. 7, 1888. Navy laxity and WCW's report: *NYT,* Dec. 5, 1885, Jan. 10, 1886; Nevins, *Cleveland,* 220; *Army & Navy Register,* Dec. 1885. Attacks on WCW: *NYTrib,* Sept. 17, Aug. 8, 1886.

Pages 11 to 13:

"I was afraid": Hirsch, 307. Mrs. Potter's recitation: Fairfax Downey, *Portrait of an Era: As Drawn by C. D. Gibson* (Scribners, 1936), 77–78; article by Mrs. Potter in

Hearst's International-Cosmopolitan, Mar. 1933, p. 149; *NYT*, Feb. 28, 1886. *NYW*'s retort: Mar. 1, 1886. Mrs. Whitney's dinner: *NYT*, June 25, 1886.

Pages 14 to 16:
Carnegie letter: *Andrew Carnegie*, by Joseph Frazier Wall (New York: Oxford, 1970), 646. WCW's orders regarding Panama: *NYT*, Mar. 19, 1895. WCW–Lamar colloquy: Quoted in WCW to Flora, Oct. 20, 1885. Watterson on Cleveland: Henry Watterson, *Marse Henry*, 2 vols. (New York: Doran, 1919), II: 117. Cleveland on Whitney: *NYT*, WCW obituary Feb. 3, 1904. WCW warns Flora: WCW to Flora, Aug. 1, 1887. Cleveland invites WCW for poker: Cleveland to WCW, Feb. 1, 1887, DWSE Prs. "Take the money": Watterson, *op. cit.*, II: 210–12.

Pages 17 to 19:
NYTrib on WCW's railroad scheme. Feb. 28, 1886; *NYT* on same, Feb. 23, and Mar. 1, 1886. Sleeping aldermen: E. J. Kahn, Jr., *The Merry Partners* (Random House: 1955), 98. *NYW*'s attack and interview of Widener: Feb. 25, 28, 1886. Urges clean hands: Mar. 1, 1886. WCW's reply: in all leading NYC papers, Mar. 3, 1886.

Pages 20 to 24:
Hard of killing: Flora to Harry, Jan. 19, 1886. "Coarse debauchee": *NYS*, Aug. 7, 1884. "Keep your dignity": To Flora, Aug. 1, 1887; reply, Aug. 5. Instructions about horses: To Flora, July 14, 1887. Kin to God: Jules Abels, *The Rockefeller Billions* (Macmillan, 1965), 84. Mrs. Stevens's background: Dixon Wecter, *The Saga of American Society* (Scribners, 1937), 411n. WCW to Flora on illness: Oct. 21, 1887; President to WCW, Oct. 27; WCW to President, Nov. 8; President's reply, Nov. 11. Rumor in *NYT*: Oct. 30; Harmony's remark, *NYT*, Nov. 2; WCW's trips to NYC, *NYT*, Nov. 1; Flora's statement, *NYT*, Nov. 20. WCW's annual report: *NYT*, Dec. 9, 1887. Cotillion at Leiters': *NYT*, Feb. 14, 1888

Pages 25 to 29:
WCW spent $80,000,000: Hirsch, 335–36. Flora's pettishness: To WCW, Sept. 22, 1887. WCW refusal to apologize: To Flora, Aug. 15, 1888. "I have always": To Flora, Sept. 24. Her long letter of accusation: Oct. 1, 1888. Her note showing repentance: Oct. 2. WCW's bitter reply: Oct. 7. His telegrams: Oct. 9, 12.

Pages 30 to 31:
Watterson's correction: Watterson, *op. cit.*, II: 209–10. Spring Rice's comment: *op. cit.*, I: 91, dated Apr. 15, 1888. "Beast of Buffalo": Robert McElroy, *Grover Cleveland, The Man and the Statesman* (Harper, 1923), 289. WCW warns Flora again: Sept. 17, 1888; urges her to rest, July 17, 1888. Flora's lawn party: *NYT*, Sept. 24; *NYH*, Sept. 20, 1888. Hewitt and the Irish: *NYTrib*, Apr. 11, 1888; also Matthew Breen, *Thirty Years of New York Politics* (New York, 1899), 767.

Pages 32 to 35:
Flora attacks lies about President: *Chicago Tribune*, Dec. 7, 1888. Cleveland thanks her: Dec. 12, 1888. Depew's defense: *NYTrib*, Dec. 8. WCW writes Depew: Hirsch, 322. Pauline Whitney at party: *NYT*, Feb. 2, 1889. David B. Hill's character: *The Au-*

tobiography of George B. McClellan Jr., ed. Harold C. Syrett (Lippincott, 1956), 84–85; Harry Thurston Peck, Twenty Years of the Republic (Dodd, Mead, 1913), 278–79. NYT on Hill and Whitney: Feb. 8, 1889. Flora weeps on leaving: NYT, Flora obituary, Feb. 6, 1893.

Pages 36 to 40:
"Act well your part": Hirsch, p. 7. Oliver Payne joins up: Mark D. Hirsch, unpublished manuscript, Flora Payne, Her Life and Times, DWSE Prs. Flora describes the Alhambra: To parents, June 10, 1863, in DWSE Prs.

Pages 40 to 44:
"Behold me": To parents, Oct. 23, 1863. Flora to "darling Ol": Nov. 13, 1863. She writes father from Paris: Oct. 16, 1864. Oliver knew they would fall in love: WCW to Flora, Mar. 4, 1869. "How you looked I plainly recall": WCW to Flora, July 5, 1877. "Mr. Whitney shall do": Flora's letter of Dec. 11, 1868. "Goethe said": To WCW, Feb. 14, 1869. "Own up and out with it": Jan. 13, 1869. Eagles and heart: To WCW, May 21, 1869. About housekeeping, money, and losing keys: From letters Apr. 25, May 9, 24. Will live handsomely: Apr. 14, 1869. "Got you into this scrape": WCW to Flora, Apr. 16. "Nine cheers": July 23. "I am utterly ashamed": Flora's letter of Apr. 22, 1869. "Starving and dying": To WCW, Mar. 2. "Live like a nun": May 24. "We have been together": June 30. "Ten pyramids crushing me": July 7. Like two birds: July 8. She blows up boiler: May 24. Father and mother's generosity: June 30. "The boys told me": Aug. 18. WCW's reply: Aug. 22. "I have decided": WCW's letter of Sept. 26, 1869.

Pages 45 to 47:
"William is in politics": Hirsch, 65. Oliver Payne joins Rockefeller: Nevins, Rockefeller, I: 362–63. "If you are working": Flora to WCW, July 3, 1874. "You, my husband": Flora to WCW, July 7, 1874. "I wish now": Flora, July 17. WCW's reply: Two of his letters combined, July 21 and 25, 1874.

Pages 48 to 51:
Beaver frock coat: Lucius Beebe, The Big Spenders (Doubleday, 1966), 234. A man of about 35: NYH, Aug. 10, 1875. NYTrib misnames him: Aug. 10. Reorganizes new office: NYH, WCW obituary, Feb. 3, 1904. "The just presumption": NYTrib, Nov. 7, 1882. "Henry B. Payne, of Ohio": NYT, June 23, 1876. "Yale commencement . . . Sioux Indians": NYT, June 23, 1876. "Thanks to Tammany": NYT, June 26, 1876. "Three genuine fights": NYTrib, June 27. Tilden-Hayes dispute: Eugene A. Roseboom, A History of Presidential Elections (Macmillan, 1957), 242–49. "I do hope": WCW to Flora, Aug. 23, 1874. "I really think": WCW to Flora, Aug. 16, 1874. Flora's gloves-and-cravats letter: Aug. 17, 1877.

Pages 51 to 54:
"I am not a quick . . .": WCW to Flora, Apr. 16, 1869. Tilden beckons Whitney: Perry Belmont, An American Democrat (Columbia University Press, 1941), 192–93. NYH on "cam-Payne": June 20, 1880. NYTrib suspects WCW motives: June 18. "The most absurd statements": NYT, June 21. Wickham and Whitney light cigars:

NYH, June 22. "These gentlemen already have the Mayor": *NYH,* June 21. Whitney on Tilden: W. C. Hudson, *Random Recollections of an Old Political Reporter* (New York: Cupples & Leon, 1911), 110.

Pages 54 to 56:
NYH on Whitney and Tammany: June 20, 1880. "Mr. Whitney proposes": *NYTrib,* Jan. 27, 1881. Kelly hints Whitney corruption: Hirsch, 163, 165. Whitney-Manning-Cleveland scene: *NYTrib,* Feb. 7, 1904. WCW resigns, claims reduction of expenses: *NYTrib,* Nov. 7, 1882.

Pages 57 to 61:
Edith Wharton on the *nouveaux: The Age of Innocence* (Appleton, 1920), 1. *NYT* on the Vanderbilt ball: Mar. 27, 1883. "Hearing of Miss Astor's plans": Wecter, *op. cit.,* 337. Description of ball: *NYT,* Mar. 27, 1883; *NYH,* same date. Description of the Whitneys: *NYW,* Mar. 27. The opera as a private club: John Briggs, *Requiem for a Yellow Brick Brewery· A History of the Metropolitan Opera* (Little, Brown, 1969), 16.

Pages 62 to 67:
WCW as railroad lobbyist: To Flora, June 4, 1883. Carnegie's role: Wall, *Andrew Carnegie,* 510 12, and Hirsch, 192–96. "There is nothing prettier": WCW to Flora, May 27, 1883. His account of his busy day: To Flora, May 25. WCW on Hurlbert and Pulitzer: To Flora, May 25, as is his "You are a curious compound" etc. Flora on Olive's death: Diary, DWSE Prs. WCW's cable is dated June 6, 1883. Flora jealous of Ellen: To WCW, Oct. 1, 1888. WCW and Gunn at Como: Gunn to WCW, n.d. Mar. 1884; Gunn's letter of thanks, Jan. 26, 1884. "I do so hope": Flora to WCW, Oct. 7, 1883.

Pages 67 to 72:
Gunn on age in high office: To WCW, Nov. 21, 1883. WCW's letter to Pulitzer about Standard Oil: Dec. 19, 1883. *NYW* on the new Whitney home: Jan. 6, 1884. Standard's and Oliver Payne's influence in Ohio: Nevins, *Rockefeller,* II: 103–4 and 112. *NYW* praises Henry B. Payne: Jan. 9, 1884. Oscar Wilde's utterance and description of house: *NYW,* Jan. 6, 1884. Poor Richard ethic, etc.: Merle Curti, *The Growth of American Thought* (Harper, 1943), 644–50; George Juergens, *Joseph Pulitzer and the New York World* (Princeton, 1966), 176–77. Henry Adams, Charles Francis Adams, and Theodore Roosevelt on success and the rich: Quoted in Matthew Josephson, *The Robber Barons* (Harcourt, 1934), 337–38. Beecher on prosperity: Quoted in E. Digby Baltzell, *The Protestant Establishment: Aristocracy and Caste in America* (Random House, 1964), 101. Sumner on the rich: Quoted in Baltzell, *op. cit.,* 103. "Yale College is a good and safe place": Harris E. Starr, *William Graham Sumner* (New York, 1925), 300–301. Rockefeller praises business: Baltzell, *op. cit.,* 101.

Pages 72 to 74:
"I watch the papers": Gunn to WCW, Jan. 26, 1884. *NYH's* puzzlement: July 5, 1884. WCW's statement: July 6. Devilish marching song: Nevins, *Cleveland,* 177. *NYS* on Cleveland: Oct. 19, 1884.

Pages 76 to 78:

NYW on the slums, the "vulgar wealthy," and on Gould: Apr. 23, 1885; May 27, 1884, Mar. 14, 1885. NYW on the Vanderbilts and Depew: Nov. 12, Oct. 13, 1883; on Huntington, Jan. 6, 1884; on "shoddy aristocracy," Oct. 29, 1883; on Caroline Astor, Nov. 19, 1884. NYW defends WCW: Jan. 18, 1885.

Pages 79 to 82:

"HARD CASH IN POLITICS": NYH, Aug. 23, 1885. Flora on baby Dorothy: in two letters to WCW, one undated, one July 16, 1887; WCW appraises children: To Flora, July 26, 1886. WCW urges Harvard on Harry in letter of Sept. 21, 1888; Flora counters with inflammatory appeal: to Harry, n.d., 1888. WCW's angry letter to her: Oct. 7, 1888. He writes of "lost feeling" in same letter. Whitney on Ryan: Burton J. Hendrick, *The Age of Big Business* (Yale, 1919), 132–34. "William C. Whitney would not soil his fingers": Burton J. Hendrick, "Street Railway Financiers," *McClure's Magazine*, Nov. 1907. Hendrick's detailed appraisal of WCW and associates continued in *McClure's*, Dec., and Jan. 1908. WCW conversation with Rainsford: W. S. Rainsford, *The Story of a Varied Life* (Doubleday, Page, 1922), 322.

Pages 83 to 97:

Flora's assertion that her marriage had injured her: WCW to her, Oct. 7, 1888. Flora on McAllister: To WCW, Dec. 9, 1885. Whitneys and Clevelands at ball: NYW, Jan. 3, 1890. Same issue commented on Whitney-Vanderbilt rivalry, on Flora's gown, and on Mrs. Burke Roche. The Vanderbilts' huge ballroom: Wayne Andrews, *The Vanderbilt Legend* (Harcourt, 1941), 346–47. WCW Linotype investment: Bingham Duncan, *Whitelaw Reid* (U. of Georgia Press, 1975), 96–98 and 136. Cleveland comment on WCW: Nevins, *Cleveland*, 211, dated Sept. 15, 1889. "I had dragged the party": WCW to Flora, Aug. 25, 1890. WCW shipboard interview: NYT and NYW, July 3, 1890. His two letters to Flora concerning Mrs. Randolph: Aug. 25 and Oct. 30, 1890. Mrs. Stevens, Minnie, and Paget: R. W. B. Lewis, *Edith Wharton* (Harper, 1975), 37–38, 40–41; Grace M. Mayer, *Once Upon a City* (Macmillan, 1958), 112–14. Mrs. Astor's "undisputed position": Chanler, *Roman Spring*, 235. The full "400" is listed in Wecter's *Saga of American Society*, 216–23. Pulitzer's melancholy: Hirsch, 376. WCW's statement on sailing: NYT, Apr. 14, 1892. His description of Paris on May Day: NYT, May 19, 1892. Fifty theater tickets for HPW: B. H. Friedman, *Gertrude Vanderbilt Whitney* (Doubleday, 1978), 132. "I found myself so uncomfortable": WCW to Flora, two letters combined, postmarked May 7 and 9, 1892. Flora's reply: May 10. WCW's coaching lessons: To Flora, postmarked May 10. He kisses Harry: To Flora, May 19. On Cleveland: NYT, May 19. His comments on Dorothy: To Flora, May 19.

Pages 98 to 103:

Cotillion favors: Flora to WCW, n.d. Cleveland wants WCW "to the front": McElroy, *op. cit.*, 337. WCW "held the fate" of the convention: Nevins, *Cleveland*, 489. Flora's letter from Bellagio was dated June 12, 1892. *Chicago Tribune*, June 21, was in error about WCW and Oliver. See McElroy, 336–41; Hirsch, 386–97; Nevins, *Cleveland*, 486–91 for WCW's work at convention. "Dear Bill Whitney": Worthington C. Ford (ed.), *Letters of Henry Adams, 1892–1918* (Boston, 1930), 12. Flora to "My dear Will": July 21, 1892. "When I am with you": Cleveland to WCW, Mar. 26, 1892.

"Truckling conciliation": Nevins, *Cleveland*, 305–6, Sept. 4, 1892. WCW's sharp note to Cleveland: Aug. 30, 1892, DWSE Prs. Parker on WCW: George F. Parker, *Recollections of Grover Cleveland* (New York, 1909), 153–54. Van Alen "second-order": Harvey O'Connor, *The Astors* (Knopf, 1941), 210. "I'll put you in for $100,000": DeAlva S. Alexander, *Four Famous New Yorkers* (Holt, 1923), 191. "I shall come to town": Flora's note is undated. Her letter to her father, also undated: Hirsch, 412.

Pages 103 to 106:

Atlanta Journal comment: Quoted in *NYT*, Nov. 26, 1892. "Mr. Cleveland asked": *NYT*, Mar. 27, 1893. Gunn to WCW: July 23, 1892. Flora's Newport party: *NYT*, Aug. 21, 1892. *NYH* and *NYW* on Pauline's debut: Both Dec. 11, 1892. "Dear Flora is ill": Hirsch, 414, dated Jan. 29, 1893. Cleveland's note: Feb. 2, DWSE Prs. Dorothy's recollection, written Feb. 2, 1959, courtesy of Michael Straight. *NYH* and *NYW* on Flora's death: Both Feb. 6, 1893. WCW's note to Cleveland: Hirsch, 413. Funeral: *NYT*, *NYH*, and *NYW*, Feb. 8, 1893.

Pages 107 to 110:

"Since the death of his wife": *NYT*, Feb. 22, 1893. *NYT* interview: Mar. 27, 1893; *NYTrib* comment on his grief: Mar. 31. Rumored quarrel with Cleveland: *NYT*, Apr. 16, 1893; *NYTrib* report WCW seeks governorship: Aug. 7. His *NYW* interview: July 27. *NYW* on Van Alen: Sept. 21, 24, 27, 1893. WCW's reply: *NYTrib*, Sept. 28. Cleveland's remark in Nevins, *Cleveland*, to Oscar Straus, 338. Gunn's journal entry: July 20.

Pages 111 to 115:

WCW at exposition: *NYT*, Nov. 2. WCW a "Medici": Burton J. Hendrick, *The Age of Big Business* (Yale, 1919), 131–32; his "passion for display": Richmond Barrett, *Good Old Summer Days* (Appleton-Century, 1941), 227. Rumored interest in Mary Curzon: Nigel Nicholson, *Mary Curzon* (Harper, 1977), 62–63. *TT* comment on Mrs. Belmont and Miss Van Alen: Quoted in article by Andy Logan, *New Yorker*, Aug. 14, 1965; "diamond garters": Quoted in Harvey O'Connor, *The Astors*, 201; *TT* on Mrs. Burke Roche: July 14, 1887. Mann on "cartloads of stories": Quoted in *New Yorker* cited above. "Jackal": George B. McClellan, Jr., *The Gentleman and the Tiger*, edited by Harold C. Syrett (Lippincott, 1956), 99. Root as a lawyer: Hendrick in *McClure's*, Dec. 1907; also Hendrick, *Big Business*, 139. "This is the way to do it": Philip C. Jessup, *Elihu Root*, 2 vols. (Dodd, Mead, 1938), I: 185. Root on representing WCW: the same, 187.

Pages 116 to 120:

Gunn's comments aboard ship: Alexander Gunn, *Hermitage-Zoar Notebook* (published by Whitney, 1903), 85, 87. About Frewen: Allan Andrews, *The Splendid Pauper* (London: Harrap, 1968), 31, 59, 175, 177. Gunn's comments on tour: In letters to Zimmermann (hereafter cited as Z), May 19, June 2, 1894, and in journal entries, June 23, July 16. WCW letter to Frewen: Andrews, *op. cit.*, 177. Further Gunn comments: His entries for June 21, June 14, June 16, July 28, Aug. 6, Aug. 8, Aug. 17, Aug. 29, Sept. 5, Sept. 17. WCW's greeting in New York: *NYTrib*, Sept. 27.

Pages 120 to 127:

Cleveland letter to WCW: Nov. 3, 1894, DWSE Prs. WCW in "control" of Tam-
many: Matthew Josephson, *The Robber Barons* (Harcourt, 1934), 385. WCW in
mayor's office: *NYTrib*, Oct. 4, 1894. Rumor about Miss Davidge, *NYTrib*, May 14,
1895. Paget and his family: [Anglesey], George C. H. V. Paget, *One-Leg: The Life and
Letters of . . . First Marquess of Anglesey* (Morrow, 1961), *passim*. Cigar and whiskey:
Gunn's journal, Dec. 5, 1894. Queen's portrait: *One-Leg*, 310. Incidents on tour:
Gunn's journal, Dec. 25, 26, 1894, and Jan. 1, 26, Mar. 1, 6, 8, 9, 16, 1895. On
WCW extravagance: Gunn to Z, July 8, 1894. On Colonel's enmity: journal, Feb. 20,
1895. WCW on *Alliance*: *NYT*, Mar. 19, 1895. *NYTrib* comment: Mar. 21. WCW to
Gresham: Hirsch, 480, Apr. 7. Further incidents on tour: In Gunn journal, Mar. 25;
Gunn to Z, Apr. 3; Gunn journal, Mar. 28, Apr. 25, May 3, 1895.

Pages 127 to 130:

WCW on Croker: *NYTrib*, May 30; *NYW* canvass quoted in *NYTrib*: Aug. 21;
NYTrib's rumors: May 25, 1895. On WCW's yacht: Gunn to Z, July 17. Venezuela
crisis: W. A. Swanberg, *Pulitzer* (Scribners, 1967), 196–200; WCW to Olney and to
Herbert: Hirsch, 480–81. Pulitzer vs. Morgan loan: *Pulitzer*, 200–201; WCW to
Lamont, Jan. 3, 1896; Hirsch, 482.

Pages 130 to 137:

Gunn to WCW on Pauline: June 10, 1895. Consuelo-Marlborough match: *The Glit-
ter and the Gold*, Consuelo Vanderbilt Balsan (Harper, 1952), 37–53; marriage contract: Gustavus Myers, *History of the Great American Fortunes* (Modern Library, 1936),
378; *NYT*, *NYW*, Nov. 7; Fairfax Downey, *op. cit.*, 116. Pauline's wedding: *NYT*,
NYH, *NYW*, Nov. 13; *TT*, Nov. 14; Gunn to WCW, Nov. 16; Gunn journal, Nov.
18, Dec. 5, 1895.

Pages 138 to 141:

"Nothing is strong": Gunn to WCW, Feb. 22, 1896. Speculation on WCW candidacy: *NYTrib* May 18, 1896. "More country saving": Gunn to Z, June 15. Gunn's
"entertainment": to Z, June 18. WCW's vigor: *NYTrib*, June 18. Dickinson suspicion,
to Cleveland, June 20: Nevins, *Cleveland*, 442. "Fool's errand": *NYTrib*, June 28. Mr.
Dooley: Quoted in Swanberg, *Pulitzer*, 211. Regan announcement: *NYTrib*, July 17.
Neily and Grace: *Gertrude Vanderbilt Whitney*, 137–43.

Pages 142 to 146:

WCW predicts McKinley landslide: *NYTrib*, Aug. 8. Hunt on architecture: Wayne
Andrews, *The Vanderbilt Legend* (Harcourt, 1941), 232. Harry's wedding: *Gertrude
Vanderbilt Whitney*, 145–47; *NYH*, *NYT*, Aug. 26: *TT*, Aug. 27, 1896; also in WCW
obituary, *NYTrib*, Feb. 3, 1904. Li Hung Chang: *NYW*, Aug. 30, 1896. Death of
Payne: Cleveland *Plain Dealer*, Sept. 10, 13, 1896. WCW marries Mrs. Randolph:
NYT, Sept. 29; *NYW*, *NYH*, *NYTrib*, Sept. 30. Violent background of Fred May,
NYT, editorial Apr. 13, 1893.

Pages 147 to 151:

Speculation about the wedding: *NYT*, *NYW*, Sept. 29, 1896; *NYH*, *NYT*, Sept. 30;
TT, Oct. 1. *NYH*, *NYT* obituaries on second Mrs. WCW: Both May 7, 1899. WCW to

Cleveland, Sept. 27, 1896: Hirsch, 570; WCW note to Harry and Gertrude, same date, *Gertrude Vanderbilt Whitney*, 152. Harry to WCW, Oct. 12, 1896. Gunn's greetings to the couple, Sept. 27. Dorothy's later account of the family schism was dated Feb. 2, 1959.

Pages 151 to 156:

Harry accepts WCW house: *Gertrude Vanderbilt Whitney*, 155–56. Dorothy on her stepmother: her 1959 account cited above. WCW's Aiken mansion: *NYT*, Jan. 16, 1898; his new 871 Fifth Ave. mansion: *NYTrib*, Nov. 25, 1896. Wallace Irwin verses: *Collier's*, Mar. 11, 1905. Edith's "wonderful tact": *NYT* obituary May 7, 1899. WCW's "religious" gathering: *NYTrib*, July 16, 1897. *NYH* comment: July 15. Sheehan's statements: *NYT*, July 16. Breen's observation: Matthew P. Breen, *Thirty Years of New York Politics* (published by author, 1899), 831–34. Van Wyck as Croker's puppet: George B. McClellan, *op. cit.*, 161.

Pages 157 to 161:

Gunn to WCW on his kindness: July 5, 1894; his journal entry: Dec. 5, 1895; on his Met stock: to WCW, n.d.; on wine from WCW: journal, Nov. 24, 1897. Mrs. WCW at Horse Show: *NYT* obituary, May 7, 1899. In Kentucky: *NYTrib*, Dec. 1, 1897. Beebe on WCW: Lucius Beebe, *The Big Spenders* (Doubleday, 1966), 198. Aiken accident: *NYTrib*, Feb. 22, 24, Apr. 19, 20, 1898; also *NYT* obituary May 7, 1899. Dorothy's recollection is from her memoir of Feb. 2, 1959. Gunn's comment: Journal, Apr. 22, 1898. Dorothy's reaction against riding: Beatrice Straight told author, May 10, 1978.

Pages 161 to 162:

Coolidge's story: Pound and Moore, eds., *More They Told Barron* (Harper, 1931), Aug. 11, 1903, 181.

Pages 162 to 165:

"I have always loved horses": *NYTrib*, June 23, 1898. Moving Edith to Maine: *NYTrib*, July 22, 1898; the return: *NYTrib*, Sept. 23, 27; Dorothy's recollection: memoir, Feb. 2, 1959; Gunn's gloom: Journal, Sept. 12, 1898; Gunn to Edith, Dec. 14. Whitney races: *NYTrib*, *NYH*, Apr. 30, 1899. Edith counsels Dorothy: Dorothy's memoir, cited above. Edith's death and funeral: *NYT*, May 7; *NYTrib*, May 10. Gunn's letter: May 9.

Pages 166 to 169:

Stables burn: *NYT*, July 14, 1899. WCW on return from Europe: *NYTrib*, Aug. 9; new stables and house, same. La Farge comment: Royal Cortissoz, *John La Farge* (Houghton Mifflin, 1911), 255–56. WCW races Belmont: Perry Belmont, *An American Democrat*, 630–31. His remark to grooms: Beebe, *op. cit.*, 171. On WCW enterprises: Hirsch, 551. WCW in tobacco: John K. Winkler, *Tobacco Tycoon* (Random House, 1942), 122. Harry as speeder: *NYTrib*, May 14, 1903.

Page 171:

Andy Logan on Mann: *New Yorker*, Aug. 21, 1965.

Pages 173 to 178:

State Trust affair: NYW, Mar. 12, 1900: TR's comment: Henry F. Pringle, *Theodore Roosevelt* (Farrar & Rinehart, 1939), 213; "my poor wife," NYW, Jan. 15; also Hendrick in *McClure's*, Jan. 1908; Hirsch, 552–55, Philip C. Jessup, *op. cit.*, I, 187–89. WCW to Pulitzer: Mar. 2, 1900, in Pulitzer Papers, Columbia University. NYW attacks Root: Mar. 12. "Mr. Whitney was saved": *NY Mail & Express*, Feb. 5, 1904. "Investors ruined": Hendrick, *McClure's*, Nov. 1907. TT on "Big Four": Mar. 22, June 7, 1900. $1,000 bill: Gunn entry, July 6, 1900. Gunn to Z: July 3, 22; sees Hannas, enjoys Louvre: To WCW, July 14, 26. Tod Sloan and WCW: *Tod Sloan By Himself* (Brentano's, 1915), 38ff. Gunn wins $775: to Z, Sept. 2; to "Anteus," Sept. 2.

Pages 178 to 180:

"I'll furnish a mansion": TT, Mar. 15, 1900. On WCW's new home: TT, Feb. 15. Col. McClure proposes: NYTrib, Nov. 13, 1899. Gunn to WCW: Nov. 1, 14, 1900. "Last night": Gunn to Z, Dec. 10. NYTrib, Feb. 18, describes WCW house, as did others, including *House Beautiful*, Aug. 1901.

Pages 181 to 185:

TT on Lehr: May 3, 10, 1900. Whitney's party: NYTrib, NYW, and NYT, Jan. 5, 1901. He leases Volodyovsky, NYTrib, Mar. 23. Gunn on his heart ailment: To WCW Apr. 3 and 9, combined; met at train: Gunn to Z, Apr. 30; Gunn to WCW from Nauheim June 8. Volodyovsky wins: NYTrib, June 6. Gunn's last letter: undated.

Pages 186 to 187:

Henry Adams on WCW: *The Education of Henry Adams* (Modern Library, 1931), 347–48. Declines to replace Washington: NYTrib, Mar. 30, Apr. 6, 1902.

Pages 188 to 194:

Nellie Bly exposé: George Waller, *Saratoga* (Prentice-Hall, 1966), 233. Two $20 bills: NYTrib, Aug. 19, 1901. Gargantuan betting: Waller, 255, 257. About Canfield: Alexander Gardiner, *Canfield* (Doubleday, 1930), 166. WCW bets for 38 friends: Hugh Bradley, *Such Was Saratoga* (Doubleday, 1940), 242–43. "Renaissance Prince": Richmond Barrett, *Good Old Summer Days* (Appleton, 1941), 226–27. WCW wins in Paris but decides to end racing in Europe: NYTrib, Oct. 1, 7, 1901. Hails Tammany candidate: NYW, Oct. 24. Assailed by Jerome: NYW, Oct. 27, 31, and Nov. 2; also Richard O'Connor, *Courtroom Warrior* (Little, Brown, 1963), 265. WCW leads singing: NYH, Nov. 18. "Fair women" and Mrs. Keppel: TT, Nov. 28. WCW entertains her: NYTrib, Nov. 18. Concerning Mrs. Keppel: Philippe Jullian, *Edward and the Edwardians* (Viking, 1967), 140; and Anita Leslie, *The Marlborough House Set* (Doubleday, 1973), 199. Mrs. Burke Roche: C. W. de Lyon Nichols, *The Ultra-Fashionable Peerage of America* (George Harjes, 1904), 47, 50. Her marriage and divorce: Obituary, NYT, Jan. 27, 1947. Frick's taste in music: Mark Sullivan, *Our Times* (Scribners, 1927), III: 353.

Pages 195 to 197:

"Roses and cream": NYW, Dec. 18, 1901. Saunterer's comment: TT, Dec. 12. "The great mansion": NYW, Dec. 18; NYH, NYTrib, NYS, NYT, same date, and TT, Dec. 19. Lispenard Stewart: In Nichols, *op. cit.*, 26.

Pages 198 to 201:
Metropolitan reorganization and capitalization: Gustavus Myers, *op. cit.*, 380. "Master mind": Hendrick in *McClure's*, Jan. 1908; also Hendrick, *Age of Big Business*, 144 and 139–40. "Stringed instrument": Peter Lyon, *Success Story* (Scribners, 1963), 315. Amory pamphlet, 1906. Choate statement: Gustavus Myers, *op. cit.*, 382. See also Harry J. Carman, *The Street Surface Railway Franchises of New York City* (Columbia University, 1919), 204–20, and McClellan, *Gentleman and Tiger*, 158–66.

Pages 202 to 205:
Payne's wedding: NYW, NYH, *Washington Post*, Feb. 7, 1902; NYT, Feb. 5. TR on "sharp practices": E. E. Morison and John Blum, eds., *Letters of Theodore Roosevelt* (Harvard, 1951–54) VII: 155. On Root: Pringle, *Roosevelt*, 255. Oliver's gift house: NYT, Mar. 8. The couplet: TT, Feb. 6.

Pages 206 to 212:
The recollection of Dorothy was told author by her classmate Susan Sedgwick, now Mrs. Paul Hammond. "My poor father!" is from Dorothy's 1959 memoir. Gold Heels won: TT, July 3, 1902. "Standing invitation": TT, May 8. Blue Girl won: TT, May 22. The Reggie scandal: Wayne Andrews, *op. cit.*, 381; verse about it: TT, May 8. *NYTrib* on WCW: Aug. 24: *World's Work*, May 1902: *The Widow in TT*, Aug. 7. Strictly private dinner: NYTrib, Aug. 26. On banning autos: Bradley, *op. cit.*, 356. "Harry Payne Whitney does the playing": NYTrib, Aug. 24. WCW praises Duke: Winkler, *op. cit.*, 149, and Hirsch, 549. Vanderbilt feuds: TT, Aug. 28, 21. WCW races in England: NYTrib, Oct. 27, 30. WCW writes Cleveland: Hirsch, 593, dated Dec. 8, 1902. Praise for WCW: *World's Work*, May 1902, article by W. J. K. Kenny.

Pages 213 to 217:
Dunne's verse: Elmer Ellis, *Mr. Dooley's America* (Knopf, 1941), 185–86. Canfield's raided: Parker Morell, *Lillian Russell* (New York, 1939), 217–18. WCW enjoys Caruso: TT, Jan. 28, 1904. His illness and death: *Evening Sun*, Feb. 2; NYTrib, New York American, NYT, NYH, Feb. 3.

Pages 217 to 221:
Comment on him, and funeral: *Nation*, Feb. 11, 1904; TT, Feb. 4; NYT, NYTrib, Feb. 3; *Fads and Fancies*: Logan article, *New Yorker*, Aug. 14, 21, 1965; NYW, Feb. 6; NYTrib, Feb. 25, 1904.

BOOK II

Pages 227 to 231:
Gertrude on being an heiress: *Gertrude Vanderbilt Whitney*, 96–97. "Little Miss Whitney": TT, Aug. 18, 1904. "Sister was waiting": Dorothy's diary (DD), Sept. 27, 1904. On Paris, Chartres, Cologne: DD, Sept. 2, 4, and Nov. 14. Gambling, automobiling: DD, Sept. 10, 11. At couturières, at church: DD, Oct. 8, 9. On St. Peter's: Dec. 13. Audience with pope: Jan. 4, 1905. May's risqué joke: To D, Jan. 21, 1905. At Taormina, at Venice: Feb. 27, May 16. More fittings: Sept. 2, 8.

Pages 231 to 235:

D named in 400: C. W. de Lyon Nichols, *The Ultra-Fashionable Peerage* . . . , 11–19; his listing of others: 47–48. The NYPL has a copy of the very rare *Fads and Fancies* (Town Topics Publishing. Co., 1905) under lock and key. Bacon shed by Morgan: George Wheeler, *Pierpont Morgan and Friends* (Prentice-Hall, 1973), 27–28; also James Brown Scott, *Robert Bacon* (Doubleday, 1923), *passim*. DPW in Washington: DD, Jan. 1, 1906. Barneys' dance: *NYH*, Jan. 23. DPW's debut, *Gertrude Vanderbilt Whitney*, 230–31.

Pages 236 to 241:

PDW and Howard Cary: DD, Jan. 28, 29, 1906. Meets Willard Straight: DD, Feb. 3, 1906. On boat with Cary: DD, Apr. 26, 27, 30. Cary's death: *NYT*, May 8; "Sally" letter to DPW: May 10. Adelaide married: DD, May 8; *NYT*, May 9. In Spain: DD, May 27, 31. In England: June 19, 20, 21, 22. In Switzerland: Aug. 16, 21, 26. Back home, gives party: Oct. 7 entry. Serramazzana letter dated Sept. 29.

Pages 242 to 245:

Her reading, dancing at Yale, skating at Payne's: DD, Jan. 21–27, 1907. At Aiken: Mar. 29; elected president of JL: Apr. 22. In Stockholm: July 22 entry; Moscow: Aug. 3. Her Venice essay on love: From her papers at Dartington School. "Shivers inside me": Nov. 13, 1910, to Willard Straight. Uncle's suicide: Nov. 14 entry.

Pages 246 to 252:

Rumor that DPW opposed Gladys's choice: unidentified clipping, DWSE Prs. Cornelius and Grace's social triumphs: Wayne Andrews, *op. cit.*, 365–66. Gladys's wedding: *NYT*, Jan. 28, 1908. Rumor of DPW's engagement: unidentified clipping in her diary. On Porfirio Diaz: DD, Mar. 30. At Falconer's: July 31. "Heavenly walk": Aug. 19 entry. GA's arrival: Sept. 1. At Vanderbilt races: Oct. 24. Symphony, tuberculosis articles, etc.: Entries for Nov. 6, 12, 16, 19. "I am filled . . .": DPW to Straight (WDS), Dec. 4, 1910. Her two meetings with WDS: DD, Jan. 6, 8, 1909. Visits Cuban president: Mar. 18 entry. "Dined at the Morgans": May 28 entry. WDS entry in *his* diary (SD): Same date.

Pages 253 to 259:

"Vividly alive": Herbert Croly, *Willard Straight* (Macmillan, 1924), 7. WDS's "chief infirmity": Croly, *Straight*, 36. "Little Willie" series: Prof. Olaf M. Brauner to DWS, 1920, n.d. Peking scene at the time: L. C. Arlington and William Lewisohn, *In Search of Old Peking* (Peking: Vetch, 1935), *passim*. "He was a good mimic": E. T. Williams, ms., "Recollections of Willard Straight," 3. "Legation quarter itself": WDS to Claude Bragdon, 1903. "I have burned my bridges": 1904 to Bragdon. "Imagine going through life," and "too much ambition in my cosmos": SD entries in 1903 and 1904, quoted in Charles Vevier, *The United States and China, 1906–1913* (Greenwood Press, 1968), 29. "I am unsound": SD, Apr. 4, 1904. See also Lloyd C. Griscom, *Diplomatically Speaking* (Little, Brown, 1937), 245, 252. Morgan on WDS: Croly, *Straight*, 135. Harriman's global dream: George Kennan, *E. H. Harriman's Far Eastern Plans* (Country Life, 1917), *passim*. "The Roosevelt party": WS to Frederick Palmer, Oct. 3, 1905. See also Alice Longworth, *Crowded Hours* (Scribners, 1933), 103.

Pages 260 to 267:

Morgan on WS and Longworths: Croly, *Straight*, 199; also Alice Longworth, 114. "First and foremost": Quoted in Croly, *Straight*, 199. "I made the trip across Siberia": WDS to Harriman, Oct. 31, 1906. WDS's impression on Harriman: George Kennan, *E. H. Harriman* (Houghton Mifflin, 1922, 2 vols.), II, 24n. Pringle on WDS: Henry F. Pringle, *Life and Times of William Howard Taft*, 2 vols. (Farrar & Rinehart, 1939), II: 681. WDS's heady punch. Marvin diary, 22. "There is a consensus": To Harriman, Nov. 15, 1906. "Fits of depression": Croly, *Straight*, 267. "Reply automatically": Marvin diary, 32. "Secretary greeted us": SD, Nov. 18, 1907. WDS as architect of Taft policy: Helen Dodson Kahn article, "Willard Straight," in *Makers of American Diplomacy*, edited by Frank J. Merli and Theodore A. Wilson, 2 vols. (Scribners, 1974), II: 41. Scene in Harbin: Marvin diary, 35. "The prospect": WDS to Harriman, Feb. 16, 1908. WDS's "Notes on the Late E. H. Harriman's Interest in the Far East" contains his description of the trip into Manchuria. "Prior to leaving Mukden": Same. Wallet at neck: Louis Graves, *Willard Straight in the Orient* (New York: Asia Publishing Co., 1922), 47. The account of Harriman rejecting WDS as son-in-law is in an unidentified newspaper clipping found in DWS's photo album and dated July 20, 1911, the date her engagement to WDS was announced.

Pages 268 to 271:

"She is a great heiress": *TT*, July 24, 1902. "Dined at Newlands" . . . "Lunched at White House": SD, June 13, 17, 1909. WDS too young for his eminence: Croly, *Straight*, 280. Harriman lauds WDS: To Knox, Feb. 5, 11, 1909. WDS said he was "delighted" by post with American Group: In letter June 3, 1909, to Mrs. Anna Cowles, Roosevelt collection at Harvard.

Pages 271 to 275:

Sister Hazel on WDS's clothes, etc.: Croly, *Straight*, 560. Attends Dorchester ball: SD, July 9, 1909. At Hamburg: SD, July 12; and on "smelly" Trans-Siberian: Aug. 8. His mansion in Peking: E. T. Williams, *op. cit.*, 3–4. "Straight was a remarkable person": Recollections of Nelson Trusler Johnson, Columbia Oral History Collection. "The press has reported": WDS to Harriman, Aug. 29.

Pages 277 to 280:

Root's letter to DPW: June 17, 1909; Hunt to Morrison: June 20. DPW on Nagoya: DD, Oct. 2; "fortunate escape": Oct. 31; saw Great Wall: Oct. 31. "Choking at the throat": SD, Nov. 15, "So sad": DD, Nov. 16.

Pages 281 to 286:

DPW to Cousin Katherine: Nov. 18; to WDS, Nov. 17. Her later confession: Croly, *Straight*, 357–58. WDS letters to DPW: Nov. 15, 21. Her "what a man" letter: Nov. 26. His letters: Dec. 15, 1909, and Jan. 5, 9, Mar. 6, 23, 1910. "Ethel and I": Two letters combined, Apr. 12, 14. DD, Apr. 9, 11, 1910. *TT* verse in June 7, 1906, issue. Walk in Florence: DD, Apr. 20, 1910; and two later entries, May 17 and Apr. 28.

Pages 287 to 291:

On Jackson biography: SD, Oct. 23, 1909. His letter to Mrs. Robinson: Apr. 21,

1910, Harvard Roosevelt collection. WDS on Trans-Siberian to DPW, Apr. 30; "I know I'm right": Apr. 21; on Rumsey: May 11. Joins TR's party: Alice Longworth, *op.cit.*, 177. "No pretenses": Croly, *Straight*, 364. DD: May 20, 21; her letter to him: May 21; his letter to her: May 22, 1910.

Pages 292 to 297:

WDS's verses: May 25, 1910; hers in reply dated same, but must be in error. His letter before sailing, May 29; her cable, n.d. WDS on his love: June 3. His letter to Mrs. Robinson: June 12, Harvard Roosevelt collection. "Without you": June 17. "It was good to be near you": July 3. Stephens to DPW: July 8, Dartington papers; "HOOROO": Aug. 5 from Madonna, Italy.

Pages 297 to 303:

D to S about KE: Sept. 5, 1910. D's worry about his removal from her circle: Croly, *Straight*, 364. "I want you so": WDS, Aug. 25. On the Roosevelts: Aug. 28. Asks her to return sooner: Aug. 26; her annoyed reply: Sept. 11. WDS to her: Aug. 31, Sept. 1, 4. His news about Davison also contains "You frighten me": Sept. 7. Was Wall St. corrupting him?: Sept. 9. The press gossip about DPW is in unidentified news clip, n.d. Her letter to WDS after conferring with Harry and Pauline: Sept. 15. "Poor Boy": Oct. 19. His letter from Moscow: Nov. 16, 1910.

Pages 304 to 306:

"This bores you": Dec. 18, 1910. "Whilst festivities": Unidentified news clip. "A merry Christmas": Dec. 25; "alone tonight": Dec. 28, 1910. The description of his party is in another unidentified clipping. "I left them all": Jan. 1, 1911—also his description of his drive.

Pages 306 to 310:

DPW wrote WDS of Mrs. Kinnicutt's remark Nov. 27, 1910. "Mutton-suet brain": to WDS, Nov. 2, 1910. Socialist vote: To WDS, Nov. 13. Edith Lindley's approval in DPW's letter of Nov. 2, her new basis with Bacon, Nov. 9. She finds Morgan lovely: To WDS Jan. 30, 1911. About Derby and Ethel: Feb. 19, Mar. 15. DPW's own panics: To WDS, Apr. 4, 1911. About TR and Alice: To WDS, Dec. 28, 1910. Twice moved to tears: To WDS, Jan. 23, 1911, and Nov. 25, 1910.

Pages 310 to 313:

Arnell to WDS: Feb. 7, 1911. "It's history": Feb. 12, 1911. WDS on Calhoun: Nov. 27, 1910, and Feb. 17, 1911. On the Chinese: To DPW, Jan. 29, 1911; on Sheng: WDS to Frank McKnight, Dec. 11, 1910. On the Japanese, the Morgan office, and loneliness: To DPW Dec. 25, 31, 1910. Atmosphere of Peking: to Davison, Jan. 5, 1911. On TR: to DPW, Jan. 11. Two slants on Calhoun: To DPW, Mar. 10 and 11. Ball at Russian Legation: To DPW, Feb. 25–26. She urges him to stick: Jan. 4, 1911; becomes profane: Jan. 14. WDS to Schoelkopf: Nov. 25, 1910. To DPW about the plague: Jan. 12, 1911. His "Dooley" effort: In unidentified news clip he sent DPW.

Pages 313 to 318:

On Gloucester fishermen: To WDS, Apr. 4, 1911. The press on WCW transit operations: NYT, Oct. 9, 11, 1907, and NYW, Oct. 19, 1907. "Perfectly furious": DPW to WDS, Jan. 4, 1911. Miss Elkins's romances: Archibald Butt, *Taft and Roosevelt: The Intimate Letters of Archie Butt* (Doubleday, 1930), 46, 57, 58, 237, 328, 329, 636–37. "I know how dreadfully hard" is beginning of quotation from six of DPW's letters ranging from Dec. 25, 1910, to Feb. 19–21, 1911. WDS's responses are from five letters ranging from Feb. 5 to Mar. 19–20, 1911. "Screamed with ennui": To DPW, Mar. 29. "The telegram went". To DPW, Apr. 15; her cabled "GRAZIA," same date. "Such a greediness": Apr. 19. "Just seven months ago": His letters May 25 and June 3 combined.

Pages 319 to 323:
"The fruition": May 30, 1911. Polo victory: DD, June 19. Ohl story: NYH, June 19. "Please be humble": June 6. "A sort of a blur": WDS to H.P. Fletcher, Aug. 7. "The surprise heard on all sides": unidentified clipping in DPW's papers, NYT, July 30. "I know it's foolish": July 28. Ceremony: unidentified clipping, and NYT, Sept. 8. TT's verse: Sept. 7, 1911.

Pages 325 to 328:
Dorothy describes domicile: Her Peking diary, n.d. Her comments on fears: Oct. 13, 29, 30, 1911. On WDS as husband: Jan. 8, 1912. Purple Cow dinner: Nov. 13, 1911. "This is all highly interesting": Graves, *Willard Straight in the Orient*, 62. American flag: DD, Nov. 8. Christmas: DD, Dec. 25. WDS describes violence: SD, Jan. 16, 1912. Quotation from Croly, *The Promise of American Life* (Harvard, 1965), 124. On Forbes: DD, Feb. 9. Bland's comment: Graves, *op. cit.*, 62.

Pages 328 to 330:
Street fighting: SD, Feb. 29, 1912. Marines arrive: DD, Mar. 3. NYH: In her papers, n.d. Also NY American, n.d.; NYT, Mar. 17. HPW cable. n.d. "Rotten polo". SD, Mar. 19.

Pages 331 to 335:
Mrs. Lawrance letter: n.d. On Taft, TR, and Wilson: DD, May 17, 22, June 23, July 3, 1912. At Cliveden: DD, July 14. Good impression made by WDS: Susan Sedgwick (Mrs. Paul Hammond) told author. WDS's polo field: Mrs. Flora Miller told author. "Winged sandals": Croly, *Straight*, 457.

Pages 337 to 338:
Spring Rice's romance: Chanler, *op. cit.*, 204. The Group distrusts Chinese: Pringle, *Taft*, 679. LaFollette's Weekly: Quoted in *Taft*, 681. Wilson statement: *Taft*, 693. "Mr. Morgan died": DD, Mar. 31, 1913. Ethel's wedding: DD, Apr. 4.

Pages 340 to 346.
Croly praises TR: *Promise*, 167–71. TR praises him in return: Charles Forcey, *The Crossroads of Liberalism* (Oxford, 1961), 125. Croly's "moral force": T. S. Matthews, *Name and Address* (Simon & Schuster, 1960), 208. Croly–WDS discussions: Croly, *Straight*, 472. Croly–DWS talk about weekly: Alvin Johnson, *Pioneer's Progress* (U. of Nebraska Press, 1960), 233. "How could it have happened": *Ibid*. WDS's letter to TR:

In Forcey, *op. cit.*, 186. Lippmann on DWS's "tainted money": from "Reminiscences of Walter Lippmann," Columbia Oral History Collection. WDS founds India House: *Japanese Advertiser*, Dec. 3, 1918. Examples of WDS's apprehension about DWS are seen in letters to her of June 25, 1913 (two that day), Sept. 12, 13, 1913, and Sept. 10, 1914. "Dined with Herbert": Sept. 10, 1914. Croly letter to Judge Hand: In Forcey, *op. cit.*, 176.

Pages 347 to 354:

Bulwark blown up: DD, Nov. 27, 1914. WDS letter on "peace propaganda" to Croly, Dec. 14. "I told Davison": WDS's "Diary for the Perusal of Whitney Straight, Esquire," (cited as "Diary Perusal"). DD entries Dec. 4, 7, 11, 14, 16, 23. "Please cable me": WDS letter Jan. 20, 1915. "H.P.D. asked": Diary of a Trip to London and Paris, 18. "Here I am all alone" and "turquoise in our wake": Undated letters. WDS pooh-poohs British virtue: London-Paris Diary. WDS and Col. House: WDS's diary; also *The Intimate Papers of Colonel House*, ed. Chas. Seymour (Houghton Mifflin, 1929), I: 397. "Partnership or nothing": "Diary Perusal," 1. "Forever dreaming dreams": Croly, *Straight*, 461–62. To Plattsburg: DD, Aug. 9, 1915.

Pages 354 to 357:

Telegrams to Wilson: Walter Millis, *Road to War* (Houghton Mifflin, 1935), 173. "Had England": Dec. 14, 1914. TR at Plattsburg: Francis Russell, "When Gentlemen Prepared for War," *American Heritage*, Apr. 1964. "Ethel and her baby": Aug. 28, 1915, in E. E. Morison and John Blum, eds., 8 vols., *Letters of Theodore Roosevelt* (Harvard, 1951–54), VIII: 964. "Ethel and Dorothy": *op. cit.*, Sept. 2, 965. "Sent me to meet Russian generals": "Diary Perusal," 20. "A great foreign trade opportunity": *NYT*, Oct. 28, 1914. LaFollette barb: Millis, *op. cit.*, 218. WDS's resignation: *NYT*, Sept. 18, 1915. "I have just seen Ted": Dec. 29, 1915, *Letters of Roosevelt*, VIII: 999. "I do not believe I overstate": *op. cit.*, 1004, Jan. 13, 1916. "Early Victorian geese," *op. cit.*, Feb. 8, 1019. "Flabby Gentiles and circumcized Jews": Reminiscences of Alvin Johnson, Columbia Oral History Research Collection.

Pages 358 to 363:

WDS joins AIC: "Diary Perusal," 4. Croly on House: Mar. 18, 1916. "Dinner with the American Ambassador": "Diary Perusal," 28. Chat with Harjes, *op. cit.*, 54. Lippmann to WDS on TR: Apr. 6, 1916. Almeric's "idea": "Diary Perusal," 120. "Fair hair": DD, Sept. 1, 1916. WDS letter against Wilson: *NR*, Oct. 28, 1916; also *NYT*, Oct. 29.

Pages 365 to 367:

Col. House to Daisy: Feb. 10, 1917. WDS to Pres. Wilson: Apr. 18. "Met Colonel House today": Mrs. J. Borden Harriman, *From Pinafores to Politics* (Holt, 1923), 221. Griscom also a major: Lloyd C. Griscom, *op. cit.*, 371. Rally for Joffre: *Gertrude Vanderbilt Whitney*, 390, and *NYH*, May 11. *Oswego Palladium*, June 28, says DWS to inherit millions.

Pages 369 to 372:

"The wind blew": Sept. 27, 1917. "He stated": Croly to WDS, Sept. 27. Lippmann to DWS, Oct. 22. "I agree with you": Croly to WDS, Sept. 27. "Dug potatoes," met FDR, dined with WDS: DD, Nov. 3, 23, 29. BB letter: Dec. 5.

Pages 373 to 379:
"D. stayed": SD, Dec. 11, 1917. On Gen. Wood: SD, Dec. 20. WDS to DWS, Dec. 16, 21. TR to Quentin: Joseph L. Gardner, *Departing Glory* (Scribners, 1973), 389. "Too much food": SD, Feb. 9, 1918. Talk with Daisy: Letter, Jan. 2, 1918. "We waited indeed": DWS to WDS, Dec. 15, 1917. New York freezing: DWS to WDS, Jan. 1 and 8, 1918, letters combined. About Hazel: to WDS, Jan. 18. On Lamont and on Wilson, Jan. 8, 10.

Pages 380 to 385:
WDS on Daisy's "irresponsibility": Feb. 12, 1918. Wedding: Mrs. Harriman, *op. cit.*, 261. Air raid: SD, Jan. 30. "I'm afraid that our friend": Jan. 30. "The YMCA": Feb. 10, 26, letters combined. Scared green: SD, Feb. 19. On MacArthur: To DWS, Feb. 19, 20, 21, 22. Contemplates combat: Feb. 22. DWS on House: Feb. 21. At Yaphank for YMCA: To WDS, Jan. 18, Feb. 6, combined. Her visit to Roosevelts: To WDS, Apr. 20. TR felt Flora and Quentin should marry: Gardner, *op. cit.*, 389. DWS on NR: To WDS, Feb. 21.

Pages 385 to 393:
WDS on Flora: To DWS, July 3; on the war: Feb. 22. Praises Murphy: Mar. 18. Raps Stimson: Mar. 24, Apr. 2. Madame Proat: SD, Feb. 28. On Hugon: To DWS, Apr. 4. Praises Morgan firm, envies Murphy: To DWS, Mar. 10, Apr. 14. To DWS on Langres: Mar. 2, May 17. Easter Sunday: Mar. 31. He will seek combat: Letter, Apr. 7. DWS visits TR: To WDS, July 4. Her diary entries: Mar. 29, Apr. 14, May 2, May 24. Croly on WDS's contradictions: Croly, *Straight*, 553. "I'm so proud of you": DWS letters, Mar. 11, Apr. 7, Apr. 20, Mar. 31, June 23, combined. "Your spirit": Her Mar. 26, May 4 letters combined.

Pages 393 to 397:
"Missed out": May 26. Letter to be sent if killed: June 2. "The house is rocking": June 4–5. "Things have not gone well": June 7. "Gracious goodness": June 9. "Poor Quentin": July 18. TR's response: Gardner, *op. cit.*, 390, and "Quinikins": *Ibid.*, 392. TR to WDS: July 14.

Pages 398 to 403:
"You're not easing off": June 10. DWS's response to his "trip" is given in fragments of hers of June 8, 12, and July 14. Chauffeurs: June 19. "Every dollar": July 24. Mitchel funeral: To WDS, July 12. At Upton: July 14. On YMCA secretaries: Aug. 23. With Ethel Derby: July 24. On Mrs. Herter: July 8. "When I think of you": July 24. On *NYH*: July 24, Sept. 20. "To say that I'd be better": June 30. DWS's response: Aug. 6. Upsetting dream: Sept. 7. "All day": WDS, June 23. Two foolish presents: Aug. 22. Murphy to DWS: Aug. 5. "Please, Best Beloved": Sept. 12, 20 letters combined.

Pages 404 to 408:
"Unbelievable thing": To DWS, Jan. 2, 1919. "It would do him good": Feb. 26. Her

reply: Mar. 24. His view: May 19. On settlement with Germany: May 5. Damn the paper: Aug. 11. Fire extinguishers: June 10. Strong stuff: Feb. 26. Fight, fight: Apr. 5. Dodoes: Feb. 10. Esoteric Buddhism: May 12. These pests: May 19. DWS's reply: July 8. Croly on WDS: Croly, *Straight*, 472. Croly to DWS: July 27, Oct. 13. "I'm getting a little restive": Apr. 20. Her answer: May 17. "The Daily Mail": May 12. On the locket and on their anniversary: To DWS May 28, June 23.

Pages 409 to 416:

No magic: SD, Mar. 12. Nesting birds: To DWS June 16. Three years ago: SD, Mar. 30. "I keep still": June 16. WDS letter to Phillips: June 2. Bennett on "the Major": To DWS, Dec. 1, 1918. Bennett's comment on WDS's reluctance to leave: Same. "You are working for the Just Cause": Aug. 20. "Quite a case of nerves": SD, Aug. 25. "I sketched all day": Aug. 23. "The sea air and sleep": Same. "Above all I wish": Aug. 25. Reads Mark Twain: Aug. 27. Regrets "monkeying": SD, Aug. 28, 30. "For two weeks": parts of letters Sept. 1, 5, 6. Recalls wedding: Sept. 7.

Pages 416 to 418:

DWS's canvass: To WDS, May 26. Contributes a million: Oct. 19. Belmont's remark: In DWS to WDS, Sept. 25. "Spoil me": May 7. "Press your wrists": Aug. 6. On his sore leg: May 17. Praises photo: June 8. On Vladivostok idea: Sept. 28. His reply: Nov. 6.

Pages 418 to 421:

On Dr. Manning: DD, Sept. 8. Schieffelin to DWS and her reply: Aug. 27, 30. On TR and Lodge: To WDS, Aug. 29. TR to Kipling: Angus Wilson, *The Strange Ride of Rudyard Kipling* (Viking, 1977), 320, dated Nov. 23. "Pouring": to WDS, Sept. 13. On Col. Batchkarova: DWS to WDS, Aug. 19. On Wilson: Sept. 28. Her three letters on influenza: Sept. 25, Oct. 6, 13.

Pages 421 to 428:

"Brilliant starts": Sept. 11. "On this road": Sept. 14. "The fire became": To DWS, Sept. 27. Bennett hurt: Sept. 29. "Chilly day": Sept. 30. On Lippmann: To DWS, Sept. 28. Lippmann comment: To DWS, Dec. 1. "Help Herbert": Oct. 8. "It's lucky for you": Oct. 1. "In one of the very best divisions": Oct. 22. "Back in Paris": Oct. 27. "More of the same": Oct. 28. "Daylight ahead": Oct. 29, 30 combined. Hard's idea: Oct. 19. Amy Lowell: Bruce Bliven, *Five Million Words Later* (John Day, 1970), 165. On marital fidelity: DWS to WDS, Oct. 13. Sees Wilson: Same. "Abused and vilified": To WDS, Oct. 31. "Your later letter": Oct. 31. On House's plans: Oct. 19.

Pages 429 to 433:

"Poor dear Daisy": To DWS, Nov. 1. "The Dagos": Oct. 31. To DWS: Nov. 4, 6, 2, 4. "Luxury of woe": Croly, *Straight*, 17. WDS to Whitney: Nov. 6. WDS's long cable to Croly: Nov. 7. His description of scene at HQ: To DWS Nov. 7.

Pages 434 to 436:

"When the armistice is signed": Nov. 10–11. Lippmann's observation: To DWS, Dec. 1. WDS on chat with Lippmann: SD, Nov. 11. Description of being in Paris on the loose: To DWS, Nov. 11. His cable: Received Nov. 15.

Pages 436 to 442:

Our troops attack: DD, Nov. 9. "It nearly drove me wild": To WDS, Nov. 15. "Heartachey time": Same. "Impossible to believe": Same. "A cable at last": Nov. 17. "I saw Clemenceau": SD, Nov. 13. Letters to DWS: Nov. 13, 14, 15, 16. "House is afraid": SD, Nov. 16. WDS's illness: Mrs. Harriman kept a diary beginning Nov. 18 and later sent it to DWS.

Pages 442 to 446:

"I have been wondering": Nov. 17. "Ill as he was": Mrs. Harriman, *From Pinafores . . .* , 298. "I sat beside Willard": Dec. 2. Her cable to Polk: Dec. 1. Dorothy's reply: Dec. 1. Greene's description of funeral: To Edith Lindley, Dec. 3. Delano's comments: In memo of Dec. 3 and letter, n.d., to DWS. Bennett letter to Dorothy: Dec. 1. Daisy's question: Dec. 3.

Pages 447 to 457:

Stephens to DWS: Dec. 2. Memorial service: NYH, Dec. 7. TR's tribute: NYTrib, Dec. 11. NYS headline: Dec. 18; correction: Dec. 20. Louisa Weinstein to Bennett: Jan. 1, 1919. TR's funeral: NYT, Jan. 9, 1919. On JL fight: *Oswego Palladium*, Feb. 23. DWS interview: NYT, Feb. 18. Poesy: TT, Feb. 20. DWS to Flora: Feb. 24. DSM for WDS: *Brooklyn Eagle*, Apr. 14. Diary entries: July 19, 24, 28, 26, Aug. 1, 7. DWS to Susan Sedgwick: Aug. 10. "Rather dreadful!" DD, Aug. 15. Talk with Daisy: DD, Aug. 23. Wilson's speech: Gene Smith, *When the Cheering Stopped* (Morrow, 1964), 51–52. Entries: Aug. 24, 26. Flora Whitney (now Mrs. Flora Miller) told author her recollections. DD: Aug. 28, 30, Sept. 5. "The horse-chestnuts are out": WDS to DWS, Apr. 14, 1918. "In spirit we are closer": To DWS, Mar. 31, 1918. DD, Sept. 6, 8, 9.

Pages 457 to 459:

"Last wonderful hour": DD, Sept. 14. At Corbie: Sept. 17. Meets Frewen: Sept. 21. In harbor and home: Sept. 26, 27. Then entries for Sept. 26, 27, 29, Oct. 1, 2.

EPILOGUE

Pages 463ff.

"Tall and slim, all in black": Leonard K. Elmhirst, *The Straight and Its Origin* (published by Willard Straight Hall at Cornell, 1975), 21, 24. LKE's background is given in this book and in "The Story of Dartington" (pamphlet, Dartington Press, 1970), 21. "Charming to look at": LKE in *The Straight*, 21–22. DWS joins Eleanor Roosevelt in promoting WTUL: Joseph P. Lash, *Eleanor and Franklin* (Norton, 1971), 280–81. DWS marries LKE: Her diary, Apr. 3, 1925. Interview with Devon farmer: "A Dartington Anthology, 1925–1975" (pamphlet, Dartington Press, 1975), 46–47. Author had conversations with Michael Young, who also supplied his written recollections. The Elmhirsts at White House and Dorothy's letter to Eleanor: Lash, 396, 398. "The pacifist position of *The New Republic*": Bliven, *Five Million Words Later*, 197. Dorothy paid $3,700,000 in support of *NR*: Forcey, *op. cit.*, 334.

Beatrice and Michael Straight told author their recollections.

ACKNOWLEDGMENTS

Acknowledgments

I WAS fortunate in having the generous cooperation of Beatrice and Michael Straight, daughter and son of Dorothy Whitney Straight. They told me their own recollections, furnished family pictures and documents, and led me to others who could add to the narrative. Flora Miller Irving, a great-granddaughter of the Whitneys, related family history, lent me valuable pictures and scrapbooks, and drove me to Old Westbury to see the Whitney domain there and to talk with her mother, Mrs. G. MacCulloch Miller. Mrs. Miller (the former Flora Whitney, who had been betrothed to the ill-starred Quentin Roosevelt) remembered well her aunt Dorothy Straight and the trip the two had made together to France in 1919, each to visit the grave of the man she had loved. Mrs. Irving had seen the value of the long-hidden diaries and letters of her famous grandmother, Gertrude Vanderbilt Whitney, and had collaborated with B. H. Friedman in the biography of the same name, a splendid work full of information useful to me.

At Dartington in England, Dorothy's daughter by her second husband, Mrs. Maurice Ash, talked to me about her mother and supplied pictures available nowhere else. Dr. Michael Young (now Lord Michael Young), whom Dorothy had taken under her wing as a child and who is now at work on a biography stressing her four decades in England, had memories and written memoirs to pass along. Robin Johnson, the Dartington librarian, produced pictures and papers concerning Dorothy, and Anthea Williams served as guide and chauffeur. In New York, Milton C. Rose, for many years Dorothy's attorney and friend, added his own recollections. So too did the only one of Dorothy's childhood friends still living—Susan Sedgwick, now Mrs. Paul L. Hammond—whose memory carried back to the Roser School days at the turn of the century and who could remember conversations and incidents of sixty and seventy years ago as if they were yesterday.

My special thanks go to Dr. Gould P. Colman, University Archivist at Cornell, who bore the brunt of my explorations of the invaluable Dorothy Whitney Straight Elmhirst Papers stored there; and to the members of his staff, especially Ingeborg Wald, Thomas Hickerson, Jane Gustafson, and Marcia Hopson. I am grateful also to Dr. Louis M. Starr, director of the Oral History Collection at Columbia University; to Harry Harrison and Judith Schiff of the Yale Library; to Richard Hill of the New York Public Library Annex on West 43rd Street; Rodney G. Dennis, Curator of Manuscripts, Houghton Library, Harvard University; John A. Gable, Executive Director, the Theodore Roosevelt Association; John A. Slonaker of the U.S. Army Military History Institute at Carlisle Barracks, Pennsylvania; and the staff of the Zoar Village State Memorial in Ohio. Elizabeth Downs of our small but fine library in Newtown, Connecticut, was ever helpful. And once again I had the advantage of conversations about the principal characters with my wise and warm but penetrating old friend, Dr. Henry Wexler of New Haven.

And thanks to the following, who supplied information, pictures, or permission to quote letters: Dwight Allen, Phyllis Barr, Esther Brumberg, S. C. Burden, Geoffrey Clements, Marjorie Delano, Richard Gachot, Karolyn Gould, Fowler Hamilton, Constance Harrison, Ann Hulbert, Herman Jervis, Francis C. Lawrance, Greta Lyons, Grayson M.-P. Murphy, Gloria Di Pietro, Susan Richman, Charles Howland Russell, and Morgan Dix Wheelock.

My friend and literary representative, Patricia S. Myrer, of McIntosh & Otis, Inc., read the manuscript and suggested many improvements. Laurie Graham, of Scribners, edited the book with a taste and discrimination often lacking in the author. And as always, my wife, Dorothy Green Swanberg—the other Dorothy to whom this book is dedicated —discussed characters and events with me, helping to bring them into such focus as they are, and gave the script a last corrective reading.

W. A. S.
Newtown, Connecticut

INDEX

Index